Henry Lansdell

Chinese Central Asia; a ride to Little Tibet

Henry Lansdell

Chinese Central Asia; a ride to Little Tibet

ISBN/EAN: 9783742845719

Manufactured in Europe, USA, Canada, Australia, Japa

Cover: Foto ©Andreas Hilbeck / pixelio.de

Manufactured and distributed by brebook publishing software (www.brebook.com)

Henry Lansdell

Chinese Central Asia; a ride to Little Tibet

BY
HENRY LANSDELL, D.D.

M.R.A.S., F.R.G.S.

AUTHOR OF "THROUGH SIBERIA," "RUSSIAN CENTRAL ASIA,"
"THROUGH CENTRAL ASIA," ETC.

With Three Maps and Eighty Illustrations

IN TWO VOLUMES

VOL. II.

London

SAMPSON LOW, MARSTON, & COMPANY, LIMITED
ST. DUNSTAN'S HOUSE, FETTER LANE, E.C.

1893

[All rights reserved]

BY THE SAME AUTHOR.

RUSSIAN CENTRAL ASIA,
INCLUDING
KULDJA, BOKHARA, KHIVA, AND MERV.
In Two Volumes, 42s.

THROUGH CENTRAL ASIA.
With a Map and Appendix on the Russo-Afghan Frontier.
In One Volume, 12s.

THROUGH SIBERIA.
In One Volume, 10s. 6d.
Library Edition, Two Volumes, 30s.

For further particulars, see Vol. I. page 457.

CONTENTS.

CHAPTER XXVIII.

THE PAMIRS AND THE REGIONS ADJOINING.

PAGES

Amphitheatre of mountains, crossed from Kashgar by four communications, 1.—Northern route through Artish, over Turgat Pass by Chadir-Kul and Narin, to Vierny, 3.—North-western route by valley of Kizil-su and Terek Pass to Osh, 5.—The Pamir; its name, boundaries, surface, peaks, localities, and rivers, 9.—Pamir lakes, and political negotiations connected therewith, 11.—Pamir climate, and nomad inhabitants, 13.—Its historical geography, and travellers thereon, 16.—Importance of Russian explorations, 17.—Recent travellers, and a political dispute, 19 . 1—19

CHAPTER XXIX.

ON SUNDRIES ZOOLOGICAL; OR SHOOTING, FISHING, AND BUTTERFLY-CATCHING.

Animals collected for science, 21.—Lessons in Taxidermy; Naturalists' instruments, 22.—Visit to zoological museums; Professor Zograf, Madame Fedchenko, and M. Oshanin, 24.—Acquaintances at Tashkend, and rifle practice, 26.—Central Asian fauna; Severtsoff's and Fedchenko's discoveries on the Tian Shan and Pamirs; English naturalists collecting from the south, 27.—Discoveries of Prjevalsky, Grum-Grjimailo, and Alpheraky in Sungaria and Mongolia, 28.—Littledale's capture of wild sheep, 29.—Author's collections; his new fish, *Diptychus Lansdelli*, 32.—Collecting at Ilisk, 34.—Specimens from Kuldja despatched by post; Paucity of animals between Kuldja and Aksu, 35.—Further captures at Kashgar, 36 . 20—36

CHAPTER XXX.

FROM KASHGAR TO YENGI HISSAR.

PAGES

Re-organisation of caravan; Despatch of parcels homewards, 37.—Sale of surplus baggage, 38.—My groom Amin, and his marriage, 39.—Sarim Sak, and plans for wife number two, 40.—Hire of three carts, 41.—Letters commendatory from *Taotai* and Consul, 42.—Farewell at Consulate, and Cossack escort out of town; Place of murder of Schlagintweit, 43.—Relics and monument, 44.—March to Yapchan; Route to Pamirs by Gez defile, 45.—Journey to Yengi Hissar, 46 .   37—46

CHAPTER XXXI.

THE HISTORY OF CHINESE TURKISTAN.

Legends of Trans-Oxiana; The wall of China, and neighbouring tribes; Migrations from Tarim valley to Tokharistan, 48.—Mission of Chang-kian to the Yuechi, and subjugation of Uigurs; Information concerning Tarim valley from Buddhist pilgrims, 49.—Divided condition of country at Arab invasion; Authority transferred to Bokhara, 50.—Uigur expansion from Kashgar; Kara-Khitai rule in Tarim valley; Conquest of Jinghiz Khan, 51.—Tamerlane's conquest, 52.—Rebellion of Wais Khan; Ababakar, Sultan Said, and Rashid, 53.—Rise of the *Khojas* and mountaineers; Invasion of Sungars, 54.—Depopulation of Sungaria; Recommencement of *Khoja* rebellions, 55.—Complications between Chinese and Khokandians, 56.—Invasion of the seven *Khojas*; Subversion of Chinese rule, 57.—Buzurg Khan and Yakub Bek; Yakub Bek's usurpation of authority, 58.—Reception of Russian and English embassies, 60.—Disaffection of people and readiness for return of Chinese, 61.—Yakub Khan's death; Three upstart successors, 62.—Reinstallation of Chinese Government; Retrocession by Russia of Ili valley, and formation of Sin Kiang province, 64   47—64

CHAPTER XXXII.

FROM YENGI HISSAR TO YARKAND.

District of Yengi Hissar, 65.—Town of Yengi Hissar, 66.—Visits to *Medresse* and *Gumbaz*; Native astonishment at photography, 68. —A starting-point for Wakhan; Route to Tash-Kurgan, 70.— Sarikol district. 71.—The Ak-tash valley and Little Pamir, 72.— Gumbaz-Bozai and its political interest; Wakhan villages, and the way thence into India, 73.—Historical associations of Yengi Hissar; Struggles of early Muhammadans and Buddhists, 74.— Tombs of Muhammadan martyrs; Ruins at Urdum Padshah, 75. —Departure from Yengi Hissar and journey to Kizil, 76.—Iron smelting; March through Kok-Robat, 77.—Arrival at Yarkand, 78 . . . . 65—78

CHAPTER XXXIII.

BUDDHISM AND OTHER EARLY RELIGIONS IN CHINESE TURKISTAN.

Earliest religion of Tarim valley, 79.—Survival of Shamanism among Kirghese and Kalmuks; Fire-worship unknown, 80. Brahmanism doubtful; Arrival of Buddhism; Missionaries sent for, 81.— Their work; Kuchar, an early seat of Buddhism, 82.—Travels of Fa-hian, Sung Yun, and Hiuen Tsiang; Buddhism at Cherchen, Han-moh, Karashar, Khotan, and in Tsung-ling Mountains, 83-85. —Hiuen Tsiang on Buddhism at Kuchar, Aksu, Badakshan, Osh, and Kashgar, 86.—Decay of Buddhism; Buddhist missionaries, 87. Persecution of Buddhists, 90.—Hiuen Tsiang among fire-worshippers, 91.—Supposed results of Buddhist teaching; Buddhist aspirations towards a beatified life, 92. Relics of Buddhism, 94. —The recently discovered Bower manuscript, 96 . 79-98

CHAPTER XXXIV.

OUR STAY IN YARKAND.

Hospitable reception, 99.—Lodged in suburbs, but photography forbidden, 100.—History of Yarkand, 101.—Forsyth's description, 104.—The old town and fortress; its population and mosques, 105.—Trade and costumes; No lunatic asylum; Visits from mullahs and merchants, 107.—Money loans offered; Medical assistance requested, 109.—Diseases prevalent in Chinese Turkistan; Servants of Dalgleish, 110.—Dalgleish's career and murder, 111.—Dalgleish's house, 115.—Letter from Leh, 116.—Negotiations for baggage horses, 117 . . . . 99—118

CHAPTER XXXV.

EARLY CHRISTIANITY IN CHINESE CENTRAL ASIA.

Christianity not mentioned by Buddhist pilgrims, 119.—Introduced into China by Olopuen; Testimony of Singan-fu monument, 120.—Testimonies from Western sources; Spread of Nestorians, 121.—Bishoprics in Central Asia, 122.—Prester John and Christians in time of Marco Polo, 124.—Roman Christianity in Central Asia; Pascal at Khiva and Almalik, 125.—Marignolli; Tangible remains of Christianity, 128.—Epitaphs and supposed monastery; Description of ruin, 129.—The *Tarikhi Rashidi*, 130.—Less certain remains; Nestorian translations; Their alphabet given to Uigurs, 131.—Search for Uigur antiquities, 132.—Character of Nestorian Christianity, 133.—Stamped out by Muhammadanism, 134 . 119—134

CHAPTER XXXVI.

FROM YARKAND TO KARGHALIK.

Escorted from Yarkand, 135.—Components of caravan, 136.—The river Yarkand, and precious stones, 137.—Arrival at Posgam, 138.—A night guard and street attendant; Journey to Yak-Shambeh, 139.—Taking photographs, 140.—Route from Yak-Shambeh, and

shooting, 142.—Welcome to Karghalik; Description of town, 143.
—My host's mausoleum; Visited by Chinese *Amban's* secretary,
144.—Antidote wanted against opium-smoking; Bad effects of
opium in Chinese Turkistan, 145.—Testimony of Forsyth, Bellew,
and Bell, 146.—Receipt of telegram; Letters from Leh, 147.—
Departure for India delayed, 148 . 135—148

CHAPTER XXXVII.

FROM KARGHALIK TO KHOTAN.

Route from Karghalik across a *chul*, 149.—Picket-stations to Haji
Langar, 150.—District of Guma; its shops, peaches, and river;
Journey to Moji, 151.—Exorcism and photography, 152-55.—From
Moji to Janghuia, 156.—Desolate route to Pialma; An ocean of
sand, 157.—Tabughaz Langar; its mosque and highwayman's
head; but few travellers; Arrival at Zawa Kurghan; its custom-
house and precautions, 159.—Palace of Habibulla; Naaki Mogul
and Mr Johnson, 160.—Route through cultivated fields to Ak-
Serai; Photographic and ornithological acquisitions, 162-63.—
Escorted into Khotan, 165 149—165

CHAPTER XXXVIII.

THE KINGDOM OF KHOTAN.

Two sources of Khotan history, 166.—Kusthana, capital of Li-yul;
Remusat's translation of Chinese records, 167.—Enlargement of
early Khotan, and its communication with China, 168.—Tchuen-
yuen on Khotan; its modern history, 169.—Exploration of Yurung-
kash and Tarim rivers, 171. Lob-Nor visited, 172.—Wild camels;
Route from Khotan to China, 173.—Prjevalsky's discovery of Altyn
Tagh, but failure to enter Tibet from Khotan; Failures of Pievtsoff
and Grombchevsky; Limits of Khotan, 174-75.—Deserts, buried
villages, and relics, 176.—A former excavator at Khotan, 177.—
Meteorology of Chinese Turkistan and Khotan, 178.—Author's
record, and statistics, 179. Khotan jade, and gold, 182.—Exchange of silver, 186 . 166—186

CHAPTER XXXIX.

OUR STAY IN KHOTAN.

Saluting a gun, and lodging in a *serai*, 187.—Call on the *Amban*, 188.—Visiting mosques and Chinese temple, 189.—Walk through the bazaar, 192.—Purchases, 193.—Carpets of silk, 194.—A beggars' breakfast-party, 195.—Difficulty of securing female portraits, and matrimony suggested as a means thereto, 197.—Not allowed to see prison; Cage for hanging by inches, 198.—The *Amban* of Yarkand; The two districts of Chinese Turkistan, 200.—Soldiers insufficiently armed, 201.—Ride round Khotan; its population, manners, and love of music, 202.—Musical instruments, 203.—Muhammadan feasts, 205.—Farewell to Khotan, 206   187—206

CHAPTER XL.

MUHAMMADANISM AND THE PRESENT RELIGIOUS CONDITION OF CHINESE TURKISTAN.

Muhammadan conquest of Bokhara and Ferghana, 207.—Samanid conquest of Turkistan, 210.—Introduction of Muhammadanism into Kashgar; Buddhist opposition, 211.—Muhammadanism in Khotan; Muhammadanism *versus* Christianity, 212.—Moral character of Muhammadan warriors, 214.—Origin and spread of Muhammadan influence, 215.—The Mullah kings and Yakub Khan; Present condition of people, 217.—Lack of education in Tarim valley, 219 .   .   207—220

CHAPTER XLI.

FROM KHOTAN TO KILIAN.

Departure from Khotan, 221.—Reading on horseback, 223.—Sunday at Chulak Langar, 224.—Return to Yarkand; Visit to *Amban*, and photography, 225.—Difficult bargaining for horses, 229.—A new obstacle, 230.—Prejudice against Afghans and danger from *dam*, 231.—Departure from Yarkand and outwitting contractors; a Hindu companion, 233.—Caravan at Besh-Aryk and commissions from natives, 235.—A trader at Bora, 236.—The village of Kilian, 238 221–238

CHAPTER XLII.

SOME REMARKS ON THE POLITICAL CONDITION OF CHINESE TURKISTAN.

Opinions and their value, 239.—Authors referred to and their opinions compared; Russian and English estimates of Chinese character; Prjevalsky and Seeland compared with Carey, Bell, and Younghusband, 240-43.—Author's experience concerning taxation, 246. —Turki estimates and complaints of Chinese, 247.—Russians reported as not in favour with Chinese, and why, 250.—Russians popular among Turkis, and examination of statements to the contrary, 251.—Author's own observations as to Russian popularity; Will Russia annex Chinese Turkistan? 253.—Easy of accomplishment; Difficulty of opposition from India, 254.— Powerless situation of Chinese soldiers; Author questioned at Peking, 255.—Insurrectionary elements in Chinese Turkistan, 256. —What are the English doing? 257.—British subjects and their trade restrictions, 259. —English popularity among Turkis, 261.— Author's reception favourable, 262 239–262

CHAPTER XLIII.

FROM KILIAN TO SHAHIDULA.

Purchases at Kilian, and departure, 263. Ascending among hills to Ak-Shor, 264.—Photographs of Afghans, Wakhis, and Haidar Haji, 265.—Sleeping in tent and bivouac, 266.— Kilian Pass surmounted on *yaks*, 268.--The *dam*, 269.—Shooting restrained, with specimens of birds secured, 270.—Descent from Kilian Pass to

Bostan, 272.- Delayed by horses, 275.—Passing the fort of Ali
Nazar, 276.—Valley of the Karakash and its Kirghese nomads,
277.—Keeping watch against robbers; Arrival at Shahidula,
278 .   263 278

CHAPTER XLIV.
CONCERNING GREAT TIBET.

Name of Tibet, 279.—Its boundaries, area, and orography, 280.—Great
Tibet; its surface, rivers, lakes, and provinces, 281.—Towns of
U-tsang, 282.—Roads, meteorology, and climate, 283.—The
northern plain, 284.—The inhabitants, and their religions, 286.
—Characteristics of Lamaism; Introduction of Buddhism, 287.—
Transmigration of lamas, 288.—Prayers and code, 289.—History
of Tibet, 291.—Notable kings, 292.—Ralpachen's patronage of
Buddhism, 293.—Rise of lamas to temporal power; The first
Dalai Lama, 294.—Tibet attacked by Mongols and Nepalese, but
finally subdued by China, 295.—Little Tibet; Contests for Ladak;
Hostilities with British on Sikkim frontier, 295-96.—Chinese
administration of Tibet through lamas, 297.   279—298

CHAPTER XLV.
OUR KNOWLEDGE OF, AND RELATIONS WITH, TIBET.

Early European travellers to Tibet; Odoric, 299.— Jesuit and Capuchin
missionaries, 300.—Van de Putte's journey through Lassa;
Exclusive policy initiated by the Chinese, 301.—Aid of Indian
Government invoked against the Bhotanese, 302.—Missions of
Bogle and Turner; Manning's journey, and Markham's *résumé*
of Tibetan travellers, 303.—Huc and Gabet, 304.—Tibetan
students; Dr Campbell and Dr Hooker, 305.—Later missionaries
at Leh and Bathang, 306.—Asiatic sources of information;
Chinese annals and surveys; Native explorers under Indian
Government, 307.—Journeys by Chandra Das and Ugyen Gyatso;
Gentlemen travellers, 309   299—312

CHAPTER XLVI.

A JOURNEY IN LITTLE TIBET.

Shahi Iula, 313.—Chang Chenmo and Karakoram routes, 314.—March to Suget, and attenuated atmosphere, 315.—Shah-Malik; Fear of robbers, 316.—Murder of Dalgleish; Karakoram Pass, 317.—Perils of route, 323.—From Chongeh Jilga to Danlatbeg Uldi, 324.—The Shyok, and glacier at Kumdan; Snowfall at Tschkum, 325.—Saser Pass, its glaciers and skeletons, 326.—Arrival at Tut Yailak, 327.—Sight from Karawal Dawan of Changlung, 328.—A broken-headed horse-leader, 329.—Nubra valley; New people and birds; Lodging at Panamik, 330.—Photographic endeavours, 331.—The *Sardar* of Taghar, 332.—Tibetan food and Luna worship, 333.—Ascent to Khardung, 334.—Tibetan characteristics, polyandry, and domestic affairs, 335.—Khardung Pass, and arrival at Leh, 336 . . . . 313—337

CHAPTER XLVII.

A MISSIONARY VIEW OF CHINESE TURKISTAN.

Author's attention drawn to Western Mongolia as a mission-field, 338.—An American Bible Society sending Scriptures from Shanghai, 339. Distribution among the Kalmuks, and at Aksu, 340.—Eager purchasers, 341.—Sales at Kashgar; Mullahs at Yarkand, 342.—Comparatively few Scriptures distributed; Lack of proper translations, 343.—Need for missionary effort, the good in Muhammadanism notwithstanding, 344.—More done for Chinese Turkistan by Buddhists and Muhammadans than by Christians; Feasibility of mission work; Muhammadanism shaky, and rulers neutral, 345.—Climate salubrious and provisions cheap, 346.—Routes through India, Russia, and China, 347. Remarks on furlough, female missionaries, and classes of workers, 348.—Suggested method of procedure, and first missionary centre, 349.—A *résumé* for the Church of Christ, 350 . . . . 338—350

CHAPTER XLVIII.

PLANS CONCERNING LASSA.

PAGES

Lassa, an appropriate *finale*, but difficult, 351. Stirred to activity by Mr Blackstone, 352.—Temporarily deterred, 354.- Help from the Archbishop of Canterbury, 355.—Assistance offered from Diplomatists, and Rev. Hudson Taylor, 356-57. Decision of *Manchester Guardian*; Books and MS. from Mr Markham, 358.—Commendatory letter from the Primate, and supplementary letter to the Dalai Lama, 359-60.—Tibetan translator unprocurable in Europe, 364.—Inquiries at Berlin and St Petersburg; Letters to Viceroy of India and Mr Redslob at Leh, 365.—Letters received at Kuldja, and abandonment of route through Kiria, 366.—Interview with Resident-designate at Lassa, 367.—Altered plans, 369 . . 351—370

CHAPTER XLIX.

THE JOURNEY HOMEWARDS.

Remainder of journey as concerned with Lassa ; Letter to Dalai Lama, 371.—Interview with Tibetan trader ; Entrance from Leh blocked ; Prospect of admission through Sikkim, 372.—Departure from Leh, 373.—The situation at Rawal Pindi ; Journey to Calcutta, 375.—Reception by Viceroy, 377.—Meeting with Chandra Das, and tidings of Mr James Hart ; Journey to Darjeeling and Kalimpong, 378.—Proposed sending of letter to Dalai Lama through Nepal, 380.—A further motive for attempting Nepal, 381. —Journey to Peking recommended ; Subsidiary schemes of usefulness, 382.—Journey to Khatmandu, 383.—Maharajah's unwillingness to forward letter, 385.—Interview with Nepalese Resident at Lassa, 386.- Distribution of Nepalese Scriptures, 387 . 371—388

CHAPTER L.

A SUCCESSFUL FAILURE.

No need for hurry to Peking ; Parting with Joseph, 389.—Official assistance at Calcutta ; Excursion from Rangoon to Mandalay,

391.—Singapore, Distribution of Scriptures in Annam, 392. Information, introductions, and experience collected at Hong Kong, Canton, and Foo Chow, 393. Interviews with Mr Stevenson at Shanghai, and Sir Robert Hart at Peking, 394-95.—Stay with British Ambassador, 396. Counsels of Sir Robert Hart and the Marquis Tseng; Preparations for return to India; Journey to Tientsin, 399.—No news at Tokio, Hong Kong, or Singapore, 400. —Concentration of efforts at Hyderabad and Bombay, 401. Journey *via* the Persian Gulf, and extinction of hope at Jerusalem, 402.—Intermediate work in Annam, Cambodia, the Philippines, and Quetta, 403.—Health impaired, 404. Visits to North African Missions, and prisons in Spain; What perhaps might have been accomplished in Lassa, and what was accomplished in the attempt, 405.—Summary of entire journey, 406.—Suggestions for the future, and lessons from the past, 407 . 389 - 408

APPENDICES

A. SOME OF THE SPECIMENS OF FAUNA COLLECTED BY DR. LANSDELL IN CENTRAL ASIA:—

	PAGE
Mammalia	409
Aves	410
Reptilia	415
Batrachia	415
Pisces	416
Coleoptera	417
Arachnida	418
Hymenoptera	418
Neuroptera	418
Orthoptera	418
Myriopoda	418
Lepidoptera	418

B. BIBLIOGRAPHY OF CHINESE CENTRAL ASIA:—

Preface	439
Chinese Central Asia (generally)	442
Manchuria	451
Mongolia	454
Turkistan (Chinese)	460
Sungaria	465
Tibet	466
Ladak	474
Maps Illustrative of Chinese Central Asia	476

ALPHABETICAL LIST OF AUTHORS . . . 477

GENERAL INDEX . . . 481

LIST OF ILLUSTRATIONS IN VOL. II.

	PAGE
MAP OF THE PAMIR REGIONS, WITH AUTHOR'S ROUTE *To face*	1
DIPTYCHUS LANSDELLI, A NEW FISH DISCOVERED BY THE AUTHOR IN LAKE ISSIK-KUL	33
A CHINESE "GUMBAZ," OR MORTUARY PILE, AT YENGI HISSAR	68
FRYING THROUGH A WINDOW	69
AT YARKAND—VIEW FROM THE ROOF OF THE HOUSE OF MR DALGLEISH	117
ZOEDA KHOJA, A TRAVELLING YARKANDI MOTHER	141
A MOTHER, AND TOKHTA KHAN, AN UNMARRIED GIRL, AT MOJI	155
THE APPROACH TO THE GOLDEN SHRINE AT KHOTAN	190
A DANCE OF DERVISHES	195
DERVISH SHAH YUSUF, OF KHOTAN	196
THE "KUDZA," OR CAGE FOR HANGING BY INCHES, WITH LICTORS	199
SOME OF THE MUSICAL INSTRUMENTS OF CENTRAL ASIA	204
AN UZBEG MUSICIAN	205
MUHAMMAD NAAKI MOGUL AND HIS DAUGHTER	222
THE "AMBAN" LEW AND HIS SUITE AT YARKAND	226
CLEARING THE CROWD AT THE OUTER ENTRANCE TO GOVERNMENT HOUSE AT YARKAND	228
JOSEPH MOUNTED, AND MUHAMMAD RAPHI, A WAKHAN YAK-OWNER	273
TRIN-LE-DOR-JE, A SHUSHOG, OR MINOR INCARNATION OF BUDDHA	290
SIMBOOTI, OUR HOSTESS AT PANAMIK	331
CROSSING THE MOUNTAINS IN LITTLE TIBET	336
MAP OF DR LANSDELL'S THREE JOURNEYS IN ASIA *At the end*	

OBSERVANDA.

In proper names the letters should be pronounced as follows:—
a as in f*a*ther; *e* as in th*e*re; *i* as in rav*i*ne; *o* as in g*o*; *u* as in l*u*nar; and the diphthongs *ai* and *ei* as *i* in pr*i*de.

The consonants are pronounced as in English, save that *tch* is guttural, as *ch* in the Scotch lo*ch*.

Unless otherwise stated:—

English weights and measures are to be understood.

Degrees of temperature are expressed according to the scale of Fahrenheit.

The Chinese *yamb* (50 *taels*) is reckoned at £11 5s. 0d. English.
", *tael*, *liang*, or *ser* of silver is reckoned at 4s. 6d. ,,
", *cash* ,, $\frac{1}{10}$d. ,,
", *catty* 1$\frac{1}{4}$ lb. ,,
", *jing* 1$\frac{1}{4}$ lb. ,,
", *li* (1825·25 English feet) $\frac{1}{3}$ mile
The Turkish *tenga* 2$\frac{1}{2}$d.
", *pul* $\frac{1}{12}$d. ,,
The Russian *rouble* (paper) ,, 2s. ..
", *verst* .. $\frac{2}{3}$ mile ..
", *pound* 14·43 oz. ,,
", *pood* 36 lbs. ,,
The Indian *rupee* 1s. 6d.

CHINESE CENTRAL ASIA:

A RIDE TO LITTLE TIBET.

CHAPTER XXVIII.

THE PAMIRS AND THE REGIONS ADJOINING.

Amphitheatre of mountains, crossed from Kashgar by four communications, 1.—Northern route through Artish, over Turgat Pass by Chadir-Kul and Narin, to Vierny, 3.—North-western route by valley of Kizil-su and Terek Pass to Osh, 5.—The Pamir; its name, boundaries, surface, peaks, localities, and rivers, 9. Pamir lakes, and political negotiations connected therewith, 11. —Pamir climate, and nomad inhabitants, 13.—Its historical geography, and travellers thereon, 16. Importance of Russian explorations, 17.—Recent travellers, and a political dispute, 19.

AS we approached Kashgar from the east there lay before us a remarkable amphitheatre of mountains—to the right the Tian Shan, to the left the Kuen Lun, and in front the Pamir. Over these stupendous masses go four principal routes radiating from Kashgar—north to Semirechia, north-west to Ferghana, south-west to Afghanistan, and south to Ladak. Each of these interested me, for, having got into a *cul-de-sac*, it was necessary to consider how best to get out.

The northern route measures on the map, in a direct line, 270 miles to Vierny, but by the road not less than

600 miles, over at least four mountain ranges rising to 13,000 feet. Members of the Forsyth expedition explored this road as far as Chadir-Kul, and the whole of it had been recently traversed by Dr Seeland when I met him, and received a translation of his notes from M. Gourdet. Something, then, should be said of this northern route.

Starting from Kashgar, the first 90 miles is on Chinese territory, the traveller riding through the village of Bezak. About ten miles beyond Bezak is Teshik-tash—the most advanced post held by Chinese soldiers in this direction.

Beyond Teshik-tash the Artish valley is left behind, and the route continues by that of the Toyan, the banks of which are, in some places, 200 feet high, and cut by rivulets into remarkable artificial-looking pillars and turrets. Chung Terek, or "Big Poplars," is the next station—a picturesque spot in a valley dotted with Kirghese tents, where grazing is favourable, and there are also patches of cultivated land.

From Chung Terek the road continues along the Toyan stream to the Mirza and Chakmak forts in a narrow gorge, and protected by inaccessible rocks, forming walls of defence. The forts were said to have been designed and built by the eldest son of Yakub Khan, in whose time they were garrisoned, so that Gordon and his party were comfortably lodged at Chakmak on their third night from Kashgar. Gordon speaks of these forts as "carefully constructed works that could give a great deal of trouble to an enemy advancing from the north." Twelve years later, Seeland, passing Chakmak, speaks of it as "a little Sart fortress, now abandoned, and never of much importance, though well situated."

About ten miles beyond Chakmak the Toyan is joined, at Gulja-bashi, by the Suok stream, flowing from a narrow Pass of that name not fit for horses, whilst the route which continues 30 miles from Gulja-bashi to the top of the Terek range at the Turgat Pass is used by laden camels throughout the year.

Between Kashgar and the Turgat Pass (12,760 feet) is a rise of nearly 9,000 feet, or about 100 feet per mile. Dr Stoliczka mentions his passing over three ranges geologically distinct—namely, the Artish, Koktan, and Terek. The first, which is nearest the Kashgar plain, is entirely composed of late Tertiary deposits. The second consists partly of basaltic and late Tertiary rocks in the northern, and older rocks in the southern, portions; whilst the third and northernmost range consists of old sedimentary rocks. Dr Stoliczka mentions also between Gulja-bashi and the Turgat Pass an interesting spot where the river banks, rising perpendicularly some hundreds of feet, bear evidence of being the crater of an extinct volcano.

At the top of the Pass, west of the road, is a small pyramid of stones, indicating, Dr Seeland says, the frontier between China and Russia. Three miles to the north there bursts suddenly on the traveller's view the lake called Chadir-Kul, about 14 miles from east to west, with an average breadth of six miles, and lying at a height (thrice determined by M. Petrovsky) of 11,570 feet. It is of considerable depth, and has no visible outlet, but rises with the melting of the snow and falls in the dry season, which may help to reconcile statements of the water being brackish, according to Gordon, and sweet, according to Seeland one passing in January, the other in September.

Beyond the lake, northwards, is quite a forest of

peaks, extending from west to east; and on the plateau, stretching east from the lake and forming the Aksai tableland, rises the Aksai stream, which flows towards Lob-Nor, whilst about equidistant from Chadir-Kul westwards are the head waters of the Arfa river, that finds its way to the Sea of Aral.

About 90 miles from the Turgat Pass is the Russian outpost and fort of Narin, the route to which, after passing the eastern end of Chadir-Kul, continues over the Tash-Rabat Pass (12,930 feet) and along the Karakain stream. On the northern side of this Pass is a depression, 11,000 feet high with mountains on three sides, of weird and deserted appearance, wherein is an archæological curiosity. It consists of what are thought to be the ruins of a Nestorian monastery, and will be alluded to hereafter. Seeland also observes that along the Karakain are found several *kurgans*, or mortuary hillocks, attributed to the Kalmuks, who once inhabited the region.

Kirghese tombs are also numerous, and their tents are sometimes met with; but it would appear from Seeland's narrative, as well as from what M. Petrovsky told me, that the traveller between Kashgar and Narin needs to have arrangements made for him beforehand among the Kirghese, on both Russian and Chinese soil, whereby he may be lodged nightly. Otherwise, he must carry tent, fuel, and equipment.

Narin takes its name from the river on which it is situated. Its fort consists of a low-walled inclosure, a diminutive rampart, a ditch, and a barrack. It contains a hundred infantry, half as many Cossacks, and a few artillery—a small affair among Europeans, but sufficiently terrible to Asiatics. Besides the fort there is a village built in Russian style, with 500 traders.

A day's march south of Narin is the village of Atbashi, with 80 houses inhabited by Sarts and Tatars, who cultivate the fruitful valley with oats, wheat, and lucerne, and trade with the Kirghese.

From Narin northwards a poor carriage road, with picket post-stations and horses, crosses the Dolun Pass, and proceeds along the bed of the Kochkur to Kutemaldi, whence I followed it to Vierny.

It was by this route my rouble and rupee notes had been forwarded by post to Narin to Colonel Larionoff, the local potentate, whence he kindly sent them on by Cossacks, either by the route just described as passing Chadir-Kul, or possibly by the almost parallel route over the Bogashta Pass. This route crosses the Terek range by the Terekti Pass, about 30 miles east of the Turgat. But I left to Mr Herbert Jones the pleasure of being the first Englishman to cover the route throughout, and he has since read a paper concerning it before the Society of Arts.

I had asked, and obtained permission, in case of need, to cross by what is called the Terek-davan route from Kashgar into Ferghana—a route which, so far as I know, no Englishman had then travelled. Of this the only detailed information within reach is that of Kuropatkin, who passed over it in 1876. Besides this, on meeting Captain Grombchevsky at St Petersburg and M. Petrovsky at Kashgar, I learned from both sundry particulars, to the following effect:—

From the fortress of Kashgar up the valley of the Kizil-su to the Russian frontier post at Irkeshtam is said to be 133 miles. On the first day's journey the gardens of Kashgar, and corn-fields surrounding it, become less numerous towards the village of Sarman, and at Langar the cultivated district ends; after which, at a distance of 29 miles from Kashgar, Min-Yul is reached, where I was recommended, if I made the journey, to sleep the first night. Min-Yul rejoices in a fort consisting of a thin quadrangular wall about 80 yards square, with flanking towers; also in a few gardens and fields. Of grazing or fuel there are none, and for these the traveller has to look to the neighbouring Kirghese of the Chun-bagish tribe.

The second stage, of 20 miles, is to the post of Kan-jugan, signifying "washed in blood," and traditionally said to have witnessed a great fight between the Mongols and Turks. The fort consists of a four-sided wall with loopholes, and on the way to it is passed a mullah's hut or small monastery.

On the third day is reached, after 32 miles, Aksalar, the lack of ordinary fuel along the route being, in some measure, supplied by coal, which is worked a few miles from Kurgashin-Kani. In one portion of this stage the road winds through a passage between vertical walls of compact clay, several hundred feet high, on a ledge from six to fifteen paces wide. In some places the walls overhang the road, which is twice continued by steps, and twice leaves the ledge altogether, on account of its impracticability.

The Salar fort stands in the middle of the valley, and is insignificant; but the post has the advantage of fuel and timber in the neighbouring valleys, though in autumn the grazing is insufficient for the most inconsiderable detachment.

From Aksalar the road ascends to the small fort of Mashrut by a narrow passage between vertical walls, the incline being so long and so steep that cannon could be brought there only by men. The clay soil, too, after trifling rain becomes so slippery as to render it advisable for horsemen to walk. In a defensive wall, run out from the fort, are gates less than 60 paces distant, through which the traveller must pass, though, as the fort is commanded by neighbouring heights, it could be easily taken by artillery.

Farther on, the road becomes more or less blocked with large masses of conglomerate. The latter portion of this day's stage is over soft ground overgrown with thorn, the road skirting the Kizil-su river. For a while it passes along a cornice, which in one place descends to the stream, where the bank is revetted with logs, and in another it overhangs the river and is guarded by a gate.

In this way Ulugchat is reached at 26 miles from Aksalar, and an altitude of 7,300 feet above the sea, the fort being on low ground and surrounded by commanding heights. It is the one station on the route where good water, grazing, and fuel are plentiful. In Yakub Khan's time it was garrisoned by 200 men; and at St Petersburg I was given to understand that I should find at Ulugchat an *amban* named Kwang.

Leaving this last Chinese fort, a fifth day's march, of 25 miles, brings the traveller, beyond a small post called Yegin, to Irkeshtam, the first Russian picket, which is guarded by a few Cossacks, whom I hoped to propitiate by presenting my passport and the Governor-General's card, which he had given me in case I desired to pass this way.

The traveller has now reached Russian territory; but he is not yet in a land flowing with milk and honey. He will yet need three days to cover the 62 miles to Gulcha, over the Terek Pass (13,000 feet) and through Sufi-Kurgan, opposite each of which points in my memoranda stands the note "nothing to be had."

The Pass, however, is not difficult in summer, and the route generally from Irkeshtam to Gulcha, if not quite fit for wheel traffic, could easily be made so; but in winter the snow has sometimes to be trampled down by *yaks*, and the help of the Kirghese secured to effect a passage. From Gulcha it is 49 miles to Osh, where begin postal and telegraphic communication.

When, therefore, the Governor-General directed Colonel Deubner that letters and telegrams sent for me to Osh were to be forwarded, it meant sending them by messenger about 250 miles to Kashgar; and, as if that were not enough, M. Petrovsky sent the one telegram I received 180 miles farther to Karghalik, or no less than 430 miles beyond the postal radius, and that without charge of any kind!

As another example of these acts of courtesy, it may be added that a postcard sent to Mr Littledale arrived in Ferghana after he had left for the Pamirs, whereupon, he tells me, this trifling communication was sent after him by messenger more than 200 miles! There may be other countries that would do more for a couple of passing travellers, but, if there are, I do not know them.

The reader has now been conducted up the valley of the Kizil-su to Irkeshtam, west of which the first Pass to be crossed is the Ten-murun (11,200 feet). East and west of this Pass rise two streams with their head waters only three miles apart on the map. One is the Kizil-su, flowing down to Kashgar; the other is the Kara-su, which flows into another Kizil-su passing west through the Alai valley, and so becoming the Surkhab or Waksh before it joins the Oxus.

Here, then, in a depression consisting of the valleys of these two streams, we have a well-defined boundary between the Pamir system on the south and the Tian Shan system northwards, the term "Tian Shan" being used generically for the whole mass north of the Kizil-su valleys up to the range of Tarbagatai ; the next system northward being the Altai.

We come now to the Pamirs, which have been variously designated the "heart" and "centre" of Asia, the orographical knot whence the mountains of high Asia spread like network towards India, China, and Turkistan. The Chinese, as they approached the heights from the east, called them Tsung-ling, or "Onion" Mountains ; whereas, approaching from the west, the people of Badakshan called them "Bam-i-duniah" ("the roof of the world"). Marco Polo, however, made known this region to Europe, saying, "The Plain is called Pamier."

This "Pamir" is nearly surrounded by a horseshoe of mountain ranges, with the open end westwards, and is bounded north and south respectively by the Tian Shan and Hindu Kush mountains, and on the west and east by Afghanistan and Chinese Turkistan. Kostenko gives its dimensions as 200 miles from north to south, and 170 from west to east; whilst Réclus estimates the area at 30,000 square miles—that is, about the size of Bavaria or Sardinia.

The plateau of the Pamir lies from 12,000 to 14,000 feet above the sea, and is crossed in various directions by ranges with a snow-line of 16,000 feet. The mountains, consisting of soft strata (principally mica and slate-schists), do not, as a rule, rise more than 3,000 or 4,000 feet above the adjoining valleys, so that the passes are relatively low and easily accessible. The roads, too, of the Pamir generally are very practicable. The valleys are not usually more than two miles wide, and have no defined direction, but deepen westwards where occupied by the Upper Oxus.

In the ranges bordering the Pamir on the north, east, and south are peaks rising to 10,000 feet above the plateau. From the Trans-Alai chain on the north, sometimes called the Great Alai, tower up the Kaufmann peak, 22,800 feet, and the triple-topped Gurumdy, 20,300 feet.

Again, from the mountains on the eastern verge, which we could see from Kashgar, and which Major Cumberland, after crossing them, calls, in his letters to *Land and Water*, the Tagharma Mustagh range, there rises Mustagh-Ata, "the father of ice-mountains," to an altitude of 25,800 feet; and this mass, Réclus says, is continued towards the south-east by the Chichiklik, itself about 20,000 feet high. There are also several high peaks in the Hindu Kush, but not so on the Pamir itself; nor is the western border so clearly defined as the others. Martin St Vivien would place it on a meridian running north from Sarhad just above the highest cultivated valleys of Wakhan, Shignan, Roshan, and Karategin.

Thus far we have spoken of the plateau generally as "the Pamir"; but its various plains, depressions, and parts have local names (artificial and colloquial, however, rather than geographical) to the number of at least eight. Thus, near Lakes Kara-Kul and Ran-Kul are the Khargosh (or Hare) and the Ran-Kul Pamirs; south-west of these are the Sares and Alichur Pamirs; and near the latter the Yashil Pamir. South-east of the Alichur are the Great and Little Pamirs; and in the Sarikol district, the Taghdumbash Pamir.

Concerning the hydrography of the Pamirs, the northern slopes of the Tian Shan drain into the Syr, and the southern slopes of the Hindu Kush form the watershed of the Indus, whilst through the various Pamirs drain a number of streams east to the Tarim and west to the Oxus. The general slope of the land is towards the west and south-west, and the water-parting lies much nearer to the Tarim basin than to that of the Aralo-Caspian. Gordon places it at the Neza-tash range, and its continuation northwards.

On the Pamirs are several lakes. The largest, Great Kara-Kul, in the north, is beautifully situated amidst a panorama of snow mountains. It appears now to have no outlet. Other lakes are the Little Kara-Kul, Ran-Kul, and Yashil-Kul. Greater interest attaches, however, to two lakes in the south : one on the Great Pamir, variously called Siri-Kul, Sari-Kul, and Lake Victoria ; and a smaller lake situated on the Little Pamir, called Oi-Kul and Gaz-Kul (that is, Goose Lake), and by the Kirghese Chakmak-Kul, under which name it is marked on Bolsheff's map.

When Wood, in 1838, followed a Pamir stream up to its source from the Siri-Kul, it was assumed, in the absence of fuller information, that he had discovered the principal source of the Oxus, and he was glorified accordingly. Moreover, the map thus amended became in 1873 the basis of a diplomatic arrangement between the English and Russian governments, the Upper Oxus from Siri-Kul to Khoja-Saleh being recognised as the boundary to be scrupulously respected by both Powers.

A visit to the Pamirs, however, by some of the Forsyth expedition in the following year brought to our knowledge the small Goose Lake of the Lesser Pamir, from the eastern end of which flows the river Aksu. The stream takes at first a north-easterly direction, and then flows due north along the Ak-tash valley, turns westwards across the Sares Pamir, changing its name to the Murghab, and then runs into the Panjah at Kila-Wamar, at a distance from its source of 253 miles.

On the other hand, a compass measurement (at an opening representing ten miles) from the Kila-Wamar up the Panjah and Pamir rivers to Siri-Kul, gives a length of 220 miles only. Hence Trotter and Kostenko argue that the principal source of the Oxus is the Aksu, whence perhaps the Oxus derives its name. In this case, however, it should be noticed that the Aksu has a close competitor as regards length in the river of Wakhan, which all but touches the western end of the Goose Lake, and runs to Kila-Wamar as the Panjah, a distance of 245 miles.

Other two rivers flowing from the Pamirs westward into the Oxus in a direction parallel to the Murghab, and about equidistant from it, are the Wanj on the north and the Suchan or Ghund on the south. These three rivers, the Wanj, Murghab, and Suchan respectively, may be said to water the western districts of the Pamir—namely, Darwaz, Roshan, and Shignan. Again, the northern skirts of the Pamir are watered by the Kizil-su, which flows through Karategin, and which, lower, becomes the Waksh. On the southern skirts of the Pamir is the upper stream of the Panjah, which waters Wakhan.

Of the foregoing districts, Karategin and Darwaz

Gordon mentions also that at less than half a mile from the head of the Goose Lake was observed a watercourse leading west down the valley, choked with ice and snow, and suggesting that the lake had once discharged in this direction, but that this outlet had been closed by *débris*, and another formed more to the east, where the shores are low and the valley unconfined.

belong to Bokhara ; Wakhan to Afghanistan ; and
the district of Sarikol, farther east, to China ; whilst
Roshan and Shignan, if they acknowledge any master,
are now said to be Afghan, though, according to Gordon,
they used formerly to receive a yearly payment from
the Chinese, similar to that made to Sarikol, Kunjut,
and Wakhan, for the protection of frontier and routes.

If now we turn to the eastern slope of the Pamir, we
have in the north another Kizil-su and the Markan-su
running down to Kashgar. Immediately south of
these are two streams receiving the eastern drainage
of the mountains of Sarikol and forming the Gez or
Yaman-yar, which is lost in the plains near Yapchan,
whilst from the Neza-tash commences a stream, flowing eastward, which is afterwards joined by affluents
from the mountains of Kunjut (one of which is called
the Tung), and becomes the river of Yarkand.

To these hydrographical features should be added
that Gordon found hot, sulphurous springs on the
banks of the Panjah 35 miles below Sarhad, and hot
springs also at Isligh between the Siri-Kul and the
Ak-tash valley.

The climate of the Pamirs is terribly severe, and the
temperature reaches extraordinary extremes. Thus, in
spring 1888, M. Bonvalot records that on March 13th
at 9 a.m. the thermometer indicated in the sun 75°,
but in the shade was 10° below freezing point ; at
2 p.m. it was in the sun nearly 100°, but 3° below
freezing in the shade ; at 6 o'clock there were 18° of
frost ; and at 9.20 p.m. the mercury had sunk several
degrees below zero. In the summer, instead of rain,
there falls granular snow, and during the nights even
of August, between the Kizilyart and Lake Kara-Kul,
Mr Littledale tells me, the small streams, four or five

inches deep, were frozen to solid ice. Towards the end of this month the winter snow begins to fall, and lasts till May.

Again, the gales from the north-east are so terrific that, in some places, the very rocks are worn by the sands beating incessantly against them. Hence most travellers complain that "the roof of the world" is extremely windy, and some have complained of the rarefaction of the air. Kostenko thinks the latter has been in some cases exaggerated, and Mr Littledale calls attention to the fact that, whereas neither he nor Mrs Littledale, my old servant Joseph, who accompanied them, nor the second interpreter, were sick, yet several of the Kirghese suffered, one man nearly all the time, owing, as they said, to the elevation.

After the foregoing remarks it will be anticipated that the Pamirs are uninhabited in winter. In summer they are frequented by nomads, chiefly Kirghese, who come up from the surrounding slopes to pasture their cattle. The only buildings visible are stone erections indicating the sites of old camping grounds, and here and there are tombs of *batyrs*, or braves, decked with fluttering rags and sheep's horns, the latter in some parts of the Pamir being strewed about by scores, not to say hundreds. On the highest ground there are, of course, no trees, and the fuel to be had is the root of a species of lavender, and *kisiak*, or the droppings of animals. Yet, in some places, up to 13,000 feet, the grass is so thick and nutritious as amply to confirm Marco Polo's statement that a lean hack may grow fat upon it in ten days. Also Bonvalot mentions *tchibaque*, a grass of which horses are fond, and which serves likewise for fuel.

Beside the Kirghese may be mentioned a certain

number of refugees from surrounding districts, who, according to M. Bonvalot, having committed murder or other crimes, escape to the Pamirs and hide during winter in the remote corners of the Ak-tash valley. When summer arrives, bringing with it the Chinese agents from one direction and the Kunjutes from another, those who are most "wanted" make for the heights of the Alichur, or centre of the "roof of the world," like sheep who live as much as they can out of the range of guns, and climb higher as the snow melts.

To dwell fully upon the inhabitants of the slopes of the Pamir would take us too far beyond Chinese Central Asia. Moreover, I have spoken of Galtchas, Tajiks, etc., as well as to some extent of the Pamirs, in *Russian Central Asia*. Much of the anthropological information there given was drawn from M. Ujfalvy, who has since visited and studied the people on the southern slopes of the Hindu Kush.

M. Ujfalvy points out, as others have done, sundry remains among these hill tribes of Zoroastrianism,—such as the Galtcha's unwillingness to blow out a light; the use of light and fire on certain social, medical, and religious occasions, as well as the observance of the feast of *taleni*, and dancing round fires by torchlight; and, lastly, the unwillingness to give a dog hot food. The foregoing facts, together with the predominance

* M. Van den Gheyn, in his admirable pamphlet *Le Plateau de Pamir*, summarising M. Ujfalvy's remarks, points out that the inhabitants surrounding the Pamir may be divided into three principal groups—namely, Aryans, Turkis, and Mongols. On the north are the Aryans called Galtchas, Tajiks, and Iranians generally, and on the south Aryans whom Ujfalvy would call Hindus of the Hindu Kush. On the north-east and east are the Kirghese, whilst on the south the Mongol element is represented by the people of Ladak and Dardistan. Of these last Dr Leitner has written in his *Languages and Races of Dardistan*.

of Aryan dialects among the languages spoken, seem to point, M. Ujfalvy thinks, to an Aryan or Iranian origin of the Pamir tribes.

We come now to the historical geography of the Pamir, and the travellers and explorers who have made it known to us. Some have thought that Sarikol may be a survival of Serica, whence came the silk in ancient times. More definitely, we have first the Buddhist pilgrims, Hwui Seng and Sung Yun, in 518, who tell us that the highlands of the Tsung-ling were commonly said to be midway between heaven and earth. Hiuen Tsiang, 120 years later, speaks of the sudden gusts of wind, and snowdrifts never ceasing winter or summer, of the frozen soil and the paucity of plants.

After this we hear nothing for six centuries, and then comes Marco Polo, but no other European for upwards of 300 years, till Benedict Goes, with great difficulty and loss of animals, crossed the plateau from Cabul to Yarkand. Once more follows a silence of more than two centuries, when Lieutenant Wood, in depth of winter 1838, pushed up to the Pamirs from Badakshan.

In 1860 the Government of India began to employ natives, partially trained in surveying, to travel in disguise through their border countries for the purpose of exploring. To these men largely belongs the honour of first making known to us scientifically the communications between India, the Pamir, and Chinese and Afghan Turkistan.

After these, Hayward, having made his way, in 1868, as did Shaw, from Ladak to Yarkand, pushed up to the south-east portion of the Pamir, discovering the sources of the Yarkand river and the Mustagh-Ata peak; but, in attempting to explore Wakhan, he was murdered near Darkot. Réclus mentions a Greek named Potagos as having, in 1871, crossed the Pamirs from Badakshan to Kashgar. In 1874 followed the Forsyth expedition, when Gordon, Trotter, and Biddulph penetrated to Kila Panj, the capital of Wakhan, examined the passes leading over the Hindu Kush, and returned past Lake Victoria and through the Great and Little Pamirs, thus completing, roughly, our knowledge of the south portion of the plateau.

Meanwhile, the Russians had been gradually approaching from the north, and the taking of Samarkand, in 1869, threw open to them the basins of the Oxus and Jaxartes. Quickly, Fedchenko, accompanied by his courageous and scientific wife, rushed in 1871 to the exploration of Ferghana, climbed its southern mountains, crossed into the Alai, or paradise of the Kirghese, and were the first Europeans to bring us a scientific account of the Trans-Alai chain which abuts on the Pamir on the north.

It was reserved, however, for Kostenko to be the first Russian author to set foot on the Pamirs, and, in 1876, he not only crossed the Alai, but pushed on to Lake Kara-Kul, and the Kizilyart plain, to within about 60 miles of the parts visited by members of the Forsyth mission. Kostenko was followed in 1877 and 1878 by scientific expeditions under Severtsoff, who corrected many cartographical errors respecting the Pamirs, especially in the central and eastern portions. To the foregoing names should be added that of Oshanin, who, in 1878, visited Karategin. In the following year the same district was visited by the geologist Mushketoff, and in 1881 Dr Regel explored Darwaz, and added considerably to our knowledge of the flora of these regions.

The last Russian traveller whom we need mention is Captain Grombchevsky, who, in the autumn of 1888, proceeded from Marghilan to the Alai by the Daraut Kurgan, continued up the Kizil-su and south to Ran-Kul, then along the Aksu to the west of the Chakmak-Kul. Thence he proceeded to the capital of Kunjut, discovering a pass over which a waggon might cross into Hunza, and returned northward to Kurgan-i-Ujadbai, and then south-east to Gil, falling short of Younghusband's route over the Muz-Tag by only about 13 miles. Compelled to turn back through lack of resources, he reached the Kizilyart plain, and again turned south-east to the Raskem, one of the affluents of the Yarkand river, after which he directed his steps towards the north, ascending on the way the Mustagh-Ata, and descending thence by the Gez, or Gioz valley to Kashgar, the first European I have heard of to reach it by this route.

Thus the credit of exploring and making known to the scientific world the northern, central, north-eastern, and north-western districts of the Pamir belongs exclusively to the Russians. Meanwhile, the English, since the Forsyth expedition, have been ostensibly doing but little. On the re-conquest of the Tarim valley by the Chinese, Mr Dalgleish, who was in the country at the time, is said (in *L'Exploration*, 30 *Mai*, 1883) to have persuaded the Chinese governor to send a garrison to the Sarikol district, and there set up afresh the Chinese standard; and the correctness of this statement is confirmed to me by one who had it more than once from the lips of Dalgleish himself.

In 1885-6, at the time of the Afghan frontier delimitation, Mr Ney Elias passed from Chinese Turkistan to Badakshan. Later, in the spring of

1888, Messrs Bonvalot, Capus, and Pepin crossed the Pamir, simply as travellers, from north to south, entering from Ferghana by the Taldik Pass, and crossing the Hindu Kush by the Baroghil depression—the first Europeans thus to pass from Russian territory into India.

A few months later Mr St George Littledale, already mentioned, bent on shooting wild sheep, and accompanied by Mrs Littledale, made his summer excursion to the Pamirs, penetrating from Osh to Kara-Kul, and returning the same way. In 1890 they went again to Kara-Kul, continued south to the Alichur Pamir at Burzila-Jai, which he mentions as the China-Afghan frontier in this direction; and then to the Great and Little Pamirs, beyond which they continued over the difficult Darkot Pass to Yasin and Gilghit—certainly one of the grandest journeys ever performed by a lady. They met, on this second journey, Major Cumberland crossing from Kashgar to Ferghana.

Lastly, mention should be made of Captain Younghusband, who, during his stay at Kashgar, in the winter of 1890-91, made some excursions to the Pamirs. On one of these occasions he had joined a party of Russian soldiers, said to have been out on a shooting expedition for the sake of practice as marksmen, with whom he had retired to rest in the vicinity of Gumbaz-Bozai. Thereupon he was told that he must turn back, which he did after protesting that he was not on Russian soil.

CHAPTER XXIX.

ON SUNDRIES ZOOLOGICAL; OR SHOOTING, FISHING, AND BUTTERFLY-CATCHING.

Animals collected for science, 21.—Lessons in Taxidermy: Naturalists' instruments, 22.—Visit to zoological museums; Professor Zograf, Madame Fedchenko, and M. Oshanin, 24.—Acquaintances at Tashkend, and rifle practice, 26.—Central Asian fauna: Severtsoff's and Fedchenko's discoveries on the Tian Shan and Pamirs; English naturalists collecting from the south, 27.—Discoveries of Prjevalsky, Grum-Grjimailo, and Alphéraky in Sungaria and Mongolia, 28.—Littledale's capture of wild sheep, 29.—Author's collections; his new fish, *Diptychus Lansdelli*, 32.—Collecting at Ilisk, 34.—Specimens from Kuldja despatched by post; Paucity of animals between Kuldja and Aksu, 35.—Further captures at Kashgar, 36.

LET me begin this chapter with the observation that I am no sportsman. Nor am I a sportsman's son. My father once, in the holidays, put a gun into my hands, thinking to please me, and I knocked over half-a-dozen sparrows; whereupon conscience inquired: "What business have you to do that? Those little creatures have done you no harm, and, now they are killed, they are not to you of the slightest use. Why, then, shoot them?" My conscience, in those days, was young and tender, and gained a hearing, with the result that I laid the gun aside, breaking my resolution once, I fear, in succeeding holidays; but after that, deeming it blameworthy to kill when it served no useful or scientific end, I touched nothing of the kind for a quarter of a century.

But now the case was different. Compiling lists of fauna in *Russian Central Asia* brought me into contact with naturalists, especially at the British Museum, who, when they heard of an intended journey to Chinese Turkistan, pointed out that it was a region little known to science; that the museums of Europe had few specimens therefrom—those of England almost none —and that, accordingly, I might be of real use in collecting almost every kind of fauna.

When, moreover, Dr Günther heard that there was a possibility of my travelling over the mountains frequented by Ovis Poli, of which at that time we had not one perfect specimen in our national collection, and of passing near the deserts inhabited by the wild horse and camel, his eyes fairly glistened; and he intimated that, if only a skin of the wild camel could be secured, it would be a greater prize than all else.

Much of this proved like the aerial castle-building of the schoolboy who goes out to catch trout and comes home with minnows; but, my attention having been drawn to the subject, it looked reasonable, and feasible too, that something should be attempted. At that date I was looking forward to crawling across Asia by caravan at the rate of 20 miles a day, which seemed to promise opportunity for leaving the track in pursuit of game, to say nothing of remaining stationary all the winter with little to do.

Moreover, there promised to be frequent occasions when having a battery in camp would make just the difference whether or not a pheasant, partridge, or other game adorned our breakfast-table, instead of tinned meat, Kirghese mutton, "the everlasting fowl," or, possibly, no meat at all.

I gave heed, therefore, to the wise men of Kensington, and, with a wild sheep in my eye, went to Mr Gerrard, Jun., of Camden Town, to witness the skinning of a wolf, taking Joseph with me, that this accomplishment might be added to our neglected education, as also the skinning of birds and fish.

I cannot say that these new studies attracted me, though, after looking on, and taking notes, I fancied I knew a little how things ought to be done; but the mental comment made upon the subject was, that if the collections of Europe waited for skins prepared by me, I feared they might be in expectation rather a long time. Fortunately, however, Joseph took to the business kindly. It was the only thing just then he could do for me; and after practising some few times at the workshops, Mr Gerrard reported well of his aptitude, and thus a foundation was laid.

Next, Gerrard packed for me a box of taxidermical instruments: a saw, butchers' knives, skinning-powder, alum, and arsenical soap, for mammals; bird-scissors, brain-spoons, forceps, pliers, wadding, needles, thread, and stuffing-irons, for ornithological work; also cyanide bottles, tweezers, test-tubes, and butterfly-nets for entomological captures, as Mr Bethune-Baker of Edgbaston had asked me to procure, if possible, some specimens of *lepidoptera*. Added to the foregoing were sundry instructions as to packing specimens, which were to be sent home from time to time to Gerrard.

But as yet I had no battery. How many of my friends, thought I, have guns and rifles enough and to spare, whilst I possess nothing of the kind! So, calling to say "Good-bye" to Mr Brankston of Blackheath, an octogenarian friend and former parishioner, it suddenly dawned upon me that he was not contemplating more partridge-shooting, and I asked him to be good enough to show cause why he should not lend me his gun. The gun was sent for, and then, taking the companion of earlier years out of its case, he playfully shook his head, saying, "I little thought my gun would ever come to that, but—there it is."

I next thought it necessary to advise my friend that I was going among gentry who had a great weakness for English firearms; that a previous traveller had been murdered, and I possibly might be robbed, in which case I hoped that, "for the good of the cause," he would not mind taking the risk. To this also he consented, with the final exhortation that if thus reduced to extremities I might sell the gun for £40 to help me along.

Thus I found myself the temporary possessor of a capital double-barrelled pin-fire breech-loader—an addition to my baggage I had never before carried, and which was soon found to be both costly, and more troublesome too, than the rest of one's kit.

First, the steamer people would not carry loaded cartridges. They looked suspiciously even at empty ones, because capped; and machines had to be bought for re-capping and re-filling. Next, the guard at the Prussian frontier seemed doubtful whether to report or not my carrying firearms, because I was to stay for a day in Berlin; and, thirdly, the question arose how to avoid carrying ammunition through Russia, and how far on my way one could be sure of procuring good powder and shot. Some thought that a stock had better be taken from the Russian capital; but experience proved that, with the exception perhaps of "dust shot," these needed not to be purchased west of Tashkend. Further, I was fortunate enough to meet a friend in St Petersburg who gave me a Berdan rifle as supplied to the Russian cavalry.

I visited there the Zoological Museum for a few words with Dr Strauch, the curator, and asked what animals it was most important to collect. M. Pleske showed me some of the large mammals brought home by Prjevalsky from regions adjacent to those whither I was going. Among them was the wild horse, of which, it appeared, one specimen only had been taken. Again, the white-clawed bear was pointed out as peculiar, and the light wolves of Tibet were said to be rare; whilst a magnificent specimen was shown of the wild *yak*, of which the skull and skin alone were said to weigh nearly a quarter of a ton.

M. Solomon Markovitch Herzenstein initiated me into the selection of Central Asian fishes, and gave me an introduction to Professor Zograf of Moscow, who, on my arriving there, helped me to get three sets of graduated spirit tins fitting inside one another, the great advantage of which lay in the aperture or capsule marked "S.O.T.B. Co., Albion Works, King's Cross. Lever this side up. Patent." This last word secured the cover from being manufactured in Russia, but, when fitted to a tin cylinder, it formed one of the best vessels I know for collecting specimens in spirit, or carrying on a rough journey semi-liquid provisions that need to be occasionally opened.

Of course I called in Moscow on Madame Olga Fedchenko, one of the most scientific ladies perhaps in Russia, who looked over for me the proof-sheets of the tables of fauna in *Russian Central Asia*, and who had recently completed her catalogue of the plants of

Turkistan. We had many topics in common, and I was furnished by her with one of the latest publications of the Imperial Society of Friends of Natural History, Anthropology, and Ethnography, as well as a few more introductions to scientific persons.

A propos of ethnography, Professor Zograf had showed me a very interesting collection of ethnographical objects from Turkistan and Siberia—a department in Russian museums in which I think they do better than we—not, perhaps, in buildings and fixtures, but in the number of exhibits, and, sometimes, in their arrangement.

In Tashkend, much useful assistance was rendered by M. Oshanin, who, since my previous visit, had joined the teaching staff of the Gymnasium, but who still delighted to fill up his leisure in scientific pursuits, especially entomology. He helped me to get a box made in partitions wherein to carry the cylinders filled with alcohol; also to get an additional store of arsenical soap, to say nothing of such homely purchases as a frying-pan with a lid for baking bread, an American axe, and linen cloth; the last procurable seemingly in Tashkend only in short lengths as supplied to the soldiers for shirting, and disposed of or exchanged by them for other material more to their taste.

M. Oshanin also showed me a method of packing *coleoptera*, for the invention of which he deserves a gold medal, as compared with the ordinary direction to pack your beetles in sawdust. "The result of that is," said M. Oshanin, "that after a thousand miles of travel by Russian post, your specimens will probably be shaken all together at the bottom of the box, with many of their legs broken, and at the best the whole covered with *débris* and dust."

The plan he suggested was, to take a piece of swansdown calico, double the size of the bottom of the box in which the specimens are to be packed. Place the beetles in rows, with their legs on the down over an area the extent of the box. Then double the remaining portion of the calico over the backs of the beetles, thus giving a soft but clinging substance above and below to prevent your specimens shaking about. The box may be filled with similar pieces of swansdown, having wadding and antiseptics between if desired, and thus the specimens will travel clean and unbroken as far as you please. I tried this plan with my 800 specimens of *coleoptera*, and found it answered perfectly.

Amongst new acquaintances made at Tashkend was Prince M. M. Cantacuzene, *aide-de-camp* to the Governor-General, who gave me an introduction to the military club, a palatial building, at which I dined daily. In its spacious saloon was a grand piano, said to have cost nearly £200; but (illustrative, some would say, of Russian lack of thoroughness or finish) when I asked for the lavatory, such a place seemed to be wanting or under repair, and a breakfast-cup of water was brought to pour over one's hands by way of washing before dinner.

Here, however, I met Colonel Lilienfeld, who was kind enough to get my rifle cleaned, and suggested that I should practise in the shooting-gallery adjoining the club, which, seeing that I had never discharged a rifle in my life, seemed reasonable enough, and I accordingly did so.

Thus far all was by way of preparation. Let me now proceed to a few general remarks as to what we know of the fauna of Chinese Central Asia, and the persons through whom our knowledge has been obtained.

Up to five-and-twenty years ago we had heard from Marco Polo of the big sheep on the Pamirs, and the Chinese traveller Chang-te had written of "horned horses with scales" in the Caspian, and sheep growing by the navel out of the ground! Once, when questioning a class of Irish boys who told me there were five "quarters" in the world, I asked, "Why are there five quarters in the world, but only four in an apple?" To which one of the Hibernian hopefuls replied, "Because, sir, the other one isn't yet discovered." So with the fauna of Chang-te, whereas Marco Polo's statement has been abundantly verified.

First, in order of time, of the naturalists of Chinese Central Asia may be mentioned M. N. A. Severtsoff, who, in 1867, explored the Tian Shan about Issik-Kul; and, later, the Pamirs and the Alai. Somewhat farther west we have Professor and Madame Fedchenko, between 1868 and 1871, exploring the valleys of the Syr and Zarafshan, as well as the mountains of Khokand and the Alai, and collecting about 57,000 zoological specimens, to say nothing of thousands of botanical specimens, belonging to about 1,800 different species of plants.

Turning next to the south, we have Dr Henderson proceeding with the first Forsyth mission in 1870, and obtaining 59 species of birds belonging to the hills and plains of Yarkand, together with a few specimens of *lepidoptera* and a collection of plants. The second Forsyth mission in 1873 added comparatively little to our zoological knowledge, owing to the death of Dr Stoliczka, the naturalist of the expedition. Dr Bowdler Sharpe, however, from Stoliczka's materials has recently written a monograph, so far as birds are concerned, on the scientific results of the second Yarkand mission.

Passing now to Sungaria and the Ili valley, there is Prjevalsky, who penetrated these regions, as well as other parts farther east and south. To him belonged the credit of bringing to Europe the first skin of the wild horse, named after him *Equus Prjevalskii*. M. Grum-Grjimailo, a later traveller from Sungaria, studied and hunted these animals for 20 days, adding to his trophies the skins of three stallions and a mare. He says that at a distance the wild horse may easily be mistaken for a *kulan* or wild ass, being distinguishable chiefly by its bearing. He noted also that the wild stallion never leads the herd, but is always behind taking care of the young, which he protects better than do the mares.*

Another naturalist who has helped to make us acquainted with the fauna of the Ili valley, especially its *lepidoptera*, is M. Serge Alphéraky, who, in 1879, collected 12,000 specimens in this department alone. But the latest collectors in this region are the brothers Grum-Grjimailo just alluded to, whose journey in

* Forsyth, speaking generally from native information, says: "The wild horse breeds in the hollows of the sandy ridges bordering the desert, and . . . not unfrequently shares the pasture with the Kirghese herds of its domesticated kindred species." I should be curious to know whether, under such circumstances, anything occurs with the wild horse such as I heard of in the Euphrates valley relating to the wild ass. My caravan saw a wild ass approaching some tame ones, whereupon my servant told me that the natives like their domesticated asses to breed from a wild sire, for it ensures a swift progeny. They therefore decoy the wild animal from the hills; but their success is attended with one strange risk, namely, that the wild animal, after consorting with the domesticated female, bites her on the nape of the neck and kills her; in anticipation of which a marksman is hid in a pit, who shoots the brute before he is able to commit the murder.

1889-90 extended along the eastern continuation of the Tian Shan, and to the Sungarian oases, as well as the district south of Turfan. Their zoological collection numbered 14,000 specimens, the vertebrates comprising 110 mammals, amongst which were two mountain sheep.

In connection with this last-named animal, Mr St George Littledale has come to the front. Writing to me in 1887, he asked if there were wild sheep in the Altai. I replied, "Why not go to the Pamirs?" This was a "happy hunting-ground" he had not presumed to aspire to. But "trying" did it. The Russians gave permission, and in 1888 he bagged a fine collection, much to the envy and admiration of Prjevalsky, who met him with the observation, "Here have I been shooting for years and years in Central Asia and have secured only five or six Poli, whilst you in a few weeks walk off with fifteen rams and two females!" In 1891 Mr Littledale shot several more.

I have seen the horns of several in his own house, but he has generously given his best to the Museum of Natural History, South Kensington, where, in a handsome glass case, they are exhibited—a typical collection of wild sheep of which I know not the equal in the world. The Russian specimens from the collections of Severtsoff, Prjevalsky, and Alphéraky are far more numerous; but their skins, so far as I can judge, are not so well stuffed and mounted, and not nearly so handsomely exhibited.

This little trophy will be gratifying to English sportsmen, but it must perforce be recognised that it is to Russian naturalists we owe nearly all our knowledge of the fauna of Chinese Central Asia, and that they have shown a zeal in acquiring and diffusing their knowledge which is worthy of the utmost commendation.

Having thus exhibited the lions, let me bring forward the mice, and continue my own little achievements, beginning with the first specimens collected, namely, a myriapod (*Scutigera coleoptrata*) and a *phalange* or venomous insect of the spider family, both given me by my host at Samarkand. Spiders in Central Asia—or at all events four of them—are not to be trifled with, for their bite is poisonous, and increasingly so in the following order : *Tarantula, Scorpion, Phalange, Karakurt.*

After the bite of the *phalange*, which makes four punctures, the bitten place swells rapidly, accompanied by agonising pain, high fever, and, sometimes, swollen stomach. In winter these insects sleep, and the specimen given me, at the end of April, had been torpid and kept in a box for six months. Such was its vitality, however, that, when immersed in spirit, it took four minutes to die.

A remarkable thing about these venomous spiders, especially the *karakurt*, is, that whilst their bite is dangerous to man, and fatal to horse, cow, or camel, sheep gobble them up and enjoy them. Verily what is one's food is another's poison ; and the Kirghese, knowing this, send in advance to pasture round their camping-place a flock of sheep, the smell of whose fleeces even is sufficient to drive the spiders away.

I began shooting on May 18th, after leaving Chimkend, when, as we drove along the steppe, under the Alexander mountains, there flew before us and settled on the telegraph wires numbers of blue crows ; and had our object been the collecting of pretty feathers, these birds might have been killed by scores.

Hawks, too, continually perched on the telegraph poles, not pretending to stir on the approach of the tarantass, though they were not always obliging enough to wait if I got out. "Why doesn't the gentleman shoot from the tarantass?" inquired the *yemstchik*. This was exactly what the gentleman wished, but feared to frighten the horses. Thus encouraged, however, I attempted it, with the result that one of the wheelers gave such a bound forward as to break his harness, and the postboy made no further suggestions in that direction.

On reaching Issik-Kul I took my first shot at a bird flying. Whether barrel number one hit I am not sure, but the second brought down the plover. A pheasant and some very handsome geese, or other waders, which we saw, would not allow themselves to be approached.

My greatest zoological "find," however, at Issik-Kul was not a bird, but a fish. Réclus says of Issik-Kul that not more than four species of fish have been discovered in its waters, and Kostenko gives their names as *usman*, *marinka*, carp, and bream.

M. Herzenstein told me the same, and added that specimens from Issik-Kul were not plentiful in European museums. He suggested my being on the look-out in Central Asian rivers at great altitudes for an interesting family of fishes, *Nemachilus* (that is, naked, or without scales), some having six barbels. He showed me a specimen of *Schizothorax*, called in Turkistan *Marinka*, with four barbels, of which it was desirable to get specimens; and another interesting mountain fish, *Diptychus*, with two barbels, called *Usman*, naked, or at most with exceedingly minute scales. One more species he named as rare in English collections, not in this instance smooth, but small, named *Cottus spinulosus*, a new species of "Miller's thumb," found in springs at Khojend.

Thus primed, I came to the post-house at Choktal, situated on a small rivulet running into Issik-Kul, less than a quarter of a mile distant. The postmaster knew of the *Usman* and *Marinka*. He mentioned, too, a smaller fish, *Piscari*, or *Usatch*, and a fourth he called *Chebak*; and, in addition, he spoke of another kind in the lake called *Sazan*, or perch-pike.

Upon asking for specimens, he took what resembled a shrimp-net, and, calling one of his boys, walked across his yard to a hole in the rivulet. Into this he thrust his net, bidding the boy beat about with a pole, and quickly lifted the net, containing, to my surprise, at least a dozen fishes—some of them three-pounders. Those pointed out as *Chebak* resembled roach, but the *Marinka* more nearly a tench, from which, when taken in the hand, exuded what looked like milt. These kinds were less numerous than the *Usman*; but I speedily filled a spirit can with at least three varieties, and afterwards obtained other specimens from streams running into the eastern end of the lake, congratulating myself on getting so good a collection of its fishes.

The "find" just alluded to consisted of several specimens of a new species of *Diptychus*, since named by Dr Albert Günther *Diptychus Lansdelli*, and pronounced by him to be the fourth species known of the genus. Kessler, in his remarks on Turkistan fishes, says that the genera *Schizothorax* and *Diptychus* (characterised by a slit sheath on the posterior part of the belly) belong exclusively to the high mountain regions of Central Asia. The only species of the genus *Diptychus* (namely, *D. maculatus Steind*), known up to the discovery of the Turkistan species, was found in Tibet at an altitude of 11,200 feet. The Turkistan species also, *Diptychus Severtzovi*, he adds, was obtained

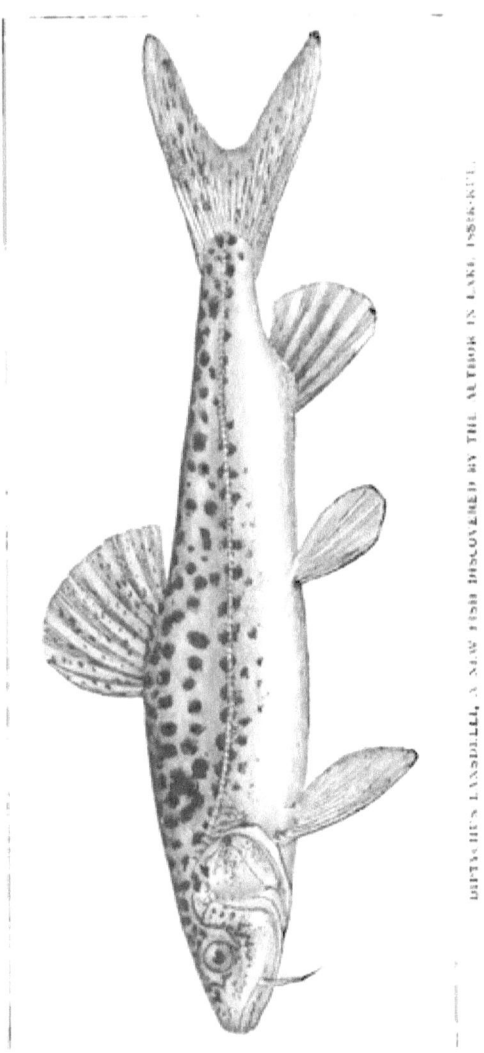

DIPTYCHUS LANSDELLI, A NEW FISH DISCOVERED BY THE AUTHOR IN LAKE ISSYK-KUL.

by Severtsoff in the rivers Ottuk and Aksai, at a height of 10,000 feet. My specimens, however, were caught at an altitude of 5,300 feet only.

On descending to the plains more fish were obtained at Uzun-Agatch (*Nemachilus Strauchii, N. labiatus*) as well as reptiles, so that, when packing at Vierny our first zoological specimens, two tins were filled with various fishes, the pigmy mouse (*Mus Wagneri*), a gerbille (*Gerbillus sp.*), frogs, toads, snakes, crickets, lizards, and snails; in all perhaps 150 specimens in spirit. Besides these were sent 30 birds, 750 beetles, and 820 butterflies.

Many of the insects were captured by children, to whom I promised a coin for any living thing, which brought, of course, many duplicates and specimens spoiled by rough handling. Moreover, one day Joseph was sent out into the steppe for a day's shooting and collecting, and not in vain; but he seemed to have no innate love for it, though ready to do my behests when the prey was caught.

At Vierny I met a Mr Urban, reputed a mighty hunter, who shot with a three-barrelled gun and rifle by Sauer. He told of snow partridge and woodcock in the Kuldja mountains, and M. Gourdet painted in glowing colours the abundance of bird life at Ilisk, mentioning a Cossack there named Dashin who would hunt with and for me, and procure all sorts of game.

Having time on our hands I telegraphed ahead, and spent a day in collecting at Ilisk with Dashin and a German introduced to me by Mr Norman, and then shot along the road to Kuldja. Thus were added to our collection a hedgehog (*Erinaceus albulus*), a sand snake (*Eryx jaculus*), a common snake (*Tropidonotus natrix*), as well as several birds, such as the kestrel (*Falco tinnunculus*), the long-legged buzzard (*Buteo ferox*), the jackdaw (*Corvus monedula*), the black-bellied sandgrouse (*Pterocles arenarius*), of which, near Borokhudsir, I secured two, if not three, at a shot; the peewit (*Vanellus vulgaris*), the redshank (*Totanus calidris*), and the black-headed wagtail (*Motacilla melanocephala*). At Ilisk, near the little river Kara-su, I brought down my first snipe and shot a diver; but we did not succeed in finding pheasants as we had been led to expect.

Arrived at Kuldja, M. Bornemann obligingly sent men to bring *Marinka* and *Usman* fishes from the Kara-su and Ili, and they brought besides a species of *Labeo*. M. de Deken also kindly proposed an afternoon's shooting. This I remember well by reason of the intense heat, which sent us home as in a bath.

Among our Kuldja specimens were the serotine bat (*Vesperugo serotinus*), a water snake (*Tropidonotus hydrus*); and of birds, the common roller (*Coracias garrulus*), the Indian grey shrike (*Lanius lahtora*), the rock dove (*Columba livia*), the turtle dove (*Turtur vulgaris*), the common and green sandpiper (*Totanus vulgaris et T. ochropus*), the eastern stonechat (*Pratincola maura*), and the white wagtail (*Motacilla alba*). Of the foregoing about 60 specimens were placed in two more spirit tins; and besides these were packed other birds, beetles, butterflies, and ethnographical objects, making up a parcel weighing nearly 60 lbs., which was sent by post to Batoum.

Between Kuldja and Aksu we were almost continually on the move, and saw very much less of animal life than we had been led to expect. The fir forests of the Uzun-Tau are said to contain herds of deer, but we saw only one specimen; nor did a mountain sheep come across our path throughout the Muz-Tag gorge. I have mentioned our butterfly-hunting on horseback and on foot, together with securing the fine specimen of the golden eagle (*Aquila chrysaëtos*) in the Muzart defile. The red-billed jackdaw, shot in the same neighbourhood, was interesting, as one of the birds frequenting high altitudes of not less, according to Kostenko, than 5,000 feet; but south of the gorge there was little vegetation, and bird life was correspondingly rare.

Of specimens taken between Kashgar and Aksu mention has been made in the narrative, whilst during our stay at Kashgar boys were invited to bring whatever they could of living things. This added to our collection several lizards (*Agama Stoliczkana, Phrynocephalus axillaris et P. versicolor, Eremias multocellata, Teratoscincus Prjevalskii*), and a green toad (*Bufo viridis*), as well as two species of fish (*Schizothorax intermedius et Nemachilus Yarkandensis*), other specimens having been obtained at Sai-Aryk and Maralbashi. My birds, marked as from Kashgar, include a starling (*Sturnus porphyronotus*), a wood sandpiper (*Totanus glareola*), and the water rail (*Rallus aquaticus*).

I sent from Kashgar in all about 2,700 specimens, which, besides those already enumerated, comprised a rat, hedgehog, snakes, a scorpion, leeches, and a few insects, such as a black bee (*Xylocopa valga*), and dragon flies (*Symphetum peridionale et S. sanguineum*). These, when packed with more ethnographical objects, were to form my last consignment sent through Russia. Henceforth my specimens were to be sent from south of the Himalayas, towards which we now set our faces.

CHAPTER XXX.

FROM KASHGAR TO YENGI HISSAR.

Re-organisation of caravan; Despatch of parcels homewards, 37.—Sale of surplus baggage, 38.—My groom Amin, and his marriage, 39.—Sariin Sak, and plans for wife number two, 40.—Hire of three carts, 41.—Letters commendatory from *Taulai* and Consul, 42.—Farewell at Consulate, and Cossack escort out of town; Place of murder of Schlagintweit, 43.—Relics and monument, 44.—March to Yapchan; Route to Pamirs by Gez defile, 45.—Journey to Yengi Hissar, 46.

BEFORE leaving Kashgar my caravan had to be re-organised. It now seemed pretty clear that we were not to wander east of Khotan, seeking from thence to enter Tibet, nor to winter in Chinese Turkistan. The question therefore arose whether the baggage could not be reduced, especially as high prices were quoted in Kashgar for horses to cross the Himalayas.

I had already despatched to Batoum, for shipment to England, three consignments from Tashkend, Vierny, and Kuldja; those from Tashkend and Vierny at the rate of four and five roubles a *pood* respectively. By favour of M. Hermann Carlovitch Kaiser—chief, I think, of the Customs—I was able to arrange that the box of ethnographical specimens should be examined in Tashkend.

This obviated its being opened in passage through Bokhara; but rather than risk any examination of zoological specimens preserved in spirit, the packages forwarded from Vierny were sent in the care of the Russian Society by camel transport some hundreds of miles farther, through Orenburg. From Kuldja the best means of transport seemed to be the Russian parcels post, by which packages up to 120 lbs. (Russian) could be sent, though the rate of 38 *kopecks*, or 9½*d.*, per pound was rather high.

From Kashgar M. Petrovsky kindly undertook to forward my parcels, by caravan, through Narin to Vierny, whence M. Gourdet was asked to send them *via* Orenburg, as before. Yet another package that the Consul was good enough to forward for me contained the rouble notes despatched from Vierny. For these I had no further use. They were therefore sent by Cossacks and post to St Petersburg, for their value to be remitted to London, and the equivalent thence to Lahore. All these packages not only went safely, but the money increased on the way, the value of the roubles since I purchased them having greatly risen.

M. Petrovsky further helped me by unexpectedly offering to purchase any of my medicines, instruments, books, or surplus baggage; and in this way were disposed of a magnetic machine, amputation and other surgical instruments, pieces of cloth and cashmere, a few books, vessels, fittings, provisions, and English stationery—the last so dear to Russian scribes; whilst M. Lutsch, the Secretary, relieved me of a set of pocket surgical instruments, and some medicines for the consular dispensary. I sold to them, besides, about 50 copies of the Scriptures in four languages for their own use and for presents; so that, what with packages sent home, Scriptures distributed, and goods disposed of, my 60 parcels were reduced to 40, to be taken forward to India.

As for the *personnel* of the caravan, experience had shown the necessity for an interpreter into Chinese to be less imperative than was anticipated, since the principal occasions when this language was needed were in calls on the mandarins, of whom I expected to visit only two more—at Yarkand and Khotan—and in every case the Chinese authorities had a staff of Turki interpreters. I did not, therefore, renew the engagement with my Chinese interpreter, but fell back upon Joseph, Amin occasionally assisting in Turki or Persian. This was somewhat of a venture, but in the end answered fairly well.

As for Amin, on our arrival at Kashgar, he turned out to be none other than a long-lost, if not prodigal, son, for my first visitor was his father, offering a present of fruit and calling down blessings on my head for bringing the truant home. Amin had been warned at Kuldja, by some of his pretended friends, against the English traveller as one who perhaps might not pay him, or, in a fit of impatience, desert him on the way. Joseph laughed when Amin confided to him his fears, telling him not to be afraid, and now Amin had come so to like his employer as to declare "he had wanted for nothing, and that I had looked after him like a father."

This little compliment was preliminary to his asking for his wages, but seemed to be not all flattery, since he expressed his readiness to accompany us to Khotan, and even to India. He received, therefore, his month's pay of thirty shillings, with which he pretended to want to purchase presents for his friends, whereas, on the strength of this sudden influx of riches, Joseph told me, to my surprise, that Amin was about to get married!

"To an old sweetard, probably," the reader may surmise, "who had been patiently waiting for years her lover's return."

Not a bit of it! Nor anything half so sentimental, for this Kashgarian *fiancée* was simply a girl of 12, whom his father wished him to marry. The union was to take place on Friday night, but was not to hinder the bridegroom's departure with me on the following Monday for Khotan, and possibly India; and indeed it seemed to be the father's device for alluring his son back again.

Having expressed a wish to see the wedding, Joseph considerately informed me that, in the case of a poor man like Amin, there would be little ceremony, which was taken to mean that I should be in the way. I therefore contented myself with offering a present to the bridegroom, and sent one also to the bride.

Another of my retinue, Sarim Sak, hearing of my inquiry for servants to go to Ladak, offered to accompany us to India for 30 roubles a month and all found, if I would pay his way back ; and when I did not, by reason of uncertainty as to our course, close with his offer at once, he professed to be so extremely pleased with my service as to volunteer to accompany me without wages to Khotan. Such disinterested attachment sounded, of course, quite touching, until by a little probing it was discovered that there was once more a lady in the case.

Sarim Sak, who was from Osh, had, in the time of Yakub Khan, married a wife who was now in Kashgar with her children, whilst he had recently been living with a second wife at Aksu, whither also he wished to bring his first love. It appeared, however, that the Chinese, wishing to put a check on the temporary marriages of the Andijanis or Russian subjects with the Kashgar women, had issued a regulation under which Sarim Sak would have difficulty in removing his Kashgar wife.

Upon my accepting his offer, Sarim Sak planned that, after his departure in my train towards Khotan, his wife and family should travel alone to Aksu, whilst he, on returning to Yarkand, instead of continuing to Kashgar, should go across country to Aksu, where, it seemed, the authorities were less strict about these matters than at Kashgar. I took the precaution, however, of writing in my note-book, "Sarim Sak agrees to accompany me to Yarkand, Khotan, and back to Yarkand, without wages, on condition that I find him and his horse food and lodging as long as he is with me." And this he readily signed.

Thus provided with interpreter, groom, and general helper, Ibrahim Bai, one of the Turki *begs*, enabled me to hire, of one Shanga, three *arbas*, to be drawn by 12 horses, and attended by four men, one of whom was the *arbakesh* who had accompanied us from Aksu. Each *arba* was to carry to Yarkand 1,500 lbs. in four days, and was to cost six *liang* of silver, or 27s.*

* If *arbas* were required to go forward to Khotan and back to Yarkand, which would take eight days each way, then each was to cost 67s. 6d. and carry 1,250 lbs. If I stayed more than five days at Yarkand, the food for the 12 horses at the rate of 3s. a day was to fall on me; whilst the drivers, besides making good anything lost, were to pay 3s. for every day they exceeded their time, Sundays being excepted as days of rest. As for payment, it was agreed that ten *liang* should be tendered in advance, and eight more at Yarkand. If the journey were continued, then ten more in advance, ten at Khotan, and the last ten on the completion of the contract.

Moreover, the *Tautai*, named Wen, furnished me with authority to require two *djiguitts* from town to town, on presentation of a letter written in Chinese and Turki, the latter being translated for me into French, and beginning with Chinese titles in Turkish letters, thus :—

"Tching Ming Erping Ding deh, Ying-u-choo, Hansu-New Line, Suleh Khun-sung, bing bedow, Janghan, Tun-shan, sini-narkhoon-ba-too-loo, Yuen.

"Know all men :—

"I have given this passport to inform you that a great foreign scholar, a government functionary, with one interpreter, six attendants, horses and vehicles, eight chests of books, eight of clothing, five of medicines, seven of provisions, a revolver, two guns, and various kinds of arms, has arrived at Kashgar from Ili.

"Now, he wishes to proceed to Yarkand and Khotan, and thence to return to his own country. Hence he asks of me to give him a passport, and, according to treaty, to provide for his safety. This, at least, is what the scholar has told me.

"Therefore, I have given the passport. I command all the local authorities to obey me, and, according to treaty, to concern themselves in his welfare. You local authorities are to give him two men for safe conduct, and not to contravene my orders. This is a very important matter.

"Having said thus much, I give the passport in the fourteenth year of the reign of Guan Sui, the twelfth day of the eighth month. Given at Kashgar."

Besides this letter from the *Tautai*, M. Petrovsky gave me a less pretentious document to a trader at Yarkand, of whom I might ask for a *djiguitt*, if needed, to Khotan. This note simply commended me as an Englishman travelling to Khotan and thence to Ladak, its pith being in the last sentence, " Do for him all you can, because he is my friend."

The Consul was minded, however, that I should go out with honours, and be sent off, literally, with colours flying. On Monday, after receiving from Madame Petrovsky some complimentary provisions (of roasted eggs among other things) for the way, I spent my farewell evening at the Consulate, my host promising, if any letters came, to send them after me.

M. Lutsch also volunteered to be of use in case of my getting into difficulty, after which the party, including Mdlle Petrovsky, accompanied me by moonlight from their house to the city gates, long since shut, but which opened to the Consul's voice, and I made my way through the deserted streets homewards.

Next morning at nine o'clock the Consul and M. Lutsch drove in a *calèche* to my lodging, accompanied by the detachment of Cossacks to escort us out of the town. In the van was a white-turbaned and a Chinese *djiguitt*, with two Cossacks bearing a silk banner displaying the colours of the regiment on one side and on the other of the Consulate.

Then came the *calèche* with the Consul, his Secretary, and myself, and next the Cossacks in full uniform, followed by our attendants and three *arbas*. Thus we drove out of the town as far as the spot where Schlagintweit was murdered, and concerning whom M. Petrovsky was able to give me certain particulars he had gathered locally.

Adolphe Schlagintweit, it will be remembered, was the first European we know of who made his way over the mountains from India to Kashgar. The cruel debauchee and despot Valikhan-tura was then besieging the Chinese in the Yengi-shahr ; and, just as Schlagintweit's caravan approached, was endeavouring to cut off from the fortress the waters of the river.

Seeing the foreigner, the despot ordered him to divert the stream, and, on his disclaiming ability to do so, demanded the papers he was carrying to the Khan of Khokand. These Schlagintweit refused to give, whereupon the monster ordered him to be put to death, and his throat was cut opposite a little half-ruined hut to the left of the third wooden culvert beyond the bridge of stone, on the way from the old to the new town.

One of the four executioners, according to Dr Seeland, is living, and M. Petrovsky shows a very long thermometer (on the scale of which may be read distinctly "Dr Schlagintweit"), which, after various inquiries for any of the murdered man's relics, was brought to him in a morocco leather case. M. Petrovsky had collected also a hundred roubles, wherewith to erect on the spot a monument bearing a plate of gilded copper, which he showed me, and whereon is written in Russian :—

"To the traveller ADOLPHE SCHLAGINTWEIT,
Who fell a sacrifice to his intense devotion to geographical science,
14/26 August, 1857.

"This memorial was erected by Nicolas Feodorovitch Petrovsky with the assistance of the members of the Imperial Russian Geographical Society in 1887."

Its erection had been delayed, and, had all been now ready, the Consul would have liked me to officiate at the inaugural ceremony with a religious service, the Cossacks being present and others *en fête* ;

but arrangements were not yet complete with the Chinese authorities respecting the ground.

At this historic spot my ornamental escort turned back, and we marched forward to the new town. Here, though only so short a distance from Kashgar, our Chinese *djiguitts* for some reason had to be changed, which delayed us a little; and then, emerging from the south gate of the Yengi-shahr, we passed along a good road for three miles through cultivated lands and over two or three river beds, the whole country being intersected by canals. After a march of four and a half tash, or about 30 miles, we reached Yapchan.

In the course of the day we were overtaken by a messenger bringing me letters, just arrived *via* Narin, but containing no news that affected my movements. We crossed at intervals about Yapchan several branches of the Gez river, which flows down off the Pamirs, from near the Mustagh-Ata Peak, through the Gez defile.*

We reached Yapchan late in the afternoon, but stayed only three hours. to rest and feed the horses; and then at eight o'clock set out to travel through the night.

The 25-foot road, lined with trees, runs through a

* I have previously spoken only of two routes, north and south, by which the Pamirs are usually reached from Kashgar, but it would appear from letters to *Land and Water*, January to June 1891, that Major Cumberland approached by the Gez defile. Leaving Kashgar, he came to Borokatai, and then to the Customs outpost at Tashmalik or Tashbalik, near to which on Bolsheff's map is marked Karaul Upal, with a track leading off to the Kizil-su valley. Beyond Tashbalik Cumberland speaks of the road to the Pamirs as good, or, at all events, better than over the Karakoram. Since my visit Colonel Grombchevsky has descended to Kashgar by the Gez defile, and Younghusband in 1891 went up by this defile, which is the route, I presume, Mr Wilkins at Tashkend suggested to me as something new to Europeans, in case I determined to cross into India by the Baroghil Pass.

well-watered and cultivated district for five miles, after which a somewhat swampy region is entered on, with good grazing ground; and so matters continue until, within six miles of Yengi Hissar, cultivation begins again.

At Yengi Hissar we came upon the sites of some of the battle-fields of the country, which reminds me that I have said little of the history of Chinese Central Asia, of which an outline, however bare, must now be attempted.

CHAPTER XXXI.

THE HISTORY OF CHINESE TURKISTAN.

Legends of Trans-Oxiana; The wall of China, and neighbouring tribes; Migrations from Tarim valley to Tokharistan, 48.—Mission of Chang-kian to the Yuechi, and subjugation of Uigurs; Information concerning Tarim valley from Buddhist pilgrims, 49. —Divided condition of country at Arab invasion; Authority transferred to Bokhara, 50.—Uigur expansion from Kashgar; Kara-Khitai rule in Tarim valley; Conquest of Jinghiz Khan, 51.— Tamerlane's conquest, 52.—Rebellion of Wais Khan; Ababakar, Sultan Said, and Rashid, 53.—Rise of the *Khojas* and mountaineers; Invasion of Sungars, 54.—Depopulation of Sungaria; Recommencement of *Khoja* rebellions, 55.—Complications between Chinese and Khokandians, 56.—Invasion of the seven *Khojas*; Subversion of Chinese rule, 57.—Buzurg Khan and Yakub Bek; Yakub Bek's usurpation of authority, 58.—Reception of Russian and English embassies, 60.—Disaffection of people and readiness for return of Chinese, 61.—Yakub Khan's death; Three upstart successors, 62.—Reinstallation of Chinese Government; Retrocession by Russia of Ili valley, and formation of Sin Kiang province, 64.

THE sources of our knowledge of Chinese Central Asia have been indicated in an earlier chapter; and in *Russian Central Asia* I have touched here and there upon the history of those portions of it that have been subjected to Russian influence, especially Sungaria, the Ili valley, and Khokand. It now remains for me to give a brief sketch of the history of the Tarim basin, or Chinese Turkistan.

In pre-historic times the Oxus was the dividing line between Iran to the west and Turan (that is, *not* Iran) on the east; or, between the civilised Persians and the wild Scythians. Persian poetry tells of battles and heroes, amongst whom Syawush is represented to have fled, about 580 B.C., from Persia to his father's enemy Afrasiab, near Bokhara. There he marries his daughter Faranghis, and receives as her dowry the provinces of Khotan and Chin. But this is all legend.

A good date with which to begin our history is 253 B.C., when Shi-Huangti, the first universal monarch of China, built the Great Wall as a defence against the marauding tribes of Mongolia. Immediately north of the wall were the Yuechi. Farther northward camped the Hiungnu or Uigurs, whilst westwards, in the Tarim valley, lived its first inhabitants known to us, called by the Persians "Saka," but in the Chinese annals "Sai" or "Se."

Somewhere about 200 B.C. the Yuechi were deprived of their lands northward by the Uigurs, and, being further pressed, the Yuechi separated into two divisions, the smaller passing into Tibet, and the larger, about 163 B.C., pushing the Saka out of the Tarim valley over the mountains westwards to the region of Balkh.

Later, about 126 B.C., the Saka were driven farther west before the Yuechi, who themselves were expelled by the Uigurs from the Tarim basin. The Yuechi then overthrew the moribund Græco-Bactrian kingdom, and ultimately established themselves as a powerful people in what was called, after their tribal appellation, Tokharistan, which included Balkh, Kunduz, Hissar, Badakshan, and Wakhan.

Meanwhile the Uigurs, who had gained possession

of the Tarim valley, conquered all the country from the borders of China to the Volga. Their headquarters were about the eastern extension of the Tian Shan, at Bishbalik, Turfan, and Hami, whence they attacked the Chinese frontier.

It was Uigur raids upon China that caused the Emperor Woo-ti to send the envoy Chang-kian in 139 B.C. to the Yuechi for help against their common enemy; but, on the enemy's arrival, more than ten years later, the Yuechi did not care to leave their lands on the Oxus to return to their eastern deserts, and the Emperor was left to fight alone. In so doing he, and afterwards his successor, succeeded so well that in 60 B.C. the Uigurs were conquered. They rebelled and were again subdued in 83 A.D.; and, soon after this, the whole country was annexed to China by the conquest of Kashgar in 94 A.D. This last success was achieved by the celebrated soldier Panchao, who also crossed the Pamirs, slew the king of the Yuechi, and pushed his victories as far as the Caspian.

The Tarim basin, thus conquered, remained subject to China for six centuries, during which period we get glimpses of its condition from the travels of the Buddhist pilgrims Fa-hian, Sung Yun, and Hiuen Tsiang. So long as the Chinese government was strong at home, the people of Kashgar were controlled by officers appointed from the imperial palace; but when the empire was weak, the inhabitants of the valley threw off allegiance, and split up into a number of petty states, each at war with the others for mastery of the whole, which mastery seems to have been held more or less firmly (and perhaps as a friendly ally of China) by the kingdom of Khotan.

The country was in this piecemeal condition when the

Arabs appeared on the banks of the Oxus at the beginning of the eighth century. In 712 their victorious general Kutaiba, having conquered Bokhara, penetrated into Ferghana, and, crossing the mountains, took Kashgar, and effected a rapid expedition along the north of the country as far as Turfan. Thence Kutaiba sent an embassy to the Chinese Emperor demanding his submission, and saying that he had sworn to tread on the soil of China.

The embassy was not harshly received, and, with his reply of non-compliance, the Emperor sent back a few shovelfuls of earth for Kutaiba to tread upon and to keep his oath. Meanwhile, the Arabs had learned the difficulties of the deserts to be crossed, which probably was the real cause of their not advancing, and, news reaching Kutaiba of the death of the Kalif Walid, he returned to Merv.

Thus far, it will be observed, the Tarim basin had been invaded, and Kashgar had taken its orders, from the east; now its politics were to be shaped by the west, where the Arabs were consolidating their conquests, and offering to fire-worshippers and Christians alike the Koran or the sword.

The most prominent of the early converts was Saman, a Zoroastrian noble of Balkh, who, on embracing Muhammadanism, regained his forfeited lands. Subsequently his four grandsons were governors of a territory that included Herat, Samarkand, Tashkend, and Ferghana. Of these Nazr, the Governor of Ferghana, became ruler of all Bokhara and Turkistan, whilst his brother and successor Ismail raised the Samani power to its highest point, so that, at his death in 907, he left an empire extending from Ispahan to Turfan and the Gobi.

The Samani dynasty came to an end in 1004, having lasted for about a century and a half. During its declining years the Bugra Khan family of the Uigurs, whose ruling chief was called Ilyik Khan, and had his capital at Kashgar, strengthened itself, so that Uigurs spread over both sides of the Pamirs from the Caspian to the Gobi. Ilyik Khan was dispossessed of his conquests west of the mountains by Sultan Sanjar of Merv, and dissensions in the Bugra Khan family opened the way for the conquest of the Tarim valley by the Mongols.

This conquest was brought about by a horde of Kara-Khitai, who came originally from the northern provinces of China and settled in Ili. They conquered all the country up to Khiva, and in 1125 their leader took the title of Gur-Khan. This Kara-Khitai rule lasted for 85 years, when it was broken up by the treachery of Koshluk, a prince of the Naiman Kirghese, who for a few years obtained power in the valley of the Tarim.

Then appeared on the scene Jinghiz Khan, who sent two of his generals to demand the submission of the Uigurs. Those in the north of the valley submitted at once. Koshluk refused, but was deserted by the Uigurs, his Naiman troops in Kashgar were cut to pieces, and Koshluk's head sent by the shepherds of Wakhan (whither he had escaped) to propitiate the Mongols. And thus in 1220 the Tarim valley (afterwards called Moghulistan) passed under the rule of Jinghiz Khan.

The Uigurs in a body now joined the standard of Jinghiz, and thus diverted from their own homes the havoc and desolation they inflicted upon other lands, so that, under the protection and toleration of Jinghiz and his immediate successors, Moghulistan is said to have enjoyed a degree of prosperity it had never before known. On the death of Jinghiz, the country fell to the lot of his son Jagatai, whose residence was at Almalik in the Ili valley, and who died in 1241.

The unity of the kingdom was then broken up, and Kashgar became a bone of contention between princes of the Jinghiz family, till it was consolidated into an independent sovereignty under Tuglak Timur, of Jagatai descent. He came to the throne in 1347, and, after restoring peace and order, died in 1363. Upon this the rule of Kashgar was usurped by its Governor, Kamaruddin Dughlat. He killed all his master's sons except an infant, Khizr Khoja, who was taken away and secreted, but recalled on the death of Kamaruddin in 1383, and set on the throne of Kashgar.

Contemporaneously with these events appears the name of Tamerlane. On becoming master of Bokhara, this renowned warrior led four expeditions into Moghulistan against Kamaruddin, and afterwards, during the supremacy of Khizr Khoja, when the Kirghese nomads repeated their raids on the Tashkend frontier, Tamerlane, in 1389, undertook his fifth and last campaign against Moghulistan. His army, advancing eastwards in four divisions, carried all before it, and completely crushed and beggared the country, which now became subject to the Uzbeg power in Samarkand. Tamerlane, however, accepted the allegiance of Khizr Khoja, married his daughter, and reinstated him as ruler.

After Khizr Khoja the government descended through a succession of Moghul Khans, whose reigns were characterised by disorder and bloodshed, more or less connected with the affairs of Bokhara and Ferghana. Among these rulers may be mentioned Muhammad Khan (a contemporary of Ulug Beg at Samarkand, and Shah Rukh in Khorasan), who was the last of the potentates governing with the style and pomp of the Jagatai court.

Then came the rebellion of Wais Khan (nephew of Muhammad Khan), who presently succeeded to the throne, and, on his death, left two youthful sons, Yunus and Eshanboga, to dispute the succession. Eshanboga was finally set on the throne, at Aksu, by Mir Said Ali, Governor of Kashgar, who subsequently seized for himself the western half of the country, and fixed his capital at Yarkand, where he was followed by his grandson Ababakar.

Against Ababakar came Sultan Said, one of the descendants of Yunus, and the last of the Moghul Khans who exercised any real authority in the country. In 1531 Said, according to the *Tarikhi Rashidi*, invaded Tibet with an army of 5,020 men, but died on his way back from *dam* (which is Persian for *breath*), or mountain sickness, at a place not far south of the Karakoram Pass, and named after him Daulat Beg Uldi, meaning "The Lord of the State died."

He was succeeded by his son Rashid, whose brother Haidar wrote the *Tarikhi Rashidi* during his government of Kashmir, upon which he entered in 1541. Rashid brought the Tarim valley, as far east as Turfan, under his dominion; but at his death dissensions prevailed, and the states fell asunder in 1572, the Jagatai dynasty having lasted upwards of 200 years since its re-establishment by Tuglak Timur.

Thus we have the Tarim valley ruled successively from the capital of China by the Celestials, from

Bokhara by the Arabs, from Karakorum by the Mongols, and from the Ili valley by the Kara-Khitai, the Uigurs being ever ready to throw off their allegiance when their distant and ultramontane masters were too weak to enforce it.

We next come to the usurpation of power by the *Khojas*, or priests. Among the mullahs and preachers who, under the Jagatai Khans, came from Samarkand to Kashgar, was the celebrated saint of the age, Makhdumi Azam, or the "Great Master." Rashid Sultan bestowed some lands upon him, and his sons were accorded a leading part in the councils of the government. This they abused to their own advantage by forming two factions among the Kirghese, which remain to this day. These parties were called the White and the Black Mountaineers, and this introduction of the Kirghese into the politics of Kashgar soon produced dissension between the spiritual aspirants for power and the several chiefs ruling the land.

At length the White Mountaineer party took the lead, and their head, *Khoja* Hidayatulla (one of the descendants of the Great Master, and afterwards known as Hazrat Aphak), aspired to the direct control of the government. The other party, however, drove Aphak from Kashgar over the mountains to Kashmir, whereupon he went to Lassa to invoke the aid of the Dalai Lama.

The Dalai Lama sent him with a recommendation to Bokoshta, the Ghaldan or chief of the Sungars, who invaded the Tarim basin, took the country for himself, and placed Aphak as Governor, aided by Kalmuk officers, at Yarkand. This was in 1678, and the Sungars, or Kalmuks, held authority over the country for 78 years, content with a money tribute of 400,000 *tengas* (£1,000) a month, and interfering but little with the administration of the *Khojas*.

In 1720 the Ghaldan Bokoshta died, and was succeeded by Ghaldan Shirin, who confirmed the pre-eminence of the Black Mountaineers in the Tarim basin which his predecessors had established, and thus intensified the struggles between the *Khojas*. In Sungaria also an attempt to gain the throne was made, later on, by Bokoshta's relative Amursana; but, not succeeding, he fled to China for help, and returned at the head of an army in 1755, by means of which he was made ruler of Sungaria. Finding that he was not to rule independently, he incited the Kalmuks to revolt, whereupon the Chinese speedily took summary vengeance, for in the following year they slew men, women, and children to the number of more than half a million, and Sungaria was completely depopulated.

The territory was then subdivided into seven circles. The Ili valley, Tarbagatai, and Kur-kara-usu (as on the map, but accurately Kara-kur-usu) formed the province of Ili; Barkul and Urumtsi were added to extra-mural Kansu; and Kobdo and Uliassutai received a separate administration. On the site of the Sungarian chief's abode the Chinese built Kuldja, and introduced into the country military colonists from Manchuria and criminals and vagabonds from China; also a tribe of Kalmuks was invited to return from the Volga valley.

Concurrently with the treachery of Amursana in Sungaria, rebellion broke out in Kashgar. Tchjao-Hoi, ruler of Ili, quickly marched thither, and subdued one town after another, driving the *Khojas* and their adherents over the mountains into Khokand, so that by the end of 1758 Chinese Turkistan was once more in the hands of the Celestials.

These successes of the Chinese caused a flutter among the Muhammadan khanates west of the mountains. To oppose the "infidel" a short-lived combination was made, including the ruler of Afghanistan, who sent an embassy to Peking to demand the restitution of Chinese Turkistan to the *Khojas*, of whom the chief was at that time one Sarim Sak.

The combination led to little, save that the inhabitants of Ush-Turfan, relying on expected help, rebelled in 1765, whereupon the Chinese massacred the entire population. After the suppression of this partial rebellion peace reigned in Chinese Turkistan for nearly 60 years, when there recommenced a series of *Khoja* rebellions extending over a large portion of the present century.

These were to a certain extent facilitated by constant trading intercourse, which afforded opportunity to the dispossessed *Khojas* living in Ferghana to hatch all sorts of sedition among the traders who came from Kashgar. To counteract this the Chinese, in 1813, subsidised the Khan of Khokand, by an annual payment of 200 *yambs* (£2,250), to control the hostility of the *Khojas*.

Amongst the *Khojas* was Jehangir, son of Sarim Sak, now dead. In 1826 he surrounded himself with a small party of Kirghese and others, marched over the mountains, drove out the Chinese, and was received with acclamation by the natives of Kashgar. Here he reigned for nine months, till the *Tsian-Tsiun* of Ili came with an army, and with considerable severity restored order, Jehangir himself being taken to Peking and exhibited in a cage, previous to being cut in pieces and thrown to the dogs.

The Chinese then attempted to punish the Khokandians for their sympathy with the *Khojas* by vexatious measures against the exportation of their goods to Kashgar. This provoked an invasion of the country by the Khokandians, who set on the throne for 90 days *Khoja* Yusuf. The Chinese on this occasion were not able to have it all their own way, and patched up the quarrel by the concession, in 1832, that the Khokandian traders residing in certain towns of the Tarim valley should pay dues for the Khan of Khokand to an *Aksakal* living in their midst, and that the foreign traders were to be under this collector's control, thus creating many times over an *imperium in imperio*.

The country now enjoyed peace till 1846 under a just and liberal Chinese governor, Zuhuruddin, in whose days were built, outside each of the large towns, the new Chinese forts called Yengi-shahr. In 1846, however, another invasion from Khokand was effected by seven *Khojas* of the Aphak family, under Katta Tura, or "Great Chief." Kashgar was taken and held for three months, after which the *Khojas* were again driven back to Khokand.

On the re-establishment of Chinese rule, the former mischievous trade and political relations with Khokand were renewed, and, in less than ten years, the people were ripe for another rebellion, this time under *Khoja* Wali Khan, who, in 1857, burst into Kashgar to receive a welcome from his Andijani compatriots, whilst the Chinese shut themselves up in their fortress till, once more, a Chinese force from Ili drove the usurpers out of the country. This was the fourth and last failure of the *Khojas* to restore their sovereignty in Kashgar.

We now come to another chapter in the history of the country, during which the Chinese were cut up root and branch. In 1862 there broke out in the provinces of Shensi and Kansu what is known as the Dungan rebellion, or insurrection of the Muhammadan Chinese. This was quite distinct from the *Khoja* machinations from Khokand, for this disaffection quickly spread westward over the whole of Sungaria and the Tarim basin, especially in such towns as were largely inhabited by Muhammadan Chinese. This brought the government at Peking to its wits' end, and, of course, weakened its hold of the distant provinces about Kashgar, whereupon the Turki Muhammadans were not slow to use the opportunity of once more casting off the Chinese yoke.

The first town to rise was Kuchar, where Rasheddin Khoja led a successful attack on the Chinese garrisons, was proclaimed Khan, and, by 1864, was acknowledged throughout the country except at Khotan. Rasheddin, however, was not one of the Aphak *Khojas*, and so not to the taste of Sadik Bek, a Kirghese Hakim or official of Kashgar, who requested the Khan of Khokand to send *Khoja* Buzurg, then living at Tashkend, and one of Aphak's descendants, that he might be placed on the throne of his ancestors.

Buzurg Khan lost no time in accepting the invitation, and took with him 50 men, and one Yakub Bek to be commander of his forces. The party appeared before the walls of Kashgar in 1865, and was gladly received by the inhabitants. Sadik Bek made over the government to Buzurg Khan, who speedily lapsed into debauchery, and the real power was gradually usurped by Yakub Bek.

Raising local forces, Yakub marched first, in the direction of Aksu, against Rasheddin, overcame him, and returned to meet a force of Dungans sent against him from Yarkand. He was again victorious, and also took Yengi Hissar. Later on, while attacking Yarkand, he discovered a treacherous movement among his followers; but by a liberal use of perjury, and by imprisoning some and killing others of the mountaineers whom he had vowed not to maltreat, he subdued the revolt, and then advanced afresh against Yarkand.

The commander of the Yarkand army was also gained over, and Yakub moved on towards Khotan. Here he enticed to his camp the ruler Habibulla Khoja, and, after swearing on the Koran to grant him a safe conduct, perfidiously slew him; so that it had come to pass, during 1866-7, that Yakub Khan had united under one sovereignty Kashgar, Yengi Hissar, Yarkand, and Khotan.

Buzurg Khan, in whose name these conquests were made, was now gradually set aside, then imprisoned, and at last sent away on pilgrimage to Mecca, after which Yakub was proclaimed Khan with the titles of Atalik Ghazi (principal champion of the faith) and Badaulet, or "the fortunate one."

His only rival now remaining in the country was Rasheddin, whose authority was still recognised by the inhabitants of Aksu, Karashar, and Kuchar. Rasheddin's court was at Kuchar, and hither Yakub hurried in 1867, enticed his rival to his camp, and had him murdered the same evening. The inhabitants of Kuchar submitted without fighting, as did those of Kurla, and thus the Turkish towns of the country were united under the new Khan.

Yakub then negotiated with the Dungan chiefs living eastwards, relative to a boundary line, which was fixed at about 30 miles east of Karashar. After this he returned *via* Aksu, where he appointed a governor, and then set out for Kashgar to consolidate the sovereignty he had set up.

Soon, however, the Dungans of Turfan, Urumtsi, and Manas violated their agreement, and, gathering a force, advanced against Karashar, Kurla, and Kuchar, pillaging the latter two. This caused Yakub to return to subjugate Dungans and Kalmuks alike, and he thereby gained possession, in 1869-70, of Urumtsi, Turfan, and the smaller towns westward.

After this Yakub Khan settled at Aksu, which he made his capital, and devoted five years to the domestic affairs of his state. In 1869 an insurrection in Sarikol was quickly subdued. Again, in 1872, the Dungans in Urumtsi rebelled, but Yakub's son, Bek-Kuli-Beg, being sent to punish them, gained possession of Manas also. After this, from 1872 to 1876, the country experienced a degree of quiet to which it had long been unaccustomed.

During this period Yakub built forts to secure his frontiers on the side of Russian Turkistan, and received from Russia—a new and highly important factor in the affairs of Central Asia—the missions of Kaulbars in 1872, of Reintal, for a second time, in 1875, and of Kuropatkin in 1876. Also, in 1870 and 1873, came the missions of Forsyth from India. Yakub tried further to strengthen his position by asking the patronage of the Sultan of Turkey, posed as a Defender of the Faith, and endeavoured to establish strong garrisons in all the towns.

But all this meant the levying of money and men from his subjects, as well as the importation of Khokandian soldiery, upon whom Yakub lavished most of his favours. The provinces were farmed out to governors, who exacted more than was due; the traders were hampered in their movements abroad, and mulcted of so-called dues; and even the mullahs were made to pay taxes, from which they had hitherto been exempt.

Thus Yakub Khan could never count on the sympathy of the people in upholding the power he had acquired by treason and treachery, perjury and murder; and the day of reckoning presently came, when the Chinese, having put down the Dungan rebellion in their western provinces, advanced in 1876 and re-occupied Manas and Urumtsi.

Many of the Dungan families fled to Yakub Khan, whose outposts during the following winter were at Turfan, Toksun, and the frontier post of Diwantchi. The *morale* of his troops was becoming weak and desertion frequent, whilst at the same time the Chinese troops were patiently biding their time, and actually sowed and reaped a crop of corn before they started afresh to the contest.

This they did in April 1877, when Fort Diwantchi surrendered without firing a shot. The Chinese commander treated his prisoners at Diwantchi with such generosity as to release them and furnish road expenses. He said he was come to deliver the country from the extortion of Yakub Khan and his Khokandian followers; and with this story of Chinese clemency some of the prisoners arrived at Karashar.

The news reached Yakub Khan at Kurla, and was not at all to his mind; so he ordered his younger son, Bek-Kuli-Beg, to stop the prisoners' power of babbling. The son obeyed by killing the greater part of them, leaving the rest to flee to the Chinese. Intelligence

of this atrocity, as it spread over the country, added to
the discontent of the people, and helped to predispose
them towards the return of the Chinese.

Kuropatkin says that the stories of Yakub Khan
dying from poison are devoid of foundation, and he
tells with much minuteness how that on May 28th,
1877, at five o'clock, Yakub Khan became greatly
exasperated with his secretary, Hamal, whom he killed
at a stroke with the butt-end of his gun. He then
began to beat his treasurer, Sabir Akhoon, who re-
taliated with a blow, which deprived the *Badaulet* of
his senses, so that he died at two o'clock the next
morning.

Upon this, Hak-Kuli-Beg, recalling the troops to
Kurla, appointed Hakim Khan Tura his deputy. He
then set out with his father's body for Kashgar,
nominally to submit to his elder brother, Bek-Kuli-
Beg, who saw in him, however, a rival, and had him
assassinated, thus securing his own authority in the
west. Meanwhile, the troops at Kurla had proclaimed
the deputy Hakim Tura as Khan, whilst at Khotan
the authority was seized by Niaz Beg.

The three upstarts now began to fight against
one another. Bek-Kuli-Beg conquered Hakim Tura,

* Lieut. Bower, who visited Karashar in 1890, was told that one day messengers "brought to Yakub Khan a letter from the Chinese, in which they asked him why he resisted when his own people were against him, and were inviting the Chinese back; and as a proof they inclosed the signatures of 272 Turkis of position who had written to them. Yakub Khan then flew in a passion, killed one of the messengers, wounded the mullah who had read the letter, and then immediately took poison and died." This was related by an old *Yuz-bashi*, who professed to have been in attendance on Yakub Khan at the time. His account, however, of the *Badaulet's* death differs entirely from that given by Kuropatkin, on the authority of Zaman Khan Effendi, who remained in a prominent position with Yakub Khan till his death, saw the fall of his monarchy, and then escaped to Russian territory.

and drove him into Russian territory; then, after resting a month in Kashgar, he set out for Khotan, whence he drove Niaz Beg into the desert towards Cherchen.

Having thus conquered the foes of his own household, Bek-Kuli-Beg heard on the 30th of October that the Chinese had advanced and captured Kurla, Kuchar, and Aksu, and that his own troops were in retreat towards Kashgar. He started, therefore, for Yarkand, whither he had caused his family to be brought, and where news came that at Kashgar the Chinese soldiers, who had been forced to turn Muhammadans, had shut themselves up in the Yengi-shahr, awaiting the arrival of their victorious compatriots.

Added to all this, the infantry whom Bek-Kuli-Beg sent from Yarkand, by the direct road to Maralbashi, deserted on the way; so that he would fain have escaped with his family in the direction of Karghalik, but was stopped and forced to attempt the recapture of the Kashgar fortress, in which dwelt many Turki wives and families.

He set out, and at Yengi Hissar, from sheer spite, slaughtered 200 Chinese menservants. The Governor of Kashgar also killed 400 Chinese who had not gone into the fortress. But all the Turki assaults on the fortress were unavailing.

On December 16th the Chinese army was reported to be close to Faizabad, and the Governor of Kashgar, shaking in his shoes, was sent out to meet the foe, which he did, and at once retreated. Then commenced a general stampede, and the Khokandians, with Bek-Kuli-Beg well to the fore, set out in the depth of winter for Russian territory, where, thanks to the kindness of the commander at Osh, many were saved from perishing, though not a few had been starved or frozen to death among the mountain snows.

On the same evening that the flight began, a small reconnoitring party, sent out from Maralbashi, entered Kashgar without a blow. The terrible massacres following reconquest on previous occasions were not forgotten, and, in addition to those who had fled from Kashgar, by the Terek-davan into Ferghana, some of the inhabitants of Yarkand tried to escape to Sarikol, but the Kirghese drove them back into the hands of the Chinese, who, this time, kept themselves under restraint.

About ten men were executed on the first day of their return; but Muhammadans were appointed head-men of the town, trial by *shariat* was permitted, and promise made that Muhammadanism should not be interfered with. Thus the people were appeased, and the country in 1877-8 once more submitted to its old masters.

China now called upon Russia to redeem her promise of restoring the Ili valley, which was honourably done in 1882, after which Russian consuls took up their residence in Kuldja; and in 1884 was formed, as already intimated, the Sin Kiang province, comprising Chinese Turkistan, and the districts of Ili and Tarbagatai.

Ili and Tarbagatai have a military organisation, but on my arrival in Kashgar in 1888 there had been established for two years a civil administration. Having thus brought matters up to the date of my visit I may continue my narrative.

CHAPTER XXXII.

FROM YENGI HISSAR TO YARKAND.

District of Yengi Hissar, 65.—Town of Yengi Hissar, 66.—Visits to *Medresse* and *Gumbaz*; Native astonishment at photography, 68.—A starting-point for Wakhan; Route to Tash-Kurgan, 70.—Sarikol district, 71.—The Ak-tash valley and Little Pamir, 72.—Gumbaz-Bozai and its political interest; Wakhan villages, and the way thence into India, 73.—Historical associations of Yengi Hissar; Struggles of early Muhammadans and Buddhists, 74.—Tombs of Muhammadan martyrs; Ruins at Urdum Padshah, 75.—Departure from Yengi Hissar and journey to Kizil, 76.—Iron smelting; March through Kok-Robat, 77.—Arrival at Yarkand, 78.

AT Yapchan we entered the division of Yengi Hissar which connects the districts of Kashgar and Yarkand. Its limits are Yapchan on the north, Ak-Robat, near Yarkand, on the south, Ighiz-Yar on the west, and Urdum Padshah on the east. The general character of the country, according to Forsyth, is arid desert, with here and there small saline pools, or more extensive reedy wastes; and everywhere the soil is highly charged with salts, which cover the ground with a white efflorescence, even under growing crops.

In the southern half of this division is a wide waste of this saline soil, covered with saltworts and a coarse reedy grass, but so soft and spongy that cattle cannot traverse it off the beaten track. Dr Bellew mentions that, dismounting on one occasion to follow some birds, he so sunk in walking that he was glad to turn back to the road.

Within the above limits the population was reckoned in Forsyth's time at 8,000 houses, congregated in about 40 agricultural settlements of at most 300 houses each. Up to Yapchan, a village of 250 houses, I rode, and there got into the *arba* for the night, which was sufficiently cold to make even my plaid an insufficient covering. We passed Khanka and Sitla—travellers' stations—our way having risen only 300 feet; Kashgar lying at an altitude of 4,043 feet, Yapchan 4,210; and, about sunrise, we approached, at an elevation of 4,320 feet, the town of Yengi Hissar.

The district belonging to the town contains 2,000 houses, and extends, says Forsyth, some 20 miles from west to east along the course of the Shahnaz river. For the town, the same authority gives about 600 houses.* The town and fort are separated from the river by an intervening ridge of sandstone and gravel hills called Kayragh. The suburbs are watered by six *ustang*, or canals, brought from the Ak-Kay reservoir at the Mazar Khoja Baglan, 30 miles west of the town, where it is filled by streams from the hills.

The main street of Yengi Hissar is lined with shops kept by Turkis, and out of this we turned into a *serai*, roomy and fairly comfortable, to spend the day,

---

* Hayward, in his itinerary, says 11,000! which I quote only to show how cautiously the figures of passing travellers—myself included —must be accepted, since they are often received from persons who do not really know; besides which the brains of uneducated Asiatics seem to fail them when they tell of reckonings of more than three figures.

previous to travelling again through the night. I mounted to the roof for a view, and secured thence a photograph of the neighbouring fort.

The fort has a side of about 500 yards long, a ditch about 50 feet wide at the top and 20 feet deep, not quite dry, fronted by a 30-foot covered way, with musketry parapet. The loopholed and crenelated walls of the fort are of mud, about 25 feet thick and high, with parapet 7 feet high and 3 feet thick. Pagoda-like buildings rise at intervals above the walls, especially over the gateways.*

In the town are three Chinese Mandarins—one civil (a *Leu*) and two military—assisted by six Turki begs of inferior rank. As my stay was to be so short, I did not think it necessary to call upon the authorities, but sent for the Russian *Aksakal*, Nazir Khoja, to whom M. Petrovsky had given me a letter. Upon my requiring small change, it appeared that the place to send for it was the *yamen*; and here for my small lumps of silver they would give at the rate of only 14 *tengas*, or 350 cash, for each *liang*, though offering to give for *yambs* 15½ *tengas*, or 387 cash—a rate considerably lower than the 475 of this coin received at Aksu.

The *Aksakal* accompanied us about the bazaar, to which a few Hindu merchants are said sometimes to come; and as I wanted to photograph public buildings I was taken to the Kulbashi (head of the brook)

* The four gateways have projections 35 by 60 yards, and inside are ramps 20 feet wide, the brick gateways being double, the outer 50 and the inner 100 feet deep. The covered way and ditch are carried round the projections. In the interior are few huts, but mud walls divide off several defensive inclosures, or quarters for troops, and storehouses. The garrison is supposed to consist of 500 Shantung cavalry.

medresse, built only a year before at a cost of 6,000 Kashgar *tengas* (£62), and containing from 30 to 40 mullahs. Before the entrance of the mosque was a broad verandah, the whole being raised on a platform within a quadrangle, round which were the humble chambers of the students.

After this they led us to a Chinese *Gumbaz*, or mortuary pile, whether covering the remains I am

A CHINESE "GUMBAZ," OR MORTUARY PILE, AT YENGI HISSAR.

not quite sure, but to the memory of some noted Chinaman, not long dead. It was simply a heap of mud in the form of a Kirghese tent, standing on a platform of mud and surmounted by a finial, the whole being surrounded with a clay open-work fence and inclosed by a wall.

Meanwhile, these photographic operations caused a good deal of astonishment among the natives, and some of the Chinese became troublesome. When, for instance, they saw me on the roof of the caravanserai, setting up my apparatus, they wanted to clamber up too; and, even when I entered my room, they came spying through the holes in the paper windows. One man had the impudence to enter my room unbidden, and seemed to think himself quite wronged when I ordered him out.

PRYING THROUGH WINDOW

The *djiguitts* also had some trouble in restraining the crowd, and I half began to wish that I had accepted a *djiguitt* from the Consulate, who would have stood no nonsense; but I observed that the Turki officials, although representatives of the Government, did not like to lay hands on a Chinaman. The courage of Joseph also considerably failed him on this occasion, which came sufficiently near to a quarrel to show me that for a foreigner, singlehanded, to deal with an excited or angry crowd of Chinese is a very ugly thing.

Had I decided upon crossing into India by the Baroghil Pass, Yengi Hissar would probably have been our point of departure. Here it was that Benedict Goes arrived from Badakshan; and hence Gordon, Trotter, Biddulph, and Stoliczka, as members of the Forsyth mission, set out for Wakhan by the most southerly of the roads I have mentioned as radiating from Kashgar to the Pamirs. Something, therefore, should be said of the south-eastern portion of these highlands, which has acquired a certain political importance for the Russians and English, and concerning which Captain Younghusband has read papers before the Geographical Society.

From Yengi Hissar the first day's journey southwards brings the traveller to the edge of the settled district at Ighiz-Yar, with 300 houses. Six miles beyond, up a river valley, the road enters the hills, which, 30 miles from the plains, present bold and precipitous cliffs. A good road continues up the valley to the Kash-kasu Pass (12,850 feet). This is reached on the fourth day, and on the south of it is Chihil (or Chegal) Gumbaz, or 40 domes, that number of clay tombs being supposed to have once been there, though Gordon found only one or two, and those not interesting. There is a road from here to Yarkand (110 miles distant), but for 35 miles it is without water.

During the fifth day's journey the Torut Pass (13,400 feet) is crossed, and two or three miles of the next day's march (in winter) is through a narrow defile, often in the bed of the stream. In this gorge with wall-like sides are several hot springs (about 116) and trees of poplar, birch, willow, and large juniper. On the next day are traversed the Chichiklik Pass (14,430 feet) and plain, to the capital of the Sarikol district, Tash-Kurgan, 125 miles from Yengi Hissar, and reached by Gordon's party on the tenth day.

The district generally slopes towards the Tarim basin, is 10,000 feet above the sea, and enjoys the alternate luxury and misery of three months of summer and nine of winter. The crops produced are beardless barley, beans, peas, carrots, and turnips. The domestic animals are camels, *yaks*, horses, cattle, sheep, and goats. A valley extends southwards across the Taghdumbash Pamir, and the river flowing through it rises in the Muztagh range of Kunjut. Between Ighiz-Yar and Tash-Kurgan, Gordon mentions Kirghese as the only inhabitants, to whom Younghusband adds Sarikolis on the Taghdumbash Pamir, and a few fugitive Wakhis.

Tash-Kurgan is inhabited by the Sarikolis, who are a different people altogether from the Kirghese. They told Gordon that they had been in the valley for seven generations as a distinct people, with a hereditary chief of their own, being descended from wanderers who came from Badakshan, Wakhan, Shignan, Hindustan, Kunjut, and Turkistan. Hence their language is a mixture of what is spoken in all these countries. But they speak Persian also. They have regular features and full beards. Their mode of salutation is different from that of the Turks, and they are Shiah Muhammadans.

During the former Chinese occupation the Sarikolis paid a nominal tribute, and secured presents yearly of

14 *yambs* (£158), which was regarded as a subsidy for the protection of the frontier and road towards Badakshan. Yakub Khan, to quell insurrection, sent hither an expedition, and deported the Sarikolis *en masse* to Kashgar in 1870, but allowed them to return two years later; and Gordon gave their number in 1874, in Tash-Kurgan and the neighbouring Muztagh-Ata plain, as 600 families.

The ruins of Tash-Kurgan are rectangular with projecting towers, apparently not ancient, but, in several of the hamlets, towers of refuge witness to the raids formerly made by the people of Kunjut and Shignan, who captured the Sarikolis and sold them as slaves.

The route from Tash-Kurgan to Wakhan continues by the Neza-tash Pass (14,900 feet) into the valley of Ak-tash, where at the foot of the Pass is a fort in ruins. M. Bonvalot, arriving here, had passed on the same day, coming south, a number of tombs—some of them in course of erection—to the memory of certain Kirghese of the family called Teits.

Through the Ak-tash valley runs the Aksu river, up the eastern bank of which the road continues through the Little Pamir to the Chakmak-Kul, marked in Walker's map as the Gaz-Kul. Gordon reached this spot on the fourth day from Tash-Kurgan. About six miles westward the party came to ruins of Kirghese huts and a burial ground, the Gumbaz-Bozai of Walker's map.*

---

* Bonvalot describes the mausoleum as of the ordinary shape—namely, four mud walls surmounted by a dome. In the lower portion are a few tombs of rectangular construction with a stone at each corner. He gives a second and generic name for it as Gumbaz-Bi, or tomb of a gentleman, presumably Bozai, who is said by Younghusband to have been a Kirghese chief who was murdered here.

About 25 miles from Chakmak-Kul there was, in Gordon's time, a deserted village, marked on Walker's map as Langar; but this and the Gumbaz-Bozai are both omitted from Bolsheff's map, and he inserts 14 miles west of the lake "Wakhan picket," as if to indicate the frontier outpost. But this does not appear in English maps (not even in Constable's recently issued map of the Pamir region), nor do I remember any such place alluded to by Bonvalot, Littledale, or Younghusband.

These details would have little interest but for the fact that it was in this neighbourhood Captain Younghusband, in September 1891, was directed by a company of Russians to turn back, as already alluded to. According to a Reuter's telegram dated February 25th, 1892, which appeared in the *Times* of the following day, it appears that "the Russian Government condemned as illegal the course taken by Captain Yanoff in expelling Captain Younghusband from the Pamir plateau, and expressed regret for the action of their officer."

From Langar the road continues 30 miles to Sarhad, a small village with a round fort and excellent grazing. Here the valley opens out, and habitations and cultivation begin and continue for five days' journey downwards among villages and intervening pasture flats to Kila Panjah, the capital. Again, from Sarhad the traveller may march without difficulty over the Baroghil Pass, which Littledale calls an extraordinary depression in the Hindu Kush, two or three miles wide, with mountains on either hand rising to a considerable height. He may then continue down the easy valley of the Yarkhun to Mastuj, as did M. Bonvalot, or he may cross, as Mr and Mrs Littledale did, the far more difficult Darkot Pass to Yasin, leading in either case to Kashmir.*

But to return whence this excursus began—to Yengi Hissar. This place has a certain attraction to the scholar, because hereabouts were fought the principal battles between Muhammadans and Buddhists by which the Muhammadans gained ascendency throughout the Tarim valley. In 1037 Hasan Bughra Khan began to reign at Kashgar with the title of Hazrat Padshah Ghazi, and upon the Buddhist forces from Khotan coming against him he opposed them with the help of his nephew Ali Arslan.

This Ali Arslan was son of Ala Nur Khanim, otherwise called Bibi Miryam, or Queen Mary, sister of the Padshah, who, whilst a virgin, was said to have miraculously given birth to this hero. The Buddhists had much ado, of course, to overcome such a prodigy, but, on their offering a reward to any one who would devise a means for his downfall, a poor old Jatlic or Nestorian priest suggested an early morning attack on the Muhammadans at the hour of prayer.

Success followed. Ali Arslan was decapitated, and his head paraded under the walls of Kashgar, before being thrown to the dogs. Hence this "martyr" has two shrines—one at Daulat Bagh, close to Kashgar, where the head is supposed to have been buried, and the other at Urdum Padshah, where his body was

---

* The Afghan merchants at Aksu gave me the following notes for the journey from Yarkand to Chitral :—

Yarkand to Siri-Kul	8 days.
Siri-Kul to Wakhan	9 ,,
Wakhan to Panja	2 ,,
Panja to Zebak (Saferbek ?)	3 ,,
Zebak to Chitral	10 ,,
	32 days.

interred. His mother, it is said, rushed into the battle-field to avenge her son's death, and, after slaying 25 of the "infidels," was herself put to death at what is now the shrine of Bibi Miryam, ten miles from Kashgar.

Some years afterwards Hasan was again attacked by the Buddhists at Yengi Hissar, and was slain. His widow, Bibi Chah Miryam Khanim, entering the field to avenge her husband's death, was pursued into the sandy desert and killed four days later. Her grave is marked by a lonely unpretending shrine called Mazar Hazrat Begum, with a poor monastery and almshouses, about 36 miles south-east of Yengi Hissar, 16 miles south of Urdum Padshah, and half a mile north of the ruins of the supposed city of Nukta Rashid.

Husen, brother of the fallen Hasan, now tried to retrieve the day, but was killed not far from the spot where his brother fell. Hence the two were buried in one grave, and the spot is now marked by the shrines and monastery of Chucham or Khojam Padshah, three miles west by south of Yengi Hissar. The entire district thereabouts is a vast cemetery, a desolate waste spreading far and wide, where several small fortified places were reduced to ruins.

Of these ruins the largest is Urdum Padshah, the site of which, Forsyth says, has been buried for centuries under the shifting sands; whilst not far distant, surrounded by a billowy sea of sand dunes, is the shrine of Ali Arslan. About 12 miles south of this latter shrine, near that of Hazrat Begum, are the indistinctly traceable fortifications of a castellated city now called Shahr-i-Nukta Rashid. It is more or less buried under sand, but the mound tops are wind-swept and thickly strewn with bits of pottery, china, and glass. North of Urdum Padshah are the ruins of Oktu, or Oktay, described as built of stone.*

These places of historic interest are all of them, it will have been noticed, away from the town; and though Yengi Hissar, or Newcastle, dates from about the eleventh century, there was nothing therein to induce one to stay, so that, worried as we were by the crowd of Chinese, I was not sorry to get away before the zeal of some of my attendants outran their discretion and culminated in a quarrel.

About five o'clock, therefore, I mounted my horse, and, with new *djiguitts*, we traversed the sandy mounds beyond the town, its gardens, and cultivation. Then we crossed a river by a bridge, and, similarly, several canals; then we ascended the flat, barren valley, a strip of cultivation being left to the northward, whilst to the southward were low sandy ridges. After proceeding for eight miles we crossed a grassy plain with a few villages, and, six miles beyond that, cultivation recommenced and continued with interruptions for 16 miles farther. Then began a sandy plain, beyond which lay the oasis of Kizil. I rode for about an hour and then turned into the *arba* for the night, which was fortunately moonlight, as the road was somewhat uneven.

We reached, at five next morning, and 31 miles from Yengi Hissar, Kizil (3,910 feet), consisting of

Forsyth quotes, as illustrative of the dry climate, that he found, near the tomb of Hasan, in the foundation of a wall, pieces of matting well preserved for 800 years—a statement I could cap by my own experience, in pieces of reed or rushes I found three times as old, and in good preservation, between the layers of sun-dried bricks at Babylon, under the mound supposed to represent the hanging gardens of Nebuchadnezzar.

300 families and a few shops, and here we rested eight hours. Here it was that Dr Bellew visited about a score of iron-smelting ovens, none, however, in blast. The ore was brought from hills two days' journey westward, and the miners and smelters were at that time said to number 200 families. Each furnace was built of clay and stone, in the centre of a round pit, roughly roofed, and with a narrow chimney six feet high, pierced round the base with air-holes. The charcoal and ore were mixed in the shaft of the chimney, and the melted metal sank into a trough below, where the nozzles of two or three bellows appeared to have been fixed.

Shaw mentions a village near Kizil named Tuplok, or Toblok, where he saw an iron furnace, with six boys and girls each blowing a skin bellows with each hand. Twenty *charaks* (16 lbs. each), he says, of ore, and the same of charcoal, were used in 24 hours, and the produce was about four *charaks* of iron, the metal being good and fine grained.

We left Kizil at about one o'clock in the day for a 30-mile stage. Riding all the afternoon across a *chul* or dreary desert of stones without verdure, we passed a ruined *langar* or rest-house with a well, and towards evening reached Ak-Robat. Here was only a picket station, inhabited by a Chinaman with a young and rather good-looking Turki wife. We asked for hot water, which proved brackish, and, after a poor cup of tea, on the *arba* coming up I got inside, and tried to sleep in crossing more desert to Kok-Robat, where we arrived a little before midnight.

Kok-Robat is a well-wooded oasis, a mile broad, with 400 families; the soil, a sandy clay, growing barley, maize, etc. We rested here through the night, and about eight o'clock next morning I started again on horseback for the remaining 25 miles to Yarkand.

I shot a few starlings and other small birds as we rode in turn through waste, grassy, partially cultivated, and well-cultivated land. Water abounded, and at 16 miles from Kok-Robat commenced the rich cultivation of the Yarkand oasis, whilst for the last three miles a wide, sandy, well-shaded broadway brought us to our goal, the city of Yarkand, 120 miles from Kashgar.

CHAPTER XXXIII.

BUDDHISM AND OTHER EARLY RELIGIONS IN CHINESE TURKISTAN.

Earliest religion of Tarim valley, 79.—Survival of Shamanism among Kirghese and Kalmuks; Fire-worship unknown, 80.—Brahmanism doubtful; Arrival of Buddhism; Missionaries sent for, 81.—Their work; Kuchar, an early seat of Buddhism, 82.—Travels of Fa-hian, Sung Yun, and Hiuen Tsiang; Buddhism at Cherchen, Han-moh, Karashar, Khotan, and in Tsung-ling Mountains, 83-85.—Hiuen Tsiang on Buddhism at Kuchar, Aksu, Badakshan, Osh, and Kashgar, 86.—Decay of Buddhism; Buddhist missionaries, 87.—Persecution of Buddhists, 90.—Hiuen Tsiang among fire-worshippers, 91.—Supposed results of Buddhist teaching; Buddhist aspirations towards a beatified life, 92.—Relics of Buddhism, 94.—The recently discovered Bower manuscript, 96.

RESPECTING the earliest forms of religious belief among the Sakas and the Yuechi during their sojourn in the Tarim basin I have met with no direct information. When Hiuen Tsiang in the seventh century has crossed out of Chinese Turkistan to the river Chu, he begins to speak of religions other than Buddhism, saying, "The Turks worship fire; they do not use wooden seats because wood contains fire, and even in worship they never seat themselves, but only spread padded mats on the ground, and so go through with it."

Again, on reaching Samarkand, he says: "The king

and people do not believe in the law of Buddha, but their religion consists in sacrificing to fire. There are here two religious (Buddhist?) foundations, but no priests dwell in them. If foreign priests seek shelter therein, the barbarians follow them with burning fire, and will not permit them to remain there."

Presently Hiuen Tsiang reaches the Oxus at Hwant'o-to (east of Balkh), where, he says, "The early kings of this country were not believers in Buddha, but sacrificed only to the spirits worshipped by unbelievers." This seems to point to Shamanism as the belief of those early rulers. Now, remembering that this was the district where the Yuechi settled after being driven out of the Tarim valley, it may be an indication of what, indeed, we should expect—that this early cult of Chinese Turkistan was in fact Shamanism.

This we know was the creed of Jinghiz Khan, and of many of the uncouth tribes that made their way westwards from the heart of Mongolia, and we doubtless see a survival of Shamanism among the Kirghese and Kalmuks in their fear of the spirits of the mountains, and in their attributing to these spirits the origin of disease.

On the other hand, I have met with no allusion showing that fire-worship ever gained a footing in the Tarim valley. North and west of the mountains, on the Chu at Su-yeh (Tokmak?), on the Zarafshan at Samarkand and Bokhara, as well as farther south at Balkh, we read of fire-worshippers. We know little about them, however, and the only relics I can indicate in Chinese Central Asia are a few lingering customs in the Pamir highlands concerning fire, and the so-called catacombs, vaguely ascribed to the time of Zoroaster which a Russian Colonel told me were still existing near Panjdeh.

Again, Dr Bellew, on the authority, seemingly, of the *Tarikhi Narshakhi*, written in 943, says that in the first century of the Christian era Hindu Brahmanism flourished vigorously in the region eastward of Bokhara. I have seen no confirmation of this, either as regards the region spoken of, or of Chinese Turkistan, so that, in the absence of fuller information, the first religion we know to have been established in Chinese Turkistan was Buddhism. The founder of this creed died about 550 B.C., and 300 years afterwards his teachings became, under Asoka—"the Constantine of the new religion"—an adopted creed in Northern India, and missionaries proceeded in various directions to spread it.

So, too, among the wonders of the West brought back by Chang-kian on his return from the Yuechi in B.C. 122, he had to tell of the worship in India and Tokharistan of Buddha; and a succeeding general, Hou Kiuping, when warring against the Uigurs, saw a golden statue of Buddha worshipped by the king of Hieou-to (perhaps Sarikol).

After this, in A.D. 62, the Chinese Emperor Ming-ti, instigated it is said by a dream and the vision of an image, despatched a mission to Tokharistan and Central India, which returned after 11 years with five Buddhist books. These were translated by imperial order about 76 A.D., and from that time Buddhism began to spread in China.

In 150 An-shi-kau, a priest of Eastern Persia, is noticed in the Chinese annals as an excellent translator. Twenty years later a priest of the Yuechi produced a translation of the *Nirvana sutra*. About

250 we find Chi Meng, a resident at Turfan, translating for the priesthood rules which he is said to have obtained from Patna.

In 290, according to Beal, a Chinese pilgrim named Chu-si-hing visited Khotan; and, in 260, we read of Fa-hou reaching China. He subsequently traversed the western countries, where he gained a knowledge of the dialects of 36 kingdoms, and brought to the imperial court at Lo-yang (Honan-fu) Buddhist and Brahmin works—of which no less than 165 were translated by the year 308.

In A.D. 335 a prince of what is now Shansi first permitted his subjects to take Buddhist vows. Hitherto natives of India had indeed been allowed to build temples in large cities; but now the people of the country were permitted to become *Shamans* or devotees; and it may be noted as a proof of the rapid growth of Buddhism that, in 350, at Lo-yang alone, there had been erected, after Indian models, 42 pagodas.

This religious movement in China proper was probably intensified in Chinese Turkistan, through which the missionaries passed, founding on their way religious establishments. We read of one of these establishments early at Kuchar (or Kucha); for the Emperor of China sent there, about the end of the fourth century, for a learned Indian priest who might supply correct versions of the chief Buddhist books known up to that time in China, where, the versions being procured, the work was helped forward alike by emperor, princes, and 800 priests.

At this period lived Chi Fa-hian (spelt also Shi Fa-hien) at Tchang'an, in Shensi. He was grieved at the imperfect rules of monastic discipline in that city, and the erroneous versions of Buddhist books. Accordingly, he set out in 399 to procure from India trustworthy texts. He was followed in 518 by Sung Yun, and in 629 by Hiuen Tsiang; and to these three we mainly owe our knowledge of contemporaneous Buddhism in Chinese Turkistan.

Placing their records side by side, and proceeding westwards from the Chinese capital, we hear first of Cherchen, where Fa-hian reports the existence of 4,000 priests, monks, or devotees—that is to say, not mere converts, but 4,000 Buddhists who had taken upon themselves vows and obligations to follow an exclusively religious life. In summer their duty was to itinerate as teachers; but in winter, or during the rainy season, they were supposed to live in forests, gardens, or secluded places, called *sangharamas*, where they could meditate and instruct their disciples.

About 500 miles west of Cherchen, Sung Yun speaks of Tso-moh (the Pi-mo, seemingly, of Hiuen Tsiang), where was a representation of Buddha; and, farther west, a city called Han-moh, with a large temple and 300 priests. Here was a full-length figure of Buddha, about 18 feet high, that was said to have translated itself hither through the air. It was reported to emit a bright light, and of course possessed miraculous powers, so that "those who have any disease, according to the part affected, cover the corresponding place on the statue with gold leaf, and forthwith they are healed." Towers were built around the image and decorated with 10,000 streamers of silk, covered with inscriptions and dates, for the most part about the year 500.

Near Karashar, Fa-hian gives the number of priests at 4,000; whilst in Hiuen Tsiang's time they are quoted at about 2,000, with ten or more monasteries, wherein the professors of the religion read their books and observed the rules with purity and strictness, partaking only of the three pure aliments.

At Khotan, according to Rockhill, the law of Buddha was introduced 170 years after the establishment of the kingdom. Sung Yun gives the story of the king's conversion by a *Bhikshu*, or Buddhist fakir, under a plum-tree; and Fa-hian numbers the priests at several tens of thousands, of whom he records some interesting details.

He says they used religious music for mutual entertainment. All had food provided for them, and dwellings were set apart for travelling priests. In one temple were 3,000 priests, who assembled to eat at the sound of the *ghanta*. "On entering the dining-hall their carriage is grave and demure, and they take their seats in regular order. All keep silence, and, when needing more food, signal for it by the hand."

Fa-hian stayed at Khotan to see the procession of images. "From the first day of the fourth month they water and decorate the streets, whilst above the city gate an awning is spread for the king, queen, and courtiers. About a mile from the city they make a four-wheeled image-car about 30 feet high, like a moving palace, adorned with the seven precious substances, and streamers of silk and curtains. The image is placed in the car, with two carved attendants, and ornaments suspended in the air. At a hundred paces from the gate, the king meets it with flowers and the burning of incense, and worships bareheaded, after which the ladies over the gate scatter flowers on the car as it passes below. This continues for 14 days, according to the number of the large religious establishments, each of which has its own car and its own day during the festival."

About three miles west of the city was said to be the royal new temple, which had been 80 years in building under three kings. It was nearly 300 feet high, adorned with carving and inlaid work, and covered with gold and silver. Above the roof were all kinds of jewels, the gifts of six kings, and the priests' apartments therein were beautiful beyond description.

Hiuen Tsiang mentions, in connection with his visit to Khotan, 100 monasteries and 5,000 followers, the king greatly venerating the law of Buddha.

West of Khotan, Fa-hian mentions the Tseu-ho country (perhaps the district of Yengi Hissar), where the king was an earnest Buddhist, surrounded by 1,000 priests. Thence our traveller came to the Tsung-ling Mountains, where the king of Kie-sha was said to keep the great quinquennial assembly.

On this occasion religious men from all quarters were congregated, and the priests were seated amid great magnificence. During several days offerings were made to them, and finally the king presented his own horse and trappings, vowing to give to the priests all he had. Much of this, however, was mere palaver, the presents being redeemed at a price, just as I have seen a Hindu in the Ganges at Allahabad offering to his god a cow, of which he has become the temporary possessor for a few pence, the animal being returned after the ceremony to its real owner.

In this country, too, were 1,000 priests and some relics of Buddha—his water-vessel and one of his teeth, a *stupa*, or monument, having been built for the tooth. This resembles what Hiuen Tsiang records

of Balkh, where he found about 100 *sangharamas* and
3,000 monks, and a *stupa* 200 feet high. In his day
Buddha's sweeping-brush would appear to have been
added to the relics, which now were brought out on
feast days to be worshipped.

In addition to the places in Chinese Turkistan
already mentioned, we are indebted to Hiuen Tsiang
for a glimpse of Buddhism at Kuchar, where some
remains and an important manuscript have been recently discovered by Lieutenant Bower. Hiuen
Tsiang found at Kuchar 100 *sangharamas* and 5,000
disciples using the literature and discipline of India.
He mentions, as near at hand, two monasteries on
the slope of a mountain and a statue of Buddha;
also, in the hall of the eastern monastery, a jade
stone, about two feet wide, bearing a foot trace of
Buddha, which emitted at the expiration of every
fast day a bright and sparkling light.

Again, outside the western gate of the chief city
were two erect figures of Buddha, about 90 feet
high. In front of these was held the quinquennial
assembly, when all the people observed a religious
fast, listening to the teaching of the law, and witnessing the procession of images. During this month
the king and his ministers, after consulting with the
priests, published their decrees.

At Aksu, Hiuen Tsiang mentions ten *sangharamas*
and about 1,000 priests, and then, crossing the mountains, he does not again remark on Buddhism until
he comes to Samarkand, where it had been stamped
out, probably by the fire-worshippers, as just now
mentioned.

On his return journey from India, Hiuen Tsiang
finds only three or four *sangharamas* in Badakshan,

and scarcely any priests in Kiu-lang-na and Ta-mo-si-tie-ti, on the Upper Oxus. As he continued eastward, however, he found at Kie-pan-to (perhaps Sarikol) a king and people greatly revering Buddha, with ten *sangharamas* and 500 followers. He mentions also Osh (which may be Osh in Ferghana or Ush-Turfan), with ten *sangharamas* and about 1,000 priests. After this he comes to Kashgar, with its several hundreds of *sangharamas* and 10,000 followers; whilst, lastly, he speaks of Cho-kiu-kia (Yarkiang), where were several tens of *sangharamas*, mostly in ruins, with some hundreds only of followers.

So much, then, for the religious condition of Chinese Turkistan between the starting of Fa-hian in 399 and the return of Hiuen Tsiang in 645. Later, we have several notices of Buddhist travellers to the west, preserved to us by a pilgrim, I-tsing, who lived about 670. He says that the travellers following Fa-hian and Hiuen Tsiang experienced difficulty in itinerating to the same spots, in consequence of there being no monasteries set apart for Chinese priests, which looks as if Buddhism in the valley had begun to wane.

Before advancing further, however, let us look more closely at these Buddhist missionaries, their principles and methods of working, and the results they were able to effect.

First, we notice that the Buddhist missionary always came to the people as a very poor man, professing to keep his body in subjection, and strictly bound to celibacy. As an individual he might possess only eight things in the world—namely, four pieces to make up his suit of clothing, an alms-bowl, a razor, a needle, and a water-strainer, the last a cubit square, through which everything he drank had to be passed, not merely to remove impurities, but to prevent the possible destruction of living creatures.

His robes were of cloths pieced together from cast-off rags ; two under-garments, one loose robe to cover the whole of the body except the right shoulder, and a fourth piece of cotton cloth for a girdle. He might not have a change of garments and might never ask for new, though if offered by the laity he might accept them.

As regards food, he was strictly under discipline. He might eat solid food only between sunrise and noon, and total abstinence from intoxicating drinks was obligatory. Morning by morning he passed from door to door, hoping to receive food, but not asking for it. When any was given he uttered in return a pious wish on behalf of the giver, but if nothing was bestowed he passed on in silence to the next house. The more strict among the devotees abstained from animal food ; ate the whole meal once a day without rising ; refused invitations to dine, and of food brought to them, and made a point of eating everything collected in the bowl, whether tasty or otherwise.

Besides the foregoing, every monk took the following vows :—1. Not to destroy life ; 2. Not to steal ; 3. To abstain from impurity ; 4. Not to lie ; 5. To abstain from intoxicating drinks ; 6. Not to eat at forbidden times ; 7. To abstain from dancing, singing, music, and stage-plays ; 8. Not to wear or use garlands, scents, unguents, or ornaments (not even his own hair, which had to be kept shaven); 9. Not to use a high or broad bed ; and 10. Not to receive gold or silver.

As to their manner of argumentation, an extract from the biographical section of the history of the

Sung dynasty, quoted by Beal, gives us a peep into their method of dealing with Sadducean opponents among the followers of Confucius.

"The instructions of Confucius," says the Buddhist assailant, "include only the single life ; they do not reach to the future state, with its interminable results. His only motive to virtue is the happiness of posterity, and the only consequence of vice that he mentions is present suffering. The rewards of the good do not go beyond worldly honours ; the recompense of guilt is nothing worse than present obscurity and poverty. Such ignorance is melancholy.

"The aims of the doctrine of Buddha are illimitable. His religion removes care from the heart, and saves men from the greatest dangers. Its one sentiment is mercy seeking to save. It speaks of hell to deter people from sin ; it points to heaven that men may desire its happiness. It exhibits the Nirvana as the spirit's final refuge, and tells us of a body to be possessed under other conditions long after our present body has passed away."

To this the Confucianist replies :—

"To be urged to virtue by the desire of heaven cannot be compared to the motive supplied by the love of doing what is right for its own sake. To avoid wrong from the fear of hell is not so good as to govern self from a sense of duty. Acts of worship, performed for the sake of obtaining forgiveness of sins, do not spring from piety. A gift made for the purpose of securing a hundredfold recompense cannot result from sincerity. To praise the happiness of Nirvana promotes a lazy inactivity. To dwell upon that form of body which we may hereafter attain to is calculated only to promote the love of the marvellous."

To this the Buddhist rejoins:—

"Your conclusions are wrong. Motives derived from a consideration of the future are necessary to lead men to virtue. Else how could we adjust the evil of the present life? Men will not act spontaneously without something to hope for. The countryman ploughs his land because he hopes for a harvest. If he had no such hope he would sit idle at home and perish."

Later on, we have an instance of Buddhist calmness in argument during a time of persecution. Under the Tang dynasty the restoring and re-editing of Buddhist books was brought to perfection; but when Kaou-Tson ascended the throne, his Confucian minister Fuh-yih induced the Emperor to call a council to deliberate on what should be done respecting Buddhism.

Fuh-yih proposed that the monks and nuns should be compelled to marry and bring up children. "The reason they adopt the ascetic life," he says, "is to avoid contributing to the revenue. What they hold about the fate of men depending on the will of Buddha is false. Life and death are regulated by a self-governing fate. The retribution of virtue and vice is the province of the prince; riches and poverty are the result of our own actions. Buddhism has caused the public manners to degenerate, whilst the theory of the metempsychosis is entirely fictitious. The monks are idle and unprofitable members of the commonwealth."

To this Siau-ü, a friend of Buddhism, replied:—

"Buddha was a sage, and, in speaking ill of a sage, Fuh-yih has been guilty of a great crime."

His opponent answered that loyalty and filial piety are the greatest virtues, and the monks, casting off as they did their prince and parents, disregarded them both; and that Siau-ü, in defending their system, was equally guilty with themselves.

Whereupon Siau-ü, joining his hands (the Buddhist mode of polite address), merely said that "hell was made for such men as his vilifier."

From this let us turn to Hiuen Tsiang and his method of procedure among the fire-worshippers at Samarkand. On his arrival he was treated disdainfully by the king, but, after the first night's rest, he discoursed for the king's sake on the destiny of men and Devas; he lauded the meritorious qualities of Buddha. He set forth, by way of exhortation, the character of religious merit. The king was rejoiced, and requested permission to receive instruction as a disciple and take the moral precepts, from which time he showed Hiuen Tsiang the highest respect.

Two young disciples went to the Buddhist place of worship, on which the fire-worshippers again pursued them with burning fire. The king directed the fire-carriers to be arrested, and, having assembled the people, ordered their hands to be cut off. The "Master of the Law," however, wishing to exhort them to a virtuous life, interceded, and they were let off with a beating.

From this circumstance all sorts of people regarded Hiuen Tsiang respectfully, and in a body sought to be instructed in the faith. Accordingly, having summoned a large assembly, he received many of them into the priesthood and established them in *sangharamas*. "It was thus that he transformed their badly disposed [heretical] hearts, and corrected their evil customs. And so it was wherever he went."

The modern reader cannot fail to be struck with the

self-denial, meekness, gentleness, and perseverance of these ancient missionaries of Buddhism; nor need we doubt that the manners and customs of the rude nations they taught were somewhat softened thereby. Fa-hian found at Palibothra hospitals for the diseased and destitute, and Hiuen Tsiang speaks of the distribution of food and medicine at the "houses of beneficence" in the Panjab.

Kublai Khan seems to have fostered Buddhism with an eye to the roughness of his quarrelsome people, so that, in setting over them a Public Instructor, he appointed a Buddhist monk, thereby endeavouring to produce among them some degree of order and love of peace.

Again, Marco Polo observes that the Mongols before their conversion to Buddhism never practised almsgiving, but that, under the priests' teaching, the Khan provided needy families with a whole year's subsistence, and established a bakery, open to all comers, where petitioners were supplied with a loaf or cake to the number of 30,000 a day.

It would appear, moreover, from Schott's essay on Buddhism in Upper Asia and China, as quoted by Yule, that Buddhist teaching led the aspirations of its followers to a future beatified life.

"In the years Yuan-yeu of the Sung (A.D. 1086–1093), a pious matron with her two servants lived entirely to the Land of Enlightenment. One of the maids said one day to her companion, 'To-night I shall pass over to the Realm of Amita.' The same night a balsamic odour filled the house, and the maid died without any preceding illness.

"On the following day the surviving maid said to the lady, 'Yesterday my deceased companion appeared to me in a dream, and said to me, "Thanks to the persevering exhortations of our mistress, I am become a partaker of Paradise, and my blessedness is past all expression in words."'

"The matron replied, 'If she will appear to me also, then I will believe what you say.'

"Next night the deceased really appeared to her, and saluted her with respect.

"The lady asked, 'May I for once visit the Land of Enlightenment?'

"'Yea!' answered the Blessed Soul; 'thou hast but to follow thy handmaiden.'

"The lady followed her (in her dream), and soon perceived a lake of immeasurable expanse, overspread with innumerable red and white lotus flowers, of various sizes, some blooming, some fading.

"She asked what those flowers might signify.

"The maiden replied: 'These are all human beings on the earth whose thoughts are turned to the Land of Enlightenment. The very first longing after the Paradise of Amita produces a flower in the Celestial lake, and this becomes daily larger and more glorious as the self-improvement of the person whom it represents advances; in the contrary case, it loses in glory and fades away.'

"The matron desired to know the name of an enlightened one who reposed on one of the flowers, clad in a waving and wondrously glistening raiment.

"Her whilom maiden answered, 'That is Yangkie.'

"Then she asked the name of another, and was answered, 'That is Mahu.'

"The lady then said, 'At what place shall I hereafter come into existence?'

"Then the Blessed Soul led her a space farther,

and showed her a hill that gleamed with gold and azure. 'Here,' said she, 'is your future abode. You will belong to the first abode of the blessed.'

"When the matron awoke she sent to inquire for Yangkie and Mahu. The first was already departed; the other was still alive and well. And thus the lady learned that the soul who advances in holiness and never turns back may be already a dweller in the Land of Enlightenment, even though the body still sojourn in this transitory world."

In this case one is surprised that the lady, who was to occupy so high a place, did not see her second self already seated on a lotus in the Land of Enlightenment; but from what has been said it is not hard to conceive that Buddhism in Chinese Turkistan may once have been a spiritual power of no little energy.

If now we ask for tangible remains of ancient Buddhism in Chinese Turkistan, I know of one place only where they are said to exist. Johnson and Carey asked in vain for vestiges of Buddhism about Kiria and Khotan, nor did I see any throughout those parts of the country I visited. An interesting testimony has come to light, however, in the pages of the Chinese mandarin Tchuen-yuen.

Speaking of Kuchar (or Kucha) he says: "At 20 *li* north of the town one may see the Siao-fo-t'oung, or cave of the great Buddha. Above and below, before and behind, in all parts of the mountain are found four or five hundred grottoes excavated in the mountain, inclosing statues of Buddha painted in all sorts of colours. In the loftiest cave stand three columns. Above, in a hollow, is the image of a great teacher in white clothing, and in Chinese characters, exactly formed, a dissertation on metempsychosis; whilst on the walls is engraved the person's life."

To this M. Gueluy adds a note from another source: "At 60 *li* west of the town, at Su-bash, there is also the Ta-fo-t'oung. . . . the grotto of Si-fan-to [the Buddha of the Tanguts], with three portions of the walls. . . . The remainder [of the inscription] is in Tangut characters. The origin of these inscriptions is unknown."

This testimony of Tchuen-yuen agrees with what Bellew was told in 1873, that near Kuchar there remained ruins of a temple and monastery, fragments of sculpture and painted galleries, together with a large figure overlooking the road to Kurla. Precious stones, also, says Forsyth, gems and trinkets, are occasionally found, and marvellous tales are told of the lustre and size of some that have been picked up here by wandering shepherds.

A still later testimony is that of Lieutenant Bower, who was at Kuchar in 1890, when a man offered to show him "a subterranean town" if he would go in the middle of the night, as the man was afraid of getting into trouble with the Chinese if they knew he had taken a European there.

Bower went, and writes: "The subterranean ruins of Mingoi are situated about 16 miles from Kuchar, on the banks of the Shahyar river, and are said to be the remains of Afrasiab's capital. The town must have been of considerable extent, but has been reduced by the action of the river. On the cliffs on the left bank, high up in mid-air, may be seen the remains of houses still hanging on the face of the cliff."

In one of the houses Bower entered he saw a tunnel

60 yards long by four broad, running through a tongue-shaped hill, with two transverse entrances and five cells, each six feet square, the walls of which had been plastered and figured with geometrical patterns.

There were said to be other similar remains in the district, as well as what Bower calls "curious old erections, generally 50 or 60 feet high, resembling somewhat in shape a huge cottage loaf, solid, and composed of sun-dried bricks with layers of beams now crumbling away." There is one also, Bower says, on the north bank of the river at Kashgar.

The natives attribute them to Afrasiab, but I suppose there can be little doubt that they are Buddhist *stupas* erected over relics. This is confirmed by Bower's guide having procured for him a packet of old manuscripts written on birch-bark, that had been dug out at the foot of one of these "curious old erections."

The manuscript thus discovered has proved to be a veritable treasure, and has been named by Dr A. F. Rudolf Hoernle "the Bower manuscript." The whole was inclosed between two wooden boards, with holes through which string was passed, its appearance thus resembling the manuscripts of India.*

Its contents consist of five portions. The first (of 31 leaves) is a medical work; the second (of 5 leaves) forms a collection of proverbial sayings; the third (of

* It is written on leaves of birch-bark, some of single thickness and others of from two to four thicknesses. Each layer is of extreme tenuity, almost transparent, the layers not being glued together, but remaining apparently in their natural state of adhesion. The shape of the leaves is different from that of all other birch-bark manuscripts hitherto known, their form being oblong and measuring about a foot in length by nearly three inches in width. The handwriting throughout is, with certain archaic forms, in the alphabet of North-western India. This points to its age being not later than 600 A.D.; and Dr Hoernle is disposed to place its date somewhere between 350 and 500 A.D.

4 leaves) contains the story of how a charm against snake-bite was given by Buddha to Ananda; the fourth part (of 6 leaves) appears to contain also a collection of proverbial sayings; and the fifth portion (of 5 leaves) contains another medical treatise.

Dr Hoernle has translated and annotated this fifth portion. It is written for the most part in verse, the metres employed exhibiting a very great variety. The language is Sanscrit.* Full information concerning the Bower manuscript is given by Dr Hoernle in the Journal of the Asiatic Society of Bengal for 1891.

Meanwhile this discovery indicates the possibility

* By way of example, I add his translation of verses 59-66, and what is written on the obverse of the fourth leaf:—

"With Dādima (pomegranate) and Tvacha (cinnamon) one should boil one-and-a-half portion of pungent (Indian mustard) oil; this causes the growth of the ears, and of the female and male genital organs. One should boil half a pala of the root of Chitraka (*Plumbago zeylandica*), likewise of Trivrit (*Ipomœa turpethum*), and Sātalā (*Stereospermum suaveolens*); and one karsha each of the roots of Danti (*Baliospermum montanum*) and . . . , and likewise of long pepper, rocksalt, asafœtida, and sorrel, and foremost 20 (karsha ?) of chebulic myrobalan. . . .

"From these one should carefully prepare ten boluses with eight pala of treacle, and take one of them on every tenth day. After it one should drink warm water for the purpose of correcting the defects of the humours; then, after the purgative has taken effect, one should bathe, and one may then return to one's ordinary diet. There should never be any hesitation with regard to this remedy, either in word, or deed, or thought. It is a purgative composed by Agasti, fit for princes, and which can be used in all seasons. It prevents old age and death; it cures all diseases; it also acts as an aphrodisiac and alterative tonic, and increases memory and health. It should never be administered to any one who has no son nor disciple; nor should it be given to an enemy of the king, nor to any other sinful liver."

Verses 81*b*-82*a* read: "Darvi (Indian barberry) and best Madhuka (liquorice), boiled in the milk of a cow or a woman, and mixed with sugar, may be applied by a good physician as a lotion in any disease due to wind, blood, and bile." And, lastly, verse 100 states that "If one laughs or eats while a plaster is applied to his face, his phlegm as well as his wind will be deranged."

of finding other manuscripts. I am told the Russians are already on the alert, and are sending experts to search. Additional manuscripts would be more valuable, since, with the exception of the ruins indicated above, the iron heel of the false prophet has seemingly stamped out every other vestige of Buddhism in Chinese Turkistan.

CHAPTER XXXIV.

OUR STAY IN YARKAND.

Hospitable reception, 98.—Lodged in suburbs, but photography forbidden, 100.—History of Yarkand, 101.—Forsyth's description, 104. —The old town and fortress; its population and mosques, 105. Trade and costumes; No lunatic asylum; Visits from mullahs and merchants, 107.— Money loans offered; Medical assistance requested, 109.—Diseases prevalent in Chinese Turkistan; Servants of Dalgleish, 110. Dalgleish's career and murder, 111. Dalgleish's house, 115 Letter from Leh, 116. Negotiations for baggage horses, 117.

AS we approached Yarkand, I felt somewhat of a stranger in a strange land. There was no friendly Consul expecting us; my only fellow-countryman, who usually lived there, had been recently murdered; and I did not expect to find a creature whom I knew, or who had ever heard of me.

It was pleasant, therefore, to meet, within about a mile of the town, a deputation come out to receive us, headed by one Mirza Muhammad Ali, calling himself *Aksakal* of the Kashmiris, and several other British subjects, as well as Mirza Jan Haji, to whom the Russian Consul had given me a letter. These were accompanied by several other Turkis arrayed in white turbans, and, for the most part, mounted, but some were on foot.

A *djignitt* had been sent forward with a letter and my card to announce our approach to the authorities, and they, Muhammad Ali informed me, had sent him, thinking I should speak Hindustani. He was desired to say that a lodging was to be prepared for me in his country house in the suburbs; but if I did not like to go there, a *serai* should be put at my disposal in the town.

I thought it best to fall in with their arrangements, and we accordingly rode forward, our cavalcade increasing as we advanced, especially by the addition of natives of India and Afghanistan, several of whom saluted, and seemed to regard us as fellow-subjects.

"Do you like the English?" said Joseph to one of the footmen running by his side.

"Why, of course I do," said the man, "or I should not have come all this distance to meet the Sahib."

And, henceforward, this seemed to be the key-note of a great deal of the attention shown to us.

We rode right through the native and Chinese portions of the town, and finally drew rein at a house about two miles out of the city in the midst of a mass of greenery. Here were gardens, flower-beds, and fruit trees in abundance, besides tall poplars that furnished specimens of starlings and small birds for my collection. In the outhouses was abundance of space for horses and retainers, whilst within the house were rooms for the storage and repacking of parcels.

The chamber set apart for my use was of large dimensions, carpeted, but not furnished, the entire end of the room consisting of a screen of carved lattice-work covered with paper. The door opened on to a spacious verandah, roofed over and supported in front by two wooden pillars. Here carpets could be spread, visitors received, and a good view obtained of the garden and grounds.

My host, Muhammad Ali, with several others, having stayed to see us comfortably settled, left us for the night in what proved the best quarters we lighted upon throughout the country. Had we been going to stay a month, nothing could have been nicer; the chief drawback was that we were entirely cut off from the native life of the city.

Next morning Muhammad Ali reappeared, saying that he had reported our arrival to the Chinese authorities, and had received permission for me to look about the town. I was preparing, therefore, about noon, to take my camera; but this put my host in a great fever, and he looked thoroughly frightened. Moreover, upon sending for permission to the *yamen*, where the *Amban* was temporarily absent, the officer next in command declined to undertake so grave a responsibility as giving me leave to photograph, and I had, for the moment, to desist. This continued throughout our early visits to the town, which extended from the 21st to the 25th of September; but things were rendered easier for us on our second visit, from the 17th to the 22nd of October, by which date the *Amban* had returned.

Before describing what we saw in the town, something should be said, I think, of Yarkand in palmier days. Bellew says, "Yarkand is one of the ancient cities of Tatary, and was in remote times a royal residence of the Turk princes of the Afrasyab dynasty"; but I have met with no trustworthy mention of it till the time of Hiuen Tsiang, and if his "Cho-kiu-kia" be Yar-kiang, then he does not say much that is suggestive of its importance.

Nor does it give one a lofty idea of its strength at the end of the eleventh century, that the place submitted to Hasan, who, after driving his Buddhist foes into the hills, returned to Kashgar, pocketing Yarkand *en route*.

In the thirteenth century Marco Polo says of the province of "Yarcan": "They have plenty of everything, particularly of cotton. The inhabitants are also great craftsmen." It does not appear, however, to have become a seat of government till made so in the early part of the sixteenth century by Mir Said Ali, grandfather of Ababakar.

This Ababakar is said to have greatly improved the city with mansions and gardens. Also he strengthened its fortification by building at a hundred paces in front of each gate two round towers for archers, and these towers were connected with the gate by a covered way, whence the defenders could shoot at those assaulting the gate. The *Tarikhi Rashidi* says that the walls were rebuilt by Ababakar, with six gates, and inclosing an area that would require 2,800 lbs. of corn to sow it. The city was supplied with water by canals from the Yarkand river, and Ababakar is said to have laid out 12,000 gardens, which probably means throughout his territory.

Yarkand was continued as capital of the country by Said; but the first detailed statement of the condition of the place in modern times we owe to Tchuen-yuen, who says:—

"They have now established there granaries wherein is stored the corn paid as taxes. These granaries occupy a vast inclosure, wherein is the official residence of the chief mandarin. The ditches of the ramparts are deep and in good condition. They form a circuit of from three to five miles. Upon the arrival of the Chinese [that is, after the depopulation of Sungaria in 1756] the chief mandarin lived at Yarkand, then at Kashgar, and later at Ush-Turfan.

"Yarkand has 8 Custom-houses and 13 military stations, the latter comprising 300 Manchu soldiers and 650 Chinese to guard the town. The Customs receipts are 35,370 *taels* of silver (£8,000), 30,540 *tan* (1,830,000 bushels) of cereals, 330 ounces of gold (£1,300), 800 lbs. of vegetable oil, besides 1,749 *taels* (£400) of communal contributions for the support of the town. For military contributions the Mussulmans give annually 57,569 pieces of cotton cloth, 15,000 lbs. of carded cotton, 1,432 linen girdles, 1,297 cords of hemp, and 3,000 lbs. of copper, of which half is sent to Ili to be made into cash.

"The governor of Yarkand has under his jurisdiction ten Mussulman towns. Yarkand has a population of from 70,000 to 80,000 families, each of the nine towns possessing about 1,000 families. Chinese merchants of Shansi, Kiang-si, Kiang-nan, and Che-Kiang, as well as the Wai-Fan, and the inhabitants of Ngansi, Touibatche, Khokand, Kashmir, and other places, have here their houses of business. The street of the Batchas is three miles long, shop after shop, and inclosing a veritable anthill of men. It is a rich country, and abounds in cattle and pasture.

"The natives in everything imitate the Chinese, whom they hold in great respect. They are by nature timid, but have among them able artisans. The native women sing and dance well, sometimes on a copper wire, stretched ten feet above the ground; but fraud is the order of the day. The Turki beks enrich themselves; the people save nothing, but all goes immediately in dissipation. Pauperism reigns everywhere. Manners are dissolute, and unnatural crime very common, just as in Fuh-kien and Kwan-tung."

The foregoing is a picture of Yarkand during the latter half of the eighteenth century, and it agrees fairly well with the description of "the good old times" under the Chinese, given to Forsyth's party during the stricter reign of Yakub Khan.

In 1874 Forsyth describes Yarkand as the largest and wealthiest city in the Tarim basin, inclosed within walls of irregular form, the length being greater than the breadth. The town stands on an open plain (3,900 feet above sea-level), and is surrounded by wide-spreading and populous suburbs, of which it was not easy to get a view as a whole. The highest eminence we could mount was a hill outside the city called Naurus Dung, whence we could see towards the east a wide extent of orchards and fields.

Besides the rice plantations there are, in their season, fields of wheat, barley, maize, millet, cotton, lucerne grass, flax (used for ropes), hemp, and a few poppies. Near the houses they make arbours overgrown with vines. There are also vineyards, but not for making wine, the grapes, whether fresh or dried, being used for food. The kitchen gardens produce melons, cabbages, onions, garlic, cucumbers, carrots, parsnips, and potatoes. These last, however, are novelties, I presume, for the Russian *Aksakal*, when supplying some for me, said that he grew a few every year to send as a present to his consul.

The city appeared to be full of trees, and towards the north was a cemetery with the tomb of one Kum-

Chicheki-ata, who was said to have died "about 500 years ago." In the same direction was seen the road leading to Aksu, and we could follow for a long distance the dilapidated old city wall, from 15 to 20 feet high, escalloped at the top, with flanking projections, and said to be four miles in circuit.

The old town is connected by a street of shops 600 yards long, with the east gate of the Chinese town or fortress, the side of which measures 800 yards. The Chinese town is fronted by a ditch 30 feet wide at top, 20 at bottom, and about 20 deep. The wall is approximately 25 feet high, with double gates. There is also a covered way 30 feet broad, with musketry wall from 7 to 8 feet high, with banquette. This is one of the three strong places in Chinese Turkistan, and may be deemed impregnable to all but European-trained troops. The garrison consists of 125 cavalry and 125 infantry.

The population of the town of Yarkand is uncertain. It was estimated by Forsyth at 35,000 as a maximum, and Roborovsky mentions from 35,000 to 40,000 as resident in the old town. Forsyth quotes, however, 32,000 houses as given formerly by the Chinese revenue returns, which is not far from 29,000 families quoted in 1877 by another authority, from the *yamen* books, for the whole district.

The city contains several large colleges—38 in all, according to Forsyth—besides mosques and a number of *serais*. Bell also mentions 120 *mahallahs* in the town. Where all these can be found I am somewhat puzzled to know, for when I asked to be shown the best of them, there appeared to be exceedingly few. We were taken first to the Yunus Van Medresse, which has a *pishtak* and gateway of rather fine proportions, with *kashi* work on the exterior, whilst within was a quadrangle surrounded by rooms for about 20 or 30 mullahs. The mosque belonging to the college was rather pretty, but the whole had a poverty-stricken appearance.

We passed on to the Friday mosque built by, and named after, Yakub Khan. The front of this verandah-like structure was supported by tall wooden pillars with carved and painted capitals, the beams also of the roof being coloured in arabesque. It was the prettiest thing of the kind we saw in Yarkand, where everything in the way of ornamentation and art was very meagre indeed.

A third *medresse* we visited was that of Abdullah Khan, with 50 or 60 mullahs, and said to have been built "more than 300 years ago by Muhammad Khan." Now, Muhammad Khan, son of Khizr Khoja, was a contemporary of Ulug Beg, who died in 1449, which would harmonise with the reputed age of the building; but it is not clear why it should be called after Abdullah Khan, the great khan, presumably, of Bokhara, who was not born until 1533.

We also visited some of the *serais*, but, as compared with those of Bokhara and Tashkend, they struck me as poor. There are said to be 1,000 Andijanis in Yarkand, most of them, to facilitate their trading, being registered as Chinese subjects. Russian cotton goods and chintzes are largely sold here. They are thick and strong, and more durable than the finer kinds which come from India. Coal is plentiful and costs two shillings a camel-load; but in summer they burn wood.

I was not greatly impressed with the commercial activity of Yarkand, for, on sending Amin into the bazaar with two or three dozen pairs of spectacles to sell for a shilling a pair, he returned saying that no merchant would take so large a venture; and the lack of demand for these optical instruments seemed to be about the same at Kashgar and Khotan.

Everywhere in the bazaar we were followed by crowds. The men were clothed in long robes, pyjamahs, and knee-boots, with skull-caps or hats of conical felt, lined and tipped with sheepskin. The women wore long chintz *khalats* of red and yellow, with wide pyjamahs; their hair, plaited in two thick tails, hung down their backs. When riding they wear knee-boots. Some of the men dye their beards red in honour of the prophet. Their ornaments are poor and confined to buttons, earrings, bracelets, finger-rings, and tassels for women's hair to adorn the ends of the plaits.

As we made our way homeward through the uninteresting streets, varied here and there by open spaces for pools of drinking water, of which there are said to be 120 in the town, we passed a house whence I heard screams. On stopping to inquire the meaning, we were shown a poor madman who had sense enough to hold out his hand for *tengas*, but for whom there existed no public asylum, as in Christian countries.

Our next day at Yarkand was Sunday, upon which I did not go into the town; but sundry visitors favoured us with calls, including mullahs from two of the *me-dresses*, to whom I gave for their colleges copies of the New Testament in Arabic, Persian, and Turki, with a Persian Bible and some text-cards.

A young mullah also presented himself, who, for some reason, did not receive a book, but he came

early next morning to ask for one, saying that he was
too poor to pay for it, even so little as 2½d. There
was about the youth an air of sincerity that pleased
me, and I presented him with a copy, whereupon he
joined his hands and devoutly offered a prayer on my
behalf; and then, with great joy, hid the volume under
his *khalat*.

Besides the mullahs, about a dozen Badakshanis,
Hindustanis, and others came to say "*Salaam*."
Among them was Turdi Akhoon, a Yarkandi merchant,
who, two days before, had arrived from India, bringing
my portrait and the card of "Mr H. Evan M. James,
C.S., Bombay." And thereon hung a tale.

On discovering the impossibility of getting letters of
credit in London on any town in Chinese Turkistan,
and on the principle of "preparing for the worst,"
I had pictured myself robbed and spoiled, and debated
how, in such a condition, I could raise money, say in
Yarkand, or on the Indian frontier.

Mr Ney Elias suggested that funds should be sent
to the Bank of India at Lahore, and he would write to
a native he knew at Leh who might cash my cheques.
He also introduced me to Mr H. E. M. James, author
of *The Long White Mountain*, who, being about to
return to India, suggested that he should take some
of my photographs, with signature at the back, to the
native Bombay merchants, who might send them to
their Yarkandi correspondents, saying that they might
expect the original some day to appear, and that if he
were in need of money his cheques were good paper.
Besides adopting these suggestions, I asked the good
offices of Lord Dufferin as Viceroy, to inform the
frontier officials of my possible appearance, and to
request their aid should I be in distress.

It was pleasant, therefore, to find that these little precautionary measures had so far succeeded, and, better still, to learn that the traders were abundantly willing to advance me money, of which, happily, not having been robbed or spoiled, I did not stand in need. The Hindus especially appeared anxious to lend; and one day, on returning to the house, no less than four men were waiting to *salaam* me, one offering to take a letter to Leh, and two to advance money.

Another Hindu on making his appearance slipped into my hand a rupee, the token in India of approaching a superior; but at that time I did not understand the custom, and regarded him as a money-changer, and, I fear, afforded him only a scant welcome. These continued offers of assistance, however, helped me to feel less of a stranger than I expected to do.

On the Monday several parents came for aid, bringing their sick and deformed children. Yarkand has been celebrated for goitre as far back as the days of Marco Polo, who says of its craftsmen, "A large proportion of them have swollen legs, and great crops at the throat, which arises from some quality in their drinking water."

How large a proportion of the inhabitants are thus afflicted may be gathered from a remark of Dr Bellew, that, in examining promiscuous groups of people about the Residency, and in attendance at his dispensary, he, on different occasions, counted seven out of ten, eleven out of thirteen, five out of seven, three out of twelve, nine out of fifteen, and, on one occasion, an entire group of seven goitrous subjects. Roborovsky says the disease appears in men at the age of puberty, and in women when they marry.

Speaking of the salubrity of the western part of the

country generally. Dr Bellew remarks as noteworthy the rarity of febrile diseases, malarious fevers and cholera being almost unknown. Diseases of the eye are frequent. Rheumatism also appears to be tolerably common, and neuralgia; also bronchitis and asthma. The frequency of skin diseases he recognises as an exponent of the people's lack of washing; whilst the last of the more prevalent afflictions he notices is dyspepsia, produced by the abuse of opium and Indian hemp.

Of the children brought to me, one had eye disease, another had a gross deformity below the abdomen, and in a third the soles of the feet were deeply cracked all over. One case seemed to me sufficiently abnormal to photograph; and, unfortunately, I could do little else.

Among the visitors who came early to *salaam* me were two who immediately excited my interest—namely, Muhammad Amin Khan and Muhammad Joo, former servants to Messrs Carey and Dalgleish. It was in the house (nominally, I suppose) of Muhammad Amin Khan, who served Dalgleish for three years, that Dalgleish lived, and this Badakshani accompanied the two Englishmen on their wonderful journey round Chinese Turkistan.

He had a huge goitre, was clad in a striped cotton *khalat*, and wore a cloth cap edged with brown fur. The lines of his face indicated a good deal of character, and he manifested great desire to serve me. He had been in India, and on my expression of the least desire, he put together his palms, raised them respectfully to his head with a profound bow, and acted to the full "your obedient servant."

Muhammad Joo was far less outwardly subservient;

he was a mixed breed, I think, between Ladak and Kashmiri parents, with probably a few other strains in his blood, corresponding, it may be, to the number of languages he spoke. He had served Dalgleish for several years in the capacity of cook, and was acting thus at the time his master was murdered, and so was able to give me authentic information on the matter, which I have since supplemented from other quarters.

On reaching Kashgar I found that M. Petrovsky had been exerting himself and spending money in a most commendable manner to catch the murderer. Not only had he drawn up a careful report to M. Zinovieff, Chief of the Asiatic department of Foreign Affairs, stating such facts as he had been able to elicit, but he summoned into my presence Osman, I think an Andijani, who was travelling in the same caravan with Dalgleish at the time of the murder, and whom the Consul was keeping under arrest. The information deposed by Osman I made notes of, and was able to compare them, later on, with the statements of Muhammad Joo; and I think it may not be uninteresting that I should briefly state the course of events as I gathered it from various sources.

Mr Andrew Dalgleish was a British trader, who in 1874, before he was 20 years of age, accompanied the first caravan of goods despatched by the Central Asian Trading Company to Yarkand, which he considered henceforward his home. He was at first agent and then liquidator of the company, after which he started in business on his own account, passing to and fro between Yarkand and the Panjab, and making along his route a number of friends and acquaintances, all of whom spoke of him with respect.

When Mr Carey performed his memorable journey,

Dalgleish was captain of his expedition, took the astronomical observations, and kept a log, the manuscript of which I waded through at the Geographical Society's house before starting. I had also a letter of introduction to Dalgleish from Mr James, who wrote to him of my intended journey.

In reply to this Dalgleish wrote of me to Mr James: "The distribution of the Scriptures in the Persian, Turki, and Chinese tongues will be received by both Tatar and Turk without prejudice, and many a blessing he will receive from the sick. But the moment he sets foot in Chinese Turkistan he must un-Russianise himself, and stand forth a pure Englishman, who, as a servant of God, has come straight from far-off England to heal the sick." He added also that he would lend me every assistance, and cash me a cheque for a goodly sum. A letter sent to me at Kuldja by Mr James contained this extract, and its date was March 13th, 1888.

A week later Dalgleish set out from Leh, bearing one or more letters for me. The caravan was a mixed one. Dalgleish was mounted on a bay horse, and accompanied by two personal servants, Muhammad Joo and a Ladaki. He had also 18 horses carrying merchandise, under the care of a caravan leader of Leh, with six attendants. Osman had 14 baggage horses, accompanied by three servants and two traders. Unconnected with the foregoing, but travelling with them, were a mounted Afghan, one Gulban, and a fakir or dervish, Said Baba, on foot.

Thus they travelled for 11 days, when, at Yartush Kin, they were overtaken at noon by an Afghan, Daud (David) Muhammad Khan, mounted on a grey horse, armed with a gun, sword, and dagger, but carrying no tent, and attended by one servant only, who forthwith returned.

Daud Muhammad Khan was no stranger to Dalgleish, for he had been known to him as an Afghan trader in Yarkand; but lately Daud had lost money, and had been put under arrest in Leh for debt. During this period Dalgleish came to Leh, and Daud sent him a dinner to his lodging, and afterwards asked a loan of 100, or even 20 rupees. This Dalgleish refused; and, having learned from Muhammad Joo how much the dinner had cost, sent the sum by him to Daud Muhammad Khan. Dalgleish was said to have befriended the debtor, however, by representing to the British Joint Commissioner that so long as the man was kept in durance he could not pay his debts, whereas, if he were released, he might be able to earn some money to do so.

When, therefore, Daud Muhammad Khan joined the caravan, his benefactor inquired whether he had broken bounds or had been liberated. The latter was said to be the case, and for five days all travelled together in harmony. Daud had no tent, and was allowed to take his tea and warm himself sometimes in that of Dalgleish. Osman expressed his suspicions to Dalgleish, saying, " Daud is not a soldier. Why, then, does he carry arms? You have said the Afghans are a bad lot, and perhaps he has bad intentions." To this Dalgleish is said to have replied, " Don't trouble; Daud will do nothing amiss."

Then, after crossing the Karakoram Pass, they came at midday to Boutai, where camp was pitched, there being 100 yards or so between the tents of Dalgleish and Osman. The ground was covered with deep snow. Tea was prepared, and towards evening Dalgleish

came across to Osman's tent (where also was Daud
Muhammad Khan), saying, "Have you drunk tea?"
"No," said Osman. "Will you join us?"

Dalgleish at first declined, saying he had had his
tea; but he ate a piece of bread for company's sake.
Presently Daud Muhammad Khan left the tent,
Dalgleish asking, "Where are you going?"

"Outside," said he; where he stayed for a long time.

Then, returning to the end of the tent, he shot at
Dalgleish, the ball whizzing past Osman. Every one
then rushed out of the tent, and the wounded Dalgleish
was struggling towards his own tent, when his brutal
murderer dealt him three or four cuts with his sword.

It was at this point, presumably, Muhammad Joo
would have me believe, that he caught Dalgleish in
his arms, saying, "Oh! my poor master!" But no
reply was made, and death quickly followed.

On subsequent examination of the body it was found
that the ball had passed through one arm, and sword-
cuts were on the other. According to a later account,
Dalgleish caught the blade in his hand; but, of course, it
was easily pulled through, and the blows that appear
to have caused death were on the back of his head,
administered probably after he had fallen.

The murderer then harangued his fellow-Muham-
madans, threatening any who manifested disapproval.

"You see," said he, "what I have done. If any of
you have aught to object, let him say so, and I'll
answer him. It was to kill this man I came here. I
tried to do so in Leh, but lacked opportunity."

Everybody was cowed before the murderer, to whom
they replied that they had nothing against him.

The wrath of the assassin then fell upon the servants
of Dalgleish, and even upon his faithful dog—the only

friend who attacked the murderer, for it seized Daud's
leg, and for this the poor animal was mercilessly thrust
through. He spoke also of killing Muhammad Joo,
taunting him with being servant to such "a dog of an
infidel," and for catching him in his arms; but ultimately he contented himself by degrading Muhammad
Joo, as a Mussulman, by cutting off his beard. When
asked if the body should be buried, he replied, "No;
let him lie as he is."

Next day all the caravan moved forward nine miles,
Daud Muhammad Khan and the dervish taking possession of the murdered man's goods, some of which
were hidden in a *cache* not far from Balti Brangsa.

Meanwhile, Muhammad Joo was in considerable
trepidation as to what his fate might be, and spared
no pains to please the murderer. On approaching a
stopping-place he ran forward to prepare a fire, and get
ready the pipe and make the tea, till, ere long, Daud
Muhammad Khan said that he and some of his fellows
might go back, which they did, and carried their
master's body to Leh.

It is not necessary for the present to trace further
the career of the murderer; but it may be imagined
that it was not without emotion that I visited the
house of poor Dalgleish in Yarkand, and saw the door
of one of his rooms sealed up, and the words written
in English on a piece of paper pasted on the lintel—

"THE GOODS OF A. DALGLEISH."

There they were, just as their owner left them; and
Muhammad Amin Khan had received instructions from
the British Joint Commissioner at Leh that he was to
keep them till sent for, which he was doing faithfully.

Of course we looked over the premises with interest,

Among its curiosities were numbers of *Ovis Poli* horns which one might have bought by the half-dozen for less than £1 a pair; but, seeing that two pairs sufficed for a horse-load, the difficulty of carriage forbade a purchase, especially as the skulls were not entire. I measured one pair, including curves, 55 inches long, and 17 inches round the thickest part.

From the top of the house we obtained a view of the neighbouring yards and gardens and roofs, on which, as Lieutenant Roborovsky says, "there is as much life as beneath them. In summer people sleep on them, work on them, clean cotton, dry fruit, receive their friends, drink, play music, and even dance."

Some of the roofs, I observed, were screened from observation by the erection of rough, leafy poles. Some are planted with tiny gardens of Indian pinks, marigolds, and asters, with which the local beauties love to decorate themselves.

Here and there a domed structure indicated some kind of religious building, as a mosque or school; but the prospect over Yarkand, seen from within the town, was anything but indicative of urban magnificence.

On our second day in Yarkand came a long-expected letter, handed me by the *Aksakal*, from Mr Redslob of Leh. He cautioned me against the danger of travelling by the route on which Dalgleish had been killed; but said that, if I persisted, he might be able to meet me in the Nubra valley. I replied that as yet I was uncertain about my movements, but, in the absence of fresh news, I expected that my way would lie over the Karakoram.

I had, in fact, already opened negotiations on the subject, first with Mirza Jan Haji, whose *serai* we visited, and who also took me to his private house.

He was willing at a day's notice to send me by horses to Osh for about eight or nine roubles per horse, each horse carrying 288 lbs.; time, 20 days; and two horses to spare. To Leh he named for the hire of each horse 240 *tengas*, or £2 10s. M. Dauvergne, he said, had recently passed and paid only 30s., but it was earlier in the season, when grass was more abundant. Each horse was to carry 225 lbs., and if

AT YARKAND—VIEW FROM THE ROOF OF THE HOUSE OF MR. DALGLEISH.

15 horses were hired, he should send five men, with five horses to spare to allow for deaths. He told me also that the journey once took him 55 days with 55 horses, of which 17 died; but that the death-rate was sometimes not more than two or three.

I had slept over this ominous intelligence, when, on the next day, came a wily-looking Badakshani, named Muhammad Hussein, who offered to take me to Leh on lower terms. His brother, he said, at Leh, wished to forward a quantity of goods to Yarkand, so that he could send me with 35 horses, and give me sundry advantages.

Upon this I called on an old mullah, Elchi Beg Haji, *Aksakal* of the Afghans and Badakshanis, who, being too infirm to come himself, had sent his son to *salaam* me. The old man showed me a letter he had received, two or three months before, from the British Joint Commissioner, announcing that I was coming from the Consul at Kashgar, and asking help if I needed it. I inquired, therefore, whether he could recommend this Muhammad Hussein, whereupon he gave him a 15-years' character, and said that he took Mr Ney Elias to Badakshan.

Meanwhile, I had not received the telegram which I expected might recall me by way of Osh, nor had I seen Khotan; and to leave the country without so doing would be only to follow in the steps of Forsyth, Shaw, Bell, and Younghusband, not one of whom, nor indeed any Englishman, had traversed the whole route thither from Yarkand, which I was anxious to do; and as Muhammad consented to keep his offer open for 25 days, I determined to hurry to Khotan and back.

Marco Polo ends his short chapter on Yarkand, "As there is nothing else worth telling, we may pass on." But he found there a Christian bishopric, which was more than we did, nor did we come across any trace of one. I have been able, nevertheless, to collect several particulars of interest concerning early Christianity in Chinese Central Asia, and these I purpose to give in the following chapter.

CHAPTER XXXV.

EARLY CHRISTIANITY IN CHINESE CENTRAL ASIA.

Christianity not mentioned by Buddhist pilgrims, 119. Introduced into China by Olopuen; Testimony of Singan-fu monument, 120. Testimonies from Western sources; Spread of Nestorians, 121. Bishoprics in Central Asia, 122. Prester John and Christians in time of Marco Polo, 124. Roman Christianity in Central Asia; Pascal at Khiva and Almalik, 125.—Marignolli; Tangible remains of Christianity, 128. Epitaphs and supposed monastery; Description of ruin, 129. The Tarikhi Rashidi, 130. Less certain remains; Nestorian translations; Their alphabet given to Uigurs, 131. Search for Uigur antiquities, 132. Character of Nestorian Christianity, 133. Stamped out by Muhammadanism, 134.

IT may have been noticed that, in the references to the travels of Fa-hian, Sung Yun, and Hiuen Tsiang, no mention is made of contact with Christians. In the case of the first two this is not so remarkable, since I am not aware that they passed through cities where, at so early a date, Christianity is known to have existed; but when Hiuen Tsiang visited Samarkand about 630, this place had been the seat of a Christian bishop, we are led to believe, for more than a century, if not so early as 411; whilst on his return to Singan-fu, the capital of his own country, in 645, he must have found a Church and Christian missionaries, who had arrived there ten years before.

According to the testimony of the Nestorian monument discovered at Singan-fu, of which the genuineness and authenticity may now be regarded as established, it appears that Christianity was introduced into China by Olopuen, or Olopan, in 635. The emperor Taitsung received him graciously, and three years later issued a decree in favour of the Christian religion, and commanded the erection of a church in his capital.

Seven years later, in the emperor Kaotsung (650—683), we have a patron of both Christianity and Buddhism together. He appointed Olopuen "Great Conservator of Doctrine for the preservation of the State," and orders were given for the erection of illustrious churches in every province. The priests all shaved their crowns and preserved their beards: they had worship and praise seven times a day, and every seventh day they were said to offer sacrifice (presumably the Lord's Supper).

Towards the end of the seventh century Buddhism prevailed; but under Hiwan Tsung (713—755) the Church recovered its ascendency, and a new missionary, named Kei-ho, or Kiho, appeared. The emperors Sutsung, Taitsung, and Tetsung continued to favour Christianity; and it was under the last of these, in 781, that the Singan-fu monument was erected.

The testimony of the monument is corroborated by an edict issued in 745 by the emperor Hiwan Tsung, enacting that throughout the empire the churches popularly known as Persian temples should be called Tathsin temples—that is, Roman, or, at least, as belonging to countries farther west than Persia.

Then times of persecution recurred, and in 845 the emperor Wutsung denounced Buddhists and Christians alike, and ordered the monks of both religions to return to secular life. We learn, however, from the Arab Abu Said that Christians formed a part of the very large foreign population at Khanfu (Hangcheu) in 878, after which for several centuries the condition of Christianity in China is shrouded in darkness.

In agreement with the foregoing dates are such scraps of history as we can gather from Western sources. For many of these we are indebted to Joseph Simon Assemanus, or Assemani, a Maronite, and keeper of the Vatican Library. He was sent by the Pope in 1715 to Egypt and Syria, where he collected Syriac and Arabic manuscripts having reference to the Eastern Churches. These he translated, edited, and annotated, and he published in four volumes a biographical account with large excerpts from the works of Syrian writers, whom he divided into Orthodox, Jacobites, and Nestorians.

He wrote his learned work on the Syrian Churches with the avowed object of helping the Roman missionaries in their efforts to subjugate these sectaries to the Papal See. The questions in debate had reference mainly to the Incarnation of our Lord; but other matters are occasionally brought forward—as, for instance, when he stigmatises a Nestorian bishop, Bubacus, as "of abandoned morals," because he lived with a lawful wife, and had presumed to say that it was "better to marry than to burn" (1 Cor. vii. 9). But whatever may be the value of his opinions, his record of facts, in view of our general ignorance on the Syrian Churches, is most valuable.

* My friend the Rev. Stilon Henning, B.D., of Plumstead, has looked through for me pretty closely volumes iii. and iv., concerning the Jacobites and Nestorians, but without discovering very much more than has already been published in Yule's *Cathay* and *Marco Polo*, though giving a few additional facts. I have also gleaned a few para-

From Assemani we learn the existence of a bishopric at Merv as early as 334. In 410 Isaac held a synod there. Merv was promoted to metropolitan rank under Jaballaha in 420, and is variously placed as seventh, tenth, and ninth among the metropolitan sees of the East. Of bishops of Merv, we note David in 520; Theodore, distinguished by Assemani as an author, in 540; another David, 550; and, in 650, Elias, who wrote books on the Holy Scriptures, and a valuable history of the Church. Then followed Joseph: John of Balad, ordained by Sergius, 860; Joseph, 900; and, in 988, Ebed Jesu, who was translated from the Church of Ispahan (Aspahan) by the primate Mares, and wrote letters to Mares, and John, his successor, on the conversion of the eastern Turks to Christ.

After the condemnation and banishment of Nestorius in 431, his followers spread extensively through Persia; and for centuries they became the chief depositaries of Greek learning in Asia. Moreover, their missionary zeal is borne witness to by their establishment of sees in Herat, China, and Samarkand.

The bishopric of Samarkand, according to one author, seems to have been founded under the patriarchs Achdeus or Silas, 411 or 503, and, under Salibazacha, in 714, to have received metropolitan rank. The same Salibazacha made a metropolitan see of Herat; and the metropolitan of this see, we are told, with those of India, took precedence of the metropolitan of China, as did the metropolitan of China of the bishop of Samarkand.

Assemani transcribes two lists, by Elias, metropolitan

graphs from a short account of the Nestorians by Professor Chvolson, published in the Russian pamphlet already referred to concerning the Nestorian cemeteries recently discovered at Pishpek and Tokmak.

of Damascus (893), and Amru (who wrote about 1340),
of 25 metropolitan and episcopal sees, subject to the
same patriarch of the East. Of these it is sufficient here
to note Merv, Herat, China, Samarkand, Turkistan,
Balkh, Tangut, Kashgar, and perhaps Almalik. "And
certainly," says Assemani, "each of these metropo-
litans had bishops under him—some 12, and some six."
Three bishops usually accompanied their metropolitan,
when a patriarch was to be elected and consecrated.

Although we cannot always safely argue from the
titles and numbers of the dignitaries of a Church that it
is equally represented by presbyters and laymen, yet
the foregoing implies a large number of Christian
communities in Western and Central Asia; so that
there is nothing improbable in the story told by
Theophylact, that, in the expedition sent against
Batwam towards the end of the sixth century, some
Turks who were deported to Constantinople as prisoners
were Christians. "They bore on their foreheads the
sign of the cross, of which the Emperor asked the
meaning, whence it transpired that in a time of pesti-
lence among the Scythians, and as a talisman, certain
of the Christians persuaded the mothers thus to tattoo
their children."

Again, in the time of the Nestorian patriarch
Timothy (778—820), we hear of successful missions in
countries adjoining the Caspian, and of the conversion
of "a Khakan of the Turks," and of several minor
princes. Assemani gives no details of the bishopric
of Turkistan, but he tells us that "Turkistan is
the region of the Turks, and embraces, according to
Eastern geographers, all the lands beyond the river
Jaxartes up to the border of Northern China."

This gives room for the supposition that the

recently discovered Nestorian cemeteries on the Chu may represent the seat of the bishop of Turkistan, in accordance with which the dates on the tombstones thus far deciphered range from 858 to 1338. Moreover, it should be observed that some of the names on the stones, though said to be those of Christian believers, are evidently of Turkish origin, as " Menkutinesh" and " Tekin," which perhaps indicates, as Professor Chvolson observes, that they were converts.

With these data, then, before us, we can better understand than could our mediæval forefathers the rumours that reached Europe of " Prester John," who, in 1145, was stated by a Syrian bishop sent to Pope Eugenius III. to be a king and Nestorian priest, claiming descent, as they said, from the three Magi.

The priest-king intended was probably the first Gur-Khan of the Kara-Khitai, who came from about Tenduk, and whose grandson in 1208, as stated in a previous chapter, sheltered Koshluk, the son of the last khan of the tribe of Naimans, or Keraits, whose Christianity is further attested by Rashid-ed-din, the Muhammadan historian of the Mongols.

To these notices of Christians in Mongolia may be added what Marco Polo records, that in the camp of Jinghiz Khan there were Christians whom the great Khan consulted as astrologers, who divined, with a split cane, the result of an impending battle, and read a portion from the Psalter. After this, Rubruquis, in 1253, makes frequent mention of the Nestorians in Central Asia, and says that they had a bishop in Singan-fu. Also Marco Polo found Christians, in 1272, in Samarkand, where, on the conversion of an uncle of Kublai Khan, they built a great church in honour of John the Baptist.

Polo speaks likewise of Christians at Kashgar, with their churches; at Yarkand, where he couples the mention of Nestorians and Jacobites; at Urumtsi, Suchan, and Kanchu, where they had three very fine churches. Tenduc he found under Chinese rulers, and it was there that the descendants of "Prester John" lived. There were Christians also, he says, nearer to China proper, as well as in Manchuria and the country bordering on Korea.

From the presence of a bishop of Kamul at the inauguration of the Catholicos Denha in 1266, Yule infers that Hami was the see of a Nestorian bishopric; and Polo's contemporary, Hayton, testifies to the number of great and noble Uigurs who held firm to the faith of Christ.

With the spread of Christianity in China proper we are not further concerned, but it should be noticed that thus far its origin and growth must be ascribed to the Eastern branch of the Church, and more especially to the Nestorians, and that down to the thirteenth century Roman Christianity did nothing whatever for Central Asia or China. The journeys, however, of Plano Carpini and Rubruquis, under the tolerant rule of the Mongol Khans, showed that something might be attempted. Accordingly, about 1336, we have Pascal, a Franciscan friar, proceeding to Urgenj, or Old Khiva, where his caravan was delayed from fear of war and plunder; and he writes :—

"Hence I was long tarrying among the Saracens, and I preached to them for several days openly and publicly the name of Jesus Christ and His Gospel. I opened out and laid bare the cheats, falsehoods, and blunders of their false prophet; with a loud voice, and in public, I did confound their barkings; and trusting in our Lord Jesus Christ, I was not afraid of them, but received from the Holy Spirit comfort and light.

"They treated me civilly, and set me in front of their mosque during their Easter (Bairam); at which mosque, on account of its being their Easter, there were assembled from divers quarters a number of their Kazis, that is of their bishops, and of their Talismani, that is of their priests. And guided by the teaching of the Holy Ghost, I disputed with them in that same place before the mosque, on theology, and regarding their false Koran and its doctrine, for five-and-twenty days; and, in fact, I was barely able once a day to snatch a meal of bread and water.

"But by the grace of God the doctrine of the Holy Trinity was disclosed and preached to them, and at last even they, in spite of their reluctance, had to admit of its truth; and, thanks be unto the Almighty God, I carried off the victory on all points, to the praise and honour of Jesus Christ and of Mother Church.

"And then these children of the devil tried to tempt and pervert me with bribes, promising me wives and handmaidens, gold and silver and lands, horses and cattle, and other delights of this world. But when in every way I rejected all their promises with scorn, then for two days together they pelted me with stones, besides putting fire to my face and my feet, plucking out my beard, and heaping upon me for a length of time all kinds of insult and abuse."

Thus far of Pascal's preaching at Old Khiva, after which he came to Almalik, and writes:—

"Thus beginning at Urgenj, all the way to Almalik, I was constantly alone among the Saracens, but by word, and act, and dress publicly bore the name of the Lord Jesus Christ. And by those Saracens I have often been offered poison; I have been cast into the water; I have suffered blows and other injuries more than I can tell in a letter. . . .

"Fare ye well in the Lord Jesus Christ, and pray for me, and for those who are engaged, or intend to be engaged, on missionary journeys; for by God's help such journeys are very profitable, and bring in a harvest of many souls. Care not, then, to see me again, unless it be in these regions, or in that Paradise wherein is our rest and comfort, and refreshment and heritage, even the Lord Jesus Christ.

"And for that He hath said that when the Gospel shall have been preached throughout the whole world, then shall the end come, it is for me to preach among divers nations, to show sinners their guilt, and to declare the way of salvation, but it is for God Almighty to pour into their souls the grace of conversion. Dated Almalik, on the feast of St Laurence 1338."

Colonel Yule adds a note: "If souls transmigrate, that of Henry Martyn was in Friar Pascal." They are certainly noble words, the utterance of which would do honour to either; and it is the more affecting to learn that within about a year after they were written Friar Pascal and his companions had their reward in martyrdom.

So well did the missionaries succeed at first, that the ruler of the Ili valley, having been cured of a cancer by one of the party, bestowed lands upon them, with full authority to preach, and made over to them his boy of seven to be baptised. This ruler, however, was poisoned, and his kingdom seized by a Saracen, who ordered that all Christians should be made Muhammadans, and that whosoever should disobey the order a third time should be put to death :—

"And so when the brethren aforesaid would not obey this order, they were bound and all tied to one rope, which was dragged along by the infuriated mob, who smote and spat upon them, stabbed and slashed them, cutting off their noses and ears, and otherwise mutilating them, till at length they fell by the sword and made a blessed migration to the Lord."

This narrative is given by Bartholomew of Pisa, and is confirmed by John de Marignolli, a papal legate sent to the khan, and who, though arriving at Almalik within a year of the martyrdom, was allowed to purchase ground, to build a church, say mass, and baptise, as well as preach. This may, perhaps, be accounted for by a remark of Bartholomew that "the aforesaid emperor before long was himself slain, and his house destroyed by fire."

Marignolli, at all events, seems to have continued his preaching as he proceeded eastwards to Hami. We learn this from an anecdote he relates regarding the payment of tithes. "A case occurred," he says, "in my own experience at Hami, when many Tatars and people of other nations, on their first conversion, refused to be baptised unless we would swear that after their baptism we should exact no temporalities from them; nay, on the contrary, that we should provide for their poor out of our means. This we did, and a multitude of both sexes in that city did then most gladly receive baptism."

The curtain now falls over Central Asian Christianity; and if we turn from book-learning to ask for tangible evidences still remaining, I know of only two—the first undoubted, the second not so clear. There is no uncertainty as to the genuineness of the recently discovered Nestorian cemeteries, and their epitaphs in

Syrian characters. One of these indicates the place of burial of "Chelikha, the renowned interpreter of Scripture, and preacher, who enlightened all the monasteries." This was in 1316, and proves the existence then in Central Asia of monastic life.

This, moreover, is confirmed, strange to say, of this very region by the Catalan map of 1375, which marks (a few miles distant to the south of Issik-Kul) an Armenian (Nestorian) monastery, said to contain the bones of St Matthew. Into the question of the bones we will not enter; but we may turn with interest to what Dr Seeland says of a ruin in this neighbourhood, where he was compelled to stop for a day at an altitude of 11,000 feet in the valley of Tash-Rabat.

"The traveller," he says, "is not a little astonished to see a stone construction, hoary with age, about 48 paces long by 36 wide, with a flat roof, from the middle of which rises a rough, half-ruined cupola, about 25 feet high.

"The entrance, fairly lofty and vaulted, conducts to an interior without windows. Under the cupola is a sort of chamber or hall, with vaulted wings, nine feet high, of rooms or cells running off in four directions in form of a Latin cross. The entrance wing has lateral corridors on one side only, and in these, as in those of the other wings, openings from 30 to 36 inches are contrived in the walls. They lead to separate cells, which are square at bottom, circular at top, and perfectly dark, except where the ceiling has, in some cases, fallen in.

"The entrances are so low as sometimes to necessitate crawling, and the interiors have no trace of chimneys, niches, or places to sit or sleep. No trace exists of refectory, kitchen, or even a fireplace throughout the building, which is constructed with mortar of fragments of local bluish and reddish schist.

"In the central hall are a few remains of plaster, but none of ornamentation. Colonel Volkhoff, in 1871, said he distinguished on the plaster rude figures of a horse with three, and a dragon with five, heads. The plaster bearing these may have since fallen, for nothing of the kind now remains but Arabic writing, evidently scribbled by passing Muhammadan traders."

Dr Seeland then asks for what purpose this building, now used by the Kirghese for folding sheep, could have been erected. Not, he says, for a fortress, or a private dwelling-house, and there are no traces of the locks and bars of a prison; nor has it any resemblance to other Central Asian rest-houses for caravans. Excavations in the vault, pointed out to the Russian traveller as the burial-place of "Sarts and Kirghese," might answer some of these questions.

Meanwhile, remembering that this building was on the direct route between the Christian see of Kashgar and the Christian settlements on the Chu, it seems not improbable that the ruin may represent the monastery indicated on the Catalan map. Mr Herbert Jones, who passed the building, told me, after reading his paper before the Society of Arts, that he heard of Nestorian remains both there and on the shores of Issik-Kul, not far from the spot now occupied by the new Russian monastery. He also mentioned the existence of ancient tombs near what I have supposed may be the monastery.

Since writing the foregoing, I have noticed Bellew's quotation from the *Tarikhi Rashidi*, that Muhammad Khan "converted the ancient Hindu temple (resembling in the massive blocks of its stone the temples of Kashmir) called Tash-Rabat, on the Pass to the Chadir-Kul, into a fortified post to protect his capital (Kashgar) from the incursions of the Kirghese." Here, then, is testimony of the existence of the building in the fifteenth century. It was supposed by the author of the *Tarikhi Rashidi* to be of Hindu origin, which may possibly have been the case, though Dr Bellew, to whom I have spoken on the subject, agrees with me in thinking that Tash-Rabat is very probably the Nestorian monastery indicated on the Catalan map.

Turning now to less certain remains of Christianity, we may remark that little is known in detail of Nestorianism as it existed in Central Asia. Professor Chvolson points out that many Nestorians were employed by the Khalifs as physicians and secretaries; and when, under the first Abbasid Khalifs, a knowledge of Greek science was desired for the Muhammadans, Nestorian scholars, who were great students of Scripture and science, were sent to Byzantium for manuscripts. They then translated into Syriac and Arabic whole shelves of Greek works on mathematics, astronomy, and rhetoric, so that by their translations and commentaries they exerted, in later days, a powerful influence in disseminating Greek culture, not only among Muhammadans, but through them among European peoples also.

Again, it should not be forgotten that the Nestorians gave an alphabet to, or modified one already existing among, the Uigurs. Professor Chvolson, quoting apparently from the *History of the Northern Courts*, and from Grigorieff's *Eastern Turkistan*, speaks of Chinese and one other form of writing as known in the fifth century in the country of the Uigurs, and adds that the latter form in the thirteenth century was modified through the introduction of the Estrangelo, or ancient Syriac alphabet, by the Nestorians.

Bretschneider, on the other hand, seems to think it impossible to fix the date of the adoption of the Syriac written characters by the Uigurs, but adds that it is a well-established fact that the Uigurs, when they first reduced the Turkish language to writing, borrowed the alphabet from the early Nestorian missionaries. Jinghiz Khan introduced the Uigur writing among the Mongols, and it is also well known, Bretschneider says, that the Uigur character was the original source of the letters still used by the Mongols and Manchus.

M. Grum-Grjimailo, speaking on what he regards as trustworthy information, says: "There are very many Uigur ruins at Syngym; parties of treasure-seekers proceed thither annually from Sukchin, and are not badly repaid for their trouble, for there are many gold and silver things there, besides copper vessels, censers, etc. In spite of all my efforts I was unable to obtain any of these Uigur antiquities; not even Uigur writings, which, as I learned, are frequently found with grains of wheat in a particular kind of earthenware vessel; leaflets with inscriptions round them, inclosed in horn and wooden boxes, are also found, but these are so brittle that on being handled they frequently fall to pieces."

It was suggested to me before I started by Dr Rost, librarian of the India Office, that in Chinese Turkistan I might possibly stumble upon Sanscrit or Uigur manuscripts, and he mentioned their being written on prepared palm-leaf as a sign of great age.

He gave me the name of Dr Radloff, as of one engaged in such studies, upon whom I called in

St Petersburg. This well-known Orientalist gave
me practical advice, thus: "If you find a manuscript
that no one in Chinese Turkistan can read, buy it;
but if it is intelligible to a Mongol, reject it." Dr
Radloff also showed me some Uigur writing, saying
that there were only about a dozen such manuscripts
in Europe. He was then at work upon the *Kudatku
Bilik*, a treatise in verse on the duties of a ruler to
his people, written in Kashgar in 1070 in Uigur. A
portion has since been published in Leipzig.

As to the character of Nestorian worship, Rubruquis
tells how on a feast day the great Khan Mangu's chief
wife with her children entered the Nestorian chapel,
kissed the right hand of the saints, and then, according
to the fashion of the Nestorians, gave her right hand
to be kissed. Mangu also was present, and with his
spouse sat on a gilt throne before the altar, and made
Rubruquis and his companions sing. They chanted
the *Veni Creator Spiritus*.

"The Emperor soon after retired, but his wife stayed
behind and gave presents to the Christians. *Terasine*,
wine, and *koumiss* were brought in. She took a cup,
knelt, asked a blessing, and while she drank the priests
chanted. They then drank till they were intoxicated.
Thus they passed the day, and towards evening the
Empress was in the same condition as the rest, and
went home in a carriage escorted by the priests still
chanting and whining."

The above, if true, would not be creditable to any
professors of Christianity. I myself have seen, in
some parts of the Eastern Church on a feast day, a
very much closer resemblance to certain features of
the foregoing than it is pleasant to write about, and
it painfully recalls the disorders condemned by the

Apostle Paul (1 Cor. xi. 21). It is, however, quite unlike other accounts I have read of the Nestorians; and it must in fairness be remembered, though Yule regards Rubruquis as a trustworthy writer, that the Westerns regarded the Nestorians as unorthodox. If, moreover, the Roman manner of speaking of sectaries in Asia in the thirteenth century were on a par with their successors' calumnies regarding Protestants, notably in Spain and Portugal, in the nineteenth century, then a very wide margin must be allowed for probable perversion and exaggeration.

But however it may be in this particular case, if judged by their fruits, these Easterns of the tenth, ninth, and earlier centuries have no need to fear comparison with those of the West: for whilst the Roman portion of the Church was sinking into the error and missionary idleness of the dark ages, the Nestorians, mindful of their Master's command, were carrying the light to the ends of the earth.

The subsequent history of Christianity in Chinese Central Asia is a melancholy one, for all was crushed by brute force under the heel of the false prophet, so that over regions where the religion of Christ, however defective in form, was obtaining a growing influence, a Christian in subsequent centuries scarcely dared to travel. Once more the tolerant rule of China makes it possible for earnest souls to preach the Christian faith where its professors have been destroyed. Who will go and rebuild the walls of this ruined Jerusalem?

CHAPTER XXXVI.

FROM YARKAND TO KARGHALIK.

Escorted from Yarkand, 135.—Components of caravan, 136.—The river Yarkand, and precious stones, 137.—Arrival at Posgam, 138.—A night guard and street attendant ; Journey to Yak-Shambeh, 139.—Taking photographs, 140.—Route from Yak-Shambeh, and shooting, 142.—Welcomed to Karghalik ; Description of town, 143.—My host's mausoleum ; Visited by Chinese *Amban*'s secretary, 144.—Antidote wanted against opium-smoking ; Bad effects of opium in Chinese Turkistan, 145.—Testimony of Forsyth, Bellew, and Bell, 146.—Receipt of telegram ; Letters from Leh, 147.—Departure for India delayed, 148.

WE started on Tuesday, September 25th, at noon, for an excursion, *via* Karghalik, to Khotan, our caravan being accompanied out of Yarkand by a complimentary escort of seven horsemen, comprising, among others, Muhammad Ali, the Kashmiri *Aksakal*, Mirza Jan Haji, the Russian *Aksakal*, and the son of old Mullah Elchi Beg, the Badakshani *Aksakal*, together with, if I remember rightly, the faithful Muhammad Amin Khan.

A ride of three-quarters of an hour brought us to a rest-house called Langar Alim Akhoon, near to the little river Zulchak, in the midst of a field of melons. Here we drew rein, and, as we had time in hand, rested for half-an-hour, feasting on half-a-dozen large and luscious melons, for which luxuries we paid a halfpenny each!

Our friendly escort then returned. It had not been thought necessary to take all our baggage to Khotan. Sixteen packages had been left sealed and numbered in charge of Mirza Muhammad Ali, who welcomed me for the purpose to his town house, and provided a *dostarkhan*. The remaining packages were put on two *arbas*, one of them being so arranged that I could turn into it and sleep when tired of riding. These *arbas* had, of course, their drivers, and, I think, an odd servant, besides which the Chinese authorities furnished two Turki *djiguitts*. The Russian *Aksakal* also sent a *djiguitt*, and the rest of our number was made up of Joseph, Amin, and Sarim Sak.

The route lay through fields of rice, maize, and melons, with a row of trees and a canal on each side of the 20-foot road, which might have passed for a good one but for the many *aryks* crossing it, and the careless manner in which the earth was replaced, after the water for irrigation had been allowed to pass through.

Not far west of the river Yarkand was a hamlet called Seh-Shambeh, or Tuesday bazaar, with a *serai*, where, on a subsequent journey, we slept. Now we passed on, and at a quarter past three, at eight miles from the city, came to the Yarkand river (known as Zarafshan), with tamarisk jungle on both banks. Dr Henderson noticed also, where he crossed, several good-sized trees of *Ailanthus glandulosa*.

The Yarkand river rises within a few miles of the Karakoram Pass, and is fed by streams descending from the glaciers of Baltistan and Kunjut, so that during the melting of the snows the stream near

Yarkand is almost a mile wide, filling its entire channel. So at least says Forsyth; whereas Henderson gives the stream, "now at its highest," from 70 to 180 yards in width, by which possibly he means the principal channel; whilst by another traveller, in August, the stream is said to be 500 yards wide with a rapid current, with eight boats for crossing. The boats measure 40 feet long by nine broad, and two and a half deep, each taking ten horses and their loads.

In September we found the volume of water scanty, and sprawling over its stony bed in many channels, the deepest of which we crossed in a ferry; but in winter, according to Forsyth, most of the rivers of Chinese Turkistan may be crossed dry-shod, stepping from one stone to another. All these rivers contain fish, and are said to be a source of food to the inhabitants. More important, however, than its fish has been, in days gone by, the yield of the Yarkand river in gold and precious stones.

Tchuen-yuen, at the close of the last century, gives some interesting particulars on this subject. "They have a river," he says, "which contains precious stones, the larger as big as a dish or a bushel, the smaller the size of the fist or a walnut, some of them weighing up to 200 or 300 lbs. They are found of various colours; some white as snow, others blue as a kingfisher, yellow like wax, black like ink, or of a shade of carmine reminding one of cinnabar, all of premier quality. One kind is streaked with bright veins, like mutton fat; another is blue and transparent, like the vegetable called *pono-sen*. The same river rolls down also nuggets of gold, which are difficult to find, because the precious morsels are lost in a mass of common stones that cumber the bed.

"A military mandarin superintends the search, causing 20 or 30 experienced Mussulmans to plunge into the river up to their shoulders, feeling the stones with their naked feet, and keeping on the move. If they come across a precious stone, they perceive it by a touch of the foot, and stoop to pick it up. A soldier placed on the bank then strikes a gong, the workmen come out of the river, the mandarin passes along a little vermilion, and the find is marked, generally with the character *che* (a stone)."

In 1870 Henderson saw marks of excavation in the sand of the Yarkand river, and was told that washing for gold was then being tried for the first time.

After crossing the Yarkand river we passed at first through a swampy country, and then a richly cultivated and well-watered district, studded with farmsteads, arriving at five o'clock at Posgam, which was said to be three and a half *tashes*, or about 17 miles, from Yarkand.

Posgam is a large village, of about 600 houses, according to Forsyth, with a street of shops. I thought some of them better stocked than in other villages of similar size. Here also we found a large Chinese station, converted to its present purpose out of a Muhammadan mosque; and to this building at first we were conducted to stay for the night. For some

---

* Tchuen-yuen adds that about 75 miles from Yarkand lies Mount Mir-t'ai, which, he says, "is full of precious stones. To get the purest, which sometimes weigh 10,000 lbs., it is necessary to climb to peaks almost inaccessible. This is done by the help of *yaks*. The Mussulmans take up machinery, by means of which they hammer the cliffs, and allow stones and tools to fall together, to be collected afterwards. Every year Yarkand furnishes in spring and autumn from 7,000 to 8,000, and sometimes 10,000 lbs. of precious stones. All are sent to Peking, and private trade in them is strictly forbidden, though among the Mussulmans it is impossible to prevent it entirely."

reason, however, my Muhammadan followers did not like this arrangement; and I was marched off instead to a Turkish *serai*, and lodged in a small, dark, and dirty room, with our beasts of burden in the quadrangle just outside.

The authorities, however, seemed mindful that no harm should befall us, and sent ten men to guard our effects through the night; and when, in the early morning, I wanted to photograph the five small and one large mile-posts, or emblems of urban rank, as well as part of a mosque, outside the *yamen*, an old *Aksakal* preceded me through the bazaar, ordering people to right and left, that my way might be unimpeded, and keeping the crowd at a distance whilst I focussed the picture. I took the opportunity at the same time to photograph my two *djiguitts* from Yarkand, Kerim Akhoon and Akhoon Khoja, in their Chinese jackets, with white breast-plates, indicating their office.

We left Posgam at 8 a.m., passing at first over a soil somewhat sandy, with cultivation, and here and there large patches of *chi* grass, but through no desert country. At two and a half miles the road passes through swampy ground for something more than a mile. Grazing is plentiful throughout the district, and hamlets are numerous. At eight miles from Posgam is forded the Tiznaf river, with firm and pebbly bed, between low, sandy banks from 80 to 100 yards apart. Ten thousand families are said to inhabit the region between this river and Posgam.

Five miles farther is Yak-Shambeh, or Sunday bazaar, with 300 houses, where, as in other chief villages of the district, a market is held once a week. On a subsequent visit we stayed here for a night, and met an obliging native official, Kudaberdi-Kazi-Bek. He was evidently the "squire" of the village, and was a keeper of falcons. When we arrived, he was about to start on a hunt.

I induced him to stand for his portrait; first with his two falconers, each of the two bearing on his wrist a hooded bird. Then I took his falconers and a good-looking *chilimchi*, or boy for making ready and handing round the pipe. Views east and west of the almost empty bazaar shaded by trees, or in some places by leafy poles stretched overhead, give a good idea of a Turkistan market-place; but my greatest triumph here, thanks to the bek's influence, was in persuading a buxom dame of Yarkand, one Zoeda Khoja, in a huge but locally fashionable *talpak* hat of brown fur, and with a child in her arms, to stand for her portrait. Next I caught her mounted astride a donkey, travelling *en famille* with a young boy clinging behind, and she holding a frightened urchin in front. The *bek's* men were induced, one to hold the donkey's head and the other to preside at the tail; and thus was posed one of my most successful of native groups.

With the men and boys I had no particular difficulty in adding to my ethnological pictures, and photographed Muhammad Yusuf Bai, aged 73; also three boys—typical street Arabs—of the locality, and Ibrahim Akhoon, the *reis* or district superintendent of morals, in huge white turban. A group of three labourers was added; another of a mullah and scholar, with a local manufacturer; and a third of two noblemen, Sadduk Beg and Kudaberdi Beg, with pipe-bearer.

This completed my taking of specimens of the male sex, and I then requested the bek to bring me some of the feminine beauties of the village who would permit their personal charms to be transferred to paper. This,

however, was not so easy a matter; but presently there appeared two old hags not far from threescore years and ten, with a third female veiled. What amount of beauty might be under this covering I knew not, but besought her to lift the veil, if only for a few seconds, that the Western world might know what could be produced in Yak-Shambeh. But my eloquence was vain; and Joseph seemed surprised that I did not know that a woman once unveiled dropped forthwith an undefined number of degrees in the social scale. I had, therefore, to photograph the two old ladies, with my assumed beauty in her *talpak* hat, but with her face covered with a kerchief.

From Yak-Shambeh the road was similar to that we travelled on the preceding day, but in some places rather more sandy. At four miles on our way we crossed the Tezab, a rapid stream 200 feet wide and 3 feet deep, in a bed of 600 yards, to the village of Kulchi, whence the well-shaded road, often 40 feet wide, traverses well-cultivated lands.

More than once I was beguiled to stalk vainly in the marshes some wild geese of brilliant hue. My gun brought me, however, here, and about Yarkand, a long-legged buzzard (*Buteo ferox*), an Isabelline shrike (*Lanius arenarius*), a white-throat (*Sylvia minuscula*), the tawny accentor (*Accentor fulvescens*), a hooded crow (*Corvus cornix*), a rose pastor (*Pastor roseus*), Brandt's shorelark (*Otocorys pallida*), and the hoopoe (*Upupa epops*). Henderson observes that the English lapwing, called *machung* in Turki, is common in the marshy ground between Karghalik and Yarkand; and on a subsequent journey I shot here a bird unknown to me, with pink feathers in the wing, and called by the natives *Tomochuk*, as well as a second species named *Tokochak*, which lives in holes in trees.

We met on the road a Kashmiri, who had a house

in Karghalik, and who, simply on the ground that I was an Englishman, regretted that he would not be at home to receive me, for he said he liked the English. This compliment was followed by another, somewhat more substantial, in the form of a *dostarkhan*, spread for me within a few miles of the town, in a government rest-house erected for such occasions. Then there came out to meet us a man sent by Aziz Bek, the chief native local authority, to bring us to his guest-house, where others of my compatriots were said to have lodged.

After a march of 24 miles in eight hours from Posgam, we reached Karghalik, a town of 1,000 families, according to Forsyth, but according to a later traveller 3,000, and at an elevation of 4,570 feet above the sea. The houses are all of mud and sun-dried bricks, the streets being covered in many places with trellis-work, on which vines and gourds are trained to give shade in summer. The people cultivate flower-gardens, in which roses predominate; whilst on the house-tops may be seen boxes of asters, marigolds, and balsams.

Passing down the long street, with shops and eating-houses in abundance, as well as places for the sale of necessaries for the outfit of caravans, we came to the guest-house of Aziz Bek, which served to remind me of the ups and downs of a traveller's life. At Yarkand I had been housed sumptuously, but slept at Posgam in what was little better than a hovel; whereas now once more I was to be lodged in a suburban villa, with a splendid garden of walnuts, apples, vines, mulberries, peaches, nectarines, and all sorts of delectable fruits.

My host was evidently a man of means; and, on the principle, I suppose, that if you wish a thing done well you should do it yourself, he had built, by means of 30 men, in 40 days, on the outskirts of the town, what he intended to be his mausoleum. It consisted of a rectangular space at the roadside, approached through an important-looking gateway, and having in the centre a small domed building for his tomb. At the side opposite the gateway was a raised verandah, or cloister, with *mihrab* and pulpit, to serve as a mosque. This was approached by a broad pathway, and the roof was supported by slender columns, all above the burnt-brick foundations being built of mud, but looking in a photograph more pretentious.

Soon after our arrival at Karghalik we were called upon by the brother of Mirza Jan Haji of Yarkand, who offered his services; and the Chinese *Amban*, who is a *Hsien* mandarin, sent me a present of fodder and maize, with an invitation to dine on the morrow. I sent return presents, including a Chinese New Testament and illuminated cards, and regretted that my haste would not permit me to stay; but, as his affable secretary could speak only Chinese, and we had no Turki interpreter, our communications were not voluble.

Next morning the secretary reappeared, this time bringing an interpreter, and a servant carrying a whatnot with five basins of cooked food. The mandarin regretted that I could not stay for a good dinner, but, failing this, he had sent some food for breakfast, and for my journey. The dishes were dressed with a delicacy and care worthy of a Parisian café; but, alas! the vinegar and garlic seasoning were so strong as to render most of them quite unpalatable to me; and when I offered them to my Muhammadan followers, they regarded the matter from another

standpoint, and would not touch food cooked by the
infidel Chinese.

After the secretary had delivered the message of
his master, he approached me with a piteous request
of his own—that I would give him medicine or something
to enable him to break off the habit of smoking
opium.

I have alluded to the emaciated Chinaman we met
at the Muzart Custom-house, and, by way of showing
how widely the habit of smoking opium has now
spread, may quote the testimony of an Englishman
who had lived long in Kansu, and who told me that
it was the exception there to meet a man who does not
smoke the drug.

In Shansi Colonel Bell was informed at several
places that 90 per cent. of the men, and many of
the women, are addicted to the habit. He found the
poppy there occupying the best garden-land, ousting
a certain and prolific wheat crop, although highly
injurious to the economy of the province, and impoverishing
the population.

Forsyth's testimony is similar. Speaking of Yengi
Hissar, he says: "Every street has its bang-shop,
generally a mean little shed, in which two or three
pipes are at the disposal of the passers-by. There
are besides several opium divans, places more like
a pawnbroker's shop than anything else—obscure
chambers, dimly lighted by a row of flickering lamps
along the floor, on which lie the somnolent devotees
of this 'thief of reason and riches.' On shelves
ranged round the walls are neatly folded and labelled
bundles of their household chattels, and even the clothes
off their backs, all kept in pawn till released by cash
payment. . . . Suffice it here to say that the abuse

VOL. II.

of these deleterious drugs is prevalent through the country."

The poppy, he says, is cultivated in Yarkand and Kashgar, but not largely, and local opium appears to be of very inferior quality, and only used to mix with the foreign and more intoxicating kind, brought from India.

I have already quoted Dr Seeland, who says that, of the lowest classes in Kashgar, half the men and four or five per cent. of the women consume opium or hemp in some form or another.

Dr Bellew also, in his medical report, speaks of the frequency of dyspepsia caused by the abuse of opium and Indian hemp. "Among the city people everywhere," he writes, "dyspepsia is met with in aggravated form, and marks very surely the destructive effects of these poisons. The haggard, hungry, dolorous, and discontented looks of these wretched victims of their passion tell but too truly the loss of all pleasure in life to them, and speak for the necessity of their continuance in the vice to eke out to its bitter end the short span of aimless existence left for them."

The last two writers, it should be observed, approach the subject, not from a moral or sentimental, but from a medical point of view. In the case of my petitioner, the opium-grower possibly, and they who share his gains, would have said: "My friend, use the opium, but do not abuse it,"—advice which, had the applicant been able to act upon it, would have rendered needless his coming to me.

This case was not a solitary one, for others had come with a similar request, as many had done to Colonel Bell. Moreover, the present was not the case of a low-born, degraded Chinaman, which would have been bad enough, but a polite young gentleman in the flower of youth, on a par with a member of our Indian Civil Service, and occupying a somewhat similar position; yet bound in chains in comparison with which the fetters and horrors of Siberia are but a trifle, and for deliverance from which, on our return journey, the poor slave came again, beseeching help.

What could I say? I recommended three things. "First," said I, "determine to give the practice up; secondly, when the craving is on, drink strong coffee" (some of which I gave him); "and, thirdly, ask help by prayer of the true God, concerning whom you may learn in this New Testament I give you."

Karghalik, though but a small town, possesses a certain importance, from its being the easternmost point of supply for caravans travelling by the Karakoram and other routes over the Himalayas to India. It was here I received from Europe my long-looked-for telegram, which the Russian authorities had been good enough to forward to me, free of charge, 450 miles beyond Osh.

I received also at Karghalik other communications. At Yarkand, on the morning of our departure, a merchant brought me a packet from Leh, inclosing two letters from Darjeeling, and one also from Mr Redslob, which had been found in the writing-case of the murdered Dalgleish, and another from Captain Ramsay, the British Joint Commissioner at Leh.

I opened this last one with some little trepidation, wondering whether he would repeat the warning conveyed by Mr Redslob against following the route of Dalgleish. In this case I should, perhaps, have chosen the Baroghil Pass; but neither Captain Ramsay

nor others said anything to dissuade my taking the
usual route; and when the telegram, received at
Karghalik, did not require my return by Osh, I
decided forthwith for the Karakoram.

As it was already September 28th, I was warned
that I ought, in anticipation of early snows, to start for
the passes at once. But all was arranged for Khotan,
and part of the money paid. I had still a reserve
of Scriptures to distribute in a district where, presumably, a printed copy had never been seen; and,
no Englishman having described the route from
Karghalik to Khotan, it was not at all to my taste
to miss this little sprig of laurel. I therefore wrote to
Yarkand to say that I hoped to be back, and ready
to start for India, by October 19th; and then we set
out for Khotan.

CHAPTER XXXVII.

FROM KARGHALIK TO KHOTAN.

Route from Karghalik across a *chul*, 149.—Picket-stations to Hajif Langar, 150.—District of Guma; its shops, peaches, and river; Journey to Moji, 151.—Exorcism and photography, 152-55.—From Moji to Janghuia, 156.—Desolate route to Pialma; An ocean of sand, 157.—Tabughaz Langar; its mosque and highwayman's head; but few travellers; Arrival at Zawa Kurghan; its custom-house and precautions, 159.—Palace of Habibulla; Naaki Mogul and Mr Johnson, 160. Route through cultivated fields to Ak-Serai; Photographic and ornithological acquisitions, 162-63.—Escorted into Khotan, 165.

WE left Karghalik about eight o'clock on Thursday morning, September 27th—a party of six cavaliers, fourteen horses, and two *arbas*. The brother of Mirza Jan Haji rode with us for half-an-hour, which sufficed to bring us through the remainder of the cultivated land we had been traversing all the way, more or less, from Yarkand.

This pleasant scenery was now exchanged for a desert of severest type, called a *chul*, where it appeared to have rained stones and boulders. The country was perfectly flat, and in keeping with what some tell us that the Tarim valley has been—namely, the bottom of an inland sea. After riding seven hours across alternate *chul* and sandy desert, and passing Egun (or Yakin) Langar, a small hamlet of four or five houses in a well-cultivated oasis, we reached Khosh Langar, the boundary between Karghalik and Guma.

Khosh Langar is a picket-station in the wilderness with a spacious rest-house, built by Yakub Khan. Here we stayed to bait the horses, and wait for the rising of the moon. Then we started about ten o'clock and I endeavoured to sleep in the *arba*, where it was rather cold, notwithstanding my fur coat and shawl. Six hours sufficed to bring us to the next station, and at four next morning we arrived at Chulak Langar, 33 miles from Karghalik.

At Chulak Langar was a well-built rest-house, also erected by Yakub Khan, on an eminence above a small walled garden and an artificial reservoir of water, whilst a few hundred yards eastward was the old rest-house, left to fall into ruin. The view from our lodging was singularly desolate, and when, after a stay of five or six hours, we plunged again, at ten o'clock, into the *chul*, stony, barren, and without a blade of verdure, it struck me as being the most thoroughly sterile and arid tract I had ever seen.

The landscape was most wearying. In the distance, southward, were barren hills; but near at hand, nothing but stones. Each mile accomplished had the same dreary aspect as the one preceding it. There was not a bird, an animal, a plant, or even an insect to be seen. The only thing that attracted my attention was an occasional cleared space, six or eight feet across and surrounded by stones. These, they said, answered for travellers' mosques, where a stone was erected for a *kiblah*, in order that passing Muhammadans, at the hour of prayer, might know which way to turn towards Mecca.

A march of nine miles, in three hours, brought us to Silak Langar, where some of us drank tea and lunched on melons, peaches, and walnuts. Five miles beyond was Hajif Langar, a rest-house built in Chinese style, and having near it tall poplars and a plantation of other trees. Then, turning into the *arba*, I crossed the bed of the river Tasgun, and, at 23 miles from Chulak Langar, arrived, soon after dark, at Guma.

The district of Guma extends from Khosh Langar about 100 miles eastward to Pialma, whilst 50 miles southward it includes the Sanju Pass. The town and district, 20 years ago, were said to possess 1,000 houses, and the bazaar 300 shops.

We left Guma next morning at eight, and, for half-an-hour, marched through the remainder of three miles of cultivation. Here I noticed many peach-trees, and, what was better, the *djiguitts* brought me a number of excellent nectarines, sun-dried in a fashion I had never seen in Europe, but very tasty for the end of September. At three miles we came to a dry bed, 200 paces broad, of a branch of the Tasgun, the main stream of which rises not far north of the Kilian Pass, and after a course of 70 miles is lost in the wilderness north of Guma.

Once more we plunged into sandy desert and *chul*, and, at nine miles, passed the hamlet of Supi Khajam; and, a mile farther on, a village of 50 houses called Chola. Two miles beyond was Mukhila Langar, and, after eight miles more, we came to a larger village called Chuda, where we rested a little while. For the remaining five miles I turned into the *arba*, and, after eight hours of desert travel, reached Moji at four o'clock on Saturday afternoon.

At Moji I intended to spend Sunday; but my

drivers wanted to go 14 miles farther to Janghuia, where, they said, was a larger village and better water; and to this I consented, partly in the hope that we might have a better opportunity of distributing Scriptures. We waited, therefore, for the rising of the moon; and orders had been given to make ready the horses, when there was heard a sound of drums and beating of tambourines.

This I learned was the preliminary stage of an exorcism, or casting the devil out of a sick woman. Now, this was an operation which, in my varied experience, I had never witnessed, but I have it on paternal testimony that very early in life I manifested an interest in such subjects. Thus, when in a little cot beside my parents' bed, I awoke early one morning, and am reported to have called out "Papa!"

"Yes, my dear," said paterfamilias.

"Papa, will you please show me Satan?"

My father, thinking perhaps to quiet me and return to his slumbers, drowsily replied, "Yes, dear."

By this time, however, my younger brother, in a cot on the other side, hearing of good things going about, put up his little head, and said, "Me too, papa?"

Again the fond parent had to say "Yes," though the family records do not say in what manner the promises were redeemed; but now that, after more than 40 years, there seemed to be a chance of witnessing an exorcism, nothing could restrain my curiosity. So the horses were ordered back to the stable, and in a few minutes Joseph and I, preceded by a *djignitt* with a lantern, were making our way to the house of one of the well-to-do men of the village, whose aged female relative was supposed to be possessed.

We were ushered into a room full of people, some

of whom were tightening a rope suspended from the beam, and fastened to a log beneath the earthen floor. A mullah was muttering prayers, presumably in Arabic, but of which Joseph could make neither head nor tail. At the same time there were passed round the rope, as if to charm it—first, some old clothes; then a pan of fire, with tea and other substances put therein; and then a bunch of twigs, with small articles attached, these twigs being afterwards placed in the rafters of the roof.

Meanwhile Jimla, a woman of 60, was leaning and panting in a very distressed condition against the wall. Upon my feeling her pulse, she seemed to have almost none. She was placed, nevertheless, at the foot of the rope, and various things were passed, first round the rope, and then four times round her head. Next, she was caused to stand astride over a brazier of fire, so as to allow the smoke to ascend her garments, tambourines and fiddles being placed against the rope, and five mullahs spitting about in various directions and galloping through formulas of which Joseph could not catch a word.

After this the fire and instruments were removed, and each was passed four times round the cord and round the woman's head. Then the instruments were taken by five men, who walked round and round the woman, banging and dinning the drum and tambourines close to the old lady's ears, after which she was made to walk round the rope till she sank exhausted.

This seemed to be the end of the first act, which had to be repeated, we were told, 14 times through the night until sunrise. A pipe of tobacco was now brought in, and handed here and there, the mullahs also taking a few whiffs. At this point we left the room, but returned at midnight to find most of the congregation asleep on the floor. As for the woman, she appeared much exhausted, telling me, in answer to my inquiry, that she felt a pain in her legs. Poor old soul! it would have been a marvel if she did not, and a great many other pains besides; but, unfortunately, I was powerless to help her.

Not that it must be taken for granted that her friends would have accepted other help; for Dr Seeland writes that the only treatment of maladies known to these natives is the muttering or reading prayers from the Koran in the presence of the patient. Dr Seeland was one night awakened by the beating of a tambourine for the purpose of driving the devil out of a sick child, and this notwithstanding that everybody knew that there was a physician staying in the next house.

Imagination, however, goes a long way in certain ailments; and on our return journey I induced Jimla, supported by an elderly male relative, to stand for her portrait, she half suspecting, I fancy, that my camera was the latest and most approved apparatus for casting out evil spirits. Whether the operation was beneficial or not to the patient I cannot say; but the old lady did me good service in being the first of her sex in that village to break the ice in allowing herself to be photographed.

After this I was able, by the help of presents, to induce others to follow suit; first two mothers with a child, and next a young woman, Tokhta Khan, said to be unmarried, but whose dress of Chinese cut suggested her being possibly the intimate of a Chinese official. Another group consisted of father and mother with baby in a Turkistan cradle, together with a mother and baby.

I photographed also at Moji the bazaar; but, as it

A MOTHER, AND TOKHTA KHAN, AN UNMARRIED GIRL, AT MOJI.

was not market day, it looked little more than a collection of empty sheds, which indeed, at such times, is the normal appearance of bazaars throughout the country. Other typical views taken in these desert villages were those of leafy bowers of cucurbitaceous plants, from which drooped the bottle-shaped gourds so well known throughout Central Asia, the dried rind of which, with the inside scooped out, serves for pails, water-vessels, powder-flasks, and even snuff-boxes.

We left Moji an hour after midnight, passed in two miles Kosha Langar, and at ten miles Kondla Langar; but the way was nearly all desert, and we did not complete the 14 miles to Janghuia before seven in the morning. Janghuia is a rather large village, with a fort built in the time of the Khotan ruler Habibulla, but not now kept up. The place has some little importance as the point where the route from the Sanju Pass joins the road to Khotan. Another route from Sanju, 15 miles long, joins the main road at Moji.

We rested at Janghuia for the remainder of the day, and in the afternoon looked about the village, which possesses a mosque of mud, with a primitive square minaret, chiefly built of sticks. The people, however, seemed to be thirsting for knowledge, so that we sold among them no less than 12 New Testaments. At Moji I had asked whether any one could read. The mullah chanting the exorcism could not, and I promised that if their *Aksakal* would come to me he should have a book—a promise which, on our return journey, I was called upon to redeem.

We left Janghuia on Monday morning at seven, passing for half-an-hour through two miles of cultivated land, the road being four inches deep, not in sand, but dust. A large house was seen on the outskirts of the village, after which we entered a sandy tract for about 20 miles without a single habitation, or, at best, a

Langar with brackish water and no provisions or fuel.

So utterly uninteresting was the way, that, in self-defence, I began for the first time to read on horseback, and so beguiled some of the tedium of ten hours spent in crossing 22 miles of sand. This brought us, at five o'clock, to a village with a small bazaar, called Piahna. Here was a fairly good *serai*, with a high pretentious-looking open-work gate, but lightly put together, against which one of my carts struck in entering, and shivered it to pieces.

Understanding that the morrow was to be our most difficult day's travel since descending from the Muzart Pass, I roused the men at three, but did not get off till six. Then, after passing through cultivation for two miles, we entered a region of sand-hills, over which our wheels drove heavily. The first building we came to was called Ak-Robat, perhaps from its white roof, covering two rooms full of manure and uncleanness. From this we passed on, and, at 15 miles from Piahna, came to Ak-Robat No. 2, or Ak-Langar.

Here was a large rest-house, having two deep wells in a courtyard 100 feet square, and surrounded by many rooms, with attendants. These wells may possibly be very old; for in the annals of the Yuan-shi we read that so far back as 1274, there were 13 water stations established by imperial order between Khotan and Yarkand. We saw also, outside but near at hand, a travellers' mosque of burnt brick, built by order of Yakub Khan, looking very bare, but substantial. As for the rest, everything around appeared as the acme of desolation; for these buildings stand in the midst of an ocean of sand, which, when blown by the wind, makes the rest-house all but invisible. Accordingly, there is erected thereon a high pole and cross-beam, serving for a bell or signal to be hung by day, or a lantern by night.

Five miles farther on we came to a place called Kum-Robat, where was the *Mazar*, or tomb, of Imam Muhammad Shah, a renowned local saint, said to have been buried (in round numbers as usual) " 500 years ago," and whose fame attracts once a year numerous pilgrims.

On the premises live five mullahs, to whom I gave five copies of the New Testament. They look after the grave of the saint, which has no ornament beyond a few poles with rags fluttering in the wind, as well as a mosque for common prayer; whilst not far from the grave is a small hut or hermitage called " Talab Kana," or the " asking-house," into which individuals may temporarily retire for a period of meditation and private prayer. This last was said to be sometimes occupied by as many as from 50 to 60 persons in the course of the year, although in some years not more than five or six came.

All around, as at the previous station, sand reigned supreme, and could not be kept out even from a small inclosure that had been railed off and planted with shrubs. A curious feature of the place consisted of hundreds of pigeons, for whose use two or three large rooms near the mosque were set apart, and I observed that our carters thought it the proper thing to scatter amongst these birds a gallon or two of corn.

Marching on from the tomb, we passed a relic of former days in a ruined but strongly-built mile-post, upon which the sand had so encroached as almost to bury it. Probably there were once houses near, now covered with sand. Then, dragging on a few miles, we passed a small rest-house called Tabughaz Langar, where was a curious little travellers' mosque constructed of posts, wattle, and daub; and, not far distant, the less pleasing spectacle of a highwayman's head in a cage on the top of a pole.

On the return journey I photographed these curious objects, and was told that the robber was formerly keeper of the rest-house, and that, after receiving his guests and learning their value in coin, he was wont to waylay or overtake them, and demand their money.

We were now approaching the end of six days' travel over what was practically a huge desert relieved by a few oases of verdure. We had met scarcely a dozen travellers, and those of the poorest, driving a few donkeys laden with produce. We overtook fewer still, but had been joined by two or three hangers-on, amongst them a man and his wife with a horse between them, which they took it in turn to ride from Karghalik, seemingly thinking it advisable to keep up with us.

Thus, after a weary march of 13 hours from Pialma over little else but sand-hills, which reminded me of those east of the Oxus near Charjui, we reached Zawa Kurghan, at seven o'clock, horses and men being thoroughly tired. Zawa Kurghan, lying at an altitude of 4,430 feet, is a neat, compact little town walled in in the time of Habibulla, and having a straight street running through it, shaded by silver poplars and closed at each end by a gate.

In this street, nearly opposite the *serai*, stands the Chinese Custom-house. An official came to make inquiries about me, although as a foreigner I was exempt from payment or examination. I was told, however, that in the case of persons coming from the opposite direction minute search was made, lest travellers should be unlawfully taking with them gold or jade, both of which are found in the district.

Under Yakub Khan the sale of gold was disallowed, but winked at. On the road between Kiria and Khotan there stood a regular searching house, where men were stripped ; and women, after being examined, were made to jump over a ditch in order that any gold they had concealed might fall out. I am not aware that any such restrictions now exist, for subsequently one of the merchants in our caravan was said to be carrying to India a considerable quantity of the precious metal.

Zawa Kurghan is the place where Yakub Khan enticed to his camp Habibulla, the ruler of Khotan. One of the men, who in returning escorted me out of Khotan (I think Naaki Mogul), remembered the event, and told me that his father tried to persuade Habibulla not to go. The wily Yakub, however, deceived the mullah by swearing on the Koran, and then perfidiously murdered him.

We turned aside, a few miles from Zawa Kurghan, to see the palace of Habibulla. It reminded me of a large English farmhouse with straggling buildings around, in which he sustained a number of dervishes and religious Muhammadans; but everything was upon a scale that denoted great simplicity, not to say poverty.

Naaki Mogul revealed another link with the past that interested me. When Mr Johnson came to the Khotan frontier in 1865, Naaki Mogul said he was one of those sent to meet the Englishman and bring him into the town. Nor was this the only reminiscence I met with of Mr Johnson, for in Yarkand a letter in the possession of a man accompanying Muhammad Ali was shown me, written thus:—

"My dear Edwin,—

"Allow me to introduce to you Sadeek Meer, trader of Ladak and Yarkand. You will find him a good man, and he may be of use to you.

"Yours very sincerely,
"W. H. Johnson.

"Srinagur, 16 11 82."

Mr Johnson read to the Royal Geographical Society a paper on his journey, from which I perceive that in returning he travelled along the Yarkand road to what he calls the village of Zilgia, where he left his luggage for three days, and pushed on by post-horses as far as Luk, 36 miles east of Yarkand.

In this case it would appear that the greater part of my route from Karghalik to Khotan had been covered by an Englishman before me, though Mr Johnson gives no information of the villages passed through. Moreover, of the only two places that he names, Zilgia and Luk, I have no record in my itinerary. Probably Luk is the same as a village eight miles east of Karghalik, and called Lob in the carefully drawn up itinerary of the Pundit Kishen Singh, printed in the Forsyth report, and to which I am indebted for some of my statistics concerning mileage, population, etc., in this region.

As for Zilgia, the name does not occur in the itinerary of Kishen Singh, nor in my own. Captain Chapman, however, from notes compiled by Ramchand (another pundit sent by Forsyth to Khotan), gives in the Forsyth report Zungoe as an alternative name for Janghuia. And this probably is the place

Johnson means by Zilgia, whence he made his way to the Sanju Pass, the first Englishman thus to have peeped from India into Chinese Turkistan.

Wishing to push forward over the remaining 25 miles from Zawa Kurghan as quickly as possible, I called the men next morning at three. We started at six to march under pleasanter conditions than on the preceding days, for henceforward our way lay through smiling fields—a cultivated country, thickly inhabited, and abounding in gardens and orchards.

East of the town we crossed by a wooden bridge, like those in Kashmir, a considerable stream 20 yards wide, whilst at ten miles from Zawa Kurghan is forded the Karakash river, flowing down from the Sanju Pass. The water of the Karakash in September was low; but so high does it rise in summer in its bed, 400 yards wide, that a rest-house is built on the bank for the accommodation of travellers temporarily detained.

At Ak-Serai we passed an empty bazaar, and also a cemetery, the latter having certain points of difference from others we had seen, in that some of the graves were railed in by fences, whilst there were standing about the ground numerous poles with fluttering rags, and the dead trunks and branches of trees similarly decorated.

I photographed both cemetery and bazaar buildings, and, in fact, kept my camera busy both going and returning between Yarkand and Khotan. For the most part the natives made no objection to my operations, not even when I photographed the tomb, prayer-house, and mosque at Mazar Imam Muhammad Shah. I am afraid I rather frightened a poor Rebecca of eight years at Janghuia, upon whom I seized as she was coming home with her waterpot, and bade her stand against a wall with the camera pointed to her face. A present, however, seemed partly to allay the fright, whilst an old lady named Tsakima, of Guma, but staying at Janghuia, drew her veil aside without compunction and permitted her charms to be carried off. And thus I was able to secure from this little-known region an interesting collection of ethnological photographs, together with views of the rough post-stations, as at Chulak Langar, Pialma, Moji, and Hajif Langar.

As we passed through the gardens of Khotan we saw some strange birds. Animal life had been scarce all the way from Karghalik, but I secured a few species in the various oases. Thus, at Chulak Langar, among the few living things to be seen were some domesticated ducks in the reservoir, and keeping company with them I perceived a couple of wild birds of smaller species. Stealing along to the edge of the water, I frightened the Chinese keeper of the rest-house, who thought I was bent on the slaughter of his property, and shouted lustily to me to desist. I was able, however, to secure as my first duck one of the wild pair, without interfering with the tame birds.

During our short stay for lunch at Silak Langar I had a chase after some *podoces*, but they ran too fast for me. Between Silak Langar and Hajif Langar several larks were seen. They appeared to be almost the only birds that made their way from out of the oases into the *chul*. Again, on leaving Pialma I secured a hawk, but saw no other birds thereabouts except larks and sparrows.

At Tabughaz Langar was a sheet of water with snipe, one of which fell to my gun, and, thinking it might be useful to have a specimen or two of Turkistan sparrows, I secured several here of the local species (*Passer montanus*), and discovered they belonged to our rarer English species; for, as Dr Henderson says, "The tree-sparrow of Europe is the house-sparrow of the city of Yarkand, where it is almost as familiar and impudent as the English or Indian house-sparrow. In Turki it is called *Chum chuk*."

Another small bird obtained in the Khotan oases was the Siberian Chat (*Saxicola pleschanka*), of which Dr Stoliczka and Colonel Biddulph found specimens near Sanju in the Kuen Lun, and at Kila Panjah on the Pamir. The Yarkandis call it *Kara chiket*, or black wheatear, and say that it breeds in the country, but disappears entirely in the winter.

I shot also an Indian starling (*Sturnus indicus*); but the birds that interested me most in Khotan were the white-winged and Severtsoff's woodpeckers (*Picus leucopterus et P. leptorhynchus*), which were numerous, and with their black, white, and reddish plumage looked pretty objects as they fluttered about in the gardens.

On approaching Do-Shambeh bazaar, seven miles short of Khotan, a *djiguitt* was sent forward with my letter. This brought out to meet us a Kandahari, Muhammad Akhram Khan, son of Jumma Khan, comprehensively styling himself "Aksakal of the Afghans, Badakshanis, Hindus, and Kashmiris"—that is to say, of all British subjects in those parts. He had among his possessions a letter addressed to him by Mr Carey, dated October 16th, 1885, and kindly offered me quarters where he said Mr Carey stayed; but as it was in the suburbs I declined, and asked to be conducted to some place in the town, if only a public *serai*.

Marching forward, we crossed one or two streams, and, as we approached the city, found the road walled in on either hand and shaded by trees, till, about two o'clock, we came in sight of our goal—the Chinese portion of the city of Khotan, 198 miles from Karghalik.

CHAPTER XXXVIII.

THE KINGDOM OF KHOTAN.

Two sources of Khotan history, 166.—Kusthana, capital of Li-yul; Remusat's translation of Chinese records, 167. — Enlargement of early Khotan, and its communication with China, 168.—Tchuen-yuen on Khotan; its modern history, 169.—Exploration of Yurung-kash and Tarim rivers, 171.—Lob-Nor visited, 172.—Wild camels; Route from Khotan to China, 173. — Prjevalsky's discovery of Altyn Tagh, but failure to enter Tibet from Khotan; Failures of Pievtsoff and Grombchevsky; Limits of Khotan, 174-75.—Deserts, buried villages, and relics, 176.—A former excavator at Khotan, 177.—Meteorology of Chinese Turkistan and Khotan, 178.—Author's record, and statistics, 179. Khotan jade, and gold, 182.—Exchange of silver, 186.

OUR knowledge of the ancient history of Khotan is derived from Tibetan and Chinese sources, not to mention the Persian legend concerning Sya-wush, who, about 580 B.C., received with his bride the provinces of Khotan and Chin as her dowry.

Tibetan legends do not go back so far, but tell more of the marvellous. Li-yul was the Tibetan name for the region about Khotan, and this, in common with some other countries, on adopting Buddhism, saw fit, Mr Rockhill says, to recast nearly all its national traditions, making the founder of Khotan to be Kus-thana, a son of Asoka, the illustrious Buddhist monarch of North India.

Kusthana means in Sanscrit "pap, or breast, of the earth," and, among the Buddhist fables and prodigies, it is stated in Tibetan writings that on the birth of Asoka's son the soothsayers foretold that he would reign in the lifetime of his father; whereupon Asoka, thinking this would involve his own deposition, ordered his queen to forsake her baby. But the friendly earth caused a breast to arise, whence the child drew his nourishment, till, after attaining the age of 19, he founded the kingdom of Li-yul, 234 years after the death of the founder of Buddhism, the capital being called Kusthana.

Chinese annals of the seventh and eighth centuries tell us that Khotan had chronicles of its own; and Rockhill thinks it probable that the Tibetan writings whence he translated his information were written in the language of Khotan; since they state that, at first, the country was half Chinese and half Indian, its spoken language being a mixture of the two, whilst its written characters resembled those of India. And this statement is corroborated by the testimony of Fa-hian, who speaks of the professed disciples of Buddha in all the countries hereabouts as using Indian books and the Indian language.

Passing now from Tibetan literature, we are indebted to Remusat, who published in 1820 from imperial records such notices as he could find concerning Khotan. Thence we learn that during the reign of Wooti, of the Han dynasty, so far back as the second century B.C., Chinese officers were first sent to Khotan, which, at that period, contained 2,300 families, or 19,300 souls, and 2,400 soldiers.

Subsequently, we get glimpses of Khotan from the mention in these imperial records of tribute received:

as when, in 202 A.D., Khotan sent to the emperor caparisoned elephants. It would appear, too, from the same source, that the kingdom of Khotan spread both westwards and northwards; for, in the third century, when China was divided at home, the states constituting Kashgar came into possession of Khotan; and to these, in the seventh century, were added Hami, Pishan, and Kurla. In 445 a punitive expedition was sent from China against Tangut, and followed its fugitive ruler to Khotan, at which period the Khotanese are spoken of as knowing neither justice nor civility.

Half a century later, however, in 509, the people are described as very ceremonious and polite, writing with pencils of wood and carrying stone seals. In 518, 541, and 632, among the tribute sent by Khotan are mentioned vases of glass, a jade image of Buddha, and a jade zone, for the last of which the emperor sent a special letter of thanks. In the reign of Kao-tsung (about 650) the king of Khotan went to the Chinese capital, seemingly as a tributary ally, with an offering of 300 camels; and in 717 the tribute included a wild camel "swift as the wind."

In the tenth century the offerings included jade and crystal, as well as an elephant captured in war against Kashgar. In 1081 there were brought from Khotan pearls, coral, ivory, camphor, and quicksilver—all sent now for the first time, and indicating an increase of trade with India. Four years afterwards a tiger was offered for the emperor's acceptance, which his Majesty declined. Later, in 1406, the king of Khotan sent envoys with tribute; and, in the Chinese annals recording the event, Khotan is described as a country which, from the time of the Han dynasty to that of the Sung, had not ceased to be in communication with China.

We know, however, that Khotan was conquered in the eleventh century by the ruler of Kashgar; and in the thirteenth century this town, with all others in the Tarim valley, submitted to Jinghiz Khan. Marco Polo, in 1274, found Khotan subject to one of the great Khan's descendants; but in the time of Benedict Goes, in 1602, it had reverted to Muhammadan rule. Nevertheless, Bretschneider, speaking generally, I suppose, of Khotan province, says that it "always sent tribute to the Chinese Court, probably either as a tributary ally or a subject state, down to the reign of Wan-li (1573—1620)."

Again, under the Kalmuk domination of the Tarim valley, Khotan was, of course, subject to the Sungars, till the Chinese once more became masters; and at the close of the last century we have Tchuen-yuen writing of Khotan as one of the six Muhammadan towns under the grand mandarin of Yarkand. The town he stated to be very populous, and the people for the most part seekers of precious stones. Their manners he described as simple, without licence, idleness, or luxury, the men cultivating the soil and the women doing needlework. The rearing of silkworms also was largely followed, and the raw silk was made into a fine sort of taffeta known as Khotan silk.

So much, then, for what may be called the ancient history of Khotan, which, if not very complete, is at least more continuous than what we know of any other province in Chinese Turkistan. In the latter half of the present century begins what may be called the modern history of Khotan, and the adjoining portions of the Tarim basin, of which we have learned more scientifically during the last 30 years than in all the centuries preceding.

For this we are indebted to travellers such as Johnson, Shaw, Forsyth, Carey, Prjevalsky, Roborovsky, and Grombchevsky, not to mention Schlagintweit, who visited Khotan, but did not survive to tell the tale, and Bonvalot, who crossed the Tarim basin somewhat east of the Khotan district. So various have been the routes followed by these travellers, that every known thoroughfare of Chinese Turkistan, I believe, with one exception, has now been described.

It was in 1865 that Johnson approached the kingdom of Khotan by the Changchenmo route from Leh, and brought back information concerning its six principal towns—of Ilchi, the capital, Karakash, and Yurung-kash, each within a day's journey, and containing, according to Forsyth, about 1,000 houses each. Besides these, east of the capital were Chira, Kiria, and Nia, the last said by Forsyth to have 500 houses. The population of the whole country Johnson gave at about a quarter of a million, which Forsyth brought down to half that number. Again, Johnson thought the country under-populated, and lacking cultivators, whereas Carey and others now report the oasis as unable to support its people, so that corn has to be imported from Karghalik, and rice from Aksu and Kuchar.

None of the European members of the Forsyth expeditions visited Khotan; but two native explorers, Ram Chand and Kishen Singh, were sent there, and I have availed myself of some of their information printed in the Forsyth report. Kishen Singh, after proceeding, as I did, from Yarkand to Khotan, continued his route to Kiria (visited also by Johnson), then struck southwards to Polu, and continued over the Tibetan plateau by Rudok and Tanksi to Leh.

It was by this route, but in the reverse direction, that Carey, in 1885, descended from Polu, a village of 60 houses, to Kiria, much to the surprise of the Chinese local authorities, who did not know of this road from India. The cultivation around Kiria, Carey says, extends for about eight miles, and there is a good bridged road from thence to Khotan, shaded with well-grown trees, and passing midway through Chira. Forsyth gives the number of houses at each of these places as 4,000, and adds that Chira produces most of the silk of the district.

Leaving Khotan, Carey followed, as did Prjevalsky a few days before, the river Yurung-kash as far as its confluence with the Kara-kash, and down the united streams known as the Khotan river to the ferry on the Tarim. No other Europeans, I believe, have travelled this route before or since. Nor need any, seemingly, wish to do so, for there are no inhabitants for the greater part of the way, and in summer the river is dry and water sometimes scarce. From the ferry Carey explored the whole of the remaining course of the Tarim to Lob-Nor.

The lower portion of this region was prospected in 1861 by a party of ten Russian *starovertsi*, or Old Believers, who were followed next year by 160 more, of both sexes. Some settled on the lower Tarim, and others at Charkalik, where they were said to have built a wooden house (perhaps a church), since swept away by floods.

The immigrants were not pleased with their newly adopted country, and, in the following spring, the Chinese Government of Turfan helped them to migrate to Ushak-tala, between Karashar and Turfan, whence they departed for Urumtsi. After this the Dungan rebellion and massacres broke out; and Prjevalsky, speaking in 1876, said nothing more had been heard of them. Nor does Carey give any fresh tidings respecting them, though he heard them spoken of; and Bonvalot, in 1889, met at Lob-Nor an old man who remembered the Russians coming.

Prjevalsky was the first European author to visit Lob-Nor, and he describes the lake as shallow, with a maximum length of 60 miles and a breadth of 12, though he himself did not advance farther than the centre of the expanse, being stopped by the reeds. A later traveller to Lob-Nor is Prince Henry of Orleans, who, in 1889, with M. de Deken, made an excursion from Bonvalot's camp down the Tarim to where the Prince alleges he strode across it, and then returned with the information that, since Prjevalsky's visit in 1876, the lake (the larger basin of which alone is spoken of in the *Encyclopædia Britannica* as four times the size of the Lake of Geneva) had dried up.

The *Encyclopædia*, quoting from Prjevalsky, gives the Tarim at the confluence of the Yarkand and Khotan rivers a depth, at low water, of from three to five feet, and a width of 190 yards, whereas towards Lob-Nor the depth is said to increase to 14 feet. If, then, the Prince could stride across this, there is abundant confirmation of the remark in the *Encyclopædia* that "the desiccation of Eastern Turkistan must have gone on, within historical times, at a much more rapid rate than geologists seem prepared to admit." Geographers, however, will probably ask, as Goethe did, for "more light" before accepting the statement that the Tarim thus dwindles away and trickles into a marsh.

Prjevalsky spoke of the deserts around Lob as the most desolate he had ever seen. The regions immediately eastward are quite unknown to science. They are the home of the wild camel, and have been so reputed for centuries. Renat's map mentions that wild camels were found in Sungaria, as, according to Mr Littledale, they continue to be, but he tells me they have to be hunted when snow is on the ground, because then only can the hunter be sure of water supply. Younghusband heard of wild camels farther east, in Mongolia, near the outlying spurs of the Altai Mountains, and Bonvalot's party talked about them with the natives at Lob, where Prjevalsky also obtained three of their skins; but no European marksman has yet brought one of them down.

West of Lob-Nor are a few miserable villages of poor inhabitants, and to the south-west are sundry ruins partially or entirely buried in the sand. One of these is probably the "city of Lop" of Marco Polo, who says that travellers rested here to prepare for a 30 days' journey over a great desert of sand to Sachu.

The desert route they followed is the one exception I referred to among the routes of Chinese Turkistan over which in modern times no European has passed. It appears to have been the way followed by Marco Polo and Benedict Goes; but when Bell, near Sachu, asked for it, he found it totally disused, and not even known, though Carey, speaking at the other end, thought he would have had no difficulty in finding a guide from Lob-Nor to Sachu for good payment.

The ordinary route from Khotan to Lob lies eastwards to Kiria, and then for about 50 miles farther to Nia, south of which are the Sorgak goldfields, and northwards the tomb of Jafer Sadek, the most frequented of the shrines about Khotan. The route then continues north-east to Cherchen (or Charchand). This was, in the times of the Buddhist pilgrims, a famous place, called Shen-shen, and Fa-hian found there 4,000 monks, who read and wrote " Indian." The way then continued to Lob—that is, if one kept to the plains.

There seems to have been an alternative route by which travellers struck into the mountains, the probable locality of which Prjevalsky was the first to point out ; for he discovered, south of Lob-Nor, the Altyn Tagh range, running like a wall along the south of the Tarim basin from the Kuen Lun, near Cherchen, and continuing as the Nan Shan range into the province of Kansu. He also discovered, not far from Cherchen, a comparatively easy pass over this range into what he called " the valley of the winds," by which, possibly, travellers proceeded in ancient times from Cherchen to China.

It was during his journey of 1884-5 that Prjevalsky discovered this valley of the winds, and after so doing crossed the Altyn Tagh to Lob-Nor, and then tried, but without success, to enter Tibet from Polu. He seems to have been determined, however, to mount the Tibetan plateau, if possible, from Khotan ; and to that end had started with Lieutenant Roborovsky, when his life was cut short at Kara-Kol.

His expedition continued its way under Colonel Pievtsoff as leader ; and from Lieutenant Roborovsky's letters we learn that they reached Khotan about a year after my visit, and entered Nia October 19th, 1889. Here it was intended the expedition should winter ; but first Roborovsky and a few others started to the mountains south-east of Nia to the tomb of Mondjalik Khanum, to reconnoitre the neighbouring passes.

Continuing past the tomb, they came to the utmost limits frequented by the Khotan shepherds, who could tell them little of the country southward beyond information they occasionally picked up from gold-seekers who pushed their way to the tableland. Having, therefore, discovered, as they thought, a route for their caravan to the plateau of Tibet, they returned to Nia, and in the following spring the attempt was made; but, owing to the enormous difficulties of the way, they were unable to explore any great tract of country.

There is another Russian name that should here be mentioned—namely, that of Colonel Grombchevsky, who, being refused permission to enter Tibet through British territory, endeavoured to do so from Chinese soil, mounting eastwards from Shahidula; but, finding himself unable to penetrate far, and through loss of horses and lack of provisions, he descended to Khotan.

Here he found one of the Pievtsoff expedition, and hastened to Nia, whence he determined to make another attempt in the direction of Lassa. He started, accordingly, on March 15th, 1890, for the goldfields at Sorgak, and then continued to Polu. Here he was thwarted by the Chinese officials of Kiria, but helped by the people of Polu, so that by May 10th he found himself on the Tibetan plateau, but too early in the season to allow of his continuing to Lassa, and he had to return to Khotan. He then continued his explorations up the basin of the Tiznaf, and passed on to the eastern slope of the mountains west of Kashgar.

Some idea will now have been formed of the former importance of what Marco Polo calls "the kingdom of Cotan," which, in the present day, appears to extend from Zawa Kurghan on the west to Nia on the east, and to take in on the south Polu and the valleys of the Khotan river, whilst on the north the district is bounded by the vast Tarim and Takla Maklan deserts.

These deserts have proved a veritable plague to many of the towns and villages of Khotan by overwhelming them with sand. Marco Polo does not allude to these buried villages; but Johnson, during his stay at Khotan, was told, with Oriental exaggeration, of 360 cities buried in four-and-twenty hours!—doubtless an enlarged edition of Muhammadan and Buddhist stories connecting the sand-storms with punishment for the neglect of religious teaching.

Johnson describes the edge of this desert, six miles north of Khotan (Ilchi), as consisting of hillocks of moving sand from 200 to 400 feet in height; and he tells of clouds of dust blown from the desert, which so darkened the air that at noon he needed a candle to enable him to read large type. Johnson brought away a sample of brick-tea believed by the natives to be of great age, and exhumed from one of these buried villages. Shaw also speaks of exhumed tea as on sale in the bazaar at Yarkand.

Forsyth directed his pundits to inquire concerning these buried towns; and one man brought him, as lately dug up, two figures—one of Buddha, and the other of Hunooman, the monkey god of India. Ram Chand also brought some gold finger-rings and nose-rings like those now worn by Hindu women, as well as an iron coin, apparently of Hermæus, and several gold coins of the reigns of Constans II., Pogonatus, Justinus, Antimachus, and Theodosius.

For my own part, I bought in Ilchi a cameo said to have been found at a buried town called Tetti, about seven miles distant, not far from Do-Shambeh bazaar. Johnson seems to have observed no ruins he thought ancient about Khotan itself.

Mr Carey tells me he made inquiries both at

Khotan and Kiria for relics of Buddhist times, such as ruins or inscriptions, but found none. At Kiria the old Kazi informed him that a large slab of stone, covered with writing in a character locally unknown, had been dug up some time previously, which he went to examine ; but, fearful that the Chinese, if they heard of it, would harass the people by requiring them to excavate and search for more such inscriptions, he commanded the stone to be broken up and destroyed, which was effectually done in his presence. The Kazi also said that ruins were known to exist in the neighbourhood of Kiria and on the road from that place to Cherchen, but that they had been covered by the drifting sand. He sent a man to show Carey the alleged site of one such ruin, but nothing of interest was visible on the surface.

Carey speaks, however, at Khotan of ruins of the wall of an older and much larger city, which included the sites of the present towns ; so that if we add these hints to the few objects of antiquity actually found, we have a presumption that the spade of the excavator might perhaps throw light on ancient Khotan.

It must be remembered, however, that one great excavator has already been in the field—namely, Ababakar, at the end of the fifteenth century. He searched and sifted the ruins and mounds about Kashgar, Yarkand, and Khotan for buried treasure. The work was carried on by gangs of convicts, and in one ruin near Khotan are said to have been found 27 jars, each big enough to hold a fully armed bowman, and filled with gold dust and *balish*, or lumps of silver.

With regard to the moving sands, under which some of these treasures are buried, Johnson's mention, just referred to, of clouds of dust corroborates, to some extent, the strong statement of Fa-hian, that in the desert east of Khotan are "sirocco winds which kill all who encounter them." Johnson says, too, of Khotan, that the climate is milder and more equable in temperature than India, with moderate rain in slight showers occasionally.

This remark calls to my mind that I have not said much of the meteorology of Khotan, nor indeed of Chinese Turkistan generally. The climate in the eastern portion of the valley is little known, except from the occasional remarks of passing travellers.

Colonel Bell, going west from Hami, met with rain in June. At Barkul he heard that showers fell frequently, the rainfall at that place being greater than at Urumtsi, and about the same in quantity as in the Ili valley. He observes, however, that the rain clouds do not pass south of the adjacent range of the Tian Shan. Even in crossing this range from Urumtsi to Toksun, he was told at Ta-bang-ching that little rain or snow fell there.

Kuropatkin, whose expedition remained in the country longer than did Bell, and travelled more especially in the northern portion, says that during the autumn of 1876 they did not see a single fall of rain, whilst during the following spring, though the sky was frequently overcast, rain only occurred four times, snow having fallen but thrice during the winter, and then melted immediately. Winds are very strong, according to the same authority, in spring from about an hour before noon to sunset. Fogs are rare between May and August, but at other times frequent.

I have mentioned the rainfalls which occurred on our journey between Aksu and Kashgar in August, but afterwards I do not remember once seeing a shower throughout the country. Between Kashgar and Khotan we were so often travelling by night that it was not possible to keep an unbroken register of maximum and minimum temperatures.

Looking, however, at my nocturnal maximum and minimum observations between August 17th and October 23rd, whilst travelling from Aksu to Khotan and back to Yarkand, the maximum temperature reached on one night at Aksu 93°, and the records of the preceding and following nights were 87° and 83° respectively, after which the highest temperature was 73°, then fell till October 23rd, when it was 60°.

As for the minimum night temperature, the highest (at Aksu) was 83° on August 17th, and this gradually diminished to 50° in October.*

* The following is my record of thermometrical observations on the journey round the western portion of Chinese Turkistan in 1888.

Date.	Locality.	Time of Reading.	Night. Maximum	Night. Minimum
Aug. 17	Aksu, chamber	8 a.m.	87	83
,, 18	,, verandah	9 a.m.	93	75
,, 20	,, ,,	...		71
,, 23	Kumbash, inner window-sill	5 a.m.	83	63
,, 24	Sai-Aryk, chamber	8 ,,	73	65
Sept. 2	Kara-Kuchar, window-sill	9 ,,	60	60
,, 4	Urdaklik, verandah	4.30 ,,	67	55
,, 5	Langur, window-sill		73	65
,, 7	Yaman Yar ,,	5.30	70	60
,, 26	Posgam, chamber		68	61
,, 29	Guma, window-sill		65	50
Oct. 1	Janghuia ,,		67	50
,, 2	Pialma, chamber		67	63
,, 3	Zawa Kurghan, window-sill		63	58
,, 6	Khotan, chamber		65	60
,, 8	,, ,,		65	58
,, 9	,, ,,		60	58
,, 10	Zawa Kurghan	—	65	50
,, 11	Pialma, window-sill		64	56
,, 21	Yarkand		63	55
,, 22	,, ,,		62	53
,, 23	Seh-Shambeh, chamber		60	51

I have already mentioned that, travelling in the *arba* between Kashgar and Khotan, the nights were chilly ; but the only places where I thought the heat overpowering were at Aksu in the middle of August, and afterwards when returning to Yarkand, at certain hours of the day towards the middle of October, when even a jacket of drill was almost too hot in the sun, though not in the shade.

METEOROLOGY OF

Month.	Barometer.			Temperature.			Relative Humidity.			(Cloud.)	Rainfall.	
	Mean.	Maximum.	Minimum.	Mean.	Maximum.	Minimum.	7 a.m.	1 p.m.	9 p.m.	Mean.	Total in Month.	Maximum on a Day.
January	25·811 / 655·6	26·048 / 661·6	25·556 / 649·1	26·78 / −2·9	54·32 / 12·4	10·76 / −11·8	86	39	70	4·2	0·00 / 0·00	—
February	25·741 / 653·8	26·091 / 662·7	25·422 / 645·7	32·36 / 0·2	60·80 / 16·0	11·18 / −11·4	78	36	61	5·3	0·00 / 0·00	—
March	25·689 / 652·5	26·048 / 661·6	25·402 / 645·2	51·08 / 10·6	73·76 / 23·2	32·36 / ·2	68	36	59	7·3	0·00 / 0·00	—
April	25·642 / 651·3	25·937 / 658·8	25·406 / 645·3	60·98 / 16·1	87·08 / 30·6	44·96 / 7·2	60	33	54	7·0	0·04 / 0·9	0·04
May	25·709 / 653·0	25·957 / 659·3	25·390 / 644·9	67·64 / 19·8	93·56 / 34·2	44·60 / 7·0	63	36	58	5·9	0·98 / 25·0	0·90 / 22·8
June	25·611 / 650·5	25·784 / 654·9	25·264 / 641·7	72·86 / 22·7	96·80 / 36·0	55·40 / 13·0	56	34	57	5·2	0·21 / 5·4	0·09 / 2·4
July	25·548 / 648·9	25·717 / 653·2	25·382 / 644·7	82·22 / 27·9	104·36 / 40·2	68·72 / 20·4	43	25	34	4·5	0·01 / 0·2	0·01 / 0·2
August	25·607 / 650·4	25·760 / 654·3	25·477 / 647·1	78·62 / 25·9	100·04 / 37·8	60·44 / 15·8	55	30	36	4·8	0·00 / 0·00	0·00 / 0·00
September	25·815 / 655·7	26·052 / 661·7	25·611 / 650·5	65·12 / 18·4	85·28 / 29·6	50·72 / 10·4	77	44	76	5·3	0·54 / 13·8	0·24 / 6·1
October	25·878 / 657·3	26·091 / 662·2	25·662 / 651·8	56·30 / 13·5	80·24 / 26·8	32·72 / 0·4	70	30	73	2·6	0·00 / 0·00	—
November	25·871 / 657·1	26·284 / 667·6	25·536 / 648·6	41·72 / 5·4	72·32 / 22·4	24·08 / −4·4	87	42	81	5·2	0·01 / 0·3	0·01 / 0·3
December	25·855 / 656·7	26·182 / 665·0	25·591 / 650·0	30·56 / −0·8	56·12 / 13·4	18·32 / −7·6	87	49	79	4·8	0·00 / 0·00	—
Annual Mean	25·733 / 653·6	—	—	55·58 / 13·1	—	—	69	36	65	5·2	1·79 / 45·6	

N.B.—The readings of the BAROMETER (corrected to zero Centigrade or 32° Fahrenheit) are in inches and millimetres. For Cloud, 10 equals a completely covered sky. RELATIVE HUMIDITY to 12 = a hurricane.

THE KINGDOM OF KHOTAN.

Better, however, than these fragmentary observations of passing travellers are the meteorological records taken at Kashgar by the Russian Consul. These are published annually in St Petersburg by Dr Wild, who has favoured me with the necessary statistics from Kashgar for the year of my visit and the following year, 1889. They concern the atmospheric pressure, temperature, relative humidity of the

KASHGAR FOR 1888.

Number of Days with							Direction and Average Force of Wind. Tri-daily Observations.												
							N.		N.E.		E.		S.E.		S.		S.W.		W.		N.W.
Rain	Snow	Hail	Thunderstorm	Clear	Overcast	Storm	Calm	Observations	Force	Obs.	Force	Obs.	Force	Obs.	Force	Obs.	Force	Obs.	Force	Obs.	Force	Obs.	Force
—	—			7	3	—	77			1	3·0			1	2·0	2	2·0	—	—		
—	—			6	6		79			3	4·3	2	4·5			2	2·0					1	2·0
—	—			1	14	—	66	3	4·0	1	4·0	6	2·7	3	3·3	1	2·0	1	4·0	2	5·0	6	4·7
1	—			2	13	—	43	14	4·1	6	3·8	3	3·3	8	3·0	2	3·0	1	2·0	3	2·9	10	3·0
4				3	8	1	42	8	4·9	4	4·2	4	2·7	10	2·9	2	2·0	1	2·0	8	5·1	11	6·0
4				6	5	3	38	7	5·4	7	3·7	9	3·3	8	2·6	3	3·3	2	3·0	2	12·0	9	8·0
1				9	6	3	42	10	4·8	4	4·0	1	4·0	5	3·4	6	3·0	2	3·5	1	2·0	13	8·8
				8	8	1	53	7	7·0	2	3·5	3	2·7	6	3·3	11	3·3	1	2·0	1	2·0	4	6·1
5	—			3	6	1	55	4	8·8	2	3·0	4	2·8	10	3·0	9	2·4	2	2·0			2	4·5
					14	2	68	3	7·3	1	4·0	3	4·0	6	2·5	3	3·0	—	—	4	2·5	4	5·5
1	1			5	7		70	1	2·0	3	2·7	1	2·0	4	2·4	5	2·5			—	—	2	4·0
				3	2	—	63			1	4·0	3	3·3	4	2·2	2	2·6	1	2·0	1	4·0	2	3·0
Tot. 16	1	—	—	67	78	11	696	57		35		39		65		48		11		25		64	—
Mean									5·3		3·7		3·1		2·9		2·8		2·8		4·3		6·1

given in inches and millimetres; TEMPERATURE in Fahrenheit and *Centigrade*; and RAINFALL is given, complete saturation being represented by 100. Force of wind is indicated by 0 = calm atmosphere, amount of cloud and rainfall, and the number of days with rain, snow, hail, and thunderstorm; as well as observations of clear, overcast, and stormy skies; together with registration of calm and directions of the wind.

Passing now from the climate of Khotan to its products, we find that for centuries the country was famous for musk and carpets, gold and jade. The

METEOROLOGY OF

Month.	Barometer.			Temperature.			Relative Humidity.			Cloud.	Rainfall.	
	Mean.	Maximum.	Minimum.	Mean.	Maximum.	Minimum.	7 a.m.	1 p.m.	9 p.m.	Mean.	Total in Month.	Maximum on a Day.
January	25.902 / 657.9	26.138 / 662.9	25.516 / 648.1	23.00 / −5.0	38.48 / 3.6	10.40 / −12.0	93	69	87	8.0	0.07 / 1.9	0.07 / 1.9
February	25.823 / 655.9	26.083 / 662.3	25.359 / 644.1	35.24 / 1.8	61.52 / 16.4	14.36 / −9.8	81	43	74	5.0	0.09 / .84	0.09 / .24
March	25.792 / 655.1	26.150 / 664.2	25.563 / 649.3	50.00 / 10.0	80.60 / 27.0	28.40 / −2.0	73	39	64	5.5	0.00 / 0.0	
April	25.026 / 650.9	25.977 / 659.8	25.347 / 643.8	65.12 / 18.4	99.50 / 37.5	46.58 / 8.1	65	37	60	6.5	1.22 / 30.9	0.68 / 17.2
May	25.689 / 652.3	26.036 / 661.3	25.343 / 644.7	64.76 / 18.2	95.00 / 35.0	47.84 / 8.8	57	32	54	4.7	0.05 / 1.3	0.05 / 1.3
June	25.579 / 649.7	25.811 / 655.6	25.347 / 643.8	80.06 / 26.7	102.56 / 39.2	64.04 / 17.8	57	30	54	5.3	0.01 / 0.2	0.01 / 0.2
July	25.528 / 648.4	25.682 / 652.3	25.734 / 644.5	82.04 / 27.8	105.08 / 40.6	65.12 / 18.4	58	33	55	4.8	0.00 / 0.0	
August	25.603 / 650.3	25.847 / 656.5	25.430 / 645.9	77.90 / 25.5	101.12 / 38.1	59.36 / 15.2	66	32	64	5.4	0.00 / 0.0	
September	25.733 / 653.6	25.934 / 658.7	25.567 / 649.4	68.18 / 20.1	93.56 / 34.2	47.48 / 8.6	68	33	65	4.0	0.00 / 0.0	—
October	25.851 / 656.6	26.237 / 666.4	25.540 / 648.7	50.72 / 10.4	74.48 / 23.6	29.12 / −1.6	69	26	63	4.5	0.00 / 0.0	
November	25.930 / 658.6	26.268 / 667.2	25.577 / 649.7	35.24 / 1.8	64.04 / 17.8	20.12 / −6.6	70	34	62	6.4	0.00 / 0.0	—
December	25.973 / 659.7	26.308 / 668.2	25.686 / 652.4	24.62 / −4.1	39.02 / 4.0	10.40 / −12.0	—	—	—	6.6	0.15 / 3.9	0.15 / 3.4
Annual Mean	25.752 / 654.1			54.08 / 12.0						5.6	1.60 / 40.6	—

N.B.—The readings of the Barometer (corrected to zero Centigrade or 32 Fahrenheit) are in inches and millimetres. For Cloud, 10 equals a completely covered sky. Relative Humidity to 12 a hurricane.

early records of Khotan frequently speak of jade; indeed, the very name of Khotan in Chinese (Yu-tian) has reference to *yu*, or jade, otherwise known as nephrite. By a strange distribution of the bounties of nature, it appears that, whilst there is an inferior kind of this stone found in Upper Burmah, the only place in the world where are found the varieties most highly esteemed is in the Kuen Lun Mountains,

KASHGAR FOR 1889.

Number of Days with							Direction and Average Force of Winds Tri-daily Observations.													
							N.		N.E.		E.		S.E.		S.		S.W.		W.		N.W.
Rain.	Snow.	Hail.	Thunderst'm.	Clear.	Overcast.	Storm.	Calm.	Observations	Force	Observations	Force	Observations	Force	Observations	Force	Observations	Force	Observations	Force	Observations	Force	Observations	Force
1	1			3	22		78	—	—	3	6·0	6	2·7	4	3·0	1	2·0					1	2·0
2	2			6	7		60	1	2·0	5	3·4	8	3·4	2	5·0	1	4·0	1	2·0	2	7·0		
				5	7	2	61	3	6·0	4	3·0	7	2·9	2	3·0	3	2·7	2	2·0	3	8·7	3	4·4
2				4	9		52	5	4·2	3	3·7	8	3·5	6	3·4	3	3·4			3	5·1	4	5·7
1				6	5	3	32	14	7·6	5	3·2	8	2·3	9	3·6	9	3·5	3	2·3	5	4·0	6	7·2
1				6	5	2	43	10	5·0	2	2·0	6	2·4	5	3·5	10	3·0			4	7·4	8	7·8
				6	6	2	34	12	6·3	5	4·4	7	2·7	5	3·0	19	3·4	2	3·0	3	5·3	3	8·7
				5	8		49	4	6·5	5	2·8	4	2·7	8	3·4	15	2·8	2	3·0	3	4·0	2	5·0
				9	2		55	6	4·3	1	3·0	5	3·0	5	3·4	6	2·8	—	—	1	4·0	5	4·8
				7	3		61	5	6·8	2	2·0	4	3·0	7	2·6	7	2·6	1	2·0	3	5·7	2	7·8
				2	9		57	2	2·0	3	2·7	10	2·6	5	2·4	4	2·0	1	4·0	1	2·0	5	4·4
2	2			2	12		58	5	2·3	7	2·6	12	2·7	2	2·0	4	2·0	1	2·0	1	2·0	3	2·0
Total 9	5			61	97	9	640	67		45		85		60		85		13		29		44	
Mean									5·3		3·3		2·7		3·2		2·9		2·5		5·4		5·8

given in inches and millimetres: Temperature in Fahrenheit and Centigrade; and Rainfall is given, complete saturation being represented by 100. Force of wind is indicated by 0 = calm and the rivers descending thence into the Tarim basin.

Chinese annals as far back as 780 tell of an imperial officer being sent to Khotan for jade ornaments, and in the tenth century the three rivers of Khotan are spoken of as containing white, green, and black jade. But, besides the smaller and more valuable pieces of this mineral found in the rivers, there are at least two jade mines near Khotan at a distance of 15 and 25 miles respectively, besides a third mine somewhat east of Shahidula.

Some of these mines were visited by Drs Cayley and Stoliczka. The latter found, at the mine he visited, more than 100 holes, pits, and galleries, where the working was seen to have been carried on in a very imperfect fashion, and with inferior instruments. Some of the veins of pale green jade, he says, were ten feet thick, but white jade rarely occupied the whole thickness of a vein. It was by no means easy to obtain large pieces, the mineral being fractured in all directions.

The common pale green variety was in general use for cups, mouth-pieces for pipes, rings, and other articles used as charms and ornaments. The more valuable, pale, transparent variety is what the Chinese used for elaborately carving into vases, some of which, looted from the Summer Palace at Peking, were said to have taken a man a lifetime to carve. Timkovski mentions, as the rarest and most highly esteemed, white jade speckled with red, and green veined with gold, which reminds me of very fine archers' rings that I have seen for wearing on the thumb, and two of which I secured in Khotan and Kuldja.

In 1882 the price of jade in Kuldja ranged from one shilling to eight guineas per Russian pound. Forsyth quotes an instance of five men obtaining a large block of good quality, weighing between 50 and 60 lbs., of which the market price fixed was 60 yambs (£675); but as no single trader was rich enough to become its possessor, it came into the hands of the governor for about one-fifth of its value.

Forsyth was informed that, under the Chinese, the jade business, in its collection and manufacture, supported several thousands of families, some of whom were Chinese emigrants skilled in carving. But all this disappeared under Yakub Khan, nor had it revived at the time of my visit to Khotan; for, on asking for articles in jade, I could find only a few insignificant objects hardly worth purchasing.

Another mineral for which Khotan has been known from remote ages is gold. In Forsyth's report gold is said to be found at 22 places, and regularly worked at Sorgak, Kappa, Cherchen, Chugguluka, and Karatagh. The mine at Sorgak was, in his time, said to be 400 feet deep. Grombchevsky, who was in 1890 the first European, I believe, to visit the place, says that gold is found in the old dried-up beds of rivulets, or by sinking shafts into the sands sometimes to the depth of 140 feet. The working is reported to be carried on in a most primitive fashion, and to be done by the poorest of the people.

I learned from a Russian official source that gold is now worked at five mines near Khotan. At Saurans, in the mountains, 400 sers (40 lbs. Russian) were obtained each month, and at Kappa, 11 days' journey from Khotan, 20 lbs. a month. There were said to be mines also at Itigak, Chadalik, and a rich one at Khodalik, in all of which are rubies. During our stay in Khotan I heard that at Cherchen the gold washings were worked by from 10,000 to 20,000 people, including their families.

In prospect of my journey to India I was recommended to exchange the remainder of my lump silver —so heavy to carry and so tempting to thieves—for a few pinches of gold dust, easily portable in one's waistbelt or breast pocket. One *ser* of gold cost 16 *sers* of silver; and Muhammad Akhram Khan and Naaki Mogul helped me through the intricacies of bargaining for and weighing 12 *sers* of gold dust, fresh and uncleaned from the mine, which I not only carried with greater comfort, but in selling the gold at Amritsar made a profit of £10 by the transaction. Forsyth mentions that a profit of one-eighth might be realised by taking gold to Ferghana or India; but in my case the profit was nearly a fifth.*

But I am anticipating what took place during our stay in the capital.

* They told me at Khotan a *ser* of gold would sell at Leh for 60 rupees, and at Lahore for 62, whereas at Amritsar it commanded nearly 65. Fifty *sers* of lump silver, they said, would sell at Leh for 165 rupees, which at 16½d., then the price of the rupee, was about the same as I had given for it at Kuldja.

CHAPTER XXXIX.

OUR STAY IN KHOTAN.

Saluting a gun, and lodging in a *serai*, 187.—Call on the *Amban*, 188 —Visiting mosques and Chinese temple, 189.—Walk through the bazaar, 192.—Purchases, 193.—Carpets of silk, 194.—A beggars' breakfast-party, 195.—Difficulty of securing female portraits, and matrimony suggested as a means thereto, 197.—Not allowed to see prison; Cage for hanging by inches, 198.—The ***Amban*** of Yarkand; The two districts of Chinese Turkistan, 200.—Soldiers insufficiently armed, 201. Ride round Khotan; its population, manners, and love of music, 202.—Musical instruments, 203.— Muhammadan feasts, 205. Farewell to Khotan, 206.

ARRIVING at Ilchi, the capital of Khotan, on Wednesday, October 3rd, and riding straight through the Chinese fort, we approached, near the farther gate, an old piece of ordnance. This was regarded, presumably, as an emblem of imperial authority, before which my escort, Akhram Khan, had to dismount as a sign of respect. I suppose he feared I might object to follow suit, for he came beforehand and solicitously asked me to salute the gun "in my own way," which I did by the easier ceremony of raising my hat.

We then passed into the Turkish town, not far distant, and were conducted to a public *serai*, which, if less comfortable and commodious than a house in the suburbs, had the great advantage of being in the midst of the people—so much so, indeed, that curious crowds swarmed into the yard, and had ultimately to be kept outside by a couple of soldiers. Almost before we were settled, sundry Afghans, Andijanis, and others called to salaam me, and I delivered a letter from Yarkand to Naaki Mogul, a Kashmiri trader, who offered me quarters in his house, and seemed anxious to be useful.

Next morning I called on the *Amban*, by name Pindarin, a good-looking mandarin of about 50. The great gates of his *yamen* were thrown open that we might pass through with honour, after which he received me kindly, and had several questions to ask when he learned that we had crossed the Muzart Pass. He had been recently promoted, he said, to office in the Ili valley, and thought to travel thither by the most direct way.

On the morrow he returned my call at the polite hour of between five and six in the morning. Fortunately he advertised me of his coming, and I took care to have all in readiness, camera included, before which he not only did not object to sit, but subsequently took a commercial view of matters and asked if I would take portraits of his wife and family.

When, however, I explained that my negatives would have to be developed in England, he did not repeat his request, and, I fear, began to think me uncanny; for subsequently, when I wished to mount the city wall, or an eminence in his garden, to get a general view of the town, I was not allowed to do so, and the *Aksakal* conducting me received a hint that he had better beware, for if my taking of photographs led to mischief, he would perhaps be imprisoned. Pindarin did not, however, neglect the practice of hospitality, for, after sending to discover my tastes, he forwarded on the day of his visit a dinner of many dishes cooked and served in excellent style.

In the afternoon and on the morrow we were conducted by Akhram Khan to some of the lions of the town. Shaw, speaking from hearsay, remarks that in Khotan were 125 mosques—an estimate I should think unduly high. The Friday mosque of burnt brick resembled others we had seen, and was said to have been built at a cost of 100 *yambs* (£1,125) by Yakub Khan. The coloured tilework over the gate was of local manufacture, and, when the Chinese reconquered the town, the Turkis paid 20 *yambs* (£227) that they should not convert the building to another purpose. Within its precincts were the mausoleum and tomb of Khoja Kalan Khojam Seid, built on a foundation of burnt brick two or three feet high, supporting open lattice-work walls. with a carved cornice above the edges of the roof.

A short distance outside the walls of the town was a low mound, to which I asked to be taken. Under Yakub Khan it was the site of a fortress, which subsequently was razed by the Chinese. From this point I managed to get a distant view of some of the streets, and of the corn bazaar near the Jumma medresse, adjoining the Jumma mosque.

Passing on, the gateway of burnt brick leading to Altyn Mazar, or "The Golden Shrine" of Hazrat Sultan, was perhaps the best attempt at architecture we saw in the town. Going through this gateway, we came to a spacious courtyard surrounded by poplars, at the farther side of which was an inner entrance to the shrine.

The mausoleum was entered through a third gateway, and here were several mullahs in attendance, who showed us, in a bare but clean room, the tomb of Hazrat Sultan, besides which, and near at hand, were about a score of dingy and dusty tombs of noblemen. Seventeen were said to be those of a father and his family, one of the tombs being built with enamelled

THE APPROACH TO THE GOLDEN SHRINE AT KHOTAN.

bricks, with Arabic letters round the cornice. There was, besides, a *medresse* or college of Hazrat Sultan, with a guest-house attached, and a small retreat or prayer-house, built by Yakub Khan. In this last, we were told, from five to twenty persons a year came to take up their temporary abode for religious purposes.

Not far from the *medresse* of Hazrat Sultan was the *Edgah*, or Festival Mosque, with a platform for grandees, used chiefly on the great feasts, when many worshippers flocking together at one time assemble in the open air. There was a *medresse* attached to this building also; after seeing which we visited the only institution of the kind I remember in Chinese Turkistan —namely, an asylum, or number of almshouses, for dervishes and the poor; but whether it was Muhammadan or supported by the Chinese I am uncertain.

After seeing so many Muhammadan structures throughout the country, it was quite a relief to visit the Chinese temple. In his bigoted zeal at his capture of Khotan, Yakub Khan destroyed the Buddhist temple, and erected in its place a building for his own creed. This in turn was destroyed by the Chinese, so that the group of religious structures we visited was quite new. They were approached by three flights of steps, the centre one leading under a roofed gateway, and those on either hand conducting to circular entrances through the outer wall. To the right, on passing through to the temple area, was a rather pretty bell-tower with ornamental cornices, and roofed with the coloured tiles so frequently seen on religious and public buildings in Peking.

On the far side of the courtyard was the temple with tiled roof, supported by two carved wooden pillars, and approached by another flight of steps. Besides this principal building, with altars or resemblances thereto to the right and left as well as in the centre, were two smaller temples or chapels with three altars, connected in some strange way, if I was rightly informed, one with the "prophet" Adam, and the other with his wife named Eve. The temple caretaker was pointed out as a Dungan, and recently a *Yengi* Mussulman, or new Muhammadan—that is, a Buddhist forced to turn Mussulman, under the persecuting rule of Yakub Khan, but who, on the return of the Chinese to power, had reverted to his old faith.

Thus far we had been followed by crowds of boys and idlers, who were kept in order by my attendant policemen and *djiguitts*. Into Muhammadan buildings of course they entered freely, but here they seemed afraid to push indiscriminately into the precincts of the Chinese temple. Some of them, however, ventured inside to see what the stranger was doing with his camera, whilst the old caretaker made not the least objection to my taking photographs of all I pleased, not excepting the sanctuary and the altar.

The altar had no image upon it, but a great deal of drapery, with lighted candles, bowls for offerings, and a bamboo root, about the size of a kidney potato, cut lengthwise in halves for divining or casting lots. I was wicked enough to covet this little object as a memento of my visit, and expressed my wish to the caretaker, who said he could not let me have it at once, but would bring it to the *serai*. He did not do so, but I afterwards obtained a similar pair at Ningpo.

When riding through the bazaar in the Chinese part of Khotan, I dismounted so as to walk from shop to shop, examining the articles for sale, which rather disconcerted Joseph and Amin, since the crowds that gathered to watch the stranger's proceedings became almost impassable, and a way had sometimes to be cleared rather unceremoniously by the *djiguitts* with their whips.

It was pleasant to see that English goods were not entirely ousted by Russian, there being cottons from Bombay and needles from Sheffield. There was no lack of Russian goods, besides native textures of cotton and silk. Again, in passing through a street in the native town, we came upon a shop kept by a Chinaman who had for sale English pictures, and who was said by his shopman to speak English. But I met no one throughout Chinese Turkistan, except my Chinese interpreter and the Russian Consul, who could do that.

In the same street I chanced to see a man making a carpet in a clumsy loom; and, asking what the price would be when finished, I gave him an earnest of the money, which was said to insure its being brought. Another small article I purchased of a Chinaman had to be brought to my *serai*, when the salesman characteristically tried a "squeeze" by asking more than was agreed. I was disposed at first to object, but my Muhammadan *Aksakal* begged me to pay and let the man go, an altercation with a Chinaman being evidently dreaded more by him than a little imposition, so that his anxiety suggested to my mind that the natives preferred to have as little to do with the Chinese as possible.

I made several purchases through Abdul Sattar, to whom I brought a letter, from the Russian *Aksakal*, I think, at Yarkand. I had heard much of the excellence of Khotan sheepskin clothing, and as I had to rig out myself as well as Joseph and Amin, Abdul Sattar brought me prepared brown and white fleeces for about eightpence each. These were for lining coats, hoods, gloves, and leggings.

A sheepskin overcoat made for my own wear, with

brown cotton exterior and of Chinese cut, cost about 25s., and proved a veritable treasure and more comfortable than my fur-lined ulster. On a par with these low prices was the cost of a live sheep—rather less than 5s.—whilst our hotel expenses and stable accommodation for six days came to 8s. only.

In native produce Khotan was formerly famous for its carpets, not only of wool, like those of Turkey and the East generally, but also with pile of silk, whilst some were made of silk and wool combined, and interwoven with threads of gold wire. These last, in the old days of Chinese prosperity, were eagerly sought for, but under Yakub Khan there was no one left to buy such luxuries, and I did not see one in the country. M. Petrovsky, at Kashgar, had made my eyes water with two specimens of silk carpets from Khotan; but when I came to inquire for the like on the spot, it was found to be difficult to get new ones quickly, there being no stock kept on hand, and the prevailing poverty, and scarcity of silk, placing such textures beyond the reach of the majority.

One curious specimen which I bought consisted of a small rug, one half of which was made of silk; and then, as if this material had run short, the other half was made of wool. It now forms part of a settee in my library; but so exactly alike are the two halves that it is not easy to perceive the difference in material. It had been suggested to me in England that I should procure, if possible, some carpets made before the invention of aniline dyes, and I was successful in obtaining at Yarkand one silk carpet of Khotan about half a century old, which, after being cleaned, turned out a greater treasure than at first it looked. In fact, the *Aksakal* said I had better not let the owner see it after

DERVISHES. *Page 195.*

cleaning, lest he should finally be unwilling to part with the family heirloom.

When visiting the medresse of Hazrat Sultan, we were besieged by a number of *Kalendars*, or dervishes, who resemble in some respects the Hindu *fakirs* and Buddhist monks. They live by religious begging, and are sometimes spoken of as great rascals who fatten in idleness on the good of the land. It struck me that they would make excellent subjects for the camera. So, instead of relieving them by alms, I invited them to come, next morning, to our *serai* for a breakfast.

I was not at all sure they would think it worth their while to come so far. They appeared, however, in force, and were stuffed with tea, bread, peaches, nectarines, and grapes, as many as they liked, and I must do them the justice to say they ate with gusto, and not at all as creatures pampered and overfed.

When they could consume no more, I called for one of their religious dances, of which the jingling of rings on a pair of wands, or, in one case, on a goat's horn, formed a part. Also two of them sang a dervish's song, holding in one hand the jingling instrument, and placing the thumb of the other hand under the ear, and bawling with all their might.

After this they stood for their portraits. A *Kalendar*, it must be remembered, glories in rags and uncleanness as outward and visible signs of inward and spiritual grace, and in this respect Dervish Shah Ismail, a beggar of 50 years, from the shrine of Hazrat Aphak in Kashgar, had evidently attained to a degree of sanctity meet for eventual canonisation. Shah Yusuf, a younger man, was a Khotanlik, who wore the proper dervish's hat and carried a goat's skin, like an Arab shepherd's scrip, suspended from his shoulder, the rest of his belongings consisting of a dervish's gourd wherein to carry the scraps he begged, and his dancing rattle.

After taking portraits of the foregoing, I continued my operations, calling in persons who would serve as ethnological types, and that with the more persistence

DERVISH SHAH YUSUF OF KHOTAN.

because I knew of no camera having been in Khotan before. In this way I photographed Muhammad Akhram Khan, our *Aksakal*, and Muhammad Naaki Mogul, aged 56, with his little daughter by a Khotan mother. My landlord at the inn, Abdullah Bai, furnished a fair type of an old man of Khotan, and of Imin Akhoon, a relative of my groom, was secured a portrait of a handsome youth of 16. To these I added a youthful son of the Kashmiri *Aksakal*, and two children who, to the age of three or four, run about the streets of Khotan in nature's robes. After this diligent use of the camera at home, I went on Saturday afternoon to take what few remaining buildings seemed worthy of representation, and thus finished a roll of 48 exposures—my highest number on any one day.

As yet, however, I had no specimens of Khotan female beauty. Naaki Mogul told me he had a wife and daughters, but he did not seem willing that I should see them, whereupon I inquired of the *Aksakal* if I could not photograph some of the fair sex, to show the people of England what the Khotan ladies were like. He said it was not permitted among the Muhammadans, but hinted that I should tell my landlord that I wanted a pretty wife, requesting him to bring me four or five for choice! "And then," said he, "as soon as they come you can take their portraits."

My first thought was, "What will Mrs Grundy say?" But I remembered that the lattice of my room opened on to a platform where I took the dervishes' portraits, and that if I posed the women there and placed within my room the *Aksakal* and other witnesses, who could see all that passed without themselves being seen, I might screen myself from the possibility of scandal.

I accordingly asked the landlord to bring some of the fair candidates; but, fortunately perhaps for my reputation, none of them came; and when I asked the old innkeeper for the reason, he said the authorities would not allow him to bring in women to be photographed! This I thought a capital instance of straining out a gnat and swallowing a camel; for had a "lawful wife," so-called, been wanted, even though to be divorced only at the end of a few days, or possibly 24 hours, the business, I presume, could have been arranged with ease—such matters, in Khotan (where women are said to exceed the men by five to four), being about as bad as in Kashgar.

On Sunday we did not go out, for, on asking to be allowed to visit the prisons, an evasive answer was returned that a new *Amban* was coming, and that his permission must be asked. I went, therefore, on Monday morning to the mandarin in charge of the old town. Here I was received by his secretary, Gompo-Nimbo, a young man, but exceedingly well dressed in satin, and with an embroidered breast-plate of exquisite needlework.

He allowed me to take his photograph, as also those of several *desakchi*, or policemen, soldiers of the guard, and lictors carrying rods, also rope presumably for hanging, chains, whips for clearing the streets, and a specimen of the *cangue*, or wooden collar. The secretary would not be induced, however, to part with any of the instruments of punishment; and when I again asked to see the prison, I was put off with a promise that it should be ready in an hour; but permission to view it never came.

To anticipate for a moment our return to Yarkand, I photographed there one prison abomination I did not see in Khotan—namely, a square cage, about seven feet high, for hanging culprits, it is said, by inches. At the top are boards with a hole, through which the neck is secured, while the feet rest on a pole, capable of being lowered, or on a pile of bricks, one being removed daily till the suspended culprit dies of exhaustion. So, at least, says common report, but I did

THE "KUEZA," OR CAGE FOR HANGING BY INCHES, WITH LICTORS.

not see it in use, nor do I know whether it was an instrument for extorting confession or for inflicting capital punishment

This Chinese cage I saw at the door of the Yarkand *yamen* when going to visit the *Amban* Lew. He was the last mandarin with whom I came into personal contact in Chinese Turkistan. He sent me rice, maize, and a couple of sheep, for which I sent presents in exchange, and he returned my call on the morrow. Lew asked many questions, betraying great ignorance of England, but seemed disposed to help me all he could, or, at all events, he was in no way obstructive, and, on the whole, was a better representative of Chinese administrators than some I had met with

I have omitted to say that for administrative purposes Chinese Turkistan is divided into two districts of four circles each,—one consisting of Karashar, Kuchar, Aksu, and Ush-Turfan ; and the other of Kashgar, Yengi Hissar, Yarkand, and Khotan. Each district is under a *Tautai*, or General, living at Aksu and Kashgar respectively, the latter being also a *Tunshan-do*, who has, besides, control over the foreign trade of the country. Both *Tautais* are under a Governor-General, resident at Urumtsi.

Down to 1866 the administration was military ; then it was made civil ; but Dr Seeland and other Russian authorities speak of many of the mandarins as banished here, and below par educationally. A second but important factor in the administration of the country are the Turki *beks*, not merely those who are *beks* by birth, but others so created by the Chinese, towards whom they act subserviently. Yet a third factor, not to be forgotten, are the interpreters ; for the Chinese do not speak Turki, and the wretched suitor for Chinese favours has frequently, it is said, to bribe these intermediaries, that his affairs may be properly stated.

The Chinese are supposed to have left the Shariat in force as they found it; but the *Kazis*, or judges, instead of being elected by the people, are now appointed by the rulers; their decisions are also sometimes questioned, and Muhammadan law practically set aside, whilst of the Chinese code the people know nothing.

The *Amban* Lew pressed me to stay a day or two longer at Yarkand that I might see some military manœuvres, which I could not do. I learned from a Russian source that the soldiery throughout Chinese Turkistan are militia, enlisted at a moment's notice, and largely made up of criminals. They are drilled for infantry, cavalry, and artillery. Each *lanza*, or battalion, should consist of 500 men, and is divided into five *sau*, and each *sau* into eight *pin*. I say should consist, because it frequently happens that the officer keeps the number down and pockets the surplus pay. Each *lanza* has a chief, who is provided with an assistant.

The soldiers should receive both food and money, infantry at the rate of four *sers* (18s.) and cavalry seven *sers* (31s. 6d.) a month; but a portion of this is frequently kept back, nominally for clothes, boots, etc.; whilst for pay to be in arrear is so common that mutiny is of frequent occurrence, just as I heard in Kuldja. The captain of a battalion receives 150 *sers* (£34) and his assistant 100 *sers* (£23) a month.

Such arms as there are (which are bad) belong to the Government, but do not suffice to allow a gun for each soldier. About one-half are armed with pikes, and in each *lanza* they have a huge blunderbuss or miniature cannon, carried and fired from the shoulders of four men. All the powder is brought from Lan-chow.*

To return, however, from this digression. As the Khotan authorities would not allow me to mount the ramparts for a general view of the whole city, I thought the next best thing would be to ride round the walls. Carey gives them as two and a half miles in circuit, and adds "badly built." This latter might well be the case, since Johnson mentions that during his stay they were building the mud wall 25 feet high and 20 feet thick, which Shaw tells us was finished by Habibulla in 14 days! Habibulla constructed similar walls, Johnson says, at Jaba, Pialma, and Guma, to secure the inhabitants against sudden attacks, the country being then in confusion.

The population of Khotan Johnson gave at 40,000. Carey says, 20 years later, 30,000. The people struck me as somewhat different from the inhabitants of the other towns we visited in Chinese Turkistan. A relic of their former autonomy lingers in the currency, the *tenga* in Khotan being in value double that in Kashgar and divided into 50 *pul*. The people appeared to me more polite and deferential to strangers than elsewhere in the country, of which I had made a note before learning that much the same had been written of them centuries before.

The Khotanese are said to be fond of music, and, in common with other inhabitants of the valley, use

* There are said to be in all Chinese Turkistan 20 *lanzas*—namely, eleven at Kashgar, three at Yarkand, one at Khotan, two at Maral-bashi, and three at Aksu—of whom 8,500 are infantry and 1,200 cavalry, or, say, in all about 10,000 men and some 400 firearms. And this small force serves to keep order in a region with an estimated population of two millions, the soldiers forming practically the Chinese population of the country.

more than a score of instruments, many of which are borrowed or adapted from the Chinese. M. Pantusoff has favoured me with his pamphlet upon these instruments as they came under his observation at Kuldja.

The stringed instrument most commonly used by the natives of Chinese Turkistan is the *doota*, resembling the Russian *balalaika*, or more remotely the English banjo. It is flat on the upper side and hemispherical below, in shape something like a pear cut in half lengthwise, with a long narrow neck, its measurement being about four feet long and eight inches at the widest part. On the neck are from eight to fifteen stops, and at the upper end handles for tightening the two catgut strings. This is the only instrument played by the women.

The *shenza* is something like the *doota*, but with three strings, and the top and bottom are of stretched fish-skin. This instrument is of Chinese origin, and has come under my notice as far eastward as the Lower Amur, where the skin of a snake was substituted for that of a fish.

The *yanshin* is a wooden box, with 48 metal strings ; and the *kalan*, or dulcimer, with 18 pairs of metal cords to be struck by a rod, might be the remote ancestor, M. Pantusoff thinks, of our grand piano.

Besides the foregoing and other stringed instruments, eight in all, the *dab*, or tambourine, of goat's skin, is in use, and the *tebil*, or kettledrum, of skins stretched over earthen pots ; as well as two drums of camel's hide, called *doombak* and *nahra*, stretched over cast-iron barrels, the larger as much as two feet in diameter, and beaten with one and two drumsticks respectively.

Amongst their wind instruments are the *nay*, a sort of flute of Chinese reed, having eight holes, and

the *surnoi*, or long flageolet, made of pear-wood,
strengthened by copper rings, which, Seeland says, is
of Persian origin. I procured on the Oxus a specimen
of this instrument, now in the British Museum. The
most imposing in appearance is the *kornay*, or copper
trumpet, five feet long, and up to ten inches in diameter
at the mouth. I heard two of them played at Kuldja
during a mandarin's dinner-party. The performers
seemed able to produce only one note, and so managed

SOME OF THE MUSICAL INSTRUMENTS OF CENTRAL ASIA.

to take breath alternately that the sound was prolonged
without a break, though not always with the same
volume, whilst variety was given to the noise by a
kettledrum. The effect was curious, and at a distance
not unpleasing.

Besides these stringed and wind instruments may be
mentioned *jang*, or copper cymbals; the *chak-chak*, a
kind of rattle; the *chong-jang*, or gong; and others, to
the number of 22 in all.

It must not be imagined, however, that the inhabitants of the Tarim valley are musical according to a European standard. They have little idea of concerted music or part-singing; though Dr Bellew, writing of a professional performance provided for his party, speaks of the music as not without merit, but somewhat monotonous. They sing, in fact, in unison, the great point being plenty of noise.

They have no written notes, nor is music taught in their schools or heard often in their streets. Unlike

AN UZBEG MUSICIAN.

the Kirghese, it is not with them deemed proper for women to play or sing in the presence of men. Whistling is also thought highly improper, not to say irreligious, and is forbidden even to children. Nevertheless, says Pantusoff, a *doota* is found in almost every house, and can be played by most of the women and half of the men.

Passing from music to feasts and dancing, I may observe that throughout the Tarim valley the usual

Muhammadan feasts are observed, and another besides, called the *Aiom*. This takes place on the fifteenth of the month Barata, that being the day, they say, when there is a revision of the lists in heaven, and the angels strike out the names of those who have died during the year. The feast is observed through the night in dancing, games, and festivities.

In addition to circumcision, marriage, and suchlike occasions of family rejoicing, they observe also in Chinese Turkistan a feast at the end of the season of mourning, and also when a woman gives birth, or is about to give birth, to her first-born. She then acquires the title of Jewan, and ever after wears upon the parts of her dress closing over the breast four short cross-bars, of green or red whilst her husband is living, but these during widowhood are covered with black.

Thus we gathered what information we could during our short but interesting stay in Khotan. As we left I turned to take a photograph of the Chinese portion of the town, with its lofty wall and pagoda-like erection over the projecting gateway. This gateway called to mind what has been said of Khotan in the fifth century, when Fa-hian describes such an elevated place on a festival as decked with ornaments and arranged for the ladies of the court, who threw down flowers upon the idol-cars passing below into the town.

These were days when Buddhism was the religion of the land, and before the rise of the devastating and persecuting Muhammadans. How Buddhism entered the valley I have already told, as well as how Christianity made its way and its influence felt in Chinese Central Asia. It remains for me now briefly to sketch the rise and spread of Muhammadanism, together with the present religious condition of Chinese Turkistan.

CHAPTER XL.

MUHAMMADANISM AND THE PRESENT RELIGIOUS CONDITION OF CHINESE TURKISTAN.

Muhammadan conquest of Bokhara and Ferghana, 207.—Samanid conquest of Turkistan, 210.—Introduction of Muhammadanism into Kashgar; Buddhist opposition, 211.—Muhammadanism in Khotan; Muhammadanism *versus* Christianity, 212.—Moral character of Muhammadan warriors, 214.—Origin and spread of Muhammadan influence, 215.—The Mullah kings and Yakub Khan; Present condition of people, 217.—Lack of education in Tarim valley, 219.

THE creed of the false prophet was scarcely half a century old when, in 673, the Caliph Muavia sent his general to the conquest of the province of Khorasan, which at that time included Bokhara. The ruler of Bokhara had recently died, leaving a beautiful, wealthy, and amorous widow, who ruled for 15 years during the minority of her bastard son, Tughshada. Consequently, when the Muhammadan Arabs crossed the Oxus, they were sternly opposed by this queen and her allies, over whom the Arabs were only partially victorious, so that they recrossed the river without taking Bokhara. In a subsequent contest Bokhara fell, and Sogdia too ; but the invaders, not being sufficiently supported from the rear, contented themselves with exacting a profession of Muhammadanism and an indemnity, and then again retired across the Oxus.

In 712 Kutaiba Bin Muslim, a succeeding viceroy of Khorasan, after five campaigns against Bokhara, established Tughshada there as governor (with whose mother he had carried on an amour), and imposed on the people a yearly tribute of 50,000 *diram*, or, say, £1,250. Mindful, too, of their morals, and owing to the frequent relapsing of the newly converted to their old forms of religion, he distributed his Arabs among the citizens—one in each household—to teach them the doctrines and obligations of Muhammadanism. He also insisted that these soldiers should share equally with the family in food and raiment, which had to be supplied at the expense of the town. Kutaiba also destroyed every emblem of idolatry, and on the site of the idol temple built a Friday mosque, annihilating opposition by the only arguments known to his creed—Islam, death, or tribute. And thus the people were cowed to submission.

But 700 families of a sect called Kashkasha ("possibly Christians," says Bellew, from *Kashisha*, a Christian priest) abandoned the city, and dwelt in huts without the walls. These, according to the authority just referred to, and to whose excellent accounts I am largely indebted for my historical information, grew into a suburb, called Kosh-Mughan, or "dwellings of fire-worshippers."

In the following year (713) Kutaiba, as previously stated, invaded Ferghana, crossed into the Tarim valley as far as Turfan, and returned quickly to Merv, where, in 716, he was killed. Nasr Bin Sayyar, a subsequent viceroy, again subjugated Ferghana, and pushed an expedition to Kashgar, but did little more than reconnoitre the country.

Presently came the mercenary conversion of Saman

the fire-worshipper, and under his descendants Muhammadanism began to grow apace. In 888 his great grandson Ismail became governor of Samarkand, whence he carried on a *ghazat*—that is, a crescentade or "holy war"—against what are now the Syr-daria and Semirechia provinces of Russian Turkistan.

In 893 he captured and annexed Taras, which Bellew understands as the equivalent for "Turkistan, a populous and wealthy frontier city that had been long frequented as a mart of exchange by Turki, Christian, Muhammadan, and Chinese merchants." I am doubtful, however, whether this should not rather be "Talas," known so well in Chinese writings; and if not in the neighbourhood of Aulie-Ata, as some think, perhaps at Pishpek, where Christian cemeteries have been discovered. In accordance with this suggestion, we read that Ismail exacted a general profession of Islam, and converted the great *Kalesiya* or church of Taras into a Friday mosque.*

Bellew also adds that during this war the Muslims attempted to spread their creed across the passes eastward. This would be a natural sequence from Pishpek, whence the direct road leads through the Buam Pass to Kashgar, whither the way for the entrance of Muhammadanism is said to have been already prepared by traders, before its forcible establishment at the point of the sword.

For more than seven years Ismail carried on a religious war on the Turkistan frontiers, acquiring, meanwhile, an undefined power over the Tarim valley. There, however, in the absence of sufficient authority, his creed made but little progress against the quiet

* I wonder whether the tower I photographed on the Burana could have been its minaret?

and resolute opposition of Buddhists and Christians, and this even in cities where its profession was more easily forced upon the inhabitants; whilst in rural districts and nomad camps it found no footing at all. Indeed, Muhammadanism was not even nominally established in Chinese Turkistan till the third quarter of the tenth century.

An account of its introduction into Kashgar is given in a record of Muhammadan saints called *Tazkira Bughra Khan*, in which, as quoted by Bellew, it appears that to a charitably disposed travelling merchant, a prince of the Bughra Khan family, one Abu Nasr Samani, Muhammad himself appeared in a vision, and bade him instruct in the faith Satuk Bughra Khan, whom he ultimately found to be a child in Kashgar.

Satuk was born in 944, and, after sundry prodigies and miracles, became the first convert to the creed of Muhammad in Chinese Turkistan. At the age of twelve years and a half, he is credited with beginning a warfare against the infidels, which he continued every summer season. The winter he spent in the worship of God. His miracles, it is said, were very many; but the two most notable were, first, his sword, when in its sheath, was like those of other men, but when he drew it against infidels it lengthened to 40 yards, and mowed down vast numbers of them. Secondly, when Satuk charged the ranks of the infidels, long flames of fire issued from his mouth, and consumed them wholesale.

If we are able to believe the records of such comprehensive warfare as this, it needs quite a moderate amount of faith to accept the statement that by the age of 96 he had subdued and converted to Muhammadism all the country, from the Oxus to Karakorum in Mongolia! He it was who introduced Muhammadanism into Kashgar, and established the same northwards as far as Turfan, leaving it to his successors to do the like southwards, among the Buddhists of Khotan.

Satuk was succeeded at Kashgar in 1037 by his son, Hasan Bughra Khan. Against him, naturally, came the Khotanese, whom Hasan drove into the hills, and, returning by way of Yarkand, forced the town to submit, before he settled awhile at Kashgar. Thence Hasan was asked for help in restoring order in Tashkend and the adjoining region. He went (marrying about this time Bibi Chah Miryam) and pushed campaigns into Persia. Thence he returned by way of the Caspian, re-establishing Muhammadanism city by city, and tribe by tribe, up to Kashgar, which town, on his arrival, he found lapsed to idolatry, and in the hands of its old masters, the Buddhists of Khotan.

Hasan now sent to Persia for assistance in a crescentade, and meanwhile effected an entrance into Kashgar, and made it once more confess the creed of Muhammad. He re-established the *shariat* in all its severity, prohibited the use of wine and flesh of dog, ass, or swine, levied a ruinous contribution for his army, and again mounted the throne as king ; but soon after he and his wife and brother were killed in battle against the Buddhists.

Shortly after the death of these so-called martyrs, the army of assistance, 2,400 strong, arrived from Persia, under Yusuf Kadir. They expelled the Buddhists from Kashgar, pursued them to Khotan, and conquered them ; and thus after various struggles, on and off for four-and-twenty years, the Muhammadans overcame this ancient seat of Buddhism, and annexed it to Kashgar.

Whilst Kashgar and Khotan were thus engaged in religious hostility, a new enemy appeared from the north in Koshluk, who appropriated both countries. Koshluk was chief of the Naiman tribe of Christians ; but on his marriage with the daughter of the Gur Khan, he became, according to Bretschneider, a Buddhist, and everywhere persecuted the Muhammadans.

At Khotan, where Yusuf Kadir and his soldiers had destroyed Buddhist temples and monasteries, Koshluk proceeded to take summary vengeance. Assembling 3,000 of the Muhammadan mullahs, he demanded a recantation of their false doctrine, and on refusal hanged their chief mullah head downwards from a bough of a tree in front of the principal mosque. He then destroyed their places of worship and desecrated their tombs.

Then appeared Jinghiz Khan, who was not Buddhist, Christian, or Muhammadan, but a pagan Shamanist, tolerating every form of religion so long as its professors submitted to himself; and this toleration was continued under his immediate successors, though not always without interference. Thus Marco Polo tells of Kublai Khan setting Muhammadan governors over the Chinese, which they could not endure : and, a plot having been discovered, Polo, speaking as an eye-witness, says :—

"These circumstances called the Kaan's attention to the accursed doctrines of the sect of Saracens, which excuse every crime, yea, even murder itself, when committed on such as are not of their religion. And seeing that this accursed doctrine had led the accursed

Achmath and his sons to act as they did without any sense of guilt, the Kaan was led to entertain the greatest disgust and abomination for it. So he summoned the Saracens, and prohibited the doing many things which their religion enjoined. Thus, he ordered them to regulate their marriages by the Tatar laws, and prohibited their cutting the throats of animals killed for food, ordering them to rip the stomach in the Tatar way."

Jagatai, who, on the death of Jinghiz in 1241, inherited Chinese Turkistan, was a bigoted Buddhist and a confirmed drunkard. One of his descendants, Mubarak Shah, was the first Mongol ruler who turned Mussulman. Then Muhammadanism, once more backed by brute force, recommenced to spread, especially in the western portions of the Tarim basin, which were nearer to its centre at Bokhara; whilst in the parts east of Kuchar, which are nearer to the influence of Buddhism in China, the religion of the prophet of Mecca has never gained so firm a hold.

In 1338 we have a Mongol ruler, Jinkshi Khan, of the Jagatai line, to whom Pope Benedict XII. addressed a letter of thanks for the protection he afforded to Christians. But during the government of his next successor but one, Ali Sultan, "the villain of a falconer," as he is called, appeared on the scene. He was a Saracen, and by his orders Friar Pascal and the Roman bishop and missionaries were martyred at Almalik.

About six years previously Toghluk Khan began to reign at Aksu, and in 1362 he also became a convert to Muhammadanism, his example being followed, it is said, by 160,000 of his people. In 1383 his successor, Khizr Khoja, enforced a strict observance of the *shariat* among the nomads, who were still mostly Buddhists. Khizr Khoja was succeeded by his son Muhammad Khan, the last of the Moghul Khans and a contemporary of Ulug Beg. Muhammad Khan converted the remainder of his people to Islam, and was so jealous of the turban, the outward emblem of the faith, being worn by any but the mullahs and his own officials, that he punished any luckless peasant who dared assume it by fastening his sheepskin cap on his head by means of a horseshoe pegged to his skull.

After this we find Muhammadanism prevailing in the Tarim valley; but in the middle of the sixteenth century we have its ruler, Mansur (who died 1542), still waging religious wars in the mountains against the Kalmuks and Kirghese, and eastwards with the Chinese.

It would be interesting to know something of the effect of these so-called religious wars upon the manners and morals of the conquerors, but it is only now and then that we get a peep into their private lives. Thus Mansur is described as a pious Mussulman and a good governor, who kept as private chaplain a *Cari*, or chanter of the Koran—the *Cari* being described, however, as slovenly in dress, filthy in habits, and disgusting in practice.

Again, in Ababakar, another ruler of Chinese Turkistan, we have a monster of cruelty. He kept Muhammad Shah, brother of the author of the *Tarikhi Rashidi*, among his eunuchs till the age of 15, and then staked him to a wall by an iron rod through the belly, and thus left him to die. His own sister he shut up in a room, and fed her with nothing but raw spirits till she died ; and he cut off the feet of thousands of his subjects, lest their discontent should tempt them to migrate and conspire against him.

Yet Ababakar affected a pious devotion to the faith, and a rigid observance of the *shariat*. Surrounding himself by mullahs and expounders of the law, he used to appeal to them for confirmation of his judgments. If they disapproved, he condemned them to death, but reprieved them out of respect for their profession, and then commuted the sentence for tasks worse than death itself.

Soon after the reign of Ababakar the dynasty of the Jagatai Khans came to an end; and in the narrative of Benedict Goes we get a peep at the religious condition of the country, when the mere fact of being a Christian was enough to endanger life; for we see this brave missionary often threatened with death, but owing his escape seemingly to the happy circumstance of his having lent money to a Muhammadan lady in distress.

Yet it was about this period that the author of *Tarikhi Rashidi* speaks of Chinese Turkistan as " well situated as a place of seclusion and spiritual meditation, noted for its saints, monks, and recluses,"— the fact being that under the Jagatai Khans, during their two centuries of rule, Muhammadanism recovered the check it had received under the invasion of Jinghiz and his successors.

Muhammadan trading mullahs now traversed the country and spread their doctrines both by persuasion and example. Hence the early Muslim champions were canonised, their graves were sought out and garnished, and the lands adjacent to these were assigned to the Muhammadan hierarchy. These in their turn, according to Bellew, palmed off on the ignorant peasantry, in the name of the patron saint, charms for the cure of diseases, professed to procure miraculous aversions of calamity, and to aid devotees in the attainment of their requests. In this way the priesthood obtained influence over the minds of the people, and soon extended it to control domestic life, and finally to usurp the direction of political affairs in Chinese Turkistan.

This brings us to the period of the mullah kings, the first of whom was Aphak, who held entire dominion, spiritual and temporal, over the Tarim valley, and had disciples even in China and India. He held a fifth of the valley in demesne, and also received tithes from his disciples abroad. Locally, he was regarded as a prophet second only to Muhammad, and, in his powers of healing and restoring the dead, was reckoned the equal of "Hazrat Isa" (the Lord Jesus), so that the people of Kashgar were attracted to him by an extraordinary devotion.

Aphak sold the country into the hands of the Sungarians or Kalmuks, who established him in authority as governor. Later, he turned his attention exclusively to spiritual functions, so that, before his death in 1693, he is said to have converted nearly 100,000 people to Islam.

On the country passing from under the dominion of the Sungars to that of the Chinese, in 1755, Muhammadanism was not greatly interfered with. Also, the *Khojas* frequently regained temporal power for brief periods; but some of them were such monsters of cruelty and lust, that for the inhabitants there was little to choose between the oppressions of the Muhammadans and the religiously tolerant rule of the infidel.

In 1865 arose Yakub Khan, who tried to support his usurpation by posing as a *Ghazi*, or defender of the faith. His personal character seems to have been anything but exemplary. He supplanted and deposed his master, poisoned his rivals, and perfidiously murdered those whom he swore on the Koran to protect. According to one of his principal officers, he scarcely ever spoke the truth; and just as he was always suspicious of others, so he in turn was trusted by none; whilst as a polygamist, with his harem of 300 women, he is said to have surpassed the Persian Fatali Shah.

Yet as a self-constituted guardian of the morals of others, he closed the licensed houses permitted under the Chinese; he built colleges and medresses, and garnished the tombs of the martyrs; whilst his friends claimed for him that, like a good Mussulman, he had not for many years omitted the scrupulous saying of his prayers five times a day.

If now we pass from this last Muhammadan ruler in Chinese Turkistan to inquire into the present religious condition of the country, I suppose a Mussulman would say that, from his point of view, things look badly. Islam flourishes best when backed by brute force, when the ruler can lead its soldiers against the "infidel," so called, forcibly to convert him and destroy every trace of his religion, or, failing this, to confiscate his property, violate his wives, and legally enslave his children.

But these "holy wars" of the crescent are no longer possible in the Tarim valley, nor under the Chinese *régime* can force be applied in sending round mullahs on Friday to drive with whips the neglectful from the bazaars to the mosques. Burnes and Vambéry testify to this custom in "Bokhara the Noble"; but from what I heard in Muhammadan countries that have fallen under Russian rule, as well as in Kashgar, it would appear that many who before needed driving to the mosques now do not go at all. Moreover, the Mussulman creed, having been so often upset or overshadowed in turn by Buddhist, Mongol, Chinese, and Kalmuk rulers, as well as by Kirghese factions, and once by the influence of a semi-Christian ruler, Koshluk, is less deeply rooted at Kashgar than in Ferghana and Bokhara. Muhammadan customs also are more lax, notably in the non-veiling of the women.

As for the moral condition of the people, one of my Russian informants, long resident in the country, writes of the mullahs: "They do not teach morality from the Koran, nor do they impart stable religious instruction; consequently, morals are exceedingly low. There is not, perhaps, in the country very much robbery on a large scale, or grave crime, but there is abundance of theft." As to what can be the condition of family life, and what we understand by social virtues, may be inferred from the testimony of this same informant, who told me he had known several girls to have 20 husbands before they were in their teens, and at the moment of saying this he instanced the case of his own *Aksakal*, who came out to meet me, having just married a girl of 12, to whom he stood in the relation of husband number four.

I recently met with the statement that these temporary marriages are not permitted by the Sunni Muhammadans; but in Kashgar, where they are Sunnis, not only is all this known to the mullahs, but they themselves officiate in cementing and unloosing these licentious unions. It is little wonder, therefore, if neither men nor women deem it sin or shame,—in keeping with which Colonel Bell says he heard of one woman who had had 36 husbands, and thought it no disgrace.

Passing on to the subject of education, I gathered from the Russian Consul at Kashgar that the lack of it throughout the country is deplorable. Dr Seeland points out that, even in more flourishing days, the inhabitants of the Tarim valley were never remarkable for intelligence. "Arabia," he says, "has produced its preachers, sages, poets, and architects; Persia its preachers, poets, and conquerors; Western Turkistan its warriors and savants; and India its thinkers and reformers. Even from among the nomad Mongols great conquerors have arisen, who by their savage energy have made the world tremble; but nothing intellectual has come out of the Tarim valley, on whose people is settled a crass ignorance and a complete lack of interest in everything ideal, unless perhaps a little in music."

There are schools attached to the mosques; but, except reading and writing, and a mechanical teaching of the Koran, the children learn nothing, and even the mullahs who teach are grossly ignorant. So, at least, says Seeland; whilst the Consul summarises thus the beau-ideal of what a Muhammadan should be—(1) he should write well, (2) dress becomingly, (3) speak clearly and advisedly, and then (4) he will please everybody.

"One may infer," Seeland continues, "how much value is set on education when in such a town as Aksu, with from 40,000 to 50,000 inhabitants, the schools are attended by only 150 children. Printing is almost unknown at Kashgar. A book-shop, if such a thing exists, is a rarity indeed. The upper classes, such as well-to-do merchants, mullahs, and *Aksakals*, do not know how to write or read." By way of illustrating this, he quotes the case of an *Aksakal* at Aksu, intelligent and experienced, but who did not know what mustard was, or mint, or turpentine, to say nothing of like ignorance of the commonest remedies for every-day ailments.

"Everything outside their own country," he says, "is for these people a prodigy and a wonder; whilst as for the details of Muhammadan theology, they neither know nor concern themselves about them; for, apart from a fanatical observance of the letter and tradition, the mullahs seem to know and teach absolutely nothing."

It seems clear, then, that Chinese Turkistan presents a wide field for Christian usefulness for the schoolmaster as well as the missionary; but of this I shall speak further in a subsequent chapter.

CHAPTER XLI.

FROM KHOTAN TO KILIAN.

Departure from Khotan, 221. Reading on horseback, 223. —Sunday at Chulak Langar, 224.—Return to Yarkand; Visit to *Amban*, and photography, 225.—Difficult bargaining for horses, 229.—A new obstacle, 230.—Prejudice against Afghans and danger from *dam*, 231.—Departure from Yarkand and outwitting contractors; a Hindu companion, 233.—Caravan at Besh-Aryk and commissions from natives, 235.—A trader at Bora, 236.—The village of Kilian, 238.

WE left Khotan on Tuesday morning, October 9th, escorted as far as Do-Shambeh by Niazi Mogul (to whom I gave presents for his wife), by Abdul Sattar, and by Muhammad Akhram Khan, our own *Aksakal*. The last I decorated with a "good service" medal; and upon my handing him a letter he had asked for, such as natives of India prize, he acknowledged the receipt with Oriental hyperbole, by saying that he valued it at more than ten thousand rupees!

We had not gone far before we were overtaken by two *djiguitts* whom the *Amban*, hearing that we had started, had sent to accompany us to Karghalik. Having brought thence two government *djiguitts* who were now returning with us, we did not need more, and I represented to the new arrivals that they had better turn back; but this they said was more than they dared to do.

On arriving at Zawa Kurghan, I discovered that Amin had coolly invited to join the caravan his relative

MUHAMMAD NAAKI MOGUL AND HIS DAUGHTER.

Imin Akhoon, bound for Kashgar, who was to ride when and how he could, and doubtless pick up his food with Amin at my expense. I was disposed at first to grumble at this addition to our company; but Imin Akhoon was a good-looking youth, "ruddy and of a fair countenance," and when, at our stopping for a meal under a tree, he took out a piece of dry bread, moistened it in the brook, and contentedly ate it, there was a simplicity about his manners that attracted me, and I thought of how youthful David might have looked when first he stood before Saul.

It was not to be expected that our journey back should be lively, since, independently of its desert character, we had exhausted its few novelties in coming. But there was no means of varying the journey to Yarkand by returning another way. I took, therefore, to regular reading on horseback, and in this fashion began plodding through Yule's *Cathay and the Way Thither*, already perused in part, with the result that the mediæval travellers in the region we were passing through appropriately beguiled some of the weary eleven hours we took in crossing the sands between Zawa Kurghan and Pialma.

The great tomes of Yule's *Marco Polo* were too bulky for horseback literature, and were reserved for perusal at stopping-places by day and by night till I had read them from title to colophon. After so doing, I put away the two works with the conviction that they are the most learned pair of geographical treatises in the English language. Their author told me that his *Marco Polo* was the outcome of five years' work.

On leaving Pialma, so warmly did St Luke begin his "little summer," that in the middle of the day I felt rather overcome, and urged the *arbakeshes* to travel by night, which they did, so that Saturday evening found us at Chulak Langar.

Chulak Langar was not a busy place, for it had no inhabitants save the Chinese station-master, to whom I sold a New Testament. But here I was to spend

Sunday. Moreover, I was not quite well, and a little the worse in body and temper for the constant travelling of the preceding days and nights; but a long morning's rest did me good, and in honour of its being our last Sunday together I gave a sheep for a feast to my eleven retainers. Usually I did not feed the *djiguitts* or the *arba* drivers; but they had served me so well, never flinching from going forward, though travel by night meant for them sitting on horseback in the cold, instead of, as with me, lying in an *arba*.

I had finished reading on Saturday the travels of Friar Odoric, and part of my Sunday's meditation was on a passage of Thomas à Kempis quoted in *Cathay*—

"*Qui peregrinantur raro sanctificantur*";

i.e., "They who do peregrination seldom reach sanctification"; which, though a trifle hard upon travellers, I could not help thinking carried a measure of truth; for my temper had been sorely tried during the week, and once I had been quite testy at the long time it took the men to get under way and start. But if the passage is to be pressed, then what becomes of the merit of so-called pilgrimages in the Greek, Roman, Buddhist, and Muhammadan communities?

On Monday we reached Karghalik, where we occupied the same lodgings as before, and where letters forwarded by the *Tautai* of Kashgar awaited me—one of them from Mr Littledale, informing me that he had left the Pamirs, where the cold had become intense. On Tuesday, as we approached Posgam, the faithful Muhammad Amin came from Yarkand to meet us, offering me the use of Dalgleish's house, and saying that all was in readiness for our departure for India.

I therefore stirred the men next morning at two, and,

after seeing them started, galloped ahead with Joseph, in haste to Yarkand to expedite leaving on the next day but one. To my great disappointment, however, the horses were not nearly ready, and the Yarkandis were not to be flurried, though I had sent two letters naming dates for leaving. There seemed nothing to be done, therefore, but to settle down quietly till the following Monday, consoling myself with the reflection that previous delays had proved to be blessings.

One of my first acts on the morrow was to take into my service Muhammad Joo, who was willing to accompany me to Leh, and perhaps Lahore, for 12 rupees a month, which was two more than he received from Dalgleish. Besides this, he wanted some warm clothing, towards the cost of which I agreed to pay half, and ten rupees in advance to leave with his wife. Then I dismissed with presents our *djiguitts*, *arba* drivers, and Sarim Sak; and in the afternoon called on Lew, the *Amban*, or chief of the three mandarins, in the city.

I found Lew agreeable and obliging. He willingly sat for his portrait near the curious octagonal entrance to his private garden, and allowed me to pose on either hand his Chinese and Turki suite. Lew even put his head under the focussing cloth of the camera to see what it was all about; not greatly, I fear, to his own enlightenment, but much to the quiet amusement of his retinue, who dared not take further liberty than to smile behind his back, and on the reappearance of the great man resume their stolidity.

After taking the *Amban's* picture, I proceeded to photograph the outer entrance of his *yamen*. The great doors, at the sides of which were painted huge figures or warders, had been thrown back that we

THE "AMBAN" LEW AND HIS SUITE AT YARKAND.

might march through with honour. This opened a view to other doors within, and improved the picture. The crowds, meanwhile, came about us like bees, but were kept back by a lictor, who with his long, heavy whip, at a word from one of us, laid about him in style, the Turkis humbly submitting, and each laughing heartily when the lash did not come down on his own back.

This lictor afterwards preceded me on my way homewards through the bazaar, making a great show with his scourge, and warning the passengers to right or left, but rarely striking them. Leave was given me to visit the prison, which I did on Sunday, distributing a few Testaments, text-cards, and *tengas*, the last after the manner of the country.

Nowhere in Chinese Central Asia did I have such trouble in bargaining for horses as at Yarkand with Muhammad Hussein. His offer before we left for Khotan was clear enough; but now he pretended that the goods for which he was to send to Leh had come, and he tried in various ways to depart from his original offer, and " squeeze " for more.

The whole of Thursday morning was spent in weighing my 21 cwt of packages, for which I agreed to hire 12 horses at 200 *tengas*, or 2 guineas each, besides giving a gratuity of 100 *tengas* to the men for looking after my four riding horses, and promising them a present if they conducted me to Leh in 25 days, which I was led to hope they might do, instead of in the usual month.

On the afternoon of the next day followed a long altercation as to when payment should be made. Muhammad Hussein and Muhammad Umar, his partner, wished for the whole 142 *sers* of silver (£32)

CLEARING THE CROWD AT THE OUTER ENTRANCE TO GOVERNMENT HOUSE AT YARKAND.

in advance. This I flatly refused; but finally consented to pay two-thirds down, leaving 50 *sers* to be paid at Leh.*

Then came a business of two or three hours on Saturday to draw up in Persian a solemn deed and contract, which my neighbour, General Tyrrell, has kindly translated for me thus:—

"We, Muhammad Hussein Bai, a Badakshi, son of Ashur Bai, and Muhammad Umar Bai, an Andijani, son of Muhammad Yusuf Bai, inhabitants of Yarkand, of our own will and pleasure subscribe as follows:—

"That we engage to let 12 pack-horses to the honourable *sahib* Henry Lansdell, gentleman, to carry various loads, the property of the *sahib*, from Yarkand to Leh.

"For the hire of the above-mentioned pack-horses, and for the feed of four saddle-horses belonging to the honourable *sahib*, the sum of 143 *sers* of pure silver, according to standard Chinese weight, has been mutually agreed upon. Of this sum we have received 93 *sers* from the honourable *sahib* in Yarkand, and the 50 *sers* remaining our agent in Leh, Maulam, *K'ushbashi*, will receive from the honourable *sahib* on safe arrival of the goods.

"Moreover, along with the 12 pack-horses we agree to furnish eight extra horses for relays and reliefs, and for the convenience of the way, as well as six men as servants and attendants, and a tent on loan

* The equivalent of 50 *sers*, they said, would be 170 paper rupees, but this form of money seemed to have no such currency at Yarkand as did the paper rouble at Kashgar, though a trader in Khotan offered to cash me paper rupees for about 25 per cent. commission. Silver rupees were said to cost in Yarkand 115 cash, but my contractors desired that I should pay the balance in lump silver.

without charge as far as Leh. The hire of *yaks* to be at the charge of the *sahib*.

"The conditions are that the above-mentioned baggage be safely delivered at Leh, and that if any article of baggage be lost we will make it good.

"This agreement is now made binding. Written on the 14th of the month of Safar al Muzaffar, in the year 1306 (1888 A.D.).

"Signed by the slaves (*i.e.*, of God) Muhammad Hussein and Muhammad Umar.

"Witness: The seal of Muhammad Ali."

Meanwhile, a new difficulty had cropped up. So far back as our stay in Kashgar, M. Petrovsky had heard that the people of Kunjut, living west of the route we were to travel, had been fighting with their neighbours, and the Consul feared they might make reprisals and render the district unsafe. I thought little of it at the time; but on our return from Khotan it appeared that the Kunjutis had meanwhile come down on caravans and the Kirghese of Shahidula, and had taken off women and children, if not some men also, as slaves to Kunjut.

By way of showing, I suppose, that the danger was not imaginary, they brought me, on the morning of our departure, two Kirghese whose wives and children had recently been stolen on the road we were to travel. Another practical outcome of this intelligence was that several native traders, especially Afghans, who were about to start for Leh, wished to tack themselves on to my caravan, so as to have the protection of our firearms, because they were not allowed to carry guns.

Now, as it was by an Afghan "hanger on" that Dalgleish had been murdered, I must confess that the

very name of Afghan had created so strong a prejudice
in my mind, that, when any one of this nationality called
even to *salaam* me, I sometimes gave him scant
attention. I therefore now asked advice of the
Badakshi *Aksakal*, especially concerning one Haidar
Khan, who had requested permission to accompany
me. Elchi Beg said Haidar Khan was a respectable
man, possessing 300 *yambs* (£3,300), and advised me,
as did others, to take him, whilst as for the Kunjutis,
"if they approach," said Elchi Beg, "shoot them
down at once!"

Yet another danger to be faced was the attenuated
air of the mountains, which I remembered killed Dr
Stoliczka and others, and I thought it prudent to
arrange beforehand in case the like should befall
myself. Muhammad Joo had told me, though subsequent events led me to doubt it, that he received no
recompense for carrying back his master's corpse to
Leh. I therefore drew up a document on the day
before starting, which I read to Joseph, Amin, and
Muhammad Joo, directing them what to do, in case
of death, with my body, and arranging for them to
receive treble pay during the carrying out of the
directions.

When the danger was past, these precautions looked
perhaps somewhat *de trop*; but on reaching the
Euphrates valley, where an Englishman had died
among a handful of Asiatics, leaving no such document
behind, I was reminded of the wisdom of preparing
for the worst, whilst hoping for the best.

Some of the Yarkandis attempted to persuade me
on the morrow to stay another day in the town; but
it was already the 22nd of October, and the best
season for crossing the passes was all but gone. I

therefore got my 49 packages and sacks on the horses, and made an afternoon start at three to Seh-Shambeh (or Tuesday) bazaar, where we found the pack-horses put up for the night, on the plea that it would be better to cross the river in the morning. Accordingly, we did so, and then, to my disgust, Maulam Bai, the caravan *bashi*, would proceed only as far as Yak-Shambeh ; no doubt because, as I afterwards discovered, he had a wife and children in the neighbourhood to whom he wished to say farewell.

A second discovery I made was of more importance ; for, happening to count the baggage horses, I perceived 22 instead of 20, as agreed, and asked the meaning of the surplus.

"Oh," said Maulam Bai, quite innocently, "they belong to an Afghan, Kurban Ali Khan, who is gone forward to Karghalik, and is there to join our caravan with three horses more."

"And who, pray, is to look after his five horses ?"

"We are."

"Thank you," said I, "but that won't do for me," and I summoned *instanter* a council.

"Now," said I to Maulam Bai, "I agreed with your employers, Muhammad Hussein and Muhammad Umar —and here is the document to prove it—that the six men they sent with 20 horses were to be my servants, and I object entirely to having an Afghan foisted on to my caravan, who is to divide your service with me. We have a holy book in England which says that 'no man can serve two masters,' and it will come to this, that, when on Sunday I want to rest, your Muhammadan master will want to go on. Please, therefore, get rid of him and his horses, and in no way let them be mixed up with mine."

Maulam Bai replied that he knew nothing of all this, and at first offered to get another servant, but said he could not send the horses separately.

I still objected, and repeated that I could not have the Afghan as part of my caravan; whereupon Maulam Bai proposed to send back to Yarkand the two surplus horses; and upon my calling into the conference Kudaberdi Kazi Bek, a local magnate of Yak-Shambeh, he agreed that the surplus animals had better be sent back.

The council then broke up, and when, next morning, I asked what Maulam Bai was going to do, Joseph said he had sent the sumpters back, his fellow-servants chuckling because they would now have only one master to serve instead of two; whilst I confessed to a feeling of satisfaction at having outwitted my slippery contractors.

On reaching Karghalik, the said Kurban Ali Khan was in waiting with his three horses, thinking, no doubt, that he had done a clever thing in thus securing, unknown to me, the protection of my guns and the work of my servants. But he pulled a long face when he found his two horses not come, and he began to tell Joseph how their return would mean to him pecuniary loss. Joseph represented, however, that his master was not a trader to be picked up as a companion on the road anyhow and unasked, and that he must make other arrangements for travel.

There was awaiting me also a Hindu, named Lakoo, of Amritsar, who, on our returning from Khotan, had met us at Posgam, and offered his *salaam*. Upon my asking him to take a letter to Leh, he not only consented, but offered to advance me money, to wait at Karghalik, and to accompany me.

At first I was suspicious of such generosity, but upon Muhammad Amin saying that he had known the man for five years, I was disposed to look upon the meeting as providential, for I did not know what I should do for interpreters when Turki ceased to be of use.

I suppose, if the truth were told, this man was a usurer, returning with money; and probably he too, in view of the Kunjuti scare, was glad to get under our protection, to say nothing of the liking of Indians generally to serve a *sahib* either for gain or glory. I had told him not to inconvenience himself, but that if he could stay, I should be glad of his company; and now he appeared, more strongly mounted than I, with a servant and three horses.

We heard also of other Afghans in Karghalik who wished to accompany us; but I had been specially put on my guard concerning Yarkand, where were said to be several Indian refugees and malcontents, ready to stir up sedition, and, if possible, drag one into a mess, so much so that my adviser, whose experience entitled his words to respect, recommended me not even to approach Yarkand till the last thing, and remain as short a time as possible. I was not conscious of having met with any of these people disaffected to the Indian Government, but, coupling these recollections with the Dalgleish affair, it seemed better to push on.

This we did after a rest of less than two hours at Karghalik, plunged at once into a *chul*, and after getting forward six miles in two hours, we came, towards six o'clock, to a village with a strip of cultivation, called Besh-Aryk, where we stayed for the night.

At Besh-Aryk I was comfortably lodged in a capital room, and celebrated our departure from the bustle of towns by giving a sheep to my attendants for dinner. Our number now consisted of Joseph, still acting as interpreter, Amin as groom, both mounted, and Muhammad Joo, who walked. In addition to these came Maulam Bai and his five fellow-servants.

The *djiguitt* who accompanied us from Yarkand was sent back from Karghalik with the injunction that he should tell the *Ambans* of both places how I had been treated by Muhammad Hussein, and, in case that worthy should complain to the magistrate, to explain the circumstances under which the two horses had been sent back.

From Karghalik two other *djiguitts* were accompanying us as far as the mountains to help in getting *yaks*, to which end the Yarkand *Amban* had also given me a letter. Besides this our two Yarkand hosts not only escorted us out of their town, but Muhammad Amin Khan, of his own free will, accompanied us to Besh-Aryk, and seemed reluctant to go back, saying that if he were not in charge of the goods of Dalgleish he would come with me to India.

As it was, he confided to me two letters, one for the British Commissioner at Leh, and the other for his old master, Mr Carey, to whom, as to other Englishmen, this man seemed decidedly partial. On the morrow I took leave of him, sending by his hand a letter to the *Amban* of Yarkand, explaining in detail what I had bidden the *djiguitt* say by word of mouth, and forwarding the letters testimonial asked for by Muhammad Ali and Elchi Beg.

Another commission confided to me was that of two Turkis, whose father, Maiman Haji, had started on pilgrimage to Mecca, taking with him a grandson of 18, four horses, nine felts, and in money two *yambs* and 35 *sers* of silver, a *ser* of gold, 14 gold *tillahs* of Khokand, and 25 rupees (say, in all, £30), and had died at Leh.

The sons asked me to deliver a letter to the British Commissioner, or his deputy, and explained that if the grandson wished to continue his pilgrimage to Mecca there should be given him one, or one and a half *yamb* (£11 or £16); but that if he did not wish to go, he should be placed under the care of a trader, and, with his grandfather's effects, be sent back to Besh-Aryk.

The receiving, writing, and translating into Persian of these documents kept me two hours after the baggage horses had started. Then, leaving, we traversed a *chul* flat for two-thirds of the way, after which we began to mount undulating ground, gradually rising to about 1,000 feet, before descending into the Bora oasis, inhabited by 150 Turki families, and situated in a ravine made verdant by a stream. The oasis is well wooded and richly cultivated, its fruits consisting of grapes, apricots, apples, and pears. Mulberry trees are cultivated and silk produced at Karghalik.

We arrived at Bora at four o'clock, after a march of 25 miles, having lunched on a carpet spread in the *chul*. Whilst so doing our caravan was overtaken by several traders, who hovered about a little way ahead or a short distance behind, but who evidently wished to keep near our company.

Also we met near Bora a trader, Muhammad Sharif, just arrived from Leh, who said Mr Redslob had come into the Nubra valley, and was waiting for me at Panamik. Nor did the trader stop there, for he said his brother at Bombay knew my friend Mr James; and Muhammad Sharif was ready to lend me on the spot horses, or anything I wanted, which fortunately was represented at that moment by a cipher; though it was pleasant to find oneself known in such an out-of-the-way place.

From Bora a route continues to Sanju up a river bed to the pass of that name. Some of the Forsyth expeditions travelled that way, but none of them by the Kilian Pass, which now, for some reason, the Chinese had decided should alone be used.

Again I stayed behind for more than an hour after the caravan had started. Then, passing through cultivation for half-an-hour, we mounted over barren sand-hills to the summit of a long and gradual ascent. Thence the broad track traversed gentle sandy undulations to Doghri Kuprik, where I stayed for lunch, and where Joseph, who had been somewhat fidgety as to whether his horse was good enough for the journey, persuaded me to give it, with 35 *tengas* to boot, in exchange for another.

And thus, after a six hours' ride, we reached Bash Langar, where we stopped for the night, the snow mountains being now well in sight. On Saturday morning we pressed forward through a series of poor oases of sandy soil, but watered by the river Tasgun, high grass mixed with tamarisk being seen at intervals.

Presently the road enters the gorge—a mile and a half wide, and bordered by sandy hills—of the river, here flowing in several rapid streams over a bed of boulders 500 yards wide. In August some of the streams are three feet deep. Now the water was low, and the narrow track, gradually rising, ascends the right bank, much cut up by small watercourses, and traverses stretches of *chi* grass, with fields of wheat here and there, whilst fine dark green poplar, apple, and apricot trees abound. The road then continues through a valley several miles wide, richly cultivated; and we arrived, after a six hours' ride, at Kilian, 28 miles from Bora, and 100 from Yarkand.

Kilian lies at an elevation of 7,000 feet, to which we had risen almost imperceptibly from Karghalik, situated 4,500 feet above the sea. Kilian is a village of 150 houses and 370 people, with a *karaul* or frontier station, guarded by ten horsemen and a score of footmen under a Turki *bek*; but there were no Chinese.

On presenting my papers, the bek procured for us accommodation; and here we rested for a Sunday, thus giving the horses a chance for a full meal in the best pasture they would see for many days. For ourselves also, Kilian was the last village we should see in Chinese Turkistan; but I must not leave the country, wherein we received so friendly a reception, without saying a few words concerning John Chinaman's rule, and upon the attitude of the people, both towards their masters and towards their neighbours, the Russians and ourselves.

CHAPTER XLII.

SOME REMARKS ON THE POLITICAL CONDITION OF CHINESE TURKISTAN.

Opinions and their value, 239.—Authors referred to and their opinions compared; Russian and English estimates of Chinese character; Prjevalsky and Seeland compared with Carey, Bell, and Younghusband, 240-43. — Author's experience concerning taxation, 246. — Turki estimates and complaints of Chinese, 247. — Russians reported as not in favour with Chinese, and why, 250.— Russians popular among Turkis, and examination of statements to the contrary, 251.—Author's own observations as to Russian popularity; Will Russia annex Chinese Turkistan? 253.—Easy of accomplishment; Difficulty of opposition from India, 254. — Powerless situation of Chinese soldiers; Author questioned at Peking, 255.—Insurrectionary elements in Chinese Turkistan, 256. —What are the English doing? 257.—British subjects and their trade restrictions, 259.—English popularity among Turkis, 261.— Author's reception favourable, 262.

HITHERTO these pages have been a record of facts rather than opinions, the value of the latter of which, as in other cases, may be tested by two trite questions: first, Does the Author know the truth? and, secondly, Is he willing to speak the truth, and nothing else? If he know not the truth the reader is at the mercy of the writer's ignorance, and if he be not scrupulous as to speaking the truth the inquirer may be led astray by the Author's deception.

Whether, then, in the foregoing pages, the reading incorporated with what I have heard and seen on the spot has placed me in a position to know the truth, the reader may be left to judge for himself; whilst, as for the rest, I can only affirm that whatever of the truth I know I wish to speak—" to extenuate nothing, nor aught set down in malice." I shall, however, as far as possible, place before the reader the data upon which my deductions are based, and thus put him in a position to draw his own conclusions.

It will have been noticed that much of my information concerning Chinese Turkistan has been either drawn from, or corrected by, the statements of other travellers. Among these should be noticed the writings of Prjevalsky and Seeland, with the verbal information given me by several Russians, including members of the Consulates of Kuldja and Kashgar, as also the records of recent travel by Carey, Bell, Younghusband, Bower, and others.

All the before-mentioned, be it observed, are men who have visited the country, and, in most cases, have seen the majority of its towns.

We will begin, accordingly, by comparing their opinions concerning the character of the local Chinese, and the imperial administration of the Tarim valley.

The Russian view of the national characteristics of the Chinese in Central Asia was once tersely summed up by a general in Tashkend, who, in bidding me farewell, said, "*Bon voyage*; but I don't envy you going amongst those pigs of Chinese." A prophet of their own, Tchuen-yuen, mentions as existing in his day, in some of the towns of Chinese Turkistan, crimes natural and unnatural; and one of the English officers named above similarly describes Lan-chow at the present day as full of abominations that cannot be mentioned.

The most painful statement, however, I heard on this point was the deliberately expressed opinion of an Englishman who had lived for many years in the north-west of China proper, and who went so far as to say that the Chinese there were the most wicked, filthy, and abominable people, he thought, upon the face of the earth. These were not the words of an enemy, for my informant said he had given his life for China. He had, moreover, exceptional facilities for knowing the Chinese of the interior in their most intimate relations.

Later on, I met with missionaries on the coast, who I am sure would draw a brighter picture of Chinese character; and so in Aksu I found the Turkis allowing that Chinese of better stamp do exist, like the *Tsian-Tsiun* of Kuldja, who is a prince; but they called their own mandarins at Aksu "black" Chinese—that is, having black hearts.

Seeland says the Chinese officials in Turkistan, civil and military, are composed of adventurers, generally very coarse and avaricious, whilst the private soldiers are recruited, for the most part, from the criminal exiles. If this be so, then, remembering that a bad tree cannot produce good fruit, we must not expect too much of the administration.

Accordingly, Prjevalsky, speaking, after his journey of 1884, of the relations of the Chinese with their subjects in the Sin Kiang, says: "Crying injustice, espionage, rapacity, grinding taxation, tyranny of officials—in a word, entire absence of all ideas of legality in all administrative or judicial matters—such are the leading characteristics of the Chinese rule. . . . We ourselves witnessed scenes of oppression that made our very blood boil; such, for example, as the seizure by the Chinese officials, nay, by their servants even, of a man's remaining beast, or whatever possession of his the taker might fancy; wives and daughters violated almost before the eyes of the parents and relatives; women subjected to corporal punishment; open robbery on the part of the soldiers, etc., etc."

To this should be added the testimony of Seeland, who writes: "As for the administration [of Chinese Turkistan] it is enough to say that it is Chinese, and of that the worst kind, by reason of its extreme distance from headquarters, and of the despotism which so easily takes root in a conquered country. Here, moreover, it is maintained with the greater severity from the fear of losing afresh this province, which the Chinese have long regarded as their own: but which has so often slipped from their hands. . . . To keep the population in salutary subjection, Chinese discipline is liberally employed. . . . The Chinese consider the Kashgarians turbulent and inclined to insurrection, . . . but the fault lies principally with the Chinese themselves, who make not the least effort to enter into the wants of the people, but, on the contrary, give them grave causes for discontent."

If now we turn to the recent testimony of Englishmen, we have Carey, who visited the country in 1885-6, and says: "At present the Chinese seem to be adopting a conciliatory policy towards the Mussulmans, due perhaps to a consciousness that their position in Turkistan is not altogether secure. Occasional instances of ill-treatment of individuals occur; but, on the whole, as far as my observation extended, their rule is not a harsh one. The tortures and detestable cruelties practised on criminals and accused persons, as described by travellers in China proper, are almost unknown in Turkistan, except that the punishment of the cage is sometimes resorted to, and severe beatings are often inflicted. Complete religious toleration is maintained."

In another paper read before the Royal Geographical Society, Colonel Bell says: "The Turks are not considered to be brave. They like the Chinese, who do not interfere with their religion or customs, and [the Turks] give them their daughters in marriage. The country needs to be fostered, and this the Chinese do not do. They take what they can, one-tenth of the produce and one-fortieth of the value of the merchandise sold, but do nothing to improve the country. Rule scarcely exists, and money is all-powerful." Elsewhere he considers them "easy masters, who do not trouble the people."

To quote from a third paper read before the Geographical Society, Captain Younghusband says: "The inhabitants [of Chinese Turkistan] seem peaceful and contented, dress simply and well, and live in houses which, though built of mud, are kept remarkably clean inside. The Turkis are, however, very much lacking in spirit, and are tame and submissive to a degree. They stand in the greatest awe of the Chinese, who, without in the least oppressing them, and without even an army of any size to cause it, yet produce an impression on the Turki mind of their overwhelming strength and importance. The Turkis accept it all in a comfortable, submissive way, and think of nothing else but how to earn a living as easily as possible."

With Bell's mention of "one-tenth of the produce and one-fortieth of the value of the merchandise sold" should be compared the following from Prjevalsky.

who says: "The condition of the country as regards taxation is no better. While, with a view to assuring their somewhat doubtful loyalty, the nomad Kirghese have been completely exempted by the Chinese from all taxation, the settled agricultural population of Eastern Turkistan, on the other hand, bear the full burden of the territorial imposts. . . .

"The sole indirect tax existing in Eastern Turkistan, that known as the *badj*—an *ad valorem* duty of 10 per cent. on all cattle sold—was last year extended by the Chinese to every article for sale in the bazaars. Thus a new burden was laid upon the agricultural class, who even without it were already paying in taxes, bribes, and other extortions at least 50 per cent. of their income; while, moreover, the general bearing of the Chinese towards the natives is one of undisguised contempt."

Again, Seeland says: "The tax fixed by the Chinese Government is heavy enough—about ten roubles each house—and is rendered in kind; but this is only a small part of what the wretched native has to pay. The husbandman, for instance, is obliged, besides these ten roubles, to give to the state officers a large part of his revenues (40 per cent. in the Aksu district), and very often the soldiers openly plunder in the bazaars. . . . For these reasons some of the landowners prefer to become daily labourers, because they are exempt from such exactions."

Yet a third Russian source, that I am not at liberty to name particularly, says that "in towns much is exacted in taxes. Payment is of three kinds—from land, trade, and forced labour. From land they take corn, straw, and wood; from trade a charge on each article sold; whilst enforced labour is worse than all, partly by reason of the exactions of the native *beks*, who, for instance, when the Government requires the labour of 100 men, proclaim that 1,000 are needed; and then, taking money from the majority to be let off, appear before their Chinese superiors with the wretched residue, who have to work for a mere subsistence allowance, or perhaps for nothing at all."

In agreement with this, Lieutenant (now Captain) Bower says: "At Kuchar the natives were loud in their complaints of the tyranny and incapacity of their masters. One subject on which they were particularly bitter was the compulsory unpaid work in the copper mines."

Thus the reader, in weighing Russian and English testimony concerning the condition of the people, will observe that the pendulum swings in one direction to Prjevalsky's "extortion of half their incomes," and on the other to Younghusband's assurance that the Chinese do not in the least oppress this peaceful and contented population. If this seems a trifle puzzling, let us return to our old test, "Are the witnesses in a position to know the truth, and are they willing to speak it?"

In connection with the first part of the question, be it remembered that all the English witnesses were, like myself, birds of passage, dependent for the most part on information from irresponsible persons, and that not one of us spoke the language of the people. On the other hand, the members of the Russian Consulates have lived in the country for years, they speak the vernacular, and have their agents in every important town. Moreover, they collect information, not for magazine articles, geographical papers, etc., but for the Emperor's eye, and then to be docketed in the imperial archives. Now, if one can get access to those reports (as in some cases I did, and the results of which I have embodied), then the reader may judge for himself where in this case the truth probably lies as between Russian and English evidence.

But let me turn to what came within my own experience, though in the matter of taxation it must be remembered that as a foreigner I was free. I recollect, in Khotan, when the weaver brought a carpet I had bespoken, he intimated, after submitting it for my approval, that he must take it to the Customhouse and pay one-twentieth of its price. Whether, if I had been a native purchaser, I should have had to pay the other half of the tenth I do not know; but I thought how strange it would seem if, on purchasing a pair of shoes in London, the salesman had first to go and pay a tax at the Custom-house!

More than once people came to me complaining about their taxation, and I sometimes invited their confidence by asking whether they preferred the old times under Yakub Khan or the present under the Chinese. At Aksu they said the country was better under Yakub Khan. They complained that, in addition to the ten per cent. on produce, and the payment of local dues, corn was taken by the Government at its own valuation, which was always low, and that if the people complained they were put into prison.

Again, they said that soldiers and Government functionaries came into the bazaar, stood at a stall and ate what they pleased, and when asked for payment administered a thrashing. If a horse sold for 100 *tengas*, six, they said, were claimed as a tax, and for every sheep kept in the mountains the tax was 16 *pul*.

They complained, too, that, whereas in Yakub

Khan's time the merchant paid one-fortieth, and that in one place only, the proportion had been raised to one-sixteenth, payable now at the Custom-house in every district through which the trader might pass. Thus, to take an extreme case, if a man started from Turfan to go round the valley, selling on the way 100 *jing* of wool purchased for 45 *tengas*, he would have to pay customs at Turfan, Karashar, Kuchar, Bai, Aksu, Kashgar, Yarkand, and Khotan, to an amount in all of 35 *tengas*. Similar complaints were uttered in Khotan, where they said Yakub Khan gave a trader a licence for six months; whereas the Chinese levied duties continuously.

As a set-off to the foregoing, I may mention that when on one occasion I asked of a Turki *djiguitt*, lent me by the Chinese, whether the people would prefer Muhammadan to Chinese rulers, he prudently replied, "Yes; but it had not pleased God to give them." Then he spoke well of the Chinese, saying that they did not tax the melons and small garden produce of the poor man, as did Yakub Khan, but took dues mainly from the rich. "The villages round Kashgar," he said, "in the time of Yakub Khan, were impoverished, whereas now they were better off; that the heart of the Chinese was good; and that they were not so exacting from the poor man."

Joseph remarked to me, however, of this informant that he thought the Muhammadan officials in Chinese employ spoke thus of their masters for fear of being reported if they spoke to the contrary. Curiously enough, he then instanced a *bek* at Kashgar who had been speaking favourably to him of the Chinese, whereas I happened to have been told of that very man that he and several others had written, and affixed their seals to, a letter, the purport of which was revolutionary, and expressed a wish for a change of government!

But besides what they had to pay, my informants of Aksu complained that they could not procure the arrest of Chinese debtors, nor get any help for the creditor. They said, too, that Chinese officials would come galloping through the bazaar, riding over those who did not get out of the way, and stop to ask no questions; whilst the Turkis were further annoyed because they had to dismount from their horses before certain officials and emblems of imperial authority.

My worthy complainants seemed quite oblivious, however, that when the English officer Burnes entered Bokhara half a century ago, he had to walk into the city merely because he was a Christian, whilst his Muhammadan servant could ride. More recently Shaw stated that, during his stay in Chinese Turkistan, a Hindu narrowly escaped punishment in Khotan for presuming to ride on horseback; and, moreover, that this kind of treatment is precisely what Muhammadans in Bokhara to this day are meting out to the Jews.

Indeed, had the Muhammadans been in power, I myself might not have been let off so easily as I was in Khotan, by merely raising my hat to a cannon! I was, therefore, wicked enough to hope that a little of their own medicine would do these Muhammadans good. By way of *finale*, they said that all were praying that the Russians or the English would come and take the country.

This brings us to a question that will interest many Englishmen, as to what the Russians are doing in the Tarim valley, and the measure of their influence there.

Colonel Bell, in his paper before the Royal Geographical Society, says, "A Russian Consul is settled in Kashgar, with an escort of 50 Cossacks under two officers"; and then he adds, "The detachment is not in favour with the people."

If by "the people" is meant the Chinese, then I should say, "Probably not; much as the schoolmaster and his cane are not popular among the boys." M. Nicolas Feodorovitch Petrovsky is a Consul who will not permit Russian subjects to be trampled upon; and how sacred he regards the persons of his soldiers the following anecdote will show.

The *Tautai* came on one occasion to pay a visit to the Russian Consulate, attended as usual by a crowd of policemen and lictors, one of whom wished to enter a door guarded by a Russian sentinel. Being forbidden to enter, the petty Chinaman struck the sentinel, which was altogether too much for the somewhat susceptible temper of his Imperial Majesty's Consul.

So, firing up immediately, he reminded the *Tautai* that now he was within the precincts of the Russian Consulate, and consequently not on Chinese soil. "I," said the Consul, "am master here, and if your Excellency does not immediately order your lictors to give that man a hundred stripes, he shall have them from the whip of one of the Cossacks." Whereupon the *Tautai* shook in his shoes, quickly gave the order for a beating, and all were taught the wholesome lesson that a Cossack on duty was a gentleman not to be struck with impunity.

M. Petrovsky also informed me how he checkmated the perversity of the *Tautai* in his attempt to enforce something irregular against Russian traders, by keeping Chinese subjects on the Russian frontier and not allowing them to enter until the *Tautai* yielded and acknowledged himself in the wrong.

But, besides examples such as these, if it is borne in mind that Russia has sliced off from the Celestial Empire an area as large as the Austrian dominions, it will not be difficult to understand that the Consul and his detachment may not be popular with the Chinese. It is obvious, too, that the Russians in Central Asia seem for the most part to be incapable of saying a good word for the Chinese, much in the same way that some Englishmen cannot speak well of Russia—a lack of impartiality that is not creditable to either.

But, if it be implied that the Russians are "not popular" with the natives of Chinese Turkistan, then this does not tally with what M. Bonvalot writes of the natives of Kurla, who are so anxious, he says, "for a fresh master that they ask us, hailing as we do from the West, if the Russians are soon coming to take them?"

I have seen the statement that the natives "fear the advent of the Russian tax-gatherer, and prefer to suffer a little injustice [from the Chinese] to the certain evils of his presence among them." But why, I would ask, should they fear the advent of the Russian tax-gatherer? With traders running to and fro every week to Ferghana and Vierny, the people of Kashgar must surely know that, whilst they are taxed at the lowest ten roubles per house, the Russian Kirghese pay only six, and no one that I am aware of ever heard of extortion on Russian soil upon such a scale as quoted from Prjevalsky and Seeland concerning Chinese Turkistan.

Dr Seeland in one place endeavours to illustrate the confidence of the natives in Russia by reference to the course on one occasion of exchange. "When," says he, "we were at our wits' end [*i.e.*, in Russia proper] to stop the depreciation of our paper rouble to the value of little more than 50 *kopecks*, the natives were giving for it in Kashgar 106 and 107 *kopecks*; that is, six and seven per cent. above its nominal value. The imbecility of the Chinese administration at this juncture was surprising. Again and again the governor of Kashgar issued mandates forbidding that Russian money should be taken for more than its real value; but, to the surprise of the honourable dignitary, his voice had an effect like that of one crying in the wilderness."

I myself, on meeting Colonel Grombchevsky in St Petersburg and asking how to carry my cash, heard of this extraordinary crisis of the money market in Kashgar, and became quite exhilarated at the prospect of my paper roubles increasing in value *en route* from 1s. 8d. to 3s.; but, unfortunately for my exchequer, things, on my arrival at Kashgar, had once more assumed their ordinary condition. I suppose the crisis alluded to was a time of panic, when, in case of flight from Kashgar, paper money would be a convenient form for carrying property to Ferghana.

Again, I have seen the statement "The Russians are not disliked where they are unknown—that is, in Urumtsi they are said by rumour to be a good people; where they are known they are not liked"—that is, so Colonel Bell says, in Kashgar; and one of the reasons given is "Cossack intrigues with the women, the Turkis not willingly (some said) giving them their daughters as temporary wives."

This reads somewhat grimly of a town where "lawful wives," each for the regulation minimum of chemise, drawers, boots, and bonnet, can be purchased by cartloads! But if Dr Seeland's testimony is to be believed, the said daughters do not wait to be given, nor even to be asked, but go themselves and offer their charms; and with this curious result.

From time to time the Chinese police-master gives orders that account be kept of the native women thus visiting the Cossacks; and then, on a given day, these damsels are marched publicly to the bazaar, and there vigorously birched; not, says Seeland, that the authorities are much concerned with their reclamation (for the most absolute licence to immorality is given under official sanction), but this is done as a sort of political demonstration, and a mild fashion of crying out, "Down with the Russians!"

Seeland further says: "The people see how much better than their own is the lot of their co-religionists in Ferghana and Semirechia; and prove their sympathy with Russia by emigrating to become Russian subjects."

But passing again from the opinions of others to what fell under my own notice, I may observe that there was given me in Kashgar a transliteration of the following native song :—

> Yarbakka Orons Keldi
> Saldatlarini baschlap
> Lodarin kopup katschti
> Yangi schahrni taschlap
> Tireret, tireret, tamascha
> Keliwat kudak Akpadschah.

This song commemorates the arrival at Kashgar of the Russian Consul and his Cossacks through the gate Yarbak, whereupon Lo, the mandarin, is pictured scuttling off and hiding himself in the new fortress; and, the Cossacks being regarded as the advance guard of the Russian army, the last two lines exclaim,

> Hip, hip, hip, hip, hurrah!
> Three jolly good cheers
> For the coming of the Czar!

And this I was told the children sang under the very noses of the Chinese in Kashgar; whilst in Aksu I have already said they told me all were praying that Russia or England would come and take the country. As for the parts farther east, General Prjevalsky, when giving me his card as an open introduction, said it would be no recommendation to the Chinese, but that everywhere he found himself liked and helped by the Turkis.

Putting together, then, what has been said concerning the northern part of the country (I say nothing at present of the south), I have no hesitation in expressing an opinion that if the Turkis of Aksu and Kashgar could have Russian rule to-morrow, they would welcome it.

A question closely allied, and of still greater interest, here arises—namely, how far these feelings are reciprocated by Russia, and whether she could, and is likely to, annex Chinese Turkistan.

I do not remember any Russian writer who has advocated such a policy; and, amongst my voluminous notes, I have nothing recalling any conversation with a Russian who spoke of such a thing as desirable. As to whether it would be possible, it would be a poor compliment to Russia to doubt it.

If, in the eleventh century, Yusuf Kadir could bring over the mountains to Kashgar a force of 24,000 men; if, during the present century, the *Khojas* of Khokand could, about half-a-dozen times, steal over the Terek Pass and secure a victory; nay, if Yakub Khan with 50 men, scarcely armed, or very badly so, could enter from Khokand and conquer the country,—it is puerile to doubt that Russia could take possession of the valley with the greatest ease.

In case of invasion, the Russians might send one detachment from Ferghana, another from Semirechia by Kara-Kol, a few more perhaps by the Muzart Pass; whilst other detachments could be sent by the Yulduz valley to Karashar, and others by the imperial road to cross the mountains at Urumtsi and towards Hami. These movements would involve the stacking of forage and depôts for supplies in certain desert places; but this, I have military authority for saying, could easily be done to meet the requirements of a considerable force.

Meanwhile, in case of an attack like this, no such counter movement, on a similar scale, by way of assistance could, I conceive, be brought over the mountains from India. It is true that Sultan Said Khan, in 1532, took 5,000 troops in the reverse direction to invade Tibet, but it was at ruinous cost of horses and men, as well as his own life; for it must be remembered that the Himalayas and Kuen Lun ranges yield no such pasture-grounds as the valleys of the Tian Shan, and the passes are much more difficult. Presumably, troops might be brought over the Baroghil, and perhaps a pass or two unknown to me eastward, as well as, with difficulty, from Badakshan; but the advance of such an army would be seriously hindered.

As for the prospects of the estimated 10,000 Chinese troops in the valley, their state would be simply hopeless. They have no telegraphs by which to send quickly to Peking for reinforcements, and even when the reinforcements started, having no railway available, it would take them nearly a year from the capital, and many months even from Kansu, to reach Kashgar.

Meanwhile the invaders would have merely to surround the Chinese forts, and if they chose to be economical with powder, they need not fire a shot, but allow the besieged to starve. The foregoing supposes the Turkis aiding or quiescent; but, even if these were obstructive, they are neither armed nor disciplined, and could do little to oppose European troops.

Almost as powerless before Europeans would be Chinese soldiers, whose drilling, as I have said, I missed seeing; but Mr Bower says, "The same sort of thing—arms, dresses, and all complete—may be witnessed in any Christmas pantomime," and he quotes Mr J. G. Scott as saying, "The Chinese army is little better than a rabble, and is hardly less a subject for jest now than it was in the old days when the warriors carried shields with hideous goblins painted on them, and beat gongs and yelled in order to scare the enemy." And this is similar to the opinions he quotes from Prjevalsky, Ney Elias, Carey, and Younghusband.

When I called the following year, at Peking, on the Marquis Tseng, he naturally asked me several questions about Chinese Turkistan. I had the honour, too, of an audience with Li Hung Chang, the Viceroy of Chi-li, at Tientsin. His Excellency put me through what was little less than a *viva voce* examination.

"Could the Russians," he asked, "make a railway from Samarkand to Kashgar?"

I said "No," thinking rather of the improbable than the impossible.

"Could an army be brought over the mountains?"

"Certainly," I replied; "it has been often done."

"Will the Russians take Kashgar?"

Now, as I was not in the confidence of the Czar, perhaps I ought not to have spoken so definitely as to his Majesty's intentions; but in conversing through a Chinese interpreter one cannot always be minute, and I answered plumply "No."

"Why not?" said his Excellency.

"Because the country would cost more to govern on a European model than the taxes would pay for."

"Was it so in the case of Russian Turkistan?"

"Yes, mainly so."

"Then why did Russia annex it?"

"Because of the turbulent tribes on their borders, whom it was necessary to circumvent and drive to a recognised frontier."

His Excellency then put to me some very pointed questions concerning my travels, but asked nothing as to the possibilities in Chinese Turkistan of another rising among the natives. One English writer speaks of the Chinese in Turkistan as not liking the Andijanis, and Dr Seeland throws light upon the subject by explaining that these are of two classes. There are first the travelling Andijanis who come trading to the country from Andijan and other towns of Ferghana, and have to be treated as Russian subjects pure and simple.

But there are besides groups of Andijanis living in the towns and villages who settled long ago from Ferghana, but were then recognised as subjects of the Khan of Khokand; and Yakub Khan continued this recognition. When the country passed once more into the hands of the Chinese, the conquerors no longer allowed the exception, but made them pay taxes, though treating them tenderly in charging only half what other inhabitants paid. The Andijanis, however, consider the impost an extortion, and claim that, as their mother country has now passed under Russia, they are consequently Russian subjects.

Hence these Andijanis form a dangerous element for the Chinese. They are ever ready to rise against local authority, and are sufficiently numerous, it is said, to drive their present masters out of the country. Seeland adds, "There is reason to suppose that they could muster 10,000 soldiers, and more than once they have let out that they possess arms concealed."

For my own part I heard nothing on the spot confirmatory of this. The expression to me of one native of Yarkand was, "They have taken away all our arms, and we are as weak as a lot of women." Seeing, then, that the natives can no longer look for help to Khokand, and apparently have no arms, and little money to get them, it seems to me that John Chinaman is likely to continue to rule over the Tarim basin for some time to come, provided neither Russia nor England interferes.

This brings us, then, to a further question as to what the English are doing in the Tarim valley, and the measure of their influence there. I have no Russian document to quote, saying that the English "are not in favour with the people"; and if it be asked what, at the time of my visit, was the attitude of the Chinese towards the English, it might be replied that there was no attitude at all, since with the murder of Dalgleish passed away the only Englishman resident in the country.

Or, looked at from another point, if the English were not popular with the Chinese, some would say they ought to be, since John Chinaman was allowed to have it all his own way, and the advantages we enjoy in Western China, compared with those of Russia, put us quite in a back seat.

Take first the permitted admission to the country. If a Russian wishes to go shooting on Chinese soil, or botanising in the Tian Shan, he simply asks for a document of the Governor at Vierny, presents it on the frontier, and in he goes ; whereas if John Bull, Esq., Junior, wants to get out of the heat of India for a month's shooting on the Pamirs, he may meekly trot round or send to Peking and ask for his passport there.

To one Russian who asked of me an explanation of this, I suggested it might partly arise from the fact that the Chinese Government had no consul or representative in India. " Whose fault but their own," said he, " is that ? In my opinion, if they do not choose to keep a representative in India, you ought to present your English passport at the Chinese frontier over the Kuen Lun, and challenge them to refuse recognition."

But I suppose the matter is regulated rather by our treaty with China, which gives us the right to travel in the interior for business or pleasure, and prescribes that passports be applied for through the British Minister at Peking.

Then, again, as to facilities for trade. I have already said that I was specially warned against being inveigled into political coteries in Yarkand. When, therefore, two men came wishing to speak to me " quite privately so that no one might hear," I was ware of them, and not quick to consent. They followed, however, among our honorary escort, and when I gave them secret audience in my chamber, they proved to be quite harmless. "We are British subjects," they said, one of them adding that he had a wife and children in Kashmir, "and we suffer at the hands of the Chinese in having to pay duties, whilst Russian native subjects pay none.

"Thus, when a Hindu, three months ago, brought from India a horseload and a half of tea, the Chinese seized and burnt it. Another horseload was confiscated five months ago from an Afghan"; and one of my complainants said that he had, at that moment, 12 bags —that is, six horseloads—of Indian tea at Kilian, but was afraid to bring it to Yarkand.

The Chinese, they said, allowed Russian subjects to bring Indian tea in transit to Ferghana, and even to sell it to Andijanis in Yarkand, but they would not allow British subjects to do so. These men looked, therefore, with envy on Russian native traders, who had their Consul at Kashgar to look after their rights, whilst they felt left out in the cold. And they wound up by expressing the wish that a British Consul might be appointed to Yarkand.

If the truth be told, I suppose that what these worthy men were pleased to regard as their rights were no rights at all; on the contrary, the Chinese have the right to forbid British subjects the importation of Indian tea, since they do not recognise Kashgar as a free port or town to the English, whatever it may be to the Russians. And concerning trade in the interior of China, it should be remembered that Russia and Great Britain do not stand on the same footing.

I have not read the treaties, but, if I am correctly informed, England enjoys rights in common with several European nations, dating from the treaties opening certain seaports of China to foreign trade,

whereas by other and subsequent treaties, such as
that of Kuldja in 1851, the treaty of Peking 1860,
and by another treaty on the retrocession of Kuldja in
1881, Russia has obtained additional concessions concerning trade on her frontier and in certain parts of
the Chinese interior. These concessions she is using
in Chinese Turkistan, Sungaria, and at various towns
along the imperial high road as far as the province
of Kansu, where there is an appointed agent, M.
Splingaerd, who mediates between Russian subjects
and the Chinese.

Hence partly, no doubt, it is that Russia is well ahead
of us in pushing her merchandise into Chinese Turkistan, Sungaria, and some parts of Mongolia. Since
my visit, Captain Younghusband, with Mr Macartney
as Chinese interpreter and assistant, have been resident
off and on in Kashgar and Yarkand ; and if this may
be regarded as an embryo consular staff, it is to be
hoped that our traders, though few in number, as I
should call them, will find it of advantage.

Colonel Bell heard in Yarkand that " some 15,000
people in Western Kashgaria look to England for help
in trading—viz., Badakshis, 8,000 ; Kashmiris, Pathans.
Hindustanis, 3,000 ; Baltis, 2,000, etc." What these
figures mean, or in what sense they look to England, I
cannot understand ; nor have I any statistics to set
against them ; but I should have estimated that the
number of traders annually passing and re-passing
from India to the Tarim valley does not exceed a few
hundreds.

When I was in Kashgar M. Petrovsky expressed
himself strongly in favour of the appointment of a
British Consul in the valley. " Together," said he,
" we could keep the Chinese in capital order, and

work in harmony to great advantage"; and he desired me (unofficially, of course), if I had the opportunity of expressing this in the proper quarter, to do so.

As to the feeling of the Turkis towards the English, I heard Dalgleish well spoken of at Kashgar, though, concerning one of his compatriots who had visited the valley, there was coupled another opinion, more wholesome than flattering, that "he was proud and haughty, like all Englishmen in India."

When, however, I asked in Khotan whether, in case of invasion, the Russians would be welcomed, they replied that some merchants had complained of rough treatment at Russian Custom-houses, and that in the southern part of the country the people had seen the English and preferred them. They added also that it would be beneficial for trade and good for persons going on pilgrimage if the country were to be annexed by the English, whose feet, they said, the people were ready to kiss, and for whom they would pull out their eyes!

How much of this was mere palaver it is difficult to estimate; but it was significant that one man, after telling me he had heard there was likely to be a British Consul at Yarkand, naively added, by way of appendix, that he would much like employment on the consular staff.

Again, I have mentioned that a certain native showed me great attention and hospitality, as he was said to have done towards other Englishmen; but it did not seem to have been altogether without purpose when the two traders, just mentioned, spoke as if they were aggrieved that this man was not recognised by the English at Leh as *Aksakal*, inas-

much as his father and grandfather before him " for
100 years " had been *Aksakals.*

Previous to Dalgleish's coming, they said, this man
used to be written to as *Aksakal*; but subsequently
another correspondent had been chosen, through the
influence, they thought, of a certain Afghan servant
in office at Leh. I could have told them that I had
been recently warned against their friend as a consum-
mate rascal ; and when one watched these intrigues,
of wheel within wheel, it tended to illustrate what
Anglo-Indians know so well—namely, the cunning
that underlies the outwardly good behaviour of the
Asiatic.

Speaking generally of my own reception throughout
the country, it was better than I expected. The
Chinese officials at Kuldja were friendly and helpful
to a degree far beyond anything I could claim ; and,
in the Tarim valley, not only were my requests usually
granted, but there was shown me an official hospitality,
a care of my person, and attention to my wishes, such
as would be shown to no ordinary traveller in any of
the states of Europe; whilst, as for the natives, they
were respectful and helpful everywhere.

How matters would have gone had I not been
recommended I cannot say; but if I were compelled
to travel unprotected either round Chinese Turkistan,
or, say, up the Euphrates valley, south of the Dead
Sea, or half-a-dozen places one could name in the
dominions of the Sultan, I should much prefer Chinese
Turkistan, where, under average circumstances, and
at ordinary times, life and property are apparently
safe.

CHAPTER XLIII.

FROM KILIAN TO SHAHIDULA.

Purchases at Kilian, and departure, 263.—Ascending among hills to Ak-Shor, 264.—Photographs of Afghans, Wakhis, and Haidar Haji, 265.—Sleeping in tent and bivouac, 266.—Kilian Pass surmounted on *yaks*, 268.—The *dam*, 269.—Shooting restrained, with specimens of birds secured, 270.—Descent from Kilian Pass to Bostan, 272.—Delayed by horses, 275.—Passing the fort of Ali Nazar, 276.—Valley of the Karakash and its Kirghese nomads, 277. —Keeping watch against robbers; Arrival at Shahidula, 278.

REFRESHED by a Sunday's rest at the village of Kilian, we left, on Monday morning, October 29th, to clamber over half-a-dozen of the high passes of the world. Our two *djiguitts* from Karghalik returned early—Hasan Akhoon, a man of 29 years, and Seid Akhoon, of 18, the latter being a son of the *Haji* of Besh-Aryk, who had died on pilgrimage.

At Kilian, we were told, was our last chance of buying provisions in quantity; so we invested in some sheep to walk in our train till needed for slaughter. Also we were able to add some apples and other fruits to our store, of which we had bought at Bash Langar grapes, melons, nectarines, and walnuts. My Turkistan cash, however, was all gone; and as our Hindu follower had been so profuse in offers of a loan, I asked him for 50 silver rupees in exchange for paper, which he readily gave without mention of commission.

We passed about nine o'clock through the village fields. Beyond, the three-foot track—a rocky and rough pathway indeed—ascends the valley, which contracts to four miles, whilst the Tasgun stream gradually narrows to a width of not many yards. We crossed it at a place called Yut-Kuduk, where were a mud hut and a little pasture; and then continued all day along the western bank.

The hills were chiefly of sand and conglomerate, but sometimes of clay-rock veined by felspar, whilst here and there we passed patches of cultivation and pasture. Wheat and barley grow from three to four feet in height, and are harvested early in August.

Beyond Yut-Kuduk was a stopping-place for caravans, called Saryk-Aryk, where we found men arrived from Ladak, and subsequently we met two or three caravans as we gradually pushed into the mountains. Here everything was bare, rugged, and ugly, with little sign of animal life save a flock of sheep. And so, about five o'clock, we were glad to reach Ak-Shor.

Ak-Shor is situated in a narrow valley between bare and uninteresting mountains ; but the place has this advantage, that, whereas I had expected to sleep under curtains, I found myself lodged in the last house we saw inhabited in Chinese Turkistan. It was owned by an *Aksakal*, Niaz Beg (of whom more hereafter), and was a semi-subterranean construction, the top of the door being on a level with the adjacent ground. Carpets were spread for me in the principal room, whilst in an out-chamber was a clumsy loom, before which sat a native making a carpet.

Our caravan was rather late next morning in starting ; and as the surroundings presented some novelties, and

the inhabitants some interesting types of faces. I set
up my camera, and took a view of Ak-Shor, looking
north, with our caravan loading; and another, looking
south, upon what the natives called the Yalakhan
Mountains in the Kuen Lun range. Close at hand
was a tent from Wakhan, anything but grand in
appearance, though possibly warm. It appeared to
be covered to a large extent with skins and odd
patches of felt, whilst near at hand was a still poorer
erection of reeds and brushwood.

The Wakhis came to this neighbourhood, according
to Bellew, about half a century ago. He heard of 50
or 60 houses of them at Tam, north of the Sanju Pass;
and Dr Henderson, when in that neighbourhood,
mentions them as unfriendly in disposition. They
speak the dialect of Wakhan and Persian, and, being
Shiah Muhammadans, do not mix with the Kirghese.
They are best known to travellers as the owners of
yaks, which they let out for crossing the Kilian and
Sanju Passes.

A group, of two Wakhis and a boy, I photographed
presents three faces of decidedly European type. My
next group was of three natives of Cabul—two men, who,
in their sheepskin hoods, looked somewhat ferocious,
and a boy of eleven, the youngest member of our
caravan. He was perched upon the horse that carried,
I was told, Haidar Haji's gold. The third group was
of Haidar Haji, of Cabul, aged 40, and Abdurrahman
Haji, of Candahar, aged 48.

Haidar Haji has been mentioned under Yarkand.
He had not started in our company; but on Sunday
caught us up at Kilian, where he arrived mounted on
a splendid horse, which, in London, I should have
valued at a hundred guineas at least. The animal

had more than once crossed and recrossed the mountains to India, and appeared quite ready to do so again. His master was a fine, good-looking Afghan, whose nationality somewhat prejudiced him in my eyes; but otherwise he looked respectable enough, and now asked permission to accompany me. Subsequently he became prodigal of promises of help in various ways, some of which I must do him the justice to say he carried out.

We left Ak-Shor about nine o'clock, our route still lying along the rapid stream, now 40 feet wide, but flowing sometimes through gorges from 50 to 100 feet deep. We crossed the river again and again; but this was not always an easy feat, the bed being often full of boulders, and the water from 2 to 3 feet deep, frozen at the banks. The track undulates considerably, passing occasionally through a little grazing land, but no longer among houses, as the few cultivators there are live in tents. Thus proceeding, we came, after a six hours' march, to Chiguluk Aghse.

Here I began sleeping under a linen tent, the smallest and least comfortable I had occupied. Putting off as long as possible the acquisition of a tent in Russian Turkistan, so as to avoid the trouble and expense of carriage, I had been told in Tashkend that I should be able to purchase a *palatka*, a light summer tent, in Vierny; but when we got there, not one was to be found in the bazaar, and the police-master, almost as a favour, sold me his, which had been a beauty in its day, lined with native silk, and just the thing for a lawn party. Indeed, I was given to understand that Governor-General Kolpakoffsky and the *élite* of Vierny had graced the same *palatka*, taking refreshment therein on more than one occasion.

I did not use it much, however, in the Tian Shan, but occupied the more roomy felt *kibitkas* set up for me by the Kalmuks; and when once over the Muzart Pass, there were generally to be found Chinese stations, though often of primitive type, which I preferred to the trouble of putting up a habitation of my own. At Kashgar the *palatka* was pronounced unsuitable for crossing the Himalayas; so at Yarkand it was agreed, verbally, with Muhammad Hussein that he should lend me two tents—a small one for Joseph and myself, and a large one for the rest of our servants.

On my missing at Chiguluk Aghse the second tent, I was told that after setting it up for me to see at Seh-Shambeh, the first night out of Yarkand, when I noticed it had a good many holes, Maulam Bai and his assistants were told that it was needless for them to hamper themselves with its carriage, and that they might each have a piece of felt to sleep under instead. This seemed to have satisfied them; and thus, to my disgust, my remaining two servants had also to bivouac nightly. This, I am bound to say, they made no fuss about; but, all the same, I put down another black mark against Muhammad Hussein, who promised the second tent, though "'twas not so writ in the bond."

Next day we continued our ride for six hours along the Tasgun valley, crossing and recrossing oftener than ever the all-but-frozen stream, which, in the course of the day, was joined by an affluent from the east. At half-past three we came to Basilik Aghse, having met several caravans. One of these informed me that Mr Redslob, having come into the Nubra valley, and waited for me five days at Panamik, had returned to Leh.

Leaving next morning between nine and ten, a

march of four hours brought us to the foot of the Kilian Pass to a place called Tschkun (or perhaps Tasgun, after the name of the river). Here the hills were steep and barren, and little grass was to be had for the horses, though *yaks* could find a better meal.

We were now at the snow-line. The Tasgun was entirely frozen over, and the thermometer in my tent had sunk during the night to many degrees below the freezing-point, in deference to which, and to avoid chapped hands and face, I resolved in these altitudes to wash only once a day, and that in the afternoon. I had been gradually adding to my clothing since leaving Kilian—a chamois leather vest and drawers, thick stockings, Alpine boots, and, lastly, a woollen helmet, that proved a great comfort. But the worst was yet to come.

We had already ascended to an altitude above that of the highest road in Europe, and had now to prepare to cross the Kilian Pass, which is so trying to horses that their loads have to be transferred to *yaks*—an animal variously described as a "tame buffalo," or a "grunting ox with a horse's tail." They are not unlike the shaggy, long-horned cattle of the Scotch highlands, but are much more strongly built. Usually they are black, and the hair is so long, particularly on the hind-quarters, that it almost touches the ground. The wild yak (*Bos grunniens*), Dr Henderson says, is almost always found just under the snow-line; and the tame *yak* is seldom employed below 12,000 feet.

The men talked at first of taking over the baggage by night; but ultimately it was deferred till the morrow, when a number of these animals were loaded and started at seven o'clock. An hour later a saddled *yak* was brought for me, the bridle consisting of a rope attached to a ring passed through the animal's nose.

The *yak* I found wonderfully sure-footed, carrying me safely over the most rugged and difficult ground; and that, too, I thought, more smoothly and with fewer jerks than a horse, especially down-hill. They progress slowly, it is true, but are capable, on occasion, of quick motion, as I found by experience: for example, one of our dogs presuming to bark in the face of the *yak*, my steed made a rapid charge at his canine impudence, which suddenly shifted my position from the saddle to the *yak's* tail, and I narrowly escaped finding myself ignominiously seated on the ground.

We had now to climb a long and steep gradient through snow more than a foot deep. Presently we reached a small platform, whence we obtained a splendid view of the surrounding snow mountains, as well as of the saddle above us, over which we were to climb. The ascent was very trying: but the sun shone, the air was clear, the ride enjoyable, and at three o'clock we reached the top, at a height of 17,000 feet.

By this time most of us, horses as well as men, were suffering more or less from *dam*, or mountain sickness, brought on by the rarefaction of the atmosphere. At what height I first began to feel this I am not quite sure. The day we approached Ak-Shor I several times dismounted to warm my feet by walking, but so soon grew tired and out of breath that I imagined my walking powers had become demoralised by having been of late so little exercised. As we approached the snow-line I had a slight headache all day (very unusual with me), and it continued through the night.

But it was not until we began to ascend to the Pass that I realised what the *dam* meant: for, on being told that there were some partridges just over a hill, 100 yards off, I took my gun, slid off my *yak*, and began running up as on ordinary occasions. Before I had proceeded many yards, however, my heart began to beat as if it would burst, and I had to sit down twice, take breath, and learn that such agility at altitudes equal to the top of Mont Blanc was quite out of place.

I now found that I must restrain my shooting, if not for my own sake, for that of Joseph, upon whom to impose the task of skinning at these altitudes would have been somewhat exacting, though he never complained, and often did not come to the tent to sleep until a long time after I had retired. Approaching the village of Kilian I had shot a hawk having a piece of string round its leg, and between Kilian and Ak-Shor we saw partridges, but on the wrong side of the river.

We, however, obtained specimens of a few small birds, such as the tawny accentor (*Accentor fulvescens*), a specimen of *Leptopœcile Sophiæ*, and Guldenstädt's redstart (*Ruticilla erythrogastra*). This last Dr Henderson found as high as 17,800 feet, and in Yarkand territory it was observed from about 15,000 feet down to the foot of the hills, but not in the plains. It frequents the neighbourhood of streams, generally where there is low jungle, hopping from twig to twig and on the ground, catching insects; but it does not appear to feed immediately at the water's edge, or to venture on the rocks and stones in mid-torrent.

Of aquatic birds I obtained specimens of the white-bellied dipper (*Cinclus leucogaster*) at Ak-Shor, and afterwards at Tschkun. We often noticed this little fisher boldly plunging in to the swiftest torrents, seeking insects in a stream the half of which was congealed to solid ice. Henderson remarks upon the difficulty of obtaining specimens of these birds because of their falling into the water when shot, and being difficult to retrieve. Fortunately, I fired up the stream, and my prey came floating down to hand like pieces of cork, the water running off their plumage "as from a duck's back." At Tschkun I shot a rock dove (*Columba livia*), and also a species of *Accentor*, of which I obtained a second specimen near the Kilian Pass.

Speaking generally of the desert region beyond, scarcely any animal life is seen. The hoopoe is met with in the barest desert and on the highest passes, busy pegging his long bill, as Hume observes, in the sand, wholly unconcerned at the desolate loneliness of the surrounding scene, and apparently unaffected by a temperature often falling during the night to many degrees below zero. It is remarkable, however, that the larger raptorial birds, especially true vultures, are conspicuous by their absence; for although on the line of march dead horses are frequent enough, yet not a vulture was seen preying upon them.

"When a horse," Hume says, "is unable to proceed, the owner cuts its throat, and, to enable its flesh to be used by future travellers, whose provisions may run short, they cut long steaks out of the haunches and lay them on stones, or suspend them on dwarf bushes, where they hang and harden, the atmosphere being too dry to allow of putrefaction." As for the partridges that lured me from my saddle on the Kilian, they were of a large species, but not obliging enough to wait for my approach, and I did not again leave my *yak* upon a similar errand.

We descended for two hours on the other side of the Pass to a spot without grass or firewood, called Kara Chaglan Aiaghe, or "foot of Kara Chaglan Pass"; and this, much to the disgust of the *yak*-owners, who thought they ought not to carry the loads so far. But Maulam Bai had taken on the horses, and there was nothing but for the *yaks* to follow. The consequence was a great deal of wrangling when the parties met—so much so, indeed, that I had to intervene and order both sides to keep the peace.

As I was not sure of another opportunity of getting a *yak* for a subject, I photographed Joseph seated on his long-horned steed, with its Wakhan owner, Muhammad Raphi, standing by,—a picture that has since become widely known; for the artist of the *Daily Graphic* took this subject for a poster when announcing my letters on "A Ride to Little Tibet"; and Joseph and his *yak* have been exhibited at hundreds of railway and advertising stations throughout England and Scotland.

There was no mistaking the fact that with the setting of the sun it became decidedly cold. Failing to gulp down at a draught the whole of a glass of hot coffee, the remainder was after a few minutes frozen. An apple placed at my bedside was also frozen, and so was my tooth-brush; whilst the ink, when I attempted to write my diary, froze between the bottle and the paper.

It was well, therefore, that I had penned in the morning my farewell letter of thanks to the *Amban* of Yarkand, telling him of our safe arrival at the Pass, and not omitting that Muhammad Hussein had added to all his other iniquities that of sending

me off minus a second tent. During the day I had
been tolerably free from headache, but it returned at
night, through which, in spite of the thermometer
descending 28 degrees below freezing-point, I slept
warmly, though not comfortably, because of the *dam*
and a slight difficulty in breathing.

JOSEPH MOUNTED, AND MUHAMMAD RAFIH, A WAKHAN YAK-OWNER.

Next morning at ten we left the southern foot of
the Pass, and began to descend by another river valley
—that of the Kilian. Our horses were a good deal
distressed, and mine on one occasion fairly dropped
under me on his knees, thinking, I fancy, to take a
nap, which, at the end of a nine hours' march, he

was allowed to do at a place called Bostan, where we camped in the bed of the river. We had now descended more than 2,000 feet, and I had walked a good deal in the course of the day without any distress; but men and animals were sufficiently tired to be glad on the morrow of a Sunday's rest.

Bostan was the most inhospitable place wherein I have ever spent a Sunday. The valley was bordered by lofty, bare, and rugged mountains, containing grey and red granite, whilst the filling in of the ravine was of granite conglomerate. Our only companions were a few ravens, who are much too wise to live in such a place, but honoured us with their presence in anticipation of a stolen meal, or a feast when our camp was broken up. Little vegetation was visible, save small bushes in the river bed. These served for fuel, and the horses were taken off to a spot where it was hoped that they might find a little grass.

Horses on this route, according to one account, are expected to eat at night only, to pick up what they can, and to do with one feed of grain a day—namely, half a nose-bag full of barley after being driven in from pasture an hour before being loaded up. Accordingly, my steeds soon began to show they were getting hungry, and of their own accord came back to the camp for their corn.

This fasting diet was strictly in keeping with the theory of the men, who, in this matter, did not preach to the horses what they failed to practise themselves. Perhaps this had something to do with their being so quarrelsome at Tschkun, where Joseph told me, to my surprise, that the men were starting for the long pull over the Pass without having taken breakfast. In deference to this procedure of older hands I restrained my own appetite, and ate less than usual before crossing the Kilian, but am not aware that I was any the better for so doing.

Some travellers say that the caravan horses are trained to fast in view of the caravan route, but this was not the case with my own; and I came to the conclusion that I made a mistake in committing their feeding to the caravan leader. Haidar Haji was wiser by far, for he sent on ahead a camel laden with forage, some of which I was glad to accept for my hungry steeds. I bethought me, too, of the remainder of our little white rolls baked at Vierny; for though they were by this time almost as hard as stones, the horses munched them with satisfaction.

Our two *djignitts* from Karghalik were replaced by Ghazim Haji and his servant, who escorted us to the Kilian Pass to help in procuring *yaks*. After seeing us safely over the Pass, these officials and sundry local helpers returned, which reduced my caravan to 10 men and 25 horses. We were favoured at Bostan with bright sunshine, so heating to my little tent as to make it stuffy and suffocating by day, whilst, by way of diversion at night, the tent was pulled down about my ears, I fancy by one of the horses sniffing about for corn.

On rising next morning, our horses had strayed, their watchman having gone to sleep, so that we did not get off till nearly noon. By that time the sun was so hot that I raised my umbrella, which the heat had not once made imperative during the previous three months since leaving Kuldja.

Our route continued down the river Kilian (called by the natives Dairmanluk) to its confluence with the Karakash, where stood, amidst a few fields, a fort, called Ali Nazar Kurgan, built by Yakub Khan. It is a solitary mud cabin inclosed by loop-holed walls, and stands under the lee of a detached rock, on the top of which Bellew noticed the ruin of an older building,—the same, probably, as that mentioned by Shaw, who heard that it was inhabited some 40 years before by a robber named Ali Nazar and his wife.

This Ali Nazar fort is situated near the junction of three routes, all converging at Karghalik, and each crossing a lofty spur of the Kuen Lun by the Kilik, the Kilian, and Sanju Passes. The Forsyth expedition crossed chiefly by the Sanju, though some of the party traversed also a fourth route from Karghalik, through Kugiar up a river valley, and joining the Karakorum route at Shahidula. The Kilian Pass seems to have been at that time closed; whereas, when I crossed it, the Chinese had for some reason forbidden travel by the Sanju Pass, which is neither so high nor so difficult as the Kilian.

As for the Kilik Pass, Forsyth says that traders were seldom or never allowed to use it; but he regards it as the shortest and the easiest, having grass and wood at every stage. The road thereto branches off from the Karakash along the Toghra-su, and then up the valley of the Kalak to the Pass; but I am not aware that any Englishman has crossed it.

About a mile beyond the Ali Nazar fort we crossed the Toghra-su, or "straight" river, running at right angles down a long, straight glen from the west into the Karakash, which has to be forded twice. My men pointed out that at certain seasons of the year the fording of these rivers is difficult, especially the Toghra-su, in which it is hard for the horses to make good their footing by reason of the large stones in the bed; and if they once stumble, they are liable to be carried away. The Karakash has much more water and is a broad stream, the valley being here from 400 to 500 yards wide and flat-bottomed.

In this valley are found a few Kirghese, who, in Bellew's time, were reckoned at 300 tents, spread in different camps, among the ravines, gullies, and river courses from Kok-Yar on the west to Sarigh-Yar on the east. They have a few camels and horses, but more *yaks*, which they hire out to caravans. These Kirghese are said to belong to the Alai tribes, and to be acquainted with routes from this district to the Pamir and Alai valleys. In the time of Yakub Khan they formed a sort of frontier guard, their chief living a greater part of the year in Kashgar.

We passed the tent of Jahn Muhammad Khan, whose wife had been stolen in the recent Kunjut raid, which further impressed upon our minds that we were, if not on enchanted ground, still in a locality by no means free from danger. Indeed, we had scarcely left Kilian, when, at Saryk-Aryk, we met a caravan, just arrived from Ladak, who told us that my coming was expected there, which, so far, was gratifying; but they went on to add that, for fear of the Kunjutis, 20 Kashmiri soldiers had accompanied caravans to Shahidula, and were stopping there.

Another report we heard was to the effect that the Kunjutis had sent a sort of apology for their recent raid to the Chinese at Yarkand, explaining that they had no feud with the Kirghese, but were in search of Indians and Kashmiris, which suggested to the mind of a fellow-subject that they might not perhaps object to an English captive! Again, Haidar Haji, having fewer horses than I, and stronger, easily kept ahead of our caravan; so that, after crossing the Pass, we saw little or nothing of him until Sunday afternoon, when he rode back to tell of information from the Kirghese that five men and six horses without baggage had been seen, who, it was thought, might be Kunjutis. Haidar Haji wished, therefore, to keep close under the protection of our guns. Two other caravans also asked similar shelter.

Accordingly, we ascended together the valley of the Karakash, and at five o'clock reached a camping-place called Aiduk, or Aibuk, where was a little grass, and our tent was set up near that of Haidar Haji, the Hindu also being not far off. The place was supposed, however, to be so liable to attack, that a guard was set to watch for the greater part of the night, consisting of Haidar Haji, Joseph, and some of the servants.

As for myself, if I felt timid concerning the matter at all, it was here; but having slept indifferently the night before, I did so the better at Aibuk; and no evil was permitted to approach. We started, therefore, the next morning at ten, and, about noon, reached the fort of Shahidula, which, though not strictly on the frontier, was the last Turki building we saw. The next houses we entered were in Tibet, of which something must now be said.

CHAPTER XLIV.

CONCERNING GREAT TIBET.

Name of Tibet, 279.—Its boundaries, area, and orography, 280.—Great Tibet; its surface, rivers, lakes, and provinces, 281.—Towns of U-tsang, 282.—Roads, meteorology, and climate, 283.—The northern plain, 284.—The inhabitants, and their religions, 286.—Characteristics of Lamaism; Introduction of Buddhism, 287.—Transmigration of lamas, 288.—Prayers and code, 289.—History of Tibet, 291.—Notable kings, 292.—Ralpachen's patronage of Buddhism, 293.—Rise of lamas to temporal power; The first Dalai Lama, 294.—Tibet attacked by Mongols and Nepalese, but finally subdued by China, 295.—Little Tibet; Contests for Ladak; Hostilities with British on Sikkim frontier, 295-96.—Chinese administration of Tibet through lamas, 297.

MANCHURIA, Mongolia, and the Sin Kiang have been already spoken of. It now remains for me to describe briefly Tibet, including the adjacent region of Koko-Nor, making up the remainder of "China beyond the Wall." The name *T'ubat* is met with in Chinese annals as early as the fifth century. In Mongolian it was called *Tubet*; in Arabic *Tubbett*; and then by Europeans in the twelfth century *Thibet*, afterwards *Tebet*, *Thabat*, and lastly *Tibet*. To the inhabitants it is now known as *Bod-yul*, or Bodland.

The country is a highly elevated region of Central Asia, bounded on the north by Chinese Turkistan and Mongolia, on the south by India, on the east by China proper, and on the west by Kashmir. Its greatest length is upwards of 1,600 miles, with a breadth towards the east of 700, in the centre of 500, and towards the west of 150, miles. Its area is estimated at 700,000 square miles, or more than Austria, France, and Spain put together.

No other country in the world can boast of such a plethora of lofty mountain ranges and plateaus. The Himalayas form its southern scarp. On the west these ranges converge and lose themselves in the Pamir tablelands, whilst on the east are the Yung Sing Mountains of China.

Besides these may be mentioned, as a continuation of the Kuen Lun, the ranges which, east of the 85th meridian, were called by their discoverer, Prjevalsky, the Moscow, Columbus, and Marco Polo Mountains, but which are spoken of by Walker in the *Encyclopædia Britannica* as the Angirtakshia, Shuga, Namohon, Burkhan Buddha, and Dzun-mo Lun ranges. These constitute the chord of an arc formed by the Altyn Tagh, Nan Shan, and Koko-Nor ranges, which project northwards and border the plains of the Lob-Nor region and Kansu; whilst between the chord and the arc are several hill ranges and some great plateaus, notably those of Tsaidam and Koko-Nor.

Speaking generally, the mountains in and around Tibet are the highest in the world. The principal chain of the Himalayas geographically dividing Tibet from India, is one of high peaks covered with perpetual snow, and culminating in Mount Everest, 29,000 feet above the sea. In the ranges of Western Tibet the peaks rise in many parts to between 20,000 and 25,000 feet—in the Muztagh range to 28,250, but rarely to more than 10,000 and often to not more than a few hundred feet above the plateaus whence they spring.

The country may be conveniently divided into Great and Little Tibet, the latter of which will be spoken of from personal observation hereafter.*

Great Tibet is broadly divisible into western and eastern regions. The western region has a considerable preponderance of tableland over hill and mountain, and of lakes over rivers. In the eastern region the reverse holds good, and the country is corrugated with ravines. Latitudinally the country may be divided into three zones, increasing in elevation from south to north — namely, a southern zone containing the centres of the settled and agricultural population, a middle zone comprising pasture lands of the nomads, and a northern zone for the most part abandoned to wild animals. The tableland of Tibet attains to 17,600 feet in the Lengzi-tang plateau of the northern zone; thence there is a gradual fall east, west, and south,—the average plateau level of the northern zone being about 13,500 feet, and that of the southern 10,000 feet.

Tibet is no less remarkable for the number of large rivers having their sources in its mountain ranges. In the west, near the sacred Lake Manasarowar, and within an area of 500 miles, rise the Indus, Sutlej, Karnali, and the Brahmaputra; whilst in Eastern Tibet are found the sources of nearly all the principal rivers that reach the coast of South-eastern Asia between Calcutta and Peking—that is to say, the Hoang-ho and Yang-tse-kiang, the Mekong, and the Salwen.

In the middle zone are many lakes, several of which

* Yule points out (*Cathay*, lxx.) that Ladak and Balti continued to a late date to be known as Great and Little Tibet, and Muhammadan writers of the sixteenth century so distinguish them. I have preferred, however, to write of Little Tibet as meaning those parts of ancient Tibet that are now under Kashmir, understanding by Great Tibet the major portion of the country, still under Tibetan rule.

lie at an altitude exceeding 15,000 feet. The largest
known of them is the Tengri-Nor, 150 miles in cir-
cumference, and 15,350 feet in elevation. About 100
miles south of this is Lake Yamdo, 120 miles round,
and 13,800 feet above the sea.

Passing now from the hydrography of Tibet to its
provinces and towns, the southern and middle zones
(which comprise Bodland proper) are divided into four
provinces—namely, Nari (or gNari) in the west, Kham
on the east, and in the centre the two provinces of U
and Tsang, but commonly united and called U-Tsang.
Nari is subdivided into Ladak and Balti (forming
Little Tibet and now a portion of Kashmir), Khorsum
(conterminous with British India), and Mang-yul
(conterminous with Nepal).

U-Tsang contains the most important portion of the
basin of the Brahmaputra, here called the Yaro-tsanpo,
and in this province are the chief towns and monasteries of the Tibetans. Entering from the west, the
first town of importance is Junglache, with a large
monastery on the south bank of the river. Eighty-
five miles lower, on the south bank also, is the city of
Shigatze, with its great monastery of Tashi-lunpo (or
Teshu-lumbo). On an affluent of the Yaro-tsanpo,
somewhat farther east, is Lassa, the chief town not
only of the U-Tsang, but of the whole country. The
capital of Kham is Chiamdo, south-east of which
are the plateaus and towns of Batang, Litang, and
Darchendo (or Ta-chienlu), which last three, though
geographically and ethnologically Tibetan, are directly
subject to China.

The Tibetans do not use carriages. Their roads, or
rather tracks, converge at Lassa. The most important are those from China—one from Sining in the

north-east, and two from Darchendo. Of these, one is called the Cham-lang, or northern road, and is 890 miles, and the other, Jung-lam, or official road, 935 miles, long. There are tracks also descending upon Lassa from Lob-Nor in the north and Ladak in the west, whilst from the south the capital is approached by paths, over the Himalayas, from Nepal, Sikkim, and Bhotan.

The climate of Tibet we infer from observations taken at Leh, and from remarks of travellers in the north, and pandits at Lassa. In Western Tibet frost prevails from October to April, and lakes and rivers down to 8,000 feet are frozen. At 15,000 feet the thermometer descends below freezing-point every night, and at 20,000 feet there is probably perpetual frost in the shade. At Lassa the mean temperature observed in February and March was 36°, and 61° in June and July. Southern Tibet is described as delightful in summer, with abundance of streams and vegetation, all nature being bright and sparkling and fresh, but in winter snow and frost reign supreme.

Of Northern Tibet Prjevalsky says : " The climate and natural character of this region are simply awful. The soil is clay mixed with sand or shingle, and almost devoid of vegetation, and in many parts coated with an efflorescence of salt. In the second half of May snow-storms are common, and frost at night reaches – 6°."

In June and July Prjevalsky experienced frosts (23°) every clear night, whilst the winter was bitterly cold and tempestuous. "Spring in Tsaidam," he says, " begins early, and is of a truly continental character. In the end of February the night frosts carried the thermometer down to – 40°, whilst in the day the temperature in the shade rose to 50°. But soon there came a recurrence of cold weather, gales, and duststorms. When these storms are at their height, the traveller can neither open his eyes in the face of the wind, nor draw breath, so charged is the air with fine dust. Even grazing camels forget their hunger and throw themselves on the ground."

The geology, flora, and fauna of Tibet proper are comparatively unknown to science. The middle and northern zones embrace the greater portion of the region called by the Tibetans the *Chang-tang*, or Northern Plain, which, for the most part, is too high and cold for anything but pastoral uses. The tracts containing valleys warm enough for cultivation they call *rong*, signifying a ravine, especially the valleys producing crops twice in the year.

The alluvial beds in the valleys are usually well watered and very fertile. The sharp needle peaks, which are highest of all and bare of soil, are met with most frequently in tracts of *rong*; so, too, are such forest-clad mountain slopes as exist.

The Chang-tang is covered to a considerable extent with succulent grass, which affords from May to August abundant pasture. Willows and tamarisk are met with on the margins of the lakes, but as a rule there is little wood or scrub of any kind.

Captain Bower stated in his paper before the Geographical Society that, during five months' march across Tibet at an altitude of 15,000 feet and upwards, the country traversed did not contain a single tree. There were collected, however, by his party 115 species of flowering plants, embracing 28 natural orders. One species was found at an altitude of 19,000 feet. Prjevalsky speaks of three or four kinds of grasses, one of which he describes as half a foot high, hard as wire, and so parched by the wind that it crackles like straw under foot and falls to powder.

Myriads of wild animals, chiefly the *yak*, wild sheep, the *kiang* or wild ass, antelope, and gazelle, roam over the vast region, but mostly congregate in the uninhabited northern portion, their dung being the only fuel procurable by the traveller for sometimes hundreds of miles. Prjevalsky distinguishes the wild from the tame *yak* by certain zoological marks, and would call the tame animal *Poëphagus mutus*.

He mentions two beautiful kinds of antelope, two varieties of mountain sheep, and a deer only found in small numbers on some of the mountains and not on the plateau itself. Speaking of the lake and basin of Koko-Nor, he saw there at the end of June a large number of widgeon, wild geese, grebe, and black-necked cranes (*Grus nigricollis*), whilst fleas and gnats so abounded, notwithstanding the altitude, as to blind one of his sheep.

In Lake Koko float some species of aquatic plants, and upon the banks grows the red onion, whilst on the surrounding sands is observed principally the silver weed—sometimes called the hundred-leaved pimpernel (*Potentilla anserina*)—one of the commonest of our wild flowers. The root tastes something like a nut. Cooked and seasoned with salt, it gives substantial nourishment, as is well known in the remote parts of Scotland, where in times of scarcity, I am told, it is not an uncommon food. The Tanguts like it much, and so do eared pheasants (*Crossoptilon auritum*, an essentially representative bird of Tibet) and moles.

The largest tributary but one of Koko-Nor, the Baleina, Prjevalsky mentions as abounding in fish. Its banks are frequented by widgeon, duck, and cormorant, whilst in the neighbouring marsh he saw the red-footed snipe, and a wild goose, named *Anser Indicus*.

Coming now to the inhabitants of Tibet, they are, ethnologically considered, of Mongol race, but not thoroughly homogeneous. On the west, as I saw them in Leh, they are short—Cunningham gave, as an average measurement, five feet two inches—whereas in Central Tibet they are described as of middle stature, and rather tall. Speaking generally, they are strong, slender in limb, with black eyes slightly oblique, no beard, and a clear, ruddy, brownish complexion, with an intelligent expression.

Besides the Tibetans, so called, there are Turki tribes in the north-west, called Hor, and Mongol tribes in the north-east, called Sok, these latter being known to the Chinese by the common name of Sifan, or "western aliens," which also includes Mongol, Tibetan, and other tribes. In the east, near the borders of China, are people called Gyarung or Chentui, whilst in the south are Lolo, Liso, and Moso, whose languages form a group cognate to the Burmese.

In the Altyn Tagh, according to A.K., savages are found living in a condition that recalls the Stone Age. In order to understand this it will be well to give a brief sketch of Tibetan history, and what is interwoven therewith—namely, the religion of the country.

The principal form of religion in Tibet is Lamaism, but there exists also an older religion called the Bonpa, which seems to have been evolved from Shamanism. The Bonpo have monasteries, especially in the central provinces, but few in the east and west. I have no recollection of seeing one in Little Tibet, but when in Leh I was taken to see Drubpa Mimi, or Old Drubpa the Sorcerer, as he was called, whom I photographed.

Lamaism is the corrupt form of Buddhism prevalent in Tibet or Mongolia, and, as pointed out by Professor Rhys Davids in the *Encyclopædia Britannica*, it is partly political, partly religious. Its ethical and metaphysical ideas, belonging to Buddhism generally, are accepted by Buddhists in some other countries; but it is the union of these ideas with a hierarchical system, and with the temporal sovereignty of the head of that system in Tibet, which constitutes Lamaism.

The central part of primitive Buddhism, says the Professor, was a system of self-culture, with a change of heart to be reached on earth, as a means of deliverance from the sorrows of life; but about the beginning of the Christian era teachers arose, who overlaid the original Buddhist Scriptures with metaphysical speculations, traditions, and new revelations. It had been revealed, they said, to the devout Buddhists of India that their lord had created the five Dyani, or celestial Buddhas, and that these had created five Buddhisatwas, or beings attaining Buddha-hood.

The Tibetans, accordingly, grasped this phase of the Buddhist creed, and their distinctive belief is that the Buddhisatwas continue to remain in existence for the good of mankind, by passing through a succession of human beings from the cradle to the grave. Accordingly, a belief was gradually inculcated in a whole pantheon of Buddhist divinities, saints, or angels. With this was incorporated a debasing belief in the efficacy of rites and ceremonies, charms and incantations, or a mixture of witchcraft, magic, and sorcery—in a word, the Tantra system, the latter books of which are said to be as immoral as they are absurd.

Buddhism thus corrupted was first introduced into Tibet by Srong Tsan Gampo early in the seventh century of our era, whilst the second introduction, as it is called, took place in 1041, under the Pandit Atisha, whose followers placed in the background the Tantra system, and adhered more nearly to the ancient faith. Moreover, the lamas, during the following 300 years, attained great power, especially under Kublai Khan, who granted to the abbot of the Sakya monastery in Southern Tibet the title of tributary sovereign of the country and head of the Buddhist Church, thus laying the foundation for the temporal sovereignty of the lamas.

In the fourteenth century a formidable rival to the Sakyas arose in Tsongkapa, whom Rhys Davids calls the "Luther" of Tibet. He appeared in Lassa as a reformer, insisted upon the return of the monks to celibacy and simplicity of dress, clothed his priests in yellow instead of red, as worn by those of the old school, and at his death had 30,000 followers in three large monasteries near the capital alone.

By the middle of the fifteenth century the yellow robes had become so powerful that the Emperor of China acknowledged the pre-eminence of two of their leaders. They were known as the Dalai Lama, who was abbot of Lassa, and the Pantshen Lama, who presided similarly at Tashi Lunpo. So great is the supposed sanctity of these lamas that they are almost regarded as gods in human form. Each is supposed to be an incarnation of some form of Buddha; the Dalai Lama, for instance, as the Dyani Buddhisatwa Chenresi. He is supposed, on dying, to effect his re-incorporation by a beam of light from his body, which enters the individual whom he selects.

Accordingly, when either of the Grand Lamas temporarily departs this life, it is necessary for the other to ascertain into whose body the celestial being (whose outward form merely has been dissolved) has been pleased again to incarnate himself. For that purpose the names of male children born just after the death of the Grand Lama are laid before the survivor. He chooses three, and throws them into a golden casket. The Chutuktus, or abbots of the great monasteries (some being considered incarnations, others as common mortals), assemble; and, after a week of prayer or religious observances, lots are drawn in their presence and in the presence of the surviving Grand Lama, as well as of the Chinese political resident, and the child whose name is drawn first is the new Grand Lama.*

Lower in grade than the Chutuktus come the Chubil Khans, or abbots of lesser monasteries, who also are incarnations. In fact, almost every monastery in Tibet claims to possess one of these living Buddhas; and I suppose it was one of this grade whom I met at Leh, named Trin-le-dor-je, who, notwithstanding his divinity, had come for aid to the Moravian medical missionary, and who allowed me to take his photograph.

Mention has just been made of the prayers of the lamas; but what we call prayer, as Schlagintweit says, is known to genuine Buddhism only in the form of hymns for honouring and glorifying the Buddhas and Buddhisatwas, for having pointed out to man, by word and example, the right path leading to Nirvana.

As for the religious code of the common people, Csoma de Körös gives it something as follows:—

1. To take refuge only with Buddha.

* This, I presume, is the theory; but Schlagintweit, whilst pointing out that the Dalai Lamas were elected by the clergy down to 1792, adds that the Court of Peking has since taken care that the sons of such persons only as are known for their loyalty and fidelity to imperial interests shall be selected for this high dignity.

2. To form in one's mind the resolution to strive to attain to the highest degree of perfection, in order to be united with the supreme intelligence.

3. To prostrate one's self before Buddha's image.

4. To bring before him offerings such as are pleasing to the senses.

TRIN-LI-DOR-JI, A SHUSBOG, OR MINOR INCARNATION OF BUDDHA.

5. To make music, sing hymns, and utter his praises.

6. To confess one's sins with contrite heart, to ask forgiveness, and to resolve not to do the like again.

7. To rejoice in the moral merits of all animated beings, and to wish that they may obtain emancipation.

8. To pray and entreat all the Buddhas now in the

world to teach their doctrines, and not leave the world too soon, but to remain here for many ages.

There are, of course, many other points of interest connected with the religion of Tibet, such as the ecclesiastical buildings, monuments, idols, and ceremonies in worship, the services and occupation of the monks, etc., some of which will be touched upon as they came under my own observation; but what has been written may suffice for the present, and will help us in passing now to Tibetan history.

So far back as the eleventh century B.C. the Chinese used to call the nomad tribes of what is now Northeastern Tibet by the name of Kiang. These wandering hordes were divided into small clans, perpetually at war with one another. Their language had not been reduced to writing; they counted by means of notched pieces of wood and knotted cords; and to these border tribes the knowledge of the Chinese was confined until the sixth century of our era.

As to what was going on in the interior of the country, there are in existence five copies of lists of kings, forming the "royal canon of Tibet," from its supposed beginnings between the fifth and second century B.C. down to the end of the Tibetan monarchy in 914 A.D. But their serious divergences (except as to later times and in general features) are thought by some writers to demonstrate their unauthentic character. Indeed, Rockhill considers that the events chronicled as taking place in Tibet before the introduction of Buddhism must be regarded not only as in great part legendary, but strongly distorted by the desire of Tibetan chroniclers to fabricate the descent of their monarchs from Buddha himself.

We are able, however, to some extent to supplement

Tibetan records by Chinese documents. Thus the annals of the T'ang dynasty inform us, with the appearance of truth, that Fanni, a scion of the Tu-bat family, fled from Kansu across the Yellow River in 433 A.D., and founded a state among the Kiang tribes ; and itwas during his reign the first Buddhist objects, from Nepal, were said to have reached Tibet.

In the reign of gNam-ri-srong-btsan, who died in 630, the Tibetans learned arithmetic and medicine from China, whilst his son Srong-btsan-sgam-po, born about 600 A.D., introduced Buddhism and the art of writing from India. He, moreover, was the founder in 639 of Sha-ldan, afterwards Lassa. He was greatly helped in proselytising by one of his wives who was a Nepalese princess, his other wife being an imperial princess of China. This king extended his sway over the whole of Tibet, in the north to Khotan, east to China, to Ladak in the west, and in the south through Nepal to the Indian side of the Himalayas, the Bay of Bengal being then called the Tibetan Sea. He also established commercial relations with China and the Tanguts, with Hindustan and Nepal. During his reign tea was first brought to Tibet from China.

The next king, Mang-srong-mang-btsam, in 663, subdued the tribes round Koko-Nor, and attacked the Chinese, who, however, subsequently invaded the country, and burnt the royal palace at Lassa. In 730 was born Khri-srong-ldeu-btsam, the most illustrious monarch of his country, according to Buddhist annals, because of his efforts for 46 years in favour of Buddhism. His son and successor thrice enacted, but in vain, the singular decree that all his subjects should be reduced to the same social level, so that there might be neither rich nor poor, great nor small.

The next important sovereign was Ralpachen, who began to reign in 816, and gained great glory by the translation of Buddhist literature. Under him a severe struggle took place with China, peace being concluded in 821, and bi-lingual tablets, which still exist, were erected at Lassa. Ralpachen seems to have been the first king to pay attention to the annals of his country. Also he enhanced the dignity of the priesthood by giving them a regular organisation and hierarchy.

Ralpachen was strangled in 838, and was followed by his brother, Glang-dar-ma—a Tibetan Julian, as he has been called—who persecuted Buddhists, but was also murdered after reigning a few years.

Then the national glory of Tibet declined, and, owing to the quarrels of the sons of the last-named king, the country was divided into eastern and western portions. Tibetan influence, moreover, fell so low at the Chinese court that, in 928, no one could be found to read a letter in Tibetan brought there.

In 1013 there arose a new power, when Dharmapala came to Tibet with several Buddhist disciples. He was followed by Atisha, already mentioned in this chapter. Atisha was the first of several chief priests whose authority subsequently became paramount, one of whom, named Sakya Pandita, paid a visit in 1246-8, by request, to the court of Kuyuk Khan. Five years later, Kublai Khan, having conquered all the east of Tibet, invited to his court Phagspa, Lodoi Gyaltshan, nephew of Sakya Pandita. Phagspa remained with the emperor 12 years, and in return for his service was invested with sovereign power over Tibet.

From this time the Sakya-pa-lamas, or priests (so called from the Sakya monastery) became Tibetan rulers, and so remained for 70 years (1270—1340), their temporal power being exercised through regents. When the power of the Sakyas began to wane that of the rival monasteries increased, and, during the troubled period which followed, appeared Chyang Chub Gyalt-shan, who subdued Tibet proper, and, with the approval of the Court of Peking, established a secular dynasty which furnished twelve successive rulers. When the Mongol dynasty in China passed away, the Mings who followed confirmed and enlarged the dominion of the Tibetan temporal rulers, recognising at the same time the pre-eminence of the chief lamas of the eight principal monasteries of the country.

In 1447 was founded the Tashi Lunpo monastery by Gedundub, of the Galdan monastery near Lassa, and who thus became the first of the great (afterwards Dalai) lamas. His immediate successor ruled from 1475 to 1541, and appointed a special officer to control the civil administration of the country. He was followed by Sodnam-r-Gyamtso, who was summoned to visit one of the Mongol princes, called in Tibetan sources King of Koko-Nor. This Mongol prince further patronised the lamas, and gave to Sodnam in 1576 the title of Vadjra Dalai Lama—the first occurrence of the now widely-known title.

Later, the Mongol king Tengir To intermeddled with and invaded Tibet. The priest bought him off, and then applied for help to the first Manchu Emperor of China. This enraged the Mongols and caused their return. They dethroned all the petty princes, subjugated the whole country, and made the fifth Dalai Lama supreme monarch of all Tibet. This was in 1645. The Chinese government confirmed the Dalai Lama in his authority in 1653. The Mongols interposed again in 1706, and the Sungarians invaded the country in 1717, interfering with the succession of the Dalai Lama, though the Chinese army finally conquered the country in 1720, and established the present system of government.

Tibet, however, did not enjoy uninterrupted peace under the Chinese; for, in 1782, the Goorkhas of Nepal, tempted by the reported wealth of the temple of Tashi Lunpo, suddenly appeared before the city. The regent and the child, Tashi Lama, escaped to Lassa, and the Goorkhas, after stripping the monastery and palace of their treasures, hurried back with their booty to Nepal. An avenging army was soon in motion from China, and within a few months the Goorkhas, having been defeated close to Khatmandu, were compelled to disgorge their plunder and undertake to pay tribute.

The Chinese are said to have turned these events to bitter account against the British in India, on the ground that they were allies of the Goorkhas and that they had trained the troops. After this a line of Chinese posts was established along the frontiers of Bhotan and Nepal. Every native of India was then expelled from Tibet, and the approach of strangers, even of the natives of Bengal and Hindustan, was strictly prohibited. This excluding regulation remains in force to this day.

We turn now for a moment from Tibet proper to the western highlands. In the tenth century, when the kingdom of Tibet broke up, several of the outlying districts were erected into independent kingdoms, and among them Ladak, whose documentary history, so far as Cunningham could learn, begins with the conquest of the country by King Chobang, about 1600. In 1685 the Ladakis, being attacked by the Sokpos, or Kalmuks, called in the assistance of the Muhammadan lieutenant of Aurungzeb ruling in Kashmir, who expelled the Sokpos and retired after establishing a mosque at Leh and arranging for the payment of tribute. Ladak was invaded also by Murad, the Chief of the Balti, who reigned from 1720 to 1750.

When the Sikhs took Kashmir, the Dogra troops, under the Vazir Zorawar Sing, in 1834 subdued Ladak, and in 1840 the Vazir advanced also to the conquest of Balti, and then threatened the neighbouring states. He even talked of invading Yarkand. The Lassan provinces of Rudok and Nari were, however, more accessible, and the Vazir, knowing that the monasteries possessed sacred vessels and instruments of gold and silver, advanced in 1841, and, like a good Muhammadan, plundered the monasteries with iconoclastic zeal, pushing his way to the holy district of Manasarovar.

But the news of the invasion soon reached Lassa ; a Chinese force approached, and Zorawar Sing and his men were slain on a battle-field 15,000 feet above the sea. Early in 1842 the Chinese reoccupied the lost territory, and besieged Leh, but the Kashmiris sent fresh troops. The Chinese and Tibetans were driven back, and had to consent to the re-establishment of the old boundary between Ladak, as a part of Kashmir, and Tibet proper.

Peace then reigned in Tibet until 1888, when the Tibetans came into collision with the British on the Sikkim frontier. On my arrival in that year at Leh, I met a Tibetan recently arrived from Lassa and asked him " How went the battle ? " to which he adroitly replied that " The Tibetans being armed with matchlocks only, not suitable for use in wet weather, and the rainy season having set in, they had suspended hostilities."

The fact was that the Indian forces had stayed further advance during the making of the convention between Great Britain and China relating to Sikkim and Tibet, ultimately signed at Calcutta, March 17th, 1890. This settled the Sikkim frontier, but left for future arrangement sundry matters concerning trade, pasturage, and the method of official communications between the British authorities and the authorities in Tibet.

This brings us to the present system of government in Tibet, which, as a dependency of China, is under the Viceroy of Szechuen. Chinese authority is represented by two imperial delegates resident at Lassa, one of whom is the assistant of the other. They direct exclusively the foreign and military administration. Subordinate to them are two great officers and two paymasters, residing at Lassa and Shigatze. Next in rank are three commanders living at different places, and, under them, three non-commissioned officers. The usual number of Manchu troops in Tibet does not exceed 4,500 men.

The civil and religious government of the country is left in the hands of the Tibetans, amongst whom the supreme authority belongs to the Dalai Lama; but he is consulted only in cases of emergency. The powers of the Dalai Lama in civil affairs are committed to a special officer for life, nominated by the Chinese government. He is known by the title of *Gyalpo*, and governs as king. He is also "Prime Minister" of the Dalai Lama, and is Regent when the latter is a minor. The "king" is selected from among the four head lamas of certain principal monasteries; and of equal rank with the "king" is the Deba Lama of the great monastery near Lassa, whose appointment, together with that of the Dalai Lama's chaplain also, has to be confirmed by the Emperor of China.

The king rules with the help of five ministers; the four for the exchequer, judicial, revenue, and home departments, being laymen, and the fifth, for ecclesiastical affairs, a lama. The four provinces of Tibet are ruled, under the king, each by a governor with minor officers. Besides these are several lesser magistrates outside the four provinces, whilst within them are four principalities under the direct government of the Chinese imperial delegates. Among these principalities is Tashi Lunpo, where resides the second Grand Lama, whose election requires the confirmation of the Emperor of China. There is likewise a Chinese officer in residence at Lassa. He superintends several minor principalities scattered over the country.

Mention should be made also, as Markham points out, not only of the Dalai Lama at Lassa and the Teshu Lama at Tashi Lunpo, but also of the Taranath Lama, an incarnation who lives at Urga and holds sway over the Mongols; but his authority is primarily ecclesiastical rather than civil.

On asking a trader from Lassa, whom I met at Leh, concerning the government of the country, he mentioned that the late *Gyalpo* or king ruled 22 years, which was indicative of his popularity; for the trader said if the people did not like the *Gyalpo*, when elected by the four monasteries, they put him to death, and substituted another in his place. Much of the information in this chapter, however, will be further illustrated by some account of the sources whence our knowledge of Tibet has been obtained.

CHAPTER XLV.

OUR KNOWLEDGE OF, AND RELATIONS WITH, TIBET.

Early European travellers to Tibet; Odoric, 299.—Jesuit and Capuchin missionaries, 300.—Van de Putte's journey through Lassa; Exclusive policy initiated by the Chinese, 301.—Aid of Indian Government invoked against the Bhotanese, 302.—Missions of Bogle and Turner; Manning's journey, and Markham's *résumé* of Tibetan travellers, 303.—Huc and Gabet, 304.—Tibetan students; Dr Campbell and Dr Hooker, 305.—Later missionaries at Leh and Bathang, 306.—Asiatic sources of information; Chinese annals and surveys; Native explorers under Indian Government, 307.—Journeys by Chandra Das and Ugyen Gyatso; Gentlemen travellers, 309.

PROBABLY the first European to visit Tibet was Friar Odoric of Pordenone, who passed through the country about 1328 on his return from Cathay. He mentions the chief city, obviously Lassa, "built with walls of black and white, where none dare shed blood of man or beast, and where dwelt the *Abassi*, or Pope of the Lamaists."

The second European approached from the south. This was Antonio Andrada, a Jesuit missionary, who, in 1624, set out from Agra to scale the appalling mountains, the snowy pinnacles of which were visible from the plains of India. After fearful sufferings he reached Lake Manasarowar, found his way to Rudok, and eventually, by way of Tangut, entered China.

The next journey, that of the Jesuit missionaries Grueber and Dorville, was in 1661, from Peking to Agra by way of Si-ning, and across the Tangut desert to Lassa. There they remained two months, and their letters describe the worship of the Grand Lama. From Lassa they crossed the Kuti Pass into Nepal, reached Khatmandu, and arrived at Agra 214 days after leaving Peking. After the foregoing, according to Schlagintweit, were the Capuchins, Joseph d'Asculi and Francisco Maria de Toun, who left Bengal in 1706, and safely reached Lassa.

Then came two more Jesuits, Hippolito Desideri and Manuel Freyre. They proceeded through Kashmir to Leh, and thence to Lassa, arriving in March 1716. Desideri remained at Lassa until 1729, when he was recalled by the Pope, owing to complaints of the Capuchin friars. We have two of Desideri's letters, and, what is more valuable, the narrative of his journey to, and residence in, Tibet, as contained in a manuscript discovered only in 1875 in a private library at Pistoia. In it Desideri says that he openly gave out at Lassa that he was a foreign lama come to convert the people, and that he was received with much toleration. There are two other documents of Desideri's in the library of the congregation of the Propaganda at Rome.

More important still for our knowledge of lamaism were the results of the Capuchin mission under Francisco Orazio della Penna, who was sent to Tibet with 12 of his brethren, and reached Lassa through Nepal in 1719. Here they established a mission that flourished for nearly a quarter of a century.

Orazio returned to Rome in 1735 for reinforcements, and once more reached Lassa in 1740.

Desideri translated into Latin a Buddhist work, called the *Tan-giur* (or *Tan-gyur*), by a great reforming lama; whilst Orazio translated into Tibetan several Christian works, and compiled besides a Tibetan-Italian dictionary. The materials brought home by the Capuchin missionaries were used by the learned linguist Giorgi in compiling his ponderous *Alphabetum Tibetanum*, published in 1762.

Thus it will be observed that the early European visitors to Tibet were, with one exception, all ecclesiastics.

This exception was a Dutchman, Samuel van de Putte, of Flushing, an LL.D. of Leyden, who, with a thirst for knowledge and adventure, left the Netherlands in 1718, crossed Asia to India, and made his way to Lassa.

After long residence there, he, in the dress of a Chinese mandarin, accompanied a deputation of lamas to Peking by the route afterwards traversed by Huc, and, passing through Lassa, returned to India in 1737. Van de Putte remains to this day the only European we know of who accomplished the journey from India through Lassa to China; but the freedom with which the Roman missionaries passed to and fro between Tibet and India seems to show that intercourse was at that time unrestrained, and that the Tibetans were at least tolerant of Christian teachers.

The exclusive policy which succeeded seems to have been initiated mainly by the Chinese authorities in Lassa, who, in 1749, put to death the Tibetan *Gyalpo*, or Regent, whereupon the people flew to arms. The tumult led to a massacre of the resident Chinese, after which the imperialists, on regaining the ascendency, strengthened their hold upon the succeeding *Gyalpos*, and in 1760 the missionaries were expelled from the country.

They retired to Nepal, and there witnessed a revolution, in the course of which the present Goorkha dynasty, under Prithi Narayan, destroyed the dynasty of the Newars ; and the Goorkhas, having conquered Nepal, so oppressed the merchants by tolls and exactions, that the once flourishing trade between Tibet and India, by way of the Nepal passes, was almost annihilated.

Whilst Prithi Narayan was thus conquering Nepal, another disturber of the peace, Deb Judhur in Bhotan, overran Sikkim, and in 1772 invaded Kuch Behar. The ruler of Kuch Behar asked help of the Government of India. Whereupon Warren Hastings organised a small force, drove the Bhotanese back to their hills, seized some of their strongholds, and forced them to sue for peace. The Teshu Lama also wrote a letter interceding for the Bhotanese, and sent it to Calcutta. British influence being thus invoked, the way was opened for other sources of information derived from political envoys, the first of whom was George Bogle.

Warren Hastings, in 1774, sent Mr Bogle (accompanied by Dr Hamilton) to the Deb Rajah of Bhotan and to the Teshu Lama. Bogle induced the Bhotan Government to allow the passage of merchants through its territory between Tibet and Bengal, and he formed a close friendship with the Teshu Lama, who took an enlightened view of matters, and wished to support trade ; but the Regent at Lassa, under the influence of Chinese agents, successfully opposed the views of the Teshu Lama as to the admission of foreigners into Tibet.

It seemed, therefore, as if the only way to counteract

this influence was to obtain through the Teshu Lama
a hearing at Peking; and the Teshu Lama promised
to endeavour to get an audience with the Emperor for
Mr Bogle, who was to go round by sea, whilst his
patron went by land. The end of these plans was
that the Teshu Lama died in 1780 at Peking of small-
pox, and Mr Bogle also died in the following year at
Calcutta.

In 1783 Warren Hastings took advantage of a
report that the Teshu Lama after his death had reappeared in the person of an infant, to send Captain
Turner through Bhotan to Shigatze to congratulate
the Regency on the renewed incarnation. Turner
visited and described the country in and around Teshu
Lunpo, and returned to India in 1784. In the following year Hastings left India, and with his retirement
all direct diplomatic intercourse between Tibet and
India ceased.

In 1811 an adventurous traveller, Thomas Manning,
made his way to Lassa, and had an interview with the
Dalai Lama—the only Englishman who has ever done
so—and returned to India in 1812.

The information preserved to us in journals, MSS.,
etc., by Bogle, Turner, and Manning has been carefully edited by Mr Clements Markham, C.B., F.R.S.,
to whose books and to whose kindness I am indebted
in several ways, and whose work on Tibet, published
in 1879, brought our knowledge of that country up to
date, and is the best of its kind.

After the visits to Tibet of Bogle, Turner, and
Manning, two French missionaries, Huc and Gabet,
in 1844, made their way from Peking by the Si-ning
route to Lassa. They were allowed to remain only a
month, during which it would appear that the Tibetan

authorities were willing to receive the strangers cordially; but Chinese jealousy and exclusiveness intervened, and a special envoy, Keshen, expelled Huc and Gabet, and sent them back by way of Bathang and Szechuen to Canton.

I was interested to hear, when I was thinking of the possibility of undertaking a journey to Lassa, that their servant, Samdadchiembo, was alive and looking about for a job, concerning whom I wrote to China, and should not have been greatly surprised to have found him awaiting me at Kuldja; but I was subsequently told at Peking that he had recently died. As a further reminiscence of Huc and Gabet, I may mention that, when I reached Leh, Mr Redslob said that he had been told by a man, who was in Lassa on the arrival of the French missionaries, that, after their expulsion, several persons were put to death for aiding their entrance into the city.

The narrative of Huc and Gabet was one of the most popular books of travel in its day, and forms a landmark among the sources of our information, because written by the last Europeans who have succeeded in entering Lassa.

We now come to a group of authorities who, if they have not actually entered Tibet proper, have in some cases lived on or approached its frontier, and also studied its literature. Foremost among them is Mr Brian Hodgson, who from 1820 lived for 23 years at the British Residency in Nepal, devoting himself to every branch of study relating to that country and to Tibet.

Next to him must be mentioned the Hungarian Alexander Csoma de Körös, who, in 1820, left Bucharest, and travelled through Bokhara and Cabul to Leh, where, content to live in the poorest manner possible, he studied Tibetan in the monasteries. He thus learned that the literature of Tibet was entirely of Indian origin. Whilst continuing his studies, he made his way to Calcutta, and in 1842 set out for Lassa, but died the same year at Darjeeling, leaving four boxes of books and papers, a few shirts, and a cooking-pot.

His dietary, according to Dr Campbell, was limited to tea, of which he was very fond, and a little plain-boiled rice. On a mat on the floor, with a box of books on four sides, he ate, slept, and studied, never undressed at night, and rarely went out during the day. He never drank wine or spirits, or used tobacco or other stimulants; and may be said to have died a literary hero, and one of the greatest Tibetan scholars.

Contemporary with Körös was Baron Schilling de Constadt, a Russian official, who from 1830 and onwards collected Tibetan books from a monastery near Kiakhta. He so ingratiated himself with the Buriat lamas, whom he employed in copying, that at the end of a year he possessed a collection of 2,000 Mongolian and Tibetan works, and afterwards obtained a copy of the *Kah-gyur*, in 101 volumes. These works, with a copy added also of the *Tan-gyur*, found their way to St Petersburg, where, among other Russian scholars, they were studied by Professor Anton von Schiefner. Mr Ralston brought some of Schiefner's studies within reach of English readers in his *Tibetan Tales*.

After the foregoing names should be mentioned that of Dr Campbell, who lived for eight years (1830—1838) as surgeon at the Residency of Khatmandu, and then became the founder of Darjeeling. He contributed much to our knowledge of the border land between

India and Tibet. In 1847 Dr Hooker explored portions of Sikkim, then comparatively unknown, reached the passes leading into Tibet, and gave us much new information in his *Himalayan Journals*.

Now we come again to missionaries, who, though not permitted to enter, have been working on the outskirts of Tibet. In 1853 two Moravian missionaries set out to penetrate into Mongolia by way of India; but being stopped on the borders by Chinese officials, they settled among the Tibetans in Kaelang. The mission was afterwards placed under Brothers Jaschke, Rechler, and Heyde.

Jaschke has given us a Tibetan-English dictionary, and I corresponded with Rechler in 1888. He was then living in a country parish in Prussia. These missionaries were afterwards joined by the Rev. F. Redslob, who, when Mr Ney Elias was British Joint Commissioner, was allowed to open a medical mission at Leh. From these two missions have resulted a translation of the New Testament, and part of the Old, as well as other Christian works.

Again, on the eastern skirts of Tibet, at Darchendo and Bathang, Roman missionaries have been labouring, one of whom, M. Desgodins, has added to our knowledge of the trade, as well as of certain departments of the fauna, of Tibet.

To the foregoing list of names must be added those of the two scholars Klaproth and Gutzlaff, who, through the study of Chinese works—Klaproth at Peking and Gutzlaff at Hong Kong—have collected much information concerning Tibet.

Thus far it will be observed I have spoken chiefly of European sources of information. We now come to information imparted by Asiatics. A Chinese work, short but interesting, especially concerning religious festivals, and called *Notice of the Provinces of Wei and Tsang*, was written by *Ma-shao-yun*, the Commissary-General of the Chinese army which expelled the Goorkhas from Tibet in 1786.

Before this date, however, when the Jesuit missionaries made a map of the country round Peking, it so pleased the Emperor Kang-hi, that he desired to have his whole empire similarly surveyed. For Tibet, two lamas were carefully trained as surveyors by the Jesuits at Peking. They were sent to Lassa *via* Si-ning, and thence to the sources of the Ganges, with the result that a map was submitted to the Jesuits in 1717, from which were prepared the maps forwarded to Du Halde, and from which D'Anville constructed his atlas of 1733. The lama survey thus became the basis of our geographical knowledge of Tibet.

This survey is now being rapidly superseded by the accomplishments of a new set of native explorers organised by Colonel Montgomerie, under General Walker. These explorers were trained in the use of surveying instruments, and despatched into regions beyond the British frontier, where Europeans could not safely penetrate. With a view to their being unknown during their time of active service, letters or numbers were substituted for their names, and they were called "pandits."

Thus, pandit A., in 1865, made his way through Nepal, and, with some difficulty, succeeded in reaching Lassa, but in the following year returned to report himself at the headquarters of the Great Trigonometrical Survey, where his observations were elaborated and mapped, and much useful information was thereby gained. Between May and November

1867, the same pandit, A., and another, C., made their way to the Tibetan gold-mines of Thok-Jalung, and returned. In 1874 a pandit, with companions, succeeded in penetrating to Lake Tengri-Nor, and then went on to Lassa.

In 1872 Colonel Montgomerie reported upon a journey undertaken by "No. 9," who approached Tibet in the footsteps of Dr Hooker, and, reaching Shigatze, paid his respects to the Teshu Lama. He got over the frontier, thanks to his successful treatment of an official's wife.

A more important journey, however, was made between July 1874 and March 1875 by the pandit Nain Sing, who, after accompanying the Forsyth expedition to Kashgar, explored the direct route from Leh to Lake Tengri, and thence to Lassa, continued down the San-po, and finally entered Assam.

The grandest journey, however, of this kind was accomplished by the pandit A-K. He was despatched in 1878 to cross Tibet from south to north into Mongolia, and return by a parallel route over new ground. He had a rosary for counting his paces, a prayer-barrel for secreting his field-books, and ample funds to stock himself as a travelling merchant.

He passed from Darjeeling to Lassa, and was detained there a year; then travelled northwards to Sachu, and was robbed. Turning back to Tsaidam, he made his way south to Darchendo, where the Roman missionaries advanced him funds, after which he turned westwards, and passed by a new route to Lassa, and so reached India after an absence of four years and a half, with all his instruments and all his field-books, having made a continuous route survey of about 2,800 miles.

I need not mention more surveying explorers; but there is another native name or two that must not be omitted, especially that of Baboo Sarat Chandra Das, and that of his companion, Lama Ugyen Gyatso, whose acquaintance I made in India, and to both of whom I was indebted for several kindnesses. Whilst living at Darjeeling, and teaching Tibetan boys, Das studied Tibetan literature, and, in 1870, by permission of the lamas, was allowed to come to Tashi Lunpo, "to study Buddhism in the places where it now flourishes." He was hospitably received by the minister of the Grand Lama, and invited to come again in the following year.

In 1881 Sir Ashley Eden obtained the sanction of the Indian Government for Das and the lama to visit Lassa, whereupon the minister was more friendly than ever, and most eager to study English among other things, and to have further intercourse with India. The lama died, however, of small-pox in 1882, and Das returned with much new information, of some of which I am in possession, and have, to a certain extent, made use.

We now come to another list of names pertaining to those who may be called "gentlemen travellers." For the most part they journeyed at their own initiative and at their own charges, being prompted by the love of adventure and desire for knowledge. Most, if not all of them, set out for Lassa, and each one failed to reach it, though penetrating far enough into various parts of the country to afford us a considerable amount of valuable information.

Foremost among these in point of time, as well as in the importance of his discoveries, was General Prjevalsky. In 1876 he reached the Altyn Tagh, or northern buttress of the Tibetan plateau. In 1879 he crossed it south of Sachu, and continued through the Tsaidam plains over the Burhan Buddha Mountains, and another range he calls the "Marco Polo" Mountains.

Then he travelled south-west to the river Nap-Chu, whence he was turned back 170 miles only from Lassa. In 1884 he crossed the Nan Shan Mountains to Koko-Nor, and, thus penetrating to the sources of the Hoang-ho, entered the basin of the Di-Chu; then, returning to Tsaidam, he marched westward along his Marco Polo, Columbus, and Moscow Mountains, to the Altyn Tagh.

That Prjevalsky intended, if possible, on his next journey to reach the Tibetan capital I make no doubt; for, although he did not tell me so, yet at our first parting in St Petersburg, in 1888, when shaking hands, he said light-heartedly, "Good-bye, till we meet at Lassa—you from the south, and I from the north." "Right," said I, "to drink afternoon tea with the Dalai Lama." This, however, was vouchsafed neither to him nor me; but, since his death, I have often thought of his words.

In the same year that Prjevalsky entered Tsaidam from the north (1879), the Hungarian Count Bela Szechenyi tried to enter Tibet, also from Sachu. Being stopped, his expedition attempted the road from Koko-Nor to Lassa; but being again baffled, they proceeded to Darchendo and Bathang. Captain Gill, two years previously, had approached Bathang through Western China, but was not allowed to proceed farther towards Lassa, whereupon he proceeded southwards by Talifu and Bhamo to India; and Count Szechenyi, being likewise prevented, did pretty much the same.

When Prjevalsky walked out of Tibet in 1885,

Carey was just preparing to walk in. In the following year Carey crossed the Altyn Tagh, south of Lob-Nor, the Machu being his farthest point southwards, whence he returned through Eastern Tsaidam.

The year 1889 saw no less than four leaders of expeditions—Grombchevsky, Pievtsoff, Bonvalot, and Rockhill, to say nothing here of myself—making their way from various quarters towards Lassa. Grombchevsky, as previously observed, tried to approach from Shahidula, and mounted the plateau, only to find himself, from want of supplies, compelled to return. In the following spring he tried to find a road from Nia *via* Sorgak, and thence towards Lassa by a route which I myself had thought to attempt. Failing in this, he tried again in May to accomplish his ends through Polu, but was stopped by physical obstacles. Prjevalsky's last expedition, to the command of which Pievtsoff succeeded, reconnoitred the passes from Nia in 1889, and attempted an entrance in the following year, but, for the same reason, also failed.

Bonvalot, accompanied by Prince Henry of Orleans and M. de Deken—the last of whom I met at Kuldja, and to whom I am indebted for revising certain portions of this book—was more fortunate. Profiting by a remark of Carey that there was a path from Lob-Nor, used by the Kalmuk pilgrims, to Lassa (of which I also heard in 1888 at the Chinese Legation in London), Bonvalot scaled the Altyn Tagh, and continued southwards by a route west of that taken by Prjevalsky in 1879-80, and descended upon Tengri-Nor, less than 100 miles from Lassa. Here, however, he was met by Tibetan officials, and made to retire eastwards to Bathang and Darchendo.

As for Mr Woodville Rockhill, Tibet has been his

life hobby, and the reaching Lassa, therefore, I suppose, his *summum bonum*. To this end he has spent years of study in learning the language; and when I reached Peking in 1889, it was reported that he had arrived at the Tibetan frontier near Si-ning.

Thence he continued north of Koko-Nor, and descended in a south-westerly direction. Difficulties of transit, however, and, to some extent, lack of funds, caused him to give up the attempt to reach Lassa, and he followed the route of A-K. to Darchendo. Rockhill, in his scholarly *Land of the Lamas*, has given an account of his journey and much useful information.

Another traveller who has since reached Darchendo is Mr Pratt. He has also published a book, called *To the Snows of Tibet through China*.

The last of these "gentlemen travellers" known to me is Captain Bower, who, on his return to India from Chinese Turkistan, started again in 1891. Accompanied by Dr Thorold, he crossed into Tibet from Chang Chenmo, struck east and south to near Lassa, then travelled somewhat northwards, and afterwards south-east to Chiamdo. He has since read a paper on his journey before the Royal Geographical Society.

Quite recently there has been announced a journey in Tibet and a near approach to its capital by Miss Taylor, whom I met at Darjeeling in 1889, and who, for missionary purposes, was there studying Tibetan. Concerning this journey we await particulars.

There still remain several points not touched upon, such as the habitations of the people, their food, occupation, language, music, and recreations; but these subjects belong equally to Little as to Great Tibet, and will in some cases at least be alluded to in continuing my route towards Ladak.

CHAPTER XLVI.

A JOURNEY IN LITTLE TIBET.

Shahidula, 313.—Chang Chenmo and Karakoram routes, 314.—March to Suget, and attenuated atmosphere, 315.—Shah-Malik; Fear of robbers, 316.—Murder of Dalgleish; Karakoram Pass, 317.—Perils of route, 323.—From Chougeh Jilga to Daulatbeg Uldi, 324.—The Shyok, and glacier at Kumdan; Snowfall at Tschkun, 325.—Saser Pass, its glaciers and skeletons, 326.—Arrival at Tut Yailak, 327.—Sight from Karawal Dawan of Changlung, 328.—A broken-headed horse-leader, 329.—Nubra valley; New people and birds; Lodging at Panamik, 330.—Photographic endeavours, 331.—The *Sardar* of Taghar, 332.—Tibetan food, and lama worship, 333.—Ascent to Khardung, 334.—Tibetan characteristics, polyandry, and domestic affairs, 335.—Khardung Pass, and arrival at Leh, 336.

ON arriving at Shahidula, the name of the place was familiar to me as the spot where Shaw, on his first visit, was kept in durance vile till Yakub Khan gave permission for him to enter his country. Shaw describes the fort in his day as "a lot of little rooms surrounding a courtyard, into which they open. A parapet with loopholes for muskets runs round the outer edge of this flat roof, whilst, at the corners, little round towers, also loopholed, command the four sides. This primitive fort stands in the centre of a small shingly plain. The Karakash, like a trout stream, runs past, a few hundred yards off, while all round rise barren, rocky mountains."

That Shaw spoke truth concerning the barren and desolate appearance of the place my photograph bears witness; the only bright spot therein being, in the centre of the picture, a distant snow peak, that was called by my men Ali Nazar Kurghan Tagh, or the mountain over the fort we had passed on the previous day of Ali Nazar.

Shahidula takes its name from a shrine on one of the neighbouring hills, the fort being built, according to Shaw, by the Maharajah of Kashmir, who, during the troubles in Chinese Turkistan in 1864, sent a few soldiers and workmen across the Karakoram range (his real boundary), and for two summers manned the fort; but when matters became settled his troops were withdrawn, and the fort was occupied, as Shaw and Hayward found on their arrival, by the soldiers of Yakub Khan.

Subsequently, Shahidula was deserted for the new fort of Ali Nazar Kurghan, 20 miles distant. At the time of our passing Shahidula, the fort was unoccupied, but I have since heard that the place is held by the Chinese. Grombchevsky, however, speaks of "a newly erected Kashmirian fortress at Shahidula Khoja," whence he addressed a letter to Kashmir. Thus, to travellers coming from India, Shahidula is now the first permanently inhabited spot they reach in Chinese Turkistan.

From this place there branches off to the east a route past some jade quarries, on to the Lingzi Plains and across the Chang Chenmo (by which name the route is generally known) to Leh; but a more direct route goes nearly due south over the Karakoram, towards which we started on the 6th of November.

From Shahidula firewood must be taken for several

days, till the Nubra valley is reached, though at most of the stages a few roots can be found. Grain can sometimes be bought, as a last resource, of the Kirghese, who at times pasture their flocks in this valley. The valley continues in a straight direction for about 20 miles.

At five miles from Shahidula, the Karakoram track leaves the valley, and turns into the hills to a place four miles beyond, called Suget, where we arrived after a march of six hours, and camped on the right bank of the Karakash.

Here a little firewood was found, and grazing was fairly plentiful, so that we stayed on the morrow to let the horses enjoy the pasture, and started about noon. The track continued up a flat, gently rising, stony valley, 500 yards wide, bordered by steep clay hills. After six hours' march we came to Khotan Jilga, in full view of the Suget Pass.

The weather had been delightful, and the sun sufficiently warm to induce the removal of one's overcoat; but in the few minutes in the shade, necessary for taking a view of the Pass, my fingers became so cold that I feared frost-bite. Added to this, we were rising again, and I was so exhausted with the trifling effort of undoing and putting away the camera, that I had to sit down and rest. The least exertion became a painful effort, and after the day's journey I could do little more than sit in my tent, rest my head on my hand, and neither write, read, nor even think.

Next morning we started soon after nine o'clock, continuing up the ravine, now narrowed to about 200 yards; and after accomplishing another four miles we performed a zigzag up the Pass through a good deal of snow to the height of 17,618 feet. We then descended gently into a wide shaded valley down the hill slope, following the course of a stream that rises under the Pass, six miles beyond which is a camping-place called Chibra, but with no vegetation and little water.

Then, after the longest march on this journey—nearly 12 hours—we arrived at dusk at Shah-Malik. Here we intended to camp, but Haidar Haji would have it that this was a favourite place for Kunjut raids on caravans, and on his untiring steed he lured us "a little farther" and "a little farther" towards some secluded place he spoke of.

This resulted in our pitching tent about ten o'clock at a place the men called Darwaz Surgut, where there was no water and only a little snow, some of which they melted for my evening meal. I was too tired to wait for "dinner," and, without even writing my diary, got to bed, and there partook of a mere apology for a meal. Everybody seemed tired out ; added to which, it was bitterly cold by reason of wind ; and though we had descended 2,000 feet below the crest, the *dam*, or rarefied air, was troublesome.

In the morning I added one more article of warm clothing to my heavy outfit, the sum-total of which was now appalling. To begin with, I had put on a thick lamb's-wool vest, with sleeves, and drawers, then ditto of chamois leather ; next a flannel shirt, and above it a chamois vest without sleeves, lined with flannel ; cloth trousers and waistcoat, with jacket of kid leather, flannel lined ; then an ulster lined with fur ; and above it, sometimes, for sleeping, my Khotan coat of sheepskin, with thick stockings and fur-lined boots, together with a woollen helmet for a nightcap.

Thus I lay down on my four trunks, whilst Joseph covered me with shawl and lambskin rug. This represented my maximum—namely, five skins besides my own, four flannels, and a thick coat; yet with all this, at Suget, it was cold, and I never got into a perspiration, though the weight of clothing and the effect of the *dam* proved a little too much; and I had to rise in the night, feeling half suffocated, to take off some of the wraps.

Yet the Hindu Lakoo had assured me at Karghalik that it "was not cold now"; and he did not intend, he said, to take a tent! Nor did the men complain of the temperature, though they had little surplus energy next morning. Joseph brought me some hot cocoa for breakfast, but I learned afterwards that the men would not go the distance to get snow to heat water for themselves.

Starting again, we continued up the mile-broad river valley, with a very little grass growing here and there. The country was now composed of broad, flat, shingly valleys between steep clay hills with a backbone of rock. Before us was the main range of the Karakoram, with masses and bands of red conglomerate, whilst the hill tops were very jagged. Whilst on the march, at an altitude of 15,000 feet, we passed Ak Tagh, where is drawn on my edition of Walker's map the frontier of Kashmir.

In the course of the day Muhammad Joo pointed out the spot where were hidden the stolen goods of Dalgleish; and, at a short distance north of the Karakoram Pass, he showed us the locality where the murder took place. Here we raised a cairn near a brook, and fixed thereon a stick with a handkerchief, on which I wrote "Dalgleish was killed here," to distinguish the place from another on which M. Dauvergne a few weeks previously had raised a heap, but which Muhammad Joo said was not the exact spot where he saw the foul deed done.*

Another camping-ground was passed at Wahabjilga.

NOTE CONCERNING THE CAPTURE OF THE MURDERER OF
MR DALGLEISH.

In Chapter XXXIV. I have put together an account of the murder as given me by two eye-witnesses; and as we travelled through the country, where the subject was still "in the air," we fell in with others who gave further accounts of the murderer.

It would appear that, after sending back Muhammad Joo, Daud Muhammad Khan and the dervish continued their journey "as thick as thieves," never leaving the stolen goods, but one guarding them with a gun when the other was temporarily absent. At Baransai, nine miles from where the murder took place, Daud remained behind, the rest of the caravan going forward, after which he rejoined them, but ultimately went away from them beyond the Chinese frontier.

On reaching the Kilian Pass, the crossing was so bad (as I heard at Ak-Shor) that some of the goods had to be left in the snow, so that for their recovery the Ak-Shor *Aksakal*, Niaz Beg, was asked to send some of his servants. He did so, and also kept the goods awhile for Daud Muhammad Khan, who, after being sheltered for three days, was shown by Niaz Beg's servants an unfrequented path, by following which he avoided the Custom-house at Kilian, where also (according to Ghasim Haji) it appeared that Osman the *karakesh* did not tell the *Bek* of the murder, but said that Dalgleish was coming after 30 days.

Meanwhile, the murderer arrived at Bora, for my host there told me that he exchanged with him a horse, which he had been since obliged to surrender. He wished me also to understand that he had taken a prominent part in the capture of the dervish, for all of which he would like part of the reward.

When I was at Khotan, the *Amban* told me he had heard that the Government of India had offered 5,000 rupees for the capture of the murderer, who (I understood him to say) had been to Khotan (though he said it was not generally known), and quickly left for Yarkand.

I turn now to the testimony of Osman, as given in M. Petrovsky's report, and which Osman in person confirmed to me.

When the major portion of the caravan arrived at Karghalik, they went to the mandarin to tell him what had happened. But he replied that Daud Muhammad Khan was not a Chinese subject, nor was it his business to institute inquiries. They had better mention it, he said, to the authorities at Yarkand.

On reaching Yarkand, the *Amban* was absent, and his assistant Loo said, "Wait till the *Amban* comes. We heard of the matter a week ago, but where the Aktagh stream flows through a cutting in slate rocks. And thus after seven hours' march over an elevated and stony plateau, impeded by a cutting

the *Amban* does not want to make inquiry." " After this," said Osman, "M. Petrovsky ordered me to Kashgar, and now I have told what I saw."

Thus far Osman : after which, in the Consul's official report, follows what he himself heard and did in Kashgar. Daud Muhammad Khan, on reaching Kashgar, lived for five days with an Afghan, Nehmet Ullah Khan, at the caravanserai of Durdabek, and then lodged for two days with an Afghan, son of Baz Tura Khan, outside the town. During these days he sent off an Afghan for his goods at Ak-Shor, which, coming to the ears of the Russian Consul, he likewise despatched a messenger to take charge of, if possible, the property of Dalgleish, and M. Petrovsky also informed both the *Tautai* and his secretary, Tun Shan, that the murderer was in Kashgar.

Meanwhile, a man of Kashgar, Muhaeddin, acting as agent for Nazar Haji, then at Ladak, to whom Daud Muhammad Khan owed money, sued him for debt in the court of the *Tautai*, who ordered the debtor not to leave the town. Nehmet and another Afghan standing surety that he should not run away. Nothing, however, appears to have been asked by the Chinese concerning the murder.

Daud Muhammad now returned to the caravanserai of Durda Bek, and on the $\frac{22 \text{ April}}{4 \text{ May}}$ pretended that he was going with Dildar Khan, the Afghan *Aksakal*, Nehmet Ullah Khan, Shah Abbas Khan, and a man named Tammim to visit the shrine of Hazrat Aphak. One of the servants of Nehmet Ullah Khan was sent to the caravanserai for the murderer's two saddle-bags ; but the landlord, as he told the Consul, refused to give them up, saying that their owner was detained for debt, whereupon Ibrahim Bek, one of the native officials of the town, came to the rescue and said the bags might go. And thus the bird escaped.

The Consul now urged the *Tautai* to arrest the four men who accompanied the murderer, and to secure from Yarkand the Afghan Gulban (who was present at the murder), to inquire with what passport Daud had escaped, and at what places it had been presented. Whether the Consul up to this point was acting on his own initiative I do not know, but his report said that, though the Afghan *Aksakal* was arrested, it was not so with the remainder of the four men, though living on the spot, and that Gulban was not arrested until after a letter had arrived from Sir Mortimer Durand, the Secretary of the Indian Government, offering, I presume, the reward of 5,000 rupees for the capture of the murderer, and, I think, 3,000 for that of the dervish.

Nor did the Chinese, according to the report, do much even then, whilst the Consul claims to have sent notices of the offered reward all over the district. And certainly I remember at Aksu, on August 19th, the *Aksakal* there bringing to me the Consul's note, ordering him not to wait for the wind, we arrived at Balti Brangsa, at an elevation once more of 17,000 feet—everything very cold, with ink, bread, potatoes, and other necessaries all frozen.

Chinese to act, but to publish abroad the matter at once. Notices, too, were sent by the Consul to the Governors-General Rosenbach and Kolpakoffsky, as well as to General Ivanoff at Vierny, and on the Russian frontiers to Colonels Diebner at Osh and Larionoff at Narin, that they might be on the look-out should the murderer approach.

Meanwhile, the Consul received a telegram, in connection with which he was about to send a letter to the *Tautai* on September 10th (the day after my reading his report), and to the following effect :—

"The Russian and English Ambassadors at Peking have expressed their thanks for my inquiries concerning Daud Muhammad Khan, which inquiries they hope may be continued, and they desire me to inform you that the *Tsung-li-Yamen* considers it a grave matter, and one that must be followed up. I therefore inform you that Daud Muhammad Khan went to Aksu with a passport belonging to the Afghan Tammim, and that Tammim afterwards left with another passport."

And here matters stood during my stay in Kashgar, where the Consul was keeping in custody Osman, the caravan leader; but his messenger to Ak-Shor, to whom he had advanced a hundred roubles for expenses, had not returned. I had heard on August 20th at Aksu, that an Afghan at Kashgar, who gave the murderer a Chinese document to help him on his way, had been arrested by or through the Russian Consul; yet, notwithstanding all this action on the part of M. Petrovsky, the mandarin at Maralbashi, through which Muhammad Khan probably passed, told me, when I arrived there on August 31st, that he had received no orders concerning the murderer from Peking, nor seemingly from anywhere else.

During my second stay at Yarkand, M. Petrovsky's messenger, Mullah Alim Jahn, called on me with a list of effects he had recovered belonging to Dalgleish, first among which my notes mention the horse ridden by Daud Muhammad Khan (the one, I suppose, taken from my host at Bora), and the skin of Dalgleish's horse, his gun and case, with many articles belonging thereto, a medicine case, teapot, and sundry articles of silver, writing materials and articles of clothing, and horse gear, to the number in all of 37 items. I understood from the mullah that the *Tautai* had examined by scourging the Afghan messenger of Daud Muhammad Khan, but failed to learn whither the murderer had gone.

Also, I heard that the *Amban* of Yarkand was detaining Niaz Beg, whom he had summoned from Ak-Shor because he had not informed him of having Dalgleish's things in his possession. In fact, Niaz Beg was brought to me, and some of the people wanted me to ask for the man's release, pretending that, if he were not at Ak-Shor when I arrived, I should have difficulty or delay in getting *yaks*. But I declined, as others told me this was merely a dodge to get their friend free, so that he might get right away.

It was on the next day, however, Saturday, 10th November, we attained our greatest altitude on the route when crossing the Karakoram Pass. The

Our latest news, therefore, on leaving Chinese Turkistan, was that the dervish had been captured, but that the murderer, after having been seen at Aksu, was supposed to have gone thence to Ush-Turfan, and taken refuge amongst the nomad Kirghese.

But the tragedy was not to end here. M. Dauvergne, being a resident of Srinagur, knew Dalgleish in his passing to and fro, and just about a year after he had raised a pile of stones the Frenchman appeared again on the Karakoram. He had with him this time a marble tablet, the cost of which had been contributed by public subscription, and this he was going to place on the spot where his friend was murdered.

Two Englishmen also accompanied him, Major Cumberland and Lieutenant (now Captain) H. Bower, the latter of the 17th Bengal Cavalry. Major Cumberland afterwards wrote some letters to *Land and Water*, Captain Bower sent an official report to the Indian Government, and to these two authorities I am indebted for most of my information of events happening after I left the country.

Dauvergne, Cumberland, and Bower reached the Karakoram on August 8th, 1889, and on that day (just 16 months after the murder) they erected the memorial to Andrew Dalgleish, Major Cumberland expressing the very natural wish that he had the head of Daud Muhammad to fix alongside.

The party then continued to the Taghdumbash Pamir, whence M. Dauvergne, after shooting wild sheep, returned into Kashmir. Cumberland and Bower travelled to Yarkand, whither the former went north in search of stags, whilst the latter proceeded to Kashgar in search of Daud Muhammad Khan.

Mr Bower had been authorised by the Indian Government so to do, and, on inquiring for the murderer at Yarkand, was told that he had been seen four days' march from Balkh. He then despatched two men by way of Tashkurgan to follow him up.

On Bower's arrival at Kashgar, M. Petrovsky was away on leave, but the secretary of the Consulate, M. Lutsch, who was then acting, gave all the information he could, but was unable to say where the murderer probably was, as rumours of his having been seen had come from almost every direction.

The Yarkand informer, however, having seemed very positive, Bower decided to send two men through Russian territory, thinking they might get ahead of the murderer should he proceed northward from Balkh; and these men he supplied with a letter addressed to Russian officers in French and English, and requesting that, in the event of the men requiring assistance, it might be afforded.

Bower himself then started for Aksu to make inquiries, but he learned whole region hereabouts was a bleak, desolate, and inhospitable waste, without fuel or forage. Leaving Brangsa, we passed through a narrow gorge, up the course of a little torrent for a mile, of slate detritus, the soil being soft and spongy. Fortunately, there was no snow on the Pass, up which we mounted by an easy track to an altitude of 18,550 feet.

My breathing was not much distressed thereby, so long as I remained in the saddle, but a very little walking sufficed to induce distress. The weather, however, was fine and fairly calm, so that in passing the natural boundary between Turkistan and India we could enjoy the thought of being 3,000 feet higher

only what was known when I was there. Just as he was about to come away, however, he heard of a man answering to the description, who had lived in the jungles near Karashar, and who entered the town on market days only to sell wood. Thither Bower went, failed to find the man, but discovered instead the ruined underground buildings near Kuchar and the Bower manuscript, referred to in Chapter XXXIII., and then returned to Kashgar.

Meanwhile, his scouts in Russian territory had been more fortunate, for one of them, going into the bazaar in Samarkand, suddenly came upon Daud Muhammad Khan keeping a pedlar's stall. The scout had known the murderer in Leh, and the latter, seeing that he was recognised, looked very uncomfortable; but the scout, fearing that his prey might get away, told him not to be afraid, for that he too had escaped from Leh and had letters for him at the *serai*, if he would await his return. The scout then went to the police, who accompanied him to the bazaar, where, instead of delivering letters, he clapped the man on the shoulder, saying, "Daud Muhammad—murderer!" after which the culprit was walked off to gaol.

On hearing this, Bower wrote to our ambassador in St Petersburg, to request that the prisoner might be handed over to him either at Batoum or Kashgar, but recommending the latter, in order that his being marched through a country where he was known might be a lesson to the natives.

Before the answer came, however, M. Lutsch sent a note to Bower, June 13th, 1890, saying, in reference to the extradition of the murderer of Mr Dalgleish, that he had just received news of the suicide of Daud Muhammad Khan, who had hanged himself in prison; and so ended the matter.

than the top of Mont Blanc, and riding over a very high pass, if not the highest in the world.

We now descended by a valley resembling that we had left, the track passing over bare gravel and clay, till, after a march of about seven hours, we arrived at Chougeh Jilga.

Again and again we had been reminded of the perils of our route by the almost numberless skeletons, chiefly of horses, lying about; whilst, among the caravans we met, one man told us that on the Saser Pass he had just lost six horses.

Moreover, on arriving at Chougeh Jilga, we found a pilgrim from Mecca with his horse dead and he himself starving. His fellow-pilgrims had declined to carry his saddle-bags, and left him to do as best he could. Also a man and woman on foot arrived at the place almost destitute. We were able to give the *Haji* some food at once, and in the morning I added some bread, cheese, tea, and a pair of gloves, after which the party in distress joined another caravan that fortunately happened to be passing, and we bade them farewell.

Having arrived at Chougeh Jilga on Saturday evening, I would fain have remained, according to our rule, to rest on the Sunday; but it was freezing, there was no fuel except the little we had brought for cooking, and no pasture for the horses. The *caravanbashi* accordingly said, and certainly with good reason, that we must go forward.

Haidar Haji now came to the fore, offering food for my riders, which I gladly accepted, or otherwise they would have had none, so badly had my contractor arranged for feeding them. By way of exchange, I served out to Haidar, and to several of both caravans, a quantity of chlorate of potash, which they seemed to appreciate, and which I read of in Dr Bellew's *Kashmir and Kashgar* as an antidote to the *dam*. From this all of us were suffering, more or less, though I enjoyed at Chougch Jilga an excellent night's rest.

At ten next morning we started in glorious weather, but experienced later a biting wind that called for still more wraps. In the course of the day we found ourselves amidst magnificent scenery, and came to Daulatbeg Uldi, where is a parting of ways—that to the left leading to the Depsang plateau, and the other to the right, by Kumdan—both meeting at the Shyok river, opposite Brangsa Saser.

At Daulatbeg Uldi was a tomb, and also three domed caves or huts, said to have been erected by a pilgrim. Beyond this point we met a solitary horseman, Abdul Aziz Khan, on his way to Kashgar, who handed me two letters—one, he said, was from Mr Redslob, and the other from the British Joint Commissioner. The wind was again blowing bitterly cold, and the situation was exposed, so that I did not stay to open the envelopes; and when, later on, I did so, I found a letter inclosed for Mr Hendriks at Kashgar, but could only carry it back to Leh.

Haidar Haji, in the course of the day, got ahead of us, so that after a march of nine hours, or fifteen miles, from Daulatbeg Uldi (rather a long Sabbath day's journey), we pitched tent by ourselves at Yapchan (or Gyapshan).

Owing to the straying of the horses during the night, we did not start on the Monday till noon, and followed down the bed of the Shyok in and out of the water, and then at nine miles passed through a narrow opening, where the river bed is nearly blocked by the end of a huge glacier. The glacier was of immense proportions, and threatened to overwhelm, by falling masses of ice and of stones, the luckless traveller who should approach too near. We waded through the cold river to a bank of loose pebbles and shingle at the foot of a lofty vertical cliff, like a wall.

This is Kumdan, and it struck me as one of the curious sights of the journey; besides which we had around us pinnacles of ice, some I judged 150 feet high, the growth of years, if not of centuries, reminding me of fountains and of trees in a variety of fantastic forms. In some places the river ice was strong enough to bear us; at others we had to scramble through the water; and thus we continued down the river course, till towards evening we crossed the stream at a place where the water was wide, and the current so rapid that our dog declined to face it; after which, at eight o'clock, we climbed to the camping-place at Saser Tschkun, or the foot of the Saser Pass.

Haidar Haji had arrived before us, and I was glad to sit by his fire whilst my tent was being pitched, and to give some more medicine to his men. We were camped in a wild, savage-looking place, and I was thoroughly tired out. Ever since we started, the clouds had threatened snow, which made me anxious, because we were hoping to reach Leh in seven or eight days, whereas, in the event of a considerable fall, we should have to make a *détour* of three or four days in addition.

When, therefore, my tent being ready, snow began to descend, my spirits sank; but recalling the many journeying mercies I had received, I was beginning to resign myself to whatever might be coming, when we were not unpleasantly surprised by Maulam Bai and his assistants. They had been quarrelling and swearing and wrangling incessantly during the day, but were now united in face of a common danger, and bursting out into a wild monotone, they repeated sundry prayers for the stopping of the snow and for propitious weather in crossing, on the morrow, the most dreaded pass on the journey.

The air was not so cold at Saser Tschkun as on the previous day, because there was less wind, and I roused the men very early next morning, though not with great success, for it was earlier than they approved, but I wished that we might have a long day before us. Previous to starting I served out medicine all round, and rubbed vaseline on the chapped and gashed faces of Amin and Muhammad Joo.

At half-past ten we began our march. Happily the fall of snow was slight, and the little that had fallen was rather to our advantage in crossing the ice. The sun, too, came out and the air was calm, so that I could heartily respond to the exclamation of one of the *Hajis*, "How good God is to give us such a fine day!"

It was not difficult, however, to understand that in bad weather the crossing would be one of the most horrible journeys in the world. "When the wind blows," said the men, "it cuts you in two." We were at an elevation of 17,800 feet, and at this altitude skeletons of dead horses were more numerous, perhaps, than on any other part of the Pass.

Riding up a rough gully for two or three miles, we crossed the watershed, and then continued up and down by an extremely difficult path between the side of an enormous glacier and the opposite hills, a narrow pass full of angular rocks and snowdrifts.

Presently we came to several colossal glaciers, the like of which I had never seen, and some of which we had to ride across. Here and there our horses had to scramble like cats up banks and inequalities of ground, to which I had become so accustomed as to have grown perhaps unmindful of danger ; for, on more than one occasion, the old *Hajis* called out to me to dismount, and not risk breaking my neck in such places as they had not dared to ride over.

On the whole I consider that day's work the most dangerous thing in travel I have ever done. I thought I had accomplished something in crossing the Muzart, but the Saser was far more difficult—the ice was of colossal proportions, and around us still towered snowy peaks to a height of more than 20,000 feet above the sea.

A nine hours' march took us through a grand piece of Nature's handiwork, but I was thoroughly tired at the end of it, partly because I was not well, so that I counted it no small mercy when we all safely reached Tut Yailak. Here we descended into the bed of a river, and camped on a gravelly flat under a glacier whence the stream issued.

There was scanty fuel, but better pasture. The night, however, was bitterly cold. A basin of water placed near the head of my bed quickly froze solid. The dogs wanted to come into my tent for warmth, and Joseph said the servants had passed a cold and comfortless night. I, too, had felt unwell and passed a restless night. We had, therefore, to comfort ourselves with the hope that possibly on the next night we might sleep under a roof instead of canvas.

Next morning we started soon after ten o'clock, and marched down the left bank of the river amidst granite rocks for three miles. Then we espied the first sign we had recently seen of man's handiwork, in the form of a rickety tree-bridge, 25 feet long, and of course without rails, across which one needed a cool head to ride a horse. Afterwards the way led down the right bank amongst huge masses of diorite by about the worst track possible. Beyond this we began a severe undulating ascent along a ledge which led us, after many halts to breathe our horses, to the summit of Karawal Dawan, 14,100 feet high.

Here we had unmistakably left behind the land of Muhammad and entered that of Buddha, for at the top of the mountain were a number of *obos*, and numerous flags with Tibetan inscriptions.

But something that interested us more was that, from this lofty height, we could distinguish, far below us, cultivated fields in the Nubra valley, and two settlements or villages—the first houses we had seen for many days, and for which now we longed. To these habitations we descended by a very steep track, and after a seven hours' march from Tut Yailak camped at Changlung, the *ultima thule* in this direction of Little Tibet.

The houses proved veritable hovels, and too bad to be preferred to the tent, but we had seen nothing of the kind since leaving Ak-Shor, and, rough as things were, it seemed like a return to civilisation. The Tibetans, or Bots, what few there were, showed a disposition to be helpful, and I was pleasantly surprised by the discovery that Muhammad Joo was linguist enough to speak not only Turki, but Tibetan, Hindu, Kashmiri, and a few words, I think, of Persian.

Presently the baggage horses and their leaders

arrived, one of the men, Tokhta Akhoon, coming to me with a broken head and a doleful tale against Maulam Bai. This *caravanbashi* had proved himself a bully of the first order, and seemed to understand so well how to hurt the feelings of his fellow-servants as well as their persons, that his abuse fairly wrung tears from them. His method of " swearing " was to insult their female relations, to say disgusting things of them, doing violence also to the memories of their parents.

On this day he had gone farther, and had struck Tokhta Akhoon when on the ground with a large stone, and made a gash in his skull; whereupon I told the bully pretty plainly that, if he could not lead the caravan without using so much filthy language to his servants, he had better go back to Yarkand; and henceforward I let him see that I was displeased with him, and not to be pacified by his making light of his cruelty.

I did my best to dress the wounded man's head, and then we celebrated our return to settled life by a good meal all round. This was more than the horses had had for many a day; but we were able now to get a few supplies for man and beast, including fodder, barley, and milk.

Next morning we were favoured with bright weather and comparative warmth, the rays of the sun in the valley being powerful. Setting out at noon, we travelled with some degree of comfort, the first sign that we were fairly in her Majesty's dominions being that we had a good pack-road, from which the large stones were cleared to either side.

We passed along the valley—from half-a-mile to a mile wide—along patches of turf and brushwood, jungle of buckthorn, tamarisk, myricaria, and roses. The stream, flowing over a bed of shingle in many channels, had to be crossed; and at seven miles from Changlung we passed through the extensive oasis of Ispangu. The hills, rising on either hand, were lofty and steep, of diorite and granite; whilst under the hills were fan-like oases formed in the felspathic sandy soil by streams, and producing wheat and barley, together with trees of willow, apricot, poplar, buckthorn, and occasionally elm.

We soon found ourselves not only among a new people, but, to some extent, among new birds also, for, in addition to rooks and magpies, we saw several smaller species, which it was useless to shoot, owing to the difficulty of retrieving them from the thorny jungle.

After a march of five hours we reached Panamik, a distance of less than 12 miles. Thence I despatched a letter to Leh to Mr Redslob, saying that, by doing three marches in two days, I hoped to arrive by the following Monday. The messenger, I was told, was to "fly," carrying the letter before him in a cloven stick, tied at the top (with red if announcing a death), and this without charge, because Joseph said I was an English *Sahib*, or gentleman; but it would not be done so for a trader.

At Panamik I slept in my first Tibetan house, typical of others I saw later on in Sikkim and elsewhere. Outside, Tibetan houses have a substantial and comfortable appearance, and are of two stories. The lower is given up to cattle, for stables, and for storage, whilst the upper is approached by a ladder. The sleeping-place assigned me was warmer, if not so clean as my own tent; but a fire was a doubtful luxury on account of the smoke, for which the only outlet was a hole in the roof.

I wished to put on paper some of our Tibetan surroundings, and had commenced by taking a view from Changlung of the head of the Nubra valley, with a grand snow mountain to the north-west. About 15

SIMBOOTI, OUR HOSTESS AT PANAMIK.

miles to the eastward is marked on Walker's map a mountain 25,170 feet high.

These interested me less, however, photographically, than the new race of inhabitants we had met, of whose beauty I cannot say much. The women were dressed in rags and sheepskins, but were unveiled, and had no objection, like the Muhammadan women, to being photographed. At Panamik my hostess, Simbooti, aged

35, was cheerful and better-looking than some of her sex, and very attentive to our wants.

One of the best photographs I took was that of the lama or parish priest at Panamik, aged 50, who presided at a Buddhist temple, and who stood before me holding in his hand a copper *kurgan*, or water-pot, and in it some peacock's feathers.

I secured views also of my lodging, as well as of the temple, and of monumental-looking erections called *chortens*, or relic repositories, which frequently inclose remains of revered lamas, sacred writings, consecrated objects, etc. No Tibetan passes these without depositing thereon some sort of oblation, if only a stone.

About a mile after leaving Panamik we passed some hot springs (the temperature of some of which Bellew found to be 167°); and here we overtook Haidar Haji, who had spent the previous day there, and remained for two hours in the water. Our broken-headed *karakesh* also would have liked to remain at Panamik for his ailments; but I urged him to come forward to Leh, and be treated by the Moravian doctor there.

We travelled accordingly with Haidar to Taghar (or Tughar), where I called on the *Sardar* Subhan, or headman, who had sent me two men to Panamik to see that the inhabitants did not refuse to sell supplies. We did not hear of any difficulties of this kind, though they said there was usually little of surplus produce in the valley to sell.

At the house of the *Sardar* we stayed to luncheon, and were regaled with sugar-candy, and, what I appreciated more, *sattu*, or parched barley, coarsely ground. They boiled it for me in milk, and I took quite kindly to this Tibetan fare, and asked for it often. This barley-meal is the staple diet of the Tibetan when on a journey,

for with a bag of *sattu*, moistened between his fingers
into dough pellets, he fares sumptuously ; his drinking
vessel for brick tea being a *koray*, or wooden basin,
which he carries in his breast as a bosom companion.

The *Sardar* we found to be a man in authority
over 40 hamlets, containing 300 houses. He had an
English gun, but wanted powder and shot, some of
which I sent him from a subsequent station. I gave
him, too, a small union-jack, several of which had been
packed up amongst my presents. Having left Panamik
at noon, in warm, sunny weather, we reached about
eight o'clock a place called Tirit, where I slept in poor
quarters, having passed during the day many *chortens*,
and observed many Buddhist erections perched on
the hills.

Hearing, on one occasion, a noise proceeding from a
house, I turned aside and entered, and found several
lamas going through a religious service. Before a
Buddhist altar, on which lights were burning, were six
lamas, ranged at right angles in two rows, beating
drums and cymbals, the leader holding in one hand a
bell, and in the other a *dorji* or *vagra*—an emblem of
the holder's power over evil spirits. There was no
congregation present, and my intrusion seemed to
attract no attention ; and they went on half singing,
half saying, what seemed the same words again and
again, having probably a certain number to get through
" to order " of the person who had called them into the
house for the benefit of their ceremonies.

On the next day we continued along the valley,
still bordered by barren hills rising 2,000 feet above
the river, and after about eight miles we halted for
luncheon, of tea and *sattu*, at Sati. Leaving this
place, our remaining dog stayed behind, the other

having succumbed to fatigue on the previous day. From Sati there are two routes to Leh: one follows the river route and crosses the Digar Pass; the other and direct route, which we followed, is by the Khardung Pass.

Beyond Sati the river is crossed in August by ferry, and the stream, flowing over a bed of boulders and sand, is then 200 feet wide, with a rapid current. But in November we were able, I think, to ford the stream, beyond which we had a long ascent, through a rugged gorge in the hills, leading to the Khardung plateau.

Patches of pasture occur at intervals in the ravine, which has a general width of 150 yards, and we met several peasants who had seemingly walked to long distances in search of fuel, and were returning with bundles of wood on their heads. In this gorge I shot a few small birds. Also, we overtook some of the Kashmiri soldiers, who had accompanied the caravans we heard of on the way to Shahidula, and we met some Buddhist devotees or dervishes, said to have come from Lassa.

Thus journeying for eight hours from Tirit we reached Khardung, at an altitude of 13,050 feet, at half-past six on Saturday evening. The village had 20 houses with a little pasture and cultivation, and here we determined to spend Sunday. They took us to what I suppose was a very rough specimen of a government bungalow, where one of our *haji* acquaintances had taken up his quarters in the best chamber, but which he gave up to me, as he intended leaving on the morrow.

What with the unglazed window, the smoke-hole in the roof, and the smoke-filled room, my abode was far from luxurious. It was pleasant, however, to spend a Sunday in rest, and quietly look at our Tibetan surroundings. I made a house-to-house visitation of the dwellings at hand, and distributed some Tibetan textcards, which were the only things of the kind I had.

Everywhere we had a kind reception, and I thought the women rather pleasing and certainly not shy, as were the women of Turkistan. They were, however, by no means numerous in this region, and although it is possible occasionally to find a man with more than one wife, it is less rare to find a woman with several husbands, not more than three, however, the *Sardar* said, in the Nubra valley. I was informed that on the other side of the river cases of polyandry exist, but not in Khardung village. Inquiring concerning the evident paucity of children, they told me there were only 15 in the village.

In the first dwelling we entered they were drying barley by the smoke of a dung fire, and in the next house the barley was being parched before grinding, whilst the housewife was making wheaten cakes something like *chupatties*, which she baked in a pan. Among other articles of food were pumpkins and onions brought from Taghar in the valley.

In the doctor's house, so-called, was a book on medicine, strapped between boards, said to have cost from 30 to 40 rupees. We also observed some earthenware and copper vessels for cooking, water being procured by melting ice. The tobacco-pipe in use resembled the *chilim* of Turkistan. Among our visitors who came to " salaam " us were several Kashmiri soldiers, one of whom said he was a tax-gatherer, who took by force what people did not pay.

Everything and everybody looked very dirty and exceedingly poor, though some in the village were said to possess as many as ten oxen or *yaks*, the latter of which cost from 15s. to 30s. each, a horse from 15s. to £4, and a calf a couple of shillings. We were more concerned, however, with the price of chicken, at from 3d. to 4d., and eggs at a farthing each.

Our stores were rapidly sinking; our native bread was all gone, and flour nearly so. Our last fowl and the last of our mutton were cooked at Khardung; added to which, the dried apricots were all eaten. It became of importance, therefore, to get forward, and we hired 15 *yaks* to take us over the Pass, each at a rupee and a half, or they were to receive two rupees if they got me to Leh by Monday night.

Haidar Haji, who knew his ground, went forward on Sunday afternoon to sleep at the foot of the Pass, and we were called on Monday morning at three for a final start at six. The rise for about ten miles was gentle, and I rode my horse, after which came a steep ascent of 1,250 feet. For this feat I was transferred to a *yak*, to whose hair I had to cling most uncomfortably and ungracefully to prevent slipping off behind.

The ascent was long, steep, and difficult. The height of the Pass, being 17,700 feet, was trying to the breath, and I voted the Khardung the most tedious Pass in some respects we had met with, besides which there was a wind, so that I felt sick, exhausted, and cold. Again, the descent was by no means easy, and there was difficulty in getting refreshment. Joseph managed half-way down to make me a cup of tea, and then, mounting my horse, I rode the remainder of a 12 hours' journey into Leh on the 29th day after leaving Yarkand.

Here I made for the Moravian mission-house, and

CROSSING THE MOUNTAIN

received a hearty welcome from Mr and Mrs Redslob
and Dr and Mrs Marex. I was put up in a simply
furnished but perfectly clean room, and never in my
life did I get with such delight between a pair of clean
sheets, for I had not been in a proper bed for five
months, and again and again, for whole weeks at a
stretch, had slept without undressing. Here, too,
after listening to Joseph's *patois* only for four months,
I heard once more English properly spoken, and enjoyed the delights of Christian society and fellowship.
I had now kindred spirits with whom to talk over
missionary matters, which we proceeded speedily to
do, and to consider my plans for Lassa.

CHAPTER XLVII.

A MISSIONARY VIEW OF CHINESE TURKISTAN.

Author's attention drawn to Western Mongolia as a mission-field, 338.—
An American Bible Society sending Scriptures from Shanghai, 339.
—Distribution among the Kalmuks, and at Aksu, 340.— Eager
purchasers, 341.—Sales at Kashgar; Mullahs at Yarkand, 342.—
Comparatively few Scriptures distributed; Lack of proper translations, 343.—Need for missionary effort, the good in Muhammadanism notwithstanding, 344.—More done for Chinese Turkistan by
Buddhists and Muhammadans than by Christians; Feasibility of
mission work; Muhammadanism shaky, and rulers neutral, 345.—
Climate salubrious and provisions cheap, 346.—Routes through
India, Russia, and China, 347.—Remarks on furlough, female
missionaries, and classes of workers, 348.—Suggested method of
procedure, and first missionary centre, 349.—A *résumé* for the
Church of Christ, 350.

I HAVE mentioned in the Introduction to this work the inquiries I made of Mr Hudson Taylor in 1883 concerning Western Mongolia as a mission-field. Four years later, my interest was rekindled and given a practical turn by Mr Crossett expressing the hope that a door would be opened for a pioneering tour from Peking, and asking me whether I would come out and lead the way.

I have told in my Introduction also the story how, when the English societies said they were unable to help, an American society came to the rescue, by means of which it was arranged that Scriptures in

Chinese and kindred languages should be sent from Shanghai to Lan-chow, and thence across the Gobi desert to meet me in Central Asia, whilst I was to collect those needed in West Asian languages as I went along.

Accordingly, I purchased in St Petersburg, at the depôt of the British and Foreign Bible Society, such Scriptures as were needed in Persian, Kalmuk, and some few other languages, which the Rev. W. Nicolson, its agent—always so kind and helpful—forwarded for me by parcel post to Kuldja. At Tiflis I had occasion to purchase a few copies in Hebrew, and at Tashkend found the last depôt of the Bible Society from which to make up my stores of Scriptures for distribution in Chinese Turkistan. Here I bought additional copies in Arabic, Hebrew, Persian, and Kirghese. Mr Bartsch, the depositary, gave me also some Chinese New Testaments which had by some means come from a bankrupt's stock into the hands of the town authorities, who, not knowing what to do with them, had presented them to him. All these Mr Bartsch kindly packed, and helped me, besides, in making sundry complementary arrangements.

At Kuldja, as I have said, I found that the American Bible Society had sent from Shanghai to my intended Chinese interpreter three boxes of Scriptures for me, or, in case we failed to meet, to be distributed by himself. One box he left at his home in China proper for lack of room in his cart, another he left at Urumtsi, to be called for on his return journey, and the third he brought forward and partially distributed during my first visit to Suiting.

Here, the people, discovering that we had books to

sell, came to the inn to purchase. One Chinaman compared our work to a certain custom of their own. "The heaven," said he, "is above us, and when our friends die, we in China go to a temple and pray to the gods, and then print a good book and give away 1,000 copies or so!" They were somewhat puzzled, however, at our charging money for the books, even though little. Still more were some of them perplexed that any Christian should come from China proper and not be a Roman Catholic, or from the west, as I had done, and not be a Russian. This was contrary to their usual experience in Suiting, and they suspected we were deceiving them.

I presented copies of the Old and New Testaments to the mandarins at Suiting; and gave or sold several copies at Kuldja to the student-interpreters at the Consulate, besides presenting others in Kalmuk to the Roman Catholic missionaries.

Upon the withdrawal of my interpreters, it was, of course, an important consideration with me, how these altered circumstances would affect the main object of my mission; but careful consideration seemed to show that it need do so less than at first sight might appear. Of the Scriptures brought from the east, about nineteen-twentieths were Chinese, and therefore suitable for Urumtsi and the towns on the northern road where Chinese populations predominated; whilst of Scriptures brought by me, four-fifths were in western languages, and were therefore needed for the Turki inhabitants of Chinese Turkistan.

Accordingly, as I moved from one camp to another of the Kalmuks, I made it a practice to leave a few copies of the Gospels printed in their language, but had no need of any other version between Kuldja and Aksu.

except in the case of the wretched opium-smoking official in his lonely abode at the Custom-house of Muzart-Kurgan, with whom I left a copy of the New Testament in Chinese.

After warnings received from the Russians as to the fanaticism of the Muhammadan Turkis, I was not at all sure how attempts to distribute the Scriptures among them at Aksu would be received. So I began, cautiously, by asking my Muhammadan host to accept two New Testaments in Kirghese and Persian, and one of Mrs Grimke's large and pretty illuminated text-cards, I think also in Persian. All of these he took with readiness, and afterwards expressed a desire for an Arabic Bible, which I gave him.

Then he set out to accompany me to the bazaar to pay visits to those who had come out on the day before to meet my caravan. We found them assembled in two parties at different *serais*, each with a *dostarkhan* spread with luscious fruits, and waiting to receive us, which they did with every sign of welcome. In the course of the visit, each was presented with a large illuminated card ; and upon my offering Kirghese and Persian Testaments each for 100 cash, to my agreeable surprise, they bought them all eagerly, and wanted more.

This eagerness to possess books received another illustration west of Aksu in a settlement of 40 families at Tum Chuk. Here a mullah came saying that he did not possess four *tengas*, but would go and get me, in exchange for my book, a piece of felt ; whilst another man came offering three *tengas*, which I took : so that afterwards a brisk trade commenced in Kirghese and Persian copies, and at last I declined to sell more, not wishing to dispose of too large a proportion of my slender store in this small place, but desiring to spread them as far as possible over the country.

At Kashgar we sold a good many copies in four languages at the Consulate, the purchasers deeming that the books would be regarded by the natives as valuable presents. Besides these, the only two Jews living in Kashgar came and bought two copies of Hebrew Scriptures. They appeared very poor, asked for a small copy of the Psalms as a present, and, on receiving the books in their "holy language," they kissed them and rubbed them against their foreheads.

The shrine of Khoja Aphak, outside Kashgar, is counted by Muhammadans the most sacred spot in Chinese Turkistan, and here I took my books almost in fear and trembling.

On the Sheikh's appearing, I informed him, as already stated, that I too was a mullah, and had brought some of our sacred books that I should like to present to the college—namely, the Bible in Arabic and Persian, and the *Inghil*, or New Testament, in Persian and Kirghese. All of these he accepted; in addition to which I left other copies at Kashgar with the Chinese mandarins.

At Yengi Hissar I pursued a similar policy on visiting the mullahs at the Kulbashi College, and also at Yarkand, where the mullahs at the colleges did not wait for me to bring the books, but themselves came out to me in the suburbs. I gave them, for two of their colleges, copies of the New Testament in Arabic, Persian, and Kirghese, with a Persian Bible and text-cards.

A young mullah of Yarkand presented himself, who, as I mentioned, did not on the first day receive a book, whereupon he came early the next morning to ask for one for himself, saying that he was too poor to pay for it even so little as $2\frac{1}{2}d$. I presented him with a copy, whereupon he joined his hands and devoutly offered a prayer on my behalf. The same sort of thing continued on our way to Khotan, as at Janghuia, where, amongst a mere handful of poor houses in the wilderness, we sold a dozen New Testaments.

It is hardly necessary to further multiply instances. Wherever we came we found the books readily bought by the people, and also accepted as presents by the mandarins, as well as by the mullahs in *medresses* and mosques, so that I can recall only one man (at Aksu) who showed any antipathy to our books, and even his opposition was passive rather than active.

Some of my friends (well meaning, no doubt) have expressed the wish that I had distributed more copies of the Scriptures, and in a certain sense I cordially wish so too. Looked at, however, from another standpoint, I think that for a pioneer journey I distributed about enough, for it should be remembered that I had not one copy in the real language of the country. Kirghese was the nearest, and the people sometimes complained that they could not understand it.

Those who could read Persian and Arabic were few and far between, and I doubt whether distribution in these languages was more appropriate than would be the distribution of French Testaments in England. The number of Chinese also who could read was small, so that were I, with my present information, starting again to do the journey in the same time, and under like circumstances, I should take just about the same stock of books as before.

Before starting I had hoped that the British and Foreign Bible Society would have had ready in time for me some of the Gospels in Uzbeg. They had one passing through the press, and I called at the depôt in Berlin, where the printing was being superintended, and saw also one of the translators at Tashkend. But I was too early. Any one going now would have the great advantage of carrying certain portions in Uzbeg, which would no doubt be nearer, if not exactly suited to, the requirements of the people, but even then the number who can read is not large.

Having now stated what I planned, and having given some idea of the distribution accomplished, let me pass to what as a pioneer I was able to learn.

In the first place, it was quite manifest that there was in Chinese Turkistan a crying need for missionary effort.

It is not necessary to attempt to minimize or to depreciate what is good in Muhammadanism. John de Marignolli bears true witness to their rigid attention to prayer, fastings, and other religious duties, as does Ricold of Monte Croce to their " reverence for the name of God, for the prophets, for the holy places, and their loving and peaceable conduct towards each other."

We can afford also to let Muhammadanism generally be judged by its best professors ; but the condition of the people of Chinese Turkistan, as sketched in the foregoing chapters, will speak for itself to such Christians as recognise their duty of obedience to their Master's injunction to make disciples of all nations (and therefore of these misguided people) by teaching them the nobler and higher truths of Christianity.

It is a saddening thought that Chinese Turkistan

should have been visited by men in tattered robes, who, by self-denial and persuasiveness, could win the country for Buddha; that in other ages the followers of the false prophet should have subjugated the valley to Muhammad; whilst the Christian Church should have done less than either to carry her greater blessings to this mountain-girt valley.

When my attention was first turned to this region, I thought no missionary from any branch of the Christian Church had been there. In this I was wrong; but it should be pointed out that this was the case for very many centuries, and for practical purposes is so now. The ground is occupied by no Christian Society, the one seeming exception to this being not so in reality.

What, then, might be said as to the possibilities there for mission work? The country has been gained for Buddha and conquered for Muhammad; why should it not again be won for Christ? In speaking upon the subject to M. Petrovsky, he was sanguine that a well-organised English or Russian mission would succeed in Chinese Turkistan, and he said that he had written on the subject to the Archbishop of Vierny.

Moreover, there are certain considerations which point to Chinese Turkistan as a favourable field for missionary effort among Muhammadans. First, the people having received Muhammadanism later than in the countries farther west, and their creed having been upset from time to time by Buddhists and others, it is not so deeply rooted as in some other countries.

Again, it is very important to remember that, though the people are Muhammadans, the rulers are not. Hence European missionaries might probably reckon upon being generally free from danger of violence and the petty persecution which in some Moslem countries forbids, and in others hinders, Christian effort, inasmuch as the Chinese mandarins would probably take up towards missionaries a position of neutrality.

Another important consideration for English missionaries is the salubrity of the climate as compared with that of India, Africa, and tropical countries. In earlier chapters I have given many statistics concerning the climate of the valley and its diseases. In regard to both Dr Bellew speaks favourably of the dryness of the atmosphere and the not inordinate heat, as well as the absence of fevers, cholera, and epidemics generally.

All these have suggested to my mind as exceedingly probable that some of the missionaries who are invalided home from the tropical regions of India, Africa, and China, might find in the high plateau of Chinese Turkistan a field of labour in which they might continue, instead of giving up, the work that many of them so unfeignedly love.

The annual necessity in India of going to the hills, often at a long distance and great expense, would hardly exist, and, if it did, might mean only a change of work from among the settled Turkis to the nomad Kirghese, and that for little more than the duration of a summer holiday or an itinerating mission.

Another consideration that might weigh with a Missionary Society is of an economic character, in that native provisions are, from an English point of view, exceedingly cheap. A sheep may be bought for less than half-a-crown, peaches 30 a penny, and other fruit in proportion. A manservant's wages, without food, cost only 10s. a month, and a gentleman's dyed sheepskin coat may be bought for 12s., though, of course, imported goods are dearer.

The country is unmistakably difficult of access. At

the same time, a would-be missionary need not picture himself getting there by either of the routes I have described, for these were about the most difficult ways of entering and leaving the country that I could possibly have selected. Now that the Indian Government have taken Kunjut in hand, and made roads, or at least bridle-paths, up to the far north of Kashmir, I suppose that the least difficult route to the Tarim valley would be from Liverpool to Karachi by steamer, rail to Rawul Pindi, thence to Srinagur by carriage (if not by rail), and so on horseback through northern Kashmir over the Baroghil, or possibly an easier pass to the eastward, and then along the Little Pamir before descending upon Yarkand.

There would be nothing very arduous about this; and if a sportsman's wife could accompany her husband across the Pamirs, by a more difficult route than this, to shoot wild sheep, I am greatly mistaken if missionaries' wives could not be found to accompany their husbands in the search for sheep of another kind.

But if this route were not practicable, there would remain the track to Kashgar from Khokand, which by Russian leave could be almost reached by the Trans-Caspian railway ending at Samarkand. If this permission were withheld, there would be the route through Western Siberia, leaving the rail at Orenburg or Tiumen, and crossing the Tian Shan from Vierny *via* Issik-Kul, or from Kuldja by one of the passes east of the Muzart.

Lastly, there would be the route overland from Peking, which, though very long and tedious, would have the great advantage of giving the missionary a peep at Chinese life; and carrying with him credentials from Peking, he would enter the country with more *prestige* than if he merely clambered over the mountains from India, even though armed with a Chinese passport.

If to the difficulty of access an objection be added as to the secluded position of the country, it should be remembered that a post reaches Kashgar two or three times a month, and that a letter or newspaper from London costs no more to go to Kashgar than it does to Paris.

The question of furlough and sending home of children would certainly be a difficult one; but I am assuming that, as far as climatic reasons go, this would scarcely be necessary, as in the case of countries farther south. The Roman Catholic missionaries at Kuldja had "burnt their boats," and were expecting never to see Europe again. "Why should we?" said they. "Our friends have forgotten us. We speak Chinese, dress as Chinese, think in Chinese, and have nearly become Chinese ourselves."

M. Petrovsky was decidedly in favour of married men, whether English missionaries or Russian popes; and I should regard it almost as a necessity that some of the members of a mission should be women. The Muhammadans do not understand the excellence or the honour of single blessedness. Male missionaries could never teach the Turki women, and without this the people would not be effectively reached.

Looking at the various classes of workers who should go, I should be disposed to mention, first, medical missionaries, whether they established hospitals or not; and next, perhaps, translators. Up to this point there would be nothing to bring the strangers into conflict with the religious prejudices of the people; and, whilst the physician's efforts were calling down many a blessing, the translator could be quietly preparing the way for the schoolmaster, and then might follow the evangelist.

This looks a more roundabout way than beginning with the New Testament method of evangelizing first: but it is instructive to bear in mind that the work of the Nestorian and Roman missionaries of the middle ages in Central Asia, who made no translations that we know of, "left not a wreck behind"; whereas, when on a change of dynasty persecution arose in Madagascar, copies of the Scriptures made by Protestant missionaries remained to keep alive the faith, and in the Trans-Baikal to this day Russian priests are using among the Buriats the translations made by Protestant missionaries who left the country half a century ago.

As to where the first missionary centre should be established, M. Petrovsky thought Kashgar would be the best. But he had never been at Yarkand; and if the missionaries were English I should be disposed to remember the words of Dalgleish, already quoted: "Many a blessing he will receive. But the moment he sets foot in Chinese Turkistan he must un-Russianise himself, and stand forth a pure Englishman, who, as a servant of God, has come straight from far-off England to heal the sick."

I cannot say that we met signs of antipathy to the Russians among the Turki inhabitants, though we certainly did among the Chinese of Kashgar. Seeing, however, that English *prestige* stands higher at Yarkand and that a British agent is resident there, I should have no hesitation in recommending that English operations be begun at Yarkand. They might then be extended successively to Aksu, Kashgar, and Khotan.

As for the Chinese inhabitants of Turkistan, I should be disposed, for some time to come, to leave them alone; for, in the first place, they are comparatively few in number; they come from so many provinces of China that I presume their variety of dialects would render work among them extremely difficult; they have no Chinese wives or children (at least very few) through whom they could be approached; besides which the missionaries at first would have quite enough to cope with in the active opposition of Muhammadans.

Such, then, are the principal features of what I thought, did, and learned in the course of my pioneer mission to Chinese Turkistan; and this *résumé* I would respectfully lay before the Church of Christ. If the results seem feeble and few, I regretfully allow that they are so; but would point out, if I may, that there is an open field for the reader to go and do more. The standing orders of our Master are not rescinded; the sleeping dust, the newly discovered tombstones, and the noble examples of Nestorian and Roman martyrs, alike call us to reconquer Central Asia for Christ.

May Christian hearts be stirred to take the matter up, to devote their lives to the work, and thus to help in making disciples among all nations!

CHAPTER XLVIII.

PLANS CONCERNING LASSA.

Lassa, an appropriate *finale*, but difficult, 351.—Stirred to activity by Mr Blackstone, 352.—Temporarily deterred, 354.—Help from the Archbishop of Canterbury, 355.—Assistance offered from Diplomatists, and Rev. Hudson Taylor, 356-57.—Decision of *Manchester Guardian*; Books and MS. from Mr Markham, 358.—Commendatory letter from the Primate, and supplementary letter to the Dalai Lama, 359-60.—Tibetan translator unprocurable in Europe, 364.—Inquiries at Berlin and St Petersburg; Letters to Viceroy of India and Mr Redslob at Leh, 365.—Letters received at Kuldja, and abandonment of route through Kiria, 366.—Interview with Resident-designate at Lassa, 367.—Altered plans, 369.

TO reach unapproachable Lassa suggested itself from the outset as an appropriate *finale* for my journey in Chinese Turkistan. The Russian officers to whom I mentioned the idea in 1882 thought it would be very difficult, and when, in the following year, I inquired at the Chinese Legation in London, I was told at once that there were political difficulties in the way.

Four years later, I learned that I should not be likely to secure the help of the Chinese Government in attempting to approach the Tibetan capital from east or south, though I did not gather that they had any particular objection to my trying it on my own responsibility from the north or west. In talking with

Mr Ney Elias, he thought that getting into Tibet was quite out of the question.

Accordingly, when I was considering the reasons for and against a pioneer mission, Tibet was not included in the programme, nor was any mention made of it in my first manifesto, which was headed simply "A Projected Tour to Eastern Turkistan."

The first person to stir me to active effort for Tibet was a gentleman I know only by correspondence, Mr William E. Blackstone, of Illinois. After perusing in 1886 my *Russian Central Asia*, then recently published, he wrote saying he was in communication with a very poor, quasi-medical missionary, who had gone to Asiatic Russia, and who, he thought, "would be very thankful if I would donate him a copy of my book."

I am afraid the wicked question stole into my mind. "Then why, my friend, don't you spend a couple of guineas and send him one?" But better thoughts, happily, succeeded. I presented a copy, as suggested, and so began my acquaintance with Mr Blackstone, to whom presently I had occasion to write, and in so doing mentioned that I was contemplating a journey to Central Asia.

In reply he wrote, in December 1887, thus: "I am glad to learn that you still hope to undertake the journey through Mongolia and Kashgar. It seems to me exceedingly important that this region should be opened up to mission work, and nothing would hasten this more than such a trip as you propose and the publication of your investigations and experiences.

"I pray that God may open the way for the funds to be provided. About what will the expense be? I should be happy to contribute my mite."

Asked as to the equivalent of his " mite " in figures, Mr Blackstone replied : " The region through which you propose to pass is one that I have long prayed might be opened to the Gospel. And in the hope that your journey might lead to such results, I wish to say that you can depend on me for £100 of the £1,000 which you say you shall need. I will forward it wherever you direct as soon as the rest is provided."

Within a month of receiving this letter, I telegraphed for the money, which came, and with it this interesting recital. " I must tell you that, coming a little sooner than I expected, I had not the money at command, but I took it to the Lord, and told my good wife it was of the Lord, and that in some way He would provide.

" The next morning a friend had some money paid in unexpectedly, and I made arrangements to use this for a time, and procured the draft ; then I went to the Christian conference in Chicago, where I was to speak last evening on the subject of the Lord's Coming and the world's evangelisation. Just as I entered the room a gentleman to whom I had loaned some money (years since), the circumstances of which were peculiar, so that I had not the least expectation of payment (at present), beckoned me and handed me a cheque for £100! I was nearly overcome with surprise and emotion, for it was plainly the hand of our blessed Lord."

I hope Mr Blackstone will pardon my making this use of private letters, but I feel sure his words and deeds will interest not a few of my readers. Other sentences that practically affected me were : " I hope your journey may be very productive, as heretofore, in seed-sowing, and especially that it may show the possibility of locating missionaries in the extremes of

Chinese territory. And, oh! my dear brother, how I do wish you could also get into Tibet!" The last sentence was very much like a spark falling upon gunpowder, and I asked straightway, "What will you give?"

Whilst waiting for the answer I was wondering whether to set about raising a further sum for Tibet, but succeeding considerations suggested that I had better make sure first of Chinese Turkistan. On November 30th I saw the late Mr Colborne Baber, an expert who gave me much information, but said that my idea of getting into Tibet was quite hopeless. "If," said he, "the Indian Government lately could not get in the friendly mission of Macaulay, what chance has an individual of doing so?" Accordingly, when sending out my circular letter on December 13th, asking for introductions, I said nothing about Tibet.

But a week later, on the anniversary of my ordination, when I usually overhaul my affairs spiritual and temporal, I considered further the proposed Tibetan appendix to my journey.

The reasons for the attempt seemed that, on finishing the journey round Chinese Turkistan, I should be near the Tibetan frontier, supplied perhaps with Tibetan Scriptures, accompanied, as I expected, by interpreters, armed probably with a Chinese passport, and though I was led to expect no official help, I was not forbidden to do what I could on my own account. In addition to this there was the glamour of trying to enter a city where no European now living has set foot, besides the, to me, higher consideration that throughout Tibet proper there is not a single missionary of any denomination whatever.

On the other hand, funds were not yet forthcoming :

and the attempt upon Tibet was an undertaking big enough in itself, without tacking it on to a previous expedition by no means insignificant: I had little information about the country; a medical missionary for whose services I had asked had been refused by his committee; and I thought I might learn much during the journey to Turkistan that would be useful if on another occasion I attempted Tibet. I concluded, therefore, unless something unforeseen should arise, not to do more at present.

But to banish the matter from my mind was not so easy. On the same day that I received from the Archbishop of Canterbury a contribution for Chinese Turkistan as "A token of good will," Mr Baber pronounced my Tibetan idea to be hopeless; but another thought had come into my mind upon my bed, and it seemed almost an inspiration.

I had been reading Turner's book on Tibet, and the exchange of letters in those early days between the Tibetan and Indian authorities, and the thought flashed into my mind: How would it do if I asked the Archbishop of Canterbury to give me a letter to the Dalai Lama, then go to the frontier, and pose as an English lama bearing a communication from the Grand Lama of the West to the Grand Lama of the East, and ask for permission to enter the country and deliver my message?

This may strike the reader as extremely visionary, but it so far influenced me on the eve of applying for my passport for Chinese Turkistan, that I wrote in my diary: "I intend to apply to-morrow to the Chinese Legation for a passport for China proper, Turkistan, *and Tibet*. The last, to all human appearances, is hopeless, but if no one tries none will succeed."

And these words became to me something like a watchword, steeling my determination against all prophecies of failure. Did not my friends, thought I, to a man, regard my attempting Siberia in 1879 as utterly useless? The Secretary of the Bible Society at that time gravely informed me that "The Committee thought I had undertaken more than I could possibly perform," and Count Schouvaloff, the Russian Ambassador, though favourable, deemed my project Utopian.

So again, in 1882, I remembered well how one member of the Bible Society's Committee, during my application for a grant of books, leaned forward and asked with surprise and incredulity, "Do you mean to say you are going to try to enter Bokhara?" and, upon my replying in the affirmative, he leaned back as if judging it hopeless to say anything further to one so quixotic.

Yet, in both cases, I succeeded. Why, then, should I not try whether God's time for opening Tibet were come? Besides which I believed I should not "toil in vain." I was undertaking service for a Master who once said, "She hath done what she could"; and I desired that something similar might be true of me.

Accordingly, on the 2nd of December, I mentioned in high quarters my thoughts concerning a letter from the Archbishop, which were not only not laughed at, but offers were tendered of diplomatic help. Then came days of alternate cloud and sunshine. I wrote to two millionaires with an eye to funds, but neither responded, and upon my seeking literary employment, thereby to raise money, two editors declined. Mr James told me on December 22nd, as did Ney Elias and Baber, that for me to attempt Tibet was hopeless.

But on the 23rd came a cablegram from Mr Blackstone—"£100 more for Tibet." On the day following he wrote a letter, adding, "I have been much in prayer for you, and we shall continue to remember you in all your journey, especially asking that God will enable you to enter and go all through Tibet, thus opening up this last stronghold of the Dragon's dominions. I suppose I little appreciate the dangers, privations, and hardships of the undertaking, and from a human standpoint one might well nigh despair of ever accomplishing it. But there is nothing too hard for God."

This generous encouragement was followed by a telegram from a medical missionary—"Yes"; namely, that he was willing to accompany me from Kashmir, and I saw extracts from a letter to Mr Hudson Taylor, that one of his agents treated it as a light matter to go round Turkistan, and said that if we got no farther than Yarkand or Khotan he should not be overjoyed.

This put me upon my mettle, and helped to unsettle the passive position I had assumed. Again, I was calling upon an octogenarian friend, and telling him I was going to Chinese Turkistan, upon which he appeared much affected, and, to my surprise, said, " I do not like your undertaking so long an expedition upon so little as a thousand pounds. If you get into any difficulty you may draw upon me for any amount up to another hundred." I pointed out that in such an eventuality to remit money to Chinese Turkistan would be extremely difficult, but if he would give me £50 I would accept, and if I had no need return it. And I made the like offer to Mr Blackstone and the editors—namely, that if I did not succeed in entering

Tibet. I would return what was not spent in the endeavour.

Whilst thus the matter was in the balance, it was kindly decided for me by the unknown writer of a paragraph in the *Manchester Guardian*, who informed the public that the Reverend Dr Lansdell was going to Tibet. This was news to me, and at first not very pleasing, for I feared that if through the press my plans reached the authorities in China, it would be just the thing, perhaps, to stop me.

The *Manchester Guardian* followed this up by spontaneously requesting me to write some articles, and offered to provide for the expedition some of the "sinews of war." I invited the help, too, on a small scale, of the Royal Geographical Society, but the Council declined. Mr Clements Markham, on the other hand, of whom as a writer on Tibet I asked advice, was very sympathetic, gave me several useful books, and, what I deemed more valuable still, a manuscript brought from Tibet by Mr George Bogle.

I hoped to make capital of this, in connection with the letter I had concocted, and which I thought to ask the Archbishop to sign, commending me to the Dalai Lama. I showed the rough draft to Mr Hudson Taylor, who approved it, as did Colborne Baber, the latter repeating that I had not the least chance of entering Lassa. In writing, I endeavoured to copy the inflated style of the Tibetan letters in Turner's book, and I went to Bethnal Green Museum to see among the Jubilee presents the form, colour, dimensions, etc., of the imperial address then recently sent to our Queen by the Emperor of China.

On sending my draft to the Archbishop, his Grace hesitated (wisely, as it afterwards proved) to sign the letter as I had written it, thinking it would be scarcely seemly for him, on the ground of being a chief officer of a Christian Church, to address a non-Christian hierarch. Wishing, however, to assist me if possible, his Grace kindly wrote a more general commendatory document, which read thus:—

"ADDINGTON PARK, CROYDON,
"19th January, 1888.

"This is to certify that the Reverend Henry Lansdell, Doctor of Divinity, and Fellow of the Royal Geographical Society, a learned and excellent clergyman of the Church of England, and a traveller of great distinction, is, with my full knowledge and approbation, undertaking a journey through the regions of Central Asia and China; his journey, however, having no political, military, or commercial object whatsoever.

"If, therefore, it should be possible and agreeable to the authorities to grant to Doctor Lansdell special facilities for visiting the ancient city of Lassa and other places of interest and importance in Tibet, I shall esteem it a kindness, tending to promote that fuller knowledge of one another's welfare which is conducive to the good of the various nations of the earth.

"(*Signed*) EDWARD CANTUAR,
*Archbishop of Canterbury; Primate of
All England and Metropolitan.*"

This letter I thought would answer my purpose, and I had it engrossed on a large sheet of paper, printed with a lithographed border of flowers. This the Archbishop signed, and permitted to be affixed thereto the archiepiscopal seal of Canterbury. The document was then mounted on a piece of rich yellow satin, placed as a scroll in a red morocco satin-lined case, and the whole inclosed for travelling in a tin cylinder—a precious document fit to send down to posterity!

Then I concocted a letter from the humble Lama Henry Lansdell, wherein I indulged freely in all the flowers of Tibetan rhetoric, and reading thus:—

"From the humble Lama Henry Lansdell, Doctor of Divinity, Member of the Royal Asiatic Society, and Fellow of the Royal Geographical Society, of London, to the illustrious Dalai Lama in Lassa, Ruler and Chief of the Lamas throughout Tibet, China, Mongolia, Siberia, Turkistan, and other countries of Asia.

"May the seas and mountains waft peace and prosperity to the Rulers, Lamas, and People of Tibet!

"Whereas I have the honour of bearing a letter from the Archbishop of Canterbury, the Chief English Lama, and my ecclesiastical superior, to the authorities in Tibet, and whereas the letter sets forth that I am a traveller, I beg leave to explain that, in one journey of 76,000 *li*, I have travelled round the world, traversing Siberia from west to east, crossing America and sailing on two oceans for 30,000 *li*. I have visited, with two exceptions, every country in Europe, as well as Russian Turkistan, Khokand, Bokhara, and Khiva, and from all these governments I have received the greatest kindness, with facilities to visit and to study their institutions, so that I have been enabled to write concerning them several large books.

"I now purpose during the coming summer to travel again in Asia, through Kuldja to Urumtsi, and round the Chinese New Dominion to Turfan, Aksu, Kashgar, Yarkand, Khotan, and other towns; after which, in the following spring, I should much like to be allowed to pass through your country and to visit the illustrious and holy cities of Lassa and Tashi Lumpo.

"I beg to say that I am furnished with a passport entitling me to travel in the Chinese dominions under the protection of the authorities, also four letters of commendation to the Governor-General of Ili, and to the Commander-in-Chief of the Chinese forces south of the Tian Shan, the letters being from the Marquis Tseng, from his successor Lew Tajen, the Chinese Minister in London, and from Hung Tajen, the Chinese Minister in Paris and St Petersburg. Also Lord Salisbury, Prime Minister of Her Majesty the Queen of England and Empress of India, has instructed the English Minister at the Court of Peking to ask for me other favours for travelling in the Celestial Empire.

"The Archbishop's letter speaks of me as a 'learned clergyman,' in keeping with which it is the great object of my life to make religion and learning flourish.

"I am hopeful, Grand Lama, that you enter into my feelings, and that your desires for the spread of knowledge accord with mine. I have learned with much satisfaction that, 114 years ago, the Teshu Lama, at that time Guardian of the Infant Dalai Lama, after sending a dignified letter, interceding for the Bhotanese to the Governor-General of Bengal, received with great hospitality and kindness two of my countrymen, Mr Bogle and a surgeon named Hamilton. So warm indeed was the friendship that grew up between the Teshu Lama and Mr Bogle, that when, five years later, the Lama was about to visit Peking, he desired Mr Bogle to go by sea to Canton, promising to obtain the Emperor's pass for him to proceed and join the Lama at the capital.

"Also the Lama gave to Mr Bogle a long scroll of Tibetan writing, describing the laws and religion of your country, a translation of which has been widely read by my countrymen. You will be interested to hear, Grand Lama, that I am bringing this very manuscript with me, which has been carefully preserved in England for more than 100 years, and concerning the meaning of which I should like to have further instruction, seeing that we know so little in England of your books and sacred writings.

"I do not intend to be accompanied by armed soldiers, but by a physician bringing many medicines wherewith, if it be the will of Heaven, to cure your sick, as well as an interpreter into Chinese, perhaps by other interpreters, if needed, and a few servants.

"I desire to collect specimens of plants useful for medicines, also animals, birds, fishes, and insects, all of which, in England, we gather from various parts of the world, admiring the Divine Wisdom with which they are made, and striving to learn in what way they may be of service to man.

"Further, I shall be thankful for any information that may be given me, or objects shown to me, connected with your religion, manners, and customs, especially ancient writings or monuments that have come down from the great and wise men of the past; whilst I shall be happy, if any desire it, to give such information as I possess concerning the manners, customs, and religion of the kingdoms of the West; also to show portraits of our Chief Lama and other great men, as well as pictures of places and buildings in England.

"I pray you then, Grand Lama, receive me whilst

passing through your country, as I have been received elsewhere, with kindness; and give me the opportunity to learn more of you and your people. Then shall my heart, like the blossoms of spring, abound with satisfaction, gladness, and joy; and let me assure you that any learned lama whom you may please to send will be heartily welcomed in England, where tens of thousands of my countrymen are anxious to know more of you and your country's welfare. Thus will peace and goodwill be established between us, and I, with many others, shall not cease to pray for the prosperity and happiness of the people of Tibet!

"I should like to enter Tibet from Ladak, because I shall probably winter there, and there live the only persons I know who can read and write a letter in Tibetan and English. I am asking them to make a translation of this letter, and to send copies by Darjeeling and other routes to Lassa. Upon receiving one of these I would ask your Holiness to send me a reply through Darjeeling, as the quickest route, in Tibetan and Chinese, or perhaps one of the languages of India or Turkistan, to the care of the British Joint Commissioner at Leh, who will forward it to me.

"Will your Holiness also kindly instruct the lamas and officials on my route to afford me facilities for travel in the early part of next year, so that by the will of Heaven I may have a prosperous journey, and pay my respects to your Holiness and to his Excellency the Chinese Resident in Lassa?

"(*Signed*) HENRY LANSDELL, D.D.

"WRITTEN IN LONDON, *February*, 1888.

"P.S.—If an official guide might be sent to me to the frontier at Leh, either through Tibet or Darjeeling and India, I would gladly pay the cost of his journey and remunerate him for his services."

This letter I showed to two diplomats, one of whom thought the document exceedingly ingenious, and the other offered sundry valuable hints and heartily wished me success. But now came the question of translation. Mr Hudson Taylor said he did not envy the man who had to translate it into Chinese, and I could hear of "Never a clerke at Oxen-forde" or elsewhere in Europe who could do it.

So, bidding farewell to my octogenarian father, who realised but too truly that he might never see me again (for he died before my return), and giving directions about my private affairs in case of death, I started forth, prepared for whatever might befall me on my pioneer mission to Chinese Turkistan. I had also in mind, as an unpublished appendix to my principal work, to enter Tibet, and even Lassa if possible, and to leave no stone unturned until it might be said that I "had done what I could."

I had made friends at the office of the Moravian Missions in London, who wrote about me to their missionaries at Leh, and, with reference to my precious scroll, packed in my trunk, I was told that perhaps Pastor Rechler, once resident in Little Tibet, could do the translation. I arranged, therefore, to stop for this purpose at Berlin, where I received a letter written by him from a remote Prussian village, dissuading me from coming to him, for that the task was too difficult and technical for his rusty Tibetan.

In speaking to the Chinese Minister at Berlin, I

was gently feeling my way to matters Tibetan, when his Excellency straitly warned me against attempting Tibet. The Governor of Szechuen, he said, some time since desired a mandarin to go into Tibet ; whereupon the Dalai Lama said that if he allowed this, the English too would want to enter, and so the mandarin was obliged to return : after which the Minister added that, in making such an attempt, I might get into difficulties.

I then pushed on to St Petersburg, where I met Prjevalsky, said nothing to him of the Archbishop's letter, but broached to him the possibility of my attempting to enter from Khotan *via* Kiria. He said it was impossible in summer to get into Tibet from Kiria, though it might be done with great difficulty in late autumn, but it would be better to enter from Ladak.

I said that an Englishman (meaning Carey) had come down from the plateau by Kiria. "Yes," he said, "but to come down a mountain is one thing, and to get up it another. I myself tried and failed." He wished me success, however, and hoped that we should meet in Lassa, adding that, with 50 soldiers, a man in Tibet might go where he pleased.

I next passed on to Kharkof, whence I wrote to Lord Dufferin as Viceroy, informing him of my plans, and praying his Excellency to smooth my way by writing on my behalf (1) to the British Resident in Kashmir ; (2) to the Joint Commissioner at Leh, that he would forward letters ; (3) and to such persons as might be able to establish my credit north of the Himalayas, with a view to the possible cashing of cheques.

This letter I posted at Batoum with two others—

one to the Rev. Rylands Brown at Darjeeling, asking him, if possible, to forward letters received from Mr Redslob to Lassa, and the all-important one to Mr Redslob at Leh.

To Mr Redslob I inclosed copies of the Archbishop's and my own letters, desiring him to translate them into Tibetan, and of my own to make five copies destined for Lassa—one through Mr Rylands Brown at Darjeeling, one through the Moravian missionary at Kaelang, one to be forwarded by himself from Leh, and two to be sent to Kuldja to me, on the chance of my being able to send one possibly by the Kalmuks from Karashar, and the other to be carried by myself *via* Kiria. I asked him also (having previously communicated with the Moravian authorities at Herrnhut) whether he could meet me at Yarkand to give information concerning Tibet generally, and possibly accompany me over the Himalayas, or even to Lassa.

My project being thus launched, I continued to Kuldja, where I found a letter from Mr Carey, wishing me success, but not concealing his opinion that the enterprise would be one of much toil and hardship, and but too likely to end in disappointment, possibly even disaster.

The supposed route through Kiria and Polu, he pointed out, would be a deeply interesting journey, but it would be exploration of the first order of difficulty, as the marching distance would be about 1,000 miles over an elevated, mountainous, and unknown country, at no point in which could I be certain of obtaining supplies. It would be absolutely necessary, therefore, to carry everything wanted for man and beast (except water, grass, and fuel) for at least six months, and this would involve very difficult and expensive arrangements.

Need I say this letter took away my breath? Prjevalsky shook my hopes of entering *via* Kiria; Carey smashed them; and seeing in the light of subsequent events that Prjevalsky's last expedition failed to enter by Kiria with £7,000 for resources, I judged it no discredit to me not to have gone forward when I had barely £500. But, added to the financial difficulties, another had cropped up of which I learned first at Kuldja—namely, that the Indian Government was at war with Tibet, having sent a military expedition and killed several Tibetans on the Sikkim frontier.

When things, however, were looking their blackest, there came suddenly a rift in the clouds which enkindled new hopes. One of the diplomats in London, whilst wishing me well, advised: "Try and make things square with the Chinese Resident at Lassa." "But how can I possibly do that?" thought I, "seeing I have not the least idea of his name or how he can be approached."

Imagine, then, my surprise when in the Ili valley I was talking to a native, and speaking of my wish to enter Lassa, he told me that the *Tsian-Tsiun Seh* had been the second Chinese official in Lassa for eight years, and had only recently come away; that the temporary Resident there was Shung, hereafter to be assistant; and that Ch'ang K'eng, the *Tutung*, or Vice-Governor, and head of the Manchu military, then in Suiting, had been newly promoted premier Resident (as I understood him) at Lassa, for which place he was to set out in a few days on an eight months' journey, from the Ili valley.

"Surely," I exclaimed, "this is the finger of God!

for of all men upon the face of the earth, this is one
I did not expect to meet with." Needless to say,
I sought an interview with Ch'ang. He struck me as
a superior man, and manifested interest in a new map
I showed him of Tibet. I gave him sundry presents
—an air cushion, whereon to rest his bones during his
long journey, a wool helmet to keep warm his shaven
head, the Old and New Testaments, and a pair of
binoculars. He asked much about my travels, when
they began, and what had been gained thereby. He
appeared pleased when I told him why I wrote books,
and I said that I strove to make religion flourish. I
showed him the Archbishop's letter, in all its glory,
told him my plans for getting a translation to the
Dalai Lama, and asked if he would help me in my
endeavour to enter Lassa.

His answer I thought very candid; but, reasonably
enough, he hesitated to make any promises. He said
he had the will to help me, but until he arrived at his
post he did not know what he could do. "As a man
of education," he said, "of course you know that the
entry of Europeans is strictly forbidden : but if, when I
get there, that rule is relaxed, then I shall do for you
the best I can. Come to me," he said, "and I will
tell you, yes or no."

This interview at Suiting I followed up by a letter
sent from Kuldja repeating my request, and asking
Ch'ang to tell the authorities in Lassa that he had
seen me and also the Archbishop's letter. I said, too,
that if I found no answer from the Dalai Lama at Leh,
I should probably go forward to Darjeeling, and about
March or April, the time I supposed he would arrive,
I might send to Lassa to ask permission to enter the
country.

I also wrote to the *Tsian-Tsiun* to the effect that it had long been a great desire of mine to visit Lassa, and that I had written to the Dalai Lama asking permission. In case I obtained it, I should like to pay my respects also to the Chinese officials. Would he, then, give me a letter to them, saying that I came properly recommended to him from the Chinese Legation in London, and that I was the bearer of a letter from the Chief Lama in England to the authorities at Lassa?

From the *Tsian-Tsiun* I received no answer, but Ch'ang sent an adjutant a distance of 50 miles to Kuldja, with a present of two pieces of satin, a fan, and two canisters of tea. My letter he returned, saying that he did not understand Manchu, and repeating that he could promise nothing, but advised me not to rely upon him, as perhaps he would have no power to help. He added, however, that we had met as friends, and he would do what he could. In addition to what had been said of Ch'ang, who was proceeding, *via* Si-ning and the Chinese official road, to Lassa, I heard also that a certain official at Lassa, No-man Khan, had sent an officer, Khan-wang, to Karashar, where he now was, and that he was to return in the eighth month by a short route to the south.

I saw no way of making use of this gentleman, or of attempting to accompany him, by the route I suppose afterwards taken by M. Bonvalot; so I wrote to Mr Redslob, telling him of our unexpected meeting with a future Lassa Resident, and announcing my altered plans to cross the Muzart Pass; but I heard nothing of Mr Redslob till September 25th, as we were leaving Yarkand for Khotan.

At this juncture my prospects did not look worse

for Tibet than I expected. The Baboo Chandra Das, though unable to accompany me, sent a sympathetic message through Mr Rylands Brown from Darjeeling; and Mr Redslob, though unable to come to Yarkand, promised to meet me at the head of the Nubra valley, saying that to go with me to Lassa would be just the thing he had been wishing to do for years. And this is how matters stood when, as I have already stated, we arrived on November 19th at Leh.

CHAPTER XLIX.

THE JOURNEY HOMEWARDS.

Remainder of journey as concerned with Lassa; Letter to Dalai Lama, 371.—Interview with Tibetan trader; Entrance from Leh blocked; Prospect of admission through Sikkim, 372.—Departure from Leh, 373.— The situation at Rawal Pindi; Journey to Calcutta, 375.—Reception by Viceroy, 377.—Meeting with Chandra Das, and tidings of Mr James Hart; Journey to Darjeeling and Kalimpong, 378. — Proposed sending of letter to Dalai Lama through Nepal, 380.—A further motive for attempting Nepal, 381. Journey to Peking recommended; Subsidiary schemes of usefulness, 382.—Journey to Khatmandu, 383.—Maharajah's unwillingness to forward letter, 385.—Interview with Nepalese Resident at Lassa, 386.—Distribution of Nepalese Scriptures, 387.

I HAVE already spoken of "a pioneer mission to Chinese Turkistan" as my work, and compared my designs upon Lassa to an appendix. The appendix in this case far exceeded the work itself; but I shall here confine myself mainly to such portions of the remainder of the journey as concern my attempt on Lassa.

On reaching Leh I lost no time in asking what had been done with my letter to the Grand Lama. The difficulty and technicalities of the translation were such that, though Mr Redslob had for years been translating the Scriptures into Tibetan, he did not feel equal to the task of translating my letter. He had found a man, however, who, for payment and with his help, had done it; but when Mr Redslob went on to ask him to deliver the missive in Lassa, he said it was more than his head was worth. And each person invited to carry it replied that a native taking to the Grand Lama such a letter would probably be put to death.

Two days later I had an interview with a trader, Munshi Palkyes, just come from Lassa, having been sent as envoy by the Maharajah of Kashmir; but he gave no hope that I should be permitted to enter the forbidden territory. He said their books commanded them to allow no foreigner to enter their country, and that the Tibetans did not promise obedience to the Chinese in religious matters, but only in secular affairs.

Further, that if I presented myself on the frontier, I should be turned back, just as some Russians were, said he, three years before, "though armed with a yellow passport from Peking." I purchased from this man several curios just brought from Lassa, whose 300,000 lamas, he said, were to a man adverse to any treaty whereby foreigners should be admitted, though the peasantry, he thought, were not opposed.

Under these circumstances there was no hope of my entering from Leh. Besides this, I was informed that the Indian Government forbade British subjects in India from attempting it, and Mr Redslob told me how he had several times been followed and watched during his summer itinerating journeys lest he should break bounds.

But there was something also to be said on the other side, for Mr Redslob had told me that Ney Elias was at that moment on the Sikkim frontier helping forward negotiations for peace, and he suggested that this friend might possibly help me to get in, or to send in letters from thence. Better than this, Mr Redslob expressed his willingness to accompany me in the following spring as interpreter; and upon his asking, by way of a feeler, Gergan, his *munshi* (a son of the former treasurer to the Dalai Lama), whether he would accompany him as servant and guide, *via* Darjeeling, the man consented, though somewhat afraid of the heat of the Indian plains.

I wrote, therefore, from Leh to the Moravian Board at Herrnhut, mentioning my singular meeting with the coming Chinese Resident at Lassa, and asking whether, if I should receive permission to enter Tibet, Mr Redslob might be free to accompany me from the opening of the passes in May till the following winter. Then I added, "As Mr Redslob is at present the only person I know who can speak English and Tibetan, I hope the Board will consider very carefully and prayerfully before they say 'No.'" Mr Redslob also wrote, pointing out how it might possibly be done, and I then made ready to depart.

I would gladly have stayed longer at Leh, to have seen more of this Moravian Mission. The simplicity, self-denial, and devotion of Moravian missionaries are proverbial, and I saw good specimens at Leh. I attended their Sunday services, saw how they lived in their homes, and can bear testimony to the tenacity with which they adhere to apostolical simplicity, zeal, and perseverance.

For another reason, too, I would fain have lingered, in that I was tired. From my arrival on Monday till nearly Saturday midnight I was quiet hardly ten minutes, so that Sunday's rest was welcome indeed. But the most serious consideration was that the season for travel was already past, and they were expecting that any day the first snow might fall, block the passes, and cut them off from the rest of the world for the winter.

The *Wazir*, or native governor, was very civil, and having been instructed by the British Joint Commissioner before his departure to aid me, he was ready to cash a cheque or lend me money; besides which the *Wazir* helped me with letters for securing relays of horses, and gave a sepoy as attendant.

Thus provided, and with a caravan reduced to eleven horses and my three servants, we started from Leh on November 26th, the ground thinly covered with newly-fallen snow. I had visited in Leh the great Lama monastery, and took occasion, at all risks, to do the same at the monastery of Lama Yuru.

On the tenth day we approached the dreaded Pass of the Zoji-la, which was now the crux of our journey. Here I was supplied with 42 men to help me through the snow. Towards afternoon a letter overtook me from the chief man at Dras, saying that he would send more men, and that I had better stop, or we might be lost, horses and all.

But I was just at that moment about to attack the Pass, and did not see its dangers, so pushed forwards, till, on rounding a corner, I perceived what a narrow ledge it was from which the snow had to be cleared before me; whilst, in addition to the danger of avalanches from above, there yawned a horrible precipice below, down which one of my *haji* companions over the Karakoram had lost a horse. It is so fatal a spot that on the melting of the snow in spring a number of corpses of men and horses, fallen during the winter, are usually found.

Here the owners of the horses entreated that I

would not compel them to take their animals across, for they might probably never get them back, to which I consented on condition that they themselves carried my baggage. My own horse was led, a man at his head, and another holding his tail, whilst I myself went on foot, clad in felt boots, and should have fallen 50 times but for being steadied in front by the *Yuzbashi* or officer, and propped up from behind by Muhammad Joo.

Once over the Pass, we pushed on in darkness, and did not arrive till about midnight at the huts of Sonamarg.

And thus I finished, with the utmost labour and discomfort, the last of seven passes (varying in height up to nearly 19,000 feet) between Kuldja and Kashmir. Three days more of comparatively smooth travelling brought us to Srinagur, where no additional hopes were kindled concerning Lassa; and the anniversary of my ordination, a few days before Christmas, found me at Rawal Pindi.

Here a review of the situation led me to record in my diary, concerning Lassa : " I have put my hand to the plough, and I dare not look back. Many say that I shall not succeed in getting there, but . . . it seems to me quite clear that my duty is to go to the Viceroy at Calcutta, and perhaps to Darjeeling, and not to stop till I am convinced it is not God's will that I should go farther."

But I had now reached a railway, and had therefore to part with Amin, my groom, who, with tears in his eyes, declared again I had been as a father to him, and that he had wanted for nothing. Joseph and Muhammad Joo continued with me to Lahore.

I am afraid we all looked rather tattered and torn, and somewhat like wild men of the woods; for a young missionary who came to the station to meet me expressed his fears whether the railway officials would allow my servants to pass out of the station with luggage, lest they might be thieves! Joseph hastened to remove this reproach, and, going to a second-hand shop, he secured what was probably an officer's cast-off morning suit. Telling me of his purchase, he said, " I could not get a black coat, sir, like yours, so I bought the nearest"—the said "nearest" being a black dress suit, the collar faced with *moiré antique*; and in this splendid array he appeared on Christmas morning, greatly to the surprise of my host, who wondered much who it could be thus doing honour in India to the Englishman's festival.

I had written from Leh to the Viceroy, also to Mr Ney Elias; and from the latter I found a letter at Lahore telling me that there was not the least hope of my getting to Lassa. Another letter of a sorrowful character informed me that my father had died two months previously, which seemed to call for my presence in England; so that it looked as if I must think of setting my face homewards after seeing the Viceroy at Calcutta.

Muhammad Joo was parted with at Amritsar, where I met some veterans of the Church Missionary Society, and among them the Rev. Robert Clark, who has had much to do with founding mission-stations along the north-west frontier of India, and who thought to encourage me by saying that "if I would give a portion of my life to stirring up interest and sending the Gospel into Central Asia, it would be a work angels might envy, and generations would rise up to call me blessed."

I then turned aside at Jeypore to talk over matters Tibetan with Mr Carey; and thence, on learning particulars of a route from Darjeeling to the Tibetan frontier, I wrote to Mr Ney Elias as to the possibility of my meeting him there.

By the kindness and influence of Mr Dunstan, a former parishioner in Eltham, I was furnished with a free pass on the entire length of railway from Agra to Calcutta, where on the day of arrival I saw the Viceroy, and afterwards was several times a guest at Government House.

The Marquis of Dufferin had just gone; the Marquis of Lansdowne was just come. His Excellency was kindness itself, and listened attentively to my plans; but he thought them hopeless, and feared that my sudden appearance on the frontier would make the Tibetans suspect that it was only a dodge of the Government to get an Englishman into the country. Sir Mortimer Durand, the Secretary of State, happened to be at Government House at the moment, and, on being appealed to, expressed a similar fear.

Now, if at this juncture the Viceroy had plainly forbidden me to go towards the frontier, I should in all probability have deemed it my duty to obey, and taken it as an intimation that I was to set my face homewards. But his Excellency was gracious enough to stop many degrees short of this, and to add that if there was anything he could do without prejudice to the negotiations then pending he was willing to be of use; and to this he gave practical effect by signing for me a letter to the authorities throughout India that proved well-nigh invaluable.

Meanwhile new rays of hope were beginning to appear. I had found on arrival at Calcutta a letter awaiting me from the Moravian board, giving permission for Mr Redslob to accompany me. On the same day, and afterwards, I met Baboo Sarat Chandra Das, who, though living at Darjeeling, happened to be staying in Calcutta.

He knew, through Mr Rylands Brown, of my designs; and it was gratifying to me to hear that he got into Lassa by a plan almost identical with my own—namely, by writing to the Grand Lama and asking permission; only that in his case he had the advantage of being an Asiatic, and of sending his letter in a time of peace. The Baboo took a more hopeful view than others of my endeavours, advised me not to go in February or March, gave me several pieces of important information, and sketched out a programme, according to which I was to wait in Calcutta for two or three months.

Presently I heard of Mr James Hart, who had passed rapidly through Calcutta, and was gone up towards the frontier to help on the Chinese side in reopening negotiations. Talking about him in one of my calls, Sir Mortimer Durand thought there would be no harm in my trying to see Mr Hart and asking for his help. A telegram sent that afternoon to Darjeeling brought reply from Mr Hart that he should be there " for some days yet," whereupon I announced my coming to Ney Elias and Rylands Brown, and within 24 hours had started once more for the snows of the Himalayas.

Arrived at Darjeeling, I disclosed my plans the same evening to Mr Hart, who thought they might prejudice the political negotiations. His position was a peculiarly delicate one. As a trusted Englishman, he was come to help the Chinese, as it were, against the Indian authorities; and it was absolutely necessary that he should be above suspicion of collusion with one of his own countrymen who wished to enter Tibet. He therefore gave me little hope of success, but said that he was expecting the arrival in about a week of a messenger from the frontier.

On the next day came letters from Mr Ney Elias at the frontier, and from Mrs Rylands Brown, who, with her husband, was staying, on the way thither, at Kalimpong, and inviting me to meet them there. Putting all together, therefore, I determined to start on the morrow, in the hope possibly of meeting Ney Elias and of hearing what Mr Brown had done respecting my letter destined for Lassa. On my way I learned that Ney Elias had just gone down, so that he must have passed me in the train; further, on my arrival Mrs Brown told me that her husband had been quite unable to forward a translation of my letter.

My going to Kalimpong, however, gave birth to fresh hopes; for Mr Sutherland, my host, a sturdy and excellent missionary, as he seemed to me, of the Scotch University Mission, took me next morning to a lamasery in the village with a painted temple within. Then we called at a house containing a chapel, where service was going on, many lamas sitting there and praying all day long, with a mug of beer standing before each, and refreshments being brought from time to time. Here an old Bhotanese governor was staying in the house of his son.

On talking to the old gentleman of my prospects, he said the Tibetans were greatly excited by the war, and that if I attempted to go now they might do me violence. His son, however, was expecting before long to go to the frontier, and Mr Sutherland suggested that perhaps he would help in getting my letter forward. Besides this, I was told of certain persons in Darjeeling who might be able to procure me a messenger to the frontier, and Mrs Brown was good enough to invite me to stay with them if I had need whilst awaiting a reply from Tibet.

I returned, therefore, to Darjeeling, and found awaiting me the card of Mr Alfred Wallis Paul, the deputy-commissioner, to whom the Lieutenant-Governor of Bengal had kindly telegraphed on my behalf, and who was closely connected with the negotiations. On broaching to him my plans, however, I got little encouragement, for he thought it would be better not to try to send my letter to Lassa.

I was walking away from his house, somewhat depressed and wondering what to do next, when I met Sarat Chandra Das coming to seek me. He took me to his house, where I met the Lama Ugyen Gyatso, chief interpreter to the Sikkim field force, and who accompanied Das to Lassa. I showed him my letters as translated for the Grand Lama, one of which he undertook to re-write on proper paper and in correct style. He pronounced my own letter "a good one," undertook to insert certain explanations in brackets, gave me sundry pieces of advice, and intimated where an interpreter could be found.

Meanwhile Mr Hart's expected messenger did not arrive, and a new idea presented itself to my mind as to whether anything could be done for my plans through Khatmandu, the capital of Nepal. Murray's guide-book had frightened me out of my wits by stating that the trip to Khatmandu was expensive and would cost from £200 to £250; besides which Anglo-Indians are aware that no Englishman can enter Nepalese territory except by invitation of the Maharajah or the British Resident. I met a man at Darjeeling who told me these figures as to expense were greatly exaggerated, and he mentioned, as one who could help me on my way, a son of Colonel Lowis, with whom I had dined at Calcutta.

On the next day it was suggested to me that if, whilst waiting for an answer from Lassa, I could make my way from Darjeeling through Nepal to Khatmandu, I might profitably distribute Scriptures, and should be breaking fresh ground over which no Englishman had passed. This commended itself strongly to my mind, and looked like an opportunity of usefulness, whether I succeeded or not in sending the letter.

Besides this I remembered I had a link, or perhaps could make one, with the British Resident, Major (now Colonel Sir Edward) Durand, in that my servant Joseph had been in his service, and it was he whom Joseph had asked to take him to England to be baptised. I wrote, therefore, telling the Colonel how well and consistently his *protégé* had served me, and inquired as to the feasibility of my visiting Khatmandu.

These desires for usefulness were further strengthened when I called on the Rev. A. Turnbull of the Scotch Mission, who told me that Mr Arthington (already known to me by correspondence) had written about a year before to ask him to try to get copies of the Scriptures into Nepal, and offering to pay the expense. Mr Turnbull, however, on applying to the authorities for leave to send in a colporteur, was not allowed to do so. But he was now abundantly willing to help me, told me what Nepalese Scriptures he had printed, what they would weigh, etc., and we so laid our plans that he might forward them quickly if I telegraphed from Calcutta.

Meanwhile, a letter had come from Mr Sutherland saying that the man he had mentioned did not expect to go to the Chinese *Amban* on the frontier until March, but that he was willing to take my letter if the authorities would permit. Accordingly, I drafted a postscript to my letter to the Dalai Lama, and also a letter to my friend Ch'ang, whom I supposed to be the new *Amban* I heard of as coming to Lassa ; and I was talking to Mr Hart about translating it into Chinese, when a messenger arrived saying that a telegram had come from the frontier summoning him there, and that an officer and four soldiers were on their way to escort him to the *Amban*.

Mr Hart then kindly promised to do for my plans anything he could without bringing himself under suspicion, and Mr Paul also expressed his willingness to do anything to further my ends that was not incompatible with his other duties ; but he was distinctly of opinion, as Mr Hart also had suggested, that my better plan for sending the letter was to attempt it from headquarters at Peking.

It was now February, and under the most favourable circumstances the opening of the snow passes on the Chinese side would hardly allow of my entering Tibet, I thought, till June. Suppose, then, in the interval, I went leisurely round the coast, visiting and preaching at mission-stations up to Peking, and there asked the authorities to forward my letter to their new Resident, my friend Ch'ang, at Lassa ; whilst I, returning to Shanghai, made my way up the Yang-tse-kiang, distributing Scriptures, and on to the Tibetan frontier at Bathang, there to wait a reply. If it were favourable, I should be ready to enter; but if it were unfavourable, or if no reply came, then by crossing into Upper Burmah I could break in upon ground which, though not absolutely new, was certainly but little known, and so proceed homewards.

Accordingly, I returned to Calcutta, got my letter to Ch'ang done into Chinese, and with this twofold idea of Nepal and Peking had a pleasant hour's chat with Sir Mortimer Durand.

From him I learned that his brother was not just then in Khatmandu, but away shooting tigers, and that my letter to him, therefore, might be delayed. He thought the Nepalese authorities would not allow me to go from Khatmandu to Darjeeling, and seemed quite sure that I should not enter Lassa, but thought the journey up the Yang-tse-kiang and into Burmah would present very much of interest. Similarly Ney Elias, whilst giving me some new ideas about action from Nepal, continued his prophecy of my failure to enter Lassa.

On the other hand, calling on Colonel Lowis, he kindly undertook to write to his son, located at the end of my railway journey through Tirhoot, and who might be able to give me information and help in getting forward to Khatmandu.

And now came several days of suspense, during which I saw Mr Wood Mason at the Calcutta Museum, and inquired of him as to what extent the fauna of Nepal and of the upper Yang-tse-kiang was known to science. A letter came from Mr Sutherland expressing his willingness to place himself at my disposal as interpreter for a journey to Nepal; but so long was an answer coming from Major Durand that, on a certain Tuesday, I had all but taken a ticket for a coasting steamer towards Singapore. Something led me to defer the purchase a day, and on the morrow I found a note awaiting me from Mr Lowis, saying that my letter to Major Durand had miscarried, but that all the arrangements were in train for my journey, and I was to be the Major's guest.

This was information, as asked for, and something more; so that, at first, I was rather taken aback at having the matter thus decided for me. I thought, however, of the words, "I have set before thee an open door," and if only on the chance of distributing Scriptures, conducting Sunday services, etc., I thought I ought to go.

This thought was strengthened at the early service next day, which was Ash Wednesday; and speed being necessary, I took it as a good sign when Mr Campbell, of the East Indian Railway, kindly promised to forward after me the Nepalese Scriptures. He afterwards sent me also a free pass on their part of the line.

Yet another providential circumstance in my favour was that, in calling on the late Rev. W. Smith, Principal of the Scotch General Assembly's Institution, he told me of a young man of 22 in their school, a Nepalese named Harkhadoz, who had expressed a wish some day to enter Nepal as a missionary, and who, he thought, might accompany me as interpreter, there being not sufficient time for me to avail myself of the services of Mr Sutherland. Harkhadoz, on being spoken to, consented, and I took him straightway to the Museum to have him taught how to skin a bird.

Then I telegraphed to Darjeeling for 300 Nepalese Scriptures to be sent to Mr Campbell, and asked Colonel Lowis to write to his son that I was due on the following Sunday morning, and would be ready if desired to take one or more services among the indigo planters of Tirhoot.

About four-and-twenty hours later we started, and in eight days, after travelling by steam, horseback, and in a *palki* on the shoulders of men, I arrived at Khatmandu, where the Resident and Mrs (now Lady) Durand accorded me a hearty welcome.

I thought the Major seemed rather surprised when I expressed my desire to go thence to Darjeeling; but he was good enough to send to the Maharajah asking him to give me an audience. This native potentate at once declined my request, saying that no European had passed that way, and that if he attempted to send any one he should move the hostility of the people against himself; further, that I might be murdered, in which case he would be held responsible.

To this I replied I would take the risk and he should be held guiltless. Then he said that such a step might cause rebellion; that the people were like savages, etc., etc., his wicked-looking old private secretary chiming in now and then, whilst I looked upon their utterances as a pack of fibs.

Then I asked whether they could send a letter for me to Lassa. But the Maharajah said it would be useless, since the authorities there would not receive a letter from the Viceroy, nor even respect Chinese orders. He suggested accordingly that I should take away my letter for the present, and when peace was restored, he might be able to forward it to the Nepalese representative in the Tibetan capital.

At this juncture he said it was time to prepare for the Durbar, which I subsequently attended with the Resident, and was placed near the Maharajah. Upon his turning to talk to me, I led the conversation to the subject of prisons, asked to see his jails, and told him how I had been through Siberia distributing books to the prisoners. "How very glad," said he, "they must have been to get them!" a remark which I did not forget, as will presently be seen.

A few days later I made the acquaintance of a Nepalese who had twice been in Lassa. He said he was residing there when some foreigners on the Tibetan frontier asked for admittance, and that he, with the Chinese Resident, both endeavoured to persuade the Tibetan authorities to allow the strangers to enter, but in vain.

Then, to illustrate their aversion to change, he pointed to a Tibetan-made coat on his back and the narrow width of the material (not more than nine inches). He had told them, he said, that they should make it wider, to which their only reply was that it was not their custom and they must keep to that.

This man gave me, however, what I thought might prove valuable information, and, among other things, the stations and approximate distance between them, from Lassa to Bathang and from Lassa to Peking. He also dissuaded me from sending my letter *via* Darjeeling, but approved the idea of going round to Peking.

Thus, with the exception of learning about routes from Lassa, I did not seem to be much nearer my goal by going to Khatmandu; but there were a few things to put in the opposite scale.

Probably I was the first English clergyman to conduct service in Khatmandu, and to administer the Holy Communion according to the English rite in Nepal. I also baptised the only English baby in the country—namely, Arthur Nepal, son of Joseph Gaze, bandmaster to the Maharajah's musicians. Moreover, if I could not regard the results of my tour as very important, I could not charge myself with not having tried my best.

Further, I was thinking what to arrange concerning the Scriptures, for the arrival of which thus far I had waited in vain. The exigencies of his official position prevented the Resident from undertaking to have them distributed if they came after my departure, and the English surgeon was already sufficiently opposed in his efforts for the people by the Nepalese authorities, without his giving them a handle for further opposition.

I therefore had to leave Khatmandu without having received the books, and had proceeded a few hours when we met men carrying my boxes of Scriptures.

I opened them immediately, and before many hours were over had distributed 300 portions to willing recipients. Where we stopped for breakfast I had many requests for the books; so that all were disposed of, not only to residents, but in many cases to coolies travelling towards Khatmandu, whence, no doubt, the books spread from the capital to distant homes in other parts of the country.

On looking back, this *finale* struck me as quite providential, and the best thing that could have happened. Had the books arrived a day earlier, I should have had, probably, to ask permission to distribute, and the Maharajah might have declined; as it was, I arranged that copies should be sent to some of the generals I met at the Durbar; and I wrote to the Maharajah, reminding him of his expression that " the Siberians must have been pleased to get my books."

Hence I had been doing the like among the people of Nepal, and asked his acceptance of a specimen copy of each kind I had distributed.

I know of no one else who has been able, before or since, thus to scatter Scriptures in Nepal, though a few copies, doubtless, trickle into the country from Darjeeling, and more, perhaps, might be thus got in from the plains. I was deeply thankful, therefore, thus to have broken new ground.

I now set my face towards Calcutta, and wrote home to England that my next postal address would be at Shanghai.

CHAPTER L.

A SUCCESSFUL FAILURE.

No need for hurry to Peking; Parting with Joseph, 389.—Official assistance at Calcutta; Excursion from Rangoon to Mandalay, 391. Singapore; Distribution of Scriptures in Annam, 392.—Information, introductions, and experience collected at Hong Kong, Canton, and Foo Chow, 393.—Interviews with Mr Stevenson at Shanghai, and Sir Robert Hart at Peking, 394-95.—Stay with British Ambassador, 396.—Counsels of Sir Robert Hart and the Marquis Tseng; Preparations for return to India; Journey to Tientsin, 399.—No news at Tokio, Hong Kong, or Singapore, 400. Concentration of efforts at Hyderabad and Bombay, 401. Journey *viâ* the Persian Gulf, and extinction of hope at Jerusalem, 402.—Intermediate work in Annam, Cambodia, the Philippines, and Quetta, 403.—Health impaired, 404.—Visits to North African Missions, and prisons in Spain; What perhaps might have been accomplished in Lassa, and what was accomplished in the attempt, 405.—Summary of entire journey, 406.—Suggestions for the future, and lessons from the past, 407.

MY twofold plan, of a journey to Peking and up the Yang-tse-kiang, demanded no particular hurry, because, if I arrived too early, the Tientsin river would still be frozen; and the passes into Tibet would be best crossed when the summer was well advanced. Seeing, therefore, that I should have time on my hands, it seemed prudent to reduce expenses as much as possible, and to part with Joseph, who could not speak Chinese. Also I thought that I could now, for economy's sake, get along without a regular servant.

Accordingly, I recommended him to Sir Donald Wallace, who was returning to England through Persia, and I think I never wrote a testimonial with greater pleasure than in the present instance, wording it as follows:—

"Seid Joseph Abbas has been my personal servant and interpreter for the past year and two months, during which he has accompanied me through Russian and Chinese Turkistan and over the Karakoram to Ladak and Kashmir. Throughout this journey I have found him truthful and scrupulously honest, and to me and my interest as true as steel. He has never shrunk from hardship or danger, and more than once has sat up the whole night skinning birds or in other work that required despatch. He superintends effectively other servants, with whom he rarely quarrels, and he can upon occasion cook, do general repairs, and make himself extremely useful. I am sorry that to the Persian, Arabic, Uzbeg, Turkish, and English languages which he speaks, he does not add Chinese, so that I might take him farther on my journey. I shall part from him with great regret, and sincerely wish him well wherever he may go.

"(*Signed*) HENRY LANSDELL."

Joseph accompanied me to the train by which I left for Nepal, and with tears told me he would go with me anywhere in the world. I was glad to hear afterwards that Sir Donald Wallace was as pleased with him as I had been.

Having now to go into parts little known to topographers, I called at the Surveyor-General's department in Calcutta, where Colonel Thuillier took great pains to afford me the latest information on Upper Burmah, and to provide me copies of the latest maps.

Colonel W. Gatacre too, of the Quartermaster-General's department, was most kind in commending me to the Commander-in-Chief, who instructed the General Officer in Burmah to afford me assistance if needed, and wrote concerning me to the Quartermaster-General in Madras. Besides these introductions, I was favoured with sundry others from civilians to various places round the coast, and then took a ticket for Singapore *via* Rangoon.

At Rangoon I had to change steamers and wait a week, and was cogitating whether in the interim to run up to Mandalay, when, going into the Chief Commissioner's office, I heard that Mr Colbourne Baber had gone up only the day before. Now, for information concerning a journey to the Upper Yang-tse-kiang, Mr Baber was one of the few Englishmen in the world who could direct me, since he had travelled there, soon after the murder of Mr Margary. Also General Gordon, commanding in Upper Burmah, was at Mandalay, and the Bishop of Rangoon assured me of a bed at the mission-house of the Society for the Propagation of the Gospel.

I quickly decided, therefore, to go, despatched ahead two or three telegrams, and within 30 hours was at Mandalay, the Rev. John A. Colbeck coming to meet me. I preached twice on the Sunday: once to a military congregation, in what was the pagoda, or Chapel Royal, of Theebaw, King of Burmah.

I also saw General Gordon, who promised to send instructions to the military outposts near the Chinese frontier, so that my arrival might not be unexpected, if I appeared there some months hence.

Mr Baber, however, had passed on to Bhamo, whither time did not allow of my pursuing him. I therefore rushed back to Rangoon, and, before leaving, dined with Sir Charles Crosthwaite, the Chief Commissioner, who kindly promised, if I would let him know when I was going to Tibet, that he would give notice to the people on the Burmese frontier that I might possibly need their assistance.

Having thus prepared my way for the eventuality of trying to pass from Bathang to Upper Burmah, I sailed down to Singapore, where it was necessary again to change steamers. At Singapore various acts of official kindness were shown me by the Governor, Sir Cecil Clementi Smith, and others; and I met Mr Haffenden, the agent of the British and Foreign Bible Society.

Mr Haffenden waxed eloquent upon the neglected spiritual condition of Tonking, saying that nothing was being done there for the Bible Society, which made me anxious to go and attempt something, especially when he went on to add that there was not a single Protestant missionary throughout the country.

When, therefore, a German, Captain Vil, hungry for passengers, called to tell me he was making a chance voyage to Cochin China, I purchased a number of Scriptures for distribution in French and Chinese—there being then no others available—and took ship for Saigon. From Saigon I proceeded by steamer along the coast, distributing my books, and spying out the spiritual nakedness of the land as far as Hanoi, the capital of Tonking.

They had told me at Rangoon that the wild tribes of the hills between Upper Burmah and Yunnan were dangerous to travel among ; and I accordingly made inquiries at Hanoi whether, if the passage into Burmah by Bhamo should not be possible, one could pass southeast through Yunnan, and so descend the Red River to Tonking. This was said to be not impossible ; so, having collected much useful information and procured introductions, I passed on to Hong Kong.

At Hong Kong, though proceeding towards Peking, I still had one eye upon Tibet ; and, in calling on Mr F. A. Morgan, of the Imperial Customs (who had heard of my coming from Mr James Hart), I was encouraged to hear that Mr Hart, on arriving at the frontier, was provided by the Tibetan authorities with a gaily-caparisoned mule, and accorded a welcome. Mr Morgan gave me some introductions to persons on the Yang-tse, as well as the Red River, and advised that the time to start for Tibet would be the end of September or the beginning of October.

This left me ample time to steam along the China coast, stopping at the principal ports, visiting missions of various sorts, collecting information, and asking advice of several authorities as to how far, apart from getting into Tibet, my visiting Western China was likely to be of use from a missionary point of view.

Mr Kenmure, the Bible Society's agent at Canton, thought I might procure some useful information for Bible work in Szechuen, Yunnan, Kwei-chau, etc., by inquiring as to the distribution of dialects, what missionaries are at work, whether European colporteurs would succeed, and which form of Bible work would answer better, the settled or the itinerating ; whether the southern tribes are approachable, and whether Yunnan could be worked best from Shanghai, Canton, or Burmah.

At Hong Kong, Mr Ost, whose guest I was, and

who, with his wife, appeared to me to be doing most admirable work for the Church Missionary Society, thought that, were he in my place, he should be disposed to go to Western China, and through Burmah, even if I could not go to Tibet ; whilst Archdeacon Wolfe, at Foo Chow, thought that, apart from the Lassa endeavour, my going to Yunnan might be decidedly useful for missionary purposes.

Another thing pointing in a similar direction was that, in Shanghai, a letter was read to me from Mr James Hart, written at Darjeeling, saying that the negotiations with the Indian Government, though slow, were looking brighter.

On the other hand, I had been industriously reading Colquhoun's *Across Chryse*—a similar journey to the one I contemplated—and I cannot say his book encouraged me to go and do likewise. Again, Mr Stevenson, the vice-director of the China Inland Mission, who had himself been to West China, and was a competent judge, did not see any very special good likely to be gained by one who could not speak the language going across China to Burmah—that is, if the authorities did not entertain my proposal of going to Tibet ; and so little chance had I, he thought, of success with them, that he did not see his way to take active steps in advance in allotting me an interpreter, though abundantly willing, immediately permission was given, to help me all he possibly could.

This interview, I confess, depressed me a little, though I could not but allow it was reasonable on his part, seeing that my own secret hopes of entering Lassa were by no means great.

In this somewhat unsettled frame of mind I steamed northward to Tientsin, where I heard that Mr W.

Rockhill had started for Tibet not many weeks previously, having studied the language for years, and hoping to get into Lassa in disguise. The British Consul was perfectly sure, he said, do what I would, that I should never get into Tibet, though he and many others were not only willing but zealous to do me service, whilst I was quite overwhelmed with offers of hospitality.

And so at last I came to Peking, where, at the Church Mission House, was a note awaiting me from Sir John Walsham, H.B.M. Ambassador, inviting me to his summer residence in the hills, but adding that it would be out of the question for him to ask for me a passport to Tibet! This was not inspiriting; but I determined to make the excursion next day, and tell my tale *vivâ voce*.

I called first, however, upon Sir Robert Hart, head of the Imperial Customs, and the Englishman most trusted, perhaps, by the Chinese Government.

Sir Robert had heard of me from his brother, and had prejudged, I fancy, that I was somewhat fanatical. He heard me patiently, however, and at the end of my story was gracious enough to say that I was more reasonable than he had expected to find me.

I confess to being somewhat taken aback at the importance he attached to my desire to enter Lassa; for he went on to say that, were they to bring forward just then my application for leave, it would imperil the pending negotiations, and that he was sure the Chinese would not allow it. Further, that even if they consented to send my letter to Lassa, it would take five months to get an answer, so that he very decidedly advised me for the present to desist.

He added that he was waiting only for the settlement

of the negotiations to go home, which he hoped to do before the winter, and he was good enough to say, though not generally sanguine, he thought matters might be settled by the autumn, and that travel in Tibet might be possible. Hence he thought I could with safety place my affairs in the hands of Sir John Walsham, and keep for the next few months within reach.

Then, hiring a Peking donkey for myself and another for a little baggage, I rode out to the Temple of Su-ping-tai, where the embassy was staying. Here Sir John received me with the courtesy and hospitality for which he is famous, and we had a pleasant talk over my journey through Chinese Turkistan (which surprised him in view of the few facilities I had) and over Sikkim affairs; but he did not approach the main point on that evening.

As I lay in bed earnestly thinking over my prospects concerning Lassa, I deemed that if Sir John took the same view of the matter as did Sir Robert Hart, my way would be tolerably clear. Accordingly, after breakfast I related my story to Sir John, not telling him at first that I had consulted Sir Robert. He took, however, precisely the same line of argument, saying that the Tibetans would be certain to regard such a request as mine merely as another move in tactics, and that if my plans were brought forward now, it would hamper them in the settlement of the Sikkim affair.

I had hitherto refused to believe in my inmost heart that so small a fly as myself could trouble the British lion, but now that Sir John re-echoed what had been said by the Viceroy and Secretary of State for India, Mr Paul, Mr James Hart, and Sir Robert, his brother, I forthwith gave in and hauled down my colours, saying that of course I would desist, for if only as an Englishman I could not think of being so unpatriotic as to allow a little private scheme of my own devising to hamper or be a cause of hindrance to negotiations of such importance as were then pending.

This seemed, as a Scotchman would say, to "fetch" Sir John, and he spontaneously remarked that he hoped the Sikkim affair would be settled by the autumn. His sympathies, he said, were with me. Further, that as I had adopted his view of matters, and came so well recommended, he would look after my interests, and if I would leave my papers with him he would keep me acquainted with the course of events and my prospects in connection therewith.

We then discussed my proposed route through China and Burmah. He thought there would be no difficulty in getting a passport, but did not anticipate that any special good would be gained thereby. According to his latest news from the Burmese frontier, the hill tribes were turbulent, and he deprecated my risking what he was pleased to call a valuable life like mine, or if it did not come to a question of life or death, there was danger of my being made prisoner.

Such an event, he said, would cause grave trouble, add to their complications with the Chinese, and make fresh difficulties. And this was practically in accord with what they had told me in the Commissioner's office at Rangoon. As for my alternative—going down the Red River to Tonking—he said the French were at that time suspicious, and he mentioned reasons, which I thought satisfactory, why just then he could not help me in that direction.

Where, then, was I to spend the next few months— the hottest in the year? I had been advised at

Shanghai not to come there in the heat of summer, for fear of fever, and Sir John advised me on the score of health against remaining long at that season in Peking.

Moreover, on leaving Foo Chow, some disease, strange to my experience, had, I fancied, tried to get hold of me, for I found myself languid and unwell, though not prevented from getting about. The missionaries at Tientsin said I had been suffering slightly from malaria, which was common there. I had suffered also slightly with a rash brought on by the heat of Tonking—all which seemed to warn me that I was not invulnerable, and had better not go towards the tropics in the hottest weather.

Sir John thought I might spend a fortnight in Korea and a month in Japan, where it would be comparatively cool. In a subsequent conversation he said that he had mentioned in his official correspondence my arrival at Peking, and that I had forborne, in the face of making more difficulties with the negotiations, to press my case; but he would keep my wish well before him, and could telegraph to his colleague in Tokio and let me know how events were proceeding.

Accordingly, I rode back to Peking, and calling again on Sir Robert Hart, he told me that a telegram had come showing Sikkim matters to be more favourable than when we last met. On mentioning my idea of going to Korea and Japan for the month of August, he thought the negotiations would hardly be cleared up by that time; but he suggested that, in any case, it would probably be easier, physically and politically, to enter Tibet from India and come out by the east instead of *vice versâ*, which seemed rather to point to my returning to India by the autumn, and there awaiting the end of the negotiations.

On asking Sir John's advice, when he came for a day or two to Peking, he thought that if I were allowed to enter Lassa at all, it would be from India. The next day Dr Dudgeon took me to call on the late Marquis Tseng, who left his sick-bed to see me, and asked several questions about the Russians and Chinese Turkistan. The Marquis seemed decidedly of opinion that from India would be the most feasible way to enter Tibet, and he thought I might get permission to do this when the Sikkim negotiations were settled.

I told him of having met his friend Ch'ang in Kuldja, which pleased the Marquis. He gave me half-a-dozen of his cards to be used as introductions for sights around Peking, but for Lassa recommended my getting introductions from Tibetans rather than from Chinese. He accepted a Chinese atlas, on which I marked my travels in red; and he promised that, if my applications were sent in to the authorities, he would do what he could to further my object.

I then left Peking, having told Sir John that my route would probably be to Korea and Japan till the beginning of September, and then to Southern India, with the hope that matters might be more settled by October. In accordance with the foregoing, I despatched my heavy luggage to Singapore, wrote home to England that my next address would be at Madras, and then, returning to Tientsin, I was favoured with an interview with his Excellency Li Hung Chang, whom I endeavoured to interest in my travels.

I had reached Tientsin *viâ* Kupeikow, turning off to the coal-mines at the head of the Chinese railway at Tang-shan, whither I had written, thinking to give the few Europeans there a Sunday service, distributing Scriptures along the route, and being accompanied by the Rev. Francis H. Sprent, of the North China Church Mission.

At Tientsin also I visited the Public Library, where I saw a copy of my *Through Siberia*, the very copy, presumably, read by Mr Crossett, which led to his asking me to come out and lead the way! I had heard of Mr Crossett at Shanghai, and was told he had just left for Tientsin, where I should probably see him. But he died on the passage, and I stood instead by his grave.

From what I heard of him he was peculiar and erratic, but a good man, and I could not help thinking by what a feeble instrument I had been led to undertake my long journey, as had previously been the case with my journey across Siberia, the first motive power in the other case being an invalid lady.

I then took steamer for Chemulpo, rode across Korea by a route undescribed by any Englishman to Fusan, and, after visiting the principal mission-stations of Japan, arrived at Tokio, where the British Minister had nothing for me from Sir John Walsham. So I took ship for Hong Kong.

At Hong Kong I heard that the Indian troops were withdrawn from the Sikkim frontier, and Mr Morgan told me he had heard from Mr James Hart that the negotiations were practically finished, though by sending for his boxes it did not look as if Mr Hart were coming away immediately. Also, Mr Morgan had heard by letter that Mr Rockhill had failed to enter Lassa.

I then pushed on to Singapore, thinking I might find a letter there or at Madras, writing at the same time to England that my next address would be at Bombay.

I received no communication at Singapore, and so wrote to Sir John asking for advice as to what to do on reaching Bombay—whether, that is, to give up further thoughts of Lassa and go home, or to hold on a few months after Christmas in the hope of getting permission, seeing that if the permission were given I could not cross the passes till the spring.

My next hope was that I should certainly find correspondence at Madras. And so I did—a packet of 25 letters—which I opened with trepidation, lest after long silence there should be bad news. But there was not one of my letters that said a word to enlighten me about Tibet. I received them, moreover, just as I was about to start for Bombay through Hyderabad.

To Hyderabad a batch of letters was sent from Bombay, and when again there was nothing to direct me concerning Tibet, I began to feel desperate. Not having one morning to rise so early as usual, I lay cogitating carefully my course, and decided that I must concentrate all my forces with a view to a final effort.

I judged that the persons intimately concerned in carrying on the negotiations would be extremely chary of imparting to me many particulars of what was going on; their business of course required secrecy, and I had no claim to being allowed to look behind the scenes. Yet I thought that, at all events, I had the goodwill of some of them, and at last I determined to write to five persons at Darjeeling, Calcutta, and Peking, asking each to send a telegram of one word, "GO" or "WAIT."

By "GO" I should understand that he thought it hopeless for me to remain in expectation of being allowed to enter Tibet during the coming summer, and from "WAIT" I should infer that he thought it might be worth my while to stay a month or two longer, whilst to Sir John Walsham I wrote more fully concerning a passport. The answer in each case was to be sent to Bombay, whither I next directed my steps.

The two lesser lights from Darjeeling telegraphed "GO," but from the three greater lights, including the Viceroy, I heard nothing. Meeting with a Scotch clergyman from Melrose who was going to Darjeeling, I sent a message to Mr Sutherland asking him to be on the look-out for a suitable interpreter who might accompany me in case I was permitted to go to Lassa, since Mr Redslob had written that he was suffering from an infirmity in his legs that would prevent his accompanying me.

At last, when the weather was getting something more than warm, I determined to go slowly homewards, but so keeping in touch with Bombay that, if a favourable letter arrived from Peking or the Viceroy, I might be recalled by telegram.

I put my heavy baggage, therefore, in the hands of an agent to await directions, and started up the Persian Gulf, intending to cross the desert to Jaffa, thinking that if by the time of my arrival there a favourable letter should reach me, I could rush round to Bombay, pick up my caravan luggage, and so get up to Tibet in suitable time for crossing the passes.

Up to the date of my reaching Baghdad no letter or telegram had overtaken me, whereupon I wrote to the Viceroy telling him of my whereabouts, nor was it till I reached Jerusalem that I received the last fell stroke that shattered my remaining hopes.

One or more of my letters to the Viceroy, it seemed, had failed to reach him, but his secretary now wrote that, although a satisfactory arrangement had been arrived at with China in reference to the relations with Sikkim and Tibet, his Excellency did not consider the moment opportune for endeavouring to procure facilities for travelling in the latter country, and he regretted that he was unable to meet my wishes. This then settled the matter.*

It merely remained for me now to continue home-

---

* Meanwhile, I had not been idle during this time of waiting and suspense. I have mentioned that at Darjeeling Mr Turnbull told me how Mr Arthington had offered to pay the expenses of a colporteur to distribute Scriptures in Nepal. When, therefore, I succeeded in doing this to some extent, I wrote to Mr Arthington, saying that the excursion (thanks to a free pass on the railway, and the hospitality of the Resident and the indigo planters) had cost only £20. This sum he kindly remitted to me on the China coast, and drew my attention to Annam and Cambodia, neither of which then had any portion of the Scriptures in the vernacular.

Accordingly, I took from Hong Kong to Singapore one of the boats of the *Messageries Maritimes*, my ticket allowing me to break the journey at Saigon, and to proceed by the next boat a fortnight later. In the interim I ran up to Pnom-penh, the capital of Cambodia, where I made inquiries, as I had done in Saigon, for any scholar who could translate the Scriptures into Annamese or Cambodian, but could hear of no one capable of so doing. Later on I went to Bangkok, where I found American missionaries to the Siamese, but none who could translate into Cambodian.

Then continuing to Singapore, on my way to Madras, Mr Haffenden asked, "When do you start?"

"The day after to-morrow," said I.

"How I wish," said he, "that you could go to Manila. We have sent two men there to endeavour to open a Bible depôt. One is dead, the other is in prison, and we are at our wits' end to know what to do."

Finally, the local committee unanimously asked me to go, which I did (they paying the fare and hotel expenses), and the man was soon afterwards released.

I was brought away from Manila by the kindness of Captain Craigie, in H.M.S. *Hyacinth*, on which I acted as quasi-Chaplain, to Borneo, and then continued to Singapore, whence I steamed to Ceylon, crossed

wards. But my health was impaired, and I was at last brought to see that I had been going too fast, and taxing my strength more than I suspected. On the whole my usual good health had supported me through the entire journey. Anxiety at Kuldja gave me for a few days a disordered digestion, after which all went well till malaria, or whatever it was, touched me going up the China coast. Then all was right up to Bombay, when I squeezed in night and day journeys to get up to Mount Aboo and down to Goa, and had hardly recovered from the fatigue before I rushed up to Quetta, again travelling night and day.

Rest on the steamer carried off this fatigue, but when, after four months daily in the saddle in Chinese Turkistan, I travelled by Ezra's route from Babylon to Jerusalem, for which he took four months and I only two, I was, to say the least, tired. Then I continued through Palestine, not with the luxury of Cook's tourists, but with a single servant and such cooking as he could do for me. On arriving at the banks of the Jordan, I slept in the open, and thought perhaps that this had disordered my digestion, whereupon at Ramoth Gilead I took too strong a pill, and travelled onwards for several days, when, had there been a house to stay in, I had better have rested.

And so I came up from Jericho to Jerusalem, where

to Tinnevelly, and travelled through Southern and Central India, visiting mission-stations, preaching, lecturing, and seeing and learning all I could.

At Karachi I waited for the succeeding steamer, and in the interim ran up to Quetta, held service for a few natives and engineers who were making the tunnel into Afghanistan, and officiated similarly at the head of the Persian Gulf. At Baghdad I preached more than once, as also at the mission-stations in Syria and Palestine, and had promised to do so a second time in Jerusalem, when—for the first time in my life—I fainted!

Dr Wheeler, of the London Jews' Society, was my good Samaritan, took me in and lodged me, gave me physic, and, though allowing that there was nothing organically wrong, thought I had better go straight home. This, however, I could not bring myself to do, but inasmuch as my mind was no longer on the stretch concerning Lassa, I thought I might recuperate my forces whilst leisurely returning and making the journey as useful as possible.

I, therefore, steamed to Malta, crossed southwards to Tripoli, and visited the stations of the North African Mission as far as Tangier.

Then I crossed into Spain, where, thanks to letters sent in advance from the English Foreign Office, I obtained permission to visit the Spanish prisons, into which I tried to introduce the Scriptures.

And so at length I reached England, to find awaiting me 30 bundles containing 1,564 postages, after an absence of 950 days, during a journey of 50,000 miles.

I have ventured to call my Tibetan appendix a "successful failure."

Had I succeeded in reaching Lassa, as I at first projected, from Chinese Turkistan, I should have had the distinction of being the only European now living to enter the holy city. I might perchance have distributed some Scriptures, taken photographs, and learned more than we now know of the capital. Also, if I had created a favourable impression upon the Grand Lama, or other influential personages, and found any opening for a mission among the Tibetans, this would perhaps have been as much as I could have expected to accomplish.

As it was, I placed before my supporters on my return a brief summary, as follows :—

The mission extended over two years and seven months, of which 525 were travelling and 425 were stationary days.

The regions visited comprised five of the kingdoms of Europe, four of Africa, and every kingdom of Asia.

The methods of travel were 18,000 miles by railway, 25,000 by water, and 7,000 by driving and riding on the backs of horses, camels, donkeys, yaks, elephants, mules, and men.

Copies of the Scriptures, or portions thereof, were distributed through five countries in eleven languages, distribution not being usually attempted where Bible agents were already at work.

Mission-stations were visited to the number of 170, in 110 localities, working under 50 societies and organisations. This brought me into personal contact with 400 missionaries. There were visited, likewise, 31 prisons in 29 towns.

I preached during the journey 75 sermons (some of them being interpreted into five languages), conducted 18 other religious services, and delivered 37 lectures or addresses, chiefly on my travels and frequently from a missionary point of view, for the encouragement of workers.

In districts little known to science (and those only) specimens were collected of fauna,—namely, 295 birds, 341 reptiles and fish, 867 beetles, and 3,586 butterflies; that is, 5,089 specimens in all.

With the camera were attempted 964 exposures (generally in duplicate), or, say, 500 photographs, whilst my diaries, journals, and notes extended to 2,509 pages.

Cash accounts were kept and presented to three

auditors in 32 kinds of currency. I brought home a small balance from the fund for Chinese Turkistan, more from the fund for Tibet, and some of the latter has been returned, as was promised, to one of the donors. The entire expense for the whole period of absence from London was, on the average, 30s. a day.

Once more—looking as a pioneer at the kingdoms passed through—I find Tibet, Nepal, Bhotan, and (perhaps) Chinese Turkistan without Christian missionaries. Missionaries (especially medical), translators, and Bible colporteurs should, I think, be set to work at once in Chinese Turkistan, but into Tibet, Bhotan, and Nepal I see no opening at present.

Next, I found the Ili valley, Cambodia, Cochin China, Annam, Tonking, and the Philippines, in the hands exclusively of Roman missionaries. Translators are needed for all these regions, and more missionaries, as also perhaps a chaplain for the European residents at Manila.

The next group of kingdoms consists of Ladak, Sikkim, and Siam, where there are Protestants and Moravians at work, but where I think Church of England missionaries would be welcomed. At Bangkok especially, both European and American residents expressed their desire for a Church of England clergyman.

To the foregoing I added my thanks to those who, by their means, sympathy, and prayers had aided me. Above all I expressed my gratitude to Him who preserved my life in many dangers and difficulties, and that without serious disaster or trying illness, throughout a very long and arduous undertaking.

I now cherish the hope that the result of my prolonged journey will eventually, by the Divine blessing, yield more for the Kingdom of God than if I had entered Great Tibet. When looking at my former successes in crossing Siberia and entering Bokhara, I learn not to give too much heed to prophecies of failure, but to go and try. Looking at my not having been permitted to enter Lassa, I learn that in *seeking* success we sometimes gain more than by acquiring it.

FINIS.

APPENDIX A.

SOME OF THE SPECIMENS OF FAUNA COLLECTED BY DR LANSDELL IN CHINESE CENTRAL ASIA.

THE following is by no means a complete record of the specimens collected by me. Proper precautions were not taken, unfortunately, before leaving England, to have all the specimens catalogued and determined on arrival. I give the lists, however, such as they are, and have to thank sundry friends for looking through them, especially Mr Dresser, F.Z.S., for classifying the birds; Mr Western, F.E.S., the beetles; Mr Bethune-Baker, F.L.S., F.E.S., for his List of Lepidoptera, and Dr Günther, F.R.S., for describing my new species of fish.

MAMMALIA (Mammals).

Latin Names.	English Name.	Place and Date of Capture.
Vesperugo serotinus	*Serotine bat*	Kuldja, 7.88
Erinaceus albulus	*Hedgehog*	Hisk, 13.6.88
Mus Wagneri	*Pigmy mouse*	Tashkend, 5.88
" "	"	Kuldja, 7.88
Gerbillus sp.	*Gerbille*	Tashkend, 5.88
Cervus maral (horns)	*Maral*	Maralbashi, 1.9.88

AVES (Birds).

FALCONIDÆ (Diurnal Birds of Prey).

Latin Names.	English Names.	Place and Date of Capture.
Falco tinnunculus	Kestrel	Sambhar, 10.1.89
" "	"	Hisk, 13.6.88
" cenchris	Lesser kestrel	
Aquila chrysaëtos	Golden eagle	South Muzart, 12.8.88
Buteo ferox	Long-legged buzzard	Borokludsir, 14.6.88
" "	" "	Srinagur, 8.12.88
" "	" "	Uri, Kashmir, 15.12.88
" "	" "	Near Yarkand, 26.12.88

MEROPIDÆ (Bee-eaters).

Merops viridis	Green bee-eater	Agra, 19.1.89

CORACIDÆ (Rollers).

Coracias indicus	Indian roller	Sambhar, 10.1.89
" "	" "	Segowlie, Tirhoot, 11.3.89
" garrulus	Common roller	Kuldja, 21.6.88

ALCEDINIDÆ (Kingfishers).

Ceryle rudis	Pied kingfisher	Jeypore, 13.1.89

PSITTACIDÆ (Parrots).

Palæornis torquatus	Rose-winged paroquet	Jeypore, 13.1.89
" "	" "	Agra, 19.1.89
" schisticeps	Slaty-headed paroquet	Murree, 23.12.88

PICIDÆ (Woodpeckers).

Latin Names.	English Names.	Place and Date of Capture.
Picus leucopterus	White-winged woodpecker.	Khotan, 3.10.88
,, ,,	,, ,,	9.10.88

CAPITONIDÆ (Barbets).

Megalaima caniceps	Common green barbet	Segowlie, 11.3.89

UPUPIDÆ (Hoopoes).

Upupa epops	Hoopoe	Kuldja, 19.7.88
,, ,,	,,	Aksu, 21.8.88
,, ,,	,,	Karghalik, 24.10.88

LANIDÆ (Shrikes).

Lanius lahtora	Indian grey shrike	Kuldja, 19.7.88
,, ,,	,, ,, ,,	Jeypore, 13.1.89
,, arenarius	Isabelline shrike	Aksu, 24.8.88
,, ,,	,, ,,	Chadir-Kul, 28.8.88
,, ,,	,, ,,	Kashgar, 28.8.88
,, ,,	,, ,,	Yarkand, 21.9.88

DICRURIDÆ (Drongo Shrikes).

Dicrurus ater	Black drongo	Agra, 19.1.89

CINCLIDÆ (Dippers).

Cinclus leucogaster	White-bellied dipper	Ak-Shor, 30.10.88
,, ,,	,, ,,	Tschkam, 1.11.88

TIMALIDÆ (Timaline Birds).

Trochalopterum simile.	Himalayan variegated laughing thrush.	Murree, 23.12.88
Trochalopterum lineatum.	Himalayan streaked laughing thrush.	Kohala, Kashmir, 19.12.88

SAXICOLIDÆ (Chats).

Latin Names.	English Names.	Place and Date of Capture.
Copsycus saularis	Magpie robin	Segowlie, 11.3.89
Ruticilla rufiventris	Indian redstart	Agra, 19.1.89
" erythronota	Eversman's redstart	" 29.10.88
" erythrogas-tra.	Güldenstädt's red-start.	Nubra Valley, 16.11.88
" " "	"	" Ak-Shor, 29.10.88
Pratincola maura	Eastern stonechat	Hisk, 13.6.88
" "	"	Kuldja, 19.7.88
Saxicola pleschanka	Siberian chat	Urdaklik, 4.9.88
" "	" "	Guma, 29.8.88

SYLVIDÆ (Warblers).

Sylvia minuscula	Dwarf whitethroat	Yarkand, 24.9.88

MOTACILLIDÆ (Wagtails).

Motacilla alba	White wagtail	Kuldja, 19.7.88
" personata	Masked wagtail	Muzart, 12.8.88
" maderas patensis.	Large pied wagtail	Segowlie, 11.3.89
" melanoce-phala.	Black-headed wagtail	Hisk, 13.6.88

PARIDÆ (Titmice).

Leptopoecile Sophiæ	Severtzoff's warbler titmouse.	Ak-Shor, 30.10.88
Parus cyanus	Azure titmouse	Muzart, 12.8.88
" "	" "	Nubra, 16.11.88

ACCENTORIDÆ (Accentors).

Accentor sp.	Accentor	Kilian Pass, 3.11.88
" fulvescens	Tawny accentor	Yarkand, 24.9.88
" "	" "	Ak-Shor, 30.10.88
" "	" "	Tschkun, 1.11.88

CORVIDÆ (Crows).

Corvus corone	Carrion crow	Nubra, 17.11.88
" cornix	Hooded crow	Yarkand, 24.10.88

Latin Names.	English Names.	Place and Date of Capture.
Corvus monedula	Jackdaw	Hisk, 13.6.88
,, collaris	Collared jackdaw	Srinagur, 8.12.88
Pica leucoptera	Magpie	Muzart, 12.8.88
Garrulus lanceolatus	Black-throated jay	Kohala, 19.12.88
Dendrocitta rufa	Indian tree pie	Segowlie, 12.2.89

STURNIDÆ (Starlings).

Sturnus indicus	Indian starling	Khotan, 10.10.88
,, porphyronotus	Starling	Charwagh, 29.8.88
,, porphyronotus	,,	Kashgar, 4.9.88
Pastor roseus	Rose pastor	Yarkand, 21.9.88
,, ,,	,, ,,	Karghalik, 24.10.88
Acridotheres tristis	Common mynah	Srinagur, 8.12.88
,, ,,	,, ,,	Sambhar, 10.1.89
,, ,,	,, ,,	Jeypore, 13.1.89
,, ,,	,, ,,	Agra, 19.1.89

FRINGILLIDÆ (Finches).

Passer ammodendri	Severtzoff's sparrow	Zawa Kurghan, 10.10.88
,, montanus	Tree sparrow	Kuldja, 19.7.88
,, ,,	,, ,,	Khotan, 10.10.88
Carpodacus erythrinus	Scarlet bullfinch	,, 12.8.88
Montifringilla Brandti	Brandt's snowfinch	South Muzart, 12.8.88

ALAUDIDÆ (Larks).

Alaudula sp.	Skylark	Guma, 28.9.88
,, Seebohmi	Seebohm's lark	Aksu, 24.8.88
Otocorys Brandti	Brandt's shorelark	Karghalik, 24.10.88
Galerita cristata	Crested lark	Chadir-Kul, 28.8.88
,, magna	,, ,,	,, ,, 29.8.88
,, ,,	,, ,,	Charwagh, 29.8.88

COLUMBIDÆ (Pigeons).

Latin Names.	English Names.	Place and Date of Capture.
Columba livia	Rock dove	Kuldja, 19.7.88
,, ,,	,, ,,	Tschkun, 1.11.88
Turtur vulgaris	Turtle dove	Kuldja, 19.7.88

PTEROCLIDÆ (Sandgrouse).

Pterocles arenarius	Black-bellied sand-grouse.	Borokhudsir, 14.6.88

PHASIANIDÆ (Pheasants).

Lophophorus impeyanus.	Impeyan pheasant	Kashmir, 15.12.88
Euplocomus albo-cristatus.	White-crested Kalij pheasant.	Uri, Kashmir, 15.12.88
Caccabis chukar var. pallescens.	Pallid Chukar Partridge.	South Muzart, 12.8.88

CHARADRIDÆ (Plovers).

Ægialites cantianus	Kentish plover	Aksu, 21.8.88
Vanellus vulgaris	Peewit	Ilisk, 13.6.88
,, ,,	,,	Aksu, 14.8.88

SCOLOPACIDÆ (Snipes).

Totanus glareola	Wood sandpiper	Aksu, 21.8.88
,,	,, ,,	Kashgar, 4.9.88
,, ochropus	Green sandpiper	Kuldja, 19.7.88
,, hypoleucus	Common sandpiper	,, 19.7.88
,, calidris	Redshank	Ilisk, 13.6.88
Himantopus candidus.	Stilt	Tschkun, 10.1.89

RALLIDÆ (Rails).

Fulica atra	Common coot	Sambhar, 10.1.89
Rallus aquaticus	Water rail	Kashgar, 15.9.88

ANATIDÆ (Ducks).

Dafila acuta	Pintailed duck	Sambhar, 10.1.89

REPTILIA (Reptiles).

Latin Names.	English Names.	Place and Date of Capture.
Eryx jaculus	Sand snake	Hisk, 13.6.88
Coluber dione	.	..
Tropidonotus hydrus	Water snake	Kuldja, 7.88
,, natrix	Common snake	Hisk, 13.6.88
Agama Stoliczkana	Lizard	Kashgar, 9.88
Phrynocephalus axillaris.	,,	..
,, versicolor.	,,	..
Eremias multocellata.	,,	
Teratoscincus Prjewalskii.	,,	

BATRACHIA (Batrachians).

Bufo viridis	Green toad	Kashgar, 9.88
Rana temporaria	Common frog	Kara-Kol, 5.88

PISCES (Fishes).

Latin Names.	Place and Date of Capture.
Diptychus Lansdelli *	Issik-Kul, 22.5.88
Schizothorax intermedius	Kashgar, 9.88
Labeo sp.	River Ili, 7.88
Nemachilus Yarkandensis	Kashgar, 9.88
" Kungessanus	Issik-Kul, 22.5.88
" Strauchii	Tian Shan Mountains, 5.88
" labiatus	" " " "

---

* In the *Annals and Magazine of Natural History* for April 1889, Dr Günther thus describes

DIPTYCHUS LANSDELLI.

D.11.   A.7.   P.18.   V.10.   L. lat., 80—90.

"Nearly the whole body is naked, the parts above the lateral line being quite scaleless; but there are a few scales between the lateral line and the root of the pectoral fin, a few scattered scales on the abdomen, and a series of larger ones running on each side of the vent and the anal fin. The scales of the lateral line are distinct enough in its anterior part, but rudimentary behind.

"The body is low, loach-like, the greatest depth being only one-sixth, or nearly one-sixth, of the total length (without caudal); the length of the head is contained four times and a quarter in it, and exceeds the length of the caudal peduncle. Interorbital space very broad, its width being equal to the length of the snout. The diameter of the eye is one-sixth of the length of the head and rather less than two-thirds of that of the snout. Mouth semi-circular, quite at the lower side of the snout. Barbel about as long as the eye. The dorsal fin is as long as high, its origin being equidistant from the end of the snout and from the end of the caudal peduncle. Caudal fin deeply forked. Pectoral fin reaching to the origin of the dorsal, ventral fin nearly to the vent. The outer ventral ray is opposite to, or a little behind the last dorsal ray.

"The upper two-thirds of the body of this species are covered with deep black spots, the largest of which are half the size of the eye.

"The largest of the species is 12 inches long; its anal rays are covered with seasonal epidermoid tubercules, arranged in a series along each ray."

COLEOPTERA (Beetles).

CARABIDÆ (Sunshiners).

Elaphrus cupreus Meg.
Carabus granulatus Linn.
 „ pumilio Küst.
Chlænius spoliatus Rossi.
Harpalus æneus Fabr.
Harpalus ruficornis Fabr.
 „ sp.
Calathus sp.
Dolichus sp.

SILPHIDÆ (Carrion Beetles).

Silpha obscura Linn. Hister sinuatus Ill.

SCARABÆIDÆ (Dung Beetles).

Onthophagus marginalis Geb.
Aphodius erraticus Linn.
 „ granarius Linn.
 „ sp.
Ceratophyus Hoffmannseggi (Dej.) Fairm.
Oxythyrea cinctella Schaum.
Cetonia aurata Linn.
 „ Karelini Zubk.

MALACODERMIDÆ.

Malachius æneus Linn. Malachius sp.

TENEBRIONIDÆ.

Anatolica gibbosa Gib. Blaps sp.
Tentyria sp. Tenebrio sp.

CANTHARIDÆ (Blister Beetles).

Cerocoma Mühlfeldi Gyll. Mylabris sp.

CURCULIONIDÆ (Weevils).

Sitones sp. Cleonus sp.
Chlorophanus vittatus Sch. Baridius sp.

CHRYSOMELIDÆ.

Chrysochares asiaticus Fab.
Lina sp.
Chrysomela sp.
Entomoscelis adonis Fab.
Agelastica alni Linn.

COCCINELLIDÆ (Lady Birds).

Coccinella septem-punctata Linn. Halyzia sp.

ARACHNIDA (Spiders).

Latin Name.	Place and Date of Capture.
Galeodes araneoides	. Samarkand, 28.4.88

HYMENOPTERA (Bees).

Latin Names.	English Names.	Place and Date of Capture.
Xylocopa valga	. Black bee .	. Kashgar, 17.9.88
Ophion luteus .		. Aksu, 14.8.89

NEUROPTERA.

Symphetrum meridionale .	. Kashgar, 10.9.88
„ sanguineum	„ „

ORTHOPTERA.

Ædipoda flavum	1888

MYRIOPODA.

Scutigera coleoptrata	. Samarkand, 28.4.88

LEPIDOPTERA (Butterflies and Moths).

I AM indebted for the following list (in which are included the specimens I brought from Chinese Central Asia) to Mr George T. Bethune-Baker of Edgbaston, who has not here attempted to make a complete catalogue of Turkistan Lepidoptera, but rather to supplement that of Erschoff given in my *Russian Central Asia*, vol. ii., p. 581. Since that list appeared Russian entomologists have explored various parts of Turkistan, and many thanks are due to His Imperial Highness the Grand Duke Romanoff for the magnificent way in which he has given the results of these and other expeditions and researches to the entomological public. To bring this list up to date Mr Bethune-Baker has had recourse mainly to these memoirs, together with a few papers of Staudinger's in the *Stettiner Entomologische Zeitung*. He has not, however, used the various papers by Christoph on the Lepidoptera of the Akhal Tekke, inasmuch as our present list deals with regions farther east. Nevertheless, there is no doubt that the whole district, together with Persia, Turkey in Asia, and the Levant, generally forms one sub-region, which has already been defined as the Mediterraneo-Persic sub-region.

The Lepidoptera I brought home, Mr Bethune-Baker says, tend to confirm the view (if such confirmation be needed) that the fauna of Chinese Turkistan is essentially Western Palæarctic in its character.

The species captured by me have an asterisk prefixed (*).

ABBREVIATIONS.

Alph	. . .	Alphéraky	Hw . .	Haworth
B .	. . .	Boisduval	Koll .	Kollar
Bergstr .	.	Bergstrasser	L . . .	Linnæus
Bkh .	. .	Borkhausen	Ld .	Lederer
Chr .	. .	Christoph	Mén . .	Ménétries
Cl .	. .	Clerck	O . . .	Ochsenheimer
Cr .	. .	Cramer	Pall . .	Pallas
Ersch .	.	Erschoff	Rott .	Rottemburg
Esp .	. .	Esper	Stgr .	Staudinger
Ev .	. .	Eversmann	Tausch .	Tauscher
F .	. . .	Fabricius	View . .	Vieweg
Feld .	. .	Felder	Vill . .	Villers
Frr .	. .	Freyer	Wernb .	Werneberg
Gn .	. .	Guenée	Z . . .	Zeller
Gr. Gr .	.	Groum-Grshimailo	Zett	Zetterstedt
Hb .	. .	Hübner	oc .	occidentalis (west)
Heyl .	. .	Heylaerts	or . .	orientalis (east)
Hfn .	. .	Hufnagel	m . . .	meridionalis (south)
H. S. .	.	Herrich-Schäffer	V. v. .	variety

RHOPALOCERA.

PAPILIONIDÆ.

Names.	Distribution in other countries.
Papilio Machaon v. Centralis Stgr.	Samarkand, etc.
Ismene Helios v. Maxima Stgr. (in litt.)	Persia, Turkistan.
Parnassius Apollonius Ev.	Turkistan.
„ Princeps	Pamirs.
„ „ Gr. Gr.	„
„ Honrathi Stgr.	„
„ Discobolus Alph.	Tian Shan.
„ Romanovi Gr. Gr.	Pamirs.
„ Actius Ev.	„
„ Rhodius Honr.	„
„ Charltonius Gray	Chinese Turkistan, Pamirs.
„ Delphius Ev.	Tian Shan, Pamirs.
„ V. Infernalis Stgr.	Alai Mountains.
„ V. Telustris Gr. Gr.	Pamirs.
„ V. Cardinal Gr. Gr.	Pamirs (Hissar Mountains).
„ V. Staudingeri Bang Haas.	Pamirs.
„ V. Hunza Gr. Gr.	Hindu Kush Mountains.
„ Simo Gray	Trans-Alai, etc., Pamirs.
„ Mnemosyne v. Gigantea Stgr.	Alai Mountains, Pamirs.

PIERIDÆ.

*Aporia Crataegi L.	Europe, Asia, etc.
Pieris Brassicæ v. Nepalensis Gray	Himalaya, Ferghana.
„ Roborowskii Alph.	Pamirs, Hindu Kush Mountains.
„ Tadjika Gr. Gr.	Pamirs.
• „ Rapæ L.	Europe, Asia, etc.
• „ V. Mannii.	Kashgar, Aksu, etc.
„ Canidia Sparm v. Palæarctica	Pamirs.

APPENDIX A.—LEPIDOPTERA.

Names.	Distribution in other countries.
Pieris Krueperi Stgr. v. Prisca Stgr.	Ferghana, Greece, Asia Minor, Persia.
„ V. Verna Gr. Gr.	Darwaz Mountains.
„ V. Mahometana Gr. Gr.	„ „
„ Napi L.	„ „ Europe, Asia, oc. Siberia
„ V. Napeae Esp.	Kashgar, Europe.
„ Ochsenheimeri Stgr.	Tian Shan.
„ Shawii Bates	Pamirs, Chinese Turkistan.
„ Iranica Bien	Persia, Kourgan.
„ Daplidice L.	Europe (except N.), Asia, etc.
„ V. Bellidice O.	„ „
„ Ab Raphani Esp.	Persia, Margellan.
„ Chloridice Hb.	Russia m., Asia, Siberia oc., Persia, Pamirs.
„ Callidice Esp. v. Kalora Moore	Tian Shan and Himalaya Mountains.
„ Leucodice Ev.	Persia, Central Asia.
„ V. Illumina Gr. Gr.	Pamirs.
Anthocharis Belia Cr.	Europe m., Asia Minor, Ferghana, etc.
„ V. Daphalis Moore	Central Asia.
„ Cardamines L.	Europe, Asia Minor, Central Asia, and Siberia.
„ Pyrothoe Ev.	Russia, Central Asia.
Zegris Fausti Chr.	Ferghana, Turkistan, Turkmenia.
Leucophasia Sinapis L.	Europe, Asia oc., Siberia oc., Ferghana.
Colias Marco Polo Gr. Gr.	Pamirs.
„ Erate Esp.	Russia, Siberia, Pamirs, Amur.
„ Hyaleoides Gr. Gr.	Hissar and Alai Mountains.
„ Pallida Stgr.	Ferghana, Pamirs.
„ Hyale v. Alta Stgr.	Pamirs.
„ Sieversi Gr. Gr.	„
„ Cocandica Ersch.	„
„ Eogene Feld.	Kashmir, Mongolia, Pamirs

Names.	Distribution in other countries.
Colias V. Erythas Gr. Gr.	Pamirs.
„ V. Elissa Gr. Gr.	„
„ Ab ♀ Cana Gr. Gr.	„
„ Staudingeri Alph. v. Pamira Gr. Gr.	Tian Shan, Pamirs.
„ Regia Gr. Gr.	Pamirs.
„ Alpherakii Stgr.	„
„ Christophi Gr. Gr.	Alai and Hissar Mountains.
„ Romanovi Gr. Gr.	Alai Mountains.
„ Thisoa Man v. Æolides Gr. Gr.	Trans-Alai.
„ Wiskotti Stgr.	Alai and Hissar Mountains, etc.
„ Ab ♀ Leuca Stgr.	Alai.
„ V. Separata Gr. Gr.	Trans-Alai.
„ V. Leucotheme Gr. Gr.	Pamirs.
„ V. Chrysoptera Gr. Gr.	„
„ V. Seres Gr. Gr.	„
Rhodocera Farinosa Zell.	Europe oc., Asia oc., Alai Mountains.

LYCÆNIDÆ.

Thecla Sassanides Koll.	Persia, Afghanistan, Pamirs, Kashmir.
„ Lunulata Ersch.	Hissar Mountains.
„ Rubi L.	Europe, Pamirs.
Thestor Fedtchenkoi Ersch.	Ferghana, Pamirs.
„ V. Alpina Gr. Gr.	Pamirs.
Polyommatus Solskyi Ersch.	Samarkand.
„ V. Fulminans Gr. Gr.	Alai Steppes.
„ Alpherakii Gr. Gr.	Kunjut Mountains.
„ Caspius v. Transiens Stgr.	Farab.
„ Sultan Stgr.	Hissar Mountains.
„ Sarthus Stgr.	Alai, Pamir.

Names.	Distribution in other countries.
Polyommatus Phœnicurus Ld.	
v. Margelanica Stgr.	Pamirs.
„ Dimorphus Stgr.	„
„ Thersamon Esp.	Europe or. m., Hyrcania, Asia oc., etc.
„ V. Alaica Gr. Gr.	Pamirs.
„ Dispar Hw. v. Rutilus Wernb.	Europe, Armenia, Central Asia.
„ Alciphron Rott.	Europe, Armenia, Central Asia.
„ Phlæas L.	Europe, etc.
„ V. Oxiana Gr. Gr.	Kabadian.
Cigaritis Acamas Klug	Syria, Persia, Central Asia.
Lycæna Bætica L.	Europe m., Africa, India, Central Asia.
„ Phiala Gr. Gr.	Kabadian.
„ Argiades Pall.	Europe, Asia, Siberia.
„ V. Decolor Stgr.	Asia.
„ Alaina Stgr.	Pamirs.
„ Elvira Ev.	Syr-daria and Amu-daria.
„ Trochylus Frr.	Europe m., Asia Minor, Central Asia.
„ Ægon	Europe, Armenia, Central Asia.
„ Dschagatai Gr. Gr.	Schir-Abad, Syr-daria.
„ Argus L.	Europe, Asia Minor, Pamirs.
„ Roxane Gr. Gr.	Pamirs.
„ Argiva Stgr.	Ferghana, Pamirs.
„ Eversmanni Stgr.	Russian Turkistan.
„ Christophi Stgr.	Kashmir, Russian Turkistan.
„ Tomyris Gr. Gr.	Pamirs.
„ Rutilans Stgr.	Alai Steppes.
„ Iris Stgr.	Alai Mountains, Pamirs.
„ Sieversi Chr.	Persia, Ferghana.
„ V. Haberhaueri Stgr.	Ferghana.
„ Bellona Gr. Gr.	Koudara.

Names.	Distribution in other countries.
Lycæna Loewii Z. v. Ferghana Stgr.	Bokhara, Ferghana.
„ Zephyrus H. S. v. Zephyrinus Stgr.	Asia Minor, Persia, Russian Turkistan.
„ Baton Bergstr.	Europe, Persia, Russian Turkistan.
„ Devanica Moore.	Pamirs, Kashmir.
„ Cytis Chr.	Russian Turkistan.
„ Panagæides Stgr.	„ „
„ V. Alaica Stgr.	Alai, Pamirs, Turkistan.
„ Tengstrœmi Ersch.	Russian Turkistan.
„ V. Carbonaria Gr. Gr.	Pamir Mountains.
„ Sinensis Alph.	Russian Turkistan.
„ Pheretes v. Lehanus Moore	Ladak, Issik-Kul.
„ Pheretiades v. Pheretulus Stgr.	Ferghana, Pamirs.
„ Miris Stgr.	Russian Turkistan.
„ Astrarche Bergstr.	Europe, Asia, etc.
„ Venus Stgr.	Russian Turkistan.
„ Eros v. Amor Stgr.	„ „
„ Hunza Gr. Gr.	Valley of River Mazar.
* „ Icarus Rott.	Europe, Asia Minor, India, Asia, etc.
* „ Amanda Schn.	Europe, Asia Minor, Russian Turkistan.
„ Magnifica Gr. Gr.	Russian Turkistan.
„ Eumedon Esp.	Europe, Asia Minor, Russian Turkistan.
„ Kogistana Gr. Gr.	Russian Turkistan.
„ Admetus v. Rippartii Frr.	Europe, Pontus, Russian Turkistan.
„ Phyllis v. Phyllides Stgr.	Russian Turkistan.
„ Poseidon v. Poseidonides Stgr.	„ „
„ Kindermanni v. Iphigenides Stgr.	„ „

Names.	Distribution in other countries.
Lycaena Actis v. Actinides Stgr.	Alai Steppes.
„ Dagmara Gr. Gr.	Khingoob-daria.
„ Argiolus L.	Europe, etc.
„ Sebrus B.	Europe, Asia Minor, Russian Turkistan.
„ Persephatta Alph.	Russian Turkistan.
„ V. Minuta Gr. Gr.	Pamirs.
„ Semiargus Rott.	Europe, Russian Turkistan, Amur.
„ Cyllarus Rott.	Europe, Russian Turkistan, Amur.
„ Chrysopis Gr. Gr.	Kunjut Mountains.
„ Charybdis Stgr.	Russian Turkistan.
„ Gigantea Gr. Gr.	Pamirs.

ERYCINIDÆ.

Polycæna Tamerlana Stgr.	Trans-Alai.
„ V. Temir Gr. Gr.	„ „

NYMPHALIDÆ.

Limenitis Trivena Moore	Russian Turkistan.
Neptis Lucilla v. Ludmilla H. S.	„ „
Vanessa C. Album v. Interposita Stgr.	„ „
„ V. Undina Gr. Gr.	„ „
„ Urticæ L.	Europe, Asia, etc.
„ Cardui L.	„ „
Melitæa Arduinna v. Rhodopensis Frr.	Pontus, Russian Turkistan.
„ V. Evanescens Stgr.	Russian Turkistan.
„ Ab Fulminans Stgr.	„ „
„ Phoebe v. Sibina	„
„ Trivia Schiff. v. Cataphelia Stgr.	„ „
„ Didyma O.	Europe, Russian Turkistan.
„ V. Turanica Stgr.	Bokhara.
„ V. Ala Stgr.	Peter the Great Mountains.
„ V. Persea Koll.	Kara-Kum.

Names.	Distribution in other countries.
Melitæa Saxatilis v. Ferghana Stgr.	Russian Turkistan.
„ V. Maracandica Stgr.	Hissar Mountains.
„ Acræina Stgr.	Margellan and Khokand.
„ Pamira Stgr.	Russian Turkistan.
„ Minerva Stgr.	Pamirs.
„ V. Palamedes Gr. Gr.	Russian Turkistan.
„ V. Pallas Stgr.	Alai Mountains.
„ Parthenie v. Sultanenis Stgr.	Samarkand.
„ Asteroida Stgr.	Osh.
*Argynnis Hegemone Stgr.	Pamirs, etc.
„ Pales v. Generator Stgr.	Turkistan.
„ Hecate v. Alaica Stgr.	Pamirs.
„ Lathonia L.	Europe (ex. Polar region).
„ Aglaja L.	„ (ex. Maur, Canar, Syria, and Persia).
„ Niobe v. Eris Meigen.	Europe, etc.
„ Jainadeva Moore	India, Pamirs.
„ Pandora Schiff	Europe, Algeria, Russian Turkistan.

SATYRIDÆ.

*Melanargia Parce Stgr.	Russian Turkistan.
„ V. Persa Gr. Gr.	„ „
„ V. Lucida Stgr.	„ „
Erebia Turanica Alph.	„ „
„ Meta Stgr.	„ „
„ V. Maracandica Ersch.	„ „
„ Hades Stgr.	„ „
„ Jordana Stgr.	„ „
„ V. Fasciata Stgr.	„ „
„ Ida Gr. Gr.	„ „
„ V. Icelos Gr. Gr.	„ „
„ Myops Stgr.	„ „
„ Mongolica Ersch.	„ „
„ Radians Stgr.	Alai and Trans-Alai.

APPENDIX A.—LEPIDOPTERA.

Names.	Distribution in other countries.
Erebia, V. Progne Gr. Gr.	Russian Turkistan.
Œneis Hora Gr. Gr.	Alai.
Satyrus Briseis v. Ferghana Stgr.	Ferghona.
„ V. Maracandica Stgr.	Russian Turkistan.
„ Heydenreichi Ld.	„ „
„ Anthe O.	Russia, Persia, Russian Turkistan, Siberia.
„ V. Enervata Alph.	Russian Turkistan.
„ Kaufmanni Ersch.	„ „
„ Staudingeri Bang Haas	„ „
„ V. Gultschensis Gr. Gr.	„ „
„ Sieversi v. Sartha Stgr.	„ „
„ Lehana Moore	„ „ and Burmah.
„ Huebneri Feld.	Kashmir, Russian Turkistan.
„ Boloricus Gr. Gr.	Kunjut Mountains.
„ Abramovi Ersch.	Russian Turkistan.
„ Leechi Gr. Gr.	Kunjut Mountains.
„ Wilkinsi Ersch.	Russian Turkistan.
„ Dissoluta Stgr.	„ „
„ Josephi Stgr.	„ „
„ Intermedius Gr. Gr.	„ „
„ Pamirus Stgr.	„
„ Stulta Stgr.	„ „
„ Parisatis Koll.	Persia, India, Mongolia.
„ Stheno Gr. Gr.	Pamirs.
„ Actaea v. Cordulina Stgr.	Russian Turkistan.
„ V. Alaica Stgr.	Alai Steppes.
Pararge Eversmanni F. v. W.	Russian Turkistan.
„ Menava Moore	Indian Mountains, Kashmir, Russian Turkistan.
Epinephele Davendra Moore	India, Russian Turkistan, etc.
„ Dysdora Ld.	Hyrcania, Russian Turkistan.
„ Narica Hb.	Coll. H. Lansdell, Turkistan.
„ Kirghisa Alph.	Russian Turkistan.
„ Haberhaueri Stgr.	Alai Mountains.

Names.	Distribution in other countries.
Epinephele V. Maureri Stgr.	Russian Turkistan.
,, Capella Chr.	,, ,, and Persia.
,, Pulchella Feld.	India, Russian Turkistan.
,, Naubidensis Ersch.	Russian Turkistan.
,, Cadusina v. Laeta Stgr.	,, ,,
,, V. Monotoma Stgr.	,, ,,
,, Lycaon v. Intermedia Stgr.	,, ,,
,, Turanica	,, ,,
,, Catamelas	,, ,,
,, Interposita Ersch.	,, ,,
Cœnonympha Nolckeni Ersch.	,, ,,
,, Iphis v. Mahometana Alph.	,, ,,
,, Pamphilus L.	Europe.
,, Sunbecca Ev.	Russian Turkistan.

HESPERIDÆ.

Spilothyrus Alceæ Esp.	Europe, Algeria, Russian Turkistan.
,, V. Australis Z.	Europe, Russian Turkistan.
,, Altheæ Hb. v. Bæticus Rambur	,, ,, ,,
,, Proteus Stgr.	Russian Turkistan.
Syrichthus V. Prometheus Gr. Gr.	,, ,,
,, Tessellum Hb.	Russia and Turkistan.
,, Nobilis Stgr.	Russian Turkistan.
,, Antonia Speyer	,, ,,
,, V. Gigantea Stgr.	,, ,,
,, Sidæ Esp.	Europe, Turkistan, Siberia.
,, Alpina Ersch.	Russian Turkistan.
,, V. Darwazica Gr. Gr.	,, ,,
,, Malvæ L.	Europe, Asia Minor, Russian Turkistan, Siberia.
,, Phlomidis H. S.	Europe, Asia Minor, Russian Turksitan.

Names.	Distribution in other countries.
Syrichthus Poggei Ld.	Syria, Russian Turkistan.
,, Lutulentus Gr. Gr.	Russian Turkistan.
,, Orbifer v. Lugens Stgr.	,, ,,
Hesperia Thaumas Hfn.	Europe, Algeria, Hyrcania, Russian Turkistan.
,, Stigma Stgr.	Russian Turkistan.
,, Sylvanus Esp.	Europe, Russian Turkistan, etc.
,, Comma L.	Europe, etc. (ex. Mauritania and Canaries).
,, Nostrodamus F.	Europe, Algeria, Russian Turkistan.
,, Ahriman Chr.	Russian Turkistan.
,, Ormuzd Gr. Gr.	,, ,,

HETEROCERA.

Sphinges.

SPHINGIDÆ.

Sphinx Convolvuli L.	Europe, Algeria, Russian Turkistan.
Deilephila Insidiosa Ersch.	Russian Turkistan.
,, Zygophylli O.	,, ,, and Russia.
,, Euphorbiae v. Centralasiae Stgr.	,, ,,
,, Livornica Esp.	Europe, Algeria, Asia Minor, Russian Turkistan.
,, Alecto L.	Europe, Russian Turkistan.
Smerinthus Kindermanni v. Orbata Gr. Gr.	Russian Turkistan.
,, Populi v. Populetorum Stgr.	,, ,,
Pterogon Proserpina Pall.	Europe, Russian Turkistan.
Macroglossa Ducalis Stgr.	Russian Turkistan.
,, Fuciformis L.	Europe, Pontus, Russian Turkistan.
,, Stellatarum L.	Europe, etc.

SESIIDÆ.

Names.	Distribution in other countries.
Sciapteron Tabaniforme v. Kungessana Alph. .	. Russian Turkistan.
Sesia Senilis Gr. Gr. .	,,
,, Ceiformis Stgr. .	,, ,,
,, Mutilata Stgr. .	,, ,,
,, Chrysidiformis v. Turanica Ersch.	

ZYGÆNIDÆ.

Ino Ambigua Stgr.	. Russian Turkistan.
,, Amaura Stgr.	,, ,,
,, Splendens Stgr.	,, ,,
,, Incerta Stgr.	,, ,,
,, Cognata v. Suspecta Stgr	,, ,,
,, Subsolana v. Solana Stgr.	,, ,,
,, Budensis v. Asiatica Stgr.	,, ,,
,, Dolosa Stgr.	,, ,,
Zygæna Pilosellæ v. Nubigena Ld. .	. Europe, Russian Turkistan.
,, Hissariensis Gr. Gr.	. Russian Turkistan.
,, Sogdiana Ersch. .	,, ,,
,, V. Separata Stgr.	,, ,,
,, Truchmena Ev. .	,, ,,
,, Kawrigini Gr. Gr.	,, ,,
,, Erschoffi Stgr.	,, ,,
,, Cocandica Ersch.	,, ,,
,, V. Karategina Gr. Gr. .	,, ,,
,, Huguenini Stgr. .	,, ,,

SYNTOMIDÆ.

Syntomis Bactriana Ersch.	. Russian Turkistan.
,, Maracandica Ersch.	,, ,,
,, V. Cocandica Ersch. .	,, ,,

BOMBYCES.

NYCTEOLIDÆ.

Names.	Distribution in other countries.
Sarrothripa Musculana Ersch.	Russian Turkistan.

LYTHOSIDÆ.

Nola Turanica Stgr.	Russian Turkistan.
Lithosia Lutarella v. Pallifrons.	,, ,, and Europe.

ARCTIIDÆ.

Deiopeia Pulchella L.	Europe, Algeria, Russian Turkistan, etc.
Nemeophila Russula v. Mortua Stgr.	Russian Turkistan.
Euarctia Proserpina Stgr.	,, ,,
Arctia Caja L.	,, ,, and Europe.
,, Intercalaris Ev.	,, ,,
,, Hebe v. Sartha Stgr.	,, ,,
,, Erschoffi v. Ferghana Stgr.	,, ,,
,, Glaphyra v. Gratiosa Gr. Gr.	,, ,,
,, Rupicola Gr. Gr.	,,
,, Guttata Ersch.	,, ,,
,, Spectabilis Tausch.	Russia and Russian Turkistan.
Ocnogyna Diva Stgr.	Russian Turkistan.
Spilosoma Fuliginosa v. Fervida	Europe, Russian Turkistan.
,, Placida Friv.	Asia Minor, Russian Turkistan.
,, Puella Stgr.	Russian Turkistan.
,, Turensis Ersch.	,,
,, Melanostigma Ersch.	,, ,,
,, Menthastri Esp.	Europe and Russian Turkistan.

COSSIDÆ.

Names.	Distribution in other countries.
Cossus Campicola Ev.	. Russian Turkistan.
„ Intractus Stgr.	„ „
Holcocerus Gloriosa Ersch.	„ „
„ Sericeus Gr. Gr.	„ „
Phragmatœcia Castaneæ Hb.	„ „ and Europe.
„ Furia Gr. Gr.	„ „
Hypopta Cæstrum Hb.	„ „ and Europe.
Stygia Æthiops Stgr.	„ „
Endagria Monticola Gr. Gr.	„ „
„ Agilis Chr.	„ „
„ Lacertula Stgr.	„ „
„ Nigritula Stgr.	„

PSYCHIDÆ.

Psyche Unicolor v. Asiatica Stgr.	Russian Turkistan, Amur.
Acanthopsyche Grummi Heyl.	„ „
Chalia Staudingeri Heyl.	„ „

LIPARIDÆ.

Orgyia Tristis Gr. Gr.	. Russian Turkistan.
„ Dubia Tausch.	„ „ and Russia.
„ Prisca Stgr.	„ „
Dasychira Selenophora Stgr.	„ „
„ Fascelina v. Nivalis Stgr.	„ „
Leucoma Flavosulphurea Ersch.	„ „
Porthesia Karghalika Moore	„ „
Ocneria Dispar L.	. Europe, etc. (ex. reg. sept. and Canaries).
„ Sarthus Ersch.	. Russian Turkistan.

BOMBYCIDÆ.

Bombyx Alpicola v. Prima Stgr.	Russian Turkistan.
„ Castrensis L.	. Europe, Asia Minor, Central Asia.

APPENDIX A. LEPIDOPTERA.

Names.	Distribution in other countries.
Bombyx Neustria v. Parallela Stgr.	Russian Turkistan.
„ Eversmanni Kind.	Russia, Russian Turkistan.
Crateronyx Sardanapalus Stgr.	Russian Turkistan.
Lasiocampa Obliquata Klug.	„ „
Megasoma Primigenum Stgr.	„ „

NOTODONTIDÆ.

Harpyia Interrupta Chr.	Russia, Russian Turkistan.
„ Erminea Esp.	Europe.
„ Przewalskii Alph.	Russian Turkistan.
„ Vinula L.	Europe, Russian Turkistan.
Pygæra Anachoreta v. Pallida Stgr.	Russian Turkistan.

NOCTUÆ.

Raphia Approximata Alph.	Russian Turkistan.
Acronycta Elæagni Alph.	„ „
„ Centralis Ersch.	„ „
„ Rumicis v. Turanica Stgr.	„ „
Bryophila Raptricula Hb.	„ „ and Europe.
„ Ab Oxybiensis Mill.	„ „ „
Agrotis Adumbrata Ev.	„ „
„ Obscura Brahm	Europe, Russian Turkistan, Siberia, Amur.
„ Degeniata Chr.	Russian Turkistan.
„ Insignata Ld.	„ „ and Russia.
„ C. Nigrum L.	Europe, Siberia, Russian Turkistan.
„ Xanthographa v. Elutior Alph.	Russian Turkistan.
„ Rubi View.	Europe (except Switzerland), Ural Mountains, Russian Turkistan, Pamirs.
„ Multangula Hb.	Europe, Ural, Russian Turkistan, Pamirs.

Names.	Distribution in other countries.
Agrotis Alpestris B.	Europe (mountains), Russian Turkistan, Pamirs.
,, Nomas Ersch.	Russian Turkistan and Pamirs.
,, Juldussi Alph.	Kuldja and Pamirs.
,, Lasciva Stgr.	Russian Turkistan.
,, Musiva Hb.	Europe, Pontus, Russian Turkistan.
,, Flammatra F.	Europe, Russian Turkistan.
,, Simulans Hufn.	,, ,, ,,
,, Citillus Alph.	Russian Turkistan.
,, Sollers Chr.	,, ,,
,, Junonia Stgr.	,, ,,
,, Signifera F.	Europe, Pontus, Russian Turkistan.
,, Rava H. S.	Iceland, Labrador, Russian Turkistan.
,, Confinis Stgr.	Russian Turkistan.
,, Birivia v. Plumbea Alph.	,, ,,
,, Exclamationis v. Serena Stgr. (in litt.).	,, ,,
,, Nigricans L.	,, ,, and Europe.
,, Islandica v. Rossica Stgr.	Russia, Russian Turkistan.
,, Tritici v. Varia Alph.	Europe, ,, ,,
,, Hilaris Frr.	Pontus, ,, ,,
,, Indigna Chr.	Russian Turkistan.
,, Basigramma Stgr.	,, ,, and Russia.
,, Conspicua ab Lycarum H. S.	Europe, Hyrcania, Russian Turkistan, etc.
,, Subconspicua Stgr.	Russian Turkistan.
,, Confusa Alph.	,, ,,
,, Multicuspis Ev.	Ural and Russian Turkistan.
,, Acuminifera Ev.	Russian Turkistan.
,, Junctimacula Chr.	,, ,,
,, Segetum v. Pallida Stgr.	,, ,,
,, Crassa v. Golickei Ersch.	,, ,,
,, Obesa v. Scytha Alph.	,, ,, and Persia.

APPENDIX A.—LEPIDOPTERA. 435

Names.	Distribution in other countries.
Chareas Graminis v. Megala Alph.	Russian Turkistan.
Neuronia Arschanica Alph.	,, ,,
Mamestra Spalax Alph.	Ural, Russian Turkistan, and Armenia.
,, Contigua Vill.	Europe, Ural, Turkistan.
,, Dissimilis Kn.	Europe, Siberia, Turkistan.
,, Brassicæ L.	Europe, Pontus, Siberia, Russian Turkistan.
,, Altaica Ld.	Russian Turkistan.
,, Oleracea L.	Europe and Turkistan.
,, Dianthi Tausch.	Russia, Pontus, Turkistan.
,, Trifolii Rott.	Europe, Russian Turkistan.
,, Reticulata v. Unicolor Stgr.	Russian Turkistan.
,, Chrysozona Bkh.	Europe, Syria, Turkistan.
,, Accurata Chr.	Russian Turkistan.
Dianthœcia Orientalis Alph.	,, ,,
Phleboëis Petersi Chr.	,, ,,
Phœbophilus Amœnus Stgr.	,, ,,
Comophorus Villosus Alph.	,, ,,
Ammoconia Cæcimacula F.	,, and Europe.
Polia Chamæleon Alph.	,, ,,
,, Tenuicornis Alph.	,, ,,
,, Centralasiæ ab Asiatica Alph.	,, ,,
Miselia Cortex Alph.	,, ,,
Luperina Siri Ersch.	,, ,,
Isochlora Viridis v. Maxima Stgr.	,, ,,
Eicomorpha Antiqua Stgr.	,, ,,
Hadena Adusta v. Vicina Alph.	,, ,,
,, Furva Hb.	Europe, Russian Turkistan.
,, Expallescens Stgr.	Russian Turkistan.
,, Leucodon Ev.	Russia, Siberia, Turkistan.
,, Gemina ab Remissa Tr.	Europe, Turkistan, Amur.
Pseudohadena Armata Alph.	Russian Turkistan, Tibet.
Rhizogramma Peterseni Chr.	Russian Turkistan.

Names.	Distribution in other countries.
Hydroecia Ochreola Stgr.	Asia Minor, Turkistan.
Mycteroplus Didymogramma Ersch.	Russian Turkistan.
Tapinostola Musculosa v. Laeta Alph.	,, ,,
Leucania Dungana Alph.	,, ,,
,, Pallens v. Infumata Alph.	,, ,,
,, Conigera F.	Europe, Ural, Turkistan.
,, Vitellina Hb.	Europe, Asia Minor, Persia, Russian Turkistan.
,, L. Album L.	Europe, Asia Minor, Russian Turkistan.
Caradrina Quadripunctata F.	Europe, Pontus, Russian Turkistan, Siberia.
,, Menetriesii v. Grisea Ev.	Russian Turkistan.
,, Vicina Stgr.	South Russia, Turkistan.
,, Ambigua F.	Europe, Russian Turkistan.
Hydrilla Gluteosa Tr.	Europe, Ural, and Russian Turkistan.
,, Cinerea Alph.	Turkistan.
Amphipyra Tragopoginis v. Turcomana Stgr.	,,
Hiptelia Grummi Alph.	,,
Cosmia Subtilis Stgr.	,,
Dyschorista Plebeja Stgr.	,,
Scoliopteryx Libatrix L.	Europe, Turkistan, Amur.
Calocampa Exoleta v. Impudica Stgr.	Russian Turkistan.
Xylomyges Conspicillaris L.	Europe, Russian Turkistan.
Pulcheria Catomelas Alph.	Russian Turkistan.
Cucullia Amota Alph.	,, ,,
,, Umbratica L.	Europe, Russian Turkistan.
,, Chamomillæ Schiff	,, ,, ,,
,, Tanaceti Schiff	Europe, Pontus, Turkistan.
,, Xeranthemi B.	Europe, Russian Turkistan.
,, Argentina F.	Russia, ,, ,,

Names.	Distribution in other countries.
Cucullia Splendida Cr.	Ural, Russian Turkistan.
Plusia Deaurata v. Semiargentea Alph.	Russian Turkistan.
„ Gutta Gn.	Europe, Asia Minor, Persia, Turkistan, Amur.
„ Pulchrina v. Monogramma Alph.	Russian Turkistan.
„ Gamma L.	Europe, Russian Turkistan.
„ Circumflexa L.	Europe, Pontus, Turkistan.
„ Ni Hb.	Europe, Algeria, Asia Minor, Turkistan.
„ Hochenwarthi Hochw.	Europe, Russian Turkistan, Labrador.
„ Divergens Hb.	Alps, Russian Turkistan.
Hypsophila Jugorum Ersch.	Russian Turkistan.
„ V. Pamira Stgr.	„ „
Heliothis Dipsaceus L.	Europe, Russian Turkistan.
„ Scutosus Schiff	„ „ „
„ Armiger Hb.	Europe, Algeria, Turkistan.
„ Incarnatus Frr.	Spain, Syria, Russia, Russian Turkistan.
Acontia Lucida v. Lugens Alph.	Russian Turkistan.
„ Ab Albicollis F.	Europe, Russian Turkistan.
Armada Hueberi Ersch.	Russian Turkistan.
„ Panaccorum Men.	„ „ and Sarepta.
Thalpochares Respersa v. Grata Tr.	Europe, Russian Turkistan, Syria.
„ Purpurina Hb.	Europe, Pontus, Turkistan.
„ Ostrina v. Æstivalis Gn.	Europe m., Syria, etc., and Russian Turkistan.
„ Chlorotica v. Viridis Stgr.	Turkistan.
Agrophila Trabealis ab Nigra Ersch.	„
Metoponia Subflava Ersch.	„
Euclidia Regia Stgr.	„
„ Catocalis Stgr.	„
„ Ab Grummi Alph.	„

Names.	Distribution in other countries.
Euclidia Mi Cl. .	. Europe, Pontus, Ural, Russian Turkistan.
„ Munita Hb. .	. South Russia, Turkistan.
„ Ab Immunita Mill.	„ „ „
Pericyma Albidentaria Frr.	„ „ „
„ Profesta Chr. .	. Russian Turkistan.
Acantholipes Regularis Hb.	. Turkistan and Russia.
Leucanitis Rada B. . .	. Armenia, Turkistan.
„ Caucasica Koll.	„ „
„ Langi Ersch. .	Russian Turkistan.
„ Obscurata Stgr.	. Asia Minor, Turkistan.
„ Sesquilina Stgr.	. Russian Turkistan.
„ Saisani Stgr.	„ „
„ Stolida F. .	. Europe, Algeria, Asia Minor, Russian Turkistan.
Palpangula Myrifica Ersch.	. Russian Turkistan.
Grammodes Algira L. .	. Europe, Algeria, Asia Minor, Syria, Russian Turkistan.
Catocala Elocata Esp.	. Europe, Algeria, Asia Minor, Syria, Russian Turkistan.
„ Neonympha Esp. .	. Russia, Armenia, Russian Turkistan.
„ Puerpera (Giorna)	. Europe, Syria, Armenia, Russian Turkistan, Siberia.
Spintherops Cataphanes v. Maculifera Stgr.	. Russian Turkistan.
„ Dilucida v. Asiatica Stgr. .	. Russia, Russian Turkistan.
Toxocampa Lusoria L.	. Europe, Pontus, Russian Turkistan.
„ Craccæ F.	. Europe, Armenia, Russian Turkistan, Amur.
Hypena Ravalis H.	. South Russia, Pontus, Russian Turkistan.

APPENDIX B.

BIBLIOGRAPHY OF CHINESE CENTRAL ASIA.

THIS bibliography is intended to be complementary to the two bibliographies published in *Through Siberia* and *Russian Central Asia*; so that works previously mentioned in them, which have reference also to parts of Chinese Central Asia, are not necessarily repeated here. Experience gained in compiling the bibliography of *Russian Central Asia* enabled me on the present occasion to go to work more directly than before, but I am not sure whether the result is quite so exhaustive.

A commencement was made by taking several catch-words * that might be expected to occur in the titles of books, papers, or articles, treating of the countries under consideration. Then, search was made through Watt's *Bibliotheca Britannica* and Low's *English Catalogue*, the latter professing to be " of books published in Great Britain, and the principal books imported from the United States of America." Next, for French books, the *Catalogue Général* of Otto Lorenz, from 1840 and onwards, was searched, and also the classified catalogues of the London Library, the India Office, and the Royal Geographical Society.

* Such as Amur, Asia (Central), Buddhism (in Tibet), China (outside the Wall), Chinese Turkistan, Gobi, Himalayas, Kalmuks, Kansu, Karakorum, Kashgaria, Khotan, Ladak, Lassa, Leh, Little Tibet, Lob-Nor, Manchuria, Mongolia, Muzart (Pass), Sungaria, Tangut, Taranchis, Tarim, Tatars, Tian Shan, Tibet, Turks, Uigurs, Yarkand, Yuechi, etc.

In this way was compiled, it is hoped, a tolerably complete list of works on Exterior China, published in English and French, as well as a few German and Russian books. After this, with the same catch-words, were searched, for articles, papers, and minor literary efforts, the indices of the journals of half-a-dozen learned Societies, namely : —

>The Royal Geographical Society of London,
>The Manchester Geographical Society,
>The Bombay Geographical Society,
>The Royal Asiatic Society of London,
>The Asiatic Society of Bengal,
>The Society of Arts of London.

The total number of titles collected in this manner was 742. These were copied to give, as far as possible, the author's name ; title of book or article ; date of the travel or information ; name of editor or translator ; name of periodical or series ; place and date of publication. The titles were then classified under the eight heads of : 1, Chinese Central Asia (generally) ; 2, Manchuria ; 3, Mongolia ; 4, Sungaria ; 5. Turkistan (Chinese) ; 6, Tibet ; 7, Ladak ; and 8, Maps ; the last being chiefly those in my own possession.

After this the titles were arranged chronologically—not necessarily according to the year of publication, but with regard rather to the date when the information was obtained —and each title, or sometimes group of titles, was then numbered. Finally, an index was made of authors' names, to each of which there was added the numbers standing in the bibliography against their respective works.

Thus informed of what has been done, and how, the reader who wishes to extend his researches may see where to begin. It is probable that a few more English and American books could be found, the titles of which do not appear in the bibliographical works of Watt or Low, whilst for minor literary contributions the entire field of popular literature may be searched. In prosecuting this work I have been largely assisted by others, especially by my wife, who has been the real compiler of this portion of my book, and to all of whom my thanks are due.

Taking now an extended view, it will be seen that my three bibliographies of Siberia, Russian Central Asia, and Chinese Central Asia cover, with more or less completeness, the whole of northern and central Asia, from the Caspian to the Pacific, and extending northwards to the Arctic Ocean. The Hon. George Curzon also has prepared a bibliography of Persia, and M. Henri Cordier of China proper. Thus the literature bearing on more than half the area of Asia has been collected and classified, and it were much to be wished that others would make bibliographies of the remainder.

"But why," it may be asked, "stop here?" Is it anything short of a blot and a shame to our nation, which possesses in the British Museum the finest library in the world, and which has a literature, we think, surpassed by none, that we remain, nevertheless, so deficient as not to possess a subject catalogue thereto? Hence it comes to pass that, if an author is about to treat of, or a traveller to visit, say, Borneo, and he wishes to know what has been penned thereon, there exists no one work of reference to which he can turn and see at a glance all that has been published upon this, or a given subject, in books, to say nothing of contributions to periodical publications.

If we ask a librarian, "What books have you by such an author?" the answer will be soon forthcoming; but ask, "What books have you on such a subject?" and the librarian is either dependent on his own knowledge or on reference to a number of incomplete bibliographical works.

As I said, then, in *Russian Central Asia*, "What a boon might be bestowed upon students and literary men, and through them, be it remembered, on their readers, and what glory added to our literature, if some generous patron of letters, assisted by enthusiastic volunteers, would compile a subject catalogue of English books! There is now in course of preparation an English dictionary that, when completed, will be the most thorough, by far, in any language; in the prosecution of which the editorial staff has been assisted by hundreds of volunteers. Could not a like effort be set on foot in the interest of bibliography? Could not some benefactors be found to bear the expense of the editorial staff? Many a fortune has been bequeathed or given for a less worthy object. The title of the work might be made to perpetuate the name of the donor, and abundance of voluntary help could be enlisted." The accomplishment of such a work would be a crown to our literature to the end of all time; and decennial appendices could hereafter be made to give information up to date.

Meanwhile, I append my little bibliography, *arranged chronologically*.

ABBREVIATIONS.

J.A.S.B., *Journal of the Asiatic Society of Bengal.*
J.B.G.S., ,, ,, ,, *Bombay Geographical Society.*
J.M.G.S., ,, ,, ,, *Manchester Geographical Society.*
J.R.A.S., ,, ,, ,, *Royal Asiatic Society (of London).*
J.R.G.S., ,, ,, ,, *Royal Geographical Society (of London).*
J.S.A., ,, ,, ,, *Society of Arts.*
P.R.G.S., *Proceedings of the Royal Geographical Society.*
P.G.M., *Petermann's Geographische Mittheilungen.*
O.S., Old series. N.S., New series.
—— signifies repetition of preceding author's name.
[ ] Square brackets inclose the known or supposed dates of travel, or time when the information was acquired.

CHINESE CENTRAL ASIA IN GENERAL.
FROM EARLIEST TIMES TO 1700.

1. **Beal, Samuel.** The Life of Hiuen Tsiang. *London.* 1888
2. **Bretschneider, E.** Notes on Chinese Travellers to the West. *Shanghai*, 1875
3. —— Notices of Mediæval Geography, etc. *London.* 1876
4. —— Mediæval Researches from Eastern Asiatic Sources. *London.* 1888
5. **Reinaud, J. T.** Relations des Voyages faits par les Arabes et les Persans dans l'Inde et à la Chine dans le XII° siècle de l'ère Chrétienne. Texte Arabe avec traduction Française. 2 vols. 1846
6. **Yule, H.** Cathay and the Way Thither. *London.* 1866
7. **Carpini, J. de Plano.** Travels in Tartary [1246]. **Kerr.** Vol. I.
8. **Rubruquis, W. de.** Travels in Tartary [about 1253]. **Kerr.** Vol. I.
9. **Haithon, Prince of Armenia.** Travels in Tartary [1254]. **Kerr.** Vol. I.
10. —— —— Histoire Orientale Arménien. **Bergeron, P.** Recueil des voyages en Asie.
11. —— —— Raccolta delle Navigationi et Viaggi. **Ramusio, G. B.** 2 vols.

APPENDIX B.—BIBLIOGRAPHY.   443

12. **Polo, Marco.** Travels in China (1260 to 1295). **Kerr.** Vol. I.
13. —— Voyage du Vénétien (1272 to 1295).
14. —— Raccolta delle Navigationi et Viaggi. **Ramusio, G. B.**
15. —— The Most Noble and Most Famous Travels into the East parts of the Worlde, as Armenia, Persia, Arabia, Tartaria, with many other Kingdoms and Provinces. 4to. *London*, 1579
16. **Oderic, of Pordenau.** Travels into China (1318). **Kerr.** Vol. I.
17. **Goes, B.** Reisen ... nach China. Voyages and Travels. Allgemeine Historie, vol. vii.
18. —— Travels from Lahore to China in 1607. **Astley.** Vol. IV.
19. —— Travels through the Tartar's Countrie. **Purchas.** Vol. III. 1603
20. —— Travels from Lahore to China. **Purchas.** Vol. III. 1603
21. —— Travels from Lahore to China. **Pinkerton.** Vol. VII. *London*
22. **Purchas, Samuel.** Relation of two Russe Cossacks Travailes out of Siberia to Catay. Vol. III. 1619
23. —— Pilgrimes. Vol. III. Fol. *London*, 1625
24. **Davies, John.** Travels and Voyages of the Ambassadors sent by Frederic Duke of Holstein to the Great Czar of Muscovy and the King of Persia; containing a complete History of Muscovy, Tartary, Persia, and other adjacent countries. Fol. *London*, 1633-9
25. **Fletcher, Giles, LL.D.** Israel Redux; an Essay on probable grounds that the Tartars are the posterity of the Ten Tribes of Israel. 8vo. *London*, 1667
26. **Anderson, George.** He travelled through Arabia, Persia, India, China, and Japan, and returned by Tartary, Northern Persia, Mesopotamia, and Palestine. An account of this was taken down by **Adam Olearius**; he was afterwards prevailed upon to revise the MS., and it was published at Sleswick by **Olearius** in German. Fol. 1669
27. **Greslon, Adrien.** Histoire de la Chine sous la Domination des Tartares. 8vo. *Paris*, 1671
28. **Settle, Elkanah.** Conquest of China by the Tartars. (A Tragedy.) 4to. *London*, 1676
29. **Morrison, John.** Voyages and Travels through Muscovia, Tartary, India, and most of the Eastern World. Translated from the Dutch. 4to. *London*, 1684
30. **Avril, P.** Voyages in various parts of Europe and Asia. 8vo. *London*, 1693
31. **D'Hauteville.** A brief history of the Tartars. Translated from the original French. *London*, 1698

1700–1800.

32. **Tooke, William, F.R.S.** Account of the burial-places of the Ancient Tartars. 1705
33. **Bergeron, Pierre.** Relations des Voyages en Tartarie du Père Rubruquis, avec un Traité des Tartares, et précède d'une intro-

duction concernant les voyages et les nouvelles decouvertes des principaux voyageurs. 8vo. *Paris*, 1734

34. **Bergeron, Pierre.** Voyages en Asie dans les 12me, 13me, 14me, et 15me siècles; accompagné de l'Histoire des Sarasins et des Tartares. 2 vols. 4to. *La Haye*, 1735

35. **Du Halde, John Baptist.** Geographical, Historical, Chronological, Political, and Physical Description of the Empire of China and Chinese Tartary. 4 vols. Fol. *London*, 1736

36. —— Description of China and Chinese Tartary; together with the Kingdoms of Korea and Thibet. With maps, etc., and notes by the translator. 2 vols. Fol. *London*, 1738-41

37. **Strahlenberg, Philip John von.** Historico-Geographical Description of the North and Eastern parts of Europe and Asia, but more particularly of Russia, Siberia, and Great Tartary, both in their ancient and modern state; with a new polyglot table of the dialects of 32 Tartarian Nations, and a vocabulary of the Kalmuck-Mongolian tongue; translated from the original German into English. 2 vols. 4to. *London*, 1736-8

38. **Cook, John, M.D.** Voyages and Travels through the Russian Empire, Tartary, and part of the Kingdom of Persia. 2 vols. 8vo. *Edinburgh*, 1770

39. **Grosier, Abbé.** Translation from the French of his general description of China; containing the topography of the 15 provinces which compose this vast Empire, that of Tartary, the Isles, and other tributary countries; the number and situation of its Cities, the state of its Population, the Natural History of its Animals, Vegetables, and Minerals. Together with the latest accounts of their Government, Religion, Customs, Arts, etc. 2 vols. 8vo. *London*, 1788

40. **Winterbotham, W.** An Historical, Geographical, and Philosophical View of the Chinese Empire; comprehending a Description of the 15 provinces of China, Chinese Tartary, Tributary States; Natural History of China; Government, Religion, Laws, Manners and Customs, Literature, Arts, Sciences, Manufactures, etc. To which is added a copious account of Lord Macartney's Embassy; compiled from original communications. 8vo. *London*, 1795

41. **Huttner, J. C.** An Account of the British Embassy through China and part of Tartary. 8vo. *Berlin*, 1797

1800—1850.

42. **Bergman, B.** Nomadische Streifereien unter den Kalmüken in den Jahren 1802-3. 4 vols. *Riga*, 1804-5

43. —— Voyage chez les Kalmuks. Trad. by **Moris**. 8vo. *Chatelain-sur-Seine*, 1825

44. **Coxe, W.** Account of Commerce between Russia and China. 1804

45. **Geissler, J. G.** Mahlerische Darstellungen, etc.; or, Picturesque

Representations of the Manners, Customs, and Amusements of the Russians, Tartars, Mongols, and other nations of the Russian Empire. With 40 coloured plates. 8vo. *Leipzig*, 1805

46. **Oollah Meer, Izzut.** Travels in Central Asia, 1812-1813. Translated by **Capt. Henderson.** *Calcutta*, 1872

47. **Rémusat, Abel B.** Nouveaux Mélanges Asiatiques. 2 vols. 8vo. 1820

48. **Klaproth, J.** Verzeichniss der Chinesischen und Mandschuischen Bücher und Handschriften der Königlichen Bibliothek zu Berlin. *Paris*, 1822

49. —— Magasin Asiatique, ou Revue Géographique et Historique de l'Asie Centrale. 2 vols. *Paris*, 1825

50. **Rosenmüller, E. F.** Biblical Geography of Central Asia. 2 vols. 12mo. *London*, 1836-7

51. **Miles, Col.** Genealogical Tree of the Turks and Tartars. 8vo. *London*, 1838

52. **De Humbold, A.** Asie Centrale. Recherches sur les chaines de montagnes et la climatologie comparée. 3 vols. 8vo. 1843

1850–1860.

53. **Huc, Abbé.** L'Empire Chinois, faisant suite aux *Souvenirs d'un Voyage, etc.* 2 vols. 8vo. 1854

54. —— The Chinese Empire; a sequel to the *Recollections, etc.* 2 vols. 8vo. 1855

55. —— Christianity in China, etc. 2 vols. 8vo. 1857

56. **Williams, S. W.** The Middle Kingdom; Chinese Empire and its Inhabitants. *New York and London*, 1848. 2nd edition, *London*, 1883

57. **Ferrier, J. P.** Caravan Journeys in Persia, Afghanistan, Turkistan, and Beloochistan, with Historical Notices of the Countries lying between Russia and India. 8vo. 1856

58. **De Saint-Martin, Vivien.** Mémoire analytique sur la carte de l'Asie Centrale et de l'Inde, construite d'après le Si-yu-ki et les autres relations Chinoises des premiers siècles de notre ère. 8vo. 1858

59. **Ewart, W.** Settlement in India and Trade with Central Asia. *London*, 1858

1860–1870.

60. **Schott.** Die Tataren des Tschingghis-Chan, von einem Chinesischen Zeitgenossen (les Tâtars de Tchinghiz-khân, par un auteur Chinois contemporain). Dans les Archives (d'Erman) für wissenschaftliche Kunde von Russland, t. xx., pp. 185-191. 1861

61. **Radlof.** Observations sur les Kirghis. Journal Asiatique, Oct., pp. 309-328. 1863

62. **Taylor, Bayard.** Central Asia. Proceedings of the American Geographical Society of New York, pp. 59-77. 1863-4

63. **Julien, Stanislas.** Mélanges de géographie Asiatique et de philologie Sinico-Indienne, extraits des livres Chinois. 8vo. 1864
64. **Golubief, Capt.** Observations on the Astronomical Points determined by the Brothers Schlagintweit in Central Asia. J.A.S.B., Part II., new series, pp. 46-50. 1866
65. **Tonnelier, Jules.** Dictionnaire géographique de l'Asie Centrale. 4to. 1869
66. Trade Routes between North India and Central Asia. *Exeter*, 1869

1870 1880.

67. **Pumpelly, R.** Across America and Asia. A five years' journey. 8vo. *London*, 1870
68. **Poltaratsky.** Journey of, for investigation of Muzart Pass in the Tian Shan. Journal of the Russian Geographical Society, pp. 175-185. 1869
69. **Kaulbars.** Journey to the Muzart Pass in the Tian Shan in 1870. Journal of the Russian Geographical Society. 1871, pp. 176-178; 1872, pp. 17-22.
70. ——— Survey in the Tian Shan. J.R.G.S., xl., p. 165.
71. **Shépéleff.** Reconnaissance of Muzart Pass in Tian Shan (Russ.). Journal of the Russian Geographical Society, pp. 113-137. 1872
72. ——— Le défilé et les glaciers de Mouzart [1871]. Extract du Journal de St Pétersbourg 13.15.20 Juillet 1872.
73. ——— Recognoscirung des Musart Passes. P.G.M., p. 400. 1872
74. **Cayley.** The Jade Quarries of the Kuen Lun. Macmillan's Magazine, vol. xxiv., p. 455. *London*, 1871
75. **Montgomerie, Major T. G.** A Havildar's journey through Chitral to Faizabad. J.R.G.S., xvi., No. 3, pp. 253-361. 1870
76. **Kropotkine, P. O.** Article on Eastern Turkistan. Encyclopædia Britannica, ninth edition.
77. **Drew, M. Fred.** Letter to Sir Roderick Murchison on the death of Mr Hayward. P.R.G.S., xv., No. 2, p. 117. 1871
78. **Veniukoff.** Das Russische Asiatische Grenzlande. *Leipzig*, 1874
79. **De Rialle, Giraud.** Mémoire sur l'Asie Centrale, son histoire, et ses populations. 8vo. *Paris*, 1874-5
80. **Stuart, A.** Les traces du chemin de fer Central Asiatique projetées par MM. F. de Lesseps et Cotard. 8vo. 1876
81. **Shaw, R. B.** On the Ghalchah languages. J.A.S.B., vol. xlv., Part I., chap. ii., pp. 138-276. *Calcutta*, 1876
82. **Gordon, T. E.** The Roof of the World. 8vo. *Edinburgh*, 1876
83. Le Chamanisme. Journal des Missions Evangeliques, pp. 275-280. 1877
84. **Shaw, Robert.** Waterpassings *versus* Ranges. Geographical Magazine. 1877
85. **Paquier, J. B.** Le Pamir; étude géographique et historique sur l'Asie Centrale. 8vo. 1877

86. **Baker, Col. V.** L'Angleterre et la Russie dans l'Asie Centrale ; Rapport politique et stratégique. 12mo. 1877
87. Recueil d'itinéraires et de voyages dans l'Asie Centrale et l'extrême Orient. 8vo. 1878
88. **Prjevalsky, N.** De Kouldja par le Tian Shan jusqu'au Lob-Nor. From *Journal de St Pétersbourg*, March. 1878
89. **Keene, H. G.** Notes on a Map of the Mughal Empire. J.A.S.B., p. 152. 1878
90. **Michell, Robert.** The Russian Expedition to the Alai and Pamir. J.R.G.S. 1878

1880—1890.

91. **Lansdell, Henry.** Through Siberia [1879]. 2 vols. 8vo.
London, 1882. 5th edition, 1 vol., *London*, 1883
92. —— Durch Sibirien [1879]. Tr. into German by **W. Müldener**. 2 vols. *Jena*, 1882
93. —— Genom Sibirien [1879]. Tr. into Swedish. 2 vols.
Stockholm, 1882
94. —— Gjennem Sibirien [1879]. Tr. into Danish. 2 vols.
Copenhagen, 1883
95. **Vambéry, H.** Die Primitive Cultur des Turko-Tartarischen Volkes.
Leipzig, 1879
96. **Raverty, H. G.** Notes on Kokan, Kashgar, Yarkand, and other places in Central Asia. J.A.S.B., xxvi., p. 257.
97. —— Tabakat-i-Nasiri : a General History of the Muhammadan Dynasties of Asia. *London*, 1881
98. **Boulger, D. C.** England and Russia in Central Asia. 2 vols. 8vo.
1879
99. **Karazine, N.** Scènes de la vie terrible dans l'Asie Centrale, 12mo.
1880
100. **Tomaschek, Wilhelm von.** Centralasiatische Studien. II. Die Pamir-Dialecte. *Wien*, 1880
(Bulletin de l'Athénée Orientale, No. 4.) 1881
101. **Reclus, Élisée.** Nouvelle Géographie Universelle. *Paris*, 1880
102. **Severtzow, Dr N.** Études sur le passage des oiseaux dans l'Asie Centrale, particulièrement par le Ferghanah et le Pamir. Avec carte. Bulletin de la Société Impériale des Naturalistes, No. 2. 1880
103. **Ujfalvy-Bourdon, Madame de.** Voyage d'une Parisienne dans l'Himalaya occidental (Le Koulou, le Cachemire, le Baltistan, et le Dras). Le Tour du Monde, 1161-3, 1197-9. 1881
104. **Koelle, S. W.** On Tartar and Turk. J.R.A.S., xiv. 1882
105. **Lansdell, Henry.** Russian Central Asia, including Kuldja, Bokhara, Khiva, and Merv [1882]. 2 vols. 8vo. *London*, 1885
106. —— Russich-Central-Asien, nebst Kuldscha, Buchara, Chiwa, und Merv ; Deutsche Ausgabe bearbeitet durch **H. von Wobeser**. Mit vielen Illustrationen im Text, vier doppelseitigen Tonbildern, Karte,

und Photographie des Verfassers sowie einem einzeln käuflichen wissenschaftlichen Anhang, enthaltend Fauna und Flora von Russisch-Turkestan und Bibliographie. 8vo. *Leipzig*, 1885
107. **Séréna, Mdme Carla.** Seule dans les Steppes : Épisodes de mon voyage aux pays des Kalmouks et des Kirghiz. 12mo. 1883
108. **Gatteyrias, J. A.** À travers l'Asie Centrale. 12mo. 1884
109. **Patagos, Dr.** Dix Années de Voyages dans l'Asie Centrale et l'Afrique Équatoriale. 8vo. 1885
110. **Boulger, D. C.** Central Asian Questions. 8vo. *London*, 1885
111. **Moser, H.** À travers l'Asie Centrale ; le Steppe Kirghize, le Turkestan Russe, Boukhara, Khiva, etc., impressions de voyage. 4to. 1885
112. **Blondus, Jean.** La lutte pour les communications avec l'Asie. Journal des Sciences Militaires. 1885
113. **R——, Capitaine.** Notes sur les routes commerciales des Russes, des Anglais, et des Français vers les frontières Chinoises.
Paris, 1885
114. **Seeland, Nicolas.** Les Kirghis. Revue d'Anthropologie, 15me Janvier. *Paris*, 1886
115. **Chvolson, D.** Die im Gebiete Semirietschie aufgefundenen syrischen Grabinschriften. Mémoires de l'Académie Impériale des Sciences de St Pétersbourg, 7 Juin, xxxiv., No. 4. 1886
116. **Pantusov, N.** Khristianskie Pamiatniki v'Semiriechenskoi Oblasti.
St Petersburg, 1886
117. **Hay, M. B.** Earthquake of 1887 in the Vierny district. P.R.G.S., October. 1888
118. **Boulangier, E.** Chemin de fer Trans-Caspien. *Paris*, 1887
119. —— Voyage à Merv. Tour du Monde, Mars 1887. *Paris*, 1887
120. **Lansdell, Henry.** Through Central Asia, with a map and appendix on the diplomacy and delimitation of the Russo-Afghan frontier.
London, 1887
121. **Prjevalsky.** Journeys and Discoveries in Central Asia. P.R.G.S., April. 1887
122. **Tchuen-yuen.** Description de la Chine Occidentale. Traduit du Chinois par **A. Gueluy.** Extract du Muséon-Louvain. 1887
123. **Pobedonostzeff, K.** Vsepoddannishii otchet ober-procurora Sviatishago Synoda za 1887. *St Petersburg*, 1889
124. **Ghern, Von.** Poyazdka na rakii Chu. *Omsk*, 1887
125. Trans-Caspian Railway, Report on the commercial importance of the. Foreign Office Miscellaneous Series. *London*, 1887
126. **Younghusband, F. E.** Journey across Central Asia. With Map. P.R.G.S., August and September. 1888
127. **Windt, Harry de.** From Peking to Calais by Land. *London*, 1888
128. **Reclus, Élisée.** (Edited by **E. G. Ravenstein** and **A. H. Keane**). The Universal Geography. *London*, 1888
129. **Cameron, V. L.** Among the Turks. With 27 illustrations. Post 8vo, 1888

130. **Bonvalot, Gabriel.** Through the Heart of Asia over the Pamir to India. Tr. by C. B. Pitman. 2 vols. *London*, 1889
131. **Ostroumoff, N. P.** Istoricheskiy ocherk vsaimneh otnosh eniy meghdu Christianstvom i Musulmanstvom. *St Petersburg*, 1888
132. —— Poslovitz tuzemnago naseleniya Turkestanskago kraia. *Tashkend*, 1888
133. **Heyfelder, D.** Transkaspien und seine Eisenbahn. *Hanover*, 1888
134. **Curzon, George N.** The Trans-Caspian Railway. P.R.G.S., May. 1889
    Russians in Central Asia. *London*, 1889
135. **Dutreuil de Rhins, J. L.** L'Asie Centrale. Thibet et régions limitrophes.) Avec Atlas. *Paris*, 1889
136. **Oliver, E. E.** The Chagatai Mughals. J.R.A.S., January. *London*, 1888
137. **Günther, Dr A.** Notice of a new fish from Issik-Kul (Diptychus Lansdelli). Annals and Magazine of Natural History, April. 1889
138. **Morgan, Delmar.** Memoir of Prjevalsky. P.R.G.S., January. 1889
139. Otchet ob Altaiskoi i Kirgizkoi Missizakh Tomskoi eparkhii za 1888 god. *Tomsk*, 1889
140. Otchet pravoslavnago Missionarskago obstchestva za 1889. *Moskva*, 1890

1890-1892.

141. **Bowman, A.** Among the Tartar Tents; or, The Lost Fathers. New ed. 12mo. *London*, 1890
142. **Radde, Gustav.** Expedition nach Trans-Caspian Band. Geolog. Soc. Lib. Zoologie. *Tiflis*, 1890
143. **Roborovsky.** Russian Expedition to Central Asia. P.R.G.S., January and March. 1890
144. **Cumberland, C.** Sport on the Pamir Steppes in Chinese Turkistan. Letters to *Land and Water*, January to June. 1891
145. **Pevtsof, Col.** The Russian Expedition to Central Asia under. Tr. by E. Delmar Morgan. P.R.G.S., February. 1891
146. **Yate, A. C.** The Tashkent Exhibition, 1890. P.R.G.S., January. 1891
147. **Groum-Grijimailo.** Expedition to the Thian Shan Oases. With Maps. P.R.G.S., April. 1891
    Forschungen in Turfan. Mitgeteilt von C. Hahn, Tiflis. Globus. lxiii., pp. 381-386. 1893
148. **Leitner, G. W.** Hunza, Nagyr, and other Pamir Regions. With Map. Imperial and Asiatic Quarterly Review, January. *London*, 1892
149. **Price, Julius M.** From the Arctic Ocean to the Yellow Sea (1891). 8vo. *London*, 1892
150. **Capus, G.** Agriculture in Sub-Pamirian Regions. Imperial and Asiatic Quarterly Review, January. *London*, 1892
151. **Steveni, W. B.** Colonel Grombchevsky's Explorations, and Recent Events on the Pamirs. With Autograph Map. Imperial and Asiatic Quarterly Review, January. *London*, 1892

152. **Johnston. C.** Derwaz and Karategin. Imperial and Asiatic Quarterly Review, January. *London*, 1892.
153. **Younghusband, F. E.** Journey in the Pamirs and Adjacent Countries. P.R.G.S., April. 1892

MISCELLANEOUS.

154. Sketch of the Revolutions in Tartary. **Kerr.** Vol. I.
155. **Severtzov, N.** Carte des routes de migration des oiseaux en Asie Centrale. Turkistan Gazette, 348. *Tashkend*
156. Asia, Central. J.B.G.S., xvii., 62, 155, 244, 259.
157. Cotton in Central Asia. J.S.A., xviii., 189.
158. Russian Commerce with Central Asia. J.S.A., xviii., 191.
159. Trade of Central Asia. J.S.A., xix. 572; xxi., 433.
160. **Gordon, T. E.** Asia : Central, East, and West. J.R.G.S., xlvi., 381.
161. Buddhism introduced into China. J.R.A.S., vi., 251, O.S. In Northern China, 275, N.S. In Bactria, ix., 169, N.S. Principal objects of worship, ii., 319, O.S. *London*
162. **Humboldt, Alexander von.** Central Asia, Analysis of, J.R.G.S., xii., 269 ; xiii., p. lxxix. Geography of, p. lxxx. Note relative to, xiii., 195. Explorations of, xii., p. xlv. The highest known tableland of, xix., 27, 28.
163. Notice of papers in the North China branch of the Royal Asiatic Society. J.R.A.S., xiv., 46, N.S.
164. **Edgeworth, M. P.** Central Asia. Abstract of a Journal kept by Mr Gardiner. With Introduction. J.A.S.B., 283.
165. The Chu River. J.R.G.S., xxxix., 319.
166. Chinese Warfare in Central Asia. J.R.G.S., xliii., 135.
167. **Piasetzky, P.** Travels through China (Russ.). Tr. by **Miss Gordon-Cumming.** 2 vols. 8vo. *London*, 1884
168. **Montgomerie, T. G.** Report of the Mirza's Exploration of the Route from Cabul to Kashgar. P.R.G.S., xv., No. 3, pp. 181-204.
169. Irtish River. J.R.G.S., xxxii., 246, 555 ; xxxv., 64 *et seq.*, 214, 215 ; xxxv., 59-62, 215 ; xlvii., 153.
170. Khitai the origin of the mediæval name Cathay. J.R.A.S., xiii., 121, N.S.
171. The Empire of Kara-Khitai. J.R.A.S., xv., 439, N.S. Conquers Khuaresm, viii., 281, N.S. History of, 262.
172. Kansuh, what it now includes. J.R.G.S., xiv., 119 ; xliii., 114 ; xlv., 172, 174 ; xlviii., 63.
173. **Khwajah Ahmud Shah Nakshbundee Synd.** Narrative of travels through Yarkund, Kokan, Bokhara, and Cabul in search of Mr Wyburd. J.A.S.B., xxv., 344.
174. Proof of physical changes in Steppes of Tartary. J.R.G.S., xxxv., 12.
175. On the name of Tartar and Turk. J.R.A.S., xiv., 126, N.S.
176. Tata, the universal form for "Tartar" adopted in the Celestial Empire. J.R.A.S., xiv., 143, N.S.

177. Tartar and Turk languages. J.R.A.S., xiv., 132, N.S.
178. Tartar and Turk mean "Nomad, Turcoman, Bedouin," etc. J.R.A.S xiv., 153, N.S.
179. Tarbagatai Mountains and District. J.R.A.S., xxxv., 67-69, 213, 215, 227-228; xxxviii., 433.
180. Massacre of Tartars by Russians. J.R.A.S., xviii., 414, O.S.
181. **Severtsoff, M. N.** A Journey to the Western Portion of the Tsung Ling Mountains. J.R.G.S., xl., 343.
182. The Tian Shan Mountain System in Central Asia. J.R.G.S., xii., 276; xxxii., 560, 562, 564; xxxv., 219, 221-223, 225-230; xxxvi., 261; xxxvii., 13; xxxviii., 434-436, 446; xxxix., 319, 321, 323, 328-331; xl., 102, 111, 112, 125, 150, 252, 259.
183. Arassan, Spring in, xxxi., 362. Its glaciers, xxxv., 228. Avalanches in, xxxix., 319. Flora of, xl., 260. Russian surveys in, xxxix., p. clxvii. Volcanic action, xl., 395.
184. **Semenoff.** First ascent of the Tian Shan in 1857. J.R.G.S., xxxi., 356; xxxix., p. clxxvii.
185. Turki language. J.R.G.S., x., 308, N.S.; xi., 94, N.S.; xvii., 153, N.S.; xviii., 178, N.S.
186. Turkish literature. J.R.A.S., xii., 104, N.S.; xiii., 146; xiv., 125; xv., 115; xvi., 110; xviii., 124, 564; xix., 178, 330, 700.
187. Notes on Turko-Tatar and Finn-Ugric. J.R.A.S., xviii., 465, N.S.
188. Turkish inscriptions. J.R.A.S., xix., 700, N.S.
189. **Gourdet, Paul.** Le tremblement de terre à Vierny. In manuscript.

MANCHURIA.

1770–1850.

190. **Kien-Long, Emperor of China.** Éloge de la Ville de Moukden et de ses Environs, Poème; accompagné de notes curieuses sur la géographie, sur l'histoire naturelle, de la Tartarie Orientale, et sur les anciens usages des Chinois. Composées par les Editeurs Chinois et Tartares; traduit en François par le **P. Amiot.** 8vo.
Paris, 1770.
191. **Amiot, Father.** A Chinese poem in praise of the City of Moukden, by the **Emperor Kien-Loug**; translated into French, with Historical and Geographical Notes and Plates. 8vo. *Paris*, 1770.
192. **Georgi, J.** Les Nations Samoyèdes et Mandshoures et les Peuples les plus Orientaux de la Sibérie. 4to. *St Petersbourg*, 1777.
193. **Langles, L.** Déatils Littéraires et Typographiques sur l'Édition du Dictionnaire et des Grammaires Tartares Mantchoux. 8vo.
Paris, 1790.
194. ——— L'Alphabet Mantchou. 3rd edition. 8vo. *Paris*, 1807.

195. **Schott, Dr W.** Verzeichniss der Chinesischen und Mandschu-Tungusischen Bücher und Handschriften der Königlichen Bibliothek zu Berlin. *Berlin*, 1840
196. Catalogue of Mongolian, Mantchurian, Tibetan, Chinese, and Sanskrit Works. Library of the Asiatic Department, St Petersburg. *St Petersburg*, 1844
197. **Palmer, A. H.** Memoir on the Present State of Manchooria. *Washington*, 1842
198. **Meadows, T. T.** Translations from the Manchu, with Original Texts. 8vo. *London*, 1849

1850-1870.

199. **Wylie, A.** Translation of the Ts'ing-wan K'e Mung. A Chinese Grammar of the Mantchu-Tartar Language. *Shanghai*, 1855
200. **Kaulen, Fr.** Linguæ Mandschuricæ Institutiones. *Ratisbonæ*, 1856
201. **Habersham, A. W.** My Last Cruise. Visits to the Mouth of the Amur. *Philadelphia*, 1857
202. **Schrenck, Dr L. von.** Reisen und Forschungen im Amur-Lande, 1854-6. *St Petersburg*, 1858
203. —— Amur-Landes: Die Völker des. *St Petersburg*, 1891
204. **Collinson, Admiral.** The Coasts of China and Tartary. 1858
205. River Explorations. (Amur.) *Washington*, 1859
206. **Furet, Père.** Lettres sur l'Archipel Japonais et la Tartarie Orientale, suivis d'un traité de Philosophie Japonaise et de plusieurs Vocabulaires. 8vo. 1860
207. **Tilley, H. A.** Japan, the Amoor, and the Pacific. A Voyage of Circumnavigation in the Russian corvette *Ryuda*. 8vo. 1861
208. **Maak, R.** Journey along the Valley of the Usuri (Russ.). *St Petersburg*, 1861
209. **Circourt, Count A. de.** The Russians on the Amur, etc. *Paris*, 1862
210. **Fleming, George.** Travels on Horseback in Mantchu Tartary. 8vo. *London*, 1863
211. **Michie, Alex.** Narrative of a Journey from Tien-tsin to Moukden in Manchuria. J.R.G.S., xxxiii., pp. 153-166. 1864
212. **Voelkel, P.** Chilkofski's Fahrt auf dem Ssungari im sommer 1866. Mittheilungen de Peterman. pp. 345-346. 1868
213. **De Furth, Camille.** Un Parisien en Asie. Voyage en Chine, au Japon, dans la Mantchourie Russe et sur les bords de l'Amour. 12mo. 1866
214. **Bouditcheff.** La région de l'Oussouri; traduit du russe par P. Voelkel. Bulletin de la Soc. de Geogr., January, p. 47. 1868
215. **Williamson, Alexander.** Notes on Manchuria. P.R.G.S., xiii., No. 1, pp. 26-34. 1869
216. —— Journeys in North China, Manchuria, etc. 2 vols. 8vo. 1870
217. —— Notes on Manchuria. J.R.G.S., xxxix., 18.

1870—1888.

218. **Palladius, Archimandrite.** An Expedition through Manchuria, from Pekin to Blagovestchensk, in 1870. Tr. by **E. Delmar Morgan** J.R.G.S., vol. xlii., pp. 142-180. 1872
219. **Summers, Rev. J.** Descriptive Catalogue of the Chinese, Japanese, and Manchu Books in the Library of the India Office. *London*, 1872
220. **Adam, Lucien.** Grammaire de la Langue Tongouse. *Paris*, 1873
221. —— Grammaire de la Langue Mandchou. *Paris*, 1873
222. **Lakarof, J.** Manchu and Russian Dictionary. *St Petersburg*, 1875
223. Les Houillères de la Mandchourie méridionale. L'Économiste Français, No. 5, p. 144. 1877
224. Mantchourie. Le Tour du Monde, No. 828. 1878
225. **Harlez, C. de.** Manuel de la Langue Mandchou. *Paris*, 1884
226. **De Mailly-Chalon, M.** Un Voyage en Mandchourie. Bulletin de la Société de Géographie. 1885
227. Manchu banners. J.R.G.S., xliv., 86, 87.
228. **James, H. E. M.** Manchuria, Notes of a recent journey. J.M.G.S., vol. iii., p. 205. 1887
229. —— The Long White Mountain. 8vo. *London*, 1888
230. **Bogdanoff, Anatolie.** Material dlia istorty manchvi i prikladnoi diatennosti v Rossii, etc. *Moscow*, 1888

MISCELLANEOUS.

231. **Abul-Ghasi.** The Genealogical History of the Tartars.
232. **Astley, T.** Ed. by **J. Green.** Vol. IV., Book II. Description of Korea, East Tartary, and Thibet.
233. Amur river. J.R.G.S., xix., 70; xxviii., 176; xxxiv., 142; xxxvii., 215; xxxix., 20-35; xliii., 179, 256, 376.
234. **Bushell, S. W.** Notes of a Journey outside the Great Wall. J.R.G.S., xliv., 73.
235. **Howorth, H. H.** The Northern Frontagers of China: Part I. Mongols, vii., 221; Part II. Manchus, vii., 305; Part III. The Kara Khitan, viii., 262; ix., 235; Part IV. Kin or Golden Tatars, ix., 243; Part V. Khitai or Khitans, xiii., 121; Part VI. Hia or Tangut, xv., 438; Part VII. The Shato Turks. J.R.A.S., N.S.
236. Origin of Manchus. J.R.A.S., v., 38, N.S.; vii., 305, N.S.
237. Manchus certainly descended from the Kin Tatars. J.R.A.S., ix., 243, N.S.
238. Conquest of China by Manchus. J.R.A.S., xv., 438. N.S.
239. Manchuria and Manchuris. J.R.G.S., xxviii., 376. Geographical progress in regard to, xxii., 111; xxvii., 161. Its boundaries, xliii., 168.
240. The burial-place of the Manchu family. J.R.G.S., xxxiii., 163.
241. **Lloyd, W. V.** Notes on the Russian Harbours on the Coast of Manchuria. J.R.G.S., xxxvii., 212.

242. Manchuria, Central and Northern. J.R.G.S., xxxix., 18.
243. Manchuria, boundary between Mongolia and. J.R.G.S., xliii., 168.
244. The Sungari river. J.R.G.S., xxxvii., 224; xxxix., 1, 19-22, 24, 26-28, 32-35; xlii., 168; xxviii., 381, 384-386, 392-395, 397, 410, 435, 438, 441.
245. The coast of Tartary. J.B.G.S., xv., 104.
246. Coast surveys of Tartary. J.R.G.S., xxvi., 118; xxvii., 126; xxviii., 110; xxx., 137; xxxvii., 224.
247. The Ussuri river. J.R.G.S., xxvii., 386, 394, 395, 410, 420, 423, 438, 440, 441; xxxvii., 215-217. 222-227; xxxix., 1, 19-22. Explorations of, by the Russians, xxxvii., 224. Meteorological observations on, 227.

MONGOLIA.

1173—1700.

248. **De Tudèle, Benjamin.** Voyage de 1173.
249. Travels of an Englishman in Tartary [1242]. **Kerr.** Vol. I.
250. Voyage of a certaine Englishman into Tartaria [1243]. Vol. I. **Hakluyt.**
251. **De Plano Carpini, J.** Travels into Tartary [1246]. **Astley.** Vol. IV.
252. —— Relations des Mongols ou Tartares pendant 1245-7.
253. —— et **Ascelin, N.** Voyage vers les Tartares, etc., 1246-7.
254. **Minori, Frate.** Due Viaggi in Tartaria [1247].
255. **Ramusio, G. B.** Raccolta delle Navigationi et Viaggi.
256. **De Rubruquis, Guillaume.** Voyage en Tartarie et la Chine [1253].
257. —— The Remarkable Travels into Tartary and China [1253]. **Harris, J.** Vol. I.
258. **Hayton, Armeno.** Dell'origine e successione de Gran Cani Imperadori Tartari [1253-1303]. **Ramusio.** Vol. II.
259. **Polo, Marco.** Travels into Tartary [1272]. **Astley.** Vol. IV.
260. —— Reisen in die Tartarie [1272]. Voyages and Travels. Allgemeine Historie, vol. vii.
261. **Mandevil, Sir J.** Voyage to Tartary [1322-55].
262. **Shah Rokh.** Embassy of, to China in 1419. **Astley.** Vol. IV.
263. **Mendez, Pinto F.** Observations of Tartary [1521-45]. **Purchas.** Vol. III.
264. —— Historia Oriental de las peregrinaciones en Tartarie.
Madrid, 1627
265. **Broniovius, Mart.** Tartarie Descriptio. 1595
266. **Vera, G. di.** De Navigationi fatte degli Olandesi nella Tartaria.
Venice, 1599
267. **Feynes, Sieur de.** Voyage faict par Terre depuis Paris jusques à la Chine. 4to. *Paris*, 1630

APPENDIX B.—BIBLIOGRAPHY. 455

268. **Ascelin, Francis.** Voyage en Tartarie. 8vo. *Paris*, 1634
269. The Travels of the Ambassadors from Holstein into Tartary. 1635
270. Voyages and Travels. The World Displayed, vols. xiii, xiv
271. **Martini, Martin.** Bellum Tartaricum; or the Conquest of the great and most renowned Empire of China, by the invasion of the Tartars. 8vo and Fol. *London*, 1654
272. —— De Bello Tartarico Historia. 18mo. *Antwerpiæ*, 1654
273. —— De Bello Tartarico Historia. Tr. into Spanish by **Dr de Aquilæ-y-Zuniga.** *Madrid*, 1665
274. **Pinto, F.** Reise nach Tartarie. Allgemeine Historie, vol. x.
275. **Olearius, Adam.** Voyages and Travels of the Ambassadors during 1633 to 1639, containing a compleat History of Muscovy, Tartary, Persia, etc. Fol. *London*, 1662; 2nd edition, 1669
276. **De Palafox, Don Juan.** Historia de la Conquista de la China par el Tartaro. 12mo. *Paris*, 1670
277. —— History of the Conquest of China by the Tartars. Tr. from the Spanish. 8vo. *London*, 1671
278. —— History of the Tartars and of their Wars with the Chinese. 8vo. 1679
279. —— Historia de la Conquista de la China par el Tartaro. Traduite en Français par le sieur **Colle.** 12mo. *Amsterdam*, 1723
280. **Struys, Jean.** Voyages en Muscovie, en Tartarie, en Perse, aux Indes, etc. 4to. *Amsterdam*, 1681
281. —— Voyages en Tartarie. *Lyons*, 1682
282. **Verbiest, Father.** Account of a Journey of the Emperor of China into the Eastern Tartary. 1682
283. **D'Orléans. Père Joseph.** Histoires des deux Conquérants Tartares qui ont subjugué la Chine. 12mo. *Paris*, 1688
284. **De L'Epy** or **Espy, Heliogenes.** A Voyage into Tartary. 8vo. *London*, 1689
285. **Avril, Father.** Travels into divers parts of Europe and Asia to discover a new way by land into China. From the French. 12mo. *London*, 1693
286. **Ides, Evart Ysbrants.** Travels through the Countries of the Mongul Tartars 1692-5. **Harris, J.** Vol. II.
287. —— Travels in China in 1693. **Astley.** Vol. III.
288. —— Three Years' Travels from Moscow to China. *London*, 1697
289. —— Journal of an Embassy from John and Peter Alexievitz, the Emperors of Muscovy, to China. 8vo. *London*, 1698
290. —— Three Years' Travels from Moscow Overland to China; through Great Ustiga, Siriana, Permia, Davur, Great Tartary, etc., to Pekin. To which is added an accurate description of China. Done originally by **Dionysius Hae,** a Chinese Author. Tr. from the Dutch. 4to. *London*, 1706
291. **Brand, Adam.** Journal of the Embassy from Muscovy to China Overland. 8vo. *London*, 1698

1700—1800.

292. **Backhoff, Feodor Iscowitz** (the Muscovite envoy). Voyage into China. Tr. from the High Dutch. 1708
293. Histoire Généalogique des Tartares, 2 vols. 12mo. *Leyden*, 1726
294. **De la Croix, Pétit.** The History of Genghizcan the Great, First Emperor of the Moguls and Tartars. 8vo. 1732
295. **Aboul-Ghazi, Béhadour.** Histoire des Mongols et des Tartares. Publiée, traduite, et annotée par le **Baron Desmaisons**. 2 vols. 8vo. 1871
296. **Du Halde, J. B.** Description de la Tartarie Chinoise. 4 vols. Fol. *La Haye*, 1735
297. —— A Description of Chinese Tartary. 2 vols. Fol. *London*. 1738
298. **Mosheim, J. L.** Historia Tartarorum Ecclesiastica. 4to. *Helms*, 1741
299. **Alcuini.** Due Viaggi in Tartaria. **Ramusio.** Vol. II. 1747
300. **Brunem.** Histoire de la Conquete de la Chine par les Tartares Manchoux. 2 vols. 16mo. *Lyons*, 1754
301. **Pallas, P. S.** Nachrichten über die Mongolischen Völkerschaften. 2 vols. 4to. *St Petersburg*, 1776
302. **De Tott, Baron.** Memoirs on the Turks and Tartars, with personal strictures. Tr. from the French. 2 vols. 8vo. 1786
303. **Langles, L.** Dictionnaire Tartare Mantchou-Français. 3 vols. 4to. *Paris*, 1789-90
304. **Radcliffe, W.** The Natural History of East Tartary. *London*, 1789
305. **Staunton, Sir George Leonard.** An Authentic Account of an Embassy from the King of Great Britain to the Emperor of China, and of a small part of the Chinese Tartary. 2 vols. 4to and 1 vol. fol. of plates. *London*, 1797

1800—1850.

306. **Timkowski, G.** Travels of the Russian Mission through Mongolia in 1820-1. 2 vols. 8vo. 1827
307. **Remusat, Abel B.** Recherches sur les Langues Tartares, etc. Vol. I. 4to. 1820
308. —— Memoires sur les Relations Politiques des Princes Chrétiens et particulièrement des Rois de France avec les Empereurs Mongols. 4to. *Paris*, 1822
309. Voyage à Peking à travers la Mongolie en 1820-21. *Paris*, 1827
310. **Ranking, J.** Historical Researches on the Wars and Sports of the Mongols and Romans; in which elephants and wild beasts were employed or slain. 4to. *London*, 1826
311. —— Historical Researches on the Conquest of Peru, Mexico, Bogota, Natchez, and Talomeco, in the 13th Century, by the Mongols, accompanied with elephants. *London*, 1827

312. **Schmidt, J. J.** Forschungen im Gebiete der Mongolen und Tibeter, mit Beleuchtung und Widerlegung von **J. Klaproth.**
St Petersburg and Paris, 1824
313. —— Grammatik der Mongolischen Sprache. 4to. *St Petersburg*, 1831
314. —— Mongolisch, Deutsch, Russiches, Wörterbuch. *St Petersb.*, 1835
315. **Du Plan Carpin, J.** Relations des Mongols ou Tartares.
Paris, 1838
316. **Hammer-Purgstall, Freiherr.** Geschichte der Ilchane, das ist der Mongolen, in Persien. 2 vols. *Darmstadt*, 1842-3
317. Catalogue of Mongolian, Manchu, Tibetan, Chinese, and Sanscrit Works in the Library of the Asiatic Department, St Petersburg (Russ.). *St Petersburg*, 1844
318. **Kowalewski, J. E.** Dictionnaire Mongol-Russe-Français. 3 vols. 4to. *Kasan*, 1844-9
319. **Popof, A.** Kalmuk Grammar (Russian). *Kasan*, 1847
320. Tartar Tribes. 18mo. *London*, 1848

1850—1870.

321. **D'Ohsson, Baron.** Histoire des Mongols, depuis Tchinguis-Khan jusqu'à Timour-Bey ou Tamerlan. 4 vols. 8vo. *Amsterdam*, 1852
322. **D'Orléans, Père P. J.** Tartar Conquerors of China. The two journeys into Tartary of Father Verbiest, and Father Pereira's journey into Tartary. Tr. from the Dutch of **R. Witsen**; ed. by the **Earl of Ellesmere.** 8vo. Hakluyt Society. 1854
323. **Strachey, H.** Physical Geography of Western Tartary. 1854
324. History of the Tartar Conquerors who subdued China. From the French of the Père **D'Orléans**, 1688. Tr. and ed. by the **Earl of Ellesmere.** With an introduction by R. H. Major, Esq. 1856
325. **Pumpelly, R.** Notice of an Account of Geological Observations in Mongolia. *London*, 1856
326. **Castrén, M. A.** Ethnologische Vorlesungen uber die Altaischen Völker nebst Samojedischen Märchen und Tartarischen, Heldensagen. 8vo. *St Petersburg*, 1857
327. **Huc, M.** Christianity in China, Tartary, and Tibet. 3 vols. 8vo.
London, 1852
328. **Thomson, J. M.** Narrative of a Voyage to Tartary. 1859
329. **Furet, P.** Lettres à M. Léon de Rosny sur l'Archipel Japonais et la Tartarie Orientale. 12mo. 1860
330. **Sprye, R.** Commerce with Tartary. 1860
331. **Poussielgue. Achille.** Relations de voyage de Shang-hai à Moscou par Pékin, la Mongolie et la Russie Asiatique, redigées d'après les notes de **M. de Bourboulon.** Tour du Monde, t. ix., pp. 81-128, t. x., pp. 33-96, 289-336. 1864
332. —— Voyage en Chine et en Mongolie de M. de Bourboulon, Ministre de France, et de Mdme de Bourboulon, 1860-61. 12mo. 1866

333. **Simon, Eugene.** Note sur les productions de la Mongolie, d'apres un mémoire de **M. E. Simon,** par **M. C. Viennot.** Bulletin de la Société Impér. d'Acclimatation, Août, t. x., pp. 480-484. 1863
334. **Grant, C. M.** Journey from Pekin to Saint Petersburg, across the Desert of Gobi. J.R.G.S., xxxiii., pp. 167-177. 1864
335. **Bowman, A.** Among the Tartar Tents. A Tale. New edition. 8vo. *London*, 1865
336. **Feer, Léon.** La Puissance et la Civilisation Mongoles au XIIIe siècle. 8vo. 1867
337. **Gulick** (Missionaire Américain). Note sur les Mongols. Journal des Missions Évangéliques. 1868
338. **Williamson, A.** Journeys in North China and East Mongolia. 2 vols, 8vo. 1870

1870-1880.

339. **Wolff, Q.** Geschichte der Mongolen oder Tartaren. *Breslau*, 1872
340. Voyages de Bruxelles en Mongolie et travaux des Missionnaires de la Congrégation de Scheutveld les Bruxelles. 2 vols. 8vo. *Bruxelles*, 1873-4
341. **Piatkanoff, K. P.** History of the Mongols. 1873
342. Communications faites à la Societé de Géographie de Saint-Petersbourg sur différents voyages dans l'intérieur de la Mongolie. Procés-verbaux de la Société. 1872-3
343. **Duret, Théodore.** Voyage en Asie: Le Japon, La Chine, La Mongolie, Java, Ceylon, L'Inde. 12mo. 1874
344. **Meignan, Victor.** De Paris à Pékin par terre; Sibérie, Mongolie. 8vo. 1876
345. **Prjevalsky, N.** Mongolia, the Tangut Country, and the Solitudes of Northern Tibet. Tr. by **E. D. Morgan,** with notes by **Col. H. Yule.** 2 vols. 8vo. 1876
346. **Howorth, H. H.** History of the Mongols from the 9th to the 19th Century. 4 vols. 8vo. *London*, 1876-90
347. **Liverani, Fr. Fra.** Giovanni da Plan di Carpine. Viaggiatore e Descrittoire di Tartaria e Mongolia. *Perugia*, 1876
348. **Orlof, A.** Mongol-Buryat Grammar (Russian). *Paris*, 1878
349. **Clark, F. C. H.** Sosnoffsky's Expedition to China. J.R.G.S., May. 1878
350. **Prjevalsky, N.** Mongolie et Pays des Tangoutes. Traduit par **G. du Laurens.** 8vo. 1880
351. Les Mongols, leur passé, leur présent. Revue Britannique, No. 12. 1880

1880-1893.

352. **Potanin.** Sketches of N. W. Mongolia (Russ.). 8vo. *St Petersburg*, 1881
353. —— Sketches of N. W. Mongolia, Notice of. J.R.G.S., p. 120. 1882
354. **Kostenko, G. N.** Ocherki severo zapadnoi Mongolia. 2 vols. 1881

355. **Jülg, Prof. B.** On the Present State of Mongolian Researches J.R.A.S., January. 1882.
356. **Piassetsky, P.** Voyage à travers la Mongolie et la Chine. Traduit par **L. A. de Ricard.** 8vo. *Paris*, 1883.
357. —— Voyage à travers la Mongolie et la Chine. Traduit par **Aug. Kuscinski.** 8vo. 1883.
358. —— Russian Travellers in Mongolia, etc. Tr. by **J. G. Cumming.** 2 vols. 8vo. *London*, 1884.
359. **Deken, Constant de.** Promenade à travers l'Asie Centrale: De Liang Tschou (Kan Sou) à Kouldja. Les Missions Catholiques, No. 792. 1884.
360. **Gilmour, J.** Among the Mongols. With Engravings from Photographs. 8vo. *London*, 1883; new edition, 1888.
361. **Meignan, V.** From Paris to Pekin over Siberian Snows. 8vo. 1885.
362. Explorations by A. K. in Great Tibet and Mongolia. Scottish Geographical Magazine. 1885.
363. **Prjevalsky, N. M.** Travels from Kiakhta to the Sources of the Yellow River (Russ.). 4to. *St Petersburg*, 1888.
364. **Molesworth, J. M.** Notes of Travel from Shanghai to St Petersburg. J.M.G.S., vol. v., p. 36. 1889.
365. **Yadrintzeff, N.** Discoveries in Mongolia. Babylonian and Oriental Record, August, vol. vi., No. 2. 1892.
366. **Bretschneider, E.** Itinéraires en Mongolie. Traduit du Russe par **M. Paul Boyer.** Journal Asiatique, ix., 1, 296-336. 1893.

MISCELLANEOUS.

367. Tartarie Chinoise. **Laharpe, J.** Vol. VIII.
368. Travels through Tibet to and from China. **Astley.** Vol. IV.
369. **Bacon, R.** Tartarian Relations. **Purchas.** Vol. III.
370. **Broniovius de Biezerfedea, M.** Description of Tartaria. **Purchas.** Vol. III.
371. Of the Tartarians and their Religion. **Purchas.** Vol. V.
372. Travels through Tartary, Tibet, and Bukharia to China. **Astley.** Vol. IV.
373. **Chaggi, Memet.** Travels and Observations in the Country of the Great Chan. **Purchas.** Vol. III.
374. The Beginning of the English Discoveries towards the North; also Voyages through Regions of Tartaria. **Purchas.** Vol. III.
375. **Guignino, A.** Descrittione della Jarmatia Europea de tutti Tartari campestri. **Ramusio.** Vol. II.
376. Relations touching the Tartars taken out of **Roger Wendover** and **Matthew Paris.** **Purchas.** Vol. III.
377. Beschreibung von der Tartarey die unter China gehöret. (Voyages and Travels.) Allgemeine Historie, vol. vii.
378. **Jordan,** ou **Jourdain Catalani, P.** Mirabilia Descripta, sequitur de Magno Tartaro. (Voyages and Travels.) Recueil, vol. iv.

379. **Bernard, John Frederic.** Recueil des Voyages au Nord, contenant divers Mémoires très-utiles au Commerce et a la Navigation; and an account of Great Tartary.
380. **Bacon, Roger de.** Observations sur les Parties Septentrionales du Monde et Relations touchant les Tartares. par **Matt. Paris.**
381. Kiakhta, town of. J.R.G.S. xxiv., 306; xxxii., 558; xxxiii., 171. 174-176, 177; xxxvi., 154. Its elevation. vi., 390; ix., 483.
382. Mongol Embassy at Peking. J.R.G.S., xxxvi., 130.
383. **Grant, Charles Michell.** Route from Pekin to St Petersburg *viâ* Mongolia. P.R.G.S., vii., 27-35; J.R.G.S., 167.
384. **Elias. Ney.** Notes of a Journey through Western Mongolia July 1872 to January 1873. J.R.G.S., xliii., 108; P.R.G.S., xxii., 184.
385. Mongolia, the present extent of. J.R.A.S., xiv., 46. N.S.
386. The Mongolian Race and their Region. J.R.G.S., ix., 193.
387. Mongolia. J.R.G.S., xxxiii., 167; xliii., 120. Maps of, xiv., 123.
388. **Hodgson, B. H.** On the Mongolian Affinities of the Caucasians. J.A.S.B., xxii., 26.
389. **Howorth, H. H.** Two Early Sources for Mongol History. J.R.A.S.
390. **Delitch. Otto von.** Urga die Hauptstadt der Mongolei. Ausallen Welttheilen.
391. Mongols, their history. J.R.A.S., xiii., 126. N.S. Numbers, xiv., 48. N.S. Once a terror to the world. xiv., 42. N.S.
392. Mongols at present divisible into—I. East Mongols; II. West Mongols; III. Buriats. J.R.A.S., xiv., 47, N.S.

TURKISTAN (CHINESE).

FROM EARLIEST TIMES TO 1850.

393. **Kingsmill, Thos. W.** The Intercourse of China with Eastern Turkestan and the Adjacent Countries in the Second Century. J.R.A.S., January, xiv. 1882
394. **Beal, Samuel.** China to India. Buddhist Travels. *London,* 1869
395. —— Buddhist Records of the Western World. 2 vols. *London,* 1890
396. **Du Halde.** A Description of Chinese Tartary. *London,* 1738
397. **Remusat, Abel.** Histoire de la Ville de Khotan. *Paris,* 1820
398. **Klaproth, Julius.** Sprache und Schrift der Uiguren. *Paris,* 1820
399. **Berghaus, H.** Asia. Memoir zur Erklärung der reduzirten Karte von . . . Katschkar, etc. *Gotha,* 1832-5

1850-1870.

400. **Prinsep, W. T.** Tibet, Tartary, and Mongolia; their Political Condition. 1851
401. **Huc.** Christianity in China and Tartary. 3 vols. *London,* 1858
402. **Valikhanoff, Capt.** A Journey to Kashgar in 1858. 1868

403. **Johnson, W. H.** Report on his Journey to Khotan. J.R.G.S. xxxvii, 1.
404. —— On Hindu Tartars. J.A.S.B., 236. 1866
405. —— On a Journey to Khotan. J.A.S.B., 182. 1866
406. **Rawlinson, Sir Henry C.** On the present journey of Mr W. P. Johnson from Leh to Ilchi. P.R.G.S., xi., pp. 6-14.
407. —— On the trade routes between Turkistan and India. Note analytique dans l'Athénæum, November, No. 2,142. p. 648. 1868
408. **Vambéry, Hermann.** Cajataische sprachstudien. *Leipzig*, 1867
409. **Montgomerie, T. G.** Report of the Mirza's exploration from Cabul to Kashgar [1868-9]. J.R.G.S., xli., pp. 132-193, Map.
410. **Hayward, G. W.** Journey from Leh to Yarkand and Kashgar [1868-9]. J.R.G.S., xl., pp. 33-166, Map. 1870
411. —— Statement of Routes between Kashgar and British Territory. 1869
412. —— Statement of Routes between Yarkand and British Territory. 1869
413. —— Statement of Routes between Khotan and British Territory. 1869
414. —— Vocabularies, iv. Recalculated Elevations of Towns.
Lahore, 1870
415. **Shaw, Robert B.** A Visit to Yarkand and Kashgar [1868]. P.R.G.S., xiv., pp. 124-137. 1870
416. —— Results of Observations taken on a Journey to Yarkand in 1870. J.R.G.S., xli., pp. 373-392. 1871
417. —— Visits to High Tartary, Yarkand, and Kashgar (formerly Chinese Tartary), and return journey over the Karakoram Pass. 8vo.
London, 1871
418. —— Letter on Yarkand Antiquities. J.A.S.B., p. 92. 1875
419. —— Prince of Kashgar on the Geography of Eastern Turkistan. P.R.G.S., xx., No. 6, pp. 482-493. J.R.G.S., xlvi., 277. 1876
420. —— Critical article in Geog. Magazine, No. 11, p. 304. 1876
421. —— On the position of Pein, Tcharchand, Lob-Nor, and other places in Central Asia. P.R.G.S., xvi., No. 3, pp. 242-253.
422. —— Miscellaneous notes on Eastern Turkistan. P.R.G.S., xvii., No. 3, pp. 195-197.
423. —— A Vocabulary of the Language of Eastern Turkistan; with two Turki Vocabularies of Birds and Plants by **Dr J. Scully.** J.A.S.B., xlvii., Part I. Extra, No. 1. A Grammar of the Language of Eastern Turkistan. J.A.S.B., xlvi., Part I., 242.
424. **Scully, J.** A Contribution to the Ornithology of Eastern Turkistan. Stray Feathers, iv., p. 41. 1876
425. **Blanford, W. T.** Description of Felis Shawiana, a new Lyncine Cat from Eastern Turkistan. J.A.S.B., xlv., Part II., 49.
426. **Forsyth, Douglas.** Despatches and Memoranda. Ordered by the House of Commons to be printed. 4to. 58 pages and Map.
London, 1869

427. **Henderson, Dr G., and A. O. Hume.** Lahore to Yarkand. Incidents of the route and natural history of the countries traversed by the Expedition of 1870 under Forsyth. 8vo. *London*, 1873
428. **Harcourt, A. F. P.** Our Northern Frontier. *London*, 1869
429. **Grigorieff.** Eastern or Chinese Turkistan (in Russ.). 2 vols. *St Petersburg*, 1869-73
430. **Walichanof.** Die reise nach Kashgar, ergänzt durch mehrere russiche Reiseberichte von F. Marthe. Zeitschrift der Gesellschaft für Erdkunde zu Berlin, No. 26, pp. 151-180. 1870
431. **Khân D'Ibbalum.** Route de Kachmir à Yarkand par Yassin. P.R.G.S., xvi., No. 3, pp. 387-392. 1870
432. **Vambéry, Herman von.** Uigurische Sprachmonumente, und das Kudatku Bilik, uigurischer Text mit Transcription und Uebersetzung, nebst einem uigurisch-deutschen Wörter-buche und lithografirten Facsimile aus dem original texte des Kudatku-Bilik. 8vo. *Innsbruck*, 1870
433. Ost-Turkestan und seine Grenzgebirge, nach Hayward, Shaw, Forsyth, und anderen neueren Reisenden. Mittheilungen de Petermann, No. 7, pp. 257-273, Carte. 1871

1870—1880.

434. Memorandum of Subjects for Scientific Observation for the Members of the Yarkand Mission. J.A.S.B., p. 123. 1873
435. Yarkand Mission. Progress and Route Report. Fol. 1873
436. **Forsyth, T. D.** Report of a Mission to Yarkand in 1873 under command of Sir T. D. Forsyth, with Historical and Geographical Information regarding the Ameer of Yarkand. Map (in cover), and Photographs. 4to. *Calcutta*, 1875
437. —— On the Buried Cities of the Great Desert of Gobi. J.R.G.S., May 25. 1878
438. Forsyth's Mission to Yarkand. J.S.A., xix., 648; xxii., 696.
439. **Bellew, H. W.** Kashmir and Kashgar. A narrative of the journey of the Embassy to Kashgar in 1873-4. 8vo. *London*, 1875
440. **Trotter, Capt. H.** Account of the Survey Operations in connection with the Mission to Yarkand and Kashgar in 1873-4. Maps (one in cover). 4to. *Calcutta*, 1875
441. **Gordon, Lieut.-Col. T. E.** The Roof of the World; being the narrative of a journey from Tibet to the Russian Frontier and the Oxus sources in Pamir. 4to. *Edinburgh*, 1876
442. Itinéraires dans l'Asie Centrale, etc. 8vo. *Paris*, 1878
443. **Blanford, W. T.** List of Mammalia collected by the late Dr Stoliczka, with description of new species. J.A.S.B., xl., 10, Part II., 105.
444. —— List of Reptilia collected by the late Dr Stoliczka in Eastern Turkistan, with description of new species. J.A.S.B., xliv., Part II., 191. On an apparently undescribed Weasel from Yarkand, xlvi., Part II., 259.

445. **Pelzeln, August.** On the species of birds collected by Dr Stoliczka in Thibet and the Himalayas. Ibis, p. 302. 1868
446. **Sharpe, R. B.** Scientific Results of the Second Yarkand Mission. *Aves*. Printed by Government of India. *London*, 1891
447. **Regel.** Expedition from Kuldja to Turfan [1879-80]. Tr. by **D. Morgan.** P.R.G.S., June. 1881
448. **Schlagintweit-Sakünlünski, H. von.** Die Pässe über die Kammlinien des Karakorum und des Künlün. 4to. *München*, 1874
449. —— Reisen in Indien und Hochasien, vols. iii. and iv. 8vo. 1872, 1880
450. **Hellwald, Fr. von.** Centralasien Landschaften und Völker in Kaschgar, Turkestan, Kaschmir, und Tibet. *Leipzig*, 1875
451. **Blockman, Henry.** Exhibitions of coins from Kashgar. J.A.S.B., 90. 1876
452. Turkestan Oriental. Le Tour du Monde. No. 727, 1874; No. 868, 1877
453. **Ujfalvy, C. E. de.** Le Kohistan . . . avec une appendice sur la Kashgarie. 186 pp. 8vo. 1878
454. **Boulger, D.** Life of Yakub Beg. *London*, 1878
455. **Prjevalsky.** (Tr. by **Morgan.**) Kuldja to Lob Nor. *London*, 1878
456. —— Le Lob Nor, et l'oasis de Cherchen. La Gazette géographique, No. 50. 1885
457. Lob Nor. J.R.G.S., xxxi., 365; xxxvi., 164; xl., 83, 125, 309; xli., 160. Elevation of, xl., 128.
458. **Kouropatkine, A. N.** Les Confins Anglo-Russes dans l'Asie Centrale; étude sur la Kachgarie. 12mo. 1879
459. —— Kashgaria (Russian). *St Petersburg*, 1879
460. —— Kashgaria; its History, Geography, Industries, etc. Tr. by **Major W. Gowan.** 8vo. *Calcutta*, 1882

1880–1893.

461. **Rockhill, W. Woodville.** The Life of the Buddha. *London*, 1884
462. **Vambéry, Hermann.** Das Turkenvolk. *Leipzig*, 1885
463. **Carey, A. D.** Journey round Chinese Turkistan. P.R.G.S., December. 1887
464. **Carey** and **Dalgleish,** Journey of (ed. by **Delmar Morgan**). Royal Geographical Society's Supplementary Paper, vol. iii., Part I. *London*, 1890
465. **Gueluy, M.** Description de la Chine Occidentale par un voyageur. Traduite du Chinois. Le Muséon, No. 1. 1887
466. **Grombchevsky, Lieut.** A journey between the towns of Kashgar, Yarkand, and Khoten. J.M.G.S., vol. iii., p. 96. 1887
Expedition to Tibet. P.R.G.S. 1891
467. **Bell, Mark S.** The Great Central Asian trade route from Peking to Kashgaria. P.R.G.S., February. 1890
468. **Bower, H.** Report of a journey in Chinese Turkistan in 1889-90. With a route Map. *Gov. Printing Office, Calcutta*, 1891

469. **Hoernle, A. F. Rudolf.** A note on the date of the Bower Manuscript. J.A.S.B., vol. lx., Part I., No. 2. 1891
470. —— The first instalment of the Bower Manuscript. Reprinted from J.A.S.B., vol. lx. *Calcutta*, 1891
471. **Walker, J. T.** Notes on Mr Dauvergne's travels in Chinese Turkistan. P.R.G.S., November. 1892
472. **Wegner, G.** Versuch einer Orographie des Kwen-Lun. 8vo. 1891

MISCELLANEOUS.

473. **Wathen, W. H.** Memoir on Chinese Tartary and Khoten. J.A.S.B., Iv., 653.
474. **Buist, Dr,** Letters from, regarding a mission to Chinese Tartary. J.B.G.S., viii., 13.
475. Hia, the Fourth Empire. J.R.A.S., xv., 439, N.S.
476. Igours, or Uighurs, emigrate from Turfan to the Irtish. J.R.G.S., i., 247.
477. **Seeland, Nicolas.** La Kashgaria et les passes du Tian-shan. Notes de voyage traduites par **Paul Gourdet.** (Manuscript.)
478. Description of Kashgar. **Astley.** Vol. IV.
479. Kashgar-Davan, a mountain range. J.R.G.S., xxxviii., 432, 435; xl. 261, 262, 264. Eastern Turkistan, xli., 137-139, 151, 170, 171, 174, 176. People of, 177. Soil of, 179. Trotter's work in, xlviii., 191. Climate of, 145, 178. Trotter, H., on the geographical results of the Mission to Kashgar under Sir T. D. Forsyth in 1873-4, xlviii., 173.
480. Kashgar, two places of this name, J.R.G.S., ix., 516. Tibetan name of. xxiii., 2, 6. City of Eastern Turkistan, xxxi., 367; xxxv., 216; xxxvi., 164, 165. Position of, 168, 169, 252, 276, 278; xxxvii., 2, 6, 7, 11, 13, 16; xxxviii., 432; xl., 75, 101. 109, 110, 168; xli., 138, 139, 143, 144. Productions of, 179. Longitude of. xl., 267. Described, 97. Position of, 122. Fort of, 96-99, 105. Russian trade with, xxxii., 556. Results of astronomical work at, xlviii., 226.
481. Kashgar river. J.R.G.S., xxxviii., 33, 344, 390, 434; xxxix., 322, 327, 330, 331; xl., 94, 96, 97, 102, 110-112, 128; xli., 183; xlvi., 281, 283, 290, 293, 295. Course of, 130.
482. Buddhism in Khotan. J.R.A.S., xix., 196, N.S.
483. Khotan, some account of, J.R.G.S., ix., 196; xxxvi., 157; xl., 48, 114; xlvi., 297; xlvii., 1. Notice of, from Moorcroft's papers. i., 235. Ancient road from Tibet to, xxiii., 67. Army of, xxxvii., 9. Grains of the country, 6. Current coins, 9. Khan of, 3, 4, 12, 16, 17. Minerals, 6. Population, 8. Position of city, xl., 121. Forest trees of. xxxvii., 6, 7. Towns of. xxxvi., 164, 165; xl., 76. Province of, xl., 4, 5, 8, 9, 12, 17. Animals of, xxxvii., 7, 8. The route to, from Leh, xlviii., 183, 184. Forsyth's visit, xlvii., 7.
484. Khotan Daria. J.R.G.S., xxxvii., 11; xl., 48-130.
485. **Radloff.** Kudatku Bilik. 2 vols. Fol. *Leipzig*

486. Taranchi language. J.R.A.S., xviii., 185, N.S.
487. Tangout, a former name for Tibet. J.R.G.S., xx., 226.
488. Tarim river. J.R.G.S., xxxvii., 5; xxxviii., 435; xl., 125, 128, xxxi 365; xlvi., 283 n.
489. An Exploring Expedition into Chinese Tartary. J.R.G.S., xvii., p. liv.
490. Uighurs, in A.D. 1001, send an Embassy seeking aid against Chao-pao-ki. J.R.A.S., xv., 449, N.S.
491. **Montgomerie, T. G.** On the Geographical Position of Yarkand and some other Places in Central Asia. P.R.G.S., x., No. 4, 162-165; J.R.G.S., xxxvi., 157, Map.
492. Yarkand. J.R.G.S., i., 234; ii., 254; xiv., 119, 120; xxxiv., 29 *et seq.*, xxxv., 64; xxxvi., 168, 260, 265, 267; xxxvii., 4, 5, 10, 12, 13, 16; xl., 33, 34, 50, 51, 69, 75, 79, 80, 82-84, 91, 94, 109, 121. Towns in, xxxvii., 7. Miles from, to Badakshan, xl., 145. Kashgar, 135. Khotan, 136. From Leh 33, 34. Trade of, xxxvii., 7. Dust in, xlvii., 21. Height above the sea, xxxvi., 164; xli., 186. First mission to, in 1870, xlvii., 1. Latitude and longitude of, xl., 90. Route to, from India, xl., 117. Goitre in, xli., 146.
493. Yarkand, city of, J.R.A.S., vii., 302, O.S. Government of, by Chinese officials, xii., 382, O.S.
494. Yarkandi language. J.R.A.S., xviii., 185, N.S.
495. Yarkand river. J.R.G.S., i., 245; xxxvi., 33, 164; xxxviii., 435; xl., 117; xli., 183; xlvi., 289, 294, 295; xlviii., 179.
496. Kleine beschreibung der Bukharey oder des Konig reichs. (Voyages and Travels.) Allgemeine Historie, etc., vol. vii.
497. Bokhara, Little. J.R.G.S., xxxv., 214-216.

SUNGARIA.

498. **Kostenko.** Dzungaria, Military and Statistical Account (Russ.). *St Petersburg*, 1887.
499. **Radloff, D.W.** Das Kudatku Bilik des Jusuf Chass Hadschib, aus Balasagun. *St Petersburg*, 1891.
500. Chuguchak, Town of, in Central Asia. J.R.G.S., xxxv., 379; xxxii., 555 *et seq.*; xxxv., 63, 68, 69, 217; xxxviii., 432, 433.
501. Djungaria, Chinese and Russian, establishment of Chinese rule in, J.R.G.S., v. Humboldt's opinions on volcanoes in, not confirmed, 228, 229.
502. Djungarian Ala-tau. J.R.G.S., xxxi., 357, 358, 362, 366, 370; xxxv., 217, 227, 228; xl., 308.
503. Djungarian "Solfatara," or smoking apertures. J.R.G.S., xxxv., 229.
504. **Michell.** Djungaria and the Celestial Mountains. Tr. from the Russian. J.R.G.S., xxxv., 213.

505. Gobi Desert. J.R.G.S., ix., 483; xii., 274; xxxiii., 177; xl., 396, xliii., 120.
506. Kalmuks of Khoten, transported by their Chinese conquerors to the cities of Ili. J.R.G.S., i., 239. Camping grounds of the Urunkhait tribe, 69. Kalmuk devotion to Lamas, xlv., 314.
507. "Kalmuk" only now used by Wolga-Kalmuks, but the true key to the ordinary Mongolian. J.R.A.S., xiv., 47, 52, N.S.
508. Flight of Torgonth Tartars to China. J.R.G.S., xxxvi., 133.

TIBET.

FROM EARLIEST TIMES TO 1800.

509. **Astley, T.** Ed. by **J. Green.** Travels through Tartary, Tibet, and Bokharia, to and from China [1246-1698].
510. **Körösi, Alexander Csoma.** Translation of a Tibetan passport, dated A.D. 1688. J.A.S.B., ii., 201.
511. Discovery of Father Ippolito Desideri's Journal in Tibet. Markham's Geograph. Magazine, No. 1, p. 21, et No. 9, pp. 253, 254. 1876
512. **Desiderius, H.** Reisen nach Tibet. (Voyages and Travels.) Allgemeine Historie, vol. vii.
513. **Du Halde, J. B.** Description ... du Tibet. 1735. Translated into English. *London*, 1738
514. **Penna, Horaz Della.** Nachricht vom Aufgange der Capucinermission in Tibet. (Voyages and Travels.) Allgemeine Historie, vol. vii.
1741
515. **Herrero, Dr D. A. M.** Representacion a la sagrada congregacion de Propaganda Fide, de la Mission del Thibet. Traducida del Toscano. 4to. *Madrid*, 1744
516. **Giorgi, Augustine Anthony.** Alphabetum Thibetanum (enriched with valuable dissertations on the Geography, Mythology, History, and Antiquities of Thibet). 4to. 1761

1800-1850.

517. **Bogle** and **Manning.** Narratives of George Bogle's Mission to Thibet in 1774, and of Thomas Manning's journey to Lhasa in 1811-12. Ed. by **C. R. Markham.** 8vo. *London*, 1876
518. **Turner, Samuel.** An Account of an Embassy to the Court of Teshoo Lama, in Tibet; containing a narrative of a journey through Bootan and part of Tibet. 4to. 1800; 2nd edition, *London*, 1806
519. —— An Account of a Journey to Tibet. J.A.S.B., i., 199, 206.
520. **Ritter, C.** Entwurf zu einer Karte vom ganzen gebirgs systeme des Himalaja nach den Quellenangaben. 4to. *Berlin*, 1832
521. **Thomson, Thos.** Western Himalaya and Thibet, 1847-8. 8vo. 1852
522. **Hoffmeister, W.** Travels in Ceylon and borders of Tibet.
Edinburgh, 1848
523. **Hooker, J. D.** Elevation of the Great Tableland of Tibet. 1849

524. **Huc, Abbé.** Souvenirs d'un Voyage dans la Tartarie, le Thibet, et la Chine; pendant les Années 1844, 1845, et 1846. 2 vols. 8vo. 1850-53
525. —— Travels in Tartary and Thibet. 2 vols. 8vo and 16mo. *London*, 1852
526. —— Recollections of a Journey through Tartary, etc. Condensed translation by **Mrs Percy Sinnett.** 12mo. 1852
527. —— Recollections of a Journey through Tartary, etc. Tr. by **W. Hazlitt.** 2 vols. 8vo. *London*, 1852

1850—1870.

528. **Prinsep, W. T.** Tibet, Tartary, and Mongols; their Social and Political Condition, and the Religion of Boodh, as there existing. 2nd edition. *London*, 1852
529. **Harvey, Mrs.** Adventures of a Lady in Tartary, Thibet, China, and Kashmir; with an account of the journey from the Punjaub to Bombay overland. 3 vols. *London*, 1853
530. **Markham, Col. F.** Shooting in the Himalayas. A journal of sporting adventures and travel in Chinese Tartary, Ladac, Thibet, Cashmere, etc. *London*, 1854
531. **Strachey, H.** Physical Geography of W. Tibet. 8vo. 1854
532. —— The Physical Geography of the Part of Tibet adjoining Kumaon and Garhwal. J.R.G.S., xxi. 57; xxiii. 1.
533. **Schlagintweit, H. A.** and **R.** Prints and Facsimiles of Objects of Buddhist Worship, and of various Thibetan Documents, collected 1854-8.
534. **Schlagintweit, E. de.** Buddhism in Thibet. Atlas of Objects of Buddhist Worship. *Leipzig and London*, 1863
535. **Schlagintweit-Sakünlunski, Hermann v.** Ueber die Salzseen des westlichen Tibet, nebst allgemeiner topographischer Erläuterung Hochasiens. Zweiter Jahresbericht der Geographischen Gesellschaft in München, pp. 24-40. 8vo. *München*, 1872
536. **Krick, Abbé.** Relations d'un Voyage chez les Abors, en 1853; suivi de quelques documents sur la même mission, par **Renou** et **Latry.** 12mo. 1854
537. **Huc, Abbé.** Le Christianisme en Chine, en Tartarie, et au Thibet. 4 vols. 8vo. 1858
538. Les Missionaires Catholiques au Thibet. Annales de la Propagation de la Foi. No. 223, pp. 420-445. 1865
539. **Huc, Abbé.** Life and Travels in Tartary, Thibet, and China. By **M. Jones.** 12mo. 1867
540. **Knight, Capt.** Diary of a Pedestrian in Cashmere and Thibet. *London*, 1863
541. **Montgomerie, T. G.** Report of the Trans-Himalayan Explorations, 1865-7. *Dehra Doon*, 1867
542. **Jaeschke, H. A.** On North Himalayan Languages. J.A.S.B., p. 190. 1866

543. **Jaeschke, H. A.** Note on the Pronunciation of the Tibetan Language. J.A.S.B., xxxiv., Part I., 91.
544. **Stewart, Dr J. L.** Notes of a Botanical Tour in Ladak, or Western Tibet. Transactions of Edinburgh Botanical Society, vol. x., pp. 207-239. 1868-9
545. **Leitner, G. W.** Results of a Tour in Little Thibet.
Lahore and London, 1868
546. **Kinloch, A. A.** Large Game Shooting in Thibet, etc. 4to. 1869; 2nd edition. 4to. London, 1876; Calcutta, 1885

1870-1880.

547. **Cooper, T. T.** Thibet and the Mishmee Hills. London, 1873
548. **Montgomerie, T. G.** Explorations in the S. W. of Thibet, by the Pundits. Highways of London, April, p. 30. 1873
549. —— Routes in the Western Himalayas, Kashmir, etc
Dehra Doon, 1874
550. —— Narrative of an Exploration of the Namcho or Tengri Nur Lake in Great Tibet, made by a Native Explorer, during 1871-2. J.R.G.S., xlv., p. 315. 1875
551. —— Memorandum on the Results of the Exploration of the Namcho or Tengri Nur Lake. J.R.G.S., xlv., p. 325. (1875) 1876
552. —— Report of a Route Survey made by Pundit . . . from Nepal to Lhasa. J.R.G.S., xxxviii., pp. 129-219; with Map, xxxix., 129.
553. —— Journey to Shigatze in Tibet and return into Nepaul in 1871, by the Native Explorer No. 9. J.R.G.S., xlv., 330. Great Tibet and Nepaul; Extracts from an Explorer's Narrative, xlv., 350.
554. **David, Armand.** Natural History of North China . . . and of Mongolia and Thibet. 4to Shanghai, 1873
555. Eine Reise im den hochsten Berg der Erde. Petermann's Mittheilungen (Carte), No. 4, pp. 147-152. 1875
556. **Blanford, W. T.** Exhibition of Skins of Tibetan Mammalia. J.A.S.B., 197. 1875
557. **Markham, C. R.** Travels in Great Tibet and trade between Tibet and Bengal. P.R.G.S., xix., No. 5, pp. 327-343. 1875
558. —— Travels in Tibet and trade with Bengal. J.R.G.S., xlv., 299.
559. —— Great Tibet. Discovery of Lake Tengri-Nor. Geographical Magazine, February, pp. 41-44. 1875
560. **Willson.** Tibet to Ind. Caucasus. London, 1875
561. **Nain Sing** (the Lhasa Pandhit). Geographical Discoveries in Tibet. Markham's Geographical Magazine, No. 5, 1875, p. 156; No. 6, 1876, pp. 141-145.
562. **Prjevalsky, N.** Troisième voyage de, en Asie Centrale. De Zaissansk au Thibet et aux sources du Hoang-Ho. Condensé par J. Biel. Tour du Monde, t. liii. 1880
563. **Tournaford, P.** Les Mines du Thibet. L'Explorateur, iv., p. 151. 1876

564. **Ganneval, A.** Le Thibet et la Chine occidentale. Bulletin de la Société de Géographie de Lyon, No. 5, pp. 385-399. 1876
565. Forschungen in Kaschmir, Nepal und Tibet. Ausland, Nos. 5 et 7. 1876
566. Geographische entdeckungen in Tibet. Ausland, No. 27, p. 537. 1876
567. **Chauveau, Mgr.** Le Thibet en 1875. Les Missions Catholiques, 8 année, pp. 79 et 92. *Lyons*, 1876
568. **Caillard, F. Roumanet du.** Voyage d'un pionnier du commerce britannique de Schangaï au Tibet oriental. L'Explorateur, iii., pp. 496, 519, 556. 1876
569. **Wordsworth, W.** The Church of Tibet and the Historical Analogies of Buddhism and Christianity. *Bombay*, 1877
570. **Desgodins, C. H.** La Mission au Thibet 1855 à 1870. 1872
571. —— Notes sur la Zoologie du Thibet. 8vo., 24 pp. Extrait du Bulletin de la Société d'Acclimatation. *Paris*, 1873
572. —— Lettres et communication sur les confins sud-est du Tibet. Bulletin de la Soc. de Géogr., Novembre 1872, p. 525, et Mars 1873, p. 335.
573. —— Le Thibet et le Bouddhisme. Les Missions Catholiques, 8 année, pp. 378, 394, 404. *Lyons*, 1876
574. —— Le Territoire de Bathang (Thibet). Bulletin de la Société de Géographie, Décembre, pp. 614 à 625. 1876
575. —— Notice sur le Thibet. Bulletin de la Société de Géographie, Septembre, pp. 315 à 326. 1876
576. —— Notes sur le Thibet. Bulletin de la Société de Géographie, Octobre, pp. 429 à 434. 1877
577. —— Du Thibet. Remarques sur un article de la Revue britannique (Intitulé Le Kashgar, le Pamir, et le Thibet). Missions Catholiques, No. 31, Août, p. 247. 1877
578. —— Le Thibet d'après la correspondance des Missionaires. 2nd edition. 8vo. 1879
579. —— On the Eastern Frontier of Thibet. J.A.S.B., p. 197. 1880
580. **Trotter, H.** Account of the Pundit's Journey in Great Tibet from Leh to Lassa. J.R.G.S., May. 1878

1880 1893.

581. **Hennessey, J. B. N.** Report on the Exploration in Great Tibet and Mongolia, made by A——k in 1879-82. *Dehra Doon*, 1884
582. **Walker, J. T.** Four Years' Journeyings through Great Tibet. P.R.G.S., February. 1885
583. L'Epigraphie Chinoise au Thibet. Inscriptions recueillis, traduites, et annotées par **Maurice Jametel**, 1ère livraison. 8vo. 1879
584. **Kreitner, G.** Im fernen Osten ; Reisen des Grafen **Bela Szchényi** in Indien, Japan, China, Tibet, und Burma 1877-80". *Wiesbaden*, 1881
585. **Geddie, J.** Beyond the Himalayas ; Travel and Adventure in Thibet. 8vo. *London*, 1881

586. Buddhism; its Introduction into Thibet, Ritual, Religious Offices, etc. J.R.G.S., xx, 217-224.
587. **Lillie, Arthur.** Buddhist Saint Worship. J.R.A.S., xiv. 1882
588. **Das, Sarat Chandra.** Narrative of a Journey to Lassa in 1881-2. *Calcutta*, 1885
589. ——— The Sacred and Ornamental Characters of Tibet. J.A.S.B., No. 2. 1882
590. ——— Contributions on the Religion, History, etc., of Tibet. The Bon (Pon) Religion. J.A.S.B., 1882, Part I., 187, 206. Early History of Thibet in the Middle Ages, 211, 235. Rise and Progress of Buddhism, Ii., Part I. The Lives of the Tasi Lamas, 15. Rise of Buddhism in Mongolia, 58. Life and Legend of the Great Buddhist Reformer, 53. Rise of Buddhism in China, 87. Ancient China, as known to the Thibetans, 99. Life of Magarjuna, 115. Buddhist Schools of Thibet, 121.
591. **Garnier, Francis.** De Paris au Thibet. Notes de Voyages. 1882
592. **Prjevalski, N. M.** Travels from Zaisan to Tibet and on the Upper Yellow River (Russ.). 4to. *St Petersburg*, 1883
Wissenschaftliche Resultate der von N. M. Przewalski nach Central-Asien unternommenen Reisen. 4to. (In course of publication.) *St Petersburg*, 1888-91
Band. I. Säugethiere, Bearbitet von **E. Buchner**; II. Vögel, **Th. Pleske**; III. Fische, **S. Herzenstein**.
On the birds of Northern Tibet. Ibis, p. 242. *London*, 1884
On the birds of Mongolia, the Tangut country, and the solitudes of Northern Tibet, Rowley's Ornithological Miscellany, vols. ii. and iii.
593. **Jaeschke, H. A.** Tibetan Grammar. *London*, 1883
594. **Prjevalsky, N. M.** Reisen in Tibet und am oberen Lauf des Gelben Flusses. Aus dem Russischen von **Stein-Nordheim**. 8vo. *Jena*, 1884
595. ——— De Zaissansk au Thibet. Tour du Monde. 1887
596. **Prouvèze, L'Abbé.** De France en Chine et au Thibet. 2 vols. 12mo. 1885
597. **Hart, V. C.** Western China; Great Buddhist centre of Mount Omei. 12mo. *Boston, Mass.*, 1888
598. **Johnstone, D. L.** Mountain Kingdom; Adventure in Thibet. Post 8vo. *London*, 1888
599. Convention between Great Britain and China relating to Tibet. Parliamentary Paper. *London*, 1890
600. Tibetan literature. Edinburgh Review, October. 1890
601. **Sandberg, Graham.** The Grand Lama of Tibet. Murray's Magazine. October. *London*, 1891
602. **Rockhill, W. W.** An American in Tibet. Century Magazine. November, December, January. 1890-91
Travels in North-East Tibet. P.R.G.S. 1892
603. ——— The Land of the Lamas: a Journey through Mongolia to Tibet. 8vo. *London*, 1891

604. **Bonvalot, Gabriel.** De Paris au Tonkin à travers le Tibet inconnu. Paris, 1892.
605. —— Across Tibet. Tr. by **C. B. Pitman.** 2 vols. London, 1891.
606. **Orléans, Henri D'.** De Paris au Tonkin par terre. Revue de Deux Mondes, Février. Paris, 1891.
607. **Pratt, A. E.** Two Journeys to Ta-tsien-lu, on the Eastern borders of Tibet. P.R.G.S., June, p. 329. 1891.
608. —— To the Snows of Tibet through China. London, 1892.
609. **Bower, Captain H.** Journey across Tibet. P.R.G.S., May, p. 316. 1892.
610. —— Journey across Tibet. Geographical Journal, vol. ii., p. 385. 1893.
611. **Bishop, J. L.** A Journey through Lesser Tibet. Scottish Geographical Journal. 1892.
612. —— Among the Tibetans. Geographical Journal, July, p. 468. 1893.
613. General Geography of Tibet. Geographical Journal, vol. ii., p. 402. 1893.

MISCELLANEOUS.

614. Description of Tibet. **Pinkerton.** Vol. VII.
615. Travels through Tibet by several Missionaries. **Pinkerton.** Vol. VII.
616. **Astley.** Travels through Tibet to, and from, China. Vol. IV.
617. Beschreibung von Tibet. (Voyages and Travels.) Allgemeine Historie, vols. vi., vii.
618. **Blanford, W. T.** On the species of Marmot inhabiting the Himalayas, Tibet, and the adjoining regions. J.A.S.B., xliv., Part II., 114.
619. —— Note on a large hare inhabiting high elevations in Western Tibet. J.A.S.B., xliv., Part II., 214.
620. **Campbell, A.** Routes from Darjeeling to Thibet. J.A.S.B., xvii. 488; xxi., 407-477.
621. —— Answers to Mr Piddington's query about winds, storms, etc., in Thibet. J.A.S.B., xix., 457.
622. —— A Journey through Sikkim to the Frontier of Thibet. J.A.S.B., xxi., 407, 477, 563.
623. —— Note on Eastern Tibet (with sketch map of route to Lassa). J.A.S.B., xxiv., 215.
624. Tibetan languages. By **Major Fryer, Capt. Forbes, Mr St Barbe**, and others. J.R.A.S., xi., 68, N.S.
625. List of Halting-places between Gartokh and Lhasa. J.R.G.S., xxxix., 208-210.
626. **Gill, W. T.** Travels in Western China and on the Eastern Borders of Tibet. J.R.G.S., xlviii., 57, 61, 62.
627. **Godwin-Austen, H. H.** Figures of the Species of Diplommatina Benson. J.A.S.B., xxxvii., Part II., 83.
628. **Gützlaff, Dr.** Tibet, projected Russian Mission into. J.R.G.S., xx., 191-222.

629. **Gützlaff, Dr.** Translation of Names from Thibetan into Chinese. J.R.G.S., xiv., 124; xix., 43. Other researches on, 66, 67.
630. **Hodgson, B. H.** On a new Species of Pheasant from Thibet. J.A.S.B., vii., 863.
631. —— Notices of the Marmot of the Himalaya and Thibet. J.A.S.B., x., 777.
632. —— Notice of the Mammals of Tibet. J.A.S.B., xi., 275.
633. —— Description of a new Species of Tibetan Antelope ; with plates. J.A.S.B., xv., 334.
634. —— On the Tibetan Badger (*Taxidia leucurus*). J.A.S.B., xvi., 763, N.S.
635. —— On the tame Sheep and Goats of the Sub-Himalayas and of Thibet. J.A.S.B., xvi., 103.
636. —— Tibetan type of Mankind. J.A.S.B., xvii., Part II., 222.
637. —— Relics of the Catholic Mission in Tibet. J.A.S.B., xvii., Part II., 225.
638. —— The Pole Cat of Tibet. J.A.S.B., xviii., 446, N.S.
639. —— On the Shou or Tibetan Stag. J.A.S.B., xix., 466, 518.
640. —— Routes of two Nepalese Embassies to Pekin, with Remarks on the Watershed and Plateau of Tibet. J.A.S.B., xxv., 473. On a new Perdicine Bird from Tibet, xxv., 165.
641. **Gray, J. E.** Catalogue of the Specimens and Drawings of Mammals, Birds, Reptiles, and Fishes of Nepal and Tibet, presented by H. B. Hodgson, Esq., to the British Museum.
    12mo, 1846 ; 2nd edition, 8vo, *London*, 1863
642. Influence of the Manchoo Dynasty in Tibet. J.R.G.S., xx., 222.
643. **Körös, Alexander Csoma de.** Geographical Notice of Tibet. J.A.S.B., i., 121.
644. —— Geographical Notice on Thibet. J.A.S.B., i., 121.
645. —— Translation of a Tibetan Fragment. J.A.S.B., i., 269.
646. —— Extracts from Tibetan Works translated. J.A.S.B., iii., 57.
647. —— Analysis of a Tibetan Medical Work. J.A.S.B., iv., 1.
648. —— Interpretation of the Tibetan Inscription on a Bhotian Banner, taken in Assam, and presented to the Asiatic Society by Capt. Bogle. J.A.S.B., v., 264.
649. —— Notices on the different systems of Buddhism, extracted from the Tibetan authorities. J.A.S.B., vii., 142.
650. —— Enumeration of Historical and Grammatical Works to be met with in Tibet. J.A.S.B., vii., 147.
651. —— Analysis of the Dulva, a portion of the Tibetan work entitled the Kah-Gyur. J.A.S.B., xx., Part I., 41.
652. —— Notices on the Life of Sakya, extracted from the Tibetan authorities. J.A.S.B., xx., Part II., 285.
653. —— Analysis of the Sher-Chin-Phalch-hen-Dkon-Seks-Do-Ne-Nyang-Das and Gynt. Being the 2nd, 3rd, 4th, 5th, 6th, and 7th divisions of the Tibetan work entitled the Kah-Gyur. J.A.S.B., xx., Part II., 393.

654. **Lydekker, Richard.** On the occurrence of the Musk-Deer in Thibet. J.A.S.B., xlix., Part II., 4.
655. —— On the Zoological Position of the Bharal, or blue sheep of Tibet. J.A.S.B., xlix., Part II., 131.
656. Lamaist system in Tibet. J.R.A.S., iv., 284, N.S.; x., 312, N.S.
657. Lama Monastery at Peking. J.R.G.S., xxxvi., 145.
658. Temples in China. J.R.G.S., xxxii., 33. Near Dolonnor, xliv., 84.
659. L'Assa. J.R.G.S., xxxii., 1-26; xxxvi., 165, 167; xxxvii., 2; xxxviii., 130 *et seq.*; xxxix., 146-148, 154; xlv., 248, 312, 324, 338. Its situation and district, xx., 214. Palace, 215. Manufactures and trade, 216, 217. City of, xxii., 3. Boundary between Lhassa and Leh, xxxviii., 165.
660. Lassa river. J.R.G.S., xxxix., 213, 214, 216, 218.
661. Leh. J.R.G.S., i., 233; iv., 60. River, i., 245 *n.* Snowfall at. xxi., 70; xxiii., 13-29. Climate, 58, 61. Temperature of earth, 63. Barometric pressure at, 64. City of, xxxiv., 44; xxxvi., 158, 159, 161, 163, 167, 169; xxxvii., 1 *et seq.*, 343, 344, 348, 355; xxxviii., 216, 217; xl., 33-36. Routes from, to Ilchi, xxxvii., 9, 10; to Yarkand, 11, 12; xl., 136-144; xlviii., 174; *viâ* Changchenmo and the Chang Lang Pass, xl., 33.
662. **Moorcroft, William.** A journey to Lake Manassarovara in Little Tibet. J.A.S.B., xii., 375.
663. **Prichard, Dr.** Tibetan type of Mankind. J.A.S.B., xvii., Part II., 580.
664. The San-poo river in Tibet. J.R.G.S., xiv., 123; xxi., 64; xxiii., 7, 9, 35; xl., 286, 287, 289, 302; xlv., 299, 316, 333.
665. **Schiefner, F. A.** (Tr. by **W. R. S. Ralston.**) Tibetan Tales derived from Indian sources. *London*, 1882.
666. **Shaw, R. B.** Stray Arians in Tibet. J.A.S.B., xlvii., Part I., 26.
667. **Des Mazures, Thomine.** Memorandum on the countries between Thibet, Yunan, and Burmah; with notes by **H. Yule.** J.A.S.B., xxx., 367.
668. Travels through Tibet to and from China by several Missioners. **Astley.** Vol. IV.
669. Disposal of the dead in Tibet. J.R.A.S., vi., 28, N.S.
670. Tibet Panjabl Mountains. J.R.G.S., vi., 345.
671. Little Tibet. J.R.G.S., 15. Height of its Mountains, ix., 515
672. Tibet, Trade with. J.R.A.S., x., 115, N.S. Various substitutes for writing used in, xvii., 420, 425.
673. Thibet. J.B.G.S., xvi., 93.
674. Thibet Trade. J.S.A., xix., 415; xxv. 118.
675. Travels through Tartary, Tibet, and Bakharia . . . to China. **Astley.** Vol. IV.
676. Tibet. J.R.G.S., xxii., 106; xxxi., 16, 18, 25; xxxii., 23, 26, 41. Milk and butter in, xlviii., 61, 62. Hue and Gabet on, xxv., 113. Mountain systems of, xxviii., 144. Great Lama visited, xxxviii.,

676. Trade of, xxxviii., 172. Observations taken in, xxxix., 182-187, 172-181.
677. Migrations of the Tibetans. J.R.G.S., xxxii., 145.
678. Tibetan mode of sleeping. J.R.G.S., xxxix., 155.

LADAK.
1819—1880.

679. **Moorcroft** and **Trebeck.** Travels in Ladak [1819 to 1825]. 1841
680. **Vigné, G. T.** Travels in Kashmir and Ladak. 2 vols. 1842
681. **Thomson, Thos.** Western Himalaya and Tibet. 1852
682. **Cunningham, A.** Ladak: Physical, Statistical, and Historical.
London, 1854
683. **Cunningham, J. D.** Notes on the limits of perpetual snow in the Himalayas. J.A.S.B., xviii., 694.
684. —— Notes on Moncroft's Travels in Ladakh, and on Girard's account of Kunawar. J.A.S.B., vol. xiii., 172, 233.
685. **Torrens, H. D.** Travels in Ladak, Tartary, and Kashmir.
London, 1862
686. ——— Travels in Ladak, Tartary, and Kashmir. 2nd edition, 8vo. 1863
687. The Diary of a Hunter from the Punjab to the Karakorum Mountains.
London and Norwich, 1863
688. **Godwin-Austen, H. H.** The Glaciers of the Mustakh Range. P.R.G.S., vol. viii., No. 2, February, pp. 34-42. 1864
689. ——— On the Glaciers of the Mustakh Range. J.R.G.S., xxxi., pp. 19-56. 1865
690. ——— On Outlining the Figures of Deities in Ladak. J.B.A.S., xxxiii., 151.
691. ——— Description of a Mystic Play as performed in Ladak. J.B.A.S., xxxiv., Part I., p. 71.
692. ——— Notes on the Pangong Lake District of Ladak. J.R.G.S., xxxvii., 343-363; and J.A.S.B., xxxvii., Part II. 1868
693. ——— The Pangong Lake District. J.B A.S., xxxviii., Part II. 1868
694. List of Passes through the Himalaya. J.R.A.S., x., 123. N.S.
695. **Montgomerie, T. G.** Report on the Trans-Himalayan Explorations [1865-7]. *Dehra Doon*, 1867
696. ——— Report of the Trans-Himalayan Explorations during 1867. P.R.G.S., xiii., No. 3, pp. 183-198; and J.R.G.S., xxxix., pp. 146-187.
1869
697. ——— Narrative Report of the Trans-Himalayan Explorations made during 1868. J.A.S.B., Part II., No. 1, pp. 47-60.
698. **Rawlinson, Sir H. C.** On trade routes between Turkestan and India. P.R.G.S., xiii., No. 1, February, pp. 10-23. 1869
699. **Schlagintweit-Sakünlünski, H. von.** Die Pässe uber die Kammlinien des Karakorum und des Künlün in Balti, in Ladak und im östlichen Turckistan. Nach unseren Beobachtungen von 1856 et 57 und den neueren Expeditionen. 4to. *München*, 1874

700. **Schlagintweit-Sakünlunski, H. von.** Klimatischer charakter der pflanzen der geographischen Regionen. Hochasiens, und vergleichung en der Daten über die angrenzenden Regionen.
München, 1877.
701. **Lambert, Cowley, and Barclay.** A Trip to Cashmire and Ladak.
London, 1877.
702. **Leitner, G. W.** The Languages and Races of Dardistan. 4to
Lahore, 1877.
703. **Biddulph, J.** Tribes of the Hindoo Koosh. Calcutta, 1880.
704. **Conway, Mr.** Glacial Explorations in the Karakorum Range under P.R.G.S., 178, 468, 557, 631, 704, 753, 768, 769. 1892.
705. —— Expedition to the Karakorum Range by. Geographical Journal, pp. 261, 291. 1893.

MISCELLANEOUS.

706. Himalaya Mountains. J.R.G.S., xxi., 14 n., 20, 21, 25-27, 30, 36, 356; xxxii., 1, 26, 304, 305; xxxiv., 22; xxxv., 226; xxxvi., 166; xxxvii., 69, 343, 349, 350; xl., 398, 399; xlv., 301, 336.
707. Himmaleh or Himalaya Mountains, journey through, by Captain Johnson. J.R.G.S., iv., 41, 63; vi., 347.
708. Karakorum Pass J.R.G.S., xii., 280; xix., 28, 29; xxxi., 20; xxxvi. 157, 160, 163, 168; xxxvii., 3, 9, 10, 13, 19, 20; xl. 33, 34, 45, 57, 58, 60, 63, 65, 114, 118, 126.
709. Karakorum Range. J.R.G.S., xxxi, 20; xxxiv., 19, 20, 21, 34, 39, 52; xxxvi., 157, 159, 161, 166; xxxvii., 10, 12; xl., 39, 41, 49, 53, 55-57, 59, 60, 62, 65, 66, 83, 115, 116, 125, 126, 163.
710. Karakorum, the capital of the Mongol Khans. J.R.G.S., xxxv., 214.
711. Ladak, Vigne's Travels in. J.R.G.S., xii., 132. Described, xx., 206-208. Its mountains and limits, xx., 203. Inhabitants and capital, 206. Connection with Eastern Tibet, 208. Province of, xxi., 58; xxiii., 4, 6, 8. Cliffs of alluvium, 18; conglomerates, 20, 22. Height of mountains, 24; of passes, 25, 26; open Indus valley, 28; gorges, 29; slopes of valley, 30; mean height, 34-40. The Indus in, 41, 42, 44-46, 52. Earthquakes, 58. Climate and meteorology, 58-65. Jungle wood in, xlvii., 80. Former province, xlvi., 203. Cunningham's work on, referred to, xxxi., 25. Line of perpetual snow, xxxix., 159. Survey of, 147.
712. **Lydekker, Richard.** Notes on some Laddak Mammals. J.A.S.B. xlix., Part II., 6.
713. City of Leh. J.R.A.S., vii., 288, O.S.
714. Report of Mission at Leh in Ladak. Periodical accounts relating to the foreign missions of the Church of the United Brethren. London
715. **Strachey, R.** On the Snow Line in the Himalayas. J.A.S.B., xviii., 287.
716. —— On Physical Geography of part of the Himalayas. J.R.G.S., xxi., 57; xxii., 106; xxiii., 68; xxv., 112; xxvii., 64.
717. **Ullah.** Travels beyond the Himalayas. J.R.A.S., vii., 283, O.S.

MAPS ILLUSTRATIVE OF CHINESE CENTRAL ASIA.

718. **Bretschneider, E.** Map of the Middle Part of Asia (in Mediaeval Researches from Eastern Asiatic Sources.) *London*, 1888
719. **Rénat.** Carte de la Dzoungarie [1716-33]. *St Petersburg*, 1881
720. **Romanovsky, G. D.**, and **Mushketoff, J. V.** Geologicheskaia karta Turkestanskago kraia 1874-80]. (Geological Map of Russian Turkistan.) *St Petersburg*, 1884
721. **Nain Singh's** Route from Ladak to Assam. J.R.G.S., xlvii. *London*, 1878
722. **Prjevalsky.** Map of Tibet to Illustrate the Travels of. P.R.G.S. *London*
723. Chart of the River Oxus. MS.
724. Karta Turkestanskago voiennago okruga. 40 versts to 1 inch. *St Petersburg*, 1882
725. **Walker.** Turkestan, etc. 32 miles to 1 inch. September. 1881
726. **Ujfalvy.** Ethnographical Map of Central Asia.
727. **A. K.** Revised Sketch Map of Explorations in Great Tibet. 3 sheets. 1884
728. —— Pundit's Explorations in Great Tibet. P.R.G.S., February. 1885
729. **Stewart, C. E.** Map of Khorasan. *London*
730. Karta Zakaspiiskago kraia. 1 inch = 20 versts. Topographical Department. *Tiflis*, 1875
731. Russian Map of Trans-Caspian Province. 1 inch = 5 versts. Topographical Department. *Tiflis*, 1885
732. Russian Map of Trans-Caspian Province. 1 inch = 20 versts. Topographical Department. *Tiflis*, 1885
733. **Lansdell, H.** Through Central Asia. Map in, to Illustrate Dr Lansdell's route, and the Russo-Afghan Frontier. *London*, 1887
734. —— Russian Central Asia, Ethnological Map in. Vol. II. *London*, 1885
735. Bolsheff's Karta Verchovey Amu Darii (Head waters of the Amur). 30 versts to 1 inch. *St Petersburg*, 1886
736. **Carey.** Map of Chinese Turkistan. P.R.G.S. *London*, 1887
737. **Younghusband, F. E.** Journey across Central Asia, and Map. P.R.G.S., September. 1888
738. **Curzon, G.** Map of Trans-Caspian Railway. P.R.G.S., May. 1889
739. **Bell, M. S.** Central Asian trade route from Peking to Kashgaria. P.R.G.S. 1890
740. **Pevtsof, M. B.**, and **Bogdanovitch, K. I.** New Map of Chinese Turkistan, showing the routes of. Geographical Journal, July. 1893
741. **Veniukoff.** Map of routes across Mongolia (Russ.).
742. —— Map of Mongolia. Tr. by **Moxon.**

LIST OF AUTHORS.

WITH REFERENCE NUMBERS TO THEIR WORKS IN THE FOREGOING BIBLIOGRAPHY.

Abul Ghasi, 231, 295
Adam, Lucien, 220, 221
A. K., 727, 728
Alenini, 299
Amiot, 190, 191
Anderson, George, 26
Aquile-y-Zuniga. D'E.,273
Aselin, Francis, 253, 268
Astley, T., 18, 232, 251, 259, 262, 287, 368, 372, 478, 509, 616, 668, 675
Avril, P., 30, 285
Ayton, 9-11, 258

Backhoff, Feodor Iscowitz, 292
Bacon, Roger de, 369, 380
Baker, V., 86
Barbe, H. St, 624
Barclay, 701
Beal, Samuel, 1, 394, 395
Bell, Mark S., 467, 739
Bellew, H. W., 439
Bergeron, Pierre, 10, 33, 34
Berghaus, 399
Bergman, B., 42, 43
Bernard, J. F., 379
Biddulph, J. D., 703
Biel, J., 562
Bishop, J. L., 611, 612
Blanford, W. T., 425, 443, 444, 556, 618, 619
Blockman, H., 451
Blondus, Jean, 112
Bogdanoff, Anatolien, 230
Bogdanovitch, K. I., 740
Bogle and Manning, 517
Bolsheff, 735
Bonvalot, G., 130, 604, 605
Bouditcheff, 214
Boulangier, E., 118, 119
Boulger, D. C., 98, 110, 454
Bourboulon, De, 331
Bower, H., 468, 609, 610
Bowman, A., 141, 335
Boyer, Paul, 366

Brand, Adam, 291
Bretschneider, E., 2-4, 366, 718
Bronjovius de Biezerfedea, 265, 370
Brunem, 300
Büchner, 592
Buist, Dr, 474
Bushell, S. W., 254

Cailland, F. R. du, 568
Cameron, V. L., 129
Campbell, A., 620-623
Capus, G., 150
Carey, A. D., 463, 464, 736
Carpini, J. de P., 7, 251-253, 315
Castrén, M. A., 326
Cayley, 74
Chaggi, Memet, 373
Chaveau, M. G. R., 567
Chvolson, D., 115
Circourt, A. de, 209
Clark, F. C. H., 349
Colle, 279
Collinson, Admiral, 204
Conway, 704, 705
Cook, John, 38
Couper, T. T., 547
Cowley, 701
Coxe, W., 44
Cumberland, C., 144
Cumming, J. Gordon, 167, 358
Cunningham, A., 682
Cunningham, J. D., 683, 684
Curzon, G. N., 134, 738

Dalgleish, A., 464
Das, Sarat Chandra, 588-590
David, A., 554
Davies, John, 24
D'Aquile-y-Zuniga, 273
De Bourboulon, 331

De Furth, Camille, 213
D'Hauteville, 31
De Humbold, A., 52
De la Croix, Pétit, 294
Deken, Constant de, 359
De Koros, Alexander Csoma, 643-653
Delitch, Otto von, 390
De Mailly-Chalon, M., 226
De Rialle, Giraud, 79
De Saint-Martin, Vivien, 58
De Tudèle, Benjamin, 248
Desgodins, Ch., 570-579
Desideri (or Desiderius, H., 511, 512
Desmaisons, 295
Des Mazures, Thomme, 667
De Windt, Harry, 127
D'Ibbalum Khan, 431
D'Ohsson, 321
D'Orléans, Henri, 606
D'Orléans, Joseph, 283, 322, 324
Drew, M. Fred., 77
Du Halde, J. B., 35, 36, 296, 297, 396, 513
Duret, Theodore, 343
Dutreuil de Rhins, 135

Edgeworth, 164
Elias, Ney, 384
Ellesmere, Earl of, 322, 324
Espy, Heliogenes de F, 284
Ewart, W., 59

Feer, Leon, 330
Ferrier, J. P., 57
Feynes, Sieur de, 267
Fleming, George, 210
Fletcher, Giles, 25
Forbes, Major, 624
Forsyth, T. Douglas, 426, 436-438
Fryer, Major, 624
Furet, 206, 329
Furth, De Camille, 213

Ganneval, A., 564
Garnier, F., 591
Gatteyrias, J. A., 108
Geddie, J., 585
Geissler, J. G., 45
Georgi, A. A., 192, 516
Ghasi, Abul, 231, 295
Ghern, Von, 124
Gill, W. J., 626
Gilmour, J., 360
Godwin-Austen, H. H., 627, 688-693
Goez, Benedict, 17-21
Golubief, Captain, 64
Gordon, T. E., 82, 160, 441
Gourdet, Paul, 189, 477
Gowan, W., 460
Grant, C. M., 334, 383
Gray, J. E., 641
Green, J, 509
Greslon, Adrien, 27
Grigorieff, 429
Grombchevsky, 466
Grosier, Abbé, 39
Groum-Grijimailo, 147
Gueluy, A., 122, 465
Guiguimo, A., 375
Gulick, 337
Gunther, A., 137
Gutzlaff, Dr, 628, 629

Habersham, A. W., 201
Hae, Dionysius, 290
Hahn, C., 147
Haithon, 9-11
Hakluyt, 250
Halde, J. B. du, 35, 36, 296, 297, 396, 513
Hammer, Purgstall, 316
Harcourt, A. F. P., 428
Harlez, C. de, 225
Harris, J., 257, 286
Hart, V. C., 597
Harvey, Mrs., 529
Hauteville, D', 31
Hay, M. B., 117
Hayton, Armeno. 9 11, 258
Hayward, G. W. J., 410-14
Hazlitt, W., 527
Heilwald, Fr. von, 450
Henderson, Capt., 46, 427
Hennessey, J. B. N., 581
Herrero, Dr A. M., 515
Herzenstein, S., 592
Heyfelder, O., 133
Hodgson, B. H., 388, 630-640
Hoernle, A. F. Rudolf, 469, 470

Hoffmeister, W., 522
Hooker, J. D., 523
Howorth, H. H., 235, 346, 389
Huc, Abbé, 53-55, 327, 401, 524-527, 537, 539
Humbold, A. von, 52, 162
Huttner, J. C., 41
Hume, A. O., 427

Ides, E. Y., 286-290
Iscowitz, 292

Jaeschke, H. A., 542, 543, 593
James, H. E. M., 228, 229
Jametel, Maurice, 583
Johnson, W. H., 403-405
Johnston, C., 152
Johnstone, D. I., 598
Jones, M., 539
Jourdan, Cataline, 378
Jülg, Prof. B., 355
Julien, Stanislas, 63

Karazine, N., 99
Kaulbars, 69, 70
Kaulen, Fr., 200
Keane, A. H., 128
Keene, H. G., 89
Kerr, 7-9, 12, 16, 154, 249
Khán, D'Ibbalum, 431
Kien, Long, 190, 191
Kingsmill, Thomas, 393
Kinloch, A. A., 546
Klaproth, J. V., 48, 49, 312, 398
Knight, Capt., 540
Koelle, S. W., 104
Koros, Alexander Csoma de, 510, 643-653
Kostenko, G. N., 354, 498
Kouropatkine (or Kuropatkin), A. N., 458-460
Kowalewski, J. E., 318
Kreitner, G., 584
Krich, Abbé, 536
Kropotkine, P. O., 76
Kuscinski. Aug., 357

La Croix. Petit de, 167
Laharpe, J., 367
Lakarof, J., 222
Lambert, Cowley, 701
Langles, L., 193, 194, 303
Lansdell, Henry, 91-94, 105, 106, 120, 733-734
Latry, 536
Laurens, G. de, 250
Leitner, G. W., 148, 545, 702

Lillie, Arthur, 587
Liveraini, Fr., 347
Lloyd, W. V., 241
Lydekker, Richard, 654, 655, 712

Maak, R., 208
Mailly-Chalon, De, 226
Major, R. H., 324
Mandevil, Sir J., 261
Markham, C. R., 517, 557-559
Markham, F., 530
Martini, Martin, 271-273
Mazures, Thomine des, 667
Meadows, T. T., 198
Meignan, Victor, 344, 361
Mendez, Pinto, 263, 264
Michell, R., 90, 504
Michie, Alex., 211
Miles, Col., 51
Minori. Frate. 254
Molesworth, J. M., 364
Montgomerie, T. G., 75, 168, 409, 491, 541, 548-553, 695-697
Moorcroft, William, 662, 679
Morgan, E. Delmar, 138, 145, 218, 345, 445-447, 464
Moris, 43
Morrison, John, 29
Moser, H., 111
Mosheim, J. L., 298
Muldener, 92
Muskketoff, J. V., 720

Oderic of Pordenau. 16
Olearius, Adam. 26, 275
Oliver, E. E., 136
Oollah, Meer, 46
Orléans, Henri d', 606
Orléans, Joseph d', 283, 322, 324
Orlof, A., 348
Ostroumoff, N. P., 131, 132

Palafox, John de, 276-279
Palladius, Archimandrite, 218
Pallas, P. S., 301
Palmer, A. H., 197
Pantusoff, N., 116
Paquier, J. B., 85
Paris, Matthew, 376, 380
Patagos, Dr, 109
Piatkanoff, K. P., 341
Paulo. Mark, 12-15, 259, 260

LIST OF AUTHORS. 479

Pelzeln, A., 445
Penna. H. de la, 514
Pétit de la Croix, 294
Pevtsof, Col., 145, 740
Piassetsky, P., 167, 356-358
Pinkerton, 21, 614, 615
Pinto, F. M., 263, 264, 274
Pitman, C. B., 130, 605
Pleske, Th., 592
Pobedonostzeff, K., 123
Polo, Marco, 12-15, 259, 260
Poltaratzky, 68
Popoff, A., 319
Potanin, G. E., 352, 353
Poussielgue, Achille, 331, 332
Pratt, A. E., 607, 608
Price, J. M., 149
Prinsep, W. T., 400, 528
Prjevalsky (or Prschewalski), N., 88, 121, 345, 350, 363, 455, 456, 562, 592, 594, 595, 722
Prichard, Dr, 663
Prouvèze, Abbé, 596
Pumpelly, R., 67, 325
Purchas, Samuel, 20, 22, 23, 263, 369-371, 373, 374, 376

R——, Capitaine, 113
Radcliffe, W., 304
Radde, Gustav, 142
Radloff, D. W., 61, 485-499
Ralston, 665
Ramusio, G. B., 14, 255, 258, 299, 375
Ranking, J., 310, 311
Ravenstein, 128
Raverty, Lieut., 96, 97
Rawlinson, H. C., 406, 407, 698
Reclus, Elisée, 101, 128
Regel, 447
Reinaud, J. T., 5
Rémusat, Abel B., 47, 307, 308, 397
Rénat, 719
Renon, 536
Rialle, Giraud de, 70

Ricard, L. A. de, 356
Ritter, C., 520
Roborovsky, 143
Rockhill, W. W., 461, 602, 603
Rokh, Shah, 262
Romanovsky, G. D., 143, 720
Rosenmuller, E. F., 50
Rubruquis, W. de, 8, 256, 257

Sandberg, Graham, 601
Scheifner, F. A., 665
Schlagintweit - Sakünlünski, E., 534
Schlagintweit, H. von, 448, 449, 533, 535, 609, 700
Schmidt, I. J., 312-314
Schott, W., 60, 193
Schrenk, L., 202, 203
Scully, Dr, 423, 424
Seeland, Nicholas, 114, 477
Semenoff, 184
Serena, Carola, 107
Settle, Elkanah, 28
Severtzoff, M. N., 102, 155, 181
Sharpe, R. B., 446
Shaw, R. B., 81, 84, 413-423, 666
Shepeleff, A., 71-73
Simon, Eugene, 333
Singh, Nain, 561, 721
Sinnett, Mrs Percy, 526
Sprye, R., 330
Staunton, G. L., 305
Stein-Nordheim, 594
Steveni, W. B., 151
Stewart, J. E., 544
Stewart, C. E., 729
Strachey, H. R., 323, 331, 532, 715, 716
Strahlenberg, P. J. von, 37
Struys, Jean, 280, 281
Stuart, A., 80
Summers, James, 219
Synd, Ahmud Shah N., 173

Taylor, Bayard, 62
Tchuen-yuen, 122

Thomson, J. M., 328
Thomson, Thomas, 521, 681
Tilley, H. A., 207
Timkovski, 306
Tomaschek, Wilhelm, 100
Tonnelier, Jules, 65
Tooke, William, 32
Torrens, H. D., 685, 686
Tott, Baron de, 302
Tournafort, P., 563
Trebeck, 679
Trotter, H., 440, 580
Tudèle, Benjamin de, 248
Turner, S., 518, 519

Ujfalvy, 453, 726
Ujfalvy-Bourdon, Madame de, 103
Ullah, 717

Valikhanoff, 402, 430
Vambéry, Hermann, 95, 408, 452, 462
Veniukoff, 78, 741, 742
Vera, G. di, 266
Verbiest, Father, 282
Viennot, 333
Vigne, G. T., 680, 711
Voekel, P., 212

Walker, J. T., 471, 582, 725
Walichanof, 402, 430
Wathen, W. H., 473
Wegner, G., 472
Wendover, Roger, 370
Williams, S. W., 56
Williamson, Alex., 215-217, 338
Willson, 500
Winterbotham, W., 40
Witsen, 322
Wobeser, H. von, 100
Wolff, O., 339
Wordsworth, W., 500
Wylie, A., 199

Yadrintzeff, 305
Yate, A. C., 140
Younghusband, F. E., 120, 153, 737
Yule, H., 6, 345, 667

ANONYMOUS.

Amur River Explorations, 205, 233
Arassan Spring, 183
Asia, Central, 156

Bokhara, 497
Buddhism, 386
— in China, 161
— in Khotan, 482

Bukharey, Kleine beschreibung, 406
Catalogue of Mongolian and Sanskrit Works, 196, 317

Central Asia, Cotton, 157
— Trade of, 158, 159
Chamanisme, 83
China, Conquest of, 238
    warfare in Central Asia,
    166
Chu (river), 165
Chuguchak, Town of, 500
Convention between
    Britain and China, 599

Desideri's Journal, Discovery of, 511
Diary of a Hunter, 687
Djungaria, 501
Djungarian Ala-tau, 502
    Solfatara, 503

English Discoveries towards the North, 374

Gartokh and Lhasa, halting-places, 625
Gobi Desert, 505

Ilia, Fourth Empire, 475
Himalaya Mountains, 706, 707
    Passes through, 694

Igours, or Uigurs, 476
Irtish (river), 169
Itinéraires dans l'Asie Centrale, 442

Kalmuk, 507
Kalmuks of Khotan, 506
Kansuh, 172
Kara Khitai, Empire, 171
Karakoram, 708-710
Kashgar, 480
    Davan, 479
    Description of, 478
    (river), 481
Kashmir, Forschungen in, 565
Khitai, Origin of, 170
Khotan, 483
    Daria, 484
Kiakhta, 381

Ladak, 711
L'Assa, 659
Lassa (river), 660
Leh, 661
— City of, 713
— Report of Mission, 714

Little Tibet, 671
Lob Nor, 457

Manchourie, Houillères, 223
Manchu banners, 227
— family burial-place, 240
Manchuria and Manchuris, 224, 239, 242. 243
Manchus, Origin, 236, 237
Mongol Embassy at Peking, 382
Mongolia, 387
    Map of, 742
— Present extent of, 385
Mongolian Race, 386
Mongolie, Voyages, 342
Mongols, East and West, 351, 391, 392

Nomad, Turcoman, and Bedouin, 178

Ost-Turkestan, 433
Otchet ob Altaiskoi, 139, 140
Oxus, Chart of the, 723

Papers in China Branch of R.A.S., 163
Peking, Lama Monastery at, 657
— Voyage à, 309

Recueil d'Itinéraires, 87
Reise in hochsten Berg, 555

San-poo (river), 664
Sungari (river), 244

Tangout, 487
Taranchi language, 486
Tarbagatai Mountains, 179
Tarim (river), 488
Tartar and Turk, 175
    languages, 177, 185
— Conquerors, 324
    tribes, 320
    Turkish, and Ugric
    literature, 186, 187
Tartarians, Of the, 372
Tartares, Histoire généalogique, 293
Tartars, Massacre of, 180
— Relations touching, 376
Tartary, Beschreibung von der, 377
— Coast of, 245. 246

Tartary, Expedition into, 489
— From Holstein to, 269
    Revolutions in, 154
    Steppes of, 174
— Travels in, 249. 250
    — through, 372
Tata, or Tartar, 176
Temples in China, 658
Thibet, 673. 676
    Epigraphie Chinoise, 583
    Geographische entdeckungen, 566
— Influence of Manchoo
    dynasty, 642
    Lamaist system in, 656
    Missionaires au, 538
    Panjahl Mountains, 670
    trade, 674
Tian Shan Mountains, 182
Tibet, beschreibung von, 617
— disposal of dead, 669
— Geography of, 613
— Explorations in, 362
— Trade with, 672
— Travels through, 368
Tibetan literature, 600
— mode of sleeping, 678
Tibetans, Migrations, 677
Torgouts, Flight of, 508
Trade routes, 66
Trans-Caspian, Map of, 731, 732
— Railway, 125
Turkestan Oriental, 452
Turkestanskago karta, 724
Turkish inscriptions, 188

Uighurs, 490
Ussuri (river), 247

Voyages and Travels, 270
    de Bruxelles en Mongolie, 340

Yarkand, 492
— City of, 493
    language, 494
    Mission, Memorandum of, 434. 437
— Progress of, 435
— (river), 495
Yuen, Tchuen, 122

Zakaspiiskago kraia karta, 730

GENERAL INDEX.

Volume I. is to be understood unless otherwise mentioned.

ABBAS, SEID JOSEPH, Author's personal servant and interpreter—*see* Joseph
Abbasid, Abdul, interpreter, 145
Abu Kadair, Visit to, 205
Acha-Tag, Kirghese at, 379
— — Village of, 378
Afghanistan, Route to, ii. 1
Afghans, Escort at Aksu, 313
— Prejudice against, ii. 231
— Scripture distribution among, 345
— trading at Aksu 314
Africa, North, Visit to Missions, ii. 405
Agra, Kindness of Mr Dunstan, ii. 377
Aibuk, Camping at, ii. 278
Akburkhan, Monastic ruin at, 257
Akhal Tekke oasis, 26
Akhoun, Tokhta, at Jarkend, 145
— Vali, Servant of, 145
Akhram Khan, escort at Khotan, ii. 187
Akir-Tiube post-station, 104
Ak-Kay reservoir, ii. 66
Ak-Langar, Mosque at, ii. 157
— — Ocean of sand at, ii. 157
— — rest-house, ii. 157
— — Wells at, ii. 157
Ak-Robat picket-station, ii. 77
Aksai river, 378 ; ii. 4
— tableland, ii. 4
— valley, Kirghese in, 380, 398
— — Younghusband in, 379
Aksalar, Fort of, ii. 6
— Fuel and timber at, ii. 6
Ak-Serai, Cemetery at. ii 162
— — Photography at, ii. 162
Ak-Shor, Carpet-weaving at, ii. 264
— — Departure from, ii. 206
— — Photography at, ii. 265
— — Village of, ii. 264
— — Wakhis at, ii. 265

Aksu, Afghan traders at, 314
— Area of, 341
— Arrival at, 341
— Bazaar of, 347 ; ii. 341, 348
— Bell, Col., at, 316
— Buddhism at ii. 86
— Buildings of, 348
— Camera repaired at, 349
— Carey, Mr. at, 316
— Cart-driver before magistrate at, 355
— Cemeteries of, 316. 348
— Chen, *Tautai* of, 349
— Coal at, 347
— Cultivation at 351
— Dalgleish's murderer in, 347
— Departure from, 381
— Escorts at, 313, 316, 381
— Feasting near, 314
— Fort at, 348
— Fruit abundant at, 348
— Funeral at, 349
— Gardens of, 348
— Granaries at, 351
— Gun factory at, 348
— History of, 340
— Houses of, 348
— Inhabitants of, 348
— Lodging at, 341
— Madamin Bai at, 312
— — House of, 311
— Manufactures of, 347
— Mausoleum at, 348
— Merchants' visits to Author, 345
— Mining near, 347
— Money changing at 342
— Mosques at, 348
— Muzart-Kurgan and, Distance, 313
— observations, Thermometrical, 312
— Official visits at, 350

VOL. II.

31

Aksu, Opium-smoking at, 409
— Osman Bai and his creditors, 314
— Panjabi workmen at, 348
— Payment of Osman Bai at, 354
— Photography at, 349
— Population of, 341 ; ii. 219
— Presents at, 312, 350, 351
— Prison inspection, 352
— Prisoners' photographs, 352
— Purchases at, 347
— Rice-fields at, 348
— river, 321, 378; ii. 12
— — Crossing the, 383
— — Shooting birds on, 383
— roads to Kashgar, 377
— Route to, 200, 305
— Scripture distribution at, 351 ; ii. 341
— — sales at, ii 341
— Shops at, 351
— Soldiers of, 304
— Tea by the wayside, 314
— Tobacco cultivation at, 347
— Tombs at, 348
— Town of, 341, 348, 351
— Traders in, 345
— Villages in district of, 341
— Welcome at, ii. 341
— Yakub Bek at, ii. 60
— Younghusband at, 316
Ak Tagh, Journey past, ii. 317
Ak-tash valley, ii. 12, 72
Akyar, Hamlet of, 378
— Kirghese at, 379
Alachain tribes of Mongolia, 163
Alai Kirghese at Karakash, ii. 277
A'ak-chu lake, 321
Alexander, Archbishop, at Vierny, 122
— Mountains, 104, 115, 289 ; ii. 30
— the Great at Old Merv, 41
Alexéef, Dr P., as railway companion, 10
— — — Hospitality of, 12
Alford, Dean, Epitaph of, 113
Ali, Mirza Muhammad, at Yarkand, ii. 99
— Nazar fort, ii. 276
— Sultan, at Hami, 326
Alikhanoff, Col., Administration of, 38
— — at Merv, 36
— — Diplomacy of, 46
— — Hospitality of, 36
— — Introduction to, 31
— — Liberation of slaves by, 46
— — and the submission of Merv, 44
Alimpiu, the ancient Almalik, 151
Almalik, Jagatai Khan at, ii 52
— Marignolli at, ii. 128
— Mediæval Christians at, 151
— Pascal at, ii. 126
— Site of, 151
Almaty Peak, 129

Alphéraky, M., on Ili fauna, ii. 28
Altai languages, Translations into, 123
— mission at Tomsk, 122
— Mountains, 153
Alti-shahr, 318
Altyn-Immel, Hindrances at, 144
— — post-station, 143
— — Tarantass repairs at, 143
Altyn Mazar at Khotan, ii. 189
Altyn Tagh, Discovery of, ii. 174
— — Savages in, ii. 286
Altyn-Tau hills, 231
Aman-el-Mulk, chief of Chitral, 346
American Bible Soc. on the Amur, 159
— — — Assistance of, 201
— Mission at Kalgan, 323
Amin Agha, groom, 176, 216 ; ii. 39
— — Marriage of, ii. 40
— — Parting with, ii. 375
Amritsar, Clark, Rev. R., at, ii. 376
— Parting with Muhammad Juo, ii. 376
Amu-daria Curious vehicle at, 58
— — Czar steamer at, 52
— — Dinner-party at, 52
— — English engineer at, 52
— — Guest of Col. Tcharykoff at, 50
— — Khilkoff, Prince, at, 50
— — Loewenhagen, Capt., at, 52
— — railway station, 49
Amur river, American authors on, 156
— — — Bible Society's work on, 159
— — Atkinson's description of, 156
— — Author's account of, 156
— — Gowing's description of, 156
— — Russian conversion of natives, 158
— — Scripture distribution on, 159
Anau, Ruins of mosque at, 32
Andijanis' escort at Aksu, 313
An-how-tzien, Kalmuks in, 397
Annam, Scripture distribution in, ii. 392
Annenkoff, Gen., Guest of, 81
— — Introduction to, 6, 31
— — Parting with, 87
Ansi-fan, Town of, 325
Anthropologie, Revue, on Kirghese, 398
Aphak monastery at Kashgar, 448
Aphekhtine, Mdlle, at Bokhara, 62
Arab invasion of Turkistan, ii. 50
— supremacy at Old Merv, 41
Arabian knowledge of the "Seres," 360
Arabic manuscripts, ii. 121
Aral, Kirghese at, 379
Arbas, or native carts, 146, 178
Archali-Karachat glacier, 263
Archæology of Central Asia, 110
Arendarenko, M., at Samarkand, 89
Arfa river, ii. 4.
Argun, Treaty of, 161
Armenian intercourse with China, 360

Arthington, Mr, Assistance of, ii. 403
Artish, District of, 380
— range, ii. 3
Artyk railway station, 32
— Salt tract near, 32
Aryans, Dr Bellew on, 406
Asia, Stanford's map of, 319
— Central, Costumes of women, 100
    Deer-stalking in, 405
— — Fox-hunting in, 405
— — Lakes of, 126
   — Minarets in, 108
   — Missionary effort in, 101
   — Mountains of, 114
   — Nestorian Christianity in, 109
— — Streets of, 418
— - Wives in, 409
   — Woman's work in, 102
— Chinese Central: Dedication, iii
— — — Authors' works on, ii. 477
— — — Bibliography of, ii. 439
— — — Bishoprics in, ii 122
    Chronology of, 454
    Contents of Author's chapters on, Vol. I., xi ; Vol. II., iii
— — Early Christianity in, ii. 119
— — — monastic life in, ii. 129
   — - travellers in, 362
   — Fauna of, ii. 27
— — — — collected by Author, ii. 409
— — Fish of, ii. 416
— — — History of, 357 ; ii. 47
  — Illustrations in Vol. I., xxii
   — — — Vol. II., ii. xv
   Inhabitants of, 396
   — Introduction to, xxxi
   — Itinerary of Author, xxiv
   — Maps of, ii. 476
— — — Meaning of, 356
— — — Nestorian banishment, ii. 122
  - — Observanda, xxx
— — — Preface to, vii
— — — Remains of Christianity, ii. 128
  — — Roman Christianity in, ii. 125
— — — Sources of our knowledge, 356
   — Spiders of, ii. 30
   — Tathsin temples, ii. 120
— — — Travellers' narratives, 364
   See also Turkistan
Askhabad, Arrival at, 30
— Interview with Governor, 32
   Introductions at, 31, 32
— - Market-place of, 30
- Military club at, 30
— Persian ice-cellar at, 30
- - Population of, 30
- Railway station at, 30
— Turkoman raid near, 45
Aski Shahr, Ruin of, 447

Assemani on Nestorians, ii. 122
Astrakhan Kalmuks' photographs, 234
Atbanof tribe in Tekes valley, 245
Atbashi, Village of, ii. 5
Attek oasis, Railway across, 32
— — Ruin at Shilgan, 32
— — Town of Luftabad, 32
Aulie-Ata, Posting through, 104
— — Ramazan fast at, 104
Auvat, Desert near, 308
— Fruit at, 307
— river, 306
— Station of, 307
Aziz Bek, Guest-house of, ii. 143

BABA-DURMAZ railway station, 32
Baba-Kul, 321
Badakshan, Buddhism at, ii. 86
— Trade of, 440
Baghchiserai railway station, 16
Baghdad, Arrival at, ii. 402
— Preaching at, ii. 404
Bagrat h lake, 321, 337
Bahrin, Hamlet of, 430
Bai, Dairy produce of, 339
- Population of, 339
Bairam Ali railway station, 48
— — Ruins of, 43
— — Water storage at, 48
Baker, Mr Bethune, entomologist, ii. 22
Baku, Arrival at, 20, 137
- Call on Governor of, 21
— Tatar porters at, 23
Bala Ishem, Oil wells of, 25
— — Salt marsh near, 25
Balauti range, 378
Balgazi, Kalmuks in, 397
Balguluk, View from, 287
Balkan Bay on the Caspian, 25
Balkash lake, Desert near, 104
Balkashin, M... in Talki defile, 140
Balti Brangsa, March to, ii. 320
Bami railway station, 26
Bangkok, Visit to, ii. 403
Baptisms by Russian missionaries, 103
Baptist Mission at Tai-yuen, 324
Baratola, Kalmuk Khan of, 209
Barin, Village of, 378
Barkhan railway station, 49
Barkul, City of, 329
— Cultivation at, 329
— Inhabitants of, 329
— Manchu troops in, 396
— Road to, 329
— Roads from, 330
— Ruined villages at, 329
— Soil of, 329
— Soldiers at, 329
- Town of, 168

Baroghil Pass, Crossing the, 345
Bartsch, M., at Tashkend, 102
— — Assistance of, ii. 339
Bash Langar, ii. 237
Bashagma, Hamlet of, 379
Basilik Aghse, Caravans at, ii. 267
Batang, Town of, ii. 282, 306
Batoum, Arrival at, 18
— Custom-house, 136
— Departure from, 18
— Joseph at, 18, 226
— Peacock, Mr. at, 137
— Specimens posted to, 206
— Visit of Consul at, 18
Batrachians, ii. 415
Bedal Mountain, 378
— Pass, Road to, 199, 379
Bees collected by Author, ii. 418
Bekler-Bek, Medresse of, 103
Belgian missionaries at Gehol, 150
— — — Hei-hsui, 159
— — — Hsi-wan-tze, 159
— — — Kuldja, 163
Bell, Col., at Aksu, 316
— — — Hami, 327
— — — Maralbashi, 417
— — — Turfan, 335
— — — Urumtsi, 331
— — in Chinese Turkistan, 373
— — on Chinese officials, ii. 243
— — opium-smoking, ii. 145
Bellew, Dr, on Aryans, 406
— — — Brahmanism, ii. 81
— — — Kashgarian diseases, ii. 109
— — — Yarkand history, ii. 101
Belowti Pass, 380
Beneslavsky, M., Governor of Baku, 21
Berg, M., police-master at Jarkend, 145
Berlin, Chinese Minister at, 2 ; ii. 364
Besac, Gen., postmaster-general at St Petersburg, 172
Besh-Aryk, Commissions from natives of, ii. 235
— — Village of, ii. 234
Besharik-Ustan, Village of, 384
Bezak, Village of, ii. 2
Bhotanese invade Kuch Behar, ii. 302
Bible in Mongolia, 163
— Society at Newchwang, 159
— — — Tashkend, 102, 170
— — — Tiflis, 20
— — in Manchuria, 159
— — — Petersburg, 10
"Bibliotheca Sinica" by Cordier, 357
Biddulph, Col., at Charwagh, 394
— — — Kila Panj, ii. 17
— — — Maralbashi, 422
— — — Yengi Hissar, ii. 70
Biisk, Hospital at, 123

Biisk, Macarius, Bishop, at, 123
Birds collected by Author, ii. 410
Birkuts, or eagles, at Kuldja, 205
Blackstone, Mr W. E., of Illinois, ii. 352
— — — — Author's project assisted by, ii. 357
Blagovidoff, Col., at Chimkend, 104
Blunoff, Capt., at Tashkend, 95
Bobrinsky, Count, Meeting with, 11
Bogashta Pass, ii. 5
Bogdo Mountains, 335
— Tian Shan range, 168
Bogus tribe in Tekes valley, 245
Bogle, Mr Geo., Tibetan MS. of, ii. 358
Bokhara, Apartments of M. Klemm at, 62
— Batchas at, 52
— Bazaar of, 64
— Capital punishment in, 52
— Cemetery of, 65
— Chinese at, 153
— Chuchugoim medresse, 79
— Circumcision at, 68
— College of Divan-beggi, 78
— Conolly, Capt., in, 71
— Conquest of, ii. 50
— Curzon, Mr, on Emir's court, 52
— Departure from, 80
— Dinner to maniacs, 67
— Driving and riding in, 61, 78
— Emir of, Palace of, 73
— — — Presents to Author, 76
— — — M. Klemm, 76
— — — Prisoners released by, 72
— — — Reception by, 74
— Executions in, 57
— Fellow-guests at, 62
— Festivities in, 73
— Finance minister of, 54
— Guest of Russian Resident at, 50
— Hebrew MSS. at, 68
— Heyfelder's medical work in, 72
— Horse-dealing in, 70
— House of the Ishan, 65
— Jewish oppression in, 69
— Jews' synagogue at, 67
— Kalan mosque at, 64
— Lepers' quarter at, 72
— Luggage sent on camels to, 137
— Madame Klemm's hospitality, 62
— Mirbadaleff, M., in, 78
— Muhammadan conquest of, ii. 207
— Mulberry trees in, 79
— Paucity of Europeans, 63
— Photography at, 64
— Prison at, 70
— Prostitution in, 52
— Railway fête at, 63
— — station, 60
— — — Inn at, 60

Bokhara, Reforms of new Emir, 51
— Russian influence in, 77
— — ladies in, 63
— — Residency at, 61
— Slavery abolished in, 51
— Stoddart, Col., at, 71
— Streets of, 79
— Superstition of natives, 73
— Suspicion of natives, 64
— Tamerlane at, ii. 52
— Treatment of maniacs, 65
— velvet at Merv, 38
— Visitors at, 60
— Zindan prison souvenir, 72
Bombay, Author's anxiety at. ii. 402
Bonney, Prof., Geological note of, 287
Bonvalot, M., Journeys of, 212; ii. 13, 19, 72, 311
Booghru, Butterfly hunt near, 233
— Kalmuk camp at, 231
— — cattle at, 231
Boots, Mr, engineer at Amu-daria, 52
Bora, Caravan visitors at, 236
— oasis, Fruit cultivation in, ii. 236
— — Turki families in, ii. 236
Bora-Burgusu, Kalmuks in, 397
Borisoff, missionary to Kirghese, 123
Bornemann, M., at Kuldja, 173; ii. 35
— — Assistance of, 196, 197
— — Linguistic abilities of, 208
Borneo, Visit to, ii. 403
Borokhoro range, 167, 229
Bostan, Camping at, ii. 274
— Horses astray at, ii. 275
Bower, Capt., at Karashar, ii. 62
— — in Chinese Turkistan, 376
— — Manuscript discovery, ii. 90
— — on Chinese rule, ii. 245
— — — Mingoi ruins, ii. 95
Brankston, Mr, Gun of, ii. 23
Bretschneider, Dr, Interview with, 5
— — on Chinese records, 364
— — — Syriac writing, ii. 132
— — Works of, 5
Brown, Rev. R., at Darjeeling, ii. 366
— Shipley, & Co., bankers, 90
Brunière, M. de la, among Gilyaks, 159
— — — — Murder of, 159
Buam defile, 114
— Stony road through Pass, 143
Buddha, Golden statue of, ii. 81
Buddhism among the Kalmuks, 258
— at Kuchar, 338
— Chinese study of, 359
— Decay of, ii. 87
— in China, 358
— — Mongolia, 162
— Relics of, ii. 96
   Schott's essay on, ii. 92

Buddhist aspirations, ii. 92
— Buriats, 163
— missionaries, ii. 87
— opposition to Muhammadanism, ii. 211
— persecution, ii. 90
— pilgrims, 359; ii. 16, 49
— temple at Kuldja, 195
Bugra Khan family, ii. 51
Bugur, Rug manufacture at, 338
Bukhtarma river, 123
Bukonsk, Kirghese station at, 122
Bulun Tokoi in Sungaria, 165
Bulundzir river, 321
Buonaparte, Prince Roland, 254
Burana tower, Excursion to the, 107, 108
Buriats of Mongolia, 162
Butterfly collection of Author, ii. 418
— hunt near Booghru, 233
— — — Tekes river, 236
— hunting on horseback, 248
Buzurg Khan at Kashgar, ii. 58

CAIN, Tomb of, at Sarakhs, 32
Calcutta, Chandra Das in, ii. 378
— Official assistance at, ii. 390
— Parting with Joseph at, ii. 390
— Railway journey to, ii. 377
— Smith, Rev. W., at, ii. 384
— Tidings of Mr James Hart, ii. 378
— Visit to Col. Lowis, ii. 383
— — — Sir Mortimer Durand, ii. 383
Cambodia, Visit to, ii. 403
Camden Town, Wolf-skinning in, ii. 22
Camel tracks from Hami, 329
Camp, First Sunday in, 222
Campbell, Dr, in Tibet, ii. 305
Cantacuzene P., at Tashkend, 94; ii. 20
Canterbury, Abp, Assistance of, ii. 355
— — Letter from, ii. 359
— Dean Alford's epitaph at, 113
Canton, Bible Society at, ii. 393
Capus, M., on the Pamirs, ii. 19
Caravan "hangers-on," 217
— Number of horses and men, 217
— Personnel of, 216
— travel by horses, 208
— — Provisions en route, 224
Carey, Mr, at Aksu, 316
— — — Hami, 327
— — — Jeypore, ii. 376
— — — Tibet, ii. 311
— — — Turfan, 335
— — — Urumtsi, 331
— — in Chinese Turkistan, 375
— — on Chinese officials, ii. 242
— — — Khotan, ii. 171
— — — — ruins, ii. 177
— — — monetary affairs, 97
   — suitable presents, 102

Carrick, Dr, *Koumiss* factory of, 253
Caspian, Crossing the, 22
— to the Oxus by rail, 22
— *See also* Trans-Caspian
"Cathay," by Sir Henry Yule, 357, 364
Cayley, Dr, at jade-mine, ii. 184
Cemeteries near Tokmak, 109
Cemetery of Bokhara, 65
— — Khiva, 65
— — Pishpek, 109
Ceylon, Embassy to China, 359
  Visit to, ii. 403
Chadalik gold and ruby mine, ii. 185
Chadir-Kul, 378
— — Bell at, 389
— — Birds at, 390
— — Cultivation at, 390
— — Deer at, 391
— — Forests at, 389
— — Forsyth expedition at, ii. 2, 3
— — Horse-flies at, 389
— — Houses of, 390
— — Jungle at, 389
— — Mausoleum at, 390
— — Pheasants at, 391
— — Photography at, 390
— — *Podocs* at, 392
— — Ruins at, 389
— — Street of, 390
— — Tamarisks at, 389
Chakmak, Gordon at, ii. 2
— Seeland at, ii. 2
— fort, ii. 2
— Kul, ii. 11
— — Gordon at, ii. 72
Chalon, M. Mailly-, in Manchuria, 156
Chaman, New, Author at, 34
Chandra Das, Journey of, ii. 309
  — meets Author in Calcutta, ii. 378
— — visits Author at Darjeeling, ii. 380
Ch'ang, Resident-designate at Lassa, ii. 368
Chang Chenmo route to Leh, ii. 314
Chang-kian, Mission of, ii. 49
Chang, Li Hung, Interview with, ii. 399
Changlung, Camp at, ii. 328, 329
Ch'ang-te, Narrative of travels of, 366
Chang, *Tu-tung* of the Ili valley, 185
Chapchal, Altitude of, 227
— — Arrival at gorge, 221
— — Exchange of dogs at, 233
— — First Sunday in camp at, 222
— — Geology of gorge, 230
— — Kalmuk tents at, 221, 228
— — Lodging in Kalmuk tent, 222
— — Pass of, 221
— — — Altitude of, 230
    — Climbing of, 229
      Descent from, 231

Chapchal, Temperature of, 228
— Trees and fruit at, 221
Charin river, 220, 310
Charjui, Artillery at, 54
— Cultivation at, 49
— Drive to, 52
— Gallows at, 57
— Murder of former *Bek* of, 54
— News of luggage at, 137
— Oasis of, 49
— Prison revisited, 55
— — Photographing criminals, 56
— Slavery at, 51
— Visit to *Bek* of, 52
Charwagh, Antiquities near, 395
— Biddulph, Col., at, 394
— Canals near, 394
— Departure from, 395
— Forsyth expedition at, 394
— Inhabitants of, 394
— Sport at, 394
Chelva, Juan de, at Bokhara, 62
Chemulpo, Journey to, ii. 400
Chen, *Tautai* at Aksu, 349
Cherchen, Buddhism at, ii. 83
— gold-mine, ii. 185
— route from Khotan, ii. 173
Cherchen-daria, 321
Chiamdo, the capital of Kham, ii. 282
Chian-da-loya, Farewell to, 305
Chibra, Camping-place of, ii. 316
Chichiklik Pass, ii. 10, 71
Chiguluk Aghse, Bivouac at, ii. 266
Chihil Gumbaz, Tombs of, ii. 70
Chikhalibekoff, M., in Turkistan, 407
Chilan, Hamlet of, 386
— Poplars at, 387
Chi-li, Province of, 324
Chimkend, Arrival at, 103
— Blagovidoff, Col., at, 104
— Departure from, ii. 30
Chimpanzee, Town of, 151
Chi-mu-sa, Chinese families at, 414
China beyond the Wall, 153
— Child marriage in, 194
  Church and stage in, 203
— Entry into, 150
— Former extent of dominion, 153
— — Inland Miss. at Kuei-hwa-cheng, 323
— — — — Lan-chow, etc., 324
— Mongol supremacy in, 362
— Nestorian missionaries in, 361
— Outer, Character of surface, 153
— — Political divisions, 154
— Passport difficulties in, 149
— Punishment in, 196
— Uigur raids on, ii. 49
— Wall of, neighbouring tribes, ii. 48
— — within the Wall, 153

GENERAL INDEX.   487

Chinaz, Arrival at, 94
Chinese Central Asia, *see* Asia
— character. English estimate, ii. 241
— — Russian estimate of, ii. 240
— conquests, 358 ; ii. 295
— defeats in Sungaria, 168
— diplomatic arrangements, 2
— historians, 357
— inhabitants of Kashgar, 197
— inn, Description of, 179
— Manners of, 204
— Minister at Berlin, 2
— money-changing, 342
— officials, Advice concerning, 301
— — at Suiting, 207
— pilgrimage to India, 359
— priests at Hei-hsui, 159
— prison tortures, 443
— Romanists at Suiting, 203
— table etiquette, 184
— temple and theatre at Suiting, 203
— travellers, 109
— troops, 412
— Untruthfulness of, 418
— victories in Sungaria, 169
Chirchik, Valley of the, 94
Chitral, Chief of, 346
— Journey from Yarkand to, ii. 74
Choktal, near Aksu, 382
— Driving through, 125
— Fish at, ii. 32
— Post-house of, ii. 32
— *Serai* at, 382
Chol Kuduk, ride to, 386
Chola, Village of, ii. 151
Chougeh Jilga, March to, ii. 323
Christianity in Central Asia, 109
— — Mongolia, 164
Christmas at Lahore, ii. 376
Chu river, 104
— — Crossing the, 113, 126
— — Kapustin, M., on, 114
Chuchugorm *madresse* at Bokhara, 79
Chuda, Village of, ii. 151
Chugguluka gold-mine. ii. 185
Chuguchak, Fort of, 166
　Houses in, 166
　Revolt of troops at. 332
— Town of, 165
— Trade of, 166
Chulak Langar, Birds at, ii. 163
— — Rest-house at, ii. 150
　— Sunday at, ii. 223
Chun-bagish tribe of Kirghese, ii. 6
Chung Terek, Kirghese at, ii. 2
Church and stage in China, 203
— of England Zenana Society. 102
Chvolson, Prof., Russian scholar, 109
— — on Chinese writing, ii. 131

Chvolson, Prof., on Nestorians, ii. 122
— — — Syriac inscriptions, 111
Circumcision at Bokhara, 68
Clark, Rev. R., at Amritsar, ii. 376
Clothing for Author's journey, 189
Cochin China, Voyage to, ii. 392
Colbeck, Rev. J. A., at Mandalay, ii. 391
Coleoptera collected by Author, ii. 417
Collins, Mr, on Amur river, 156
Cologne, Detention at, 2
Confucians in Sungaria. 169
Conolly, Capt., in Bokhara, 71
Constadt, Baron de, works of, ii. 305
Constantinovsk, Halt at, 126
Coombell, in Muzart valley, 288
Cordier's " Bibliotheca Sinica," 357
Craigie, Capt., of *Hyacinth*, ii. 403
Crimea, Arrival in the, 17
Cromie Lieut, Translation work by, 109
Crossett, Mr, on missions, ii. 338
— — Death of, ii. 400
Crosthwaite, Sir C., Visit to, ii. 392
Csoma de Korös, Tibetan student, ii. 304
— — — Death of, ii. 305
Cumberland, Major, at Kashgar, ii. 19
— — — Maralbashi, 423
— — in Chinese Turkistan. 376
— — on the Pamirs, ii. 10
Curzon, Mr. on court of Bokhara, 52
Czar, Author's present to, 4
— Presents of, to Gur Jemal, 40
Czar steamer at Amu-daria, 52

Dalai Lama at Lassa, ii. 288, 294. 297
— — Author's letter to, ii. 360
Dalgleish, Mr, Caravan of, ii. 112
— — Career of, ii. 111
— — Effects of, ii. 320
— — House of, ii. 115
— — in Chinese Turkistan. 375
— — Locality of murder, ii. 317
— — Murder of, 134, 346 ; ii. 114
— — on Scripture distribution, ii. 112
— — Servants of, ii. 110
Dam, or mountain sickness, ii. 269
Damarchi, Hospitality at, 220
— Village of. 219
Darchendo, Roman mission at, ii. 300
— Town of, ii. 282
" Dardistan, Languages of," ii. 15
Darjeeling, Brown, Rev. R., at, ii. 380
— Death of Csoma de Koros at, ii. 305
— Founder of. ii. 305
— Journey to, ii. 378
— Paul, Mr A. W., at, ii. 380
— Turnbull, Rev. A., at, ii. 381
— Visit of Chandra Das, ii. 380
Darkot, Murder of Hayward at, ii. 17
Darwaz, Dr Regel at, ii. 17

Darwaz district, ii. 12
— Surgut, Camping at, ii. 316
Daud M. Khan murders Dalgleish, ii. 114
— — — Capture of, ii. 318
— — — — Reward for, 346 ; ii. 318
— — — Suicide of, ii 322
Daulatbeg Uldi, Domed caves at, ii. 324
Davids, Prof Rhys, on Lamaism, ii. 287
Deibner, Col., at Osh, 99
Deken, M. de, at Kuldja, 193
— — — — Lob-Nor, ii. 172
— — — Journeys of, 212
— — — on Manchu language, 158
— — — — Manchurians in Ili, 218
— — — — Mongolians, 160
— — — Sport with, ii. 35
Dervishes at Kashgar, 447
Desgodins, M., on fauna of Tibet, ii. 306
— — — trade of Tibet, ii. 306
Deubner, Col., ii 8
Dilke, Mr Ashton, in Ili valley, 374
— — — — Talki Pass, 168
Diptychus, Author's new specimen, ii. 32
Divan-beggi college at Bokhara, 78
Diwantchi fort, ii. 61
Djil-Aryk post-station, 113
Dmitrieff, M., exile at Jarkend, 144
Doghri Kuprik, Horse exchange, ii. 237
Dolan shepherds' hospitality, 423
Dolans at Yarkand, 423
— Character of, 424
— Dwellings of, 423
— Manufactures of, 423
Dolun Pass ii. 5
Dorga glacier, 271
Do-Shambeh bazaar, ii. 164
Dudgeon, Dr, at Peking, ii. 399
Dufferin, Lord, Assistance of, ii. 108
Dungan mosque at Kuldja, 213
— rebellion, ii. 58
— women, Dress of, 219
Dungans from Ili valley, 113
— subjugation of, ii. 60
Dunstan, Mr, at Agra. ii. 377
Durand, Col., Letter to, ii. 381
— Sir M. on Author's journey, ii. 377
— — — Visit to, ii. 383
Durbuljin, Kalmuk troops at, 166
Durun, Ice-cellars at, 28
— Native dwellings at, 28
— railway station, 28
Dushak railway station, 32
Dyspnœa, Kirghese treatment of, 124

EARTHQUAKE at Vierny, 130
Easter in Tashkend, 96
Eden, Sir A., helping Chandra Das, ii. 309
Egun Langar, Hamlet of, ii. 149
Elias, Mr Ney, at Badakshan, ii. 18

Elias, Mr Ney, at Leh, ii. 306
— — — on Chinese Turkistan, 149
— — — — Sikkim frontier, ii. 372
Erbu lu, luggage porter at Jarkend, 145
Eshik-bashi range, 308
Esther, MS. roll of Book of, 69
" Etat Major " at St Petersburg, 8
— — — — — Kindness of officers, 10
— — — Tiflis, Dinner with chief of, 19

FA-HIAN, Travels of, ii. 83
Faizabad, Bazaar at, 429
— Chinese barracks at, 430
— Cultivation at, 430
— Dungan cavalry at, 430
— Houses of, 428
— Road to, 428
— — — Kashgar, 430
— Visit of Chinese general, 428
Fan-tek, Gov.-General of Sin Kiang, 333
Farab, Journey to, 60
— railway station, 60
Fazul, Author's former servant, 89
Fedchenko, Explorations of, ii. 17, 27
— Madame, Visit to, ii. 24
Feodoroff, M., at Tashkend, 95
Ferghana, Arabs in, ii. 50
— Cumberland, Major, in, ii. 19
— Fedchenko's explorations in, ii. 17
— Mountains, 290
— Muhammadan conquests of, ii. 208
— route from Kashgar, ii. 1, 5
— Trade of, 439
Fife, Duke of, at St Petersburg, 5
Fleming, Mr, on South Manchuria, 156
Foo Chow, Archdeacon Wolfe at, ii. 394
Food for Author's journey, 188
Foo-Shan, interpreter at Kashgar, 187
Forsyth expedition at Chadir-Kul, ii. 2
— — — Charwagh, 394
— — — Kashgar, 375
— — — Maralbashi, 422
— — on the Pamirs, ii. 11, 17
— — at Yarkand, ii. 104
— — — Yengi Hissar, ii. 66, 70
— on opium-smoking, ii. 145
Friday mosque at Yarkand, ii. 106
Fritsche, M., on Mongolian climate, 160
Fuh-Khan, Chinese families at, 414
Furniture for Author's journey, 190
Fusan, Ride to, ii. 400

GABET in Tibet, ii. 303
Gagarine, Prince, 369
Gam-i-sang, Grapes at, 430
— — — Village of, 430
Gataere, Col., Introductions by, ii. 391
Gaz-Kul on the Little Pamir, ii. 11
Geduonoff, M., at Pishpek, 106

GENERAL INDEX.   489

Geelan, Arrival at, 236
— Impracticable ford at, 237
Gehol, Belgian missionaries at, 159
— Chinese priests at, 159
Geok Tepe fortress, 28
— — railway station, 28
German Bible-class at Tiflis, 19
Germans at Kharkof, 15
Gerrard, Mr, naturalist, ii. 22
Gez river, ii. 13, 45
Ghaljas, Kalmuk encampment at, 218
— Shooting grouse at, 219
— valley, 218
Gheyn, M. van den, on Pamirs, ii. 15
Giaour Kala, Ruins of city of, 41
Giaurs, End of Akhal oasis at, 32
— railway station, 32
Gill, Capt., Journey of, ii. 310
Gilmour, Mr, in Mongolia, 161, 163
Gilyaks, Baptisms among, 158
- - Brunière. M. de la, among, 159
Gobi plain, 324
Goes, Benedict, at Hami, 327
— — — Maralbashi, 422
— — — Yengi Hissar, ii. 70
— — on Pamirs, ii. 16
— — Travels of, 364
Go-gil-ga mountain, 286
Go'di tribe of Manchuria, 158
— — Baptisms among, 158
Good Friday in Tashkend, 96
Goorkha invasion of Tibet, ii. 295
Goose lake on the Pamirs, ii. 11
Gordon, Gen., at Chadir-Kul. ii. 3
— — — Chakmak, ii. 2, 72
— — — Kila Panj, ii. 17
— — — Mandalay, ii. 391
— — — Tash-Kurgan, ii. 71
— — — Yengi Hissar, ii. 70
Goujouss. Capt., at Jizak, 93
Gourdet, M., Hospitality of. 133, 139
— — on birds of Ilisk, ii. 34
— — — Vierny earthquake, 130
— — Seismic records of, 135
Gowing, Mr L. F., on Amur river. 156
Gramenitsky. M., Vierry earthquake, 132
Graphic, Author's photographs in, 44
Grierson, Mr, Consul at Sevastopol, 17
Gromke, Mrs, cards of. 219 ; ii. 341
Grombchevsky, Col., at Polu, ii. 175
— — fails to enter Tibet, ii. 175
— — in Chinese Turkistan, 376
— — Information of, 9
— — on the Pamirs, ii. 18
— — Tibetan journey of. ii. 311
Grum-Grjimailo, M., at Turfan, 335
— — — in Sungaria, ii. 28
— — — on Uigur antiquities, ii 132
— — Urumtsi trade, 332

Guchen, Cattle at, 330
— Garrison of, 414
— Inhabitants of. 330
— Manchu town of, 397
— Shops of, 330
— Soldiers at. 330
— Town of, 168, 330
— Trade of. 330
Gufur Khan, Afghan *Aksakal*, 340
Guillaume, M., Drive with, 39
Gulcha, Route to, ii. 7
Gulja-bashi, Suok stream at, ii. 3
Guma, Cultivation at, ii. 151
— District of, ii 151
— Houses of, ii. 151
- Shops at, ii. 151
— Town of, ii 151
Gumbaz, or mortuary pile, ii. 68
Gumbaz-Bozan, Mausoleum of, ii. 72
— — Younghusband at, ii. 19. 73
Gu-medi. Hunan braves at, 414
Gunther, Dr, on Ovis Poli, ii. 21
Gur-Emir at Samarkand, 90
Gur Jemal, Pension of, 40
— — Reception by. 40
Gurumdy Peak, ii. 10
Gutzlaff on Tibet, ii. 306

HABIBULLA, ruler of Khotan, ii. 160
— Murder of, ii. 160
— Palace of, ii. 160
Haffenden. Mr. at Singapore, ii. 392
Haidar Haji at Kilian, ii. 265
— — Travelling with, ii. 332
Haji, Mirza Jan. at Yarkand, ii. 90
Hajif Langar. Birds at. ii. 163
— — Rest-house at. ii. 151
Hami, Ali. Sultan, at, 326
- Bazaar of, 328
— Bell, Col., at, 327
— Camel tracks from, 329
— Carey, Mr, at, 327
-- Chinese at, 326, 329
— European visitors at, 326
— Fertility of. 327
- Gardens of, 328
  Goes, Benedict, at, 327
  History of, 326
- Horses at. 326
- Journey from Su chow to, 325
  Mausoleum at, 328
-- Potanin at, 327
— Present condition of, 327
— Prjevalsky at, 327
- Road to, 168
- Roads from, 329
-- Russian merchandise at, 328
— Shah Rukh's embassy at. 326
  Sosnovsky at. 327

Hami, Tombs of, 328
— Trade of, 328
— Turfanese at, 326
— Uigurs at, 326
— Uspensky's account of, 327
— Younghusband at, 323, 327
Han-moh, Buddhism at, ii. 83
Hanoi, Journey to, ii. 392
Harfeld Mrs. at Askhabad, 32
Harford, Capt., at Sevastopol, 17
— Mr, at St Petersburg, 5
Harkhadoz. a Nepalese, ii. 384
Hart, Mr, tidings of, at Calcutta, ii. 378
— Sir Robert, at Peking, ii. 395
— — — Counsel of, ii. 396
Hasan. Tomb of, ii. 76
Hastings and the Bho'anese, ii. 302
Hay, Miss, at Tashkend, 94
— — Translation work by, 132
Hayward, Mr, at Kashgar, 374
— — Murder of, 374 ; ii. 17
— on the Pamirs, ii. 16
— — — Yengi Hissar, ii. 66
Hazrat Aphak, Shrine of, 446
— Sultan, "Golden Shrine" of, ii. 189
Hebrew Scriptures bought at Tiflis, 20
— manuscripts at Bokhara, 68
Hedjouboff, M., at Tiflis, 20
Hei-hsui, Belgian missionaries at, 159
— — Chinese priests at, 159
Henderson, Dr, with Forsyth, ii. 27
Henning, Rev. S., on Nestorians, ii. 121
Herat, Nestorians in, ii. 122
Herbert, Col., at St Petersburg, 5
Hermitage at Mazar-bash, 276
Herrnhut, Moravian Board at, ii. 373
Herzenstein, M, on fishes, ii. 24
Heyfelder, Dr, in Bokhara, 72
— — on Turkmenia, 84
"Himalayan Journals" on Tibet, ii. 306
— range. 153
Hindu Kush, M. Ujfalvy on the, ii. 15
Hiongnu subdued by Chinese, 358
— Turkish race of, 358
Hiuen Tsiang, Chinese author, 108; ii. 83
— — among fire-worshippers, ii. 91
— — in the Muzart Pass, 279
— — on Buddhism, ii. 86
— — — early religions, ii. 79
— — — Pamirs, ii. 16
Hodgson, Mr, Tibetan student, ii. 304
Hoernle, Dr, on Bower MS., ii. 96
Holdich, Col, Introduction from, 19
Hong Kong, Guest of Mr Ost at, ii. 393
— — Introductions at, ii. 393
— — Visit to, ii. 400
Hooker, Dr, in Sikkim, ii. 306
Hoshoits of the Kunges valley, 397
Howell, Mr. in Mongolia, 161

Howorth, Sir Henry, 113
— — — "Mongols" of. 109
Hsi-wan-tze, Belgian missionaries at, 159
— — — Chinese priests at, 159
Huc in Tibet, ii. 303
— and Gabet, Narrative of, ii. 304
Hunan, Soldiers of, 328, 414
Hung Ta-jen at Berlin, 2
"Hungry" Steppe. Crossing the, 93
— — Wells in the. 93
Hunt, Mr, Consul at Kertch, 18
Hussein, M., Loan of tents by, ii. 267
Hyacinth, H.M.S., Chaplain on, ii. 403
Hyderabad, Tibetan efforts at, ii. 401

Ice cavern near Mazar-bash, 279
— cellars on Persian frontier, 28
— — cliff, Horses hauled up, 276
— — tables in Muzart Pass, 272
— — wells in Muzart Pass, 273
I-crow, Village of, 384
Ighiz-Yar, Houses of, ii. 70
Ilchi. capital of Khotan, ii 187
Ili Muhammadans in Manchuria, 218
— river at Kuldja. 214, 215
— — Bivouacking on, 215
— — Departure from, 216
— — Fording the. 217
— — Horse-shoeing on bank of, 216
— — Whipping the ferryman, 214
— valley, Dilke, Ashton, in, 374
— — Fauna of. ii. 28
— — Field for missionary work, 170
— — Inhabitants of. 169
— — Jagatai Khan in, ii. 52
— — Kalmuks in, 169
— — Manchus in. 218, 396
— — Mineral oil in, 230
— — Morgan, Delmar. in. 374
— — Native Christians in, 218
— — restored to China, ii. 64
— — Roman mission in, 194
— — Russia in possession, 370
— — Schuyler in, 374
— — Scripture distribution in, 170
— — Taranchis in, 219
— — Temperature of, 228
— — View from Chapchal, 229
— — Villages in. 229
Ilisk post-station, 140
— Altitude of, 142
— Bird life at. ii. 34
— Fauna collected at, ii. 34
— Meeting an Englishman at, 140
— Siberian exiles at, 141
Ilyik Khan at Kashgar, ii. 51
India. Chinese ambassadors in, 359
— Viceroy of, Interview with, ii. 377
— — — Letter to, ii. 365

GENERAL INDEX.   491

Indus, Watershed of the, ii. 11
Irish Presbyterians in Manchuria, 160
Irkeshtam, Russian frontier at, ii. 5
Irtish, Black, Valley of the, 165
Ishan at Bokhara, House of, 65
Iskander Kala ruins of city of, 41
Isligh hot-springs, ii. 13
Ismail, caravan servant, 217
Ispangu oasis, Cultivation in, ii. 330
— — New people and new birds, ii. 330
Issik-Kul, New fish from, ii. 33
— — Basin of, 115
— — Fauna of, ii. 31
— — Geology of, 287
— — Kara-Kirghese at, 120
— — Narrow escape near, 116
— — Russian monastery at, 121
Issygaty defile, near Tokmak, 121
Iswa Chenza, 325
Itigak gold and ruby mine, ii. 185
Ivanoff, Gen., Governor of Semirechia, 133
— Park at Samarkand, 91
Ivanoffsky, M., engineer at Bokhara, 60

JACOBITES, Rev. S. Hemming on, ii. 121
Jagasai Khan in Ili valley, ii. 52
Jai-tugrak-ustang river, 310
Jaii-a, Huts at, 386
Jalyn-Khatsyr glacier, Kaulbars on, 268
Jam, Aquatic birds at, 310
— Cultivation at, 308
— Death of a horse at, 311
— Soldiers at, 304
— Village of, 308
James, Mr H. E. M., Author of " Long White Mountain," 156; ii. 108
— — — — Letter from, ii. 112
Janart river, Fording the, 382
Janghuia, Cultivation at, ii. 156
— Scripture distribution at, ii. 152
— — sales at, ii. 156, 343
— — Village of, ii. 152, 156
Japan, Visit to mission stations, ii. 400
Jarkend, Arrival at, 144
— Departure from, 148
— Dmitrieff, M., at, 144
— Geology of road to, 143, 144
— Hospitality at, 144
— Interpreter at, 205
— Kindness of police-master at, 145
— Luggage forwarded to, 139
— Modes of conveyance from, 146
— Money arrangements, 146
— — changing at, 342
— Prjevalsky's guides in, 145
— Purchase of cart and horses at, 146
— Rich native of, 145
— Visit to *Nachalnik's* house, 144

Jdanow, Gen., at Tiflis, 19
Jehangir at Kashgar, ii. 56
— Execution of, ii. 56
Jergalan river, 119
Jericho, Visit to, ii. 404
Jerusalem, Indisposition at, ii. 404
— — Kindness of Dr Wheeler at, ii. 405
— — Plans frustrated at, ii. 402
Jewish illumination of MSS., 68
— oppression in Bokhara, 69
Jews of Samarkand, Synagogue of, 91
— — Visits from, 91
— synagogue at Bokhara, 67
— — — — Circumcision in, 68
Jeypore, Mr Carey at, ii. 376
Jing, *alias* " Monkey-face," 234
— Pretensions of, 213, 214
Jinghiz Khan, Christians in camp. ii. 124
— — Conquests of, 362; ii. 51
— — Death of, ii. 52
— — in Tarim valley, ii. 51
Jinho military station, 167
Jiti-shahr, 318
Jizak, Capt. Gonjouss at, 93
— Route to, 93
— Smarguloff, Col., at, 92
Johnson, Dr L., Camera selected by, 295
— Mr, at Khotan, ii. 160
— — Yarkand, ii. 161
— — in Kashmir, 374
Jones, Mr H., on Kashgar route, ii. 5.
— — — Nestorian remains, ii. 130
Jou, M., Linguistic capabilities of, ii. 328
— — Parting with, ii. 376
Jordan river, Sleeping in open at, ii. 404
Joseph, Accident to, 278
— Antecedents of, 226
— at Blackheath, 226
— Strangers' Home, E. London, 225
— Bread made by, 225
— in charge of baggage, 226
— meets Author at Batoum, 226
— Narrow escape from gun accident, 299
— Parting with, ii. 390
— Recommended by Sir West Ridgeway, 225, 226
— shipped to Batoum, 226
— Taxidermical skill of, 298; ii. 22
— Testimonial from Author, ii. 300
Jubilee sovereigns in Turkistan, 97
Jumma mosque at Khotan, ii. 189
Junglache, Monastery at, ii. 282
Junker's bank at Petersburg, 97
Jun-Wang at Karashar, 187

KAELANG, Moravian mission at, ii. 300
Kafiristan, Thoughts of, 444
Kah-i-chang at Suiting, 182
— Agility of, 183

Kah-i-chang, Breakfast with, 182, 203
— Presents to, 184, 186
— — from, 207
— Visit from, 184
Kailek, Arrival at, 294
— Eagles at, 297
  Horse-shoeing at, 296
— Poultry at, 295
  Soldiers at, 304
  Taking possession at, 295
— and Tuprak, Distance between, 303
Kainuk, Taranchis at, 219
— Village of, 219
Kaiser, M., at Tashkend, ii. 37
Kakshal, Kirghese at, 378
Kalan mosque at Bokhara, 64
Kalendars at Kashgar, 447
Kalgan, American mission at, 323
Kalimpong, Journey to, ii. 379
— Lama service at, ii. 379
— Sutherland, Mr, at, ii. 379
Kalmuks, Administration of, 256
— Agriculture among, 259
— at Shartoo, 246
— — Udungei, 250
— Baratola, Khan of, 209
— Beverages of, 251
— Buddhism among, 258
— Camels on the Volga, 231
— Camp at Booghru, 231
— — Chapchal, 221
— — Ghaljat, 218
— Lodging in tent of, 222
— Cattle of, 231
— Dogs of, 232
— Dress of, 254
— Education of, 256
— Evangelisation of, 170
— Food of, 250
— in An-how-tzien, 397
— — Balgazi, 397
— — Bora-Burgusu, 397
— — Karashar, 397
— — Khobak, 397
— — Sarin, 397
— — Sungaria, 397
— Intellectual capacities of, 257
  Interpreter at Suiting, 207
— Jewellery of, 259
— Marriage customs of, 258
  Morals of, 258
— near Karashar, 337
— — Toksun, 337
— Nomad life of, 259
— Number of, 256
— Objects of worship, 258
  of Astrakhan steppes, 254
— — Mongolia, 102
— the Volga, 169, 254

Kalmuks on Muzart river, 250
— Photographs of, 236, 254
— Polygamy among, 259
— Poverty of, 258
— Roman mission work among, 193
— School at Vierny, 256
— Scripture distribution among, 218, 398 ; ii. 340
— — translations, 169
— Shamanism among, ii. 80
  Subjugation of, ii. 60
  Tents at Chapchal, 228
— Tribal quarrels of, 169
— Troops at Durbuljin, 166
— Visit to tent, 253
— Women, 258
Kalpak-tash Mountain, 286
Kalpin, Desert of, 386
Kamensky Brothers, carriers, 137
Kan, Village of, 220
Kan-chow, Lazarites at, 325
Kan-jugan, Battle at, ii. 6
— — Fort of, ii. 6
— — Monastery at, ii. 6
Kansu, Administration of, 325
— Rebellion in, ii. 58
— Superstition in, 193
Kappa gold-mine, ii 185
Kapustin, M., Camp of, 114
Karabo-Ata railway station, 35
Karabagh, Sulphur springs at, 347
Karachi, Visit to, ii. 404
Kara-davan Mountain, 286
Karakain river, ii. 4
Karakash river, ii. 162, 277
— — Camping on bank, ii 315
— valley, ii. 276
— — Kirghese nomads in, ii. 277
— — Robbers in, ii. 277
Kara-Khitai rule in Tarim valley, ii. 51
Kara-Kirghese at Kara-Kol, 119
— — Costumes of, 120
— — Districts of, 120
— — Origin of, 120
— — Orthodox Church Mission to, 122
— — Religious condition of, 121
— — Seeland, Dr, on, 119
Kara-Kol, Arrival at, 116
— — Change of plans at, 119
— — Climate of, 117
— — Garrison at, 119
— — Guest of *Nachalnik*, 118
— — Kara-Kirghese at, 119
— — Korolkoff, Col., at, 118
— — Morgan, Mr Delmar, at, 117
— — Prjevalsky's death at, ii. 174
— — Scenery of, 117
— — Vaouline, Col., at, 118
— watershed, 289

Karakoram Pass, ii. 317
— — Dalgleish, Mr, at, ii. 113
— — Perils of ii 323
— route, Preparations for, 446
— — to Leh. ii. 314
Kara-Kuchan, Sunday at, 425
Kara-Kul on the Pamirs, ii. 11
Kara-kur-usu district. Lakes of. 167
— — — — Towns of, 167
Karashar, Bower, Lieut., at. ii 62
— Buddhism at, ii. 83
— Colleges formerly at. 397
— Houses of. 397
— Kalmuks at. 169, 337, 397
— Population of, 337
— river, 338
— Roads to and from, 199, 337, 338
— Ruins at. 337
— Shops of, 397
— Town of, 337, 397
Kara-su stream, ii. 8
Kara-Tag range, 220
Karatagh gold-mine, ii. 185
Karategin. Oshanin at, ii. 17
Karaul-Kuyn, Drifting sands at, 49
Karawul, Kirghese at, 379
— Dawan, Summit of, ii. 328
Karghalik, Arrival at, ii. 143
— Crossing the desert from, ii. 149
— Cultivation at, ii. 143
— Departure from. ii. 148, 234
— Elevation of. ii. 143
— Fruit at, ii. 143
— Hindu seeking protection at, ii. 233
— Hospitality at, ii. 143
— Houses of, ii. 143
— Letters at, ii. 147
— Lodging at, ii. 143
— Mausoleum at, ii. 144
— Mulberry trees in. ii. 236
— Opium-smoking at, ii. 145
— Presents at, ii. 144
— Route to, ii 136
— Shops at, ii 143
— Silk manufacture at, ii. 236
— Telegram at, ii 147
— Town of, ii. 143
— Visit of Chinese official, ii. 144
Karkara river, 309
Kash river, 229
— — Roman mission work on, 193
Kashgar, Area of, 434
— as centre for mission work, ii. 349
— Bazaar at, 439
— Buddhism at, ii. 87
— Buddhist forces at, ii. 74
— Buddhists expelled from, ii. 211
— Capture by Arabs, ii. 50
— **Caravanserai at, 438**

Kashgar, Carts engaged, 446 ; ii. 44
— Cemetery at, 447
— Chinese inhabitants of, 197, 414
— — prison torture, 443
— — victory at, ii. 57
— City wall of, 434
— Conquest of, ii. 49
— Contest for sovereignty, ii. 52
— Corn-fields around. ii. 5
— Cumberland at, ii. 19
— Departure from, ii. 43
— District of. 430
— Escort from, ii. 43
— European residents in. 436
— Excavation of ruins, ii. 177
— Foo-Shan, interpreter, 187
— Former travellers from, ii. 45
— Forsyth's missions to, 375
— from Kuldja, Expense of journey, 60
— Fruit at, 436
— Gardens of, ii 5
— Golden mosque of, 451
— Grave of Yakub Khan, 449
— Guest of the *Tautai*, 432
— Hayward, Mr, at, 374
— Hemp-smoking in, 408
— History of. 446
— Homeward despatch of parcels. ii. 37
— Houses of. 430
— Industry of, 438
— Interview with *Tautai*, 440
— Kalendars, or dervishes, 447
— Kashi work at, 450
— Kaulbars at, 375
— *Khoja* invasion, ii. 57
— Letters at, 437 ; ii. 42
— Mausoleum at, 449
— Meteorology of. ii 180
— Moghul rulers ii 53
— Money forwarded to, 134
— Mosque at, 438
— Mountains at, ii. 1
— Muhammadanism in, ii. 210
— Opium-smoking in, ii. 146
— Osman Bai paid at, 446
— Packing specimens at, 451
— Petrovsky, M., at, 134, 435
— Petrovsky's, Miss, journey to, 405
— Photography at, 438
— Population of, 430
— Presents at, 441
— Prison inspection, 441
— — instruments, 442
— — Photography in, 442
— — Scripture distribution in, 444
— Rebellion in, ii. 55
— Reintal, Capt., in, 374
— Reorganisation of caravan, ii. 57
— Ride to Russian Consulate, 433

Kashgar, Rising of mountaineers, ii. 54
— Roads from Aksu, 377
— Route to Pamirs, 45
— Ruins at, 447
— Russian Consulate at, 435
— — Embassy at, 374
— — escort at, 432
— — travellers at, 370
— Sale of surplus baggage at, ii. 38
— Schlagintweit's murder at, ii. 43
— Scripture sales at, ii. 38, 342
— Seeland's route from, ii. 2
— Shaw, Mr, at, 374
— Shops of, 438
— Shrine of Hazrat Aphak, 447
— Soldiers at, 414
— Sunday in, 438
— Sungarian exactions at, 168
— *Tautai* of, 380 ; ii. 42
— — Visit of to Author, 440
— Town population of, 435
— Uigur expansion from, ii. 51
— Visit of officials, 437
— Yakub Khan at, 374
— Younghusband's route, 378
Kashgar-daria, 321
Kashgaria, 318
— Defences of, 420
Kash-kasu Pass, ii. 70
Kashmir, Mr Johnson in, 374
" Kashmir and Kashgar," 406
Kastek Pass, 113
Katte Kurgan, Drive to, 85
Kaufmann, Gen., War-horse of, 212
— Peak, ii. 10
Kaulbars' embassy to Kashgar, 375
— mission to Yakub Khan, ii. 60
Kaushid Khan Kala, Turkomans at, 35
Kayragh hills at Yengi Hissar, ii. 66
Kazandjik, Village of, 25
Kazangul, Hamlet of, 430
Ketoin, Great, river, 113
— Little, river, 113
Kenmure, Mr. Bible Society's Agent at Canton, ii 393
Kent-Shlentchi, Soldiers at, 304
Kertch, Visit to Consul at, 18
Kessler on Turkistan fishes, ii. 32
Ketmen, Pass of, 221
Khair-Samun, Sibo village of, 217
Khala-chi lake, 321
Khalik-Tau range, 308
Khalkhas of Mongolia, 162
Khamil, City of, 328
— *see also* Hami
Khan, Daud Muhammad, *see* Daud
Khan Tengri ta ge, 118, 243, 308
— — Altitude of, 308
— — Photographs of, 309

Khan-Yailak, Attendants depart, 260
— — Chinese picket-station, 259
— — Road to, 252
— — and Taingha-tash, Distance, 303
Khanakai, Arrival at, 235
— March to, 233
— Pass of, 221
— Photographs of Kalmuks at, 236
— river, 233
— Storms at, 235
Khanka, Travellers' station at, ii. 66
Khardung, Ascent to, ii. 334
— Houses of, ii. 334
— Pass, Ascent of, ii. 336
— Paucity of children at, ii. 335
— Visit to natives, ii. 335
Kharkof, Arrival at, 14
— Departure from, 16
— Dondukoff-Korsakoff, Prince, at, 15
— Germans at, 15
— Hôtel de l'Europe at, 14
— Luggage mishap at, 16
— Lutheran church at, 15
— Population of, 15
— Railway routes from, 16
— Visit to town prison, 15
Khatmandu, Campbell, Dr, at, ii. 305
— Goorkha defeat at, ii. 295
— Journey to, ii. 385
— Maharajah's unwillingness to assist Author, ii. 385
— Service conducted by Author at, 386
— Welcome at, ii. 385
Khilkoff, Prince, at Amu-daria, 50
— Railway experience of, 58
Khiva, Benoist-Méchin, Baron, at, 44
— Cemetery of, 65
— Executions in, 57
— Gallows at, 57
— Melons as tribute to China, 153
— Pascal at, ii. 125
Khobak, Kalmuks in, 397
Khodalik gold and ruby mine, ii. 185
Khojak tunnel, 34
Khojas, Rebellion of, ii. 54, 55
Khorgos, Russo-Chinese boundary, 148
Khosh Langar picket-station, ii. 150
Khotan, Almshouses in, ii. 191
— Arrival at, ii. 165
— bazaar, Purchases in, ii. 193
— Beggars' breakfast-party, ii. 195
— Buddhism at, ii. 84
— Buddhist defeat at, ii. 211
— Carpet manufacture, ii. 194
— Chinese bazaar, ii. 192
— — temple in, ii. 191
— Convicts as excavators, ii. 177
— Corn bazaar at, ii. 189
— Dancing dervishes, ii. 195

GENERAL INDEX.

Khotan, Departure from, ii. 221
— Early people of, ii. 168
— Escort from, ii. 221
— Exchange of silver, ii. 186
— Gardens of, ii. 163
— Gold-mines of, ii. 185
— "Golden Shrine" at, ii. 189
— Habibulla, ruler of, ii. 160
— History of, ii. 166
— Hospitality at, ii. 189
— Jade-mines near, ii. 183
— Jilga, ii. 315
— Limits of, ii. 175
— Lodging in a *serai*, ii. 187
— Meteorology of, ii. 178
— Mosques of, ii. 189
— Muhammadanism in, ii. 211
— Photography at, ii. 118, 192, 195, 196, 198
— Population of, ii. 170, 202
— Products of, ii. 182
— Ride round walls of, ii. 202
— river, 321
— Saluting a gun at, ii. 187
— Sandy deserts *en route*, ii. 176
— Shepherds of, ii. 174
— Streets of, ii. 189
— Travellers in, ii. 170
— Turkish town at, ii. 187
— Villages sand-buried, ii. 176
— Visit to *Amban*, ii. 188
Khua-khaitsi lake, 321
Khuidu-gol river, 397
Kia-yu-kuan, Town of, 325
Kiakhta, Gilmour's journey to, 161
— Tea route at, 161
— Town of, 161
Kila Panj, capital of Wakhan, ii. 17
Kila-Wamar, Panjah river at, ii. 12
Kilian, Cultivation around, ii. 237
— Elevation of, ii. 238
— Fruit at, ii. 263
— Houses of, ii. 238
— Pass, Birds secured in, ii. 270
— — Crossing the, on *yaks*, ii. 268
— — Descent from, ii. 272
— — Shooting restrained, ii. 270
— — Suffering from *dam*, ii. 269
— Provisions at, ii. 263
— Road to, ii. 237
— village population, ii. 238
Kinsu, Village of, 396
Kirghese, Anthropological characteristics, 398
— at Bukonsk, 122
— — Chung Terek, ii. 2
— — Tokmak, 402
— — Ush-Turfan, 398
— Beverages of, 251

Kirghese, Capital of the, 104
— Chinese difficulties with, 405
— Chun-bagish tribe of, ii. 6
— Crimes of, 404
— Cultivation by, 404
— Diseases among, 402
— Education of, 257
— food in Semirechia, 251
— in Aksai valley, 398
— — Ak-tash valley, ii. 72
— — Chinese Turkistan, 368
— — Siri country, 398
— manner of living, 403
— mission in Tomsk, 122
— Missionary work among, 123
— modes of treating disease, 124
— Morals of, 404
— Muhammadanism among, 258
— Occupations of, 404
— on Pamirs, ii. 14
— Pillage by, 405
— raided by Kunjutis, ii. 239
— Seeland, Dr. on, 398
— Shamanism among, ii. 80
— tombs near Tash-Rabat, ii. 4
— Visit to tents of, 125
Kiria, Route through, ii. 366
Kirin, Population of, 155
Kiskilensk defile, Earthquake in, 132
— Escort from, to Vierny, 128
— post-station, 128
Kizil, Families in, ii. 77
— Iron-smelting at, ii. 77
— Journey to, ii. 76
— Shops of, ii. 77
Kizil Arvat railway station, 26
Kizil-Bulak, Cultivation at, 306
— — Curious geological formation, 306
— — Dust columns near, 305
— — Soldiers at, 304
Kizil-Kuegai river, 378
Kizil-su stream, ii. 8
Klaproth on Tibet, ii. 306
Klemm, M, at Bokhara, 62
— Madame, Hospitality of, 62
Kludolf, Russian artist, 271
Knox, Mr, on Amur river, 156
Kobdo, Kalmuks in, 169
— Opening for mission at, 164
— Roads to, 329
— Russian shops at, 329
Kochkur, Bed of, ii. 5
Kodj railway station, 26
Kor-Jarligan Mountains, 126
Kokjar river, 309
Kok-Mainak post-station, 115
Kok-Robat, Cultivation at, ii. 77
— — Families at, ii. 77
— — Journey to, ii. 77

Kokshaal range. Altitude of, 310
Koktan range, ii. 3
Kok-Teke range, 308
Kolpakovsky, Gen., Welcome by, 105
Koluch, Author's former servant, 89
Kondla Langar, Hamlet of, ii. 156
Komurolen post-station, 144
Koo-Kah, one of Author's escort, 213
— — Return home of, 260
Kopa river, Source of, 127
Korea, Ride across, ii. 400
Korolkoff, Col., at Kara-Kol, 118
Korsakoff, Prince Dondukoff-, 6, 15
Kosha Langar, Hamlet of, ii. 156
Koshluk, a Kirghese prince, ii 51
— Decapitation of, ii. 51
Kostenko, Gen., in Muzart Pass, 263
— Measurements of, 303
— on source of Oxus, ii. 12
— — the Pamirs, ii. 9, 17
— — Tian Shan range, 243, 263
— Route of 246
— "Turkistan Region" by, 9
Koumiss, a Central Asian beverage, 253
— cure at Samara, 253
— establishment at Orenburg, 253
Kublai Khan, Buddhism fostered by, ii. 92
— — Conquests of, ii. 293
— — Tibetan lamas under, ii. 288
Kuch Behar, Bhotanese invasion of, ii. 302
Kuchar, Buddhism at, ii. 82, 86, 338
— Forsyth's account of, 338
— Minerals at, 339
— Population of, 339
— Rebellion at, ii. 58
— Sculpture at, 338
— Shops in, 339
— Town of, 338
— Troops at, 339
— Yakub Bek at, ii. 59
Kuei-hwa-cheng, Mission at, 323
Kuen Lun range, 324; ii 1, 265
Kuhlberg, Col., Hospitality of, 19
Kulchi, Village of, ii. 142
Kuldja, Arrival at, 151
— Baptism at, 177
— Belgian missionaries at, 163
— Birds of, ii. 34
— Bornemann, M., at, ii. 35
— Brigandage near, 178
— Buddhist temple at, 195
— Child marriage in, 194
— Chinese bazaar at, 195
— Cossack escort to, 150
— Cost of fodder at, 177
— Crossing the Ili at, 215
— Danger of night travel, 178

Kuldja, Deken, M. de, at, 193; ii. 35
— Departure from, 211
— Despatch of luggage to, 145
— Dog presented to Author, 212
— Dungan mosque at, 213
— Eagles at, 205
— Escort from, 213
— Excursions to Suiting, 178, 202
— Executioners at, 196
— Farewell to officials at, 212
— Gifts to Roman missionaries in, 194
— Horses at, 176
— Ili river at, 214
— Illness of Author at, 202
— Impedimenta at, 188
— Instruments of punishment at, 196
— Interpreter at, 197
— Kaufmann's war-horse at, 212
— Letter from Mr Carey, ii. 366
— Lodgings at, 171
— Lutheran postmaster at, 177
— Magistrate's procession at, 195
— Mandarin administration at, 176
— Mattie's visit to Author, 207
— Official visitors in, 178
— Polyglot character of, 208
— Price of jade in, ii. 184
— Provisions and fodder at, 211
— Return to, from Suiting, 205
— Roman mission in, 169, 193, 195
— Routes from, 199
— Russian *Aksakal* in, 205
— Sale of horse and cart at, 205
— Scriptures for, ii. 339
— Service at, 177
— Sibo village near, 217
— Specimen collecting at, ii. 35
— Specimens posted to Batoum, 206
— Steenemann, M., Work of, 193
— Suburbs of, 178
— Taranchi market at, 174
— — mosque at, 177
— Tatar hostess at, 206
— Thermometrical observations at, 312
— to Kashgar, Cost of journey, 99
— Tombs of the Khans at, 177
— Turki interpreter resigns, 199
— under the Chinese, 174
— Visit from blind native, 192
— Visiting in, 192
"Kuldja," our caravan dog, 233
— Death of, 312
Kuldja Bashi Mountains, 127
Kulkevitch M., Introduction to, 31
Kum-bash, Station of, 384
Kum-Robat, Pigeons at, ii. 158
— — — Tomb at, ii. 158
Kum Tagh, Sands of, 321
Kumdan, Glacier at, ii. 325

GENERAL INDEX.

Kungei Ala-Tau range, 114, 287
Kunges river, 229
— valley, Hoshoits of, 397
Kunia Urgenj, Destruction of, 108
Kunjut Mountains, ii. 13
Kurban-Bairam, Feast of, 345
Kurgashin-Kani, Coal near, ii. 6
Kurla, Population of, 338
  · Road from, 338
    Town of, 308, 338
  · Yakub Khan at, ii. 61
Kuropatkin on Chinese forts, 420
  - — Terek-davan route, ii. 5
Kursk, Arrival at, 14
Kurtu river, 127
Kusthana, capital of Li-yul, ii. 166
Kutaiba, Victories of, ii. 50
Kutemaldi, Village of, 115, 125 ; ii. 5
Kutuktu, The, at Urga, 162
Kuyuk Mazar railway station, 80

LADAK, Bibliography of, ii. 474
    Contests for, ii. 295
    Route to, ii. 1
Lahore, Bad news at, ii. 376
— barber at Maralbashi, 417
— Christmas at, ii. 376
— Letter from Mr Ney Elias, ii. 370
Lama Yuru, Monastery at, ii. 374
Lamaism, Characteristics of, ii. 287
Lamaists of Mongolia, 162
  · — Sungaria, 169
Lan-chow, City of, 324
    Missions at, 324
    Romanists at, 324
Land and Water, Letters to, ii. 10
Langar, Village of, ii. 5, 73
Langar Alim Akhoon rest-house, ii. 133
Langton & Son's present to Author, 223
Lansdowne, Marquis of, Interview with,
  ii. 377
Lao-tsao-ghoo, Chinese town of, 151
Larionoff, Col., at Narin, 134 ; ii. 5
Lassa, Capuchin mission at, ii. 300
  - Chinese delegates at, ii. 298
    Curios from, ii. 372
    Dalai Lama at, ii. 288, 294, 297
    Eden, Sir Ashley, at, ii. 309
    Endeavours to enter, ii. 368
    Entrance from Leh blocked, ii. 372
  - Expulsion of missionaries from, ii. 302
    Galdan monastery near, ii. 294
    Interview with Chinese Resident-
      designate, ii. 368
        Nepalese Resident at, ii. 380
    Jesuit mission at, ii. 300
    Manning's journey to, ii. 303
    Massacre of Chinese at, ii. 301
    Mongol pilgrimages to, 162

Lassa, Plans concerning, ii. 351
— Sungar capture of, 168
— Town of, ii. 282
— Van de Putte's journey through, ii. 301
Lazarites at Kan-chow, 325
  — — Liang-chow, 325
Leh, Arrival at, ii. 336
  · Dalgleish, Mr, at, ii. 112
    Departure from, ii. 374
  — Lama monastery at, ii. 374
    Letter to Mr Redslob at, ii. 366
— Lodging at, ii. 337
    Medical mission at, ii. 306
  - Moravian mission at, ii. 336, 373
    Redslob, Mr, at, ii. 116
    Welcome at, ii. 337
Leitner, Dr, on "Languages and Race-
    of Dardistan," ii. 215
Lengzi-tang plateau, ii. 281
Lepidoptera, ii. 418
Lepsinsk to Urumtsi, Road from, 165
Levashoff, Gen., at Askhabad, 32
  - — — Tashkend, 98
Lew, *Amban* of Yarkand, ii. 200, 225
  - Taking portrait of, ii. 225
Li, Gen., at Faizabad, 428
Li-yul, Kingdom of, ii. 167
Liang-chow, Mission at, 325
— — Lazarite bishopric at, 325
    — Manchu garrison at, 158
      Population of, 325
  · · Town of, 325
Lieven, Princess, Luncheon with, 10
Lilienfeld, Col., at Tashkend, 96 ; ii. 26
Lingzi plains, ii. 314
Litang, Town of, ii. 282
Littledale, Mr St George, 95
—   in Sungaria, 374
—   — on tent-life, 223
      the Pamirs, ii. 14, 19
      — wild-sheep hunting, ii. 20
Lob-Nor, Deken, M. de, at, ii. 172
    lake, 321
    Orleans, P. Henry of, at, ii. 172
  — Prjevalsky at, ii. 172
— — Villages near, ii. 173
— — Wild camels at, ii. 173
Loewenhagen, Capt., at Amu-daria, 52
London, Author's departure from, 2
- - Missionary Society's work in Mon-
    golia, 163
Low-chen, *see* Hami
Lowis, Col., Visit to, ii. 383
Luftabad, Town of, 32
Lungur, Dearness of fodder at, 427
Lutheran church at Kharkof, 15
— postmaster at Kuldja, 177
— service at Tashkend, 96
Lutsch, M., at Kashgar, ii. 58

MACARTES, Bishop, at Biisk, 123
Madamin Bai at Aksu, 312
— House of, 316
Madras, Letters at, ii. 401
Mai-boulak stream, 249
Maldabaevskaia post-station, 101
Malo-Narinsk, District of, 105
Malta, Journey to, ii. 405
Mammalia, ii. 400
Manas district, Fertility of, 168
  military station, 107 ; ii. 61
Manchester Guardian, Help of, ii. 358
Manchu agility, 185
  interpreter at Suiting, 207
  troops in Tibet, ii. 297
Manchuria, Bible Society's work in, 159
  Bibliography of, ii. 451
  Boundaries of, 155
  Chinese colonisation in, 158
  Classic language of, 158
  Efforts to Christianise, 158
  Fleming's description of. 159
  Government of, 155
  Hi Muhammadans in, 218
  James, Mr, in, 156
  Manyargs of, 156
  Méchin, Baron Benoist, in, 156
  Mountains of, 155
  Nomad tribes of, 159
  Population of, 155
  Presbyterians in, 160
  Provinces of, 155
  Rivers of, 155
  Roman missionaries in, 159
  Shamanists of, 158
  Williamson, Mr, on, 156
Manchus in Ili valley, 218, 396
  Pe-lu towns, 396
Mandalay, Colbeck, Rev. J., at. ii. 391
  Excursion from Rangoon to, ii. 391
— Gordon, Gen., at, ii. 391
  Preaching at, ii. 391
Manila, Visit to, ii. 403
Manning's journey to Lassa, ii. 303
Manyargs of Manchuria, 156
Maralbashi, Arrival at, 395
  Bell, Col., at, 417
  Birds near, 425
  Chinese fort at, 418
  Departure from, 424
  District of, 386
  Dolan shepherds near, 423
  European travellers in, 422
  Female prisoner at, 410
  Fort at, 416
  Garrison of, 422
  Goes, Benedict, at, 422
— Houses of, 422
  Indian merchants at, 416

Maralbashi, Lahore barber at, 417
  Mandarin's visit to Author, 417
  Mussulman attendants at, 418
  Photography at, 418
  Population of, 422
  Shops of, 416
  Visit to bazaar, 416
  — Mandarin, 416
— — prison, 416
  Yakub Khan at, 418
Maralty tributary of the Muzart, 252
Marco Polo, Christians in time of, ii. 124
  — on Pamirs, ii. 9, 16
— — — Yarkand, ii. 102
— — — Travels of, 362
" Marco Polo," by Sir Henry Yule, 364
Marex, Dr. at Leh, ii. 337
Marignolli, John de, at Almalik, ii. 128
  — — — — Hami, 326
Markham, Mr C., Assistance of, ii. 358
  — on Tibet, ii. 303
Mashrut, Fort of, ii. 6
Mattie at Suiting, 186, 203
  on Chinese officialism, 302
Mazar tomb at Turfan, 337
Mazar-bash, Arrival at, 275
— — Fort at, 276
— — — Hermitage at, 276
  — — Route from, 279
  — — Soldiers at, 304
Méchin, Baron Benoist, at Khiva, 44
— — — — Merv, 44
—   in Manchuria, 156
Merke, Arrival at, 105
Merv, Bokhariot manufactures at, 38
  Caravanserais of, 37
  Cathedral contemplated at, 37
  Departure from, 47
  Fortress at, 36
  Governor's administration of, 38
  Kutaiba at, ii. 50
— Méchin, Baron Benoist, at, 44
  Mouravieff, Col., at, 36
  Murghab river at, 35
  oasis, Entry by rail, 35
  Old, Alexander the Great at, 41
— — Arab supremacy at, 41
— — Archbishop's seat at, 41
— — Christianity in, 41
— — Monuments of, 41
  — Persian investment of, 42
  — Ruins on site of, 41
  Yusuf Khan's dwelling in, 39
— Persian carpets at, 38
  Railway favours at, 47
—   station and bridge at, 35
  — Russian annexation of, 43
— Shops of, 37
  Submission of, 44

GENERAL INDEX.   499

Merv, Sultan Sanjar of, ii. 51
— Tassel work of Sariks, 38
— Tekke carpets at, 38
— Trade of, 37
— Turkoman bazaar at, 36
— — inclosure at, 35
— Visit to Governor of, 36
Mestchertsky, Princess, Tea with, 12
Michie, Mr. in Mongolia, 161
Mikhailovsk railway station, 25
— Water distillation at, 25
Milne, Prof. John, in Mongolia, 161
Min-Yul, Fort of, ii. 6
Ming-bulak, Region of, 105
Mingoi ruins, Lieut. Bower on, ii. 95
Mirbadaleff, M., at Bokhara, 62
Mirkhovitz, Gen., Invitation of, 10
Mirza fort, ii. 2
Moghul rulers of Kashgar, ii. 53
Moji, Exorcism at, ii. 152
— Journey to, ii. 151
— Photography at, ii. 154
Mongol supremacy in China, 363
Mongolia, Alachain tribes of, 163
    Bibliography of, ii. 454
    Buriat tribes in, 163
    Christianity in, 164; ii. 124
    Climate of, 160
    Dimensions of, 160
    Divisions of, 161
    Elias, Mr Ney, in, 374
— Inhabitants of, 160
    Missionary work in, 163
    Parker, Mr, in, 163
    Prjevalsky's travels in, 371
    Towns of, 161
    Trade routes in, 161
— Travellers in, 161
    Tribes of, ii. 48
    Western, as a mission field, ii. 338
    Winter in, 160
" Mongols, Among the," by Gilmour, 163
— in Tarim valley, ii. 51
    Russian contact with, 368
— and Turks, Battle between, ii. 6
Montgomerie, Col., in Tibet, ii. 307
Montpensier, Duchess of, at Bokhara, 62
Moravian mission at Leh, ii. 336
— missionaries in Little Tibet, ii. 306
Morgan, Mr Delmar, at Kara-Kol, 117
— — — in Ili valley, 374
— — — on Talki Pass, 168
Morgan, Mr F. A., at Hong Kong, ii. 393
Morier, Sir Robert, at St Petersburg, 4
— — — Introductions through, 5
Moscow, Arrival at, 11
— Banking arrangements at, 11
    Hospitality at, 12
    Preaching in, 11

Moscow, Tea with Princess Mestchertsky, 12
— Visit to Madame Fedchenko, ii. 24
— Visitors from, at Bokhara, 62
— Zograf, Prof., at, ii. 24
Moths collected by Author, ii. 418
" Mountain, The Long White," by Mr James, 156
Mouravieff, Col., Companionship of, 36
Mouravieff, Count, Drive with, 39
— — Introduction to, 31
Muhammad Joo, see Joo
Muhammadan feasts and dancing, ii. 205
— festivities in Bokhara, 73
— martyrs' tombs, ii. 74
— prejudice against photography, 451
Muhammadanism among Kirghese, 258
— Degradation of, 412
— in Chinese Turkistan, ii. 207
— — Kashgar, ii. 210
— — Sungaria, 169
— — the desert, ii. 150
Mukden, Town of, 153
Mukhila Langar, Village of, ii. 151
Mulla Kara railway station, 25
Mullah-Khoja on the Muz-davan, 271
Murghab river, 35; ii. 12
Murza-Rabat in the Steppe, 93
Mushketoff, Geological map of, 287
— on the Pamirs, ii. 17
Mustagh-Ata Peak, ii. 16
Muz-davan, Accident on glacier, 275
— — Meeting a stranger on, 271
— — Pass, Arrival at Mazar-bash, 275
— — — First European over, 281
— — Photograph on crest of, 270
— — Scrambling down the, 276
Muz-Tag range, 243
Muzaffar-ed-din, Emir of Bokhara, 51
Muzart forest, Shrubs and flowers, 248
— gorge, Basin in, 265
— literature, 280
— Pass, Agate in, 273
— — Animal suffering in, 269
— — Bridges in, 249
— — Butterfly hunt in, 248
— — Coloured marble in, 273
— — Crest of, 270
— — Crevasses, 273
— — Dangers of, 260, 268
— — Departure for, 240
— — Difficulties of pack animals, 274
— — Entrance to, 245
    Forest zone of, 247, 266
— Glaciers in, 265, 274
— — Height of, 270
— — Hiuen-Tsiang's description of, 279
— — Ice grottoes, 274
— — hummocks, 273

Muzart Pass, Ice tables, 272
— — Jasper in, 273
— — Length of, 308
— — Marble block in, 249
— — Paucity of animal life in, 273
— — Ravens and kites in, 271
— — Russian accounts of, 263
— — Stony roads of, 272
— — Trees of, 248
— — View of *mer-de-glace*, 273
— — " White Mountain " in, 267
— river, Bed of, 262
— — Crossing the, 252
— — Kalmuks on, 250
— — Lesser, Wading across, 248
— — Tosti tributary, 250
— valley, Geology of, 288
— — Marble monument in, 286
— — Photography in, 266
Muzart-Kurgan, Arrival at, 299
— — Customs examination at, 301
— — Departure from, 305
— — Inspection of, 304
— — Lodging at, 300
— — Nimrod's strategy at, 304
— — Opium-smoking at, 303
— — Soldiers at, 304
— — Visit of Customs official, 303
— — and Aksu, Distance, 303, 313
Muzart-nin-su, Accident in fording, 292
— — — Camera washed away, 292
Myriopoda, ii. 418

NAAKI MOGUL, of Khotan, ii. 160, 188
Naiman Kirghese, ii. 51
Nan-lu route, 325
Nankow Pass, 323
Narim, Great, Cossack school at, 123
— — Kirghese settlement at, 123
Narin, Cossacks at, ii. 4
— Fort of, ii. 4
— Houses of, ii. 5
— Larionoff, Col., at, 134 ; ii. 5
— river, ii. 4
— Sarts at, ii. 5
— Tatars at, ii. 5
— Traders at, ii. 4
— Village of, ii. 4
Narin-Kol, Cossacks at, 238
— — Ride to 238
— — Russian picket at, 238
— — Thunderstorm at, 239
Nepal, Baptism of infant in, ii. 387
— Fauna of, ii. 383
— Holy Communion in, ii. 386
— Revolution in, ii. 302
— Scripture distribution in, ii. 387, 403
Nepalese invasion of Tibet, ii. 295
Nertchinsk, Treaty of, 154

Nestorian alphabet given to Uigurs, ii. 131
— cemeteries, ii. 122
— Christianity in Central Asia, 109
— missionaries in China, 361
— monument at Singan-fu, ii. 120
— ruins at Tash-Rabat, ii. 4
— translations ii. 131
— worship, Character of, ii. 133
Nestorians at Samarkand, ii. 122
— Chvolson, Prof., on, ii. 122
— Henning, Rev. Stilon, on, ii. 121
— in Herat, ii. 122
— — Persia, ii. 122
— Spread of, ii. 121
— Yule on, ii. 121
Neuroptera, ii. 418
Newchwang, Bible Society at, 159
Newton, Prof., of Cambridge, 391
Ney, Mr Elias, at Yarkand, 375
— — — in Mongolia, 374
Neza-tash Pass, ii. 72
— — river, ii. 11, 13
Nia, Pievtsoff's expedition at, ii. 174
Niaz Beg, House of, ii. 264
Nicolaivitch, M., Introductions of, 31
Nicolson, Rev. W., at St Petersburg, 109, 173 ; ii. 339
Norman, Mr John, at Ilisk, 140
Nubra valley, Cultivation of, ii. 328
— — Villages in, ii. 328

OBOLENSKY, Prince Dmitry, Meeting with, 14
Obrucheff, Gen., Visit to, 6
Oi-Kul on the Little Pamir, ii. 11
Okhotsk, Sea of, 153
Okta, Ruins of, ii. 76
Olga, Madame, at Bokhara, 62
Olopuen, Christianity introduced into China by, ii. 119
Onion Mountains, ii. 9
Opium-smoking at Muzart-Kurgan, 303
Ordos of Mongolia, 162
Orenburg, *Koumiss* establishment at, 253
Oriel railway station, 14
Orleans, P. Henry of, at Lob-Nor, ii. 172
— — — — Journeys of, 212
— — — — Tibetan journey of, ii. 311
Orochons of Manchuria, 156
— Baptisms among, 158
Orthodox Missionary Society, 123
Orthoptera, ii. 418
Ortus country, Romanists from, 193
— Mongols, Mission to, 163
Osh, Buddhism at, ii. 87
— Deibner, Col., at, 99
— Post and telegraph at, ii. 8
Oshanin, M., Assistance of, ii. 25

Oshanin, M., on the Pamirs, ii. 17
— — — Vierny earthquake, 132
— — — Postal information by, 106
Osman Bai, caravan leader, 200
— — Contract with, 210
— Linguistic abilities of, 208
— — Negotiations with, 210
— — Payment of, 342, 354, 446
Otar, Breakdown near, 126
— Exiles to Siberia at, 128
Oxus river, Arabs on the, ii. 50
— — Bridge over the, 58
— — Crossing the, 59
— — Old bed of, 25
— — Source of the, ii. 12

PALESTINE, Visit to missions in, ii. 404
Pamir, The, Boundaries of, ii. 9
— Communications, ii. 16
— Historical geography of, ii. 16
— Nomenclature of, ii. 9
— Peaks of, ii. 10
— Plateau of, ii. 9
— Roads of, ii. 9
Pamirs, Buddhist pilgrims on, ii. 16
— Climate of, ii. 13
— Flora of, ii. 17
— Forsyth expedition on, ii. 11, 17
— Geology of, 290
— Hydrography of, ii. 10
— in winter, ii. 14
— Kirghese on, ii. 14
— Lakes of, ii. 11
— Littledale, Mr, on, 227
— Nomad inhabitants of, ii. 15
— Origin of tribes, ii. 16
— Regions adjoining, ii. 1
— Route from Kashgar, ii. 45
— Russian explorations, ii. 17
— Severtsoff's discoveries, ii. 27
— Travellers on, ii. 16, 18
— Wild sheep on, 95
— Younghusband expelled from, ii. 73
Panamik, Author's hostess at, ii. 331
— Buddhist priest at, ii. 332
— — temple at, ii. 332
— Haidar Haji at, ii. 332
— Hotsprings near, ii. 332
— Lodging at, ii. 330
— Photography at, ii. 331
— Redslob, Mr, at, ii. 267
Panchao, Victories of, ii. 49
Panjabi workmen at Aksu, 348
Panjah river, ii. 12
— sulphur springs, ii. 13
Panjdeh, Catacombs at, 39
— Russian rule at, 38
— Work of Sariks of, 38
Pantusoff, M., at Vierny, 109

Pantusoff, M., on gravestone inscriptions, 111
— — — musical instruments, ii. 203
Parker, Mr, among the Mongols, 163
Pascal, Friar, at Almalık, ii. 126
— — — Khiva, ii. 125
Pau-ting, Town of, 324
Paul, Mr A. W., at Darjeeling, ii. 380
Pchigodski, Dr, at Tokmak, 402
Peacock, Mr, Consul at Batoum, 18, 137
" Peking to Calais by Land," 161
— Hospitality of British Ambassador, ii. 396
— Interview with Sir R. Hart, ii. 395
— Jehangir executed at, ii. 56
— Russian embassy to, 368
Pe-lu route, 325
— towns, Manchus in, 396
Pembroke, Mr, Kindness of, 226
Pepin, M., on the Pamirs, ii. 19
Persia, Nestorians in, ii. 122
Persian carpets at Merv, 38
— Gulf, Journey up, ii. 402
— intercourse with China, 360
Persians in Old Merv, 42
Pesky railway station, 49
Peter the Great, Cupidity of, 369
Petersburg, St, Arrival at, 3
— Bible Society in, 10, 173 ; ii. 339
— British Embassy, Call at, 4
— — — Dinner at, 5
— Departure from, 10
— " Etat Major " at, 8
— Fife, Duke of, at, 5
— Gazette on slavery at Bokhara, 51
— Geographical Society at, 5
— Grombchevsky, Capt., at, 9
— Harford, Mr, at, 5
— Herbert, Col., at, 5
— Interview with Postmaster-General, 172
— — — Prjevalsky, Gen., ii. 365
— — — Vlangali, M., 6
— Kindness of officials, 4
— Korsakoff, Prince Dundukoff, at, 6
— Kostenko, Gen., at 9
— Lieven, Princess, Luncheon with, 10
— Mirkhovitz, Gen., at, 10
— Objects of visit to, 3
— Obrucheff, Gen., at, 6
— Parade of troops at, 10
— Scientists visited at, 5
— Social gatherings at, 5
— Zoological Museum at, ii. 24
Petrovsky, M., at Chadir-Kul, ii. 3
— — — Kashgar, 134 ; ii. 38
— — Hospitality of, 436
— — Intellectual tastes of, 430
— Miss, at Kashgar, 405

Petrovsky, Miss, at Tashkend, 99
Pfennig, M., at Tashkend, 96
Pialma, Birds of. ii. 163
— Desolate route to, ii. 157
— Reading on horseback near, ii. 223
 Village of, ii. 157
Pievtsoff, Col., Expedition of, ii. 174
Pindarun, *Amban* of Khotan, ii. 188
Pishan. Garrison at, 334
— Oasis of, 334
— Route to, 333
— Shops of, 334
Pishpek. Archæological researches, 109
— Arrival at. 105
— Cemetery at. 109, 110 ; ii. 122
— Departure from, 107
— Gedionoff. M., at, 106
— Pushebin, Col., at, 105. 126
Pleske, M., zoologist, ii. 24
Plevé, M., Visit to, 4
Pnom-penh, capital of Cambodia, ii. 403
Pobedonostzeff, M., Assistance of, 4
Podolsk railway station, 14
Poltaratsky on the Muz-davan 263
Polu, Gromhchevsky at, ii. 175
Pomerantzoff, M., at Tashkend, 98
Popoff, Col., at Bokhara, 60
Portohalgasun, Mongolian town of, 164
Posgam, Houses and shops of, ii. 138
— Lodging at, ii. 139
— Photography at, ii. 139
— Population of district. ii. 139
— Village of, ii. 138
Potagos, M., on the Pamirs, ii. 17
Potanin at Hami, 327
Poukaloff, Col., at Samarkand, 88
Preobajensk, Arrival at, 124
— Fishing at, 124
— Kirghese doctors at, 124
Presbyterians in Manchuria, 160
" Prester John," ii. 124
Price, Mr Julius, in Mongolia, 161
Prjevalsky, Gen., at Hami, 327
— — — Jarkend, 145
— — — Lob-Nor, ii. 172
— — Death of, ii. 174
— — Discoveries of, ii. 28
— — Fails to enter Tibet, ii. 174
— — in Mongolia, 371
— — on Chinese officials, ii. 241
— — Tibetan journey of. ii. 309
— — Zoological specimens of, ii. 24
Pskoff, Stay at, 3
Ptolemy, Geography of. 357
Pushchin, Col., at Pishpek, 105
— — Parting with, 115

QUETTA. Author at, 34
— Service at, ii. 404

RADDE, Dr, and Tiflis Museum. 20
Radloff, Dr, Visit to, ii. 132
Ramoth Gilead, Visit to, ii. 404
Ramsay, Capt., Letter from, ii. 147
Ran-Kul on the Pamir, ii. 11
Rangoon, Crosthwaite, Sir C., at, ii. 392
— to Mandalay, Excursion from, ii. 391
Rashid in Tarim valley, ii. 53
Ravenstein. M., on Christianity in Manchuria. 159
Rawal Pindi, Review of situation at, ii. 375
Rawlinson, Sir H., Translation by, 67
Rechler. Pastor, at Berlin, ii. 364
Réclus' account of Muzart Pass, 270
— on Sungarian routes, 165
— — the Pamirs, ii. 9
Redjap, porter at Jarkend, 145
Redslob, Rev. F., at Leh, ii. 306, 337
— — — — Panamik, ii. 267
— — — Correspondence with, ii. 116, 147, 366   [372
— — — on inaccessibility of Lassa, ii.
Regel, Dr, at Darwaz, ii. 17
— — — Turfan, 335
— — — Urumtsi, 331
Reintal, Capt., at Kashgar, 374
Remusat on Khotan history. ii. 167
Repetek railway station, 49
Reptiles collected by Author, ii. 415
Ridgeway, Sir West, Introductory letter from, 19
— — — recommends Joseph, 226
Roborovsky, Lieut., at Khotan, ii. 174
Rockhill, Mr W., journey of, ii. 311
Roman mission at Tai-yuen, 324
— missionaries in Kuldja, 193
— — — Mongolia. 163
Romanadt, M., at Kuldja, 177
Romanovsky's geological map, 287
Rosenbach, Gen., at Tashkend, 94
— Garden of, 102
Roshan district, ii. 12
Rubenstein, M., 84
Rubruquis on Nestorian worship, ii. 133
Russian Church Mission to Kirghese, 123
— conversions on the Amur, 158
— extirpation of slavery, 51
— favours. Review of, 147
— hospitality, 14
— influence in Bokhara, 77
— missionary work on the Amur, 158
— monastery at Issik-Kul, 121
— parcels post, 173
— post-office censorship, 172
— public meetings, 5
— railway dangers, 13
— Society for Transport, 137
— temperance movement, 11

GENERAL INDEX.

SABLER, M., Sec. to Holy Synod, 4
— — Assistance of, 136
Sabouroff, M., Introduction to, 31
Safr Bai, Kirghese at, 379
— — Road to, 379
Sai-Aryk, Butterfly hunt at, 384
— — Fruit at, 384
— Gardens at, 384
— Hailstorm at, 385
— Night march from, 385
— Ride to, 384
— — Turki families at, 384
Saian Mountains, 153
Said, Sultan, Rule of, ii. 53
Saigon, Scripture distribution at, ii. 392
Saik, Hamlet of, 378
St Vivien, Martin, on Pamirs, ii. 10
Sairam lake, 167
Sam-Su post-station, 128
Samanid conquest of Turkistan, ii. 200
— power in Turkistan, ii. 50
Samara, *Koumiss* cure at, 253
Samarkand, Arrival at, 88
— Bridges near, 88
— Dalgleish's murderer captured, ii. 322
— Departure from, 92
— Fête at, 85
— Fire-worship in, ii. 80
— Former acquaintances, 88
— Government House at, 88
— Ivanoff Park at, 91
— Jews' synagogue at, 91
— Nestorians in, ii. 122
— Poplar-trees in, 88
— Road to, 88
— Scripture sales at, 91
— Tamerlane's mausoleum at, 80
— Tolpygo, M., engineer at, 88
— Visits from Jews of, 91
Sandjar Kala, Ancient monuments of, 41
Sanjar, Sultan of Merv, ii. 51
Sanju Pass, ii. 151, 162, 237
Santai, Chinese families at, 414
Santash Pass, 118
Sarakhs, Tomb of Cain at, 32
Sares Pamir, ii. 12
Sarhad, Village of, ii. 73
Sari-Kamish lake, 321
Sari Kul on the Pamirs, ii. 11
Sariasi river, 383
Saribeli, Village of, 380
Sarikol district, ii. 71
— Revolt in, ii. 60
Sariks, Tassel work of, 38
Sarim Sak and his wives, ii. 40; ii. 56
Sarin, Kalmuks in, 397
Sarman, Village of, ii. 5
Sart, A wealthy, 145
— fortress at Chakmak, ii. 2

Sarts at Narin, ii. 5
— Depravity of, 409
— Immorality of, 404
Sary-jassy Mountains, Altitude of, 310
— — river, Source of, 310
Saryk-Aryk, Caravans at, ii. 264
— Sheep at, ii. 264
Saser Pass, Elevation of, ii. 326
— Glaciers and skeletons, ii. 326
— Tschkun, Camping at, ii. 325
Sati, Halt at, ii. 333
Saurans gold-mine, ii. 185
Schlagintweit in Chinese Turkistan, 374
— Monument to, ii. 44
— Murder of, ii. 43
Schott's essay on Buddhism, ii. 92
Schultz, M. von, Introduction to, 32
Schuyler in Ili valley, 374
— on "Turkistan," 109
Scotch Presbyterians in Manchuria, 160
Scott, Mr J. G., on Chinese army, ii. 255
Scripture distribution to Afghans, 345
— Kalmuks, 398; ii. 340
— at Aksu, 351; ii. 341
— — Janghuia, ii. 152
— Kharkof, 15
— Kuldja, ii. 339
— — Saigon, ii. 392
— — Suiting, 204, 207; ii. 339
— — Yarkand, ii. 227, 342
— — Dalgleish, Mr, on, ii. 112
— in Annam, ii. 392
— — Chinese Turkistan, ii. 339
— — Ili valley, 170
— Kashgar prison, 444
— — Nepal, ii. 387, 403
— — on the Amur, 159
— sales at Janghuia, ii. 156
— — Kashgar, ii. 38
— translations into Kalmuk, 169
Seeland, Dr, at Chadir-Kul, ii. 3
— — Chakmak, ii. 2
— — Vierny, 119
— on Chinese officials, ii. 241
— — Kirghese, 119, 398
— — education, 257
— — — food, 250
— — — opium-smoking, ii. 146
Seh-Shanabeh bazaar, ii. 232
Seid Abdul Ahad, Emir of Bokhara, 51
Selenginsk, Missionary school at, 163
Seletsky, Madame, at Jarkend, 144
Semirechia, Capital of, 130
" Christian Monuments in," 109
— Governor of, 133
— Kirghese food in, 251
— Route to, ii. 1
— Trade of, 439
"Seres," Arabian knowledge of, 360

"Seres," Land of the, 37
— Region of the, 357
"Serica" of Ptolemy, 357
Serpukhov railway station, 14
Sevastopol, Departure from, 18
— Drive through, 17
— Harford, Capt., at, 17
  Sunday labour at, 17
— — service at Consulate, 17
Severtsoff, M., on Pamirs, ii. 17, 27
Shadman-Malik, Bridge of, 92
Shafidul, Rest-house at, 430
Shah-Malik, Kunjut raids at, ii. 316
Shahidula, Arrival at, ii. 278
 - Fort of, ii. 313
  Jade-mine at, ii. 184, 314
  Kunjuti raid on, ii. 230
Shahnaz river, ii. 66
Shamanism in Manchuria, 158
Shamanist Buriats, 163
Shanghai, American Bible Society at, 201 ; ii. 339
  Stevenson, Mr, at, ii. 394
Shansi, Opium-smoking in, ii. 145
— Province of, 324
Shantung cavalry, 414
Shara-muren river, 155
Sharbo-Guchi, Pass of, 221
Sharpe, B., on Yarkand birds, ii. 27
Shattoo, Arrival at, 245
  Granite rock at, 247
  Kalmuks at, 246
  Road from, 248
  Russians at, 246
Shaw, Mr, at Kashgar, 374
— on the Pamirs, ii. 16
Shensi, Rebellion in, ii. 58
Shepeleff at Mazar-bash, 276
 - in the Muzart Pass, 246
  Measurements of, 303
  on the Muz-davan, 263
Sheppard, Capt. W., in Mongolia, 161
Sheremetieff, Gen., at Tiflis, 19
Shigatai, Fortress of, 334
Shigatze, Monastery at, ii. 282
Shignan district, ii. 12
Shiho coal-fields, 168
— gold-washings, 168
 - military station, 167
  Naphtha lake of, 168
  Salt-beds of, 168
Shilgan, Ruin at, 32
Shing-shing-she, 325
Shinking, Population of, 155
 - Province of, 155
Shirbadan, Emir's palace at, 73
Shlengir, Houses at, 313
Shor Kuduk, Hamlet of, 386
Shugeh, Ride to, 425

Shyok river, ii. 324
Siam, American missionaries in, ii. 403
"Siberia, Five Thousand Miles in a Sledge across," 156
Siberian exiles at Ilsk, 141
  Otar, 128
 - Chains and costume of, 142
"Siberian Overland Route from Peking to St Petersburg," 161
Sibo exiles in Ili valley, 218
 - village near Kuldja, 217
Sikkim, Bhotanese in, ii. 302
— Hooker, Dr, in, ii. 306
 - Hostilities with British, ii. 296
— Rani of, Tea with, 251
Silak Langar, Birds at, ii. 163
 - — Halt at, ii. 151
Simbooti, hostess at Panamik, ii. 331
Sin-cheng, Fortress of, 327
 - - Hunan soldiers at, 328
 - — see also Hami
Sin Kiang, Alashan route, 323
— - Area of, 320
 - Boundaries of, 319
 - Headquarters of, Urumtsi, 332
 - Lakes of, 321
 - Mountains of, 320
 - - Province of, 318 ; ii. 64
 - Rivers of, 321
 - — Roads of, 322
 - - — Towns of, 322
Singan, Population of, 324
— Town of, 324
Singan-fu, Nestorian monument, ii. 120
Singapore, Bible Society at, ii. 392
— Journey to, ii. 400
 - Official kindness at, ii. 392
Sirt country, 380
 - - Kirghese in, 398
Sitla, travellers' station, ii. 66
Smith, Rev. W., at Calcutta, ii. 384
— Sir C. C., at Singapore, ii. 392
Solon colonists, 217
— exiles in Ili valley, 218
 - tribes in Manchuria, 156
Solyan defile, 109
Sonamarg, Arrival at, ii. 375
Sorgak gold-mine, ii. 173, 185
Sosnovsky expedition at Hami, 327
Spain, Prison visiting in, ii. 405
Spiders collected by Author, ii. 418
 - of Central Asia, ii. 30
Sprent, Rev. H. F., at Peking, ii. 400
Srinagur, Arrival at, ii. 375
Stallybrass, Mr, in the Trans-Baikal, 164
Stapley, Mr, 192
Staro-Tokmak, Journey through, 113
Steppe, Route over the, 165

Stevenson, Mr, at Shanghai, ii. 394
Stewart, Col., at Tiflis, 18
— — on Persian slavery, 51
— — recommends Joseph to Author. 225
Stoddart, Col., in Bokhara, 71
Stoliczka, Dr, at jade-mine, ii. 184
— — Yengi Hissar, ii. 70
  Death of, ii. 27
  in Belowti Pass, 380
— — — Turgat Pass, ii. 3
Stremoukhoff, M., on Bokharan slave-trade, 51
Su-chow to Hami, Journey from, 325
Su-ping-tai, Temple of, ii. 396
Sua-Chow, Defile of. 229
— — river, 229
Suashu Pass, 221
Subhan, *Sardar*, Hospitality of, ii. 332
Suchan river, ii. 12
Suget, Arrival at. ii. 315
— Pass. View of, ii. 315
Suiting, Apricots at, 203
  Bazaars of. 179
  Breakfast at. 182
— Call on Mattie, 203
  Chinese Romanists at, 203
— Departure for Kuldja. 205
— Farewell to, 207
— Feasting at, 182
— Garden at. 203
  Houses of, 179
— Inns at, 179
  Interpreters at, 207
  Intruders at, 181
  Invitation from Commissary, 182
— Journey from Kuldja to. 178
  Mattie's advice at, 302
— Money-changing at, 342
— Official favours at, 204
  Population of, 179
— Presents at, 207
  Return to Kuldja from, 187
  Russian post-house at, 203
— — Scripture distribution at, 204; ii. 339
— Teh'ai Kuan, Controller at, 204
— Temple and theatre at, 203
— Town of, 179
  Tsian-Tsiun at, 174
  — — — Interview with, 185
— Visiting at, 184
Sulphur mines near Aksu, 347
— springs at Karabagh, 347
Sumbe river, 257
Sunarguloff, Col., at Jizak, 92
Sung Yun, Travels of, ii. 83
Sungari river, 155
Sungaria, Bibliography of, ii. 405
— — Chinese victories in, 169
— — Confucians in, 169

Sungaria, Depopulation of, ii. 55
— Districts of, 165
— English explorers in, 374
— Exiles in, 168
— Fauna of, ii. 28
— Grum-Grjimailo in, ii. 28
— - Kalmuks in, 397
— Lamaists in, 169
— Military stations of, 165
  Muhammadans in, 169
  Opening for mission work in, 170
— Prjevalsky's discoveries in, ii. 28
  Renat's map of, 372
  Repeopling of, 169
— Russian pioneers in, 370
— Surface of, 165
— Territorial division, ii. 55
  Wild camels in, ii. 173
Sungars, History of, 168
Sunnite Muhammadans, 121
Suok stream at Gulja-bashi, ii. 3
Supi Khajam, Hamlet of, ii. 151
Surkhab river, ii. 8
Sutherland, Mr. at Kalimpong, ii. 379
Syngym, Uigur ruins at, ii. 132
Syr-daria, Crossing the, 94
Syr river, ii. 10
Syria. Visit to missions in, ii. 404
Syriac manuscripts, ii. 121
Szechenyi, Count, Journey of, ii. 310
Szechuen, Governor of, ii. 365
Szen-i-cnien, Chinese families at, 414

TAEUGHAZ LANGAR, Highwayman's head at, ii. 159
— — Mosque at, ii. 159
  — Photography at, ii. 159
  Shooting at, ii. 163
Taghar, Houses of, ii. 333
  Sardar of, ii. 332
Tagharma Mustagh range, ii. 10
Tai-yuen. Missions at, 324
  — Population of, 324
— — Town of, 324
Takla Makan desert, 321
Ta-la-sze, Ancient city of, 100
Tal-Cheku Peak, 114
Talab Kana, Hermitage of, ii. 158
Talgar Peak, 129
Talki Pass, 165
  — Balkashin's journey through. 146
  — — Bridges of, 167
  Dangers of, 146
  — — Photographs of, 168
Tamerlane at Bokhara, ii. 52
  Conquests of, ii. 52
— Marriage of, ii. 52
— mausoleum at Samarkand, 80
Tamgha-tash, Glaciers near, 286

Tamgha-tash, Osman Bai's arrival, 285
— — Picket of, 282
— — Remarkable day at, 284
— — Route to, 279
— — Soldiers at, 304
— — Waiting for baggage at, 283
- Yakub Khan at, 285
— and Kailek, Distance, 303
Tang-shan, Chinese railway at, ii. 309
Tangier, Visit to, ii. 405
Taranchis at Damarchi, 219
— — Kuldja, 174
  Dress of women, 219
- in Ili valley, 219
Tarbagatai district of Sungaria, 165
— Kalmuks in, 169
— range, ii. 9
Tarikhi Rashidi, Bellew's quotation from, ii. 130
Tarim basin, History of, ii. 47
— desert, 321
- river, 321
- valley, Buddhist pilgrims in, ii. 49
—   Conquest of, ii. 49
—   Early religions in, ii. 79
—   Education in, ii. 219
—   English influence in, ii. 257
— — Jinghiz Khan's conquest, ii. 51
— —   Kalmuks in, ii. 169
    Kara-Khitai rule in, ii. 51
— Migrations from, ii. 48
— Money-changing in, 97
- — Muhammadan ascendency in, ii. 74
-   — feasts in, ii. 205
    Rashid's rule in, ii. 53
—   Russian influence in, ii. 248
Ta-gan river, ii. 237, 264
— Crossing bed of, ii. 151
- valley, Ride through, ii. 267
Tash-Kurgan, Gordon at, ii. 71
— — Route to, ii. 70
— — Ruins of, ii. 72
Tash-Liangar, Lodging at, 310
— Soldiers at, 304
  Suburbs of, 310
Tash-Rabat Pass, Kirghese tombs, ii. 4
Tash-Tube Mountains, 236
Tashi Lunpo monastery, ii. 282, 294
Tashkend, Arrival at, 94
— Banking arrangements at, 96
— Bartsch, M., at, 102
— Bazaar at, 99
  Bible Society at, 170; ii. 339
- Blinoff, Capt., at, 95
  Cantacuzene, Prince, at, 94; ii. 26
— Cathedral service at, 96
— Departure from, 103
— Easter in, 96
  Feodoroff, M., at, 95

Tashkend, Garden of Governor, 102
— Good Friday in, 96
— Hay, Miss, at, 94
— Hospitality of Governor, 95
— Levashoff, Gen., at, 98
— Lilienfeld, Col., at, 96; ii. 26
  Lutheran service at, 96
  Observatory at, 98
- Old, Station of, 94
  Open-air fête at, 102
  Oshanin, M., Assistance of, ii. 25
  Parting amenities, 102
  Passion week in, 95
  Petrovsky, Miss, at, 99
- Photographs of native women, 100
— Postal service at, 99
  Purchases in, 99
  Reception at Government House, 96
  Romanoff Street, 94
- Rosenbach, Gen., at, 94
- Service at, 96
- Strawberries in, 102
- — Sungar exactions at, 169
  Tcharykoff, Col., at, 96
- Vziemskiy, Princess, at, 99
Tasma range, 118
Tatar hostess at Kuldja, 206
— porters at Uzun Ada, 23
Tatars at Narin, ii. 5
Tathsin temples, ii. 120
Taxidermy, Lessons in, ii. 22
Taylor, Rev. Hudson, Assistance of, ii. 338, 357
- — — on passport difficulty, 149
Tch'ai Kuan, Controller at Suiting, 204
Tch'ang Te, Chinese traveller, 109
Tcharykoff, Col., at Bokhara, 62
— — Tashkend, 96
— — Dinner-party of, 52
— — Guest of, 50
Tching Tchang, M., Counsel of, 301
Tcho-gah, one of Author's escort, 213
— — Return home of, 260
Tchuen-yuen on Khotan, ii. 169
— — — Yarkand, ii. 102
— — — — river, 137
— — Travels of, 368
Tea route in Mongolia, 161
Teits tribe of Kirghese, ii. 72
Tekes river, 220, 229
— — Arrival at, 236
— — Bivouac on banks, 240
— — Fording the, 239
— — Rise and course of, 236
— valley, Absence of Kirghese in, 243
— — Canals in, 259
— — Mineral oil in, 230
— — Monastic ruins in, 257
Tekke carpets at Merv, 38

Ten-murun Pass, ii. 8
Tengri-Nor lake, ii. 282
Terek range at Turgat Pass, ii. 3
Terek-davan route to Ferghana, ii. 5
Terekti Pass, 378
Terskei Ala-Tau range, 117
Teshik-tash, Chinese station, ii. 2
Teshu Lama, Death of, ii. 303
Tezab river, ii. 142
Thok-Jalung gold-mines, ii. 308
"Through Siberia" in Tientsin, ii. 400
Thuillier, Col., Assistance of, ii. 390
Tian Shan Mountains, 114, 153
— — Avalanches in, 286
— — Geology of, 287
— — Glaciers of, 242
— — Kostenko's remarks on, 263
— — Orography of, 241
— — Severtsoff's discoveries, ii. 27
— — Snow bridges, 286
— — Sources of our knowledge of, 243
— — View from Jam, 308
Tibet, Animals of, ii. 285
— Area of, ii. 280
— Asiatic information anent, ii. 306
— Bibliography of, ii. 466
— Boundaries of, ii. 279
— Buddhism introduced, ii. 287
— Campbell, Dr, in, ii. 305
— Capuchin friars in, ii. 300
— Chinese administration, ii. 297
— — annals and surveys, ii. 307
— — conquest of, ii. 295
— Climate of, ii. 283
— Dalai Lama at Lassa, ii. 297
— European travellers to, ii. 299
— Expulsion of Huc and Gabet, ii. 304
— — Indian natives, ii. 295
— Fauna and flora of, ii. 284, 306
— French missionaries in, ii. 303
— Gentlemen travellers in, ii. 309
— Geology of, ii. 284
— Gold-mines of, ii. 308
— Government of, ii. 297
— Grand Lama of, 162
— History of, ii. 291
— Hostilities with British, ii. 296
— Houses of, ii. 330
— Indian Government explorers, ii. 307
— Inhabitants of, ii. 286
— Jesuit missionaries in, ii. 300
— Ladak, Contests for, ii. 295
— Lakes of, ii. 281
— Lama prayers, ii. 289
— — rule in, ii. 297
— — sovereignty in, ii. 288
— — worship in, ii. 333
— Lamaism, Characteristics of, ii. 287
— Legends of, ii. 166

Tibet, Literary students of, ii. 304
— Manchu troops in, ii. 297
— Markham's work on, ii. 303
— Missions of Bogle and Turner, ii. 302
— Mongol supremacy in, ii. 294
— Moravian missionaries at, ii. 306
— Name of, ii. 279
— Nepalese invasion, ii. 295
— Northern plains of, ii. 284
— Notable kings of, ii. 292
— Orography of, ii. 280
— Provinces of, ii. 282
— Religions in, ii. 286
— Religious code of the people, ii. 289
— Rivers of, ii. 281
— Roads of, ii. 282
— Sakya monastery, ii. 288
— Sanctity of lamas, ii. 288
— Sungarian invasion, ii. 294
— Surface of, ii. 281
— Trade of, ii. 306
— Translation difficulty, ii. 364
— Transmigration of lamas, ii. 288
— Van de Putte's journey in, ii. 301
— War with, 197
Tibetan food, ii. 332
— English dictionary, ii. 306
— women, ii. 335
Tientsin, Crossett's, Mr, grave at, ii. 400
— Journey to, ii. 394, 399
— Public library at, ii. 400
Tiflis, Arrival at, 18
— Bible Society at, 20
— Departure from, 20
— Geographical Society at, 19
— German Bible-class at, 19
— Hebrew Scripture purchase, ii. 330
— Hedjouboff, M., at, 20
— Hoijer's, M., Bible-class at, 19
— Hotel de Londres at, 18
— Introductions at, 19
— Jdanow, Gen., at, 19
— Kuhlberg's, Col., hospitality at, 19
— Museum at, 20
— Photography at, 20
— Sheremetieff, Gen., at, 19
— Stewart, Col., at, 18
— Sunday service in hotel, 19
— Wolff, Sir Drummond, at, 19
— Zelenoy, Gen., at, 19
Tinnevelly, Journey to, ii. 404
Tirit, Lodging at, ii. 333
Tiznaf river, ii. 139
Toga Sulookh, Sport at, 427
Togharasu, Crossing the, ii. 276
Toghri-su, Camp at, 263
Tokhta, caravan assistant, 217
Tokio, Journey to, ii. 400
Tokmak, Accident near, 107

Tokmak, Cemeteries near, 100
— Departure from, 113
  Hiuen Tsiang in, 108
— — Kara-Kirghese at, 402
— Nestorian cemetery at, ii. 122
— Pchigodski, Dr, at, 402
  Village of, 107
Toksun, Garrison of, 414
— Inhabitants of, 337
  Kalmuks near, 337
— Population of, 337
  Road from, 337
— Route to, 333
Tolpygo, M., Guest of, 88
— — House of, 88
Tolstoi, Count Leo, Visit to, 11
Tomsk mission to the Kirghese, 122, 123
— Russian Church mission at, 123
Tonking, Visit to, ii. 392
Tor-jee, one of Author's escort, 213, 234, 354, 381
Torgout Kalmuks in Volga region, 169
Torut Pass, Crossing the, ii. 70
Tosti tributary of the Muzart, 250
Toyan river, ii. 2
— valley, Cultivation in, 404
Trans-Caspian railway, 22
— Amu-daria station, 49
— Anau on the, 32
— — Artyk station, 32
— — Askhabad station, 30
— — — Attek oasis crossed by, 32
— — — Baba-Durmaz station, 32
— — — Bairam Ali station, 48
  Bala Ishem station, 25
— — Bami station, 26
  Barkhan station, 49
  Bokhara station, 60
  Desert route of, 48
  Durun station, 28
  Dushak station, 32
  Farab stopping-place, 60
  Geok Tepe station, 28
— — Giaurs station, 32
— — Introduction to controller, 32
— — — Karab-Ata station, 35
— — Kermine station, 80
— Kizil Arvat station, 26
— Kodj station, 26
— Kuyuk Mazar station, 80
— — Malik station, 80
— — — Merv, Official favours at, 48
— — — station, 35
— — Mikhailovsk station, 25
— — Mulla Kara station, 25
— — Oxus, Crossing the, 59
— — — Pesky station, 49
— — Repetek station, 49
  Sand-drifts *en route*, 49

Trans-Caspian railway, Sixty hours of travel on, 50
— — — Terminus of, 22
— — — — Tugai Robat, end of line, 81
  — — Ushak station, 25
Trans-Ilian Ala-Tau range, 114, 129
Trans-Oxiana, Legends of, ii. 48
Tripoli, Journey to, ii. 405
Trotter, Capt., at Kila Panj, ii. 17
— — — Yengi Hissar, ii. 70
— — in Belowti Pass, 380
— — on source of Oxus river, ii. 12
Tsagma river, 229
Tsakhars of Mongolia, 162
Tseng, Marquis, Counsel of, ii. 399
Tsen-ho country, Buddhism in, ii. 85
Tsi-tai-hsien, Troops at, 414
Tsian-Tsiun at Suiting, 174
— — Jurisdiction of, 185
— — — Presents from, 187
— — — to, 186
— — Secretary of, 186
Tsitsihar, Province of, 155
— — Population of, 155
Tsung-ling Mountains, 153
— — Buddhism in, ii. 85
Tugai Robat, 81
Tugh-balshi Mountains, 287
Tula, Arrival at, 14
Tulta, in Sungaria, 165
Tum Chuk, Arrival at, 393
— — Cultivation at, 393
— — Houses at, 393
— — Ruins near, 393
— — Scripture sales at, 393 ; ii. 341
— — Tiger at, 391
— — Turki families at, 393
Tung river, ii. 13
Tuplok, Village of, ii. 77
Tuprak, Departure from, 299
— Joseph's narrow escape at, 299
— Ornithological specimens at, 297
— Partridges at, 299
  Shooting at, 296
— and Muzart-Kurgan, Distance, 303
Tura-Aigir post-station, 115
Turfan, Beli, Col., at, 335
— Carey, Mr, at, 335
— Chinese quarter at, 336
  Cultivation at, 336
  History of, 334
— Mazar tomb at, 337
  Muhammadan pilgrims at, 337
— Population of, 336
— Regel, Dr, at, 335
— Route to, 333
— Ruins near, 336
— Sacred mountain of, 335
  Shops at, 336

Turfan, Town of, 334
— Travellers at, 335
— Troops at, 336
-- Turkis at, 336
— Wells at, 337
—- Yakub Bek at, ii. 60
— Younghusband at, 335
Turfanese at Hami, 326
Turgat Pass, Terek range at, ii. 3
Turki agriculture in Sungaria, 169
— depravity, 408
— estimate of Chinese rule, ii. 247
— families at Sai-Aryk, 385
— — — Tum Chuk, 393
 — in Bora oasis, ii. 236
— fanaticism, ii. 341
— honesty, 408
— industry, 408
— inhabitants of plains, 405
— inscription in Muzart valley, 280
— leaning to Russian rule, ii. 253
- narcotic abuse, 408
— shops at Yengi Hissar, ii. 60
— uncleanliness, 408
Turkistan, Chinese, Administration of, ii. 200
— Area of, 320
— — Author well received, ii. 262
— — — on taxation, ii. 246
— — — questioned at Peking concerning, ii. 255
— — Bibliography of, ii. 460
— — Boundaries of, 318
— — Buddhism in, ii. 81
— — — Relics of, ii. 94
— — Buddhist missionaries in, ii. 82
— — Climate of, ii. 246
— — Depravity in, 409
— — Desert route, ii. 173
— — Diseases prevalent in, ii. 110
— — Disaffection in, ii. 61
— — Districts of, ii. 200
— — Early religions in, ii. 79
 English popularity in, 261
 Exports of, 439
— — Feasibility of mission work in, ii. 345
 Feasting and dancing in, ii. 205
 Female missionaries for, ii. 348
 Fish of, ii. 32
 Four months in the saddle, ii. 404
— Garrisons in, 414
— Geography of, 317
— Glasses in, scarcity of, 340
— History of, ii. 47
 Horses for transport, 439
 Hospitals for natives, 100
 Hydrography of, 321
 Inhabitants of, 396, 406

Turkistan, Chinese, Insurrectionary elements, ii. 257
— Interpreter difficulty, 201, 227
— — Jubilee sovereigns in, 97
 Kalmuks in, 169
 Khoja rebellions in, ii. 56
 Khokandian quarrels, ii. 57
 Kirghese in, 398
— Length of, 320
— Mandarins in, 412
 Medical missionaries for, ii. 348
 Meteorology of, ii. 178
— Military population of, 414
— Missionary need in, ii. 344
 - view of, 338
— Morals of conquerors, ii. 214
- Mountain roads, 199
 Muhammadan influence, ii. 207, 215
 Mullah kings of, ii. 216
 Musical instruments of, ii. 203
— Names of, 318
— Opinions concerning, ii. 240
— Political condition of, ii. 239
— - Population of, 414
— - Post roads, Safety of, 94
— Present religious condition, ii. 217
— Provisions cheap, ii. 346
 Religious wars in, ii. 211
 Rivers in winter, ii. 137
— Routes, 199, 444; ii. 347
- Russian invasion practicable, ii. 254
 popularity in, ii. 250
 trade in, 439
 Samanid conquest of, ii. 209
- Schlagintweit in, 374
- Scripture distribution, 201; ii. 339
— — translations wanted, ii. 343
— — Seeland, Dr, on natives of, 400
 officials, ii. 241
 Shamanism in, ii. 80
 Soldiers of, ii. 201, 255
 Thermometrical observations, ii. 179
 Trade of, 439
 - restrictions, ii. 259
 Traders in, 414
 Travellers in, 376
 Turki beks in, ii. 200
 Will Russia annex it ? ii. 253
 Yak owners in, ii. 205
 See also Asia and Sin Kiang
Turkmenia, Dr Heyfelder on, 84
Turkoman bazaar at Merv, 30
 fortress at Geok Tepe, 28
 inclosure at Merv, 35
 lady, Interview with, 40
 oasis, Slavery in, 46
 raid near Askhabad, 45

Turkoman traffic in Persian girls, 51
Turley, Mr R., at Newchwang, 159
Turnbull, Rev. A., at Darjeeling, ii. 381
Tushkan river, 378
Tut Yailak, Camping at, ii. 327
Tyrrell, Gen., translation by, ii. 229

U-Tsang, Towns of, ii. 282
Udungei, Arrival at, 250
  Butter and milk at, 250
  Chinese picket at, 250
  Kalmuks at, 250
  and Khan-Yailak, Distance, 303
Ugyen Gyatso, Journey of, ii. 309
— Meeting with, ii. 380
Ui-Tul, Fishing at, 125
Uigurs, Antiquities of, ii. 132
  at Hami, 326
  Expansion of, ii. 51
  Nestorian alphabet given to, ii. 131
  Raids of, ii. 49
— Ruins at Syngym, ii. 132
— Subjugation of, ii. 49
— Tribe of, ii. 48
Ujfalvy, M., on the Hindu Kush, ii. 15
— — Ili Kalmuks, 254
Ulianghai tribes of Mongolia, 162
Uliassutai, Missionary need at, 164
  Roads to, 329
  Russian shops at, 329
Ulugchat, Altitude of, ii. 7
  Garrison of, ii. 7
Upga-tash Mountain, 287
Urban, Mr. at Vierny, ii. 34
Urdaklik, Photographs of, 426
— Quagmire at, 426
  Trot to, 425
Urdum Padshah, Ruins of, ii. 75
— — Shifting sands at, ii. 75
Urga, Kutuktu at, 162
— Manchu and Chinese troops at, 166
  Opening for mission at, 164
Urten Muzart, Fording the, 244
Urumtsi, Bell, Col., at, 331
  Carey, Mr, at, 331
— Chinese reoccupation of, ii. 61
— shopkeepers at, 414
  Coal and coke at, 332
— Governor-General at, 332
  History of, 330
  Importance of, 332
— Population of, 332
  Rebuilding of, 333
  Regel, Dr. at, 331
  Road from Lepsinsk to, 165
  route, Objections to, 191
  Shops of, 332
  Situation of, 331
  Soldiers at, 332

Urumtsi, Town of, 332
— Trade of, 332
  Yakub Bek at, ii. 60
Ush-Turfan, Cattle exportation, 347
— Chinese massacre at, 379 ; ii. 56
  Cultivation of district, 378
— — Fortress at, 379
— Houses of, 379
  Kirghese at, 398
  Market at, 379
  Road through, 377
— — Route to, 199
— — Shops at, 379
— — Taranchis at, 379
— Town of, 378
— — valley, 378
— — Cattle in, 379
— — Farmsteads in, 379
— — Horses in, 379
— — — Population of, 378
— — Sheep in, 379
  Wool trade of, 347
— — Yakub Khan at, 379
Ushak railway station, 25
Uspensky, M., on Hami, 327
— — Visit to, 173
Ussuri river, Description of, 156
Ust Kamenogorsk district, 123
Uzun Ada, Arrival at, 22
— — Departure from, 23
Uzun-Agatch, Fishing at, 128 ; ii. 34
— Reptiles of, ii. 34
— — village, 128
Uzun-Tau forests, ii. 35
— — Mountains, 220
— — Geology of, 229
Uzboi river bed at Mikhailovsk, 25

Van, a Kalmuk Khan, 209
Vaouline, Col., at Kara-Kol, 118
Victoria lake on the Pamirs, ii. 11
Vierny, Archbishop Alexander at, 122
  Arrival of luggage at, 139
  Author at Governor's abode, 133
— Butler at, 225
— Cathedral at, 130
— Departure from, 140
— Earthquake at, 107, 130
  Anniversary of, 135
  Destruction around town, 131
— — Gourdet's description, 130
— — Gramenitsky's account of, 132
  Memorial chapel, 135
  Oshanin's account of, 132
  Removal of inhabitants, 133
— — Victims of, 132
— Financial arrangements at, 134
- Gourdet's seismic records, 135
  Government offices at, 130

GENERAL INDEX.   511

Vierny, Hospitality of M. Gourdet, 133, 139
  Houses at, 129
  Kalmuk school at, 256
— Luggage delay at, 136
 - Mountains of, 129
  Packing of specimens at, ii. 34
  Palaces at, 130
  Pantusoff, M., in, 109
 - Population of, 130
  Public schools in, 130
  Purchase of tent at, ii. 266
— Route to, 107
  — Kashgar, ii. 1
  Seeland, Dr, at, 119
  Situation of, 129
  Start for, 126
  Streets of, 130
Vishnegradsky, M., Assistance of, 130
Vladivostock, Manchurian travellers, 156
Vlangali, M., at St Petersburg, 6, 95
Voisekovitch, Col., at Katte Kurgan, 86
Volga, Kalmuks of the, 169, 231, 254
Vuinos ceremony in Tashkend, 96
Vziemskiy, Princess, at Tashkend, 99

WADE, SIR THOMAS, on Chinese passports, 149
Wahabjilga, Slate rocks at, ii. 319
Wais Khan, Rebellion of, ii. 53
Wakhan, Exploration of, ii. 16
  Start for, ii. 70
Wakhis at Ak-Shor, ii. 265
Wallace, Sir Donald, Joseph recommended to, ii. 390
Walsham, Sir John, Counsel of, ii. 396
— — Hospitality of, ii. 396
Wanj river, ii. 12
Wheeler, Dr, at Jerusalem, ii. 405
Whyte, Mr Athenry, in Mongolia, 161
Wild, Dr, Meteorological statistics by, ii. 181
Williams, Wells, on Sungaria, 165
Williamson, Mr, on Manchuria, 156
Windt, Mr H. de, in Mongolia, 161
Wirkallen, Arrival at, 3
Wolfe, Archdeacon, at Foo Chow, ii. 394
Wolff, Sir Drummond, at Tiflis, 19
Wood, Lieut., on Pamirs, ii. 11, 16
Wylie, Mr, on Mongolian tea route, 161

YABLONOI Mountains, 153
Yak-Shambeh, Bird-shooting at, ii. 142
  — Contractors outwitted, ii. 233
  — Houses of, ii. 139
  — Market of, ii. 139
    Photography at, ii. 140
— — Village of, ii. 139
Yaka-Arak, Village of, 338

Yaka Kuduk, Chinese official at, 387
— — Houses at, 387
— — Pheasants at, 389
— — — Population of, 387
  — Scripture sales at, 387
    Sunday at, 387
    Undesirable companions at, 388
Yakoob, Death of, 89
Yakub Khan at Aksu, 348
— — — — Kashgar, 374 ; ii. 58
—   Khotan, ii. 191
—   Kurla, ii. 61
    Marabashi, 418
—   Tamgha-tash, 285
— Character of, ii. 217
 — Death of, ii. 62
  — Embassies to, ii. 60
— — Grave of, 449
    Immorality of, 411
— Upstart successors of, ii. 62
    Usurpation of, ii. 59
— — Victories of, ii. 59
    Waning power of, ii. 61
Yalakhan Mountains, ii. 265
Yalta, Steaming to, 18
Yaman Yar, Fuel at, 430
— — Stay at, 430
Yamdo lake, ii. 282
Yangi-Awat, Desert of, 380
— — Village of, 428
Yanushkovosky, M., Guest of, 85
Yapchan, Arrival at, ii. 45
— Camp at, ii. 324
— Village of, ii. 66
Yaphimovitch, Gen., at Samarkand, 88
Yarkand, Arrival at, ii. 78
— Baggage horses at, ii. 117
— Bargaining for horses, ii. 227
— Bazaar of, ii. 107
  Birds at, ii. 100
— Cage for hanging culprits, ii. 198
— Colleges in, ii. 105
— Cultivation at, ii. 104, 136
— Dalgleish, Mr, at, ii. 111
— — House of, ii. 115
 - Dolans at, 423
  Elias, Mr Ney, at, 375
— Escort from, ii. 135
  Excavation of ruins, ii. 177
— Fruit at, ii. 100
  Gardens of, ii. 100, 102
  Garrison of, ii. 105
  Goitre at, ii. 109
 - History of, ii. 101
  Hospitable reception at, ii. 99
  Houses in, ii. 105
  Inspection of prison, ii. 227
  Journey to Chitral, ii. 71
  Khotan to, ii. 225

Yarkand, Lodging at, ii. 100
— Mansions at, ii. 102
   Medical assistance requested, ii. 109
   Money loans offered, ii. 109
   Mosques in, ii. 105
— Naturalists at, ii. 27
   Old town of, ii. 105
   Photography at, ii. 101. 225
   Population of, ii. 105
   Ride through, ii. 100
 - river, ii. 136
   - - Fish of, ii. 137
      Gold in, ii. 137
      Precious stones in, ii. 137
   - - Source of, ii. 16
      Tchuen-yuen on, ii. 137
— Scripture distribution at, ii. 227. 342
—   presents at, ii. 107
   Shops of, ii. 105
— Sungar exactions at, 169
   Trade of, ii. 106
   Trees at, ii. 104
   Visit to *Amban*, ii. 200, 225
— Visits from mullahs, ii. 107
   Water supply at, ii. 102
   Yakub Bek at, ii. 59
Yarkand-daria, 321
Yashil-Kul on the Pamirs, ii. 11
Yasin, Murder of Mr Hayward at, 374
Yassa Bulak, Deer at, 427
   — Melon gardens at, 427
   - - Picket-station at, 427
   - Water-birds at, 427
   — Wild boars at, 427
Yaz-jigda, Hamlet of, 378
Yegin picket, ii. 7
Yengi Hissar, Battle-fields at, ii. 46
   — Bazaar of, ii. 67
 - - Cavalry at, 414
      District of, ii. 65
   — Forsyth mission at, ii. 70
   - Fort of, ii. 67
      Gumbaz at, ii. 68
      Hindu merchants at, ii. 67
      Historical associations of, ii. 74
— - Houses of, ii. 66
   - Kayragh hills at, ii. 66
      Mandarins at, ii. 67
      Money-changing at, ii. 67
      Opium-smoking at, ii. 145
      Photography at, ii. 67. 68
      Population of, 338 ; ii. 66
-     Tombs of Muhammadan martyrs,
         ii. 74
      Town of, ii. 66

Yengi Hissar, Travellers at, ii. 70
   Turki shops at, ii. 66
   Yakub Bek at, ii. 59
Yengi-shahr, Escort returns from, 382
 - Fortress of, 431
    Population of, 431
    Shops in, 432
Yermakoff, M., at Tiflis, 20
Yondama, Saltpetre at, 430
   Village of, 430
Younghusband, Capt., at Aksu, 316
— - - — Gumbaz-Bozai, ii. 19
— - - ··· Hami, 323, 327
  -       - Turfan, 335
         in Aksai valley, 379
   — — Chinese Turkistan, 376
   — - Sirt country, 380
   — Kashgar route of, 378
   — Muz-Tag route of, ii. 18
      on Chinese rule, ii. 243
—   - the Pamirs, ii. 19
Yuechi tribe, ii. 48
Yuldasheff, M., Jarkend merchant, 145
— · Kindness of, 147
Yule, Sir Henry, 106
   — - - on Cathay, 357, 364
   - — — — Marco Polo, 364
   — - - - - Nestorians, ii. 121
Yunnan province, 153
Yusuf Khan, *Aul* of, 39
— — - - Alikhanoff, Col., at, 46
   - - Dwelling of, at Old Merv, 39
   — - Pension of mother of, 40
Yut-Kuduk, Cultivation at, ii. 264
 - — Tasgun stream at, ii. 264

ZARAFSHAN river, Crossing the, 92
Zauka Pass, 379
Zawa Kurghan, Altitude of, ii. 159
 - Arrival at, ii. 222
    Cultivation around, ii. 102
- - Custom-house of, ii. 159
- - Habibulla's palace at, ii. 160
- - - Town of, ii. 159
Zelenoy, Gen., Dinner with, 19
Zia-eddin, Town of, 80
Zindau prison at Bokhara, 70
—   Souvenir of, 72
Zograf, Prof., of Moscow, ii. 24
Zoji-la Pass, Dangers of, ii. 374
Zoological Museum at St Petersburg, ii.
      24
   sundries, ii. 20
Zoroastrianism among hill tribes, ii. 15
Zulchak river, ii. 135

Printed by Hazell, Watson, & Viney, Ld, London and Aylesbury.

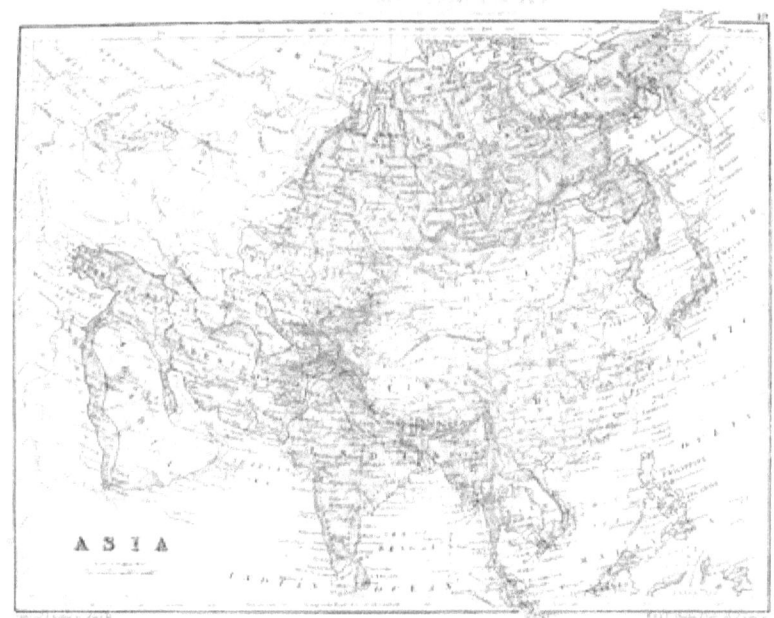

THROUGH SIBERIA.

FIFTH EDITION. IN ONE VOLUME, DEMY OCTAVO, 800 PAGES. 10.6.

Illustrated with Engravings and Map.

By HENRY LANSDELL, D.D., M.R.A.S., F.R.G.S.

A journey of 8,000 miles from the Urals to the Pacific, on the rivers Obi, Amur, and Ussuri, and by the hire of a thousand horses. The Author travelled privately on an expedition of a philanthropic and religious character to the penal establishments of Siberia, and describes his visits to nearly all its hospitals, prisons, and mines, giving a mass of authentic information concerning the exiles such as has never been published before. The book treats of all parts of the country, as to its geography, natural history, and inhabitants, both Russian and aboriginal; whilst 3,000 miles of the Amur and Ussuri are here described by an English Author as an eyewitness for the first time.

Extracts from 200 Notices of the English, Irish, Scotch, American, Australian, French, Finnish, German, and Swedish Press.

The Times. (*One column.*)—"The Reader will . . . find in Mr. Lansdell's volumes all that can interest him about Siberia."

The Athenæum. (*Five columns.*)—"With the exception of Mr. Mackenzie Wallace's 'Russia,' the best book on a Rusian subject which has appeared of late years is Mr. Lansdell's 'Through Siberia'."

Fraser's Magazine. (*Thirteen pages.*)—"His testimony . . . is simply the best that exists." O.K. . . . (a *Russian* writer.)

The Academy. *Four columns.*—"We are of opinion that 'Through Siberia' is much more entertaining, and certainly more readable, than many novels."

The Church Times. (*Two columns.*)—"Englishmen have every reason to be proud of this work; for it . . . can only result in making the name of our country more honoured and respected than any mere victory of arms would do."

Church Missionary Intelligencer. (*Four pages*)—"It is altogether different from even the higher class of books of travel. It teems with information of every possible kind."

Harper's Monthly Magazine. (*One column.*)—"Since the time of Howard, no one has given us so full and fair an account of Russian prisons as is now presented to us by Mr. Lansdell."

Revue des deux Mondes. (*Twelve pages.*)—"Qu'on n'aille pas s'imaginer après cela que M. Lansdell soit un fanatique . Il estime qu'une sage philosophie et une piété sincère ne sont irreconciliables ni avec la belle humeur ni avec ces honnêtes petits plaisirs que assaisonnent la vie."

The Baptist. (*Two columns.*)—"A man who undertakes to set matters in a true light before the eyes of the world deserves the gratitude of all parties. This Mr. Lansdell has done."

The Guardian. (*Two columns.*)—"It touches upon political and social questions of great interest, and offers information upon the internal administration of the Russian empire, which is not readily obtained elsewhere."

LONDON: SAMPSON LOW & CO., 188, FLEET STREET, E.C.
AMERICA: HOUGHTON, MIFFLIN, & CO., BOSTON.
GERMAN TRANSLATION: HERMANN COSTENOBLE, JENA.
SWEDISH TRANSLATION: ALBERT BONNIER, STOCKHOLM.
DANISH TRANSLATION: O. H. DELBANCO, COPENHAGEN.

BY THE SAME AUTHOR.

RUSSIAN CENTRAL ASIA:
INCLUDING
KULDJA, BOKHARA, KHIVA, AND MERV,

Illustrated with Photographic Frontispiece; Seventy Engravings; and with Route and Ethnological Maps.

In Two Volumes.   Demy Octavo, 1,500 Pages.   Price Two Guineas.

A journey of 12,000 miles—5,000 by rail, 3,500 by water, and 3,500 on wheels, horses, or camels—through Western Siberia to Kuldja: thence through Russian Turkistan and the Kirghese Steppes to Tashkend, Khokand, and Samarkand. Crossing into Bokhara, the Author travelled through the Khanate as guest of the Emir, floated 300 miles down the Oxus to Khiva, and then continued by a new route across the land of the Turkomans and north of Merv to Krasnovodsk. One of Dr. Lansdell's objects (as before in Siberia) was the distribution in prisons and hospitals of the Scriptures, on the Patriarchal and Persian customs of which the work throws light in references to 350 texts. In 77 chapters the book treats more or less fully of all parts of Russian Turkistan, Kuldja, Bokhara, Khiva, and Turkmenia, down to the frontier of Afghanistan; describes many hundreds of miles of country not previously visited by an English Author; gives 4,300 species of fauna and flora in about 20 lists, with introductions; adds a bibliography of 700 titles, and an index of 5,000 entries.

Extracts from Notices of the Press.

"Altogether Dr. Lansdell has reason to be proud of a work which is really monumental."—*The Times.*

"Since the father of history [Herodotus] . . . . we doubt whether a more complete book after its kind has been written. . . . At Bokhara, the description of the Emir's reception, and the author's stay at Kitab, his summer residence, is one of the most graphic bits of Oriental reading which the western world has seen."—*Church Quarterly Review.*

"Upon Russian Central Asia there is no book in the English language, and probably not in any language, to be compared with it."—*Church Missionary Intelligencer.*

"The journey of which this book is a complete record is a wonderful achievement, and worthy to be placed among the great travels of the world . . . . . ."—*British Quarterly Review.*

"His two volumes deserve the warmest commendation. They are real monuments of courage, and of patience, and of knowledge."—*Whitehall Review.*

"Two large volumes . . . . which we venture to say will take a distinguished place in the historical literature of our country."—*Ecclesiastical Gazette.*

"In a word, the ethnologist, geologist, and naturalist will find these volumes not only very pleasant reading, but also most valuable for reference."—*Nature.*

"The record of his travels is a work which does credit to our literature . . . interesting adventures follow each other like other episodes in a well-constructed drama."—*Athenæum.*

"He is full of fun as well as of information."—*Graphic.*

"Entirely free from political bias."—*Globe.*

"The book is an excellent one . . . and it is a first-rate model to those who wish to know how a book of travel should be written."—*Academy.*

"It cannot but raise the reputation of Dr. Lansdell as a great traveller, a careful observer, and an attractive writer."—*Medical Times.*

LONDON : SAMPSON LOW & Co., 188, FLEET STREET, E.C.
AMERICA : HOUGHTON, MIFFLIN, & Co, BOSTON.
GERMAN TRANSLATION : FERDINAND HIRT & SON, LEIPZIG.

www.ingramcontent.com/pod-product-compliance
Lightning Source LLC
Chambersburg PA
CBHW031945290426
44108CB00011B/681